Carmina Gadelica

by
Alexander Carmichael

Ortha nan Gàidheal

Urnan agus Ubagan

Le Solus air Facla Gnàtha agus Cleachdana a Chaidh air Chùl; Cnuasaichte bho Bhialachas feadh Gàidhealtachd na h–Alba agus Tionndaichte bho Ghaidhlig gu Beurla, le Alastair MacGilleMhìcheil

Charms of the Gaels

Hymns and Incantations

With Illustrative Notes on Words, Rites and Customs, Dying and Obsolete; Orally Collected in the Highlands and Islands of Scotland by Alexander Carmichael

Lindisfarne Press

This arrangement, edited by C J Moore,
first published in 1992 by
Lindisfarne Press, RR4, Box 94A–1, Hudson, NY 12534
Reprinted with revisions, 1994, 1997

ISBN 0–940262–50–9

Printed in Great Britain
by Redwood Books, Trowbridge, Wilts

Contents

Preface

For the best part of a hundred years Alexander Carmichael's great collection of Gaelic verse and prose, characterized by archaic charms and incantations, which we know as *Carmina Gadelica,* has dominated its own sector of the field of Gaelic literature. Carmichael's interests, both as collector and littérateur, extended well beyond the sphere of the purely religious, as indeed the six volumes that *Carmina* eventually became were so richly to demonstrate. But there is no doubt that his deepest concern was with hymns and charms and prayers, for this is the kind of material that he selected for the first two volumes of *Carmina Gadelica,* the only ones edited by himself and published in his own lifetime.

These religious texts with their strange blend of pagan and Christian imagery, witnesses to the spirituality of a vanished age, their complement of mysterious words and phrases, apparently unknown outside this repository of incantations, and their dignified, almost liturgical, style, fascinate the reading public, Gaelic and English alike. Here it would seem was a lost lexicon of piety which almost miraculously had survived into modern times. It had been discovered on the verge of extinction, in remote places and in an obscure tongue; it was now, at the last possible moment, being revealed to the world at large. The publication of *Carmina Gadelica* was a signal triumph, an outstanding literary achievement, and an event of the greatest moment to the whole of Gaelic Scotland.

What of the collector and editor? Alexander Carmichael was born in 1832 in the Island of Lismore — *Lios Mór,* the "Great Garden" — off the coast of Argyll. The kindred from which he sprang had of old held lands in Lismore, the head of the family being known as the Baron of Sguran House. At least as significant, however, was the connection of Clann Mhic Gille Mhicheil (the Carmichaels) with the Columban church established in Lismore by St Moluag who died, according to the Annals of Ulster, in 592. Specifically, there was kinship with An t–Easbaig Bàn, the Fair–Haired Bishop, remembered in Gaelic tradition as the builder of the cathedral of the island. Genealogical claims such as these are commonplace in Gaelic society and central to the construction of its kinship systems. They are not a matter of mere pretentiousness let alone snobbery in its commonly accepted meanings. They have little to do with consciousness of "class" — though they may convey a vestigial sense of caste — but they function in such a way that they give the individual a place, historically and psychologically, in the vision of his own people. Family tales of an ancestral connection with the church of Columba and its later history cannot have failed to exercise an influence on the young Carmichael and may well have prepared his mind and imagination for what was to be his life's work: the preservation for posterity of the spiritual heritage of the Gaelic church of Columba and its missionaries.

Alexander Carmichael's daily bread, however, came from the more mundane source of the Civil Service of the United Kingdom. After formal education in

Greenock Academy and collegiate school in Edinburgh, Alexander was accepted by the Commissioners of the Civil Service for work in Customs and Excise. No better choice could have been made. Carmichael's duties took him, among other places, to Skye, to Uist, to Oban, and then back to Uist again. In these areas, in the middle of the nineteenth century, when Gaelic was still the dominating everyday speech and English for thousand of Gaels simply a foreign language, Alexander Carmichael was introduced to "Gaelic oral literature ...," as he tells us, "widely diffused, greatly abundant, and excellent in quality."

From that great abundance, largely between 1855 and 1899 and particularly from 1865 to 1882 when the family's permanent residence was in the Hebrides, Carmichael drew the major texts of his collection. Even as late as 1910, when he was in his late seventies, we have a report of a "collecting pilgrimage" throughout the northern counties. The enthusiasm was characteristic for, as one of his obituary notices puts it: "What he failed to get in Uist he searched for in Glengarry; what he lost in Kintyre he tracked in Sutherland." During all that time he received no financial help from any institution. In the Introduction to *Carmina I,* he sums it up himself thus: "Three sacrifices have been made — the sacrifice of time, the sacrifice of toil, and the sacrifice of means. These I do not regret."

Alexander Carmichael contributed folk tales, proverbs, etc. and papers on antiquarian and other topics to a variety of journals, and to books such as John Francis Campbell's *Popular Tales of the West Highlands* (1860–62) and Alexander Nicolson's *A Collection of Gaelic Proverbs and Familiar Phrases* (1881). Among those texts are a heroic ballad from the Isle of Skye (still known there in substantially the same form) and an orally transmitted version of the great medieval Gaelic prose epic, "The Cattle Raid of Cuailnge" *(Táin Bó Cuailnge).* An oral recension of the ancient tragic story of Deirdre, taken down from a storyteller in Barra, was presented, first in Gaelic, then in English, to the Gaelic Society of Inverness and printed in their *Transactions,* Vols. 13 and 14 (1886–87; 1887–88); later these were published in book form.

The title *Carmina Gadelica,* Latin for "Gaelic songs/hymns/incantations, etc." was not, it would appear, Carmichael's own first choice but was urged upon him by one or more of his friends; the Gaelic title is *Ortha nan Gaidheal* ("Charms/Incantations of the Gaels"); both English and Gaelic have lengthy subtitles. There are six volumes: 1 and 2, as already noted, edited by the collector, with substantial help from others, and published in 1900. In 1928 Volumes I and II were reprinted with minor alterations by his daughter Ella (Mrs W.J. Watson). Volume III (1940) and Volume IV (1941) were edited by her son, Alexander Carmichael's grandson, James Carmichael Watson; Volume V (1954), consisting for the most part of secular poetry, and Volume VI, with comprehensive indexes and bibliographical information (1971) by Angus Matheson. The material in these volumes and in Alexander Carmichael manuscripts in the University of Edinburgh has been classified in broad terms under the following headings: invocations (e.g. prayers for protection, prayers before going to sleep); addresses to the saints; seasonal hymns, including genuine Christmas carols; blessings for everyday tasks (banking up the fire for the night, reaping, grinding, milking, herding, and hunting); incantations used in healing; prayers to the sun and the moon; rhymes about animals and birds; blessings on cattle and other livestock; miscellaneous songs, e.g. praise–songs, love–songs, milking songs, fairy songs, waulking songs; auguries, with notes on the augurers' methods; and much incidental information on custom and belief in general.

From any point of view that is an extraordinary assemblage consisting as it does of formally structured items, verse and prose, curious and arcane knowledge, and miscellaneous lore of great variety and often unique nature. Here is a fine sweep of the landscape of the Gaelic imagination now apparently for the first time revealing its mysteries.

It was therefore natural that publication of what was really no more than a sample of Carmichael's material (Volumes I and II) earned the collector immediate and unqualified praise. Writing in 1901, Dr Alexander MacBain, one of the leading Gaelic scholars of his day, expressed the view that "Mr Alexander Carmichael's *Carmina Gadelica, Ortha nan Gaidheal* is one of the most important books ever published in connection with Gaelic." High praise indeed from a man who was noted for his lack of sentimentality in such matters.

In 1906 Carmichael received jointly with his wife, a Civil List pension; three years later the University of Edinburgh conferred on him the honorary degree of LL.D. These honours were primarily bestowed in recognition of his literary work but it is important to note that that work could and did have a bearing upon the everyday life of the people who had given Carmichael so unstintingly of their own literary inheritance. The writer of the obituary in the *Celtic Review* of October 1912 (presumably the editor, Mrs W.J. Watson, Carmichael's daughter) records the following item of information:

"When Dr Skene was preparing his *Celtic Scotland*, he asked Mr Carmichael to write the chapter on old Highland land customs. This paper first turned the attention of Lord Napier and Ettrick to the condition of the crofters, and led to Mr Carmichael being asked to write a more elaborate paper of a similar nature for the Crofter Royal Commission Report. Lord Napier used to say that these two papers had more to do with the passing of the Crofters Act than people knew."

The Act in question, passed in 1886, won security of tenure for crofters, who had formerly been only tenants-at-will, liable to be turned off their holdings at a landlord's whim or that of a landlord's servant. Alexander Carmichael knew the economic aspects of life in crofting communities as well as the spiritual and aesthetic aspects (his paper for the Royal Commission is still an authoritative source) and his concern was not limited to the prayers of the people.

According to some of his friends, Carmichael was himself "one of the folk." One would think that his profession of Excise Officer can scarcely have endeared him to those who saw no harm in distilling their own whisky (and selling it at a sensible profit) or who considered that divine favour could be measured by the riches of the flotsam cast up on the beaches. Yet Carmichael's success as a collector of arcane spells and the like argues that his informants confided in him as a trusted friend.

One of his intimates and admirers was the Rev Dr Kenneth MacLeod, composer of the words to "The Road to the Isles" and collaborator with Margiory Kennedy-Fraser in *The Songs of the Hebrides* (1909). In an appreciation published shortly after Carmichael's death (and reprinted in *Carmina IV,)* MacLeod has this to say: "[Others] could get the heroic tales and ballads, the things which were recited in public at the *ceilidh;* only Alexander Carmichael could have got the hymns and the incantations, the things which were said when the door was closed, and the lights were out ... Not all of what he learned was written down, or if written down, has been preserved; many curious rites, embodied in unusual language ... were revealed to him under a strict pledge of secrecy ... A characteristic instance is within the writer's knowledge. One evening a venerable Islesman, carried out of himself for the time being, allowed Dr Carmichael to take down from him a singularly beautiful 'going in to sleep' rune; early next morning, the reciter travelled twenty-six miles to exact a pledge that his 'little prayer' should never be allowed to appear in print. 'Proud, indeed, shall I be if it give pleasure to yourself, but I should not like cold eyes to read it in a book.'

"In the writer's [i.e. Dr Kenneth MacLeod's] presence, the manuscript was handed over to the reciter, to be burnt there and then — but for days and nights after, the music of that rune haunted two men!"

A kind, generous, sensitive man, then, according to all accounts, Carmichael also had, as we have seen, a robust awareness of the everyday life of crofters and the demands of their daily round of work. It was due to his representations that the Inland Revenue was persuaded to abolish the tax on horse-drawn carts in crofting townships and on dogs kept for purposes of herding. These were by no means trivial measures for those whose lives were cast in a harsh environment, bound by the constraints of a subsistence economy. Carmichael's perceptions of Gaelic society certainly were not those of an Ivory Tower artist.

Nevertheless, he obviously had his critics. The Rev Dr Kenneth MacLeod again: "It is sometimes said that Dr Carmichael idealized us; not merely our past, which was allowable, being borne out by the beautiful material he had collected, but also our present, which itself contradicts his picture of it; that he idealized, at any rate, such of us as had passed the three score years, and more particularly such of them as had a tale to tell or a rune to chant. One does not care to deny so pleasant a charge. Every man makes his own world, to the extent, at any rate, of unconsciously reading himself into it; and thus the worse the reality idealized, the better the man who idealizes ..."

These last are significant words and to some readers might seem to verge on the casuistical.

Earlier in the same appreciation, Kenneth MacLeod had drawn a highly suggestive contrast between Alexander Carmichael and two of "our other great ones": Alexander MacBain, about whom "one could never quite get rid of the feeling that in temperament he was Teutonic rather than Celtic"; and John Francis Campbell of Islay, pioneer collector and scholar in the study of Gaelic folktales. Campbell, Dr MacLeod says, "was never quite one of us — he could never altogether hide the fact that he had learnt his art with other peoples and in other schools. And though he doubtless loved our tales and our beliefs for their own sake, yet: 'The following collection is intended to be a contribution to this new science of "Storyology." It is a museum of curious rubbish about to perish, given as it was gathered in the rough'." Campbell is referring here to his *Popular Tales of the West Highlands.*

Kenneth MacLeod may seem to us unduly sensitive to Campbell's "curious rubbish" — the science of folklore was in its infancy — for, in another place, as MacLeod well knew, Campbell insists on the *value* of "this despised old rubbish." But the telling phrase is "given as it was gathered in the rough." Neither Kenneth MacLeod nor Alexander Carmichael, nor the great majority of their kind, would for a moment have agreed with the propriety of doing that. Yet it is this phrase that enshrines the principle by which henceforth the work of all collectors of oral literature would be judged.

It was John Francis Campbell himself, characteristically, who first expressed a disquiet about Alexander Carmichael. In 1861 Carmichael, who was then living in Skye, wrote to Campbell to thank him for printing some of his (Carmichael's) contributions. He continued to send material, including texts of heroic ballads. From such poetry James MacPherson (1736–96) had "translated" his *Ossian,* which was itself then translated into Gaelic verse as part of the campaign to vindicate MacPherson's claims. For Campbell, as for others who knew the primary sources, authentic and spurious "Ossianic" ballads were usually not difficult to tell apart. But at least at this stage in his career, Alexander Carmichael apparently could not or would not draw that crucial distinction. Of his notes to one of the ballads, Campbell observes: "The remarks of Carmichael are very curious. The Lay which he sends is a genuine ballad ... Nevertheless the collector is so impressed with the authenticity of *Ossian* that he makes game of the genuine ballad." And of Carmichael's version of a folktale *A' Chaora Bhòidheach Ghlas* (The Pretty Grey Sheep), Campbell remarks: "It is Ossianic book Gaelic in places, the scribe being a firm believer in MacPherson's *Ossian.*"

Throughout this century more than one Gaelic reader felt some degree of uneasiness as he or she read through the volumes of *Carmina Gadelica,* especially Volumes I to IV. Few of these readers, however, were tradition–bearers themselves or, indeed, had ever heard a genuine Gaelic incantation. For those who had, or had access to comparative material in print, there was a sufficient amount of patently genuine material on the pages of *Carmina* to make them conclude that Carmichael, working amidst the abundance of an earlier age, had the good fortune to discover fuller and more elegant versions than the fragmentary variants that they knew themselves. If other collectors had printed specimens of Gaelic charms that lacked the amplitude and dignity of those in *Carmina,* that surely was due to Carmichael's greater skill and assiduity in searching, as well as to the trust which the "Folk" reposed in him.

Calum Maclean, then a collector at the School of Scottish Studies at the University of Edinburgh, reviewed Volume V in the Swedish journal *Arv* (Vol. 11, 1955). Maclean had worked in Uist and Barra, the communities of which had been Carmichael's richest sources, and was an expert in Gaelic folklore. He writes as follows: "It has been said that Carmichael's work was vitiated by the romanticism of MacPherson's *Ossian* and the sentimentalism of the Celtic Twilight. *It was, but to a surprisingly small degree* [my italics]. In some instances tradition bearers in the course of common, informal narration appear to use the somewhat florid style of formal heroic narrative and literary manuscript tradition."

Maclean grants that the introductory narrative passages ascribed to informants "are not, I think, the product of the tradition bearers themselves"; but he argues that "Carmichael can hardly be accused of taking liberties with the actual texts of lays, songs, hymns, charms, prayers, etc." And, while Carmichael's "texts in verse are remarkable in that they have an almost suspicious polish ... in many cases versions identical with the texts of *Carmina Gadelica* and even superior to them have been recorded within recent years, e.g. Volume V, songs on pp 28, 36." [Nos.488, 490 in the present edition.] Songs, however, be it noted; not incantations. Carmichael, he concludes, "was in a sense more of a littérateur than a student of folk tradition, but his main interest was in the literature of the folk."

Twenty-one years later, these judgements were to be seriously challenged.

In 1976, Hamish Robertson published an analysis of Carmichael's collection, manuscript and printed, in the journal *Scottish Gaelic Studies.* Here he accused the collector-editor of consistent, large-scale fabrication. Charms and incantations that were "incomplete" or "inferior" in Carmichael's estimation were simply re-made. In some instances, "words are substituted, lines are shortened or lengthened, new lines appear, verses are switched round and what was one poem-piece in the Appendix [to the Royal Commission Report — texts given by Carmichael] can swell to two or three in *Carmina.*" Moreover, Carmichael tried "and sometimes obviously, to draw a spurious sanctity of age about his collections, ... resurrecting Gaelic words of doubtful provenance."

According to these arguments, Carmichael was a literary forger and the stylistic elegance that had evoked so much admiration little more than a meretricious gloss. Dr Kenneth MacLeod's anecdote about the venerable Islesman and his "little prayer" is seen in a new and quite different light by Mr Robertson: "The man who walked miles to ask Carmichael to destroy a copy of the charm he had just previously given him had more to fear than intrusion into a secret, but also — had he only known — the threat of being labelled father to a pious rigmarole composed by a romantic dilettante."

From a consideration of the volumes edited by Carmichael himself Robertson moves to those edited by James Carmichael Watson and finds the material there suspect also. For instance, several charms in Volumes III and IV "seem to be full and flowery elaborations of charms or themes of charms evident in Volumes I and II." Robertson lists a number of points that Carmichael's grandson-editor must have been aware of: "In spite of these deterrents, he chose to publish. But it is doubtful if he became a happier man for having decided to do so."

Although Hamish Robertson scores a number of palpable hits in his investigation of Carmichael and *Carmina,* certain of his observations remain speculative. He explains why this is so: "Our chances of ascertaining the original form of charms in *Carmina* seem remote, for there is no trace of material existing for Volumes I and II among the manuscripts of the Carmichael-Watson collection, except for a few rare passages ... There is also a scarcity of manuscript material for Volume III." All this makes him raise the possibility of there having been "something to hide in the event of any posterior scrutiny into the texts."

A strong rejoinder to many of Robertson's points came from an expert in Gaelic folklore, Dr John Lorne Campbell. While the tone of Mr Robertson's contribution was critical but somewhat hostile, that of Dr Campbell's was critical but rather sympathetic. Campbell makes two very important points, one about editorial methods, the other about motives. He quotes from Carmichael's letters to show how the great collector was driven by intense idealism and concern for his fellow Gaels. To Fr Allan MacDonald of Eriskay, for instance, in June 1905: "Everything Highland is becoming of interest. Let us try to meet this interest and to show the world that our dearly beloved people were not the rude, barbarous, creedless, godless, ignorant men and women that prejudiced writers have represented them. It is to me heart–breaking to see the spiteful manner in which Highlanders have been spoken of."

Campbell comments that these motives were "entirely honourable. Contemporary critics of today do not always realize the strong anti–Highland feeling that existed in various 'Anglo–Saxon' circles in Victorian times."

As for the charges of fabrication, it had long been known to Campbell that Carmichael edited the raw materials of his collection; an Irish reviewer of *Carmina V*, in fact quotes him on this very point: "Carmichael's texts often surprise Irish readers ... Their literary excellence as compared with recordings by other collectors is probably explained by Mr John Lorne Campbell's suggestion in his booklet on Fr Allan MacDonald of Eriskay (1954) (p.29) that Carmichael's practice 'seems to have been to dovetail different versions of traditional poems, etc., in order to produce *the best possible literary version' [Eígse,* VIII, 167. (My italics).] This was no more than normal editorial practice of the time. Carmichael had been quite open about his methods. Of a certain song text, for instance, he says: 'I have some ten or twelve versions of that, all differing more or less. How to deal with them all is hard to say. I cannot give all the versions separately. To give all the versions of all poems separately would be ruinous. I must therefore collate them all and give the result alone — not at all an easy matter.'

"Or on a particular prayer, he comments 'the IV and V verses were not in the first version of this beautiful hymn. I am not sure that they originally formed part of it'."

Robertson declared that this prayer (printed in the Appendix to the Royal Commission Report) "has been split into two for *Carmina* [Nos.68, 88 here] and the two fragments polished, lines inflated or curtailed according to which of two differing metrical schemes Carmichael saw fit to squeeze them into." Campbell dismisses this criticism with the tart comment that: "From the purist point of view, Carmichael did rightly when he separated these verses from the others and printed them separately in *Carmina* ..."

But in general John L. Campbell acknowledges that "much of the first three volumes of *Carmina* must be taken as a literary and not as a literal presentation of Gaelic folklore" and furthermore that "Carmichael Watson perpetuated a style of editing in the third and fourth volumes of *Carmina,* which by 1940 was out of date." Campbell also brings to our attention that "neither Carmichael nor James Carmichael Watson was sufficiently acquainted with Catholic devotional literature to realize that some of the items they were printing were Gaelic versions of well–known Catholic hymns ..." Campbell's assessment is that Volumes V and VI alone are adequately edited. In a word, the shortcomings of *Carmina Gadelica* are not due to any kind of literary forgery but to the fact that "[Alexander] Carmichael's love for the Highlands coloured the early volumes of *Carmina* with a sentimentalism which is rather irritating at times" and that James Carmichael Watson "was handicapped for editing *Carmina* by (1) an excessive *pietas* regarding his grandfather's work, (2) lack of direct acquaintance with the oral tradition of South Uist and Barra, and (3) the fact that he was working under heavy pressure of time."

But the controversy was not to end there. In 1984 Alan Bruford carried out a comparison of the story of Deirdre as published by Carmichael and a transcript of field notes of the tale as it was told to Carmichael in 1867 by John MacNeill at

Buaile nam Bodach in Barra. The results of Bruford's enquiry into Carmichael's methods here show that "he revised every sentence, almost as if he were trying to evade copyright restrictions." *Deirdire* is not part of *Carmina Gadelica,* but Alan Bruford's conclusion has a bearing upon that work: "There is reason enough here to apply stringent critical standards to everything that Carmichael published or prepared for publication ... we are entitled to accept, if not expect, the possibility of 'improvement' or even forgery."

Readers of *Carmina Gadelica,* whether in English or Gaelic, cannot expect to be given a final answer on the fine detail of this controversy until all the evidence (including Carmichael's missing field notes) is assembled. But some general statements can be made. The texts of non-religious songs, in Volume V for instance, seem to be on the whole free of gross invention though obviously they are sometimes conflated versions of a number of variants, according to Carmichael's own explicit declaration.

To pass judgement on the charms and prayers is more difficult. Gaelic incantations do seem now to be very rare in genuine popular tradition. There are however two papers in the *Transactions of the Gaelic Society of Inverness* (Alexander MacBain "Gaelic Incantations," Vol.XVII, 1890–91, pp.222–26; and Wm. MacKenzie *Gaelic Incantations, Charms, and Blessings of the Hebrides,* Vol. XVIII, 1891–92, pp.97–182) which give a good basis for comparison with some of the material in *Carmina.* The charms are drawn from more than one source — Carmichael himself contributed indirectly to each paper, though neither paper is mentioned in *Carmina* — but there is no question here of re-working or collation of texts.

William MacKenzie (p.121) has a charm of "The Genealogy of St Bride," which he received from Fr Allan MacDonald of Eriskay, and which he translates as follows:

St Bridget, the daughter of Dughall Donn,
son of Hugh, son of Art, son of Conn.
Each day and each night
I will meditate on the genealogy of St Bridget
[whereby] I will not be killed
I will not be wounded,
I will not be bewitched;
Neither wili Christ forsake me;
Satan's fire will not burn me;
Neither water nor sea shall drown me;
For I am under the protection of the Virgin Mary,
And my meek and gentle foster-mother, St Bridget.

Alexander Carmichael's version (I:70 in the present edition) opens with what is clearly the title though it is printed as two lines of verse and its diction is ornate enough to make it seem a slightly exotic graft:

The genealogy of the holy maiden Bride,*
Radiant flame of gold, noble foster-mother of Christ.

* "Woman" would be a sufficient translation; there is no suggestion of a "maiden."

Bride the daughter of Dugall the brown,
Son of Aodh, son of Art, son of Conn,
Son of Crearar, son of Cis, son of Carmac, son of Carruin.

Carmichael's "Aodh" and "Dugall the brown" and MacKenzie's "Hugh" and "Dughall Donn" are identical names in the Gaelic text. Some at any rate of the names in line 5 are known in other charms. Carmichael does not seem to have added much here.

Probably the single most famous charm in the whole of *Carmina Gadelica* is the "Invocation of the Graces" *(Ora nam Buadh)* of Volume I (I:3 in the present edition) which opens:

I bathe thy palms
In showers of wine
In the lustral fire,
In the seven elements ...

Hamish Robertson points out that the "Invocation of the Graces" section in Volume III "all seem to elaborate on certain themes in the famous *Ora nam Buadh* ... Such a genre of charm probably existed," he writes, and goes on to assert that "several of the phrases and some of the tone of the *Carmina Gadelica* version [of *Ora nam Buadh]* could well be genuine."

Carmichael has a verse in the *Ora nam Buadh* as follows:

Dark is yonder town,
Dark are those therein,
Thou art the brown swan,
Going in among them.
Their hearts are under thy control,
Their tongues are beneath thy sole,
Nor will they ever utter a word
To give thee offence.

In William MacKenzie's "Charm to Obtain Justice" (pp.111–13), there are related lines. MacKenzie's translation of his charm is as follows:

I go forth in the name of Gods;
In the likeness of iron; in the likeness of the horse;
In the likeness of the serpent; in the likeness of the deer;
Stronger am I than each one [or "than any one else"]
Black to yonder town;
And black to those who reside therein;
[May] Their tongues be under my soles [or "feet"]
Till I again return.
May I be the white swan,
As a queen above them.
I will wash my face
That it may shine like the nine rays of the sun,
As the Virgin Mary washes her Son with boiled milk.
May restraint be on my tongue,

Love on my countenance;
The palm of Mary round my neck,
The palm of Christ on my face,
The tongue of the Mother of Jesus in my mouth,
The eye of the Protector between them;
And may the taste of honey be of every word
I utter till I return."

The much more elaborate invocation in *Carmina I* interprets this section very differently — the swan symbolizes a young girl, according to Carmichael's conjecture — but it suggests that the Invocation was put together from a number of shorter charms to which other elements were added, for instance the name *Eimir,* glossed in Carmichael's notes (II p.284) as "the wife of Cuchulainn. She is the type of beauty in Gaelic story." The form is however a literary mistranscription and is most unlikely to have been transmitted in oral tradition.

Some lines in the Carmichael's "Invocation":

An island art thou at sea,
A fortress art thou on land,
A well art thou in the desert,
Health art thou to the ailing ...

are paralleled by lines in the "Charm of Protection" [III:246 in the present edition]:

An island art thou in the sea,
A hill art thou on land,
A well art thou in wilderness,
Health art thou to the ailing ...

A variant of this charm was recorded by Calum Maclean in South Uist and published in the Swedish *Saga och Sed* (1959, pp.75–78). According to Maclean's informant, Donald Macintyre, this was the charm pronounced over Allan, chief of Clanranald who was killed in 1715.*

Donald Macintyre's version runs as follows in translation:

A charm that Brigit set upon Her Fosterling,
A charm that Mary set upon Her Son,
A charm that Michael set upon his shield,
A charm that the Son of God set around the City of Heaven.
A charm against sword,
A charm against arrow,
A charm against fits of anger and of foolishness.
A charm against fairy folk,
A charm against magic folk,
A charm against pitiless folk,

* Allan had rendered the charm useless by saying "If I come back [from battle],..." thereby implying doubt in the power of the spell. Carmichael's traditions about Allan are found in the note to II:134 in the present edition.

A charm against the peril of drowning.
A charm against the hurt of the red bog–myrtle,
A charm against the wounding of the impetuous Fiann.

The mantle of Columba be with you,
The mantle of Michael the Valiant be about you,
The mantle of Christ, my love, be around you
To protect you behind,
To protect you behind and before,
From the crown of your head to your brow
And to the black sole of your foot.

An island you are in the sea,
A hill you are on land,
A well you are in the waste,
Health are you to the ailing.

Great shall be the danger to him
Who sees the charmed body,
For the aid of Columba is with you,
And the mantle of Michael valiant is about you
And his great shield protecting you.

Compare this with Carmichael's text of the "Charm of Protection" [III:246]. It is immediately obvious that the *Carmina* text and the mid–twentieth century texts are reasonably close variants and that there is nothing in Carmichael's version to cause us to doubt its genuineness. Furthermore, in both variants Michael, the Archangel, has the epithet *mil* ("soldier," but given a variety of meanings in the *Carmina* translations). This effectively destroys Mr Robertson's argument that: "The form *Micheal mil* probably represents an ingenious antiquarian's guess, which is phonetically feasible, but should be treated as one of Carmichael's inventions."

In spite of many unanswered questions, it is now clear that *Carmina Gadelica* is not a monumental exercise in literary fabrication nor, on the other hand, is it a transcript of ancient poems and spells reproduced exactly in the form in which they survived in oral tradition. There are elements of fabrication undoubtedly: perhaps few texts in *Carmina* are totally free of some editorial repair–work and some, including the "Invocation of the Graces," may have it to a very high degree. But throughout the collection, the core of the material is the treasure–trove of oral literature that Carmichael discovered in Gaelic Scotland.

He himself tells in his Introduction to Volume I: "Although these compositions have been rescued chiefly among Roman Catholics and in the islands, they have been equally common among Protestants and on the mainland," for until the Evangelical Movement (c.1800 onwards) there was little or no difference between different religious confessions in their attitude towards the secular arts. The ancestry of some of the invocations and prayers for protection must in some cases link up with the ancient *Loricae,* of which the so–called "Breastplate of St Patrick" is probably the best known example. Their perspective is not that of the later medieval, Romanized church: St Andrew, "patron saint of Scotland" is only mentioned twice: Calum/Colum–Cille, Columba, is still the dominating figure, with Bride, St Brigit, a complex figure — pagan goddess, Christian saint, and foster-mother of Christ — taking a leading role.

The latest comment on *Carmina Gadelica* ("The Trouble with *Carmina,"* Raghnall MacilleDhuibh, West Highland Free Press, May 29, 1992) comes from Mr Ronald Black of the University of Edinburgh. He is well aware that Alexander Carmichael's writings can lead astray the unwary. Even so, he declares that "*Carmina Gadelica* is by any standards a treasure house ... a marvellous and unrepeatable achievement. There will never be another *Carmina Gadelica."*

John MacInnes
June 1992

For all bibliographical references, see *The Companion to Gaelic Scotland,* ed. Derick S. Thomson (1983; ISBN 0-631-12502-7). See especially under: Carmichael, Alexander; *Carmina Gadelica.* See also "Folklore Elements in *Carmina Gadelica,"* by F G Thompson, FRSA, FSA (Scotland), in *Transactions of the Gaelic Society of Inverness,* Vol.XLIV, 1964-66, pp.226-55.

Editor's note

References to items in the present edition are given as, for example, III:246. Here the Roman numerals identify the volume where the item occurs in the original six-volume bilingual edition; the Arabic numerals give the item number within the new consecutive sequence of this edition.

For a fuller account of the differences between the present edition and the original edition, readers are referred to the editorial note on p.573. For ease of cross-referencing, a concordance with the original edition is provided on p.675.

CJM

Introduction to the original edition

This work consists of old lore collected during the last forty–four years. It forms a small part of a large mass of oral literature written down from the recital of men and women throughout the Highlands and Islands of Scotland, from Arran to Caithness, from Perth to St Kilda.

The greater portion of the collection has been made in the Western Isles, variously called "Eileana Bride," Hebrid Isles, Outer Hebrides, Outer Isles, "Eilean Fada," "Innis Fada," Long Island, and anciently "Iniscead," "Innis Cat," Isle of the Cat, Isle of the Catey. Probably the Catey were the people who gave the name "Cataibh," Cat Country, to Sutherland, and "Caitnis," Cat Ness, to Caithness.

The Long Island is composed of a series of islands, separately known as Barra, South Uist, Benbecula, North Uist, and Harris and Lewis. This chain is one hundred and nineteen miles in length, varying from a few yards to twenty–five miles in width. Viewed from the summit of its highest link, the Long Island chain resembles a huge artificial kite stretched along the green Atlantic Ocean, Lewis forming the body, the disjointed tail trending away in the blue haze and terminating in Bearnarey of Barra.

This long series of islands is evidently the backbone of a large island, perhaps of a great continent, that extended westward beyond the Isle of the Nuns, beyond the Isle of the Monks, beyond the Isle of St Flann, beyond the Isle of St Kilda, beyond the Isle of Rockall, probably beyond the storied Isle of Rocabarraidh, and possibly beyond the historic Isle of Atlantis.

This backbone is now disarticulated like the vertebrae of some huge fossil fish, each section having a life of its own. These joints are separated by rills and channels varying from a few feet to eight miles in width.

The Atlantic rushes through these straits and narrows into the Minch, and the Minch rushes through the straits and narrows into the Atlantic, four times every twenty–four hours. The constant rushing to and fro of these mighty waters is very striking.

Many of the countless islands comprising the Outer Hebrides are indented with arms of the sea studded with rocks and islands dividing and ramifying into endless mazes, giving in some cases a coast–line of over four hundred miles within their one–mile entrance. No mind could conceive, no imagination could realise, the disorderly distribution of land and water that is to be seen in those Outer Islands, where mountain and moor, sand and peat, rock and morass, reef and shoal, fresh–water lake and salt–water loch, in wildest confusion strive for mastery. Viewing this bewildering scene from the summit of Ruaival in Benbecula, Professor Blackie exclaimed:

O God–forsaken, God–detested land!
Of bogs and blasts, of moors and mists and rain;
Where ducks with men contest the doubtful strand,
And shirts, when washed are straightway soiled again!*

The formation of the Long Island is Laurentian gneiss, with some outcrops of Cambrian at Aoi, Lewis, and four examples of trap at Lochmaddy, Uist. The rocks everywhere show ice action, being smoothed and polished, grooved and striated from hill to sea — the grooves and striae lying east and west or thereby.

There are no trees in the Long Island except some at Rodail, Harris, and a few at Stornoway, Lewis. The wind and spray of the Atlantic are inimical to trees under present climatic conditions. There are evidences, however, that there were trees in historic and prehistoric times.

It is said that a prince of Lewis forsook a Norse princess and married a native girl. The princess vowed by Odin, Thor, and Frea, and by all the other gods and goddesses of her fathers, to avenge the insult, and she sent her witch to burn the woods of Lewis. The tradition of the burning of these woods is countenanced by the presence of charred trees in peat–moss in many places. It is on record that a Norse prince married a native Barra girl, but whether or not this was the prince of Lewis is uncertain.

There are many evidences that the sea has gained upon the land in the Long Island. In the shore and in the sea, peat–moss, tree–roots, sessile reeds, stone dykes, dwellings and temples may be seen, while pieces of moss, trees and masonry have been brought up from time to time by hooks and anchors in from ten to twenty fathoms of water. I do not know anything more touching yet more fascinating than these submerged memorials of bygone times and of bygone men.

Immense stretches of sandy plains run along the Atlantic border of the Outer Hebrides. These long reaches of sessile sand are locally called machairs — plains. They are singularly bleak, barren, and shelterless in winter, giving rise to the saying:

Is luath fear na droch mhnatha
Air a mhachair Uibhistich.

Fast goes the man of the thriftless wife
Upon the machair of Uist.

The inference is that the man is ill clad. In summer, however, these "machairs" are green and grassy, comforting to the foot, pleasing to the eye, and deliciously fragrant, being covered with strongly aromatic plants and flowers.

* On Sunday, 21st July 1875, Professor Blackie, Mr William Jolly, and I ascended the hill of Ruaival, in Benbecula. From the summit of this hill, 409 feet high, we had an extensive view of our extraordinary surroundings, striking to the eye and instructive to the mind. On returning home to Creagorry, where we then lived, Professor Blackie wrote the lines composed on Ruaival on the flyleaf of *Burt's Letters,* which he gave to me. The day that Professor Blackie and Mr Jolly were to have left our house some mishap befell their linens, and these had to be rewashed. Mr Jolly alleged that I had bribed the servant in charge of the linens to bring about the accident in order to prolong the stay of our well–beloved guests!

But the charm of these islands lies in their people — goodly to see, brave to endure, and pleasing to know.

The population of the Long Island is about forty–four thousand. Of these, about forty–four families occupy two–thirds of the whole land, the crofters, cottars, and the poor who exist upon the poor, being confined to the remaining third. These are crowded upon one another like sheep in a pen:

Na biasta mor ag itheadh nam biasta beag,
Na biasta beag a deanamh mar dh'fhaodas iad.

The big beasts eating the little beasts,
The little beasts doing as best they may.

There are no intermediate farms, no gradation holdings, to which the industrious crofter might aspire, and become a benefit to himself, an example to his neighbour, and a lever to his country.

The people of the Outer Isles, like the people of the Highlands and Islands generally, are simple and law–abiding, common crime being rare and serious crime unknown among them. They are good to the poor, kind to the stranger, and courteous to all. During all the years that I lived and travelled among them, night and day, I never met with incivility, never with rudeness, never with vulgarity, never with aught but courtesy. I never entered a house without the inmates offering me food or apologising for their want of it. I never was asked for charity in the West, a striking contrast to my experience in England, where I was frequently asked for food, for drink, for money, and that by persons whose incomes would have been wealth to the poor men and women of the West. After long experience of his tenants, the late Mr John Gordon said: "The Uist people are born gentlemen — Nature's noblemen."

Gaelic oral literature was widely diffused, greatly abundant, and excellent in quality — in the opinion of scholars, unsurpassed by anything similar in the ancient classics of Greece or Rome.

Many causes contributed towards these attainments — the crofting system, the social customs, and the evening "ceilidh." In a crofting community the people work in unison in the field during the day, and discuss together in the house at night. This meeting is called "ceilidh" — a word that throbs the heart of the Highlander wherever he be. The "ceilidh" is a literary entertainment where stories and tales, poems and ballads, are rehearsed and recited, and songs are sung, conundrums are put, proverbs are quoted, and many other literary matters are related and discussed. This institution is admirably adapted to cultivate the heads and to warm the hearts of an intelligent, generous people. Let me briefly describe the "ceilidh" as I have seen it.

In a crofting townland there are several story–tellers who recite the oral literature of their predecessors. The story–tellers of the Highlands are as varied in their subjects as are literary men and women elsewhere. One is a historian narrating events simply and concisely; another is a historian with a bias, colouring his narrative according to his leanings. One is an inventor, building fiction upon fact, mingling his materials, and investing the whole with the charm of novelty and the halo of romance. Another is a reciter of heroic poems and ballads, bringing the different characters before the mind as clearly as the sculptor brings the figure before the eye. One gives the songs of the chief poets, with interesting accounts of their authors, while another, generally a woman, sings, to weird airs, beautiful old songs, some of them Arthurian. There are various other narrators, singers, and speakers, but I have never heard aught that should not be said nor sung.

The romance school has the largest following, and I go there, joining others on the way. The house of the story–teller is already full, and it is difficult to get inside and away from the cold wind and soft sleet without. But with that politeness native to the people, the stranger is pressed to come forward and occupy the seat vacated for him beside the houseman. The house is roomy and clean, if homely, with its bright peat fire in the middle of the floor. There are many present — men and women, boys and girls. All the women are seated, and most of the men. Girls are crouched between the knees of fathers or brothers or friends, while boys are perched wherever — boy–like — they can climb. The houseman is twisting twigs of heather into ropes to hold down thatch, a neighbour crofter is twining quicken roots into cords to tie cows, while another is plaiting bent grass into baskets to hold meal.

Ith aran, sniamh muran,
Is bi thu am bliadhn mar bha thu'n uraidh.

Eat bread and twist bent,
And thou this year shalt be as thou wert last.

The housewife is spinning, a daughter is carding, another daughter is teazing, while a third daughter, supposed to be working, is away in the background conversing in low whispers with the son of a neighbouring crofter. Neighbour wives and neighbour daughters are knitting, sewing, or embroidering. The conversation is general: the local news, the weather, the price of cattle, these leading up to higher themes — the clearing of the glens (a sore subject), the war, the parliament, the effects of the sun upon the earth and the moon upon the tides. The speaker is eagerly listened to and is urged to tell more. But he pleads that he came to hear and not to speak, saying:

A chiad sgial air fear an taighe,
Sgial gu la air an aoidh.

The first story from the host,
Story till day from the guest.

The stranger asks the houseman to tell a story, and after a pause the man complies. The tale is full of incident, action, and pathos. It is told simply yet graphically, and at times dramatically — compelling the undivided attention of the listener. At the pathetic scenes and distressful events the bosoms of the women may be seen to heave and their silent tears to fall. Truth overcomes craft, skill conquers strength, and bravery is rewarded. Occasionally a momentary excitement occurs when heat and sleep overpower a boy and he tumbles down among the people below, to be trounced out and sent home. When the story is ended it is discussed and commented upon, and the different characters praised or blamed according to their merits and the views of the critics.

If not late, proverbs, riddles, conundrums, and songs follow. Some of the tales, however, are long, occupying a night or even several nights in recital. *"Sgeul Coise*

Cein," the story of the foot of Cian, for example, was in twenty–four parts, each part occupying a night in telling. The stork is mentioned by Macnicol in his *Remarks* on Johnson's *Tour.*

The hut of Hector Macisaac, Ceannlangavat, South Uist, stood in a peat–moss. The walls were of *riasg,* turf, and the thatch of *cuilc,* reeds, to the grief of the occupants, who looked upon the reed as banned, because it was used on Calvary to convey the sponge with the vinegar. The hut was about fifteen feet long, ten feet broad, and five feet high. There was nothing in it that the vilest thief in the lowest slum would condescend to steal. It were strange if the inmates of this turf hut in the peat–morass had been other than ailing. Hector Macisaac and his wife were the only occupants, their daughter being at service trying to prolong existence in her parents. Both had been highly endowed physically, and were still endowed mentally, though now advanced in years. The wife knew many secular runes, sacred hymns, and fairy songs; while the husband had numerous heroic tales, poems, and ballads.

I had visited these people before, and in September 1871, Iain F. Campbell of Islay and I went to see them. Hector Macisaac, the unlettered cottar who knew no language but his own, who came into contact with no one but those of his own class, his neighbours of the peat–bog, and who had never been out of his native island, was as polite and well–mannered and courteous as Iain Campbell, the learned barrister, the world–wide traveller, and the honoured guest of every court in Europe. Both were at ease and at home with one another, there being neither servility on the one side nor condescension on the other.

The stories and poems which Hector Macisaac went over during our visits to him would have filled several volumes. Mr Campbell now and then put a leading question which brought out the story–teller's marvellous memory and extensive knowledge of folklore.

It was similar with blind old Hector Macleod, cottar, Lianacuithe, South Uist, and with old Roderick Macneill, cottar, Miunghlaidh, Barra. Each of those men repeated stories and poems, tales and ballads, that would have filled many books. Yet neither of them told more than a small part of what he knew. None of the three men knew any letters, nor any language but Gaelic, nor had ever been out of his native island. All expressed regret in well–chosen words that they had not a better place in which to receive their visitors, and all thanked them in polite terms for coming to see them and for taking an interest in their decried and derided old lore. And all were courteous as the courtier.

During his visit to us, Mr Campbell expressed to my wife and to myself his admiration of these and other men with whom we had come in contact. He said that in no other race had he observed so many noble traits and high qualities as in the unlettered, untravelled, unspoiled Highlander.

In 1860, 1861, and 1862, I took down much folklore from Kenneth Morrison, cottar, Trithion, Skye. Kenneth Morrison had been a mason, but was now old, blind, and poor. Though wholly unlettered, he was highly intelligent. He mentioned the names of many old men in the extensive but now desolate parish of Minngnis, who had been famous story–tellers in his boyhood — men who had been born in the first decade of the eighteenth century. Several of these, he said, could recite stories and poems during many nights in succession — some of the tales requiring several nights to relate. He repeated fragments of many of these. Some of them were pieces of poems and stories published by Macpherson, Smith, the Stewarts, the MacCallums, the Campbells, and others.

Kenneth Morrison told me that the old men, from whom he heard the poems and stories, said that they had heard them from old men in their boyhood. That would carry these old men back to the first half of the seventeenth century. Certainly they could not have learnt their stories or poems from books, for neither stories nor poems were printed in their time, and even had they been, those men could not have read them.

Gaelic oral literature has been disappearing during the last three centuries. It is now becoming meagre in quantity, inferior in quality, and greatly isolated.

Several causes have contributed towards this decadence — principally the Reformation, the Risings, the evictions, the Disruption, the schools, and the spirit of the age. Converts in religion, in politics, or in aught else, are apt to be intemperate in speech and rash in action. The Reformation movement condemned the beliefs and cults tolerated and assimilated by the Celtic Church and the Latin Church. Nor did sculpture and architecture escape their intemperate zeal. The risings harried and harassed the people, while the evictions impoverished, dispirited, and scattered them over the world. Ignorant school-teaching and clerical narrowness have been painfully detrimental to the expressive language, wholesome literature, manly sports, and interesting amusements of the Highland people. Innumerable examples occur.

A young lady said: "When we came to Islay I was sent to the parish school to obtain a proper grounding in arithmetic. I was charmed with the schoolgirls and their Gaelic songs. But the schoolmaster — an alien like myself — denounced Gaelic speech and Gaelic songs. On getting out of school one evening the girls resumed a song they had been singing the previous evening. I joined willingly, if timidly, my knowledge of Gaelic being small. The schoolmaster heard us, however, and called us back. He punished us till the blood trickled from our fingers, although we were big girls, with the dawn of womanhood upon us. The thought of that scene thrills me with indignation."

I was taking down a story from a man, describing how twin giants detached a huge stone from the parent rock, and how the two carried the enormous block of many tons upon their broad shoulders to lay it over a deep gully in order that their white-maned steeds might cross. Their enemy, however, came upon them in the night-time when thus engaged, and threw a magic mist around them, lessening their strength and causing them to fail beneath their burden. In the midst of the graphic description the grandson of the narrator, himself an aspirant teacher, called out in tones of superior authority: "Grandfather, the teacher says that you ought to be placed upon the stool for your lying Gaelic stories." The old man stopped and gasped in pained surprise. It required time and sympathy to soothe his feelings and to obtain the rest of the tale, which was wise, beautiful, and poetic, for the big, strong giants were Frost and Ice, and their subtle enemy was Thaw. The enormous stone torn from the parent rock is called "Clach Mhor Leum nan Caorach," the big stone of the leap of the sheep. Truly "a little learning is a dangerous thing"! This myth was afterwards appreciated by the Royal Society of Edinburgh.

After many failures, and after going far to reach him, I induced a man to come to the lee of a knoll to tell me a tale. We were well into the spirit of the story when two men from the hill passed us. The story–teller hesitated, then stopped, saying that he would be reproved by his family, bantered by his friends, and censured by his minister. The story, so inauspiciously interrupted and never resumed, was the famous *"Sgeul Coise Cein,"* already mentioned.

Having made many attempts, I at last succeeded in getting a shepherd to come to me, in order to be away from his surroundings. The man travelled fifty–five miles, eight of these being across a stormy strait of the Atlantic. We had reached the middle of a tale when the sheriff of the district came to call on me in my rooms. The reciter fled, and after going more than a mile on his way home he met a man who asked him why he looked so scared, and why without his bonnet. The shepherd discovered that he had left his bonnet, his plaid, and his staff behind him in his flight. The remaining half of that fine story, as well as much other valuable Gaelic lore, died with the shepherd in Australia.

Ministers of Lewis used to say that the people of Lewis were little better than pagans till the Reformation, perhaps till the Disruption. If they were not, they have atoned since, being now the most rigid Christians in the British Isles.

When Dr William Forbes Skene was preparing the third volume of *Celtic Scotland,* he asked me to write him a paper on the native system of holding the land, tilling the soil, and apportioning the stock in the Outer Hebrides. Being less familiar with Lewis than with the other portions of the Long Island, I visited Lewis again. It was with extreme difficulty that I could obtain any information on the subject of my inquiry, because it related to the foolish past rather than to the sedate present, to the secular affairs rather than to the religious life of the people. When I asked about old customs and old modes of working, I was answered: "Good man, old things are passed away, all things are become new"; for the people of Lewis, like the people of the Highlands and Islands generally, carry the Scriptures in their minds and apply them in their speech as no other people do. It was extremely disconcerting to be met in this manner on a mission so desirable.

During my quest I went into a house near Ness. The house was clean and comfortable if plain and unpretending, most things in it being home–made. There were three girls in the house, young, comely, and shy, and four women, middle–aged, handsome, and picturesque in their homespun gowns and high–crowned mutches. Three of the women had been to the moorland pastures with their cattle, and had turned in here to rest on their way home.

"Hail to the house and household," said I, greeting the inmates in the salutation of our fathers.

"Hail to you, kindly stranger," replied the housewife. "Come forward and take this seat. If it be not ill–mannered, may we ask whence you have come to–day? You are tired and travel–stained and probably hungry?"

"I have come from Gress," said I, "round by Tolasta to the south, and Tolasta to the north, taking a look at the ruins of the Church of St Aula, at Gress, and at the ruins of the fort of Dunothail, and then across the moorland."

"May the Possessor keep you in His own keeping, good man! You left early and have travelled far, and must be hungry." With this the woman raised her eyes towards her daughters standing demurely silent, and motionless Greek statues, in the background. In a moment the three fair girls became active and animated. One ran to the stack and brought in an armful of hard, black peats, another ran to the well and brought in a pail of clear spring water, while the third quickly spread a cloth, white as snow, upon the table in the inner room. The three neighbour women rose to leave, and I rose to do the same.

"Where are you going, good man?" asked the housewife in injured surprise, moving between me and the door. "You must not go till you eat a bit and drink a sip. That indeed would be a reproach to us that we would not soon get over. These slips of lassies and I would not hear the end of it from the men at the sea, were we to allow a wayfarer to go from our door hungry, thirsty, and weary. No! no! you must not go till you eat a bite. Food will be ready presently, and in the meantime you will bathe your feet and dry your stockings, which are wet after coming through the marshes of the moorland."

Then the woman went down upon her knees, and washed and dried the feet of the stranger as gently and tenderly as a mother would those of her child.

"We have no stockings to suit the kilt," said the woman in a tone of evident regret, "but here is a pair of stockings of the houseman's which he has never had on, and perhaps you would put them on till your own are dry."

One of the girls had already washed out my stockings, and they were presently drying before the bright fire on the middle of the floor. I deprecated all this trouble, but to no purpose. In an incredibly short time I was asked to go "ben" and break bread.

Through the pressure of the housewife and of myself the other three women had resumed their seats, uneasily it is true. But immediately before food was announced the three women rose together and quietly walked away, no urging detaining them.

The table was laden with wholesome food sufficient for several persons. There were fried herrings and boiled turbot fresh from the sea, and eggs fresh from the yard. There were fresh butter and salt butter, wheaten scones, barley bannocks, and oat cakes, with excellent tea, and cream. The woman apologised that she had no *aran coinnich* — moss bread, that is, loaf bread — and no biscuits, they being simple crofter people far away from the big town.

"This," said I, taking my seat, "looks like the table for a *reiteach,* betrothal, rather than for one man. Have you betrothals in Lewis?" I asked, turning my eyes towards the other room where we had left the three comely maidens.

"Oh, indeed, yes, the Lewis people are very good at marrying. Foolish young creatures, they often marry before they know their responsibilities or realise their difficulties," and her eyes followed mine in the direction of her own young daughters.

"I suppose there is much fun and rejoicing at your marriages — music, dancing, singing, and merry-making of many kinds?"

"Oh, indeed, no, our weddings are now quiet and becoming, not the foolish things they were in my young days. In my memory weddings were great events, with singing and piping, dancing and amusements all night through, and generally for two and three nights in succession. Indeed, the feast of the *bord breid,* kertch table, was almost as great as the feast of the marriage table, all the young men and maidens struggling to get to it. On the morning after the marriage the mother of the bride, and failing her the mother of the bridegroom, placed the *breid tri chearnach,* three-cornered kertch, on the head of the bride before she rose from her bed. And the mother did this *an ainm na Teoire Beannaichte,* in name of the

Sacred Three, under whose guidance the young wife was to walk. Then the bride arose and her maidens dressed her, and she came forth with the *breid beannach,* pointed kertch, on her head, and all the people present saluted her and shook hands with her, and the bards sang songs to her, and recited *rannaghail mhora,* great rigmaroles, and there was much rejoicing and merrymaking all day long and all night through. *Gu dearbh mar a b'e fleadh na bord breid a b'fhearr, chan e gearr bu mheasa* — Indeed, if the feast of the kertch table was not better, it was not a whit worse.

"There were many sad things done then, for those were the days of foolish doings and of foolish people. Perhaps, on the day of the Lord, when they came out of church, if indeed they went into church, the young men would go to throw the stone, or to toss the cabar, or to play shinty, or to run races, or to race horses on the strand, the young maidens looking on the while, ay, and the old men and women."

"And have you no music, no singing, no dancing now at your marriages?"

"May the Possessor keep you! I see that you are a stranger in Lewis, or you would not ask such a question," the woman exclaimed with grief and surprise in her tone. "It is long since we abandoned those foolish ways in Ness, and, indeed, throughout Lewis. In my young days there was hardly a house in Ness in which there was not one or two or three who could play the pipe, or the fiddle, or the trump. And I have heard it said that there were men, and women too, who could play things they called harps, and lyres, and bellow–pipes, but I do not know what those things were."

"And why were those discontinued?"

"A blessed change came over the place and the people," the woman replied in earnestness, "and the good men and the good ministers who arose did away with the songs and the stories, the music and the dancing, the sports and the games, that were perverting the minds and ruining the souls of the people, leading them to folly and stumbling."

"But how did the people themselves come to discard their sports and pastimes?"

"Oh, the good ministers and the good elders preached against them and went among the people, and besought them to forsake their follies and to return to wisdom. They made the people break and burn their pipes and fiddles. If there was a foolish man here and there who demurred, the good ministers and the good elders themselves broke and burnt their instruments, saying:

Is fearr an teine beag a gharas la beag na sithe,
Na'n teine mor a loisgeas la mor na feirge.

Better is the small fire that warms on the little day of peace,
Than the big fire that burns on the great day of wrath.

"The people have forsaken their follies and their Sabbath–breaking, and there is no pipe, no fiddle here now," said the woman in evident satisfaction.

"And what have you now instead of the racing, the stone–throwing, and the cabar–tossing, the song, the pipe, and the dance?"

"Oh, we have now the blessed Bible preached and explained to us faithfully and earnestly, if we sinful people would only walk in the right path and use our opportunities."

"But what have you at your weddings? How do you pass the time?"

"Oh! the carles are on one side of the house talking of their crops and their nowt, and mayhap of the days when they were young and when things were different. And the young men are on the other side of the house talking about boats, and sailing, and militia, and naval reserve, perhaps of their own strength, and of many foolish matters besides.

"And where are the girls? What are they doing?"

"Oh, they, silly things! are in the *culaist,* back-house, perhaps trying to croon over some foolish song under their breath, perhaps trying to amble through some awkward steps of dancing on the points of their toes, or, shame to tell, perhaps speaking of what dress this or that girl had on at this or that marriage, or worse still, what hat this girl or that girl had on on the Day of the Lord, perhaps even on the Day of the Holy Communion, showing that their minds were on the vain things of the world instead of on the wise things of salvation."

"But why are the girls in the *culaist*? What do they fear?"

"May the Good Being keep you, good man! They are in the *culaist* for concealment, *agus eagal am beatha agus am bais orra gun cluinnear no gum faicear iad* — and the fear of their life and of their death upon them, that they may be heard or seen should the good elder happen to be passing the way."

"And should he, what then?"

"Oh, the elder will tell the minister, and the good minister will scold them from the pulpit, mentioning the girls by name. But the girls have a blanket on the door and another blanket on the window to deafen the sound and to obscure the light."

"Do the young maidens allow the young men to join them in the *culaist?*"

"Indeed, truth to tell, the maidens would be glad enough to admit the young men were it not the fear of exposure. But the young men are so loud of voice, and so heavy of foot, and make so much noise, that they would betray the retreat of the girls, who would get rebuked, while the young men would escape. The girls would then be ashamed and downcast, and would not lift a head for a year and a day after their well-deserved scolding. They suffer most, for, sad to say, the young men are becoming less afraid of being admonished than they used to be."

"And do the people have spirits at their marriages?"

"Oh yes, the minister is not so hard as that upon them at all. He does not interfere with them in that way unless they take too much, and talk loudly and quarrel. Then he is grieved and angry, and scolds them severely. Occasionally, indeed, some of the carles have a nice *frogan,* liveliness, upon them and are very happy together. But oh, they never quarrel, nor fight, nor get angry with one another. They are always nice to one another and civil to all around them."

"Perhaps were the minister to allow the people less drink and more music and dancing, singing and merry-making, they would enjoy it as much. I am sure the young girls would sing better, and dance better, with the help of the young men. And the young men themselves would be less loud of voice and less heavy of heel, among the maidens. Perhaps the happiness of the old people too, would be none the less real nor less lasting at seeing the joyousness of the young people."

To this the woman promptly and loyally replied: "The man of the Lord is untiring in work and unfailing in example for our good, and in guiding us to our heavenly home, constantly reminding us of the littleness of time and the greatness of eternity, and he knows best, and we must do our best to follow his counsel and to imitate his example."

A famous violin-player died in the island of Eigg a few years ago. He was known for his old style playing and his old-world airs which died with him. A preacher denounced him, saying: "Thou art down there behind the door, thou miserable man with thy grey hair, playing thine old fiddle with the cold hand without, and the devil's fire within."

His family pressed the man to burn his fiddle and never to play again. A pedlar came round and offered ten shillings for the violin. The instrument had been made by a pupil of Stradivarius, and was famed for its tone.

"It was not at all the thing that was got for it that grieved my heart so sorely, but the parting with it! the parting with it! and that I myself gave the best cow in my father's fold for it when I was young." The voice of the old man faltered and a tear fell. He was never again seen to smile.

The reciters of religious lore were more rare and more reticent than the reciters of secular lore. Men and women whom I knew had hymns and incantations, but I did not know of this in time. The fragments recalled by their families, like the fragments of Greek or Etruscan vases, indicated the originals.

Before dictating, the reciter went over the tale or poem, the writer making mental notes the while. This was helpful when, in the slow process of dictating, the narrator lost his thread and omitted passages. The poems were generally intoned in a low recitative manner, rising and falling in slow modulated cadences charming to hear but difficult to follow.

The music of the hymns had a distinct individuality, in some respects resembling and in many respects differing from the old Gregorian chants of the Church. I greatly regret that I was not able to record this peculiar and beautiful music, probably the music of the old Celtic Church.

Perhaps no people had a fuller ritual of song and story, of secular rite and religious ceremony, than the Highlanders. Mirth and music, song and dance, tale and poem, pervaded their lives, as electricity pervades the air. Religion, pagan or Christian, or both combined, permeated everything — blending and shading into one another like the iridescent colours of the rainbow. The people were sympathetic and synthetic, unable to see and careless to know where the secular began and the religious ended — an admirable union of elements in life for those who have lived it so truly and intensely as the Celtic races everywhere have done, and none more truly or more intensely than the ill-understood and so-called illiterate Highlanders of Scotland.

If this work does nothing else, it affords incontestable proof that the Northern Celts were endowed, as Renan justly claims for Celts everywhere, with "profound feeling and adorable delicacy" in their religious instincts.*

The Celtic missionaries allowed the pagan stock to stand, grafting their Christian cult thereon. Hence the blending of the pagan and the Christian religions in these poems, which to many minds will constitute their chief charm. Gaelic lore is full of

* *Poetry of the Celtic Races, and Other Studies.* Ernest Renan.

this blending and grafting — nor are they confined to the literature of the people, but extend indeed to their music, sculpture, and architecture. At Rodail, Harris, is a cruciform church of the thirteenth century. The church abuts upon a broad square tower of no great height. The tower is called *Tur Chliamain,* tower of Clement (Great Clement of Rodail). Tradition says that the tower is older than the church, and the masonry confirms the tradition.

There are sculptures within the church of much originality of design and of great beauty of execution, but the sculptures without are still more original and interesting. Round the sides of the square tower are the figures of birds and beasts, reptiles and fishes, and of men and women representing phallic worship. Here pagan cult joins with Christian faith, the East with the West, the past with the present. The traveller from India to Scotland can here see, on the cold, sterile rocks of Harris, the petrified symbols of a faith left living behind him on the hot, fertile plains of Hindustan. He can thus in his own person bridge over a space of eight thousand miles and a period of two thousand years.

There are observances and expressions current in the West which savour of the East, such as sun, moon, star, and fire worship, once prevalent, nor yet obsolete.

Highland divinities are full of life and action, local colour and individuality. These divinities filled the hearts and minds of the people of the Highlands, as their deities filled the hearts and minds of the people of Greece and Rome. The subject of these genii of the Highlands ought to be investigated and compared with those of other lands. Even yet, on the verge of disappearance, they would yield interesting results. Though loving their haunts and tenacious of their habitats, the genii of the Highlands are disappearing before the spirit of modernism, as the Red Indian, once bold and courageous, disappears before the white man. Once intrusive, they are now become timid as the mullet of the sea, the shrew of the grass, or the swift of the air — a glimpse, a glint, and gone for ever. They are startled at the crack of the rifle, the whistle of the steamer, the shriek of the train, and the click of the telegraph. Their homes are invaded and their repose is disturbed, so that they find no rest for their weary feet nor sleep for their heavy eyes; and their native land, so full of their love, so congenial to their hearts, will all too soon know them no more. Let an attempt be made even yet to preserve their memories ere they disappear for ever.

Whatever be the value of this work, it is genuine folklore, taken down from the lips of men and women, no part being copied from books. It is the product of faraway thinking, come down on the long stream of time. Who the thinkers and whence the stream, who can tell? Some of the hymns may have been composed within the cloistered cells of Derry and Iona, and some of the incantations among the cromlechs of Stonehenge and the standing-stones of Callarnis. These poems were composed by the learned, but they have not come down through the learned, but through the unlearned — not through the lettered few, but through the unlettered many — through the crofters and cottars, the herdsmen and shepherds, of the Highlands and Islands.

Although these compositions have been rescued chiefly among Roman Catholics and in the islands, they have been equally common among Protestants and on the mainland.

From one to ten versions have been taken down, differing more or less. It has been difficult to select. Some examples of these variants are given. Several poems and many notes are wholly withheld, while a few of the poems and all the notes have been abbreviated for want of space.

I had the privilege of being acquainted with Iain F. Campbell of Islay during a quarter of a century, and I have followed his counsel and imitated his example in giving the words and in recording the names of the reciters. Some localisms are given for the sake of Gaelic scholars. Hence the same word may be spelt in different ways through the influence of assonance and other characteristics of Gaelic compositions.

With each succeeding generation Gaelic speech becomes more limited and Gaelic phraseology more obscure. Both reciter and writer felt this when words and phrases occurred which neither knew. These have been rendered tentatively or left untranslated. I can only hope that in the near or distant future some competent scholar may compare these gleanings of mine with Celtic writings at home and abroad, and that light may be shed upon what is to me obscure.

I have tried to translate literally yet satisfactorily, but I am painfully conscious of failures. Although in decay, these poems are in verse of a high order, with metre, rhythm, assonance, alliteration, and every quality to please the ear and to instruct the mind. The translation lacks these and the simple dignity, the charming grace, and the passionate devotion of the original. I see faults that I would willingly mend, but it is easier to point to blemishes than to avoid them:

Is furasda dh'an fhear eisdeachd
Beum a thoir dh'an fhear labhairt.

It is easy for the listening man
To give taunt to the speaking man.

Again and again I laid down my self-imposed task, feeling unable to render the intense power and supreme beauty of the original Gaelic into adequate English. But I resumed under the inspiring influence of my wife, to whose unfailing sympathy and cultured ear this work owes much.

My daughter has transcribed the manuscripts and corrected the proofs for press, and has acted as amanuensis throughout; while my three sons have helped in various ways.

The Celtic letters in the work have been copied by my wife from Celtic MSS, chiefly in the Advocates' Library. This has been a task of extreme difficulty, needing great skill and patient care owing to the defaced condition of the originals. The letters have been prepared for the engraver with feeling and insight by Mr John Athel Lovegrove, of H.M. Ordnance Survey.

The Rev Father Allan Macdonald, Eriskay, South Uist, generously placed at my disposal a collection of religious folklore made by himself. For this I am very grateful though unable to use the manuscript, having so much material of my own.

Mr John Henry Dixon, Inveran, Lochmaree, offered to publish the work at his own expense. That I have not availed myself of his generous appreciation does not lessen my gratitude for Mr Dixon's characteristic liberality.

My dear friend Mr George Henderson, M.A. Edin., Ph.D. Leipzig, B.Litt. Oxon., has helped and encouraged me throughout.

These, and the many others whose names I am unable to mention through want of space, I ask to accept my warm, abiding thanks.

Three sacrifices have been made — the sacrifice of time, the sacrifice of toil, and the sacrifice of means. These I do not regret. I have three regrets — that I had not been earlier collecting, that I have not been more diligent in collecting, and that I am not better qualified to treat what I have collected.

These notes and poems have been an education to me. And so have been the men and women reciters from whose dictation I wrote them down. They are almost all dead now, leaving no successors. With reverent hand and grateful heart I place this stone upon the cairn of those who composed and of those who transmitted the work.

Alexander Carmichael
Edinburgh, St Michael's Day, 1899

Carmina Gadelica

Invocations

1 Rune before prayer

I am bending my knee
In the eye of the Father who created me,
In the eye of the Son who purchased me,
In the eye of the Spirit who cleansed me,
  In friendship and affection.
Through Thine own Anointed One, O God,
Bestow upon us fullness in our need,
    Love towards God,
    The affection of God,
    The smile of God,
    The wisdom of God,
    The grace of God,
    The fear of God,
    And the will of God
To do on the world of the Three,
As angels and saints
Do in heaven;
  Each shade and light,
  Each day and night,
  Each time in kindness,
  Give Thou us Thy Spirit.

2 God with me lying down

God with me lying down,
God with me rising up,
God with me in each ray of light,
Nor I a ray of joy without Him,
  Nor one ray without Him.

Christ with me sleeping,
Christ with me waking,
Christ with me watching,
Every day and night,
  Each day and night.

God with me protecting,
The Lord with me directing,
The Spirit with me strengthening,
For ever and for evermore,
  Ever and evermore, Amen.
    Chief of chiefs, Amen.

3 The invocation of the graces

I bathe thy palms
In showers of wine,
In the lustral fire,
In the seven elements,
In the juice of the rasps,
In the milk of honey,
And I place the nine pure choice graces
In thy fair fond face,
  The grace of form,
  The grace of voice,
  The grace of fortune,
  The grace of goodness,
  The grace of wisdom,
  The grace of charity,

The grace of choice maidenliness,
The grace of whole-souled loveliness,
The grace of goodly speech.

Dark is yonder town,
Dark are those therein,
Thou art the brown swan,
Going in among them.
Their hearts are under thy control,
Their tongues are beneath thy sole,
Nor will they ever utter a word
To give thee offence.

A shade art thou in the heat,
A shelter art thou in the cold,
Eyes art thou to the blind,
A staff art thou to the pilgrim,
An island art thou at sea,
A fortress art thou on land,
A well art thou in the desert,
Health art thou to the ailing.

Thine is the skill of the Fairy Woman,
Thine is the virtue of Bride the calm,
Thine is the faith of Mary the mild,
Thine is the tact of the woman of Greece,
Thine is the beauty of Emir the lovely,
Thine is the tenderness of Darthula delightful,
Thine is the courage of Maebh the strong,
Thine is the charm of Binne-bheul.

Thou art the joy of all joyous things,
Thou art the light of the beam of the sun,
Thou art the door of the chief of hospitality,
Thou art the surpassing star of guidance,
Thou art the step of the deer of the hill,
Thou art the step of the steed of the plain,
Thou art the grace of the swan of swimming,
Thou art the loveliness of all lovely desires.

The lovely likeness of the Lord
Is in thy pure face,
The loveliest likeness that
Was upon earth.

The best hour of the day be thine,
The best day of the week be thine,
The best week of the year be thine,
The best year in the Son of God's domain be thine.

Peter has come and Paul has come,
James has come and John has come,
Muriel and Mary Virgin have come,
Uriel the all-beneficent has come,
Ariel the beauteousness of the young has come,
Gabriel the seer of the Virgin has come,
Raphael the prince of the valiant has come,
And Michael the chief of the hosts has come,
And Jesus Christ the mild has come,
And the Spirit of true guidance has come,
And the King of kings has come on the helm,
To bestow on thee their affection and their love,
To bestow on thee their affection and their love.

4 A general supplication

God, listen to my prayer,
Bend to me Thine ear,
Let my supplications and my prayers
Ascend to Thee upwards.
Come, Thou King of Glory,
To protect me down,
Thou King of life and mercy
With the aid of the Lamb,
Thou Son of Mary Virgin
To protect me with power,
Thou Son of the lovely Mary
Of purest fairest beauty.

5 God be with us

God be with us
On this Thy day,
    Amen.
God be with us
On this Thy night,
    Amen.
To us and with us,
On this Thy day,
    Amen.
To us and with us,
On this Thy night,
    Amen.
It is clear to be seen of us,
Since we came into the world,
That we have deserved Thy wrath,
    Amen.
O Thine own wrath,
Thou God of all,
    Amen.
Grant us forgiveness,
    Amen.
Grant us forgiveness,
    Amen.
Grant to us Thine own forgiveness,
Thou merciful God of all,
    Amen.
Anything that is evil to us,
Or that may witness against us
Where we shall longest be,
Illume it to us,
Obscure it to us,
Banish it from us,
Root it out of our hearts,
Ever, evermore, everlastingly.
  Ever, evermore, everlastingly.
    Amen.

6 Jesu, Thou Son of Mary

Jesu, Thou Son of Mary,
Have mercy upon us,
    Amen.
Jesu, Thou Son of Mary,
Make peace with us,
    Amen.
Oh, with us and for us
Where we shall longest be,
    Amen.
Be about the morning of our course,
Be about the closing of our life,
    Amen.
Be at the dawning of our life,
And oh! at the dark'ning of our day,
    Amen.
Be for us and with us,
Merciful God of all,
    Amen.
Consecrate us
Condition and lot,
Thou King of kings,
Thou God of all,
    Amen.
Consecrate us
Rights and means,
Thou King of kings,
Thou God of all,
    Amen.
Consecrate us
Heart and body,
Thou King of kings,
Thou God of all,
    Amen.
Each heart and body,
Each day to Thyself,
Each night accordingly,

Thou King of kings,
Thou God of all,
Amen.

7 Holy Father of glory

Thanks be to Thee, Holy Father of glory,
Father kind, ever–loving, ever–powerful,
Because of all the abundance, favour, and deliverance
That Thou bestowest upon us in our need.
Whatever providence befalls us as thy children,
In our portion, in our lot, in our path,
Give to us with it the rich gifts of Thine hand
And the joyous blessing of Thy mouth.

We are guilty and polluted, O God,
In spirit, in heart, and in flesh,
In thought, in word, in act,
We are hard in Thy sight in sin.
Put Thou forth to us the power of Thy love,
Be thou leaping over the mountains of our transgressions,
And wash us in the true blood of conciliation,
Like the down of the mountains, like the lily of the lake.

In the steep common path of our calling,
Be it easy or uneasy to our flesh,
Be it bright or dark for us to follow,
Thine own perfect guidance be upon us.
Be Thou a shield to us from the wiles of the deceiver,
From the arch–destroyer with his arrows pursuing us,
And in each secret thought our minds get to weave,
Be Thou Thyself on our helm and at our sheet.

Though dogs and thieves would reive us from the fold,
Be Thou the valiant Shepherd of glory near us.
Whatever matter or cause or propensity

That would bring to us grief, or pains, or wounds,
Or that would bear witness against us at the last,
On the other side of the great river of dark shadows,
Oh! do Thou obscure it from our eyes,
And from our hearts drive it for ever.

Now to the Father who created each creature,
Now to the Son who paid ransom for His people,
Now to the Holy Spirit, Comforter of might:
Shield and sain us from every wound;
Be about the beginning and end of our race,
Be giving us to sing in glory,
In peace, in rest, in reconciliation,
Where no tear shall be shed, where death comes no more.
Where no tear shall be shed, where death comes no more.

8 A prayer

O God,
In my deeds,
In my words,
In my wishes,
In my reason,
And in the fulfilling of my desires,
In my sleep,
In my dreams,
In my repose,
In my thoughts,
In my heart and soul always,
May the blessed Virgin Mary,
And the promised Branch of Glory dwell.
Oh! in my heart and soul always,
May the blessed Virgin Mary,
And the fragrant Branch of Glory dwell.

9 Rune of the *muthairn**

Thou King of the moon,
Thou King of the sun,
Thou King of the planets,
Thou King of the stars,
Thou King of the globe,
Thou King of the sky,
Oh! lovely Thy countenance,
Thou beauteous Beam.

Two loops of silk
Down by thy limbs,
Smooth-skinned;
Yellow jewels
And a handful
Out of every stock of them.

10 Bless, O Chief of generous chiefs

Bless, O Chief of generous chiefs,
Myself and everything anear me,
Bless me in all my actions,
Make Thou me safe for ever,
Make Thou me safe for ever.

From every brownie and ban-shee,
From every evil wish and sorrow,
From every nymph and water-wraith,
From every fairy-mouse and grass-mouse,
From every fairy-mouse and grass-mouse.

From every troll among the hills,
From every siren hard pressing me,
From every ghoul within the glens,
Oh! save me till the end of my day.
Oh! save me till the end of my day.

* Little mother, dear little mother.

11 The guiding light of eternity

O God, who broughtst me from the rest of last night
Unto the joyous light of this day,
Be Thou bringing me from the new light of this day
Unto the guiding light of eternity.
　Oh! from the new light of this day
　Unto the guiding light of eternity.

12 A prayer for grace

I am bending my knee
In the eye of the Father who created me,
In the eye of the Son who died for me,
In the eye of the Spirit who cleansed me,
　In love and desire.

Pour down upon us from heaven
The rich blessing of Thy forgiveness;
Thou who art uppermost in the City,
　Be Thou patient with us.

Grant to us, Thou Saviour of Glory,
The fear of God, the love of God, and His affection,
And the will of God to do on earth at all times
As angels and saints do in heaven;
Each day and night give us Thy peace.
　Each day and night give us Thy peace.

13 Prayer for protection

As Thou art the Shepherd over the flock
Tend Thou us to the cot and the fold,
Sain us beneath Thine own glorious mantle;
　Thou Shield of protection, guard us for ever.

Be Thou a hard triumphant glave
To shield us securely from wicked hell,
From the fiends and from the stieve snell gullies,
   And from the lurid smoke of the abyss.

Be my soul in the trustance of the High King,
Be Michael the powerful meeting my soul.

14 Jesu who ought to be praised

It were as easy for Jesu
To renew the withered tree
As to wither the new
Were it His will so to do.
   Jesu! Jesu! Jesu!
   Jesu! meet it were to praise Him.

There is no plant in the ground
But is full of His virtue,
There is no form in the strand
But is full of His blessing.
   Jesu! Jesu! Jesu!
   Jesu! meet it were to praise Him.

There is no life in the sea,
There is no creature in the river,
There is naught in the firmament,
But proclaims His goodness.
   Jesu! Jesu! Jesu!
   Jesu! meet it were to praise Him.

There is no bird on the wing,
There is no star in the sky,
There is nothing beneath the sun,
But proclaims His goodness.
   Jesu! Jesu! Jesu!
   Jesu! meet it were to praise Him.

15 The Rock of rocks

On the Rock of rocks,
The peace of Peter and Paul,
Of James and John the beloved,
And of the pure perfect Virgin,
  The pure perfect Virgin.

The peace of the Father of joy,
The peace of the Christ of pasch,
The peace of the Spirit of grace,
To ourselves and to our children,
  Ourselves and our children.

16 The Lightener of the stars

Behold the Lightener of the stars
On the crests of the clouds,
And the choralists of the sky
  Lauding Him.

Coming down with acclaim
From the Father above,
Harp and lyre of song
  Sounding to Him.

Christ, Thou refuge of my love,
Why should not I raise Thy fame!
Angels and saints melodious
  Singing to Thee.

Thou Son of the Mary of graces,
Of exceeding white purity of beauty,
Joy were it to me to be in the fields
  Of Thy riches.

O Christ my beloved,
O Christ of the Holy Blood,
By day and by night
  I praise Thee.

17 The cross of the saints and the angels

The cross of the saints and of the angels with me
From the top of my face to the edge of my soles.

O Michael mild, O Mary of glory,
O gentle Bride of the locks of gold,
Preserve ye me in the weakly body,
The three preserve me on the just path.
Oh! three preserve me on the just path.

Preserve ye me in the soul–shrine poor,
Preserve ye me, and I so weak and naked,
Preserve ye me without offence on the way,
The preservation of the three upon me tonight.
Oh! the three to shield me tonight.

18 The guardian angel

Thou angel of God who hast charge of me
From the dear Father of mercifulness,
The shepherding kind of the fold of the saints
To make round about me this night.

Drive from me every temptation and danger,
Surround me on the sea of unrighteousness,
And in the narrows, crooks, and straits,
Keep thou my coracle, keep it always.

Be thou a bright flame before me,
Be thou a guiding star above me,
Be thou a smooth path below me,
And be a kindly shepherd behind me,
Today, tonight, and for ever.

I am tired and I a stranger,
Lead thou me to the land of angels;
For me it is time to go home
To the court of Christ, to the peace of heaven.

19 Desires

May I speak each day according to Thy justice,
Each day may I show Thy chastening, O God;
May I speak each day according to Thy wisdom,
Each day and night may I be at peace with Thee.

Each day may I count the causes of Thy mercy,
May I each day give heed to Thy laws;
Each day may I compose to Thee a song,
May I harp each day Thy praise, O God.

May I each day give love to Thee, Jesu,
Each night may I do the same;
Each day and night, dark and light,
May I laud Thy goodness to me, O God.

20 Invocation for justice

I will wash my face
In the nine rays of the sun,
As Mary washed her Son
In the rich fermented milk.

Love be in my countenance,
Benevolence in my mind,
Dew of honey in my tongue,
My breath as the incense.

Black is yonder town,
Black are those therein,
I am the white swan,
Queen above them.

I will travel in the name of God,
In likeness of deer, in likeness of horse,
In likeness of serpent, in likeness of king:
Stronger will it be with me than with all persons.

21 Invocation for justice

God, I am bathing my face
In the nine rays of the sun,
As Mary bathed her Son
  In generous milk fermented.

Sweetness be in my face,
Riches be in my countenance,
Comb–honey be in my tongue,
  My breath as the incense.

Black is yonder house,
Blacker men therein;
I am the white swan,
  Queen over them.

I will go in the name of God,
In likeness of deer, in likeness of horse,
In likeness of serpent, in likeness of king,
  More victorious am I than all persons.

22 Prayer for victory

I bathe my face
In the nine rays of the sun,
As Mary bathed her Son
  In the rich fermented milk.

Honey be in my mouth,
Affection be in my face;
The love that Mary gave her Son
  Be in the heart of all flesh for me.

All–seeing, all–hearing, all–inspiring may God be,
To satisfy and to strengthen me;
Blind, deaf, and dumb, ever, ever be
  My contemners and my mockers.

The tongue of Columba in my head,
The eloquence of Columba in my speech;
The composure of the Victorious Son of grace
  Be mine in presence of the multitude.

23 The lustration

I am bathing my face
In the mild rays of the sun,
As Mary bathed Christ
In the rich milk of Egypt.

Sweetness be in my mouth,
Wisdom be in my speech,
The love the fair Mary gave her Son
Be in the heart of all flesh for me.

The love of Christ in my breast,
The form of Christ protecting me,
There is not in sea nor on land
That can overcome the King of the Lord's Day.

The hand of Bride about my neck,
The hand of Mary about my breast,
The hand of Michael laving me,
The hand of Christ saving me.

24 Bathing prayer

A palmful for thine age,
  A palmful for thy growth,
A palmful for thy throat,
  A flood for thine appetite.

For thy share of the dainty,
  Crowdie and kail;
For thy share of the taking,
  Honey and warm milk.

For thy share of the supping,
   Whisked whey and milk–product;
For thy share of the spoil,
   With bow and with spear.

For thy share of the preparation,
   The yellow eggs of Easter;
For thy share of the treat,
   My treasure and my joy.

For thy share of the feast
   With gifts and with tribute;
For thy share of the treasure,
   Pulset of my love.

For thy share of the chase
Up the face of the Beinn–a–cheo;*
For thy share of the hunting
   And the ruling over hosts.

For thy share of palaces,
In the courts of kings;
For thy share of Paradise
   With its goodness and its peace.

The part of thee that does not grow at dawn,
May it grow at eventide;
The part of thee that does not grow at night,
   May it grow at ridge of middle–day.

   The three palmfuls
   Of the Secret Three,
   To preserve thee
   From every envy,
   Evil eye and death;
   The palmful of the God of Life,
   The palmful of the Christ of Love,
   The palmful of the Spirit of Peace,
      Triune
      Of Grace.

* Mount of mist. Probably a particular name and not a general term.

25 God guide me

God guide me with Thy wisdom,
God chastise me with Thy justice,
God help me with Thy mercy,
God protect me with Thy strength.

God fill me with Thy fullness,
God shield me with Thy shade,
God fill me with Thy grace,
For the sake of Thine Anointed Son.

Jesu Christ of the seed of David,
Visiting One of the Temple,
Sacrificial Lamb of the Garden,
Who died for me.

26 Sleep blessing

Be Thy right hand, O God, under my head,
Be Thy light, O Spirit, over me shining.
And be the cross of the nine angels over me down,
From the crown of my head to the soles of my feet,
From the crown of my head to the soles of my feet.

O Jesu without offence, crucified cruelly,
Under ban of the wicked Thou wert scourged,
The many evils done of me in the body!
That I cannot this night enumerate,
That I cannot this night enumerate.

O Thou Ring of the blood of truth,
Cast me not from Thy covenant,
Exact not from me for my transgressions,
Nor omit me in Thy numbering,
Nor omit me in Thy numbering.

Be the cross of Mary and of Michael over me in peace,
Be my soul dwelling in truth, be my heart free of guile,
Be my soul in peace with thee, Brightness of the mountains.
Valiant Michael, meet thou my soul,
  Morn and eve, day and night. May it be so.

27 Come I this day

Come I this day to the Father,
Come I this day to the Son,
Come I to the Holy Spirit powerful;
Come I this day with God,
Come I this day with Christ,
Come I with the Spirit of kindly balm.

God, and Spirit, and Jesus,
From the crown of my head
To the soles of my feet;
Come I with my reputation,
Come I with my testimony,
Come I to Thee, Jesu;
  Jesu, shelter me.

28 The soul plaint

O Jesu! tonight,
Thou Shepherd of the poor,
Thou sinless person
Who didst suffer full sore,
By ban of the wicked,
And wast crucified.

Save me from evil,
Save me from harm,
Save Thou my body,
Sanctify me tonight,
O Jesu! tonight,
Nor leave me.

Endow me with strength,
Thou Herdsman of might,
Guide me aright,
Guide me in Thy strength,
O Jesu! in Thy strength
Preserve me.

29 Sleeping prayer

I am placing my soul and my body
On Thy sanctuary this night, O God,
On Thy sanctuary, O Jesus Christ,
On Thy sanctuary, O Spirit of perfect truth;
The Three who would defend my cause,
Nor turn Their backs upon me.

Thou, Father, who art kind and just,
Thou, Son, who didst overcome death,
Thou, Holy Spirit of power,
Be keeping me this night from harm;
The Three who would justify me
Keeping me this night and always.

30 The gifts of the Three

Spirit, give me of Thine abundance,
Father, give me of Thy wisdom,
Son, give me in my need,
Jesus beneath the shelter of Thy shield.

I lie down tonight,
With the Triune of my strength,
With the Father, with Jesus,
With the Spirit of might.

31 Sleep prayer

O Jesu without sin,
King of the poor,
Who wert sorely subdued
Under ban of the wicked,
Shield Thou me this night
 From Judas.

My soul on Thine own arm, O Christ,
Thou the King of the City of Heaven,
Thou it was who bought'st my soul, O Jesu,
 Thou it was who didst sacrifice Thy life for me.

Protect Thou me because of my sorrow,
For the sake of Thy passion, Thy wounds, and Thine own blood,
And take me in safety tonight
 Near to the City of God.

32 Resting blessing

In name of the Lord Jesus,
And of the Spirit of healing balm,
In name of the Father of Israel,
 I lay me down to rest.

If there be evil threat or quirk,
Or covert act intent on me,
God free me and encompass me,
 And drive from me mine enemy.

In name of the Father precious,
And of the Spirit of healing balm,
In name of the Lord Jesus,
 I lay me down to rest.

God, help me and encompass me,
From this hour till the hour of my death.

33 Sleep consecration

I lie down tonight
With fair Mary and with her Son,
With pure-white Michael,
And with Bride beneath her mantle.

I lie down with God,
And God will lie down with me,
I will not lie down with Satan,
Nor shall Satan lie down with me.

O God of the poor,
Help me this night,
Omit me not entirely
From Thy treasure-house.

For the many wounds
That I inflicted on Thee,
I cannot this night
Enumerate them.

Thou King of the blood of truth,
Do not forget me in Thy dwelling-place,
Do not exact from me for my transgressions,
Do not omit me in Thine ingathering,
In Thine ingathering.

34 Bed blessing

I am lying down tonight as beseems
In the fellowship of Christ, son of the Virgin of ringlets.
In the fellowship of the gracious Father of glory,
In the fellowship of the Spirit of powerful aid.

I am lying down tonight with God,
And God tonight will lie down with me,
I will not lie down tonight with sin, nor shall
Sin nor sin's shadow lie down with me.

I am lying down tonight with the Holy Spirit,
And the Holy Spirit this night will lie down with me,
I will lie down this night with the Three of my love,
And the Three of my love will lie down with me.

35 The sleep prayer

I am now going into the sleep,
Be it that I in health shall waken;
If death be to me in the death–sleep,
Be it that on Thine own arm,
O God of Grace, I in peace shall waken;
Be it on Thine own beloved arm,
O God of Grace, that I in peace shall waken.

Be my soul on Thy right hand, O God,
Thou King of the heaven of heavens;
Thou it was who bought'st me with Thy blood,
Thou it was who gavest Thy life for me,
Encompass Thou me this night, O God,
That no harm, no evil shall me befall.

Whilst the body is dwelling in the sleep,
The soul is soaring in the shadow of heaven,
Be the red–white Michael meeting the soul,
Early and late, night and day,
Early and late, night and day.
Amen.

36 Sleep consecration

I am lying down tonight,
With Father, with Son,
With the Spirit of Truth,
Who shield me from harm.

I will not lie with evil,
Nor shall evil lie with me,
But I will lie down with God,
And God will lie down with me.

God and Christ and Spirit Holy,
And the cross of the nine white angels,
Be protecting me as Three and as One,
From the top tablet of my face to the soles of my feet.

Thou King of the sun and of glory,
Thou Jesu, Son of the Virgin fragrant,
Keep Thou us from the glen of tears,
And from the house of grief and gloom,
  Keep us from the glen of tears,
  From the house of grief and gloom.

37 Bed blessing

I am lying down tonight,
With Mary mild and with her Son,
With the Mother of my King,
Who is shielding me from harm.

I will not lie down with evil,
Nor shall evil lie down with me,
But I will lie down with God,
And God will lie down with me.

God and Mary and Michael kindly
And the cross of the nine angels fair,
Be shielding me all Three and as One,
From the brow of my face to the edge of my soles.

I beseech Peter, I beseech Paul,
I beseech Mary, I beseech the Son,
I beseech the trustful Apostles twelve
To preserve me from hurt and harm;
O from dying tonight,
From dying tonight!

O God! O Mary of Glory!
O Jesu! Son of the Virgin fragrant,
Sain Ye us from the pains everlasting,
And from the fire fierce and murky,
From the pains everlasting,
And from the fire fierce and murky!

38 The soul shrine

God, give charge to Thy blessed angels,
To keep guard around this stead tonight,
A band sacred, strong, and steadfast,
That will shield this soul-shrine from harm.

Safeguard Thou, God, this household tonight,
Themselves and their means and their fame,
Deliver them from death, from distress, from harm,
From the fruits of envy and of enmity.

Give Thou to us, O God of peace,
Thankfulness despite our loss,
To obey Thy statutes here below,
And to enjoy Thyself above.

39 Soul–shrine

Thou angel of God who hast charge of me
From the fragrant Father of mercifulness,
The gentle encompassing of the Sacred Heart
To make round my soul–shrine this night,
   Oh, round my soul–shrine this night.

Ward from me every distress and danger,
Encompass my course over the ocean of truth,
I pray thee, place thy pure light before me,
O bright beauteous angel on this very night,
   Bright beauteous angel on this very night.

Be Thyself the guiding star above me,
Illume Thou to me every reef and shoal,
Pilot my barque on the crest of the wave,
To the restful haven of the waveless sea,
   Oh, the restful haven of the waveless sea.

40 I lie in my bed

I lie in my bed
As I would lie in the grave,
Thine arm beneath my neck,
   Thou Son of Mary victorious.

Angels shall watch me
And I lying in slumber,
And angels shall guard me
   In the sleep of the grave.

Uriel shall be at my feet,
Ariel shall be at my back,
Gabriel shall be at my head,
   And Raphael shall be at my side.

Michael shall be with my soul,
The strong shield of my love!
And the Physician Son of Mary
Shall put the salve to mine eye,
The Physician Son of Mary
Shall put the salve to mine eye!

41 Morning prayer

Thanks be to Thee, Jesus Christ,
Who brought'st me up from last night,
To the gladsome light of this day,
To win everlasting life for my soul,
Through the blood Thou didst shed for me.

Praise be to Thee, O God, for ever,
For the blessings Thou didst bestow on me:
My food, my speech, my work, my health.

And I beseech Thee
To shield me from sin,
To shield me from ill,
To sain me this night,
And I low and poor,
O God of the poor!
O Christ of the wounds!
Give me wisdom along with Thy grace.

May the Holy One claim me,
And protect me on sea and on land,
And lead me on from step to step,
To the peace of the Everlasting City,
The peace of the Everlasting City!

42 The dedication

Thanks to Thee, God,
Who brought'st me from yesterday
To the beginning of today,
Everlasting joy
To earn for my soul
With good intent.
And for every gift of peace
Thou bestowest on me,
My thoughts, my words,
My deeds, my desires
I dedicate to Thee.
I supplicate Thee,
I beseech Thee,
To keep me from offence,
And to shield me tonight,
For the sake of Thy wounds
With Thine offering of grace.

43 A resting prayer

God shield the house, the fire, the kine,
Every one who dwells herein tonight.
Shield myself and my beloved group,
Preserve us from violence and from harm;
Preserve us from foes this night,
For the sake of the Son of the Mary Mother,
In this place, and in every place wherein they dwell tonight,
On this night and on every night,
  This night and every night.

44 House protecting

God, bless the world and all that is therein.
God, bless my spouse and my children,
God, bless the eye that is in my head,
And bless, O God, the handling of my hand;
What time I rise in the morning early,
What time I lie down late in bed;
  Bless my rising in the morning early,
  And my lying down late in bed.

God, protect the house, and the household,
God, consecrate the children of the motherhood,
God, encompass the flocks and the young;
Be Thou after them and tending them,
What time the flocks ascend hill and wold,
What time I lie down to sleep;
  What time the flocks ascend hill and wold,
  What time I lie down in peace to sleep.

45 Blessing of house

God bless the house,
From site to stay,
From beam to wall,
From end to end,
From ridge to basement,
From balk to roof-tree,
From found to summit,
  Found and summit.

46 To whom shall I offer oblation

To whom shall I offer oblation
In name of Michael on high?
I will give tithe of my means
To the forsaken illustrious One.

Because of all that I have seen,
Of His peace and of His mercy,
Lift Thou my soul to Thee, O Son of God,
Nor leave me ever.

Remember me in the mountain,
Under Thy wing shield Thou me;
Rock of truth, do not forsake me,
My wish it were ever to be near Thee.

Give to me the wedding garment,
Be angels conversing with me in every need,
Be the holy apostles protecting me,
The fair Mary and Thou, Jesu of grace,
The fair Mary and Thou, Jesu of grace.

47 Hail, Mary

Hail, Mary! hail, Mary!
Queen of grace, Mother of mercy;
Hail, Mary, in manner surpassing,
Fount of our health, source of our joy.

To thee we, night and day,
Erring children of Adam and Eve,
Lift our voice in supplication,
In groans and grief and tears.

Bestow upon us, thou Root of gladness,
Since thou art the cup of generous graces,
The faith of John, and Peter, and Paul,
With the wings of Ariel on the heights of the clouds.

Vouchsafe to us, thou golden branch,
  A mansion in the Realm of peace,
Rest from the perils and stress of waves,
  Beneath the shade of the fruit of thy womb, Jesu.

48 Hail to thee, Mary

Hail to thee, Mary, Mother!
Thou art full of loving grace,
The Lord God is always with thee,
Blessed art thou Mary among women,
Blessed is the fruit of thy womb, Jesus,
Blessed art thou, Queen of grace;
Thou holy Mary, thou Mother of Jesus,
Plead for me a miserable sinner,
Now and at the hour of death,
  Now and at the hour of death.

49 The battle to come

Jesus, Thou Son of Mary, I call on Thy name,
And on the name of John the apostle beloved,
And on the names of all the saints in the red domain,
To shield me in the battle to come,
  To shield me in the battle to come.

When the mouth shall be closed,
When the eye shall be shut,
When the breath shall cease to rattle,
When the heart shall cease to throb,
  When the heart shall cease to throb.

When the Judge shall take the throne,
And when the cause is fully pleaded,
O Jesu, Son of Mary, shield Thou my soul,
O Michael fair, acknowledge my departure.
  O Jesu, Son of Mary, shield Thou my soul!
  O Michael fair, receive my departure!

50 The baptism blessing

Thou Being who inhabitest the heights,
Imprint Thy blessing betimes,
Remember Thou the child of my body,
In Name of the Father of peace;
When the priest of the King
On him puts the water of meaning,
Grant him the blessing of the Three
   Who fill the heights.
The blessing of the Three
   Who fill the heights.

Sprinkle down upon him Thy grace,
Give Thou to him virtue and growth,
Give Thou to him strength and guidance,
Give Thou to him flocks and possessions,
Sense and reason void of guile,
Angel wisdom in his day,
That he may stand without reproach
   In Thy presence.
He may stand without reproach
   In Thy presence.

51 The soul leading

Be this soul on Thine arm, O Christ,
Thou sing of the City of Heaven.
      Amen.

Since Thou, O Christ, it was who bought'st this soul,
Be its peace on Thine own keeping.
      Amen.

And may the strong Michael, high king of the angels,
Be preparing the path before this soul, O God.
      Amen.

Oh! the strong Michael in peace with thee, soul,
And preparing for thee the way to the kingdom
of the Son of God.
Amen.

52 The death blessing

God, omit not this woman from Thy covenant,
And the many evils which she in the body committed,
That she cannot this night enumerate.
The many evils that she in the body committed,
That she cannot this night enumerate.

Be this soul on Thine own arm, O Christ,
Thou King of the City of Heaven,
And since Thine it was, O Christ, to buy the soul,
At the time of the balancing of the beam,
At the time of the bringing in the judgment,
Be it now on Thine own right hand,
Oh! on Thine own right hand.

And be the holy Michael, king of angels,
Coming to meet the soul,
And leading it home
To the heaven of the Son of God.
The Holy Michael, high king of angels,
Coming to meet the soul,
And leading it home
To the heaven of the Son of God.

53 Soul peace

Since Thou Christ it was who didst buy the soul —
At the time of yielding the life,
At the time of pouring the sweat,
At the time of offering the clay,
At the time of shedding the blood,
At the time of balancing the beam,
At the time of severing the breath,
At the time of delivering the judgment,
Be its peace upon Thine own ingathering;
Jesus Christ Son of gentle Mary,
Be its peace upon Thine own ingathering,
O Jesus! upon Thine own ingathering.

And may Michael white kindly,
High king of the holy angels,
Take possession of the beloved soul,
And shield it home to the Three of surpassing love,
Oh! to the Three of surpassing love.

54 The new moon

In name of the Holy Spirit of grace,
In name of the Father of the City of peace,
In name of Jesus who took death off us,
Oh! in name of the Three who shield us in every need,
If well thou hast found us tonight,
Seven times better mayest thou leave us without harm,
Thou bright white Moon of the seasons,
Bright white Moon of the seasons.

Seasons

55 Christmas hail

Hail to the King, hail to the King,
Blessed is He, blessed is He,
Hail to the King, hail to the King,
Blessed is He who has come betimes,
Hail to the King, hail to the King,
Blessed be the house and all therein,
Hail to the King, hail to the King,
'Twixt stock and stone and stave,
Hail to the King, hail to the King,
Consign it to God from corslet to cover,
Be the health of men therein,
Hail to the King, hail to the sins,
Blessed is He, blessed is He,
Hail to the King, hail to the King,
Blessed is He, blessed is He,
Hail to the King, hail to the King,
Lasting round the house be ye,
Hail to the King, hail to the King,
Healthy round the hearth be ye,

Hail to the King, hail to the King,
Many be the stakes in the house,
And men dwelling on the foundation,
Hail to the King, hail to the King,
Blessed is He, blessed is He,
Hail to the King, hail to the King,
Blessed is He, blessed is He.

Hail to the King, hail to the King,
This night is the eve of the great Nativity,
Hail to the King, hail to the King,
Blessed is He, blessed is He,
Hail to the King, hail to the King,
Born is the Son of Mary the Virgin,
Hail to the King, hail to the King,
Blessed is He, blessed is He,
Hail to the King, hail to the King,
The soles of His feet have reached the earth,
Hail to the King, hail to the King,
Blessed is He, blessed is He,
Hail to the King, hail to the King,
Illumined the sun the mountains high,
Hail to the King, hail to the King,
Blessed is He, blessed is He.
Shone the earth, shone the land,
Hail to the King, hail to the King,
Blessed is He, blessed is He,
Hail to the King, hail to the King,
Heard was the wave upon the strand,
Hail to the King, hail to the King,
Blessed is He, blessed is He,
Blessed is He, blessed is He,
Hail to the King, hail to the King,
Blessed the King,
Without beginning, without end,
To everlasting, to eternity,
To all ages, to all time.

56 Christmas carol

Hail King! hail King! blessed is He! blessed is He!
Hail King! hail King! blessed is He! blessed is He!
Hail King! hail King! blessed is He, the King, of whom we sing,
All hail! let there be joy!

This night is the eve of the great Nativity,
Born is the Son of Mary the Virgin,
The soles of His feet have reached the earth,
The Son of glory down from on high,
Heaven and earth glowed to Him,
All hail! let there be joy!

The peace of earth to Him, the joy of heaven to Him,
Behold His feet have reached the world;
The homage of a King be His, the welcome of a Lamb be His,
King all victorious, Lamb all glorious,
Earth and ocean illumed to Him,
All hail! let there be joy!

The mountains glowed to Him, the plains glowed to Him,
The voice of the waves with the song of the strand,
Announcing to us that Christ is born,
Son of the King of kings from the land of salvation;
Shone the sun on the mountains high to Him,
All hail! let there be joy!

Shone to Him the earth and sphere together,
God the Lord has opened a Door;
Son of Mary Virgin, hasten Thou to help me,
Thou Christ of hope, Thou Door of joy,
Golden Sun of hill and mountain,
All hail! let there be joy!

57 Christmas chant

Hail King! hail King! blessed is He! blessed is He!
Hail King! hail King! blessed is He! blessed is He!
  Ho, hail! blessed the King!
  Ho, hi! let there be joy!

Prosperity be upon this dwelling,
On all that ye have heard and seen,
On the bare bright floor flags,
On the shapely standing stone staves,
  Hail King! hail King! blessed is He! blessed is He!

Bless this house and all that it contains,
From rafter and stone and beam;
Deliver it to God from pall to cover,
Be the healing of men therein,
  Hail King! hail King! blessed is He! blessed is He!

Be ye in lasting possession of the house,
Be ye healthy about the hearth;
Many be the ties and stakes in the homestead,
People dwelling on this foundation,
  Hail King! hail King! blessed is He! blessed is He!

Offer to the Being from found to cover,
Include stave and stone and beam;
Offer again both rods and cloth,
Be health to the people therein,
  Hail King! hail King! blessed is He! blessed is He!
  Hail King! hail King! blessed is He! blessed is He!
  Ho, hail! blessed the King!
  Let there be joy!

  Blessed the King,
  Without beginning, without ending,
  To everlasting, to eternity,
  Every generation for aye,
  Ho! hi! let there be joy!

58 Hey the Gift

Hey the Gift, ho the Gift,
Hey the Gift on the living.

The fair Mary went upon her knee,
It was the King of glory who was on her breast.

The side of the sack, the side of the sark,
The hide is struck upon the spar

To tell to us that Christ is born,
The King of kings of the land of salvation.

I see the hills, I see the strand,
I see the host upon the wing.

I see angels on clouds,
Coming with speech and friendship to us.

59 Hey the Gift, ho the Gift

Hey the Gift, ho the Gift,
Hey the Gift on the living.

Son of the dawn, Son of the clouds,
Son of the planet, Son of the star,
Hey the Gift, etc.

Son of the rain, Son of the dew,
Son of the welkin, Son of the sky,
Hey the Gift, etc.

Son of the flame, Son of the light,
Son of the sphere, Son of the globe,
Hey the Gift, etc.

Son of the elements, Son of the heavens,
Son of the moon, Son of the sun,
Hey the Gift, etc.

Son of Mary of the God–mind,
And the Son of God first of all news,
Hey the Gift, etc.

60 The Gift of Power

I am the Gift, I am the Poor,
I am the Man of this night.

I am the Son of God in the door,
On Monday seeking the gifts.

Noble is Bride the gentle fair on her knee,
Noble the King of glory on her breast.

Son of the moon, Son of the sun,
Great Son of Mary of God–like mind.

A cross on each right shoulder,
I am in the door, open thou.

I see the hills, I see the strand,
I see angels heralding on high.

I see the dove shapely, benign,
Coming with kindness and friendship to us.

61 The Virgin and Child

Behold the Virgin approaching,
Christ so young on her breast.

O Mary Virgin! and O Holy Son!
Bless ye the house and all therein.

Bless ye the food, bless ye the board,
Bless ye the corn, the flock and the store.

What time to us the quarter was scarce,
It is thou thyself, Virgin, who wast mother to us.

Thou art brighter than the waxing moon
Rising over the mountains.

Thou art brighter than the summer sun,
Under his fullness of joy.

Since the bard must not tarry,
Place ye alms in the bag with a blessing.

Servant am I of God the Son on the threshold,
For the sake of God, arise thyself and open to me.

62 The Shepherd of the Flock was born

That night the star shone
Was born the Shepherd of the Flock,
Of the Virgin of the hundred charms,
 The Mary Mother.

The Trinity eternal by her side,
In the manger cold and lowly.
Come and give tithes of thy means
 To the Healing Man.

The foam–white breastling beloved,
Without one home in the world,
The tender holy Babe forth driven,
 Immanuel!

Ye three angels of power,
Come ye, come ye down;
To the Christ of the people
 Give ye salutation.

Kiss ye His hands,
Dry ye His feet
With the hair of your heads;
And O! Thou world–pervading God,
And Ye, Jesu, Michael, Mary,
 Do not Ye forsake us.

63 Hogmanay of the sack

Hogmanay of the sack,
Hogmanay of the sack,
 Strike the hide,
 Strike the hide.
Hogmanay of the sack,
Hogmanay of the sack,
 Beat the skin,
 Beat the skin.
Hogmanay of the sack,
Hogmanay of the sack,
 Down with it! up with it!
 Strike the hide.
Hogmanay of the sack,
Hogmanay of the sack,
 Down with it! up with it!
 Beat the skin.
Hogmanay of the sack,
Hogmanay of the sack.

64 Hogmanay carol

I am now come to your country,
To renew to you the Hogmanay,
I need not tell you of it,
It was in the time of our forefathers.

I ascend by the door lintel,
I descend by the doorstep,
I will sing my song becomingly,
Mannerly, slowly, mindfully.

The Hogmanay skin is in my pocket,
Great will be the smoke from it presently.

The house–man will get it in his hand,
He will place its nose in the fire;
He will go sunwards round the babes,
And for seven verities round the housewife.

The housewife it is she who deserves it,
The hand to dispense to us the Hogmanay,
A small gift of the bloom of summer,
Much I wish it with the bread.

Give it to us if it be possible,
If you may not, do not detain us;
I am the servant of God's Son at the door,
Arise thyself and open to me.

65 The song of Hogmanay

Now since we came to the country
To renew to you the Hogmanay,
Time will not allow us to explain,
   It has been since the age of our fathers.

Ascending the wall of the house,
Descending at the door,
My carol to say modestly,
   As becomes me at the Hogmanay.

The Hogmanay skin is in my pocket,
Great the fume that will come from that;
No one who shall inhale its odour,
   But shall be for ever from it healthy.

The house–man will get it in his grasp,
He will put its point in the fire;
He will go sunwise round the children,
   And very specially round the goodwife.

The wife will get it, she it is who deserves it,
The hand to distribute the Hogmanay,
The hand to bestow upon us cheese and butter,
The hand without niggardliness, without meanness.

Since drought has come upon the land,
And that we do not expect rarity,
A little of the substance of the summer,
Would we desire with the bread.

If that we are not to have it,
If thou mayest, do not detain us;
I am the servant of God's Son on Hogmanay,
Arise thyself and open the door.
Hogmanay here! Hogmanay here!

66 Hogmanay

We are come to the door,
To see if we be the better of our visit,
To tell the generous women of the townland
That tomorrow is Calendae Day.

After being entertained the guisers go sunwise round the fire singing:

May God bless the dwelling,
Each stone, and beam, and stave,
All food, and drink, and clothing.
May health of men be always there.

Should the guisers be inhospitably treated, they file round the fire withershins and walk out, and raise a cairn in or near the door, called carnan mollachd (cairn of malison), *carnan cronachd* (scathe, or evil, cairn).

They tramp loudly, shaking the dust of the place off their feet, and intoning with a deep voice the following and other maledictions:

The malison of God and of Hogmanay be on you,
And the scathe of the plaintive buzzard,

Of the hen–harrier, of the raven, of the eagle,
And the scathe of the sneaking fox.

The scathe of the dog and of the cat be on you,
Of the boar, of the badger, and of the *brugha,*
Of the hipped bear and of the wild wolf,
And the scathe of the foul foumart.

67 The blessing of the New Year

God, bless to me the new day,
Never vouchsafed to me before;
It is to bless Thine own presence
Thou hast given me this time, O God.

Bless Thou to me mine eye,
May mine eye bless all it sees;
I will bless my neighbour,
May my neighbour bless me.

God, give me a clean heart,
Let me not from sight of Thine eye;
Bless to me my children and my wife,
And bless to me my means and my cattle.

68 Christ the Priest above us

Christ the Priest above us,
Ordained of God for all living.
Christ the Priest above us.

Tonight, the night of the cross of agony,
The cross of anguish to which Christ was crucified.
Christ the Priest above us.

Noble the Gift! noble the Poor!
Noble the Man of this night.
Christ the Priest above us.

It was Bride the fair who went on her knee,
It is the King of glory who is in her lap.
Christ the Priest above us.

I hear the hills, I hear the seas,
I hear the angels heralding to earth
Christ the Priest above us.

I hear Cairbre of the shapely, rounded limbs,
Coming softly in friendship to us.
Christ the Priest above us.

Great the assemblage upon this knoll,
Without the envy of man to another.
Christ the Priest above us.

I am servant of God the Son at the door,
Oh! arise thou thyself and open to me.
Christ the Priest above us.

69 The day of St Columba

Thursday of Columba benign,
Day to send sheep on prosperity,
Day to send cow on calf,
Day to put the web in the warp.

Day to put coracle on the brine,
Day to place the staff to the flag,
Day to bear, day to die,
Day to hunt the heights.

Day to put horses in harness,
Day to send herds to pasture,
Day to make prayer efficacious,
Day of my beloved, the Thursday,
Day of my beloved, the Thursday.

70 Genealogy of Bride

The genealogy of the holy maiden Bride,
Radiant flame of gold, noble foster–mother of Christ.
Bride the daughter of Dugall the brown,
Son of Aodh, son of Art, son of Conn,
Son of Crearar, son of Cis, son of Carmac, son of Carruin.

Every day and every night
That I say the genealogy of Bride,
I shall not be killed, I shall not be harried,
I shall not be put in cell, I shall not be wounded,
Neither shall Christ leave me in forgetfulness.

No fire, no sun, no moon shall burn me,
No lake, no water, nor sea shall drown me,
No arrow of fairy nor dart of fay shall wound me,
And I under the protection of my Holy Mary,
And my gentle foster–mother is my beloved Bride.

71 Bride the aid–woman

There came to me assistance,
Mary fair and Bride;
As Anna bore Mary,
As Mary bore Christ,
As Eile bore John the Baptist
Without flaw in him,
Aid thou me in mine unbearing,
  Aid me, O Bride!

As Christ was conceived of Mary
Full perfect on every hand,
Assist thou me, foster–mother,
The conception to bring from the bone;
And as thou didst aid the Virgin of joy,
Without gold, without corn, without kine,
Aid thou me, great is my sickness,
  Aid me, O Bride!

72 Magnus of my love

O Magnus of my love,
Thou it is who would'st us guide.
Thou fragrant body of grace,
Remember us.

Remember us, thou Saint of power,
Who didst encompass and protect the people,
Succour thou us in our distress,
Nor forsake us.

Lift our flocks to the hills,
Quell the wolf and the fox,
Ward from us spectre, giant, fury,
And oppression.

Surround cows and herds,
Surround sheep and lambs;
Keep from them the water-vole,
And the field-vole.

Sprinkle dew from the sky upon kine,
Give growth to grass, and corn, and sap to plants,
Watercress, deer's-grass, *ceis,* burdock,
And daisy.

O Magnus of fame,
On the barque of the heroes,
On the crests of the waves,
On the sea, on the land,
Aid and preserve us

73 The Beltane blessing

Bless, O Threefold true and bountiful,
Myself, my spouse, and my children,
My tender children and their beloved mother at their head.
On the fragrant plain, on the gay mountain sheiling,
  On the fragrant plain, on the gay mountain sheiling.

Everything within my dwelling or in my possession,
All kine and crops, all flocks and corn,
From Hallow Eve to Beltane Eve,
With goodly progress and gentle blessing,
From sea to sea, and every river mouth,
  From wave to wave, and base of waterfall.

Be the Three Persons taking possession of all to me belonging,
Be the sure Trinity protecting me in truth;
Oh! satisfy my soul in the words of Paul,
And shield my loved ones beneath the wing of Thy glory,
  Shield my loved ones beneath the wing of Thy glory.

Bless everything and every one,
Of this little household by my side;
Place the cross of Christ on us with the power of love,
Till we see the land of joy,
  Till we see the land of joy.

What time the kine shall forsake the stalls,
What time the sheep shall forsake the folds,
What time the goats shall ascend to the mount of mist,
May the tending of the Triune follow them,
  May the tending of the Triune follow them.

Thou Being who didst create me at the beginning,
Listen and attend me as I bend the knee to Thee,
Morning and evening as is becoming in me,
In Thine own presence, O God of life,
  In Thine own presence, O God of life.

74 The Beltane blessing

Mary, thou mother of saints,
Bless our flocks and bearing kine;
Hate nor scathe let not come near us,
Drive from us the ways of the wicked.

Keep thine eye every Monday and Tuesday
On the bearing kine and the pairing queys;
Accompany us from hill to sea,
Gather thyself the sheep and their progeny.

Every Wednesday and Thursday be with them,
Be thy gracious hand always about them;
Tend the cows down to their stalls,
Tend the sheep down to their folds!

Every Friday be thou, O Saint, at their head,
Lead the sheep from the face of the bens,
With their innocent little lambs following them,
Encompass them with God's encompassing.

Every Saturday be likewise with them,
Bring the goats in with their young,
Every kid and goat to the sea side,
And from the Rock of Aegir on high,
With cresses green about its summit.

The strength of the Triune be our shield in distress,
The strength of Christ, His peace and His Pasch,
The strength of the Spirit, Physician of health,
And of the precious Father the King of grace;

And of [saint];
And of [saint];
And of every other saint who succeeded them
And who earned the repose of the kingdom of God.

Bless ourselves and our children,
Bless every one who shall come from our loins,
Bless him whose name we bear,
Bless, O God, her from whose womb we came.

Every holiness, blessing, and power,
Be yielded to us every time and every hour,
In name of the Holy Threefold above,
Father, Son, and Spirit everlasting.

Be the Cross of Christ to shield us downward,
Be the Cross of Christ to shield us upward,
Be the Cross of Christ to shield us roundward,
Accepting our Beltane blessing from us,
  Accepting our Beltane blessing from us.

75 Hymn of the procession

Valiant Michael of the white steeds,
Who subdued the Dragon of blood,
For love of God, for pains of Mary's Son,
Spread thy wing over us, shield us all,
  Spread thy wing over us, shield us all.

Mary beloved! Mother of the White Lamb,
Shield, oh shield us, pure Virgin of nobleness,
And Bride the beauteous, shepherdess of the flocks.
Safeguard thou our cattle, surround us together,
  Safeguard thou our cattle, surround us together.

And Columba, beneficent, benign,
In name of Father, and of Son, and of Spirit Holy,
Through the Three-in-one, through the Trinity,
Encompass thou ourselves, shield our procession,
  Encompass thou ourselves, shield our procession.

O Father! O Son! O Spirit Holy!
Be the Triune with us day and night,
On the machair plain or on the mountain ridge
Be the Triune with us and His arm around our head,
  Be the Triune with us and His arm around our head.

BARRA FISHERMEN
O Father! O Son! O Spirit Holy!
Be thou, Three–One, with us day and night,
And on the back of the wave as on the mountain side
Our Mother shall be with us with her arm under our head.
  And on the back of the wave as on the mountain side
  Our Mother shall be with us with her arm under our head.

76 The feast day of Mary

On the feast day of Mary the fragrant,
Mother of the Shepherd of the flocks,
I cut me a handful of the new corn,
I dried it gently in the sun,
I rubbed it sharply from the husk
  With mine own palms.

I ground it in a quern on Friday,
I baked it on a fan of sheepskin,
I toasted it to a fire of rowan,
And I shared it round my people.

I went sunways round my dwelling,
In name of the Mary Mother,
Who promised to preserve me,
Who did preserve me,
And who will preserve me,
In peace, in flocks,
In righteousness of heart,
In labour, in love,
In wisdom, in mercy,
For the sake of Thy Passion.
Thou Christ of grace

Who till the day of my death
Wilt never forsake me!
  Oh, till the day of my death
  Wilt never forsake me!

77 Michael the victorious

Thou Michael the victorious,
I make my circuit under thy shield,
Thou Michael of the white steed,
And of the bright brilliant blades,
Conqueror of the dragon,
Be thou at my back,
Thou ranger of the heavens,
Thou warrior of the King of all,
  O Michael the victorious,
  My pride and my guide,
  O Michael the victorious,
  The glory of mine eye.

I make my circuit
In the fellowship of my saint,
On the machair, on the meadow,
On the cold heathery hill;
Though I should travel ocean
And the hard globe of the world
No harm can ever befall me
'Neath the shelter of thy shield;
  O Michael the victorious,
  Jewel of my heart,
  O Michael the victorious,
  God's shepherd thou art.

Be the sacred Three of Glory
Aye at peace with me,
With my horses, with my cattle,
With my woolly sheep in flocks.
With the crops growing in the field

Or ripening in the sheaf,
On the machair, on the moor,
In cole, in heap, or stack.
   Every thing on high or low,
   Every furnishing and flock,
   Belong to the holy Triune of glory,
   And to Michael the victorious.

78 The blessing of the *struan*

Each meal beneath my roof,
They will all be mixed together,
In name of God the Son,
   Who gave them growth.

Milk, and eggs, and butter,
The good produce of our own flock,
There shall be no dearth in our land,
   Nor in our dwelling.

In name of Michael of my love,
Who bequeathed to us the power,
With the blessing of the Lamb,
   And of His Mother.

Humble us at thy footstool,
Be thine own sanctuary around us,
Ward from us spectre, sprite, oppression,
   And preserve us.

Consecrate the produce of our land,
Bestow prosperity and peace,
In name of the Father the King,
   And of the three beloved apostles.

Dandelion, smooth garlic,
Foxglove, woad, and butterwort,
The three carle–doddies,
   And marigold.

Gray *cailpeach* plucked,
The seven–pronged seven times,
The mountain yew, ruddy heath,
   And madder.

I will put water on them all,
In precious name of the Son of God,
In name of Mary the generous,
   And of Patrick.

When we shall sit down
To take our food,
I will sprinkle in the name of God
   On the children.

79 The poem of the Lord's Day

The poem of the Lord's Day, O bright God,
Truth under the strength of Christ always.

On the Lord's Day Mary was born,
Mother of Christ of golden yellow hair,
On the Lord's Day Christ was born
   As an honour to men.

The Lord's Day, the seventh day,
God ordained to take rest,
To keep the life everlasting,
Without taking use of ox or man,
Or of creature as Mary desired,
Without spinning thread of silk or of satin,
Without sewing, without embroidery either,
Without sowing, without harrowing, without reaping,
Without rowing, without games, without fishing,
Without going out to the hunting hill,
Without trimming arrows on the Lord's Day,
Without cleaning byre, without threshing corn,
Without kiln, without mill on the Lord's Day.

Whosoever would keep the Lord's Day,
Even would it be to him and lasting,
From setting of sun on Saturday
Till rising of sun on Monday.

He would obtain recompense therefrom,
Produce after the ploughs,
Fish on the pure salt-water stream,
Fish excelling in every river confluence.

The water of the Lord's Day mild as honey,
Whoso would partake of it as drink
Would obtain health in consequence
From every disease afflicting him.

The weeping on the Lord's Day is out of place,
A woman doing it is untimely;
Let her weep betimes on Monday,
But not weep once on the Lord's Day.

The wood of the Lord's Day is too soon.
In the pool it is pitiful,
Though its head should fall in char,
It would till Monday be dormant.
About noon on the Monday,
The wood will arise very quickly,
And by the great flood without
Hasten the story of my trouble.
Without any searching for lamb, sheep, kid or goat
That would not belong to the King in the cause.
It is now it ought to be burnt,
Without listening to the clamour of the stranger,
Nor to the blind babbling of the public.

To keep corn on a high hillock,
To bring physician to a violent disease,
To send a cow to the potent bull of the herd,
To go with a beast to a cattle-fold,

Far or near be the distance,
Every creature needs attention.
To allow a boat under her sail from land,
From land to the country of her unacquaintance.

Whoso would meditate my lay,
And say it every Monday eve,
The luck of Michael would be on his head,
And never would he see perdition.

80 Hymn of the Sunday

On the holy Sunday of thy God
Give thou thine heart to all mankind,
To thy father and thy mother loving,
Beyond any person or thing in the world.

Do not covet large or small,
Do not despise weakling or poor,
Semblance of evil allow not near thee,
Never give nor earn thou shame.

The ten commands God gave thee,
Understand them early and prove,
Believe direct in the King of the elements,
Put behind thee ikon–worship.

Be faithful to thine overlord,
Be true to thy king in every need,
Be true to thine own self besides,
True to thy High King above all obstacles.

Do not thou malign any man,
Lest thou thyself maligned shouldst be,
And shouldst thou travel ocean and earth,
Follow the very step of God's Anointed.

81 Poem of the flood

On Monday will come the great storm
Which the airy firmament will pour,
We shall be obedient the while,
  All who will hearken.

On Tuesday will come the other element,
Heart paining, hard piercing,
Wringing from pure pale cheeks
  Blood, like showers of wine.

On Wednesday will blow the wind,
Sweeping bare strath and plain,
Showering gusts of galling grief,
  Thunder bursts and rending hills.

On Thursday will pour the shower,
Driving people to blind flight,
Faster than the foliage on the trees,
  Like the leaves of Mary's plant in terror trembling.

On Friday will come the dool cloud of darkness,
The direst dread that ever came over the world,
Leaving multitudes bereft of reason,
  Grass and fish beneath the same flagstone.

On Saturday will come the great sea,
Rushing like a mighty river;
All will be at their best
  Hastening to a hill of safety.

On Sunday will arise my King,
Full of ire and tribulation,
Listening to the bitter talk of each man,
  A red cross on each right shoulder.

Labour

82 Blessing of the kindling

I will kindle my fire this morning
In presence of the holy angels of heaven,
In presence of Ariel of the loveliest form,
In presence of Uriel of the myriad charms,
Without malice, without jealousy, without envy,
Without fear, without terror of any one under the sun,
But the Holy Son of God to shield me.
  Without malice, without jealousy, without envy,
  Without fear, without terror of any one under the sun
  But the Holy Son of God to shield me.

God, kindle Thou in my heart within
A flame of love to my neighbour,
To my foe, to my friend, to my kindred all,
To the brave, to the knave, to the thrall,
O Son of the loveliest Mary,
From the lowliest thing that liveth,
To the Name that is highest of all.
  O Son of the loveliest Mary,
  From the lowliest thing that liveth,
  To the Name that is highest of all.

83 Kindling the fire

I will raise the hearth–fire
As Mary would.
The encirclement of Bride and of Mary
On the fire, and on the floor,
And on the household all.

Who are they on the bare floor?
John and Peter and Paul.
Who are they by my bed?
The lovely Bride and her Fosterling.
Who are those watching over my sleep?
The fair loving Mary and her Lamb.
Who is that anear me?
The King of the sun, He himself it is.
Who is that at the back of my head?
The Son of Life without beginning, without time.

84 Smooring the fire

The sacred Three
To save,
To shield,
To surround
The hearth,
The house,
The household,
This eve,
This night,
Oh! this eve,
This night,
And every night,
Each single night.
Amen.

85 Smooring the fire

I will build the hearth,
As Mary would build it.
The encompassment of Bride and of Mary,
Guarding the hearth, guarding the floor,
Guarding the household all.

Who are they on the lawn without?
Michael the sun–radiant of my trust.
Who are they on the middle of the floor?
John and Peter and Paul.
Who are they by the front of my bed?
Sun–bright Mary and her Son.

The mouth of God ordained,
The angel of God proclaimed,
An angel white in charge of the hearth
Till white day shall come to the embers.
An angel white in charge of the hearth
Till white day shall come to the embers.

86 Blessing of the smooring

I am smooring the fire
As the Son of Mary would smoor;
Blest be the house, blest be the fire,
  Blest be the people all.

Who are those down on the floor?
John and Peter and Paul.
On whom is the vigil tonight?
  On the fair gentle Mary and on her Son.

The mouth of God said,
The angel of God spake,
An angel in the door of the house,
To guard and to keep us all
  Till comes daylight tomorrow.

Oh! may the angels of the Holy One of God
Environ me all this night,
Oh! may the angels of the Anointed One of God
Encompass me from harm and from evil,
  Oh! encompass me from harm this night.

87 Smooring blessing

I will smoor the hearth
As Mary would smoor;
The encompassment of Bride and of Mary,
On the fire and on the floor,
  And on the household all.

Who is on the lawn without?
Fairest Mary and her Son,
The mouth of God ordained, the angel of God spoke;
Angels of promise watching the hearth,
  Till white day comes to the fire.

88 The consecration of the seed

I will go out to sow the seed,
In name of Him who gave it growth;
I will place my front in the wind,
And throw a gracious handful on high.
Should a grain fall on a bare rock,
It shall have no soil in which to grow;
As much as falls into the earth,
The dew will make it to be full.

Friday, day auspicious,
The dew will come down to welcome
Every seed that lay in sleep
Since the coming of cold without mercy;

Every seed will take root in the earth,
As the King of the elements desired,
The braird will come forth with the dew,
It will inhale life from the soft wind.

I will come round with my step,
I will go rightways with the sun,
In name of Ariel and the angels nine,
In name of Gabriel and the Apostles kind.

Father, Son, and Spirit Holy,
Be giving growth and kindly substance
To every thing that is in my ground,
Till the day of gladness shall come.

The Feast day of Michael, day beneficent,
I will put my sickle round about
The root of my corn as was wont;
I will lift the first cut quickly;
I will put it three turns round
My head, saying my rune the while,
My back to the airt of the north;
My face to the fair sun of power.

I shall throw the handful far from me,
I shall close my two eyes twice,
Should it fall in one bunch
My stacks will be productive and lasting;
No Carlin will come with bad times
To ask a palm bannock from us,
What time rough storms come with frowns
Nor stint nor hardship shall be on us.

89 Reaping blessing

God, bless Thou Thyself my reaping,
Each ridge, and plain, and field,
Each sickle curved, shapely, hard,
Each ear and handful in the sheaf,
  Each ear and handful in the sheaf.

Bless each maiden and youth,
Each woman and tender youngling,
Safeguard them beneath Thy shield of strength,
And guard them in the house of the saints,
  Guard them in the house of the saints.

Encompass each goat, sheep and lamb,
Each cow and horse, and store,
Surround Thou the flocks and herds,
And tend them to a kindly fold,
  Tend them to a kindly fold.

For the sake of Michael head of hosts,
Of Mary fair-skinned branch of grace,
Of Bride smooth-white of ringleted locks,
Of Columba of the graves and tombs,
  Columba of the graves and tombs.

90 Reaping blessing

On Tuesday of the feast at the rise of the sun,
And the back of the ear of corn to the east,
I will go forth with my sickle under my arm,
And I will reap the cut the first act.

I will let my sickle down
While the fruitful ear is in my grasp,
I will raise mine eye upwards,
I will turn me on my heel quickly,

Rightway as travels the sun
From the airt of the east to the west,
From the airt of the north with motion calm
To the very core of the airt of the south.

I will give thanks to the King of grace
For the growing crops of the ground,
He will give food to ourselves and to the flocks
According as He disposeth to us.

James and John, Peter and Paul,
Mary beloved, the fullness of light,

* * *

On Michaelmas Eve and Christmas,
We will all taste of the bannock.

91 The blessing of the parching

Thou flame grey, slender, curved,
Coming from the top pore of the peat,
Thou flame of leaps, breadth, heat,
Come not nigh me with thy quips.

A burning steady, gentle, generous,
Coming round about my quicken roots,
A fire fragrant, fair, and peaceful,
Nor causes dust, nor grief, nor havoc.

Heat, parch my fat seed,
For food for my little child,
In name of Christ, King of the elements,
Who gave us corn and bread and blessing withal,
  In name of Christ, King of the elements,
  Who gave us corn and bread and blessing withal.

92 The quern blessing

On Ash Eve
We shall have flesh,
We should have that,
  We should have that.

The cheek of hen,
Two bits of barley,
That were enough,
  That were enough.

We shall have mead,
We shall have spruce,
We shall have wine,
We shall have feast.
We shall have sweetness and milk produce,
Honey and milk,
Wholesome ambrosia,
Abundance of that,
  Abundance of that.

We shall have harp,
We shall have pedal,
We shall have lute,
We shall have horn.
We shall have sweet psaltery
Of the melodious strings
And the regal lyre,
Of the songs we shall have,
  Of the songs we shall have.

The calm fair Bride will be with us,
The gentle Mary mother will be with us.
Michael the chief
Of glancing glaves,
And the King of kings
And Jesus Christ,
And the Spirit of peace
And of grace will be with us,
  Of grace will be with us.

93 Milking croon

Come, Brendan, from the ocean,
Come, Ternan, most potent of men,
Come, Michael valiant, down
And propitiate to me the cow of my joy.
  Ho my heifer, ho heifer of my love,
  Ho my heifer, ho heifer of my love.
  My beloved heifer, choice cow of every shieling,
  For the sake of the High King take to thy calf.

Come, beloved Colum of the fold,
Come, great Bride of the flocks,
Come, fair Mary from the cloud,
And propitiate to me the cow of my love.
  Ho my heifer, ho heifer of my love.

The stock–dove will come from the wood,
The tusk will come from the wave,
The fox will come but not with wiles,
To hail my cow of virtues.
  Ho my heifer, ho heifer of my love.

94 Milking croon

The charm placed of Mary of light,
Early and late going to and from home,
The herdsman Patrick and the milkmaid Bride,
Be saining you and saving you and shielding you.
  Ho hi holigan, ho my heifer,
  Ho hi holigan, ho my heifer,
  Ho hi holigan, ho my heifer,
  My calving kine on each side of the river.

A shackle of lint on my elfish heifer,
A shackle of silk on my heifer of calves,

A shackle of straw on the cows of the townland,
But a brand new shackle on my heifer beloved.
  Ho hi holigan, ho my heifer.

Seest thou that cow on the plain
With her frisky calf before her?
Do, thou lovable one, as she did erstwhile,
Give thou thy milk, O calf of Fiannach.
  Ho hi holigan, ho my heifer.

95 Milking blessing

Columba will give to her progeny,
Coivi the propitious, will give to her grass,
My speckled heifer will give me her milk,
And her female calf before her.
  Ho my heifer! heifer! heifer!
  Ho my heifer! kindly, calm,
  My heifer gentle, gentle, beloved,
  Thou art the love of thy mother.

Seest yonder thriving bramble bush
And the other bush glossy with brambles,
Such like is my fox-coloured heifer,
And her female calf before her.
  Ho my heifer! heifer! heifer!

The calm Bride of the white combs
Will give to my loved heifer the lustre of the swan,
While the loving Mary, of the combs of honey,
Will give to her the mottle of the heather hen.
  Ho my heifer! heifer! heifer!

96 Ho hoiligean, ho my heifers

My treasure thou, and thou art of the sea kine,
Red eared, notch eared, high horned;
Urine was sprinkled on the rump of thy grandsire,
And thou shalt not win from me on Monday nor Saturday.
  Ho hoiligean, ho my heifers!
  Ho hoiligean, ho my heifers!
  Ho hoiligean, ho my heifers!
  My kindly kine on each side of the stream.

My treasure thou, and thou art of the land kine,
Thou wilt give me milk produce, thou wilt give me dainty;
Thou wilt give me milk from the top of the club-moss,
And not the grey water of the sand-drift.
  Ho hoiligean, ho my heifers!

My treasure thou, and thou art of the world's kine,
Thou wilt give me milk from the heather tops;
Not grey milk of the taste of the rowan berries,
But honey milk and white as the sea-gull.
  Ho hoiligean, ho my heifers!

The melodious Bride will give thee offspring and young,
The lovely Mary will give thee colour to cover thee,
The lustrous Michael will give thee a star to guide thee,
And Christ Jesu will give thee peace and joy.
  Ho hoiligean, ho my heifers!

97 Ho, my heifer!

The night the Herdsman was out
No shackle went on a cow,
Lowing ceased not from the mouth of calf
Wailing the Herdsman of the flock,
  Wailing the Herdsman of the flock.

Ho my heifer! ho my heifer!
Ho my heifer! my heifer beloved!
My heartling heart, kind, fond,
For the sake of the High King take to thy calf.

The night the Herdsman was missing,
In the Temple He was found.
The King of the moon to come hither!
The King of the sun down from heaven!
King of the sun down from heaven!

98 Give thy milk

Give thy milk, brown cow,
For what reason should I conceal?
The skin of the calf of yonder cow on the partition,
While the calf of my love is on another grange.
Oh! ho! another grange.

Give thy milk, brown cow,
Give thy milk, brown cow,
Give thy milk, brown cow,
Heavily flowing.

My beloved shall get white-bellied calves,
And a fetter fine that shall go kindly round her legs;
No fetter of hair, nor of heather, nor of lint refuse,
But a dear fetter that men bring from Saxon land.
Oh! ho! from Saxon land.

And my queen maiden of beauty shall get
A fetter smooth to go softly round her legs;
No fetter of cord, nor of lint, nor lint refuse,
But a fetter of silk up from Saxon land.
Oh! ho! from Saxon land.

My beloved shall get grass and shelter,
She shall get hill, heath, and plain,
She shall get meadow grass, club–rush, and stubble,
And she shall get the wine from the steep bens.
  Oh! ho! the steep bens.

99 Milking song

Come, Mary, and milk my cow,
Come, Bride, and encompass her,
Come, Columba the benign,
And twine thine arms around my cow.
  Ho my heifer, ho my gentle heifer,
  Ho my heifer, ho my gentle heifer,
  Ho my heifer, ho my gentle heifer,
  My heifer dear, generous and kind,
  For the sake of the High King take to thy calf.

Come, Mary Virgin, to my cow,
Come, great Bride, the beauteous,
Come, thou milkmaid of Jesus Christ,
And place thine arms beneath my cow.
  Ho my heifer, ho my gentle heifer.

Lovely black cow, pride of the shieling,
First cow of the byre, choice mother of calves,
Wisps of straw round the cows of the townland,
A shackle of silk on my heifer beloved.
  Ho my heifer, ho my gentle heifer.

My black cow, my black cow,
A like sorrow afflicts me and thee,
Thou grieving for thy lovely calf,
I for my beloved son under the sea,
  My beloved only son under the sea.

100 Herding blessing

The keeping of God and the Lord on you,
The keeping of Christ always on you,
The keeping of Carmac and of Columba on you,
The keeping of Cairbre on you going and coming,
And the keeping of Ariel the gold–bright on you,
  The king of Ariel the gold–bright on you.

The keeping of Bride the foster–mother on you,
The keeping of Mary the yellow–haired on you,
Of Christ Jesus, the Son of peace,
The King of kings, land and sea,
And the peace–giving Spirit, everlasting, be yours,
  The peace–giving Spirit, everlasting, be yours.

101 Herding blessing

I will place this flock before me,
As was ordained of the King of the world,
Bride to keep them, to watch them, to tend them,
On ben, on glen, on plain,
  Bride to keep them, to watch them, to tend them,
  On ben, on glen, on plain.

Arise, thou Bride the gentle, the fair,
Take thou thy lint, thy comb, and thy hair,
Since thou to them madest the noble charm,
To keep them from straying, to save them from harm,
  Since thou to them madest the noble charm,
  To keep them from straying, to save them from harm.

From rocks, from drifts, from streams,
From crooked passes, from destructive pits,
From the straight arrows of the slender ban–shee,
From the heart of envy, from the eye of evil,

From the straight arrows of the slender ban–shee,
From the heart of envy, from the eye of evil.

Mary Mother, tend thou the offspring, all,
Bride of the fair palms, guard thou my flocks,
Kindly Columba, thou saint of many powers,
Encompass thou the breeding cows, bestow on me herds,
Kindly Columba, thou saint of many powers,
Encompass thou the breeding cows, bestow on me herds.

102 Herding blessing

Travelling moorland, travelling townland,
Travelling mossland long and wide,
Be the herding of God the Son about your feet,
Safe and whole may ye home return,
Be the herding of God the Son about your feet,
Safe and whole may ye home return.

The sanctuary of Carmac and of Columba
Be protecting you going and coming,
And of the milkmaid of the soft palms,
Bride of the clustering hair golden brown,
And of the milkmaid of the soft palms,
Bride of the clustering hair golden brown.

103 The protection of the cattle

Pastures smooth, long, and spreading,
Grassy meads aneath your feet,
The friendship of God the Son to bring you home
To the field of the fountains,
Field of the fountains.

Closed be every pit to you,
Smoothed be every knoll to you,
Cosy every exposure to you.
Beside the cold mountains,
 Beside the cold mountains.

The care of Peter and of Paul,
The care of James and of John,
The care of Bride fair and of Mary Virgin,
To meet you and to tend you,
 Oh! the care of all the band
 To protect you and to strengthen you.

104 Guarding the flocks

May Mary the mild keep the sheep,
May Bride the calm keep the sheep,
May Columba keep the sheep,
May Maolruba keep the sheep,
May Carmac keep the sheep,
From the fox and the wolf.

May Oran keep the kine,
May Modan keep the kine,
May Donnan keep the kine,
May Moluag keep the kine,
May Maolruan keep the kine,
On soft land and hard land.

May the Spirit of peace preserve the flocks,
May the Son of Mary Virgin preserve the flocks,
May the God of glory preserve the flocks,
May the Three preserve the flocks,
From wounding and from death–loss,
 From wounding and from death–loss.

105 A herding croon

The cattle are today going a–flitting,
   Hill–i–ruin is o h–ug o,
   Ho ro la ill o,
   Hill–i–ruin is o h–ug o,
Going to eat the grass of the burial–place,
   Hill–i–ruin is o h–ug o,
Their own herdsman there to tend them,
      Ho ro la ill o,
   Hill–i–ruin is o h–ug o,
Tending, them, fending them, turning them,
   Hill–i–ruin is o h–ug o,
Be the gentle Bride milking them,
   Hill–i–ruin is o h–ug o,
Be the lovely Mary keeping them,
   Hill–i–ruin is o h–ug o,
And Jesu Christ at the end of their journey,
Jesu Christ at the end of their journey.
   Hill–i–ruin is o h–ug o,

106 Hatching blessing

I will rise early on the morning of Monday.
I will sing my rune and rhyme,
I will go sunwise with my cog
To the nest of my hen with sure intent.

I will place my left hand to my breast,
My right hand to my heart,
I will seek the loving wisdom of Him
Abundant in grace, in broods, and in flocks.

I will close my two eyes quickly,
As in blind–man's buff moving, slowly;
I will stretch my left hand over thither
To the nest of my hen on yonder side.

The first egg which I shall bring near me,
I will put it withershins round my head.
[I will lift the egg down in my right hand,
There shall then be one in the cog.]

I will raise my left hand on high,
I will stretch it without halt quickly,
I will lift two eggs down hither,
There shall be then three in the cog.

I will stretch my right hand again,
I will lift with it at the time three,
I will seek ruling from the King,
Then verily there shall be six in the clutch.

I will raise my left hand the second time,
I will lift four with it down,
In name of Christ, King of power,
There shall then be ten in the cog.

The right fist of strongest claim,
I will lift with it two in my fingers,
Thus at ceasing my brood will be complete,
Beneath the breast of the speckled big hen.

I will put soot on their two ends,
And I dumb as the dumb the while,
In name of Creator of sea and hill,
In name of saints and apostles all.

In name of the most Holy Trinity,
In name of Columba kindly,
I will set the eggs on Thursday,
The gladsome brood will come on Friday.

107 Marking the lambs

My knife will be new, keen, clean, without stain,
My plaid beneath my knee with my red robe,
I will put sunwise round my breast the first cut for luck,
The next one after that with the sun as it moves.

A male lamb without blemish, of one colour, without defect,
Allow thou out on the plain, nor his flowing blood check,
If the froth remains on the heather with red top,
My flock will be without flaw as long as I change not the name.

The Three who are above in the City of glory,
Be shepherding my flock and my kine,
Tending them duly in heat, in storm, and in cold,
With the blessing of power driving them down
From yonder height to the sheiling fold.

The name of Ariel of beauteous bloom,
The name of Gabriel herald of the Lamb,
The name of Raphael prince of power,
Surrounding them and saving them.

The name of Muriel and of Mary Virgin,
The name of Peter and of Paul,
The name of James and of John,
Each angel and apostle on their track,
Keeping them alive and their progeny,
  Keeping them alive and their progeny.

108 The clipping blessing

Go shorn and come woolly,
Bear the Beltane female lamb,
Be the lovely Bride thee endowing,
And the fair Mary thee sustaining,
  The fair Mary sustaining thee.

Michael the chief be shielding thee
From the evil dog and from the fox,
From the wolf and from the sly bear,
And from the taloned birds of destructive bills,
From the taloned birds of hooked bills.

109 The chant of the warping

Thursday of beneficence,
For warping and waulking,
A hundred and fifty strands there shall be
To number.

Blue thread, very fine,
Two of white by its side,
And scarlet by the side
Of the madder.

My warp shall be very even,
Give to me Thy blessing, O God,
And to all who are beneath my roof
In the dwelling.

Michael, thou angel of power,
Mary fair, who art above,
Christ, Thou Shepherd of the people,
Do ye your eternal blessing
Bestow

On each one who shall lie down,
In name of the Father and of Christ,
And of the Spirit of peacefulness,
And of grace.

Sprinkle down on us like dew
The gracious wisdom of the mild woman,
Who neglected never the guidance
Of the High King.

Ward away every evil eye,
And all people of evil wishes,
Consecrate the woof and the warp
  Of every thread.

Place Thou Thine arm around
Each woman who shall be waulking it,
And do Thou aid her in the hour
  Of her need.

Give to me virtues abundant,
As Mary had in her day,
That I may possess the glory
  Of the High King.

Since Thou, O God, it is who givest growth,
To each species and kind,
Give us wool from the surface
  Of the green grass.

Consecrate the flock in every place,
With their little lambs melodious, innocent,
And increase the generations
  Of our herds.

So that we may obtain from them wool,
And nourishing milk to drink,
And that no dearth may be ours
  Of day clothing.

110 Loom blessing

Thrums nor odds of thread
My hand never kept, nor shall keep,

Every colour in the bow of the shower
Has gone through my fingers beneath the cross,

White and black, red and madder,
Green, dark grey, and scarlet,

Blue, and roan and colour of the sheep,
And never a particle of cloth was wanting.

I beseech calm Bride the generous,
I beseech mild Mary the loving,
I beseech Christ Jesu the humane,
That I may not die without them,
  That I may not die without them.

111 Setting the *iomairt*

The black by the white,
The white by the black,
The green in the middle of the red,
The red in the middle of the black.

The black in the middle of the red,
The red in the middle of the white,
The white in the middle of the green,
The green in the middle of the white.

The white in the middle of the blue,
The blue in the middle of the scarlet;
...
...

The scarlet to the blue,
The blue to the scarlet,
The scarlet to the black,
The black to the scarlet.

A thread to two threads
Of two colours,
Two threads of black
To one thread of white.

Seven threads to five,
Five to three,
Three to two,
Two to one,
In each border.

112 Loom blessing

Bless, O Chief of generous chiefs,
My loom and everything anear me,
Bless me in my every action,
Make Thou me safe while I live.

From every brownie and fairy woman,
From every evil wish and sorrow,
Help me, O Thou helping Being,
As long as I shall be in the land of the living.

In name of Mary, mild of deeds,
In name of Columba, just and potent,
Consecrate the four posts of my loom,
Till I begin on Monday.

Her pedals, her sleay, and her shuttle,
Her reeds, her warp, and her cogs,
Her cloth–beam, and her thread–beam,
Thrums and the thread of the plies.

Every web, black, white, and fair,
Roan, dun, checked, and red,
Give Thy blessing everywhere,
On every shuttle passing under the thread.

Thus will my loom be unharmed,
Till I shall arise on Monday;
Beauteous Mary will give me of her love,
And there shall be no obstruction I shall not overcome.

113 The consecration of the cloth

Well can I say my rune,
Descending with the glen;
One rune,
Two runes,
Three runes,
Four runes,
Five runes,
Six runes.
Seven runes,
Seven and a half runes,
Seven and a half runes.

May the man of this clothing never be wounded,
May torn he never be;
What time he goes into battle or combat,
May the sanctuary shield of the Lord be his.
What time he goes into battle or combat,
May the sanctuary shield of the Lord be his.

This is not second clothing and it is not thigged,
Nor is it the right of sacristan or of priest.

Cresses green culled beneath a stone,
And given to a woman in secret.
The shank of the deer in the head of the herring,
And in the slender tail of the speckled salmon.

114 Hunting blessing

From my loins begotten wert thou, my son,
May I guide thee the way that is right,
In the holy name of the apostles eleven
In name of the Son of God torn of thee.

In name of James, and Peter, and Paul,
John the baptist, and John the apostle above,
Luke the physician, and Stephen the martyr,
Muriel the fair, and Mary mother of the Lamb.

In name of Patrick holy of the deeds,
And Carmac of the rights and tombs,
Columba beloved, and Adamnan of laws,
Fite calm, and Bride of the milk and kine.

In name of Michael chief of hosts,
In name of Ariel youth of lovely hues,
In name of Uriel of the golden locks,
And Gabriel seer of the Virgin of grace.

The time thou shalt have closed thine eye,
Thou shalt not bend thy knee nor move,
Thou shalt not wound the duck that is swimming,
Never shalt thou harry her of her young.

The white swan of the sweet gurgle,
The speckled dun of the brown tuft,
Thou shalt not cut a feather from their backs,
Till the doom-day, on the crest of the wave.

On the wing be they always
Ere thou place missile to thine ear,
And the fair Mary will give thee of her love,
And the lovely Bride will give thee of her kine.

Thou shalt not eat fallen fish nor fallen flesh,
Nor one bird that thy hand shall not bring down,
Be thou thankful for the one,
Though nine should be swimming.

The fairy swan of Bride of flocks,
The fairy duck of Mary of peace.

115 Consecrating the chase

In name of the Holy Threefold as one,
In word, in deed, and in thought,
I am bathing mine own hands,
In the light and in the elements of the sky.

Vowing that I shall never return in my life,
Without fishing, without fowling either,
Without game, without venison down from the hill,
Without fat, without blubber from out the copse.

O Mary tender-fair, gentle-fair, loving-fair,
Avoid thou to me the silvery salmon dead on the salt sea,
A duck with her brood an it please thee to show me,
A nest by the edge of the water where it does not dry.

The grey-hen on the crown of the knoll,
The black-cock of the hoarse croon,
After the strength of the sun has gone down,
Avoid, oh, avoid thou to me the hearing of them.

O Mary, fragrant mother of my King,
Crown thou me with the crown of thy peace,
Place thine own regal robe of gold to protect me,
And save me with the saving of Christ,
  Save me with the saving of Christ.

116 Prayer for travelling

Life be in my speech,
Sense in what I say,
The bloom of cherries on my lips,
Till I come back again.

The love Christ Jesus gave
Be filling every heart for me,
The love Christ Jesus gave
Filling me for every one.

Traversing corries, traversing forests,
Traversing valleys long and wild.
The fair white Mary still uphold me,
The Shepherd Jesu be my shield,
The fair white Mary still uphold me,
The Shepherd Jesu be my shield.

117 Fishing blessing

The day of light has come upon us,
Christ is born of the Virgin.

In His name I sprinkle the water
Upon every thing within my court.

Thou King of deeds and powers above,
Thy fishing blessing pour down on us.

I will sit me down with an oar in my grasp,
I will row me seven hundred and seven strokes.

I will cast down my hook,
The first fish which I bring up

In the name of Christ, King of the elements,
The poor shall have it at his wish.

And the king of fishers, the brave Peter,
He will after it give me his blessing.

Ariel, Gabriel, and John,
Raphael benign, and Paul,

Columba, tender in every distress,
And Mary fair, the endowed of grace.

Encompass ye us to the fishing–bank of ocean,
And still ye to us the crest of the waves.

Be the King of kings at the end of our course,
Of lengthened life and of lasting happiness.

Be the crown of the King from the Three on high,
Be the cross of Christ adown to shield us,
  The crown of the King from the Three above,
  The cross of Christ adown to shield us.

118 The ocean blessing

O Thou who pervadest the heights,
Imprint on us Thy gracious blessing,
Carry us over the surface of the sea,
Carry us safely to a haven of peace,
Bless our boatmen and our boat,
Bless our anchors and our oars,
Each stay and halyard and traveller,
Our mainsails to our tall masts
Keep, O King of the elements, in their place
That we may return home in peace;
I myself will sit down at the helm,
It is God's own Son who will give me guidance,
As He gave to Columba the mild
What time he set stay to sails.

Mary, Bride, Michael, Paul,
Peter, Gabriel, John of love,
Pour ye down from above the dew
That would make our faith to grow,
Establish ye us in the Rock of rocks,
In every law that love exhibits,
That we may reach the land of glory,
Where peace and love and mercy reign,
All vouchsafed to us through grace;

Never shall the canker worm get near us,
We shall there be safe for ever,
We shall not be in the bonds of death
Though we are of the seed of Adam.

On the Feast Day of Michael, the Feast Day of Martin,
The Feast Day of Andrew, band of mercy,
The Feast Day of Bride, day of my choice,
Cast ye the serpent into the ocean,
So that the sea may swallow her up;
On the Feast Day of Patrick, day of power,
Reveal to us the storm from the north,
Quell its wrath and blunt its fury,
Lessen its fierceness, kill its cold.

On the Day of the Three Kings on high,
Subdue to us the crest of the waves,
On Beltane Day give us the dew.
On John's Day the gentle wind,
The Day of Mary the great of fame,
Ward off us the storm from the west;
Each day and night, storm and calm,
Be Thou with us, O Chief of chiefs,
Be Thou Thyself to us a compass–chart,
Be Thine hand on the helm of our rudder,
Thine own hand, Thou God of the elements,
Early and late as is becoming,
 Early and late as is becoming,

119 Ocean blessing

God the Father all–powerful, benign,
Jesu the Son of tears and of sorrow,
With thy co–assistance, O Holy Spirit!

The Three–One, ever–living, ever–mighty, everlasting,
Who brought the Children of Israel through the Red Sea,
And Jonah to land from the belly of the great creature of the ocean,

Who brought Paul and his companions in the ship,
From the torment of the sea, from the dolour of the waves,
From the gale that was great, from the storm that was heavy.

Sain us and shield and sanctify us,
Be Thou, King of the elements, seated at our helm,
And lead us in peace to the end of our journey.

With winds mild, kindly, benign, pleasant,
Without swirl, without whirl, without eddy,
That would do no harmful deed to us.

We ask all things of Thee, O God,
According to Thine own will and word.

120 Ruler of the elements

The Children of Israel, God taking them,
  Through the Red Sea obtained a path,
They obtained the quenching of their thirst
  From a rock that might not by craftsman be hewn.

Who are they on the tiller of my rudder,
  Giving speed to my east bound barge?
Peter and Paul and John the beloved,
  Three to whom laud and obeisance are due.

Who are the group near to my helm?
  Peter and Paul and John the Baptist;
Christ is sitting on my helm,
  Making guidance to the wind from the south.

To whom does tremble the voice of the wind?
  To whom become tranquil strait and ocean?
To Jesus Christ, Chief of each saint,
  Son of Mary, Root of victory,
  Son of Mary, Root of victory.

121 Sea prayer

HELMSMAN
Blest be the boat.

CREW
God the Father bless her.

HELMSMAN
Blest be the boat.

CREW
God the Son bless her.

HELMSMAN
Blest be the boat.

CREW
God the Spirit bless her.

ALL
God the Father,
God the Son,
God the Spirit,
Bless the boat.

HELMSMAN
What can befall you
And God the Father with you?

CREW
No harm can befall us.

HELMSMAN
What can befall you
And God the Son with you?

CREW
No harm can befall us.

HELMSMAN
What can befall you
And God the Spirit with you?

CREW
No harm can befall us.

ALL
God the Father,
God the Son,
God the Spirit,
With us eternally.

HELMSMAN
What can cause you anxiety
And the God of the elements over you?

CREW
No anxiety can be ours.

HELMSMAN
What can cause you anxiety
And the King of the elements over you?

CREW
No anxiety can be ours.

HELMSMAN
What can cause you anxiety
And the Spirit of the elements over you?

CREW
No anxiety can be ours.

ALL
The God of the elements,
The King of the elements,
The Spirit of the elements,
Close over us,
Ever eternally.

Incantations

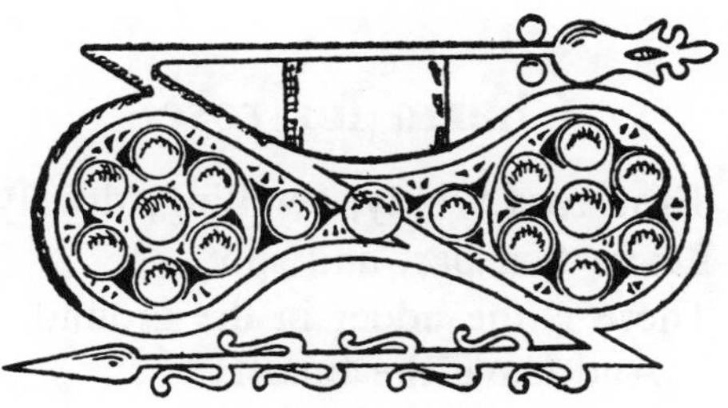

122 **Charm for rose**

Behold, Son and Christ,
The breast of Thy Mother swollen;
Give Thou peace to the breast,
Subdue Thou the swelling;
  Give Thou peace to the breast,
  Subdue Thou the swelling.

Behold it thyself, Queen,
Since of thee the Son was born,
Appease thou the breast,
Subdue thou the swelling;
  Appease thou the breast,
  Subdue thou the swelling.

See Thou it, Jesu,
Since Thou art King of life;
Appease Thou the breast,
Subdue Thou the udder;
  Appease Thou the breast,
  Subdue Thou the udder.

I behold, said Christ,
And I do as is meet,
I give ease to the breast,
And rest to the udder;
  I give ease to the breast,
  And rest to the udder.

123 Charm for rose

Thou rose windy, swelling, deadly,
Leave that part and spot,
There is the udder in the ground,
  And leave the breast.

See, Christ, the woman
And her breast swollen,
See her thyself, Mary,
  It was thou didst bear the Son.

Thou rose windy, deadly, thirsty,
Leave the breast and the spot,
And take thyself off;
  Healed be the breast,
    Withered be the swelling.

Flee thieving red one,
Flee quickly thieving one,
Swelling that was in the breast,
  Leave the udder and the breast,
    And flee hence.

124 Charm for rose

Thou rose deathly, deadly, swollen,
Leave the udder of the white–footed cow,
Leave the udder of the spotted cow,
Leave, leave that swelling,
And betake thyself to other swelling.

Thou rose thrawn, obstinate,
Surly in the udder of the cow,
Leave thou the swelling and the udder,
Flee to the bottom of the stone.

I place the rose to the stone,
I place the stone to the earth,
I place milk in the udder,
I place substance in the kidney.

125 Charm for swollen breast

The charm made by Gillecaluim,
On the one cow of the carlin,
For rose, for hardness, for pain,
For swelling, for lump, for growth,
For uzzening, for udder, for milking,
For the three *corracha crith,*
For the three *corracha cnamh,*
For the three *corracha creothail,*
Do not deny it to beast,
Do not refuse it to wife,
Do not withhold it on Sunday.
The charm made of generous Fionn,
To his very sister,
For rose, for hardness,
For swelling of breast.

126 Toothache charm

The incantation put by lovely Bride
Before the thumb of the Mother of God,
On lint, on wort, on hemp,
For worm, for venom, for teeth.

The worm that tortured me,
In the teeth of my head,
Hell hard by my teeth,
The teeth of hell distressing me.

The teeth of hell close to me;
As long as I myself shall last
May my teeth last in my head.

127 Charm for jaundice

For the jaundice, for the spaul, for the bloody flux,
For the red disease, for the withering disease,
For the bot disease, for the skin disease,
For the brown disease, for the foot disease,
And for every disease that might be
In the constitution of cow
Or adhering to stirk.

128 Charm for a bursting vein

The rune made by the holy maiden Bride
To the lame mariner,
For knee, for crookedness, for crippleness,
For the nine painful diseases, for the three venomous diseases,
Refuse it not to beast, deny it not to dame.

Christ went on a horse,
A horse broke his leg,
Christ went down,
He made whole the leg.

As Christ made whole that,
May Christ make whole this,
And more than this,
If it be His will so to do.

The charm made by Columba,
On the bottom of the glen,
For bursting of vein, for dislocation of bone:
Thou art ill today, thou shalt be well tomorrow.

129 Charm for bursting vein

Rosary of Mary, one,
Rosary of Mary, two,
Rosary of Mary, three,
Rosary of Mary, four,
Rosary of Mary, five,
Rosary of Mary, six,
Rosary of Mary, seven,
Seven Rosaries of Mary ever
Between pain and ease,
Between sole and summit,
Between health and grave.

Christ went on an ass,
She sprained her foot,
He came down
And healed her foot;
As He healed that
May He heal this,
And greater than this,
If it be His will to do.

130 Charm of the sprain

Bride went out
In the morning early,
With a pair of horses;
One broke his leg,
With much ado,
That was apart,
She put bone to bone,

She put flesh to flesh,
She put sinew to sinew,
She put vein to vein;
As she healed that
May I heal this.

131 Charm for sprain

Christ went on the cross,
Sprained the leg of a horse;
Christ came to the ground,
Whole became the leg.

As that was made whole
May this become whole,
If His will be so to do,
Through the bosom of the God of life,
And of the Three of the Trinity,
The God of life,
The Three of Trinity.

132 Charm for sprain

Christ went out
In the morning early,
He found the legs of the horses
In fragments soft;
He put marrow to marrow,
He put pith to pith,
He put bone to bone,
He put membrane to membrane,
He put tendon to tendon,
He put blood to blood,
He put tallow to tallow,

He put flesh to flesh,
He put fat to fat,
He put skin to skin,
He put hair to hair,
He put warm to warm,
He put cool to cool,
As the King of power healed that
It is in His nature to heal this,
If it be His own will to do it.
  Through the bosom of the Being of life,
  And of the Three of the Trinity.

133 Fath–fith

Fath–fith
Will I make on thee,
By Mary of the augury,
By Bride of the corslet,
From sheep, from ram,
From goat, from buck,
From fox, from wolf,
From sow, from boar,
From dog, from cat,
From hipped–bear,
From wilderness–dog,
From watchful *scan,**
From cow, from horse,
From bull, from heifer,
From daughter, from son,
From the birds of the air,
From the creeping things of the earth,
From the fishes of the sea,
From the imps of the storm.

* Probably some animal.

134 Charm of the lasting life

I place the charm on thy body,
And on thy prosperity,
The charm of the God of life
For thy protection.

The charm that Bride of the kine
Put round the fair neck of Dornghil,
The charm that Mary put about her Son,
Between sole and throat,
Between pap and knee,
Between back and breast,
Between chest and sole,
Between eye and hair.

The host of Michael on thy side,
The shield of Michael on thy shoulder,
There is not between heaven and earth
That can overcome the King of grace.

No spear shall rive thee,
No sea shall drown thee,
No woman shall wile thee,
No man shall wound thee.

The mantle of Christ Himself about thee,
The shadow of Christ Himself above thee,
From the crown of thy head
To the soles of thy feet.
The charm of God is on thee now,
Thou shalt never know disgrace.

Thou shalt go forth in name of thy King,
Thou shalt come in in name of thy Chief,
To the God of life thou now belongest wholly,
And to all the Powers together.

I place this charm early on Monday,
In passage hard, brambly, thorny,
Go thou out and the charm about thy body,
And be not the least fear upon thee.

Thou shalt ascend the crest of the hill,
Protected thou shalt be behind thee,
Thou art the calm swan in battle,
Preserved thou shalt be amidst the slaughter,
Stand thou canst against five hundred,
And thine oppressors shall be seized.

The charm of God about thee!
The arm of God above thee!

135 The charm of the lasting life

I will place the charm of the lasting life,
Upon your cattle active, broad, and full,
The knoll upon which the herds shall lie down,
That they may rise from it whole and well.

Down with success, and with blessing,
Up with activity and following,
Without envy, without malice, without ill-will,
Without small eye, without large eye,
Without the five eyes of neglect.

I will suck this, the sucking of envious vein
On the head of the house, and the townland families,
That every evil trait, and every evil tendency
Inherent in you shall cleave to them.

If tongue cursed you,
A heart blessed you;
If eye blighted you,
A wish prospered you.

A hurly-burlying, a topsy-turvying,
A hard hollying and a wan withering
To their female sheep and to their male calves,
For the nine and the nine score years.

136 St Bride's charm

The charm put by Bride the beneficent,
On her goats, on her sheep, on her kine,
On her horses, on her chargers, on her herds,
Early and late going home, and from home.

To keep them from rocks and ridges,
From the heels and the horns of one another,
From the birds of the Red Rock,
And from Luath of the Feinne.

From the blue peregrine hawk of Creag Duilion,
From the brindled eagle of Ben–Ard,
From the swift hawk of Tordun,
From the surly raven of Bard's Creag.

From the fox of the wiles,
From the wolf of the Mam,
From the foul–smelling fumart,
And from the restless great–hipped bear.

From...
From...
From every hoofed of four feet,
And from every hatched of two wings.

137 Sain

The sain put by Mary on her Son,
Sain from death, sain from wound,
Sain from breast to knee,
Sain from knee to foot,
Sain of the three sains,
Sain of the five sains,
Sain of the seven sains,
From the crown of thy head

To the soles of thy feet.
Sain of the seven paters, one,
Sain of the seven paters, two,
Sain of the seven paters, three,
Sain of the seven paters, four,
Sain of the seven paters, five,
Sain of the seven paters, six,
Sain of the seven paters, seven
  Upon thee now.
From the edge of thy brow,
To thy coloured soles,
To preserve thee from behind,
To sustain thee in front.

Be the helmet of salvation about thine head,
Be the corslet of the covenant about thy throat,
Be the breastplate of the priest upon thy breast,
To shield thee in the battle and combat of thine enemies.

If pursued, oh youth, from behind thy back,
The power of the Virgin be close to succour thee,
East or west, west or east,
North or south, south or north.

138 Love charm

It is not love knowledge to thee
To draw water through a reed,
But the love of him [her] thou choosest,
With his [her] warmth to draw to thee.

Arise thou early on the day of the Lord,
To the broad flat flag,
Take with thee the foxglove
And the butterbur.

Lift them on thy shoulder
In a wooden shovel,
Get thee nine stems of ferns
Cut with an axe,

The three bones of an old man,
That have been drawn from the grave,
Burn them on a fire of faggots,
And make them all into ashes.

Shake it in the very breast of thy lover,
Against the sting of the north wind,
And I will pledge, and warrant thee,
That man [woman] will never leave thee.

139 Love charm

A love charm for thee,
Water drawn through a straw,
The warmth of him [her] thou lovest,
With love to draw on thee.

Arise betimes on Lord's day,
To the flat rock of the shore
Take with thee the butterbur
And the foxglove.

A small quantity of embers
In the skirt of thy kirtle,
A special handful of sea-weed
In a wooden shovel.

Three bones of an old man,
Newly torn from the grave,
Nine stalks of royal fern,
Newly trimmed with an axe.

Burn them on a fire of faggots
And make them all into ashes;
Sprinkle in the fleshy breast of thy lover,
  Against the venom of the north wind.

Go round the *rath* of procreation,
The circuit of the five turns,
And I will vow and warrant thee
  That man [woman] shall never leave thee.

140 Thwarting the evil eye

Who shall thwart the evil eye?
I shall thwart it, methinks,
In name of the King of life.
Three seven commands so potent,
Spake Christ in the door of the city;
  Pater Mary one,
  Pater King two,
  Pater Mary three,
  Pater King four,
  Pater Mary five,
  Pater King six,
  Pater Mary seven;
Seven pater Maries will thwart
  The evil eye,
Whether it be on man or on beast,
  On horse or on cow;
Be thou in thy full health this night,
  [The name]
In name of the Father, the Son, and the Holy Spirit.
    Amen.

141 Exorcism of the eye

I trample upon the eye,
As tramples the duck upon the lake,
As tramples the swan upon the water,
As tramples the horse upon the plain,
As tramples the cow upon the *iuc,*
As tramples the host of the elements,
As tramples the host of the elements.

Power of wind I have over it,
Power of wrath I have over it,
Power of fire I have over it,
Power of thunder I have over it,
Power of lightning I have over it,
Power of storms I have over it,
Power of moon I have over it,
Power of sun I have over it,
Power of stars I have over it,
Power of firmament I have over it,
Power of the heavens
And of the worlds I have over it,
Power of the heavens
And of the worlds I have over it.

A portion of it upon the grey stones,
A portion of it upon the steep hills,
A portion of it upon the fast falls,
A portion of it upon the fair meads,
And a portion upon the great salt sea,
She herself is the best instrument to carry it,
The great salt sea,
The best instrument to carry it.

In name of the Three of Life,
In name of the Sacred Three,
In name of all the Secret Ones,
And of the Powers together.

142 Counteracting the evil eye

An eye covered thee,
A mouth spoke thee,
A heart envied thee,
A mind desired thee.

Four made thee thy cross,
Man and wife,
Youth and maid;
Three will I send to thwart them,
  Father,
  Son,
  Spirit Holy.

I appeal to Mary,
Aidful mother of men,
I appeal to Bride,
Foster-mother of Christ omnipotent,
I appeal to Columba,
Apostle of shore and sea,
And I appeal to heaven,
To all saints and angels that be above.

If it be a man that has done thee harm,
With evil eye,
With evil wish,
With evil passion,
Mayest thou cast off each ill,
Every malignity,
Every malice,
Every harassment,
And mayest thou be well for ever,
While this thread
Goes round thee,
In honour of God and of Jesus,
And of the Spirit of balm everlasting.

143 Spell for evil eye

The fair spell that lovely Mary sent,
Over stream, over sea, over land,
Against incantations, against withering glance,
Against inimical power,
Against the teeth of wolf,
Against the testicles of wolf,
Against the three crooked cranes,
Against the three crooked bones,
Against the three crooked *creothail,*
And against the long lint of the ground.

Whoso made to thee the eye,
May it lie upon himself,
May it lie upon his house,
May it lie upon his flocks,
May it lie upon his substance,
May it lie upon his fatness,
May it lie upon his means,
May it lie upon his children,
May it lie upon his wife,
May it lie upon his descendants.

I will subdue the eye,
I will suppress the eye,
And I will banish the eye,
The three arteries inviting
And the tongue of death completely.
Three lovely little maidens,
Born the same night with Christ,
If alive be these three tonight,
Life be anear thee, poor beast.

144 Charm for the eye

I place this charm to mine eye,
As the King of life ordained,
From the bosom of Peter and Paul,
The third best amulet under the sun.

Pour Mary, pour Bride,
Pour Patrick, king of laws,
Pour Columba the kindly,
Pour Ciaran, saint of power.

For victory in battle, for hardness of hand,
In battle of defence, in battle of offence,
On every son with whom it shall go well,
The Son of God will be with him in full armour.

From the bosom of Father,
From the bosom of Son,
From the bosom of Holy Spirit.
Amen.

145 Charm for the evil eye

Whoso laid on thee the eye,
May it lie upon himself.
May it lie upon his house,
May it lie upon his flocks,
On the shuffling carlin,
On the sour–faced carlin,
On the bounding carlin,
On the sharp–shanked carlin,
Who arose in the morning,
With her eye on her flocks,
With her flocks in her *seoin,**
May she never own a fold,
May she never have half her desires,

* Thoughts or mind

The part of her which the ravens do not eat,
May the birds devour.

Four made to thee the eye,
Man and dame, youth and maid;
Three who will cast off thee the envy,
The Father, the Son, and the Holy Spirit.

As Christ lifted the fruit,
From the branches of the bushes,
May He now lift off thee
Every ailment, every envy, every jealousy,
From this day forth till the last day of thy life.

146 Charm

Peter and James and John,
The three of sweetest virtues in glory,
Who arose to make the charm,
Before the great door of the City,
By the right knee of God the Son.

Against the keen-eyed men,
Against the peering-eyed women,
Against the slim, slender, fairy-darts,
Against the swift arrows of furies.

Two made to thee the withered eye,
Man and woman with venom and envy,
Three whom I will set against them,
Father, Son, and Spirit Holy.

Four and twenty diseases in the constitution of man and beast,
God scrape them, God search them, God cleanse them,
From out thy blood, from out thy flesh, from out thy fragrant bones,
From this day and each day that comes, till thy day on earth be done.

147 A malediction

There came two out
From the City of Heaven,
A man and a woman,
To make the *oisnean.*

Curses on the blear-eyed women,
Curses on the sharp-eyed men,
Curses on the four venomous arrows of disease,
That may be in the constitution of man and beast.

148 Spell of the evil eye

Trample I upon the eye,
As tramples the swan on a bare strand,
Power of wind I have over it,
The power of the Son of the King of Heaven
And of earth I have over it,
A portion of it on the grey stones,

* * *

And a portion on the great sea,
She herself is the instrument most able to bear it.

149 Incantation for the eye

Incantation of the seeing eye,
Incantation of the guiding star,
Incantation of the King of all kings,
Incantation of the God of life,
Incantation of the King of all kings,
Incantation of the God of life.

Incantation of Bride of the locks of gold,
Incantation of the beauteous Mary Virgin,
Incantation of the Virtue of all virtues,

Incantation of the God of glory,
Incantation of the Virtue of all virtues,
Incantation of the God of glory.

Incantation of Peter and of Paul,
Incantation of Ariel and John of love,
Incantation of the God of all gods,
Incantation of the God of grace,
Incantation of the God of all gods,
Incantation of the God of grace.

Feast of Mary, Feast of God,
Feast of cleric and of priest,
Feast of Christ, Prince of power,
Who established the sun with strength,
Feast of Christ, Prince of power,
Who endowed the sun with strength.

150 Spell of the eye

I place this spell to mine eye,
As the King of life ordained,
Spell of Peter, spell of Paul,
Spell of James, spell of John,
Spell of Columba benign,
Spell of Patrick, chief of saints,
Spell of Bride, tranquil of the kine,
Spell of Mary, lovely of the joys,
Spell of cows, spell of herds,
Spell of sheep, spell of flocks,
Spell of greatness, spell of means,
Spell of joy, spell of peace,
Spell of war, spell of the brave,
The third best spell under the sun,
The powerful spell of the Three Powers,
Father, Son, Spirit everlasting.

151 Spell of the eye

The spell fair–white,
Sent of Mary Virgin,
To the daughter of Dorail,
Of the golden–yellow hair,
Hither on mainland,
Hither on coastland,
Hither on lakeland,
Hither on ocean,
To thwart eye,
To thwart net,
To thwart envy,
To thwart hate.
To repel *breotaich,*
To repel *greotaich,*
To repel *sreotaich,*
To repel rose.

152 Spell of the eye

The spell the great white Mary sent
To Bride the lovely fair,
For sea, for land, for water, and for withering glance,
For teeth of wolf, for testicle of wolf.

Whoso laid on thee the eye
May it oppress himself,
May it oppress his house,
May it oppress his flocks.

Let me subdue the eye,
Let me avert the eye,
The three complete tongues of fullness,
In the arteries of the heart,
In the vitals of the navel.

From the bosom of Father,
From the bosom of Son,
From the bosom of Holy Spirit.

153 Spell of the counteracting

I will pluck the gracious yarrow
That Christ plucked with His one hand.

The High King of the angels
Came with His love and His countenance above me.

Jesus Christ came hitherward
With milk, with substance, with produce,
With female calves, with milk product.

On small eye, on large eye,
Over Christ's property.

In name of the Being of life
Supply me with Thy grace,
The crown of the King of the angels
To put milk in udder and gland,
With female calves, with progeny.

May you have the length of seven years
Without loss of calf, without loss of milk,
Without loss of means or of dear friends.

154 The counting of the stye

Why came the one stye,
Without the two styes here?
Why came the two styes,
Without the three styes here?
Why came the three styes,
Without the four styes here?
Why came the four styes,
Without the five styes here?
Why came the five styes,
Without the six styes here?
Why came the six styes,
Without the seven styes here?

Why came the seven styes,
Without the eight styes here?
Why came the eight styes,
Without the nine styes here?
Why came the nine,
Or one at all here?

155 The *fionn–faoilidh*

I place the *fionn–faoilidh** on me,
To drain wrath empty,
To preserve to me my fame,
While I shall live on earth.

O Michael! grasp my hand,
Vouchsafe to me the love of God,
If there be ill–will or ill–wish in mine enemy,
Christ be between me and him,
Oh, Christ between me and him!

If there be ill–will or ill–wish concerning me,
Christ be between me and it,
Oh, Christ between me and it!

156 Envy spell

Whoso made to thee the envy,
Swarthy man or woman fair,
Three I will send to thwart it:
Holy Spirit, Father, Son.

* A plant, the English name of which I do not know.

157 The red stalk

Pluck will I the little red–stalk of surety,
The lint the lovely Bride drew through her palm,
For success of health, for success of friendship,
  For success of joyousness,
For overcoming of evil mind, for overcoming of evil eye,
  For overcoming of bewitchment,
For overcoming of evil deed, for overcoming of evil conduct,
  For overcoming of malediction,
For overcoming of evil news, for overcoming of evil words,
  For success of blissfulness,
  For success of blissfulness.

158 The tree–entwining ivy

I will pluck the tree–entwining ivy,
As Mary plucked with her one hand,
As the King of life has ordained,
To put milk in udder and gland,
With speckled fair female calves,
As was spoken in the prophecy,
On this foundation for a year and a day,
Through the bosom of the God of life, and of all the powers.

159 The charm of the figwort

I will pluck the figwort,
With the fruitage of sea and land,
The plant of joy and gladness,
The plant of rich milk.

As the King of kings ordained,
To put milk in pap and gland,
As the Being of life ordained,
To place substance in udder and kidney,

With milk, with milkiness, with buttermilk,
With produce, with whisked whey, with milk–product,
With speckled female calves,
Without male calves,
With progeny, with joy, with fruitage.
With love, with charity, with bounty;

Without man of evil wish,
Without woman of evil eye,
Without malice, without envy, without *toirinn,*
Without hipped bear,
Without wilderness dog,
Without *scan foirinn,* *
Obtaining hold of the rich dainty
Into which this shall go.
Figwort of bright lights,
Fruitage to place therein,
With fruit, with grace, with joyance.

160 The figwort

I will pluck the figwort,
With the fullness of sea and land,
At the flow, not the ebb of the tide,
By thine hand, gentle Mary.

The kindly Colum directing me,
The holy Oran protecting me,
Whilst Bride of women beneficent
Shall put fruitage in the kine.

As the King of kings ordained,
To put milk in breast and gland,
As the Being of life ordained,
To put sap in udder and teat.

* A wild animal "of the border land."

In udder of badger,
In udder of reindeer,
In udder of sow,
In udder of mare.

In udder of sow,
In udder of heifer,
In udder of goat, ewe, and sheep,
Of roe, and of cow.

With milk, with cream, with substance,
With rutting, with begetting, with fruitfulness,
With female calves excelling,
With progeny, with joyance, with blessing.

Without man of evil wish,
Without woman of evil eye,
Without malice, without envy,
Without one evil.

In name of the apostles twelve,
In name of the Mother of God.
In name of Christ Himself
And of Patrick.

161 The charm of the figwort

I will cull the figwort,
Of thousand blessings, of thousand virtues,
The calm Bride endowing it to me,
The fair Mary enriching it to me,
The great Mary, aid-Mother of the people.

Came the nine joys,
With the nine waves,
To cull the figwort,

Of thousand blessings, of thousand virtues:
  Of thousand blessings, of thousand virtues.

The arm of Christ about me,
The face of Christ before me,
The shade of Christ over me,
My noble plant is being culled:
  My noble plant is being culled.

In name of the Father of wisdom,
In name of the Christ of Pasch,
In name of the Spirit of grace,
Who in the struggles of my death,
Will not leave me till Doom:
  Who in the struggles of my death,
  Will not leave me till Doom.

162 The fairy wort

Pluck will I the fairy wort,
With expectation from the fairy bower,
To overcome every oppression,
As long as it be fairy wort.

Fairy wort, fairy wort,
I envy the one who has thee,
There is nothing the sun encircles,
But is to her a sure victory.

Pluck will I mine honoured plant
Plucked by the great Mary, helpful Mother of the people,
To cast off me every tale of scandal and flippancy,
Ill–life, ill–love, ill–luck,
Hatred, falsity, fraud and vexation,
Till I go in the cold grave beneath the sod.

163 The yarrow

I will pluck the yarrow fair,
That more benign shall be my face,
That more warm shall be my lips,
That more chaste shall be my speech,
Be my speech the beams of the sun,
Be my lips the sap of the strawberry.

May I be an isle in the sea,
May I be a hill on the shore,
May I be a star in waning of the moon,
May I be a staff to the weak,
Wound can I every man,
Wound can no man me.

164 The yarrow

I will pluck the yarrow fair,
That more brave shall be my hand,
That more warm shall be my lips,
That more swift shall be my foot;
May I an island be at sea,
May I a rock be on land,
That I can afflict any man,
No man can afflict me.

165 Saint John's wort

I will cull my plantlet,
As a prayer to my King,
To quiet the wrath of men of blood,
To check the wiles of wanton women.

I will cull my plantlet,
As a prayer to my King,
That mine may be its power
Over all I see.

I will cull my plantlet,
As a prayer to the Three,
Beneath the shade of the Triune of grace.
And of Mary the Mother of Jesu.

166 St Columba's plant

I will pluck what I meet,
As in communion with my saint,
To stop the wiles of wily men,
And the arts of foolish women.

I will pluck my Columba plant,
As a prayer to my King,
That mine be the power of Columba's plant,
Over every one I see.

I will pluck the leaf above,
As ordained of the High King,
In name of the Three of glory,
And of Mary, Mother of Christ.

167 St Columba's plant

Plantlet of Columba,
Without seeking, without searching,
Plantlet of Columba,
Under my arm for ever!

For luck of men,
For luck of means,
For luck of wish,
For luck of sheep,
For luck of goats,
For luck of birds,
For luck of fields,

For luck of shellfish,
For luck of fish,
For luck of produce and kine,
For luck of progeny and people,
For luck of battle and victory,
On land, on sea, on ocean,
Through the Three on high,
Through the Three a–nigh,
Through the Three eternal,
Plantlet of Columba,
I cull thee now,
 I cull thee now.

168 Saint John's wort

Saint John's wort, Saint John's wort,
My envy whosoever has thee,
I will pluck thee with my right hand,
I will preserve thee with my left hand,
Whoso findeth thee in the cattle fold,
Shall never be without kine.

169 The aspen

Malison be on thee, O aspen tree!
On thee was crucified the King of the mountains,
In whom were driven the nails without clench,
And that driving crucifying was exceeding sore;
 That driving crucifying was exceeding sore.

Malison be on thee, O aspen hard!
On thee was crucified the King of glory,
Sacrifice of Truth, Lamb without blemish,
His blood in streams downpouring;
 His blood in streams downpouring.

Malison be on thee, O aspen cursed!
On thee was crucified the King of kings,
And malison be on the eye that seeth thee,
If it maledict thee not, thou aspen cursed;
If it maledict thee not, thou aspen cursed!

170 Shamrock of luck

Thou shamrock of good omens,
Beneath the bank growing
Whereon stood the gracious Mary,
The Mother of God.

The seven joys are,
Without evil traces,
On thee, peerless one
Of the sunbeams:

Joy of health,
Joy of friends,
Joy of kine,
Joy of sheep,
Joy of sons, and
Daughters fair,
Joy of peace,
Joy of God!

The four leaves of the straight stem,
Of the straight stem from the root of the hundred rootlets,
Thou shamrock of promise on Mary's Day,
Bounty and blessing thou art at all times.

171 The shamrock of power

Thou shamrock of foliage,
Thou shamrock of power,
Thou shamrock of foliage,
Which Mary had under the bank,

Thou shamrock of my love,
Of most beauteous hue,
I would choose thee in death,
To grow on my grave,
I would choose thee in death,
To grow on my grave.

172 The *mòthan*

I will pluck the gracious *mòthan,*
As plucked the victorious King of the universe;
In name of Father and of Son and of Spirit everlasting,
  Bride, and Mary, and Michael, before me.

I in the field of red conflict,
In which every wrath and fury are quelled,
The cause of all joy and gladness,
  The shield of the Lord protecting me.

173 The *mòthan*

Pluck will I the *mòthan,*
Plant of the nine joints,
Pluck will I and vow me,
  To noble Bride and her Fosterling.

Pluck will I the *mòthan,*
As ordained of the King of power,
Pluck will I and vow me,
  To great Mary and her Son.

Pluck will I the *mòthan,*
As ordained of the King of life,
To overcome all oppression,
  And the spell of evil eye.

174 The *mòthan*

I will pluck the gracious *mòthan,*
Plant most precious in the field,
That mine be the holiness of the seven priests,
And the eloquence that is within them.

* * *

That mine be their wisdom and their counsel,
While the *mòthan* is mine.

175 The passion–flower of virtues

Thou passion–flower of virtues beloved,
Sanctified by the holy blood of the Lamb,
Son of Mary fair, Foster Son of Bride of kine,
Son of Mary great, helpful Mother of the people.

There is no earth, no land,
There is no lake, no ocean,
There is no pool, no water,
There is no forest, no steep,
That is not to me full safe,
By the protection of the passion–flower of virtues,
  But is to me full safe,
  By the protection of the passion–flower of virtues.

176 The club–moss

The club–moss is on my person,
No harm nor mishap can me befall;
No sprite shall slay me, no arrow shall wound me,
No fay nor dun water–nymph shall tear me.

177 The red–palmed

Christ walking with His apostles,
And breaking silence He said:
"What is the name of this plant?"
"The name of this plant is
The red–palmed,
The right palm of God the Son
And His left foot."

178 The catkin wool

I will pluck the catkin wool,
As plucked the Mother of Christ through her palm,
For luck, for kine, for milking,
For herds, for increase, for cattle,
Without loss of lamb, without loss of sheep,
Without loss of goat, without loss of mare,
Without loss of cow, without loss of calf,
Without loss of means, without loss of friends,
From the bosom of the God of life,
And the courses together.

179 The catkin wool

Pluck will I myself the catkin wool,
The lint the lovely Bride culled through her palm,
For success, for cattle, for increase,
For pairing, for uddering, for milking,
For female calves, white bellied,
As was spoken in the prophecy.

180 Incantation of the red water

In name of the Father of love,
In name of the Son of sorrow,
In name of the Sacred Spirit.
Amen.

Great wave, red wave,
Strength of sea, strength of ocean,
The nine wells of Mac–Lir,
Help on thee to pour,
Put stop to thy blood,
Put flood to thy urine.
[The name.]

181 Red water charm

I am now on the plain,
Reducing wrath and fury,
Making the charm of the red water,
To the beauteous black cow.

For milk, for milk substance, for milk produce,
For whisked whey, for milk riches,
For curdled milk, for milk plenty,
For butter, for cheese, for curds.

For progeny and prosperity,
For rutting time and rutting,
For desire and kine,
For passion and prosperity.

The nine wells of Mac Lir,
Relief on thee to pour,
Put stop to thy blood,
Put run to thy urine,
Thou cow of cows, black cow.

Great sea,
Red cascade
Stop blood,
Flow urine.

182 The gravel charm

I have a charm for the gravel disease,
For the disease that is perverse;
I have a charm for the red disease,
For the disease that is irritating.

As runs a river cold,
As grinds a rapid mill,
Thou who didst ordain land and sea,
Cease the blood and let flow the urine.

In name of Father, and of Son,
In name of Holy Spirit.

183 The strangles

"A horse in strangles,"
Quoth Columba.

"I will turn it,"
Said Christ.

"On Sunday morning?"
Quoth Columba.

"Ere rise of sun,"
Said Christ.

"Three pillars in the well,"
Quoth Columba.

"I will lift them,"
Said Christ.

"Will that heal him?"
Quoth John the Baptist.

"Assuredly,"
Said Christ.

184 The spell of the fox

Be the spell of the wood–dog,
On the feet of the fox,
On his heart, on his liver,
On his gullet of greediness,
On his surpassing pointed teeth,
On the bend of his stomach.

Be the charm of the Lord upon the sheep–kind,
The charm of Christ kindly–white, mild–white,
The charm of Mary lovely–fair, tender–fair,
Against dogs, against birds, against mankind,
Against fairy dogs, against world dogs,
Of the world hither, of the world thither.

185 Prayer of the cattlefold

I drive the kine within
The gateway of the herds,
On voice of the dead,
On voice of bull,
On voice of pairing,
On voice of grayling cow
White–headed, strong–headed, of udder.
Be the big stone of the base of the couple

Without ceasing, without decreasing,
As a full-weighted tether
Trailing from the hunch of your rump,
Till bright daylight comes in tomorrow.

The Father, the Son, the Holy Spirit,
Save you, and shield you, and tend you,
Till I or mine shall meet you again.

186 The ditch of Mary

Ditch of Mary,
Ditch of Mary;
Heron legs,
Heron legs;
Ditch of Mary,
Ditch of Mary;
Heron legs under you,
Bridge of warranty before you.

Mary placed a wand in it,
Bride placed a hand in it,
Columba placed a foot in it,
Patrick placed a cold stone.

Ditch of Mary,
Ditch of Mary;
Heron legs,
Heron legs;
Ditch of Mary,
Ditch of Mary;
Heron legs under you,
Bridge of warranty before you.

Muirel placed myrrh in it,
Uriel placed honey in it,
Muirinn placed wine in it,
And Michael placed in it power.

Ditch of Mary,
Ditch of Mary;
Heron legs,
Heron legs;
Ditch of Mary,
Ditch of Mary;
Heron legs under you,
Bridge of warranty before you.

187 The hind

Peter and Paul were passing by,
While a hind in the path was bearing a fawn;
"A hind is bearing there," said Peter;
"I see it is so," said Paul.

"As her foliage falls from the tree,
So may her placenta fall to the ground,
In name of the Father of love and of the Son of grace,
And of the Spirit of loving wisdom;
Father of love and Son of grace,
And Spirit of loving wisdom."

188 Columba, Peter, and Paul

A day as I was going to Rome,
I forgathered with Columba, Peter, and Paul,
The talk that they had and that happened in their mouths,
Was loud-lunged, white-bellied, female calves,
As was spoken in the prophecy,
On this foundation for a year and a day,
Through the bosom of the God of life and all the hosts,
Chief of chiefs and of the everlasting Powers above.

189 The indigestion spell

The spell made of Columba,
To the one cow of the woman,
For the *cailleach,* for the gum disease,
For the bag, for the *colg,*
For the indigestion;

For the flux disease,
For the cud disease,
For the *mir* disease,
For the *tolg* disease,
For the surfeit;

For the *cil* disease,
For the *mil* disease,
For the water disease,
For the red disease,
For the madness;

I will cleave the *crailleach,*
I will cleave the gum disease,
I will cleave the bag,
I will cleave the *colg,*
And I will kill the indigestion;

I will cleave the flux,
I will cleave the cud,
I will cleave the *mir,*
I will cleave the *tolg,*
And drive away the surfeit;

I will cleave the *cil,*
I will cleave the *mil,*
I will cleave the water,
I will cleave the red,
And wither will the madness.

190 Cud chewing charm

If thou hast eaten the grass of the nine bens,
Of the nine fells, of the nine hillocks,
If thou hast drunk the water of the nine falls,
Of the nine streams, of the nine lakelets,
Poor "Gruaigein" of the hard paunch,
Loved one, chew thou thy cud.
Poor "Gruaigein" of the hard paunch,
Loved one, chew thou thy cud.

191 Charm of the churn

Come will the free, come;
Come will the bond, come;
Come will the bells, come;
Come will the maers, come;
Come will the blade, come;
Come will the sharp, come;
Come will the hounds, come;
Come will the wild, come;
Come will the mild, come;
Come will the kind, come;
Come will the loving, come;
Come will the squint, come;
Come will he of the yellow cap,
That will set the churn a–running.

The free will come,
The bond will come,
The bells will come,
The maers will come,
The blades will come,
The sharp will come,
The hounds will come,
The wild will come,
The mild will come,

The kind will come,
The loving will come,
The devious will come,
The brim–full of the globe will come,
To set the churn a–running;
The kindly Columba will come in his array,
And the golden–haired Bride of the kine.

A splash is here,
A plash is here,
A plash is here,
A splash is here,
A crash is here,
A squash is here,
A squash is here,
A crash is here,
A big soft snail is here,
The sap of each of the cows is here,
A thing better than honey and spruce,
A bogle yellow and fresh is here.

A thing better than right is here,
The fist of the big priest is here,
A thing better than the carcase is here,
The head of the dead man is here,
A thing better than wine is here,
The full of the cog of Caristine
Of live things soft and fair are here,
  Of live things soft and fair are here.

Come, thou churn, come;
Come, thou churn, come;
Come, thou life; come, thou breath;
Come, thou churn, come;
Come, thou churn, come;
Come, thou cuckoo; come, thou jackdaw;
Come, thou churn, come;
Come, thou churn, come;

Come will the little lark from the sky;
Come will the little carlin of the black–cap.

Come, thou churn, come;
Come, thou churn, come;
Come will the merle, come will the mavis;
Come will the music from the bower;
Come, thou churn, come;
Come, thou churn, come;
Come, thou wild cat,
To ease thy throat;
Come, thou churn, come;
Come, thou churn, come.

Come, thou hound, and quench thy thirst;
Come, thou churn, come;
Come, thou churn, come;
Come, thou poor; come, thou naked;
Come, thou churn, come;
Come, thou churn, come;
Come, ye alms–deserver
Of most distressful moan;
Come, thou churn, come;
Come, thou churn, come;
Come, each hungry creature,
And satisfy the thirst of thy body.
Come, thou churn, come;
Come, thou churn, come;
It is the God of the elements who bestowed on us,
And not the charm of a carlin with plant.
Come, thou churn, come;
Come, thou churn, come;
Come, thou fair–white Mary,
And endow to me my means;
Come, thou churn, come;
Come, thou churn, come;
Come, thou beauteous Bride,
And bless the substance of my kine.

Come, thou churn, come;
Come, thou churn, come;
The churning made of Mary,
In the fastness of the glen,
To decrease her milk,
To increase her butter;
Buttermilk to wrist,
Butter to elbow;
   Come, thou churn, come;
   Come, thou churn, come.

192 The charm sent of Mary

The charm sent of Mary Virgin
To the nun who was dwelling
On the floor of the glen,
On the cold high moors:
   On the floor of the glen,
   On the cold high moors.

She put spell to saliva,
To increase her butter,
To decrease her milk,
To make plentiful her food:
   To increase her butter,
   To decrease her milk,
   To make plentiful her food.

193 The wicked who would me harm

The wicked who would do me harm
May he take the throat disease,
Globularly, spirally, circularly,
Fluxy, pellety, horny-grim.

Be it harder than the stone,
Be it blacker than the coal,
Be it swifter than the duck,
Be it heavier than the lead.

Be it fiercer, fiercer, sharper, harsher, more malignant,
Than the hard, wound–quivering holly,
Be it sourer than the sained, lustrous, bitter, salt salt,
Seven seven times.

Oscillating thither,
Undulating hither,
Staggering downwards,
Floundering upwards.

Drivelling outwards,
Snivelling inwards,
Oft hurrying out,
Seldom coming in.

A wisp the portion of each hand,
A foot in the base of each pillar,
A leg the prop of each jamb,
A flux driving and dragging him.

A dysentery of blood from heart, from form, from bones,
From the liver, from the lobe, from the lungs,
And a searching of veins, of throat, and of kidneys,
To my contemners and traducers.

In name of the God of might,
Who warded from me every evil,
And who shielded me in strength
From the net of my breakers
   And destroyers.

194 Augury of Mary

God over me, God under me,
God before me, God behind me,
I on Thy path, O God,
Thou, O God, in my steps.

The augury made of Mary to her Son,
The offering made of Bride through her palm,
Sawest Thou it, King of life?
Said the King of life that He saw.

The augury made by Mary for her own offspring,
When He was for a space amissing,
Knowledge of truth, not knowledge of falsehood,
That I shall truly see all my quest.

Son of beauteous Mary, King of life,
Give Thou me eyes to see all my quest,
With grace that shall never fail, before me,
That shall never quench nor dim.

Miscellaneous

195 The first miracle of Christ

Joseph and Mary went
To the numbering up,
And the birds began chorusing
In the woods of the turtle–doves.

The two were walking the way,
Till they reached a thick wood,
And in the wood there was fruit
Which was as red as the rasp.

That was the time when she was great,
That she was carrying the King of grace,
And she took a desire for the fruit
That was growing on the gracious slope.

Then spoke Mary to Joseph,
In a voice low and sweet:
"Give to me of the fruit, Joseph,
That I may quench my desire."

And Joseph spoke to Mary,
And the hard pain in his breast:
"I will give thee of the fruit, Mary,
But who is the father of thy burthen?"

Then it was that the Babe spoke,
From out of her womb:
"Bend ye down every beautiful bough,
That my Mother may quench her desire."

And from the bough that was highest,
To the bough that was lowest,
They all bent down to her knee,
And Mary partook of the fruit
In her loved land of prophecy.

Then Joseph said to Mary,
And he full of heavy contrition:
"It is carrying Him thou art,
The King of glory and of grace.
Blessed art thou, Mary,
  Among the women of all lands.
Blessed art thou, Mary,
  Among the women of all lands."

196 The Virgin and child

The Virgin was seen approaching,
Christ so young on her breast,
Angels making them obeisance,
The King of glory saying it is just.

The Virgin of gold-bedewed locks,
The Jesu whiter than snow,
Seraphs of song singing their praise,
The King of glory saying it is just.

197 God of the moon

God of the moon, God of the sun,
God of the globe, God of the stars,
God of the waters, the land, and the skies,
Who ordained to us the King of promise.

It was Mary fair who went upon her knee,
It was the King of life who went upon her lap,
Darkness and tears were set behind,
And the star of guidance went up early.

Illumed the land, illumed the world,
Illumed doldrum and current,
Grief was laid and joy was raised,
Music was set up with harp and pedal-harp.

198 God of the moon, God of the sun

God of the moon, God of the sun,
Who ordained to us the Son of mercy.
The fair Mary upon her knee,
Christ the King of life in her lap.
I am the cleric established,
Going round the founded stones,
I behold mansions, I behold shores,
I behold angels floating,
I behold the shapely rounded column
Coming landwards in friendship to us.

199 Safety of the generous

Columba tells to us, that
To hell the generous shall never go;
But those who steal and those who swear,
They shall lose their right to God.

200 Mother's consecration

Be the great God between thy two shoulders,
To protect thee in thy going and in thy coming,
Be the Son of Mary Virgin near thine heart,
And be the perfect Spirit upon thee pouring:
Oh, the perfect Spirit upon thee pouring!
[Aodh [Una
[Torquil [Light
[Tascal [Health.

201 He who was crucified

Thou who wert hanged upon the tree,
And wert crucified by the condemnation of the people,
Now that I am grown old and grey,
Take to my confession–prayer, O God! pity.

No wonder to me great is my wickedness,
I am a poor clattering cymbal,
In my youth I was profane,
In my age I am forlorn.

A time ere came the Son of God,
The earth was a black morass,
Without star, without sun, without moon,
Without body, without heart, without form.

Illumined plains, illumined hills,
Illumined the great green sea,
Illumined the whole globe together,
When the Son of God came to earth.

Then it was that spoke the Mary of grace,
The Virgin always most kindly and wise,
When Joseph gave to her his love,
He desired to be often in her presence.

A compact there was between Joseph and Virgin,
In order well-becoming and just,
That the compact might be confirmed
By the seal of the Great King of virtues.

They went with him to the Temple of God,
Where the clerics sat within;
As ordained of the Great High King,
They married ere they came out.

An angel came afterwards:
"Joseph, why excited thou?"
"I got a woman from the clerics,
It is not natural for me to be calm."

"Joseph, abide thou by thy reason,
Not enlightened of thee to find fault,
What thou hast gotten is a virgin pure,
On whom man never put hand."

"How can I believe that from thee?
I myself, my grief! have knowledge:
When I laid me down by her shoulder
A living child beneath her girdle throbbed."

202 That cock

It was then spoke the rude woman:
"It was the wicked who made my ruin,
Drive the liar down below the beam,
And thou shalt be welcome to my house.

"That cock thou hast in the pot,
Chopped as broken as the kail,
The liar shall not go to the pit
Till he shall crow upon the spar."

The cock went upon the spar,
He placed his two wings to his body,
He crew sweetly, melodiously,
And my King came from the tree.

The people not liked of God
Are those who lie and those who swear;
Rather would He have the genuine prayer
And water from the eyelids flowing swiftly.

203 Omens

Early on the morning of Monday,
I heard the bleating of a lamb,

And the kid-like cry of snipe,
While gently sitting bent,

And the grey-blue cuckoo,
And no food on my stomach.

On the fair evening of Tuesday,
I saw on the smooth stone,
The snail slimy, pale,

And the ashy wheatear
On the top of the dyke of holes,

The foal of the old mare
Of sprauchly gait and its back to me.

And I knew from these
That the year would not go well with me.

204 Early Easter Monday

Early on the day of Easter Monday,
I saw on the brine
A duck and a white swan
Swim together.

I heard on Tuesday
The snipe of the seasons,
Bleating on high
  And calling.

On Wednesday I had been
Cutting the channelled fucus,
And then saw I the three
  Arising.

I knew immediately
That a flitting there was,
Blessing there would not be
  After that.

The girth of Bride calm,
The girth of Mary mild,
The girth of Michael strong,
Upon me and mine,
  Upon me and mine.

205 Omen of the swans

I heard the sweet voice of the swans,
At the parting of night and day,
Gurgling on the wings of travelling,
  Pouring forth their strength on high.

I quickly stood me, nor made I move,
A look which I gave forth to see
Who should be guiding in front?
  The queen of fortune, the white swan.

This was on the evening of Friday,
My thoughts were of the Tuesday:
I lost my means and my kinsfolk,
  A year from that Friday, for ever.

Shouldst thou see a swan of Friday,
In the joyous morning dawn,
There shall be increase on thy means and thy kin,
   Nor shall thy flocks be always dying.

206 Omens

I heard the cuckoo with no food in my stomach,
I heard the stock-dove on the top of the tree,
I heard the sweet singer in the copse beyond,
And I heard the screech of the owl of the night.

I saw the lamb with his back to me,
I saw the snail on the bare flagstone,
I saw the foal with his rump to me,
I saw the wheatear on a dyke of holes,
I saw the snipe while sitting bent,
And I foresaw that the year would not
   Go well with me.

207 The incense

In the day of thy health,
Thou wilt not give devotion,
Thou wilt not give kine,
   Nor wilt thou offer incense.

Head of haughtiness,
Heart of greediness,
Mouth unhemmed,
   Nor ashamed art thou.

But thy winter will come,
And the hardness of thy distress,
And thy head shall be as
   The clod in the earth.

Thy strength having failed,
Thine aspect having gone,
And thou a thrall,
On thy two knees.

208 Poem of the beetles

When the Being of glory was in retreat,
And wicked men in pursuit of Him,
What said the groveller of blindness,
To the beetle and the butterfly?

"Saw ye passing today or yestreen,
The Son of my love — the Son of God?"
"We saw, we saw," said the black beetle,
"The Son of freedom pass yesterday."

"Wrong! wrong! wrong art thou,"
Said the sacred beetle earthy;
"A big year it was yestreen
Since the Son of God passed."

209 Poem of the beetles

When Christ was under the wood,
And enemies were pursuing Him,
The crooked one of deception,
Said to the black beetle and the butterfly:

"Saw ye pass today or yesterday,
The Son of my love, the Son of God?"
"We saw! we saw!" said the black beetle,
"The Son of redemption pass yesterday."

"False! false! false!"
Said the little clay beetle of horses,
"A full year yesterday,
The Son of God went by."

210 Poem of the beetle

Little beetle, little beetle,
Rememberest thou yesterday?
Little beetle, little beetle,
Rememberest thou yesterday?
Little beetle, little beetle,
Rememberest thou yesterday
The Son of God went by?

211 Lullaby

Thou white swan,
Hu hi! ho ho!

Sad thy condition,
Hu hi! ho ho!

Pitiful thy state,
Hu hi! ho ho!

Thy blood flowing,
Hu hi! ho ho!
Hu hi! ho ho!

Thou white swan,
Hu hi! ho ho!

Far from thy friends,
Hu hi! ho ho!

Dame of thy converse,
Hu hi! ho ho!

Remain near me,
  Hu hi! ho ho!
  Hu hi! ho ho!

Leech of gladness thou,
  Hu hi! ho ho!

Sain my little child,
  Hu hi! ho ho!

Shield him from death,
  Hu hi! ho ho!

Hasten him to health,
  Hu hi! ho ho!

As thou desirest,
  Hu hi! ho ho!
  Hu hi! hi ho!

Pain and sorrow
  Hu hi! ho ho!

To thine injurer,
  Hu hi! ho ho!
  Hu hi! hi ho!

A thousand welcomes to thee,
  Hu hi! ho ho!

Life and health be thine,
  Hu hi! ho ho!

The age of joy be thine,
  Hu hi! ho ho!

In every place,
  Hu hi! ho ho!
  Hu hi! hi ho!

Peace and growth to him,
  Hu hi! ho ho!

Strength and worth to him,
  Hu hi! ho ho!

Victory of place,
  Hu hi! ho ho!

Everywhere to him,
  Hu hi! ho ho!
  Hu hi! hi ho!

The Mary Mother,
  Hu hi! ho ho!

Fair white lovely,
  Hu hi! ho ho!

Be fondling thee,
  Hu hi! ho ho!

Be dandling thee,
  Hu hi! ho ho!

Be bathing thee,
  Hu hi! ho ho!

Be rearing thee,
  Hu hi! ho ho!

Be shielding thee
  Hu hi! ho ho!

From the net of thine enemy;
  Hu hi! ho ho!
  Hu hi! ho ho!

Be caressing thee,
  Hu hi! ho ho!

Be guarding thee,
  Hu hi! ho ho!

Be filling thee
  Hu hi! ho ho!

With the graces;
  Hu hi! ho ho!
  Hu hi! hi ho!

The love of thy mother, thou,
Hu hi! ho ho!

The love of her love, thou,
Hu hi! ho ho!

The love of the angels, thou,
Hu hi! ho ho!

In Paradise!
Hu hi! ho ho!
Hu hi! hi ho!

212 The melodious lady–lord

Who is she the melodious lady–lord,
At the base of the knoll,
At the mouth of the wave?

Not the alc,
Not the duck,
Not the swan,
And not alone is she.

Who is she the melodious lady–lord,
At the base of the knoll,
At the mouth of the wave?

Not the lark,
Not the merle,
Not the mavis,
On the bough is she.

Who is she the melodious lady–lord,
At the base of the knoll,
At the mouth of the wave?

Not the murmuring ptarmigan
Of the hill is she.

Who is she the melodious lady–lord,
At the base of the knoll,
At the mouth of the wave?

Not the grilse of the stream,
Not the seal of the wave,
Not the sea maiden
Of May is she.

Who is she the melodious lady–lord,
At the base of the knoll,
At the mouth of the wave?

Not the dame of the distaff,
Not the damsel of the lyre,
Not the golden–haired maid
Of the flocks is she.

Who is she the melodious lady–lord,
At the base of the knoll,
At the mouth of the wave?

Melodious lady–lord,
God–like in loveliness,

Daughter of a king,
Granddaughter of a king,
Great–granddaughter of a king,
Great–great–granddaughter of a king,
Great–great–great–granddaughter of a king,
Wife of a king,
Mother of a king,
Foster–mother of a king.,
She lullabying a king,
And he under her plaid.

From Erin she travelled,
For Lochlann is bound,
May the Trinity travel with her
Whithersoever she goes,
  Whithersoever she goes.

213 Queen of grace

Smooth her hand,
Fair her foot,
Graceful her form,
Winsome her voice,
Gentle her speech,
Stately her mien,
Warm the look of her eye,
Mild the expression of her face,
While her lovely white breast heaves on her bosom
Like the black-headed sea-gull on the gently heaving wave.

Holy is the virgin of gold-mist hair,
With tenderest babe at the base of the bens,
No food for either of them under the arch of the sky,
No shelter under the sun to shield them from the foe.

The shield of the Son of God covers her,
The inspiration of the Son of God guides her,
The word of the Son of God is food to her,
His star is a bright revealing light to her.

The darkness of night is to her as the brightness of day,
The day to her gaze is always a joy,
While the Mary of grace is in every place,
With the seven beatitudes compassing her,
The seven beatitudes compassing her.

214 Killmoluag

FIRST BOY
Uill! hill! uill! O!
In what kill shall this go?

SECOND BOY
In Killmoluag of Lismore,
Where the maggots grow!

Uill! hill! uill! O!
In what kill shall this go?

In Killmoluag of Lismore,
Fairest 'neath the sun.

Uill! hill! uill! o!
In what kill shall this go?

In Killmoluag of Lismore,
I vow he shall not rise!

215 The kertch

A thousand hails to thee beneath thy kertch,
During thy course mayest thou be whole,
Strength and days be thine in peace,
Thy paradise with thy means increase.

In beginning thy dual race, and thou young,
In beginning thy course, seek thou the God of life,
Fear not but He will rightly rule
Thine every secret need and prayer.

This spousal crown thou now hast donned,
Full oft has gotten grace to woman,

Be thou virtuous, but be gracious,
Be thou pure in word and hand.

Be thou hospitable, yet be wise,
Be thou courageous, but be calm,
Be thou frank, but be reserved,
Be thou exact, yet generous.

Be not miserly in giving,
Do not flatter, yet be not cold,
Speak not ill of man, though ill he be,
If spoken of, show not resentment.

Be thou careful of thy name,
Be thou dignified yet kind,
The hand of God be on thine helm,
In inception, in act, and in thought.

Be not querulous beneath thy cross,
Walk thou warily when thy cup is full,
Never to evil give thou countenance,
And with thy kertch, to thee a hundred thousand hails!

216 Fragment

As it was,
As it is,
As it shall be
Evermore,
O Thou Triune
Of grace!
With the ebb,
With the flow,
O Thou Triune
Of grace!
With the ebb,
With the flow.

Birth and Baptism

Birth and death, the two events of life, had many ceremonies attached to them. Many are now obsolete, and those that still live are but the echoes of those that were current in the past. The customs connected with life and death were so many that only a few can be mentioned.

When a child was born it was handed to and fro across the fire three times, some words being addressed in an almost inaudible murmur to the fire–god. It was then carried three times sunwise round the fire, some words being murmured to the sun–god. These dedications to the fire– and sun–gods are indicative of faraway lands and faraway times; but of what land and of what time?

The first water in which the child is washed after it is born into the world, the bathing–woman puts a gold piece or a coin of silver into the vessel of water in which the child is being washed. And the woman does this for love of peace, for love of means, for love of wealth, for love of joyousness by day and by night, for grace of goodness, for grace of fortune, for grace of victory on every field.

After the child is born it is baptized by the nurse; this is called *baisteadh breith* (birth baptism), or *baisteadh ban–ghlùin* (knee–woman's baptism).

The reciter said: "When the image of the God of life is born into the world I put three little drops of water on the child's forehead. I put the first little drop in the name of the Father, and the watching–women say Amen. I put the second little drop in the name of the Son, and the watching–women say Amen. I put the third little drop in the name of the Spirit, and the watching–women say Amen. And I beseech the Holy Three to lave and to bathe the child and to preserve it to Themselves. And the watching–women say Amen. All the people in the house are raising their voices with the watching–women, giving witness that the child has been committed to the blessed Trinity. By the Book itself! Ear has never heard music more beautiful than the music of the watching–women when they are consecrating the seed of man and committing him to the great God of life. No seed of fairy, no seed of the hosts of the air, no seed of the world's people, can lift away the happy tranquil little sleeper for whom is made the beneficent prayer of the baptism; eye cannot lie on him, envy cannot lie on him, malice cannot lie on him; the two arms of the mild Mary of grace and the two arms of gentle Christ are to free him, shielding and surrounding and succouring the joyous little sleeper of the baptism."

Peigidh Nic Cormaig, Peggy MacCormack, née MacDonald, is now an old woman, but a fine woman still, mentally and physically. She said: "I am two score and fifteen years a knee–woman, and never has loss or mishap befallen a woman about whom were my two hands; and the praise of that be to the God of life and not to me. I was always doing my best, but I was always praying to Jesus the Son of Mary to keep my two eyes and to guide my two hands in every difficulty and in every step. I was weak, but He was strong; and the glory be to Him and to none other."

Were the child to die unbaptized, it would not be allowable to bury the body with Christian rites in consecrated ground. Stillborn or unbaptized infants were buried in a place by themselves, often in a very inaccessible place among rocks. If there were no such place available, a sunless spot outside the churchyard was used. Adjoining old places of burial there was often a special place for the burial of unbaptized infants, suicides and murderers. Such a place was called *torran* (little mound). What is now the parish church of Lismore was in pre–Presbyterian times the chancel of the Cathedral Church of the See of Argyll and the Isles, and was called Eaglais Mhor Mo–Luag, the Great Church of Mo–Luag. Beside the church are Cill Mo–Luag and Cladh Mo–Luag, Mo–Luag's Cell and Burial Place. Near the latter is a place known as Cladh na Cloinne, the Burial Place of the Children, and Cladh na Cloinne gun Bhaisteadh, the Burial Place of the Unbaptized Children. The remains of the enclosing wall were visible some years ago. Cladh Mo–Luag itself formerly extended about two hundred yards further down the field than it does at present. While this disused part was being drained and trenched, some beautifully carved stones were discovered. On the farm of West Cralacan there is a shelf among the rocks where unbaptized infants were buried, and that within the memory of persons still living. In many districts such infants were buried between sundown and sunrise, "without beam of sun or ray of moon, on a night black and dark, where no eye could see and no man could discern." It was thought that such a child had no soul; but it had a spirit, and this spirit, *taran,* entered into a rock and abode there, and became *mac talla* (son of rock), which is the Gaelic term for "echo." As to the manner and time of burial, compare Psalm 58.8: "like the untimely birth of a woman that they may never see the sun." What relationship these spirits had with the sprites known as *iridich nan creag,* the gnomes of the rocks, I am not sure.

The father of an unbaptized or stillborn child was not allowed to attend the funeral on pain of having no more children. Instead, he must go about his usual work in his usual clothes as if nothing untoward had occurred, leaving his friends to do their friendly work. This often necessitated travelling long distances, and often difficult climbing, when the burying–ground for these children was situated in a remote and rocky hillside.

Should a child, born alive, die in a few days without having received either lay or clerical baptism, the father was considered to be at fault and his negligence was much resented by the community. Not always is it so easy to obtain clerical baptism as it might seem to the dwellers in cities. In one of the small islands of the Long Island I have seen, on one of the minister's infrequent visits, children ranging up to seven years being baptized, and on one occasion I saw a boy of fourteen years being baptized, not because his parents desired adult baptism, but from lack of previous opportunity. That, however, was about thirty years ago.

I have known a minister detained for seven weeks on a small island whither he had gone to preach for a Sunday; and the late Father Allan MacDonald once went to Mingulay to hold service, meaning to return in the evening and to marry a young couple in Barra next day. Over seven weeks passed before he could get back. He spent the time in religious exercises among the people, and in collecting old lore; and the marriage party spent it in dancing, singing, and composing songs on the anxious bride and groom. So we need not wonder that some remote islands might remain without visits from the clergy for several years.

Eight days from birth the child is baptized by the clergy and received formally into the Christian Church. This baptism is variously called *baisteadh cléirich* (clerical baptism); *baisteadh mór* (great baptism); *baisteadh eaglais* (church baptism); *baisteadh pears eaglais* (baptism of the churchman); *baisteadh sagairt* (baptism of the priest), *baisteadh ministeir* (baptism of the minister); and by other names according to the form prevailing in the place. The clerical baptism is a social function, when friends and neighbours celebrate the reception of the child into the Christian Faith. The meeting is called *féisd baistidh* and *cuirm baistidh* (feast of baptism). At this function and feast the child is handed from person to person around the company, going *deiseil,* in a sunwise direction. Every person who takes the child is required to express a wish for its welfare. The wish may be in prose or in verse, but preferably in verse, and original if possible. Verse lives when prose has perished. This is why Gaelic sayings and proverbs are commonly in rime. Prose wishes at the clerical baptism are indeed rare; rimed wishes are most usual.

217 Birth baptism

When a child was born the midwife would put three small drops of water upon the forehead of the little one in name of Father, in name of Son, in name of Spirit, and she would say in this wise:

The little drop of the Father
On thy little forehead, beloved one.

The little drop of the Son
On thy little forehead, beloved one.

The little drop of the Spirit
On thy little forehead beloved one.

To aid thee from the fays,
To guard thee from the host;

To aid thee from the gnome,
To shield thee from the spectre;

To keep thee for the Three,
To shield thee, to surround thee;

To save thee for the Three,
To fill thee with the graces;

The little drop of the Three
To lave thee with the graces.

Then the midwife would give the child to a nurse to wash it, and the nurse would put a small palmful of water on the poor little infant, and she would sing the sweetest music that ever ear heard on earth, and she would say in this wise:

A wavelet for thy form,
A wavelet for thy voice,
A wavelet for thy sweet speech;

A wavelet for thy luck,
A wavelet for thy good,
A wavelet for thy health;

A wavelet for thy throat,
A wavelet for thy pluck,
A wavelet for thy graciousness;
Nine waves for thy graciousness.

218 Birth baptism

In name of Father,
  Amen.
In name of Son,
  Amen.
In name of Spirit,
  Amen.

Three to lave thee,
  Amen.
Three to bathe thee,
  Amen.
Three to save thee,
  Amen.

Father and Son and Spirit,
  Amen.
Father and Son and Spirit,
  Amen.
Father and Son and Spirit,
  Amen.

219 The prayer of baptism

When the woman is bathing the child who bas been born into the world, she puts nine little wavelets of water on the pretty little infant who has come home from the bosom of the everlasting Father. While she is doing this, she herself and the serving–women sing the baptismal verse.

The little wavelet for thy form,
The little wavelet for thy voice,
The little wavelet for thy sweet speech.

The little wavelet for thy means,
The little wavelet for thy generosity,
The little wavelet for thine appetite.

The little wavelet for thy wealth,
The little wavelet for thy life,
The little wavelet for thine health.

Nine waves of grace to thee,
The waves of the Physician of thy salvation.

The little palmful for thy form,
The little palmful for thy voice,
The little palmful for thy sweet speech.

The little palmful for thine eating,
The little palmful for thy taking,
The little palmful for thy vigour.

The little palmful of the Father,
The little palmful of the Son,
The little palmful of the Spirit.

Nine little palmfuls for thy grace
(In name of) the Three in One.

220 The baptism by the knee–woman

When the child comes into the world, the knee–woman puts three drops of water on the forehead of the poor little infant, who has come home to us from the bosom of the everlasting Father. And the woman does this in the name and in the reverence of the kind and powerful Trinity, and says:

In name of God,
In name of Jesus,
In name of Spirit,
The perfect Three of power.

The little drop of the Father
On thy little forehead, beloved one.

The little drop of the Son
On thy little forehead, beloved one.

The little drop of the Spirit
On thy little forehead, beloved one.

To aid thee, to guard thee,
To shield thee, to surround thee.

To keep thee from the fays,
To shield thee from the host.

To sain thee from the gnome,
To deliver thee from the spectre.

The little drop of the Three
To shield thee from the sorrow.

The little drop of the Three
To fill thee with Their pleasantness.

The little drop of the Three
To fill thee with Their virtue.

O the little drop of the Three
To fill thee with Their virtue.

221 A small drop of water

A small drop of water
To thy forehead, beloved,
Meet for Father, Son and Spirit,
The Triune of power.

A small drop of water
To encompass my beloved,
Meet for Father, Son and Spirit,
The Triune of power.

A small drop of water
To fill thee with each grace,
Meet for Father, Son and Spirit,
The Triune of power.

Morning Prayers

222 Prayer at dressing

Bless to me, O God,
My soul and my body;
Bless to me, O God,
My belief and my condition;

Bless to me, O God,
My heart and my speech,
And bless to me, O God,
The handling of my hand;

Strength and busyness of morning,
Habit and temper of modesty,
Force and wisdom of thought,
And Thine own path, O God of virtues,
Till I go to sleep this night;

Thine own path, O God of virtues,
Till I go to sleep this night.

223 Prayer at rising

Thou King of moon and sun,
Thou King of stars beloved,
Thou Thyself knowest our need,
O Thou merciful God of life.

Each day that we move,
Each time that we awaken,
Causing vexation and gloom
To the King of hosts Who loved us.

Be with us through each day,
Be with us through each night;
Be with us each night and day,
Be with us each day and night.

224 Prayer

Thanks to Thee ever, O gentle Christ,
That Thou hast raised me freely from the black
And from the darkness of last night
To the kindly light of this day.

Praise unto Thee, O God of all creatures,
According to each life Thou hast poured on me,
My desire, my word, my sense, my repute,
My thought, my deed, my way, my fame.

225 Thanksgiving

Thanks to Thee, O God, that I have risen today,
To the rising of this life itself;
May it be to Thine own glory, O God of every gift,
And to the glory of my soul likewise.

O great God, aid Thou my soul
With the aiding of Thine own mercy;
Even as I clothe my body with wool,
Cover Thou my soul with the shadow of Thy wing.

Help me to avoid every sin,
And the source of every sin to forsake;
And as the mist scatters on the crest of the hills,
May each ill haze clear from my soul, O God.

226 Prayer at rising

Bless to me, O God,
Each thing mine eye sees;
Bless to me, O God,
Each sound mine ear hears;
Bless to me, O God,
Each odour that goes to my nostrils;
Bless to me, O God,
Each taste that goes to my lips;
Each note that goes to my song,
Each ray that guides my way,
Each thing that I pursue,
Each lure that tempts my will,
The zeal that seeks my living soul,
The Three that seek my heart,
The zeal that seeks my living soul,
The Three that seek my heart.

227 Petition at rising

Thou holy Father of verity,
Thou kindly Father of mercy,
Deliver me from the spells,
Deliver me from the charms.

Do Thou Thyself sain me on this day,
And on each single day;
Do Thou Thyself sain me on this night,
And on each single night.

Father everlasting and God of life,
Do Thou grant us Thy forgiveness
In my wild thought,
In my foolish deed,
In my rough talk,
In my empty speech.

Father everlasting and God of life,
Do Thou grant us Thy forgiveness
In my false desire,
In my hateful doing,
In my destructive courses,
In my worthless liking.

O Lord and God of life,
Ward off from me the bane of the silent women.

O Father and God of life,
Ward off from me the bane of the wanton women.

O Father everlasting and God of life,
Ward off from me the bane of the fairy women.

O Father everlasting and God of life,
Ward off from me the bane of the false women.

O Father everlasting and God of life,
Crown Thou me with the crown of Thy love.

Nor allow stain to my soul,
Nor allow spot to my body,
Nor allow taint to my breath,
O Father of humanity.

As Thou wert before
At the beginning of my life,
Be Thou again
At the end of my course:

Now and henceforth,
In my life, in my death,
O Son and O Father,
O Spirit of grace!

228 Morning prayer

I believe, O God of all gods,
That Thou art the eternal Father of life;
I believe, O God of all gods,
That Thou art the eternal Father of love.

I believe, O God of all gods,
That Thou art the eternal Father of the saints;
I believe, O God of all gods,
That Thou art the eternal Father of each one.

I believe, O God of all gods,
That Thou art the eternal Father of mankind;
I believe, O God of all gods,
That Thou art the eternal Father of the world.

I believe, O Lord and God of the peoples,
That Thou art the creator of the high heavens,
That Thou art the creator of the skies above,
That Thou art the creator of the oceans below.

I believe, O Lord and God of the peoples,
That Thou art He Who created my soul and set its warp,
Who created my body from dust and from ashes,
Who gave to my body breath, and to my soul its possession.

Father, bless to me my body,
Father, bless to me my soul,
Father, bless to me my life,
Father, bless to me my belief.

Father eternal and Lord of the peoples,
I believe that Thou hast remedied my soul in the Spirit of healing,
That Thou gavest Thy loved Son in covenant for me,
That Thou hast purchased my soul with the precious blood of Thy Son.

Father eternal and Lord of life,
I believe that Thou didst pour on me the Spirit of grace at the bestowal of baptism.

* * *

Father eternal and Lord of mankind,
Enwrap Thou my body and my soul beloved,
Safeguard me this night in the sanctuary of Thy love,
Shelter me this night in the shelter of the saints.

Thou hast brought me up from last night
To the gracious light of this day,
Great joy to provide for my soul,
And to do excelling good to me.

Thanks be to Thee, Jesu Christ,
For the many gifts Thou hast bestowed on me,
Each day and night, each sea and land,
Each weather fair, each calm, each wild.

I am giving Thee worship with my whole life,
I am giving Thee assent with my whole power,
I am giving Thee praise with my whole tongue,
I am giving Thee honour with my whole utterance.

I am giving Thee reverence with my whole understanding,
I am giving Thee offering with my whole thought,
I am giving Thee praise with my whole fervour,
I am giving Thee humility in the blood of the Lamb.

I am giving Thee love with my whole devotion,
I am giving Thee kneeling with my whole desire,
I am giving Thee love with my whole heart,
I am giving Thee affection with my whole sense;
I am giving Thee my existence with my whole mind,
I am giving Thee my soul, O God of all gods.

My thought, my deed,
My word, my will,
My understanding, my intellect,
My way, my state.

I am beseeching Thee
To keep me from ill,
To keep me from hurt,
To keep me from harm;

To keep me from mischance,
To keep me from grief,
To keep me this night
In the nearness of Thy love.

May God shield me,
May God fill me,
May God keep me,
May God watch me.

May God bring me
To the land of peace,
To the country of the King,
To the peace of eternity.

Praise to the Father,
Praise to the Son,
Praise to the Spirit,
The Three in One.

229 The path of right

My walk this day with God,
My walk this day with Christ,
My walk this day with Spirit,
The Threefold all-kindly:
Ho! ho! ho! the Threefold all-kindly.

My shielding this day from ill,
My shielding this night from harm,
Ho! ho! both my soul and my body,
Be by Father, by Son, by Holy Spirit:
By Father, by Son, by Holy Spirit.

Be the Father shielding me,
Be the Son shielding me,
Be the Spirit shielding me,
As Three and as One:
Ho! ho! ho! as Three and as One.

230 Thoughts

God's will would I do,
My own will bridle;

God's due would I give,
My own due yield;

God's path would I travel,
My own path refuse;

Christ's death would I ponder,
My own death remember;

Christ's agony would I meditate,
My love to God make warmer;

Christ's cross would I carry,
My own cross forget;

Repentance of sin would I make,
Early repentance choose;

A bridle to my tongue I would put,
A bridle on my thoughts I would keep;

God's judgment would I judge,
My own judgment guard;

Christ's redemption would I seize,
My own ransom work;

The love of Christ would I feel,
My own love know.

231 God's aid

God to enfold me,
God to surround me,
God in my speaking,
God in my thinking.

God in my sleeping,
God in my waking,
God in my watching,
God in my hoping.

God in my life,
God in my lips,
[God in my hands],
God in my heart.

God in my sufficing,
God in my slumber,
God in mine ever–living soul,
God in mine eternity.

232

Supplication

O Being of life!
O Being of peace!
O Being of time!
O Being of eternity!
O Being of eternity!

Keep me in good means,
Keep me in good intent,
Keep me in good estate,
Better than I know to ask,
Better than I know to ask!

Shepherd me this day,
Relieve my distress,
Enfold me this night,
Pour upon me Thy grace,
Pour upon me Thy grace!

Guard for me my speech,
Strengthen for me my love,
Illume for me the stream,
Succour Thou me in death,
Succour Thou me in death!

233 Charm against venom

Be the eye of God betwixt me and each eye,
The purpose of God betwixt me and each purpose,
The hand of God betwixt me and each hand,
The shield of God betwixt me and each shield,
The desire of God betwixt me and each desire,
The bridle of God betwixt me and each bridle,
And no mouth can curse me.

Be the pain of Christ betwixt me and each pain,
The love of Christ betwixt me and each love,
The dearness of Christ betwixt me and each dearness,
The kindness of Christ betwixt me and each kindness,
The wish of Christ betwixt me and each wish,
The will of Christ betwixt me and each will,
And no venom can wound me.

Be the might of Christ betwixt me and each might,
The right of Christ betwixt me and each right,
The flowing of Spirit betwixt me and each flowing,
The laving of Spirit betwixt me and each laving,
The bathing of Spirit betwixt me and each bathing,
And no ill thing can touch me.

234 Prayer

Pray I this day my prayer to Thee, O God,
Voice I this day as voices the voice of thy mouth,
Keep I this day as keep the people of heaven,
Spend I this day as spend Thine own household,

Go I this day according to Thy laws, O God,
Pass I this day as pass the saints in heaven.

Thou loving Christ Who wast hanged upon the tree,
Each day and each night remember I Thy covenant;
In my lying down and rising up I yield me to Thy cross,
In my life and my death my health Thou art and my peace.

Each day may I remember the source of the mercies
Thou hast bestowed on me gently and generously;
Each day may I be fuller in love to Thyself
...

Each thing I have received, from Thee it came,
Each thing for which I hope, from Thy love it will come,
Each thing I enjoy, it is of Thy bounty,
Each thing I ask, comes of Thy disposing.

Holy God, loving Father, of the word everlasting,
Grant me to have of Thee this living prayer:
Lighten my understanding, kindle my will, begin my doing,
Incite my love, strengthen my weakness, enfold my desire.

Cleanse my heart, make holy my soul, confirm my faith,
Keep safe my mind and compass my body about;
As I utter my prayer from my mouth,
In mine own heart may I feel Thy presence.

And do Thou grant, O God of life,
That Thou be at my breast, that Thou be at my back,
That Thou give me my needs as may befit the crown
Thou hast promised to us in the world beyond.

And grant Thou to me, Father beloved,
From Whom each thing that is freely flows,
That no tie over–strict, no tie over–dear
May be between myself and this world below.

Place I in Thee my hope, O God,
My living hope in the Father of the heavens,
My great hope to be with Thyself
In the distant world to come.

Father and Son and Spirit,
The One Person of the Three,
Perfect, world without end,
Changeless through life eternal.

235 The Three

In name of Father,
In name of Son,
In name of Spirit,
Three in One:

Father cherish me,
Son cherish me,
Spirit cherish me,
Three all–kindly.

God make me holy,
Christ make me holy,
Spirit make me holy,
Three all–holy.

Three aid my hope,
Three aid my love,
Three aid mine eye,
And my knee from stumbling,
My knee from stumbling.

Prayers for Protection

236 Petition

O Holy God of truth,
O loving God of mercy,
Sign me from the spells,
Sign me from the charms.

Compassionate God of life,
Forgiveness to me give,
In my wanton talk,
In my lying oath,
In my foolish deed,
In my empty speech.

Compassionate God of life,
Screen from me the bane of the silent women;
Compassionate God of life,
Screen from me the bane of the wanton women;
Compassionate God of life,
Screen from me the bane of the fairy women;
Compassionate God of life,
Screen from me the bane of the false women.

As Thou wast before
At my life's beginning,
Be Thou so again
At my journey's end.

As Thou wast besides
At my soul's shaping,
Father, be Thou too
At my journey's close.

Be with me at each time,
Lying down and arising,
Be with me in sleep
Companioned by dear ones.

Be with me a–watching
Each evening and morning,
And allure me home
To the land of the saints.

237 Prayer

O Father of truth,
O Son of mercy,
Free us at this time,
Free us at every time.

Thou Son of God, grant me forgiveness
In my false swearing,
In my foolish deed,
In my empty talk.

Sain me from the hurt of the quiet women,
Sain me from the hurt of the wanton women,
Sain me from the hurt of the fairy women,
Sain me from the hurt of the world–women.

As Thou wert afore at my life's beginning,
Be Thou again at my time's ending;
Nor let into my body nor into my being
One thing that is harm to my soul beloved.

238 Prayer

O God, hearken to my prayer,
Let my earnest petition come to Thee,
For I know that Thou art hearing me
As surely as though I saw Thee with mine eyes.

I am placing a lock upon my heart,
I am placing a lock upon my thoughts,
I am placing a lock upon my lips
And double-knitting them.

Aught that is amiss for my soul
In the pulsing of my death,
Mayest Thou, O God, sweep it from me
And mayest Thou shield me in the blood of Thy love.

Let no thought come to my heart,
Let no sound come to mine ear,
Let no temptation come to mine eye,
Let no fragrance come to my nose,

Let no fancy come to my mind,
Let no ruffle come to my spirit,
That is hurtful to my poor body this night,
Nor ill for my soul at the hour of my death;

But mayest Thou Thyself, O God of life,
Be at my breast, be at my back,
Thou to me as a star, Thou to me as a guide,
From my life's beginning to my life's closing.

239 Prayer of distress

May the cross of the crucifixion tree
Upon the wounded back of Christ
Deliver me from distress,
From death and from spells.

The cross of Christ without fault,
All outstretched towards me;
O God, bless to me my lot
Before my going out.

What harm soever may be therein
May I not take thence,
For the sake of Christ the guileless,
For the sake of the King of power.

In name of the King of life,
In name of the Christ of love,
In name of the Holy Spirit,
The Triune of my strength.

240 Jesus the encompasser

Jesu! Only–begotten Son and Lamb of God the Father,
Thou didst give the wine–blood of Thy body to buy me from the grave.
My Christ! my Christ! my shield, my encircler,
Each day, each night, each light, each dark;
My Christ! my Christ! my shield, my encircler,
Each day, each night, each light, each dark.

Be near me, uphold me, my treasure, my triumph,
In my lying, in my standing, in my watching, in my sleeping.

Jesu, Son of Mary! my helper, my encircler,
Jesu, Son of David! my strength everlasting;
Jesu, Son of Mary! my helper, my encircler,
Jesu, Son of David! my strength everlasting.

241 Prayer to Jesus

I say the prayer from my mouth,
I say the prayer from my heart,
I say the prayer to Thee Thyself,
O Healing Hand, O Son of the God of salvation;

O Son of Mary the benign,
Together with Pater and Credo,
The Prayer of Mary thereafter,
And Thine own Prayer, O Son of the God of grace;

To magnify the greatness of heaven,
To magnify the greatness of God,
To magnify Thine own greatness,
And Thy glory, O Son of God of the Passion;

To give praise to Thee, Jesus,
Lord of sea and of land,
Lord of sun and of moon,
Lord of the beautiful stars.

Fountain of life to the righteous,
Faithful Brother of helpfulness,
Take Thou my prayer availing
To my soul and to my body.

Thou Lord God of the angels,
Spread over me Thy linen robe;
Shield me from every famine,
Free me from every spectral shape.

Strengthen me in every good,
Encompass me in every strait,
Safeguard me in every ill,
And from every enmity restrain me.

Be Thou between me and all things grisly,
Be Thou between me and all things mean,
Be Thou between me and all things gruesome
Coming darkly towards me.

O glorious Master of the stars,
O glorious Master of the skies,
O glorious Master of the heavens,
Blest by Thee has been every tribe and people.

Intercede Thou for me
With the Lord God of life,
With the kind Father of glory,
With the great Chief of the nations.

O Master endeared,
O Master bright, fragrant,
O Master beloved,
O Master bright, kindly,
I beseech Thee with earnestness,
I beseech Thee with humbleness,
I beseech Thee with lowliness,
I beseech Thee with tearfulness,
I beseech Thee with kneeling,
That Thou not forsake me
In the passion of my death;

But that I might find rest everlasting
In the repose of the Trinity,
In the Paradise of the godly,
In the Vine–garden of Thy love.

Put thy salve to my sight,
Put Thy balm to my wounds,
Put Thy linen robe to my skin,
O Healing Hand, O Son of the God of salvation.

O God of the weak,
O God of the lowly,
O God of the righteous,
O shield of homesteads:

Thou art calling upon us
In the voice of glory,
With the mouth of mercy
Of Thy beloved Son.

O may I find rest everlasting
In the home of Thy Trinity,
In the Paradise of the godly,
In the Sun-garden of Thy love.

242 Thou, my soul's healer

Thou, my soul's Healer,
Keep me at even,
Keep me at morning,
Keep me at noon,
On rough course faring,
Help and safeguard
My means this night.
I am tired, astray, and stumbling,
Shield Thou me from snare and sin.

243 Fragment

May the Holy Spirit distil on me
Down from out of heaven,
To aid me and to raise me,
To bind my prayer firmly
At the throne of the King of life.

* * *

In the befitting state of grace,
As is Thine own will that I should do,
O Lord God of life.

In the love of God,
In the affection of God,
In the will of God,
In the eye of God,
In the purpose of God,
In the charge of God.

As Thine own angels,
As Thine own saints,
As Thine own household
Desire in heaven,
So may I desire on earth!

244 Holy Spirit

O Holy Spirit of greatest power,
Come down upon us and subdue us;
From Thy glorious mansion in the heavens,
Thy light effulgent shed on us.

Father beloved of every naked one,
From Whom all gifts and goodness come,
Our hearts illumine with Thy mercy,
In Thy mercy shield us from all harm.

Without Thy divinity there is nothing
  In man that can earn esteem;
Without Thyself, O King of kings,
  Sinless man can never be.

In succour Thou art of all the best
  Against the soul of wildest speech;
Food art thou sweeter than all;
  Sustain and guide us at every time.

The knee that is stiff, O Healer, make pliant,
  The heart that is hard make warm beneath Thy wing;
The soul that is wandering from Thy path,
  Grasp Thou his helm and he shall not die.

Each thing that is foul cleanse Thou early,
  Each thing that is hard soften Thou with Thy grace,
Each wound that is working us pain,
  O Best of healers, make Thou whole!

Give Thou to Thy people to be diligent
  To put their trust in Thee as God,
That Thou mayest help them in every hour
  With thy sevenfold gift, O Holy Spirit generous!

245 The Three

The Three Who are over me,
The Three Who are below me,
The Three Who are above me here,
The Three Who are above me yonder;
The Three Who are in the earth,
The Three Who are in the air,
The Three Who are in the heaven,
The Three Who are in the great pouring sea.

246 Charm of protection

The charm placed of Brigit about her Foster–son,
The charm placed of Mary about her Son,
The charm placed of Michael militant about his shield,
The charm placed of God's Son about the city of heaven.

Charm against arrow,
Charm against sword,
Charm against spears,
Charm against bruising and against drowning.

Charm against firebrand,
Charm against adder,
Charm against levin,
Charm against harm in fields of battle.

Charm against child of faery,
Charm against child of earth,
Charm against hostile one,
Charm against deadly peril.

Be the cowl of Columba over thee,
Be the cowl of Michael militant about thee,
Christ's cowl, beloved, safeguard thee,
The cowl of the God of grace shield thee;

To guard thee from thy back,
To preserve thee from thy front,
From the crown of thy head and thy forehead
To the very sole of thy foot.

An isle art thou in the sea,
A hill art thou on land,
A well art thou in wilderness,
Health art thou to the ailing.

* * *

The succour of Columba is with thee,
  And his own cowl around thee;
The aiding of Michael militant is about thee,
  And his great shield protects thee.

247 Prayer

I am appealing to God,
And to Mary the Mother of Christ,
To Paul and the Apostles twelve,
To aid me and to shield me.

I am beseeching the Lord,
And Mary ever a Virgin,
To succour me and to aid me
From evil and evildoing.

May God be aiding me,
May God be succouring me,
May God be aiding me
When near the reefs.

May God safeguard me
When among the lepers,
May God safeguard me
When in narrow course.

The Son of God be shielding me from harm,
The Son of God be shielding me from ill,
The Son of God be shielding me from mishap,
The Son of God be shielding me this night.

The Son of God be shielding me with might,
The Son of God be shielding me with power;
Each one who is dealing with me aright,
So may God deal with his soul.

May God free me from every wickedness,
May God free me from every entrapment,
May God free me from every gully,
From every tortuous road, from every slough.

May God open to me every pass,
Christ open to me every narrow way,
Each soul of holy man and woman in heaven
Be preparing for me my pathway.

May God lift me up from the state of death,
From the state of torments to the state of grace,
From the earthly state of the world below
To the holy state of the high heavens.

May the fragrant Father of heaven
Be taking charge of my soul,
With His loving arm about my body,
Through each slumber and sleep of my life.

248 Encompassing

The compassing of God and His right hand
Be upon my form and upon my frame;
The compassing of the High King and the grace of the Trinity
Be upon me abiding ever eternally,
Be upon me abiding ever eternally.

May the compassing of the Three shield me in my means,
The compassing of the Three shield me this day,
The compassing of the Three shield me this night
From hate, from harm, from act, from ill,
From hate, from harm, from act, from ill.

249 Encompassing

The compassing of God be on thee,
The compassing of the God of life.

The compassing of Christ be on thee,
The compassing of the Christ of love.

The compassing of Spirit be on thee,
The compassing of the Spirit of Grace.

The compassing of the Three be on thee,
The compassing of the Three preserve thee,
The compassing of the Three preserve thee.

250 Encompassment

The holy Apostles' guarding,
The gentle martyrs' guarding,
The nine angels' guarding,
Be cherishing me, be aiding me.

The quiet Brigit's guarding,
The gentle Mary's guarding,
The warrior Michael's guarding,
Be shielding me, be aiding me.

The God of the elements' guarding,
The loving Christ's guarding,
The Holy Spirit's guarding,
Be cherishing me, be aiding me.

251 Prayer of protection

Thou Michael of militance,
Thou Michael of wounding,
Shield me from the grudge
Of ill–wishers this night,
  Ill–wishers this night.

Thou Brigit of the kine,
Thou Brigit of the mantles,
Shield me from the ban
Of the fairies of the knolls,
  The fairies of the knolls.

Thou Mary of mildness,
Thou Mary of honour,
Succour me and shield me
With thy linen mantle,
  With thy linen mantle.

Thou Christ of the tree,
Thou Christ of the cross,
Snatch me from the snares
Of the spiteful ones of evil,
  The spiteful ones of evil.

Thou Father of the waifs,
Thou Father of the naked,
Draw me to the shelter–house
Of the Saviour of the poor,
  The Saviour of the poor.

The Nativity

252 Christmas carol

This night is the long night,
Hù ri vi ho hù,
It will snow and it will drift,
Hù ri vi ho hù,
White snow there will be till day,
Hù ri vi ho hù,
White moon there will be till morn,
Hù ri vi ho hù.
This night is the eve of the Great Nativity,
Hù ri vi ho hù,
This night is born Mary Virgin's Son,
Hù ri vi ho hù,
This night is born Jesus, Son of the King of glory,
Hù ri vi ho hù,
This night is born to us the root of our joy,
Hù ri vi ho hù,
This night gleamed the sun of the mountains high,
Hù ri vi ho hù,
This night gleamed sea and shore together,

Hù ri vi ho hù,
This night was born Christ the King of greatness,
Hù ri vi ho hù.
Ere it was heard that the Glory was come,
Hù ri vi ho hù,
Heard was the wave upon the strand,
Hù ri vi ho hù;
Ere 'twas heard that His foot had reached the earth
Hù ri vi ho hù,
Heard was the song of the angels glorious,
Hù ri vi ho hù.
This night is the long night,
Hù ri vi ho hù.

Glowed to Him wood and tree,
  Glowed to Him mount and sea,
Glowed to Him land and plain,
  When that His foot was come to earth.

253 The Virgin

The Virgin was beheld approaching,
Christ so young on her breast,
Angels bowing lowly before them,
And the King of life was saying, 'Tis meet.

The Virgin of locks most glorious,
The Jesus more gleaming–white than snow,
Seraphs melodious singing their praise,
And the King of life was saying, 'Tis meet.

O Mary Mother of wondrous power,
Grant us the succour of thy strength,
Bless the provision, bless the board,
Bless the ear, the corn, the food.

The Virgin of mien most glorious,
The Jesus more gleaming–white than snow,
She like the moon in the hills arising,
He like the sun on the mountain–crests.

254 The Child of glory

The Child of glory,
The Child of Mary,
Born in the stable,
  The King of all,
Who came to the wilderness
And in our stead suffered;
Happy they are counted
  Who to Him are near.

When He Himself saw
That we were in travail,
Heaven opened graciously
  Over our head;
We beheld Christ,
The Spirit of truth,
The same drew us in
  'Neath the shield of His crown.

Strengthen our hope,
Enliven our joyance,
Keep us valiant,
  Faithful and near;
O light of our lantern,
Along with the virgins,
Singing in glory
  The anthem new.

Supplication of the Saints

255 Prayer to Mary Mother

O Mary Maiden,
  Never was known
One who was placed
  'Neath thy generous care,

Who asked thy mercy,
  Who asked thy shielding,
Who asked thy succour
  With truthful heart,

Who found not thy solace,
  Who found not thy peace,
Who found not the succour
  For which he sought.

That gives unto me
  The hope excelling
That my tears and my prayer
  May find guest–room with thee.

My heart is content
  To kneel at thy footstool,
My heart is content
  In thy favour and hearing;

To come into thy presence,
  Beauteous one of smiles,
To come into thy presence,
  Beauteous one of women;

To come into thy presence,
  Queen-maiden of mankind,
To come into thy presence,
  Queen-maiden of the worlds;

To come into thy presence,
  O flower-garland of branches,
To come into thy presence,
  Bright garland of the heavens;

To come into thy presence,
  O Mother of the Lamb of Grace,
To come into thy presence,
  O Mother of the Paschal Lamb;

To come into thy presence,
  O river of seed,
To come into thy presence,
  O vessel of peace;

To come into thy presence,
  O fountain of healing,
To come into thy presence,
  O well-spring of grace;

To come into thy presence,
  Thou dwelling of meekness,
To come into thy presence,
  Thou home of peace;

To come into thy presence,
  Thou jewel of the clouds,
To come into thy presence,
  Thou jewel of the stars;

To come into thy presence,
  O Mother of black sorrow,

To come into thy presence,
  O Mother of the God of glory;

To come into thy presence,
  Thou Virgin of the lowly,
To come into thy presence,
  Thou Mother of Jesus Christ;

With lament and with sorrow,
  With prayer and supplication,
With grief and with weeping,
  With invoking and entreaty;

That thou mayest have me spared
  Shame and disgrace,
That thou mayest have me spared
  Flattery and scorn;

That thou mayest have me spared
  Misery and mourning,
That thou mayest have me spared
  Anguish eternal;

That thou mayest help my soul
  On the highway of the King,
That thou mayest help my soul
  On the roadway of peace;

That thou mayest help my soul
  In the doorway of mercy,
That thou mayest help my soul
  In the place of justice.

Since thou art the star of ocean,
  Pilot me at sea;
Since thou art the star of earth,
  Guide thou me on shore.

Since thou art the star of night,
  Lighten me in the darkness;
Since thou art the sun of day,
  Encompass me on land.

Since thou art the star of angels,
  Watch over me on earth;
Since thou art the star of paradise,
  Companion me to heaven.

Mayest thou shield me by night,
  Mayest thou shield me by day,
Mayest thou shield me by day and night,
  O bright and gracious Queen of heaven.

Grant me my prayer of love,
  Grant me my entreaty for shielding,
Grant me my supplication of pain
  Through the shed blood of the Son of thy breast.

Count me not as naught, O my God,
  Count me not as naught, O my Christ,
Count me not as naught, O kind Spirit,
  And abandon me not to eternal loss.

256 Praise of Mary

I say the prayer
That was given with anointing
To the Mary Mother
  Of joy;

Along with Pater and Credo,
The Prayer of Mary besides,
And the Prayer of God's Son
  Of the Passion;

To magnify thine own honour,
To magnify the glory of God's Son,
To magnify the greatness of the God
  Of grace.

Plead with thy gracious Son
That He make my prayer avail
My soul, and thereafter
  My body.

Thou Queen of the angels,
Thou Queen of the kingdom,
Thou Queen of the city
  Of glory:

* * *

Thou shining Mother of gentleness,
Thou glorious Mother of the stars,
Blessed hast thou been of every race
  And people.

O thou, alone praised, worthy of praise,
Make fervent prayer for me
With the Lord of the worlds,
  The God of life.

Thou Mary, gentle, fair, gracious,
I pray that thou forsake me not
In the sharp pang
  Of my death.

Shield of every dwelling, shield of every people
That are sorely calling
On the gracious mercy
  Of thy dear Son:

Thou art the Queen–maiden of sweetness,
Thou art the Queen–maiden of faithfulness,
Thou art the Queen–maiden of peacefulness
And of the peoples.

Thou art the well of compassion,
Thou art the root of consolations,
Thou art the living stream of the virgins
  And of them who bear child.

Thou art the tabernacle of Christ,
Thou art the mansion of Christ,
Thou art the ark of Christ :
  Of Him alone.

Thou art the Queen–maiden of the sea,
Thou art the Queen–maiden of the kingdom,
Thou art the Queen–maiden of the angels
In effulgence.

Thou art the temple of the God of life,
Thou art the tabernacle of the God of life,
Thou art the mansion of the God of life
And of the forlorn.

Thou art the river of grace,
Thou art the well–spring of salvation,
Thou art the garden and the paradise
Of the virgins.

Thou art the star of morning,
Thou art the star of watching,
Thou art the star of the ocean
Great.

Thou art the star of the earth,
Thou art the star of the kingdom,
Thou art the star of the Son of the Father
Of glory.

Thou art the corn of the land,
Thou art the treasury of the sea,
The wished–for visitant of the homes
Of the world.

Thou art the vessel of fullness,
Thou art the cup of wisdom,
Thou art the well–spring of health
Of mankind.

Thou art the garden of virtues,
Thou art the mansion of gladness,
Thou art the Mother of sadness
And of clemency.

Thou art the garden of apples,
Thou art the lull–song of the great folks,

Thou art the fulfilment of the world's desire
  In loveliness.

Thou art the sun of the heavens,
Thou art the moon of the skies,
Thou art the star and the path
  Of the wanderers.

Since thou art the full ocean,
  Pilot me at sea;
Since thou art the dry shore,
  Save me upon land.

Since thou art the gem of the jewel,
  Save me from fire and from water,
Save me from sky–hosts of evil
  And from fairy shafts.

There is none who utters my song
  Or puts it into use,
But Mary will show herself to him
  Three times before his death and his end.

257 Praise of Mary

Flower–garland of the ocean,
  Flower–garland of the land,
Flower–garland of the heavens,
  Mary, Mother of God.

Flower–garland of the earth,
  Flower–garland of the skies,
Flower–garland of the angels,
  Mary, Mother of God.

Flower–garland of the mansion,
  Flower–garland of the stars,
Flower–garland of paradise,
  Mary, Mother of God.

258 I send witness
(a fragment)

I send witness to Mary,
Mother who aids men;
I send witness to Brigit,
Pure tender Nurse of the Lamb;

I send witness to Peter,
Apostle of fear and of sleep;
I send witness to Columba,
Apostle of shore and sea;

I send witness to Heaven,
To the City on high;
I send witness to Michael,
Noble warrior triumphant;

I send witness to Father,
Who formed all flesh;
I send witness to Christ,
Who suffered scorn and pain;

I send witness to Spirit,
Who will heal my wound,
Who will make me as white
As the cotton–grass of the moor.

259 Michael Militant

O Michael Militant,
Thou king of the angels,
Shield thy people
With the power of thy sword,
Shield thy people
With the power of thy sword.

Spread thy wing
Over sea and land,
East and west,
And shield us from the foe,
East and west,
And shield us from the foe.

Brighten thy feast
From heaven above;
Be with us in the pilgrimage
And in the twistings of the fight;
Be with us in the pilgrimage
And in the twistings of the fight.

Thou chief of chiefs,
Thou chief of the needy,
Be with us in the journey
And in the gleam of the river;
Be with us in the journey
And in the gleam of the river.
Thou chief of chiefs,
Thou chief of angels,
Spread thy wing
Over sea and land,
For thine is their fullness,
Thine is their fullness,
  Thine own is their fullness,
  Thine own is their fullness.

260 Michael of the angels

O Michael of the angels
And the righteous in heaven,
Shield thou my soul
With the shade of thy wing;
Shield thou my soul
On earth and in heaven;

From foes upon earth,
From foes beneath earth,
From foes in concealment
Protect and encircle
My soul 'neath thy wing,
Oh my soul with the shade of thy wing!

261 Angel guardian

O angel guardian of my right hand,
Attend thou me this night,
Rescue thou me in the battling floods,
Array me in thy linen, for I am naked,
Succour me, for I am feeble and forlorn.

Steer thou my coracle in the crooked eddies,
Guide thou my step in gap and in pit,
Guard thou me in the treacherous turnings,
And save thou me from the scaith of the wicked,
Save thou me from scaith this night.

Drive thou from me the taint of pollution,
Encompass thou me till Doom from evil;
O kindly Angel of my right hand,
Deliver thou me from the wicked this night,
Deliver thou me this night!

262 Prayer

I pray and supplicate
Cuibh and Columba,
The Mother of my King,
Brigit womanly,
Michael militant,
High-king of the angels,
To succour and shield me
From each fay on earth.

263 Womanhood of Brigit or Praises of Brigit

Brigit daughter of Dugall the Brown
Son of Aodh son of Art son of Conn
Son of Criara son of Cairbre son of Cas
Son of Cormac son of Cartach son of Conn.

Brigit of the mantles,
Brigit of the peat–heap,
Brigit of the twining hair,
Brigit of the augury.

Brigit of the white feet,
Brigit of calmness,
Brigit of the white palms,
Brigit of the kine.

Brigit, woman–comrade,
Brigit of the peat–heap,
Brigit, woman–helper,
Brigit, woman mild.

Brigit, own tress of Mary,
Brigit, Nurse of Christ —
Each day and each night
That I say the Descent of Brigit,

I shall not be slain,
I shall not be wounded,
I shall not be put in cell,
I shall not be gashed,
I shall not be torn in sunder,
I shall not be despoiled,
I shall not be down–trodden,
I shall not be made naked,
I shall not be rent,
Nor will Christ
Leave me forgotten.

Nor sun shall burn me,
Nor fire shall burn me,
Nor beam shall burn me,
Nor moon shall burn me.

Nor river shall drown me,
Nor brine shall drown me,
Nor flood shall drown me,
Nor water shall drown me.

Nightmare shall not lie on me,
Black-sleep shall not lie on me,
Spell-sleep shall not lie on me,
Luaths-luis shall not lie on me.

I am under the keeping
Of my Saint Mary;
My companion beloved
Is Brigit.

264 Blessing of Brigit

Brigit daughter of Dugall the Brown, etc.

Each day and each night
That I say the Descent of Brigit,

I shall not be slain,
I shall not be sworded,
I shall not be put in cell,
I shall not be hewn,
I shall not be riven,
I shall not be anguished,
I shall not be wounded,
I shall not be ravaged,

I shall not be blinded,
I shall not be made naked,
I shall not be left bare,
Nor will Christ
Leave me forgotten.

Nor fire shall burn me,
Nor sun shall burn me,
Nor moon shall blanch me.

Nor water shall drown me,
Nor flood shall drown me,
Nor brine shall drown me.

Nor seed of fairy host shall lift me,
Nor seed of airy host shall lift me,
Nor earthly being destroy me.

I am under the shielding
  Of good Brigit each day;
I am under the shielding
  Of good Brigit each night.

I am under the keeping
  Of the Nurse of Mary,
Each early and late,
  Every dark, every light.

Brigit is my comrade-woman,
  Brigit is my maker of song,
Brigit is my helping-woman,
  My choicest of women, my guide.

265 Rune of the well

The shelter of Mary Mother
Be nigh my hands and my feet,
To go out to the well
And to bring me safely home,
And to bring me safely home.

May warrior Michael aid me,
May Brigit calm preserve me,
May sweet Brianag give me light,
And Mary pure be near me,
And Mary pure be near me.

Journey Prayers

266 **Petition**

Be Thou a smooth way before me,
Be Thou a guiding star above me,
Be Thou a keen eye behind me,
This day, this night, for ever.

I am weary, and I forlorn,
Lead Thou me to the land of the angels;
Methinks it were time I went for a space
To the court of Christ, to the peace of heaven;

If only Thou, O God of life,
Be at peace with me, be my support,
Be to me as a star, be to me as a helm,
From my lying down in peace to my rising anew.

267 The prayer

I am praying and appealing to God,
The Son of Mary and the Spirit of truth,
To aid me in distress of sea and of land:
May the Three succour me, may the Three shield me,
May the Three watch me by day and by night.

God and Jesus and the Spirit of cleansing
Be shielding me, be possessing me, be aiding me,
Be clearing my path and going before my soul
In hollow, on hill, on plain,
On sea and land be the Three aiding me.

God and Jesus and the Holy Spirit
Be shielding and saving me,
As Three and as One,
By my knee, by my back, by my side,
Each step of the stormy world.

268 The aiding

May Brigit shield me,
May Mary shield me,
May Michael shield me,
On sea and on land:
To shield me from all anguish
  On sea and on land,
  To shield me from all anguish.

May Father aid me,
May Son aid me,
May Spirit aid me,
On sea and on land:
In the shielding of the City everlasting
  On sea and on land,
  In the shielding of the City everlasting.

May the Three succour me,
May the Three follow me,
May the Three guide me,
On sea and on land,
To the Vine–garden of the godlike
  On sea and on land,
  To the Vine–garden of the godlike.

269 Prayer

Relieve Thou, O God, each one
In suffering on land or sea,
In grief or wounded or weeping,
And lead them to the house of Thy peace
  This night.

I am weary, weak and cold,
I am weary of travelling land and sea,
I am weary of traversing moorland and billow,
Grant me peace in the nearness of Thy repose
  This night.

Beloved Father of my God,
Accept the caring for my tears;
I would wish reconcilement with Thee,
Through the witness and the ransom
  Of Thy Son;

To be resting with Jesus
In the dwelling of peace,
In the paradise of gentleness,
In the fairy–bower
  Of mercy.

270 The journey prayer

God, bless to me this day,
God, bless to me this night;
Bless, O bless, Thou God of grace,
Each day and hour of my life;
   Bless, O bless, Thou God of grace,
   Each day and hour of my life.

God, bless the pathway on which I go,
God, bless the earth that is beneath my sole;
Bless, O God, and give to me Thy love,
O God of gods, bless my rest and my repose;
   Bless, O God, and give to me Thy love,
   And bless, O God of gods, my repose.

271 The journey blessing

Bless to me, O God,
The earth beneath my foot,
Bless to me, O God,
The path whereon I go;
Bless to me, O God,
The thing of my desire;
Thou Evermore of evermore,
Bless Thou to me my rest.

Bless to me the thing
Whereon is set my mind,
Bless to me the thing
Whereon is set my love;
Bless to me the thing
Whereon is set my hope;
O Thou King of kings,
Bless Thou to me mine eye!

272 The Gospel of Christ

May God bless thy cross
Before thou go over the sea;
Any illness that thou mayest have,
It shall not take thee hence.

May God bless thy crucifying cross
In the house–shelter of Christ,
Against drowning, against peril, against spells,
Against sore wounding, against grisly fright.

As the King of kings was stretched up
Without pity, without compassion, to the tree,
The leafy, brown, wreathed topmost Bough,
As the body of the sinless Christ triumphed,

And as the woman of the seven blessings,
Who is going in at their head,
May God bless all that are before thee
And thee who art moving anear them.

Grace of form,
Grace of voice be thine;
Grace of charity,
Grace of wisdom be thine;
Grace of beauty,
Grace of health be thine;
Grace of sea,
Grace of land be thine;
Grace of music,
Grace of guidance be thine;
Grace of battle–triumph,
Grace of victory be thine;
Grace of life,
Grace of praise be thine;
Grace of love,
Grace of dancing be thine;

Grace of lyre,
Grace of harp be thine;
Grace of sense,
Grace of reason be thine;
Grace of speech,
Grace of story be thine;
Grace of peace,
Grace of God be thine.

A voice soft and musical I pray for thee,
And a tongue loving and mild:
Two things good for daughter and for son,
For husband and for wife.

The joy of God be in thy face,
Joy to all who see thee;
The circling of God be keeping thee,
Angels of God shielding thee.

Nor sword shall wound thee,
Nor brand shall burn thee,
Nor arrow shall rend thee,
Nor seas shall drown thee.

Thou art whiter than the swan on miry lake,
Thou art whiter than the white gull of the current,
Thou art whiter than the snow of the high mountains,
Thou art whiter than the love of the angels of heaven.

Thou art the gracious red rowan
That subdues the ire and anger of all men,
As a sea-wave from flow to ebb,
As a sea-wave from ebb to flow.

The mantle of Christ be placed upon thee,
To shade thee from thy crown to thy sole;
The mantle of the God of life be keeping thee,
To be thy champion and thy leader.

Thou shalt not be left in the hand of the wicked,
Thou shalt not be bent in the court of the false;
Thou shalt rise victorious above them
As rise victorious the arches of the waves.

Thou art the pure love of the clouds,
Thou art the pure love of the skies,
Thou art the pure love of the stars,
Thou art the pure love of the moon,
Thou art the pure love of the sun,
Thou art the pure love of the heavens,
Thou art the pure love of the angels,
Thou art the pure love of Christ Himself,
Thou art the pure love of the God of all life.

273 The Gospel of the God of life

The Gospel of the God of life
To shelter thee, to aid thee,
Yea, the Gospel of beloved Christ
The holy Gospel of the Lord;

To keep thee from all malice,
From every dole and dolour;
To keep thee from all spite,
From evil eye and anguish.

Thou shalt travel thither, thou shalt travel hither,
Thou shalt travel hill and headland,
Thou shalt travel down, thou shalt travel up,
Thou shalt travel ocean and narrow.

Christ Himself is shepherd over thee,
Enfolding thee on every side;
He will not forsake thee hand or foot,
Nor let evil come anigh thee.

274 The Gospel of Christ

I set the keeping of Christ about thee,
I send the guarding of God with thee,
To possess thee, to protect thee
From drowning, from danger, from loss,
  From drowning, from danger, from loss.

The Gospel of the God of grace
Be from thy summit to thy sole;
The Gospel of Christ, King of salvation,
Be as a mantle to thy body,
  Be as a mantle to thy body.

Nor drowned be thou at sea,
Nor slain be thou on land,
Nor o'erborne be thou by man,
Nor undone be thou by woman,
  Nor undone be thou by woman!

275 The pilgrims' aiding

  God be with thee in every pass,
Jesus be with thee on every hill,
  Spirit be with thee on every stream,
Headland and ridge and lawn;

  Each sea and land, each moor and meadow,
Each lying down, each rising up,
  In the trough of the waves, on the crest of the billows,
Each step of the journey thou goest.

276 Charm for protection

Thou shalt take to God,
God shall take to thee,
Surrounding thy two feet,
His two hands about thy head.

To thorns of trees or hollies;
A rock thou art at sea,
A fortress thou art on land.

Michael's shield is about thee,
Christ's shelter is over thee,
The fine–wrought breastplate of Columba
Preserves thee from the fairy shafts.

Against the screeching cranes,
Against the gnawing cranes,
Against the troubling of the world here,
Against the evil of the world beyond.

The woman on her knee,
The woman at her evil eye,
The woman with her spleen,
The woman with her envy;

The woman at the cattle of her herd,
The woman at the young of her cows,
The woman at the rearing of her flocks,
Until it reach the fibres of her heart.

* * *

Each woman who is full of spleen and envy,
Who sunders her blood, her flesh and gore,
On herself be her spleen and her severing,
From this day to the final day of the world.

Blessings

277 **Blessings**

May the Spirit satisfy you
With the water of grace.

The blessing of God and the Lord be yours,
The blessing of the perfect Spirit be yours,
The blessing of the Three be pouring for you
Mildly and generously,
Mildly and generously.

The peace of God be to you,
The peace of Christ be to you,
The peace of Spirit be to you
And to your children,
To you and to your children.

The eye of the great God be upon you,
The eye of the God of glory be on you,
The eye of the Son of Mary Virgin be on you,
The eye of the Spirit mild be on you,
To aid you and to shepherd you;
  Oh the kindly eye of the Three be on you,
  To aid you and to shepherd you.

May the everlasting Father Himself take you
In His own generous clasp,
In His own generous arm.
May God shield you on every steep,
May Christ keep you in every path,
May Spirit bathe you in every pass.

May the everlasting Father shield you
East and west wherever you go.

May Christ's safe–guard protect you ever.

May God make safe to you each steep,
May God make open to you each pass,
May God make clear to you each road,
And may He take you in the clasp of His own two hands.

Oh may each saint and sainted woman in heaven,
O God of the creatures and God of goodness,
Be taking charge of you in every strait
Every side and every turn you go.

Be each saint in heaven,
Each sainted woman in heaven,
Each angel in heaven
Stretching their arms for you,
Smoothing the way for you,
When you go thither
Over the river hard to see;
Oh when you go thither home
Over the river hard to see.

May the Father take you
In His fragrant clasp of love,
When you go across the flooding streams
And the black river of death.

May Mary Virgin's Son Himself
Be a generous lamp to you,
To guide you over
The great and awful ocean of eternity.

The compassing of the saints be upon you,
The compassing of the angels be upon you;
Oh the compassing of all the saints
And of the nine angels be upon you.

The grace of the great God be upon you,
The grace of Virgin Mary's Son be upon you,
The grace of the perfect Spirit be upon you,
Mildly and generously.

May God's blessing be yours,
And well may it befall you.

May God's goodness be yours,
And well and seven times well
May you spend your lives.

The love of your creator be with you.

May Brigit and Mary and Michael
Shield you on sea and on land,
Each step and each path you travel.

Be the eye of God dwelling with you,
The foot of Christ in guidance with you,
The shower of the Spirit pouring on you,
Richly and generously.
God's peace be to you,
Jesus' peace be to you,
Spirit's peace be to you
And to your children,
Oh to you and to your children,
Each day and night
Of your portion in the world.

The compassing of the King of life be yours
The compassing of loving Christ be yours,
The compassing of Holy Spirit be yours
Unto the crown of the life eternal
Unto the crown of the life eternal.

My own blessing be with you,
The blessing of God be with you,
The blessing of Spirit be with you
  And with your children,
With you and with your children.

My own blessing be with you,
The blessing of God be with you,
The blessing of saints be with you
And the peace of the life eternal,
Unto the peace of the life eternal.

The guarding of the God of life be on you,
The guarding of loving Christ be on you,
The guarding of Holy Spirit be on you
Every night of your lives,
  To aid you and enfold you
  Each day and night of your lives.

The love and affection of the angels be to you,
The love and affection of the saints be to you,
The love and affection of heaven be to you,
To guard you and to cherish you.
May God shield you on every steep,
May Christ aid you on every path,
May Spirit fill you on every slope,
On hill and on plain.

May the King shield you in the valleys,
May Christ aid you on the mountains,
May Spirit bathe you on the slopes,
In hollow, on hill, on plain,
Mountain, valley and plain.

The shape of Christ be towards me,
The shape of Christ be to me,
The shape of Christ be before me,
The shape of Christ be behind me,
The shape of Christ be over me,
The shape of Christ be under me,
The shape of Christ be with me,
The shape of Christ be around me
On Monday and on Sunday;
  The shape of Christ be around me
  On Monday and on Sunday.

The love and affection of heaven be to you,
The love and affection of the saints be to you,
The love and affection of the angels be to you,
The love and affection of the sun be to you,
The love and affection of the moon be to you,
  Each day and night of your lives,
  To keep you from haters, to keep you from harmers,
    to keep you from oppressors.

The peace of God be with you,
The peace of Christ be with you,
The peace of Spirit be with you
And with your children,
From the day that we have here today
To the day of the end of your lives,
Until the day of the end of your lives.
The grace of God be with you,
The grace of Christ be with you,
The grace of Spirit be with you
And with your children,
For an hour, for ever, for eternity.

God's grace distil on you,
Christ's grace distil on you,
Spirit's grace distil on you
Each day and each night
Of your portion in the world;
Oh each day and each night
Of your portion in the world.

God's blessing be yours,
And well may it befall you;
Christ's blessing be yours,
And well be you entreated;
Spirit's blessing be yours,
And well spend you your lives,
Each day that you rise up,
Each night that you lie down.

May the eye of the great God,
The eye of the God of glory,
The eye of the Virgin's Son,
The eye of the gentle Spirit
Aid you and shepherd you
  In every time,
Pour upon you every hour
  Mildly and generously.

Invocation of the Graces

278 **Invocation of the graces**

The grace placed by Brigit,
Maiden of graces,
In the daughter of the king,
Gile–Mhin the beauteous.

Form of Christ before thee,
Form of God behind thee,
Stream of Spirit through thee
To succour and aid thee.

Grace upwards over thee,
Grace downwards over thee,
Grace of graces without gainsaying,
Grace of Father and of Lord.

Grace of form,
Grace of fortune,
Grace of voice,
Grace of Jesus Christ be ever thine,
Grace of the image of the Lord be thine.

Excellence of men,
Excellence of women,
Excellence of lover,
Excellence of sons and of daughters be thine.

Excellence of corn,
Excellence of drink,
Excellence of music,
Excellence of guiding,
Excellence of sea and land be thine.

Excellence of sitting,
Excellence of journeying,
Excellence of cattle,
Excellence of churning,
Excellence of curds and butter be thine.

Excellence of the duck of Mary,
Excellence of the swan of the fountain,
Excellence of sheep and of wool,
Excellence of kids and of goats,
Lasting excellence by day and night be thine.

Grace of the love of the skies be thine,
Grace of the love of the stars be thine,
Grace of the love of the moon be thine,
Grace of the love of the sun be thine,
Grace of the love and the crown of heaven be thine.

279 Charm of grace

The charm placed by Brigit,
Maiden of graces,
On the white daughter of the king,
Gile–Mhin the beauteous.

The form of God is behind thee,
The form of Christ is before thee,
The stream of Spirit is through thee,
To succour and aid thee.

The bloom of God is upon thee,
The bloom of Christ is upon thee,
The bloom of Spirit is upon thee,
To bathe thee and make thee fair.

Grace is upwards over thee,
Grace is downwards over thee,
Grace of graces without gainsaying,
Grace of Father and of Lord.

Excellence of men,
Excellence of women,
Excellence of council,
Excellence of lover,
Excellence of sons and of daughters.

Excellence of dells,
Excellence of knolls,
Excellence of hollows,
Excellence of hills,
Excellence of horses and of heroes.

Excellence of travel,
Excellence of journey,
Excellence of small town,
Excellence of great town,
Excellence of sea and of shore.

Excellence of beauty,
Excellence of radiance,
Excellence of goodness,
Excellence of heaven,
Excellence of day and of night.

Excellence of form,
Excellence of voice,
Excellence of complexion,
Excellence of cattle,
Excellence of curd and of butter.

Thou art the star of each night,
Thou art the brightness of each morn,
Thou art the tidings of each guest,
Thou art the enquiry of every land.

Thou shalt travel a rough ground
And thou shalt not redden thy foot:
Jesus is guarding thee,
Jesus is by thy hand.

The crown of the King is around thy head,
The diadem of the Son is around thy brow,
The might of the Spirit is in thy breast:
Thou shalt go forth and come homeward safe.

Thou shalt journey upward
And come again down,
Thou shalt journey over ocean
And come again hither;

No peril shall befall thee
On knoll nor on bank,
In hollow nor in meadow,
On mount nor in glen.

The shield of Michael is over thee,
King of the bright angels,
To shield thee and to guard thee
From thy summit to thy sole.

Nor shall man
Nor shall woman

Nor shall son
Nor shall daughter

Make glance nor wish,
Hate nor jealousy,
Love nor eye,
Envy nor durance

That shall sunder thee,
That shall lie upon thee,
That shall subdue thee,
That shall wound thee.

Host shall not make,
False one shall not make,
Fairy shall not make,
World shall not make

Sling nor catapult,
Spear nor shaft,
Axe nor javelin,
Hook nor sword,

That shall affect thee,
That shall afflict thee,
That shall wound thee,
That shall overpower thee.

No smith shall make,
No craftsman shall make,
No mason shall make,
No wright shall make

Gear nor tool,
Weapon nor device,
Tackle nor instrument,
Frame nor invention,

Of copper nor stone,
Of brass nor iron,
Of wood nor bronze,
Of gold nor silver,

That shall check thee,
That shall enclose thee,
That shall rend thee,
That shall bridle thee,
Thither nor hither,
Earth nor land,
Here nor yonder,
Down nor up,

Above nor below,
Sea nor shore,
In the sky aloft,
In the deep beneath.

Thou nut of my heart,
Thou face of my sun,
Thou harp of my music,
Thou crown of my sense;

Thou art the love of the God of Life,
Thou art the love of tender Christ,
Thou art the love of Spirit Holy,
Thou art the love of each living creature,
Thou art the love of each living creature.

280 Charm for the face of a maiden

The beauty of God is in thy face,
The Son of God is protecting thee
From the wicked ones of the world,
The King of the stars is before thee.

The beauty of Mary of the deep love,
A tongue mannerly, mild, modest,
Fair hair between thy two eyebrows —
Fionn son of Cumhall between these.*

Since it is Mary and Jesus her Son
Who set this pleasantness in thy face,
May the taste of mild honey be upon thee
And upon every word thou speakest,

To simple and to noble,
To men and to tender women,
From this day that we have here
Till the day of the ending of thy life,
In reliance on the beloved and the powers eternal,
In reliance on the God of life and the shielding of
His Son.

281 Grace

Grace of love be thine,
Grace of floor be thine,
Grace of castle be thine,
Grace of court be thine,
Grace and pride of homeland be thine.

The guard of the God of life be thine,
The guard of the loving Christ be thine,
The guard of the Holy Spirit be thine,

To cherish thee,
To aid thee,
To enfold thee.

* *Fionn* means "fair."

The Three be about thy head,
The Three be about thy breast,
The Three be about thy body
Each night and each day,
In the encompassment of the Three
Throughout thy life long.

Good Wishes

282

Good wish

Power of raven be thine,
Power of eagle be thine,
  Power of the Fiann.

Power of storm be thine,
Power of moon be thine,
  Power of sun.

Power of sea be thine,
Power of land be thine,
  Power of heaven.

Goodness of sea be thine,
Goodness of earth be thine,
  Goodness of heaven.

Each day be joyous to thee,
No day be grievous to thee,
  Honour and compassion.

Love of each face be thine,
Death on pillow be thine,
  Thy Saviour's presence.

283 Prayer

Each day be glad to thee,
No day be sad to thee,
Life rich and satisfying.

Plenty be on thy course,
A son be on thy coming,
A daughter on thine arriving.

The strong help of the serpent be thine,
The strong help of fire be thine,
The strong help of the graces.

The love-death of joy be thine,
The love-death of Mary be thine,
The loving arm of thy Saviour.

284 Good wish

Thine be the might of river,
Thine be the might of ocean,
The might of victory on field.

Thine be the might of fire,
Thine be the might of levin,
The might of a strong rock.

Thine be the might of element,
Thine be the might of fountain,
The might of the love on high.

285 Prayer

Power of eye be thine,
Power of element be thine,
Power of my heart's desire.

Power of surf be thine,
Power of swell be thine,
Power of the sap of my reason.

Power of king Cù Chulainn be thine,
Power of the king of the world be thine,
Power of the king of the Fiann.

286 Good wish

The good of eye be thine,
The good of liking be thine,
The good of my heart's desire.

The good of sons be thine,
The good of daughters be thine,
The good of the sap of my sense.

The good of sea be thine,
The good of land be thine,
The good of the Prince of heaven.

287 Prayer

I pray for thee a joyous life,
Honour, estate and good repute,
No sigh from thy breast,
No tear from thine eye.

No hindrance on thy path,
No shadow on thy face,
Until thou lie down in that mansion,
In the arms of Christ benign.

288 Good wish

Wisdom of serpent be thine,
Wisdom of raven be thine,
Wisdom of valiant eagle.

Voice of swan be thine,
Voice of honey be thine,
Voice of the Son of the stars.

Bounty of sea be thine,
Bounty of land be thine,
Bounty of the Father of heaven.

289 Prayer

Be each day glad for thee,
No day ill for thee,
A life joyful, satisfied.

Be thine the success of every meeting,
Be thine the grace of the Virgin Mary,
Be thine the fullness of the King of grace.

290 Prayer

The love of the Mary Mother be thine,
The love of Brigit of flocks be thine,
The love of Michael victorious be thine,
With their arm each hour surrounding thee.

The great bounty of the sea be thine,
The great bounty of earth be thine,
The great bounty of heaven be thine,
Thy life be hale and fruitful.

The mild grace of the Father be thine,
The loving grace of the Son be thine,
The loving grace of the Spirit be thine,
Laving thee with the graces.

291 Good wish

The arm of Mary Mother be thine,
The arm of Brigit of flocks be thine,
The arm of Michael victorious be thine,
To save thee from all sorrow.

The arm of Apostle John be thine,
The arm of Apostle Paul be thine,
The arm of Apostle Peter be thine,
To guard thee from all mischief.

The arm of the God of life be thine,
The arm of Christ the loving be thine,
The arm of the Spirit Holy be thine,
To shield thee and surround thee.

292 The mother's parting blessing

The benison of God be to thee,
The benison of Christ be to thee,
The benison of Spirit be to thee,
And to thy children,
To thee and to thy children.

The peace of God be to thee,
The peace of Christ be to thee,
The peace of Spirit be to thee,
During all thy life,
All the days of thy life.

The keeping of God upon thee in every pass,
The shielding of Christ upon thee in every path,
The bathing of Spirit upon thee in every stream,
In every land and sea thou goest.

The keeping of the everlasting Father be thine
Upon His own illumined altar;
The keeping of the everlasting Father be thine
Upon His own illumined altar.

293 The pilgrim's hope

I will bathe my face
In the nine rays of the sun,
As Mary washed her Son
In the milk of the generous *brac*.

May mildness be on my lips,
May kindness be on my face,
May chasteness be on my desire,
May wisdom be in my purpose.

The love that Mary gave to her one Son
May all the world give me;
The love that Jesus gave to John Baptist
Grant that I give to whoso meets me.

May the Son of God be at the outset of my journey,
May the Son of God be in surety to aid me;
May the Son of God make clear my way,
May the Son of God be at the end of my seeking.

294 The mother's blessing

Where thou shalt bring the crown of thy head,
Where thou shalt bring the tablet of thy brow,
Strength be to thee therein,
Blest be to thee the powers therein;
Strength be to thee therein,
Blest be to thee the powers therein.

Lasting be thou in thy lying down,
Lasting be thou in thy rising up,
Lasting be thou by night and by day,
And surpassing good be heaven to my dear one;
Lasting be thou by night and by day,
And surpassing good be heaven to my dear one.

The face of God be to thy countenance,
The face of Christ the kindly,
The face of the Spirit Holy
Be saving thee each hour
In danger and in sorrow;
Be saving thee each hour
In danger and in sorrow.

295 The mother's blessing

The joy of God be in thy face,
Joy to all who see thee,
The circle of God around thy neck,
Angels of God shielding thee,
Angels of God shielding thee.

Joy of night and day be thine,
Joy of sun and moon be thine,
Joy of men and women be thine,
Each land and sea thou goest,
Each land and sea thou goest.

Be every season happy for thee,
Be every season bright for thee,
Be every season glad for thee,
And the Son of Mary Virgin at peace with thee,
The Son of Mary Virgin at peace with thee.

Be thine the compassing of the God of life,
Be thine the compassing of the Christ of love,
Be thine the compassing of the Spirit of Grace,
To befriend thee and to aid thee,
[Donald]
Thou beloved one of my breast.

(Oh! to befriend thee and to aid thee,
[Mary]
Thou beloved one of my heart.)

Prayer before Confession

296 Prayer before confession

Jesu, give me forgiveness of sins,
Jesu, keep my guilt in my memory,
Jesu, give me the grace of repentance,
Jesu, give me the grace of forgiveness,
Jesu, give me the grace of submission,
Jesu, give me the grace of earnestness,
Jesu, give me the grace of lowliness,
To make a free confession at this time,
To condemn myself at the chair of confession
Lest I be condemned at the chair of judgment;
Jesu, give me strength and courage
To condemn myself at the chair of confession
Lest I be condemned at the chair of judgment.
It is easier for me to go under subjection for a brief while
Than to go to death during eternity.
Jesu, give me to confess my guilt
As earnestly as were this the moment of my death.

Jesu, take pity upon me,
Jesu, have mercy upon me,
Jesu, take me to Thee,
Jesu, aid my soul.

A cause of grief is sin,
A cause of anguish is death,
A cause of joy is repentance
And cleansing in the river of health.

* * *

There will be joy among the angels of heaven
That I am laved in the pool of confession.

O my soul, be joyful,
God is willing to be reconciled to thee,
Seize His hand while it is stretched out
To announce to thee a loving reconcilement.

Refuse not Thy hand to me, O my God,
Refuse not Thy hand, O Lord of lords,
For the sake of my Saviour Jesus Christ,
Let me not go to death everlasting.

The Cross of Christ

The crucifixion

The bellows

From — MacDonald, a tinker woman, Castlebay, Barra.

After they had brought Christ to the cross they found that they had no nails to put into Him, and that neither had they bellows with which to blow the fire to heat the iron to make nails. There was no knowing under the white sun what to say or what to do in the confusion that was there. But the tinker woman lifted her skirt and blew the fire, and the iron was heated, and the tinker made the nails with which Christ was nailed to the tree of crucifixion. It was then that Jesus Christ the Son of the living and eternal God, up on the cross, said to the tinker woman down at the foot:

"Thou and thy kind from generation to generation, from age to age, shall be walking the ways and travelling the wilderness, without rest of night, without peace of day, because of the work of thy hand and thine ill deed."

It is not right to aid evil nor to help in ill–doing even though we should be asked and though we could do it; no, not at all (said the narrator).

In consequence of the tinker woman's action, it is forbidden in the Isles to blow the fire with one's skirt or apron. It is also forbidden to turn the peat burning side upwards in the fire, for the smith who made the nails did so.

The whitesmith

When Christ was being taken to the tree of crucifixion, in the hurry the black Jews forgot to provide themselves with nails. They went to the blacksmith and asked him to make nails to nail the hands and the feet of the Saviour to the cross. But the blacksmith refused to make nails for such a purpose. The Jews went to the whitesmith (tinsmith, tinker) and asked him to make nails to nail the hands and the feet of the Saviour to the cross. The whitesmith did the work as the Jews asked of him, and the hands and the feet of Christ the blessed Saviour were nailed to the tree of crucifixion. This is why the blacksmith is esteemed and honoured among men, while the whitesmith is contemned and despised, and this is why the race of the whitesmith is spread and scattered here and there throughout the great world.

Cross of prostration

Crosses of prostration were common throughout the Highlands and Islands. These were called *crois sleuchdaidh* or *sliachdaidh.* They had a special purpose. The cross stood afar from all buildings and habitations, and was a conspicuous feature in the landscape. When he reached the cross the pilgrim was in sight of a temple of worship or of sanctuary. He prostrated himself at the cross and sang his pilgrim–

song or hymn; thereafter he went to the church within sight and there made his offering and said his prayer.

There is a *crois sleuchdaidh* at Cnoca Breaca, South Uist. People from the south end of the island prostrated themselves there, being within sight of the church at Hógh Mór. There was another on Sunnamal, a small sandy tidal island between Benbecula and North Uist. When the traveller came to Sunnamal (which was formerly not an island) he was within sight of Teampall na Trianaid, the Temple of the Trinity, at Càirinis.

There was another *crois sleuchdaidh* at Dalmally. Another stood on the hill from Inveraray to Clàdaich, Cladich, which could be seen from afar by travellers from Inveraray. When the cross was reached the church on the island of Innis Eil could be seen.

Innis Eil is a small low grassy island towards the northern end of Loch Awe. A house of nuns stood here, and there is a burial place containing singularly beautiful carved stones. Until the early half of last century there was a change-house, which was perhaps established for the convenience of those attending funerals on the island after the house of nuns had been dissolved.

297 The cross of Christ

Be the cross of Christ between me and the fays
That move occultly out or in,
Be the cross of Christ between me and all ill,
All ill-will, and ill-mishap.

Be the angels of heaven shielding me,
The angels of heaven this night,
Be the angels of heaven keeping me
Soul and body alike.

Be the compassing of Christ around me
From every spectre, from every evil,
From every shame that is coming harmfully
In darkness, in power to hurt.

Be the compassing of the might of Christ
Shielding me from every harm,
Be keeping me from everything ruinous
Coming destructively towards me this night.

Peace

298

Peace

The peace of God, the peace of men,
The peace of Columba kindly,
The peace of Mary mild, the loving,
The peace of Christ, King of tenderness,
  The peace of Christ, King of tenderness,

Be upon each window, upon each door,
Upon each hole that lets in light,
Upon the four corners of my house,
Upon the four corners of my bed,
  Upon the four corners of my bed;

Upon each thing my eye takes in,
Upon each thing my mouth takes in,
Upon my body that is of earth
And upon my soul that came from on high,
  Upon my body that is of earth
  And upon my soul that came from on high.

299 Peace

Peace between neighbours,
Peace between kindred,
Peace between lovers,
In love of the King of life.

Peace between person and person,
Peace between wife and husband,
Peace between woman and children,
The peace of Christ above all peace.

Bless, O Christ, my face,
Let my face bless every thing;
Bless, O Christ, mine eye,
Let mine eye bless all it sees.

300 Peace

The peace of joys,
The peace of lights,
The peace of consolations.

The peace of souls,
The peace of heaven,
The peace of the virgins.

The peace of the fairy bowers,
The peace of peacefulness,
The peace of everlasting.

The Voice of Thunder

"The old people had runes which they sang to the spirits dwelling in the sea and in the mountain, in the wind and in the whirlwind, in the lightning and in the thunder, in the sun and in the moon and in the stars of heaven. I was naught but a toddling child at the time, but I remember well the ways of the old people. Then came notice of eviction, and burning, and emigration, and the people were scattered and sundered over the world, and the old ways disappeared with the old people. Oh, they disappeared indeed, and nothing so good is come in their stead — naught so good is come, my beloved one, nor ever will come."

301 The voice of thunder

O God of the elements,
O God of the mysteries,
O God of the fountains,
O King of kings!
O King of kings!

Thy joy the joy,
Thy light the light,
Thy war the war,
Thy peace the peace,
Thy peace the peace.

Thy pain the pain,
Thy love the love,
That lasts for aye,
To the end of ends,
To the end of ends.

Thou pourest Thy grace
On those in distress,
On those in straits,
Without stop or stint,
Without stop or stint.

Thou Son of Mary of the Pasch,
Thou Son of Mary of the death,
Thou Son of Mary of the grace,
Who wast and shalt be
With ebb and with flow;
Who wast and shalt be
With ebb and with flow!

302 Thunder

The voice of the great God,
And none is great but He.

New Moon

Moon worship

There are many traces of moon beliefs and of moon homage still current in the Western Isles. An old man surnamed Robertson in Eigg said:

"The men of old would not kill a pig nor sheep nor goat nor axe–cow at the wane of the moon. The flesh of an animal is then without taste, without sap, without plumpness, without fat. Neither would they cut withes of hazel or willow for creels or baskets, nor would they cut tree of pine to make a boat, in the black wane of the moon. The sap of the wood goes down into the root, and the wood becomes brittle and crumbly, without pith, without good. The old people did all these things at the waxing or at the full of the moon. The men of old were observant of the facts of nature, as the young folk of today are not."

He continued: "The new moon was propitious for clipping hair, for cutting peats, for reaping corn, for shearing sheep, and for many things of that nature. Upon seeing the new moon a person puts the right hand round the left foot and makes the cross of Christ upon his palm with the spittle of his mouth, saying:

In the holy name of the Father,
In the holy name of the Son
In the holy name of the Spirit,
The holy Three of mercy.

In some districts old and young kept a coin in their pocket to hail rioghainn na h–oidhche, the queen of the night. The coin was called *peighinn pisich* (propitious penny), and was turned thrice in the pocket when the new moon was seen.

Any journey or undertaking was hurried on or delayed in order to be under the influences of the moon — *rath gealaich.* Men and women went to the highest hill or knoll near them to look for *éiteag nan reul* or *rioghainn na h–oidhche.* They began their scrutiny in the west, turning slowly sunwise upon the right heel, till the object of their search was seen. Then they called out: *"Fhaic! fhaic! fhaic!"* ("See! see! see!") There was much emulation as to who should see the new moon first. Herdboys and herdgirls were wont to whisper softly in the ear of the cows: "There is the new moon, thou beloved one among cows!"

When a man comes out at night to see what the night is doing, he looks at the moon and at the stars, especially the constellations, and says:

Glory to thee for ever,
Thou bright moon, this night;
Thyself art ever
The glorious lamp of the poor.

303 Beauteous fair one of grace

Hail to thee, thou new moon,
  Beauteous guidant of the sky;
Hail to thee, thou new moon,
  Beauteous fair one of grace.

Hail to thee, thou new moon,
  Beauteous guidant of the stars;
Hail to thee, thou new moon,
  Beauteous loved one of my heart.

Hail to thee, thou new moon,
  Beauteous guidant of the clouds;
Hail to thee, thou new moon,
  Beauteous dear one of the heavens!

304 New moon

She of my love is the new moon,
  The God of life illumining her;
Be mine a good purpose
  Towards each creature in the creation.

Be my prayer, O God,
  In accord with Thy sanctifying;
Be my heart, O God,
  In accord with Thy loving care.

Be my deed on land
  In accord with Thy satisfying;
Be my wish on sea
  In accord with Thy directing.

Be my hope on high
  In accord with Thy requiring;
Be my purpose below
  In accord with Thy satisfying.

Let my desire, O God,
  Seek after Thy repose;
Be my rest, O God,
  With the Son of Thy tranquillity.

305 The new moon

Hail to thee, thou new moon,
  Guiding jewel of gentleness!
I am bending to thee my knee,
  I am offering thee my love.

I am bending to thee my knee,
  I am giving thee my hand,
I am lifting to thee mine eye,
  O new moon of the seasons.

Hail to thee, thou new moon,
  Joyful maiden of my love!
Hail to thee, thou new moon,
  Joyful maiden of the graces!

Thou art travelling in thy course,
  Thou art steering the full tides;
Thou art illuming to us thy face,
  O new moon of the seasons.

Thou queen–maiden of guidance,
  Thou queen–maiden of good fortune,
Thou queen–maiden my beloved,
  Thou new moon of the seasons!

306 New moon

When I see the new moon,
  It becomes me to lift mine eye,
It becomes me to bend my knee,
  It becomes me to bow my head,

Giving thee praise, thou moon of guidance,
  That I have seen thee again,
That I have seen the new moon,
  The lovely leader of the way.

Many a one has passed beyond
  In the time between the two moons,
Though I am still enjoying earth,
  Thou moon of moons and of blessings!

307 The new moon

When I see the new moon,
  It becomes me to say my rune;
It becomes me to praise the Being of life
  For His kindness and His goodness;

Seeing how many a man and woman have gone hence
  Over the black river of the abyss,
Since last thy countenance shone on me,
  Thou new moon of the heavens!

308 New moon

I am lifting to thee my hands,
I am bowing to thee my head,
I am giving thee my love,
Thou glorious jewel of all the ages.

I am raising to thee mine eye,
I am bending to thee my head,
I am offering thee my love,
Thou new moon of all the ages!

309 New moon

There, see, the new moon,
The King of life blessing her;
Fragrant be every night
Whereon she shall shine!

Be her lustre full
To each one in need;
Be her course complete
To each one beset.

Be her light above
With every one in straits;
Be her guidance below
With every one in need.

May the moon of moons
Be coming through thick clouds
On me and on every one
Coming through dark tears.

May God's hand on me dwell
In every strait that me befalls,
Now and till the hour of my death,
And till the day of my resurrection.

310 New moon

There, there, the new moon!
The King of life making her bright for us;
Be mine a good intent
Towards all who look on her.

Be mine eye upward
To the gracious Father of blessings,
And be my heart below
To the dear Christ Who purchased me.

Be my knee bent down
To the queen of loveliness;
Be my voice raised up
To Him Who made and blessed her.

311 The new moon

She of my love is the new moon,
  The King of all creatures blessing her;
Be mine a good purpose
  Towards each creature of creation.

Holy be each thing
  Which she illumines;
Kindly be each deed
  Which she reveals.

Be her guidance on land
  With all beset ones;
Be her guidance on the sea
  With all distressed ones.

May the moon of moons
  Be coming through thick clouds
On me and on every mortal
  Who is coming through affliction.

May the virgin of my love
  Be coming through dense dark clouds
To me and to each one
  Who is in tribulation.

May the King of grace
  Be helping my hand
Now and for ever
  Till my resurrection day.

312 Queen of the night

Hail unto thee,
Jewel of the night!

Beauty of the heavens,
Jewel of the night!

Mother of the stars,
Jewel of the night!

Fosterling of the sun,
Jewel of the night!

Majesty of the stars,
Jewel of the night!

313 Jewel of virtues

Hail to thee, thou new moon,
Jewel of guidance in the night!
Hail to thee, thou new moon,
Jewel of guidance on the billows!
Hail to thee, thou new moon,
Jewel of guidance on the ocean!

Hail to thee, thou new moon,
Jewel of guidance of the virtues!
Hail to thee, thou new moon,
Jewel of guidance of my love!
Thou jewel of heaven!

314 New moon

May thy light be fair to me!
May thy course be smooth to me!
If good to me is thy beginning,
Seven times better be thine end,
Thou fair moon of the seasons,
Thou great lamp of grace!

He Who created thee
Created me likewise;
He Who gave thee weight and light
Gave to me life and death,
And the joy of the seven satisfactions,
Thou great lamp of grace,
Thou fair moon of the seasons.

The Sun Prayer

Old men in the Isles still uncover their heads when they first see the sun on coming out in the morning. They hum a hymn not easily caught up and not easily got from them.

The reciter said: "There was a man in Arasaig, and he was extremely old, and he would make adoration to the sun and to the moon and to the stars. When the sun would rise on the tops of the peaks he would put off his head–covering and he would bow down his head, giving glory to the great God of life for the glory of the sun and for the goodness of its light to the children of men and to the animals of the world. When the sun set in the western ocean the old man would again take off his head–covering, and he would bow his head to the ground and say:

I am in hope, in its proper time,
That the great and gracious God
Will not put out for me the light of grace
Even as thou dost leave me this night.

"The old man said that he had learned this from his father and from the old men of the village when he was a small child. Mannerless children would be mocking Iain, thinking that he was not all there, but it is not clear to me that poor Iain was doing anything wrong."

315

Sun

The eye of the great God,
The eye of the God of glory,
The eye of the King of hosts,
The eye of the King of the living,

Pouring upon us
At each time and season,
Pouring upon us
Gently and generously.

Glory to thee,
Thou glorious sun.

Glory to thee, thou sun,
Face of the God of life.

316 The sun

Hail to thee, thou sun of the seasons,
As thou traversest the skies aloft;
Thy steps are strong on the wing of the heavens,
Thou art the glorious mother of the stars.

Thou liest down in the destructive ocean
Without impairment and without fear;
Thou risest up on the peaceful wave–crest
Like a queenly maiden in bloom.

Thanks for Food

317 The meal

Give us, O God, of the morning meal,
Benefit to the body, the frame of the soul;
Give us, O God, of the seventh bread,
Enough for our need at evening close.

Give us, O God, of the honey–sweet foaming milk,
The sap and milk of the fragrant farms,
And give us, O God, along with Thy sleep,
Rest in the shade of Thy covenant Rock.

Give us this night of the corn that shall last,
Give us this night of the drink that shall hurt not;
Give us this night, anear to the heavens,
The chalice of Mary mild, the tender.

Be with us by day, be with us by night,
Be with us by light and by dark,
In our lying down and in our rising up,
In speech, in walk, in prayer.

318 Grace before food

Be with me, O God, at breaking of bread,
Be with me, O God, at the close of my meal;
Let no whit adown my body
That may hurt my sorrowing soul.
  O no whit adown my body
  That may hurt my sorrowing soul.

319 Thanks after food

Thanks be to Thee, O God,
Praise be to Thee, O God,
Reverence be to Thee, O God,
For all Thou hast given me.

As Thou hast given life corporeal
To earn me my worldly food,
So grant me life eternal
To show forth Thy glory.

Grant me grace throughout my life,
Grant me life at the hour of my death;
Be with me, O God, in casting off my breath,
O God, be with me in the deep currents.

O! in the parting of the breath,
O! be with my soul in the deep currents.
O God, be with my soul in sounding the fords,
In crossing the deep floods.

Night Shielding

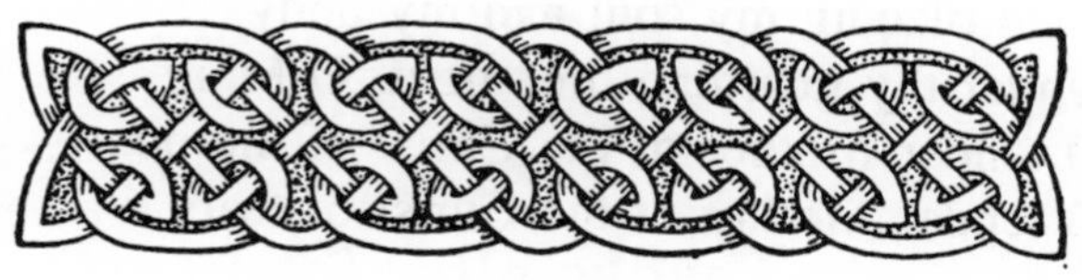

320 Charm for fear by night

God before me, God behind me,
God above me, God below me;
I on the path of God,
  God upon my track.

Who is there on land?
Who is there on wave?
Who is there on billow?
Who is there by door–post?
Who is along with us?
  God and Lord.

I am here abroad,
I am here in need,
I am here in pain,
I am here in straits,
I am here alone,
  O God, aid me.

321 The pilgrims' safeguarding

I am placing my soul and my body
Under thy guarding this night, O Brigit,
O calm Foster-mother of the Christ without sin,
O calm Foster-mother of the Christ of wounds.

I am placing my soul and my body
Under thy guarding this night, O Mary,
O tender Mother of the Christ of the poor,
O tender Mother of the Christ of tears.

I am placing my soul and my body
Under Thy guarding this night, O Christ,
O Thou Son of the tears, of the wounds, of the piercings,
May Thy cross this night be shielding me.

I am placing my soul and my body
Under Thy guarding this night, O God,
O Thou Father of help to the poor feeble pilgrims,
Protector of earth and of heaven,
  Protector of earth and of heaven.

322 Shielding of God

Thou Lord and God of power,
Shield and sustain me this night,
Thou Lord, Thou God of power,
This night and every night.

Sain and deliver me from fault,
Sain and deliver me from sin,
Sain my soul and my body,
Each dark and each light.

Bless to me the land whither I am bound,
Bless to me the thing mine eye shall see,
Bless to me the thing my purpose discerns,
Thou God of life, bless my condition.

Bless the journey whereon I go,
Bless the earth that is under my foot,
Bless the matter which I seek,
Thou King of glory, bless my condition.

323 Smooring the hearth

I will smoor the hearth
As Brigit the Foster–mother would smoor.
The Foster–mother's holy name
Be on the hearth, be on the herd,
Be on the household all.

324 Smooring the fire

I smoor this night my fire
As Mary's Son would smoor;
God's compassing be to myself and the fire,
God's compassing to myself and to all;
God's compassing to myself and the hearth,
God's compassing to myself and the floor,
And upon each herd and flock,
And upon the household all.

325 Smooring the fire

I smoor the fire this night
As the Son of Mary would smoor it;
The compassing of God be on the fire,
The compassing of God on all the household.

Be God's compassing about ourselves,
Be God's compassing about us all,
Be God's compassing upon the flock,
Be God's compassing upon the hearth.

Who keeps the watch this night?
Who but the Christ of the poor,
The bright and gentle Brigit of the kine,
The bright and gentle Mary of the ringlets.

Whole be house and herd,
Whole be son and daughter,
Whole be wife and man,
Whole the household all.

326 Night prayer

In Thy name, O Jesu Who wast crucified,
I lie down to rest;
Watch Thou me in sleep remote,
Hold Thou me in Thy one hand;
Watch Thou me in sleep remote,
Hold Thou me in Thy one hand.

Bless me, O my Christ,
Be Thou my shield protecting me,
Aid my steps in the pitful swamp,
Lead Thou me to the life eternal;
Aid my steps in the pitful swamp,
Lead Thou me to the life eternal.

Keep Thou me in the presence of God,
O good and gracious Son of the Virgin,
And fervently I pray Thy strong protection
From my lying down at dusk to my rising at day;
And fervently I pray Thy strong protection
From my lying down at dusk to my rising at day.

327 I lie down this night

I lie down this night with God,
And God will lie down with me;
I lie down this night with Christ,
And Christ will lie down with me;
I lie down this night with the Spirit,
And the Spirit will lie down with me;
God and Christ and the Spirit
Be lying down with me.

328 Sleep invocation

I lie down this night
With Brigit of the mantles,
With Mary of peace,
With Jesus of the poor.

I lie down this night
With Brigit of calmness,
With Mary revered,
With Michael of my love.

I lie down this night
Near the King of life,
Near Christ of the destitute,
Near the Holy Spirit.

I lie down this night
With the nine angels,
From the crown of my head
To the soles of my feet;
  From the crown of my head
  To the soles of my feet.

329 Going to rest

The poor, aged, and lonely reciter said: I do now as I saw my mother doing when I was a child. Before going to my bed I place the bar upon the leaf of the door, and I make the cross of Christ on the bar and on the door and I supplicate the great God of life, the Father of all living, to protect and comfort me this night:

May no wrong come unto me,
Through the crucifying–tree of Christ;
May no rapine come to me,
Through the precious blood of Jesus.

May no ill–doing come to me
Through door–leaf nor through bar;
Nor may I see oppression,
While the King of glory leads me.

After that I put out my light, and then I go to bed, and when I lie down on my pillow I make the cross of Christ upon my breast, over the tablet of my hard heart, and I beseech the living God of the universe:

May the Light of lights come
To my dark heart from Thy place;
May the Spirit's wisdom come
To my heart's tablet from my Saviour.

Be the peace of the Spirit mine this night,
Be the peace of the Son mine this night,
Be the peace of the Father mine this night,
The peace of all peace be mine this night,
Each morning and evening of my life.

330 Rest benediction

Bless to me, O God, the moon that is above me,
Bless to me, O God, the earth that is beneath me,
Bless to me, O God, my wife and my children,
And bless, O God, myself who have care of them;
Bless to me my wife and my children,
And bless, O God, myself who have care of them.

Bless, O God, the thing on which mine eye doth rest,
Bless, O God, the thing on which my hope doth rest,
Bless, O God, my reason and my purpose,
Bless, O bless Thou them, Thou God of life;
Bless, O God, my reason and my purpose,
Bless, O bless Thou them, Thou God of life.

Bless to me the bed–companion of my love,
Bless to me the handling of my hands,
Bless, O bless Thou to me, O God, the fencing of my defence,
And bless, O bless to me the angeling of my rest;
Bless, O bless Thou to me, O God, the fencing of my defence,
And bless, O bless to me the angeling of my rest.

331 Repose

Thou Being of marvels,
Shield me with might,
Thou Being of statutes
And of stars.

Compass me this night,
Both soul and body,
Compass me this night
And on every night.

Compass me aright
Between earth and sky,
Between the mystery of Thy laws
And mine eye of blindness;

Both that which mine eye sees
And that which it reads not;
Both that which is clear
And is not clear to my devotion.

332 Repose of sleep

O God of life, darken not to me Thy light,
O God of life, close not to me Thy joy,
O God of life, shut not to me Thy door,
O God of life, refuse not to me Thy mercy,
O God of life, quench Thou to me Thy wrath,
And O God of life, crown Thou to me Thy gladness,
O God of life, crown Thou to me Thy gladness.

333 Thou great God

Thou great God, grant me Thy light,
Thou great God, grant me Thy grace,
Thou great God, grant me Thy joy,
And let me be made pure in the well of Thy health.

Lift Thou from me, O God, my anguish,
Lift Thou from me, O God, my abhorrence,
Lift Thou from me, O God, all empty pride,
And lighten my soul in the light of Thy love.

As I put off from me my raiment,
Grant me to put off my struggling;
As the haze rises from off the crest of the mountains,
Raise Thou my soul from the vapour of death.

Jesu Christ, O Son of Mary,
Jesu Christ, O Paschal Son,
Shield my body in the shielding of Thy mantle,
And make pure my soul in the purifying of Thy grace.

334 Prayer

My God and my Chief,
I seek to Thee in the morning,
My God and my Chief,
I seek to Thee this night.
I am giving Thee my mind,
I am giving Thee my will,
I am giving Thee my wish,
My soul everlasting and my body.

Mayest Thou be chieftain over me,
Mayest Thou be master unto me,
Mayest Thou be shepherd over me,
Mayest Thou be guardian unto me,
Mayest Thou be herdsman over me,
Mayest Thou be guide unto me,
Mayest Thou be with me, O Chief of chiefs,
Father everlasting and God of the heavens.

335 Prayer

Father, bless me in my body,
  Father, bless me in my soul;
Father, bless me this night
  In my body and in my soul.

Father, bless me in my life,
  Father, bless me in my creed;
Father, bless me in my tie
  To my life and to my creed.

Father, sanctify to me my speech,
  Father, sanctify to me my heart;
Father, sanctify to me every whit
  In my speech and in my heart.

336 Encompassing of family

Bless, O God, the fire,
As Thou didst bless the Virgin;
Bless, O God, the hearth,
As Thou didst bless the Sabbath.

Bless, O God, the household,
According as Jesus said;
Bless, O God, the family,
As becomes us to offer it.

Bless, O God, the house,
Bless, O God, the fire,
Bless, O God, the hearth;
Be Thyself our stay.

May the Being of life bless,
May the Christ of love bless,
May the Spirit Holy bless
  Each one and all,
  Every one and all.

337 Rest blessing

Bless Thou, O God, the dwelling,
And each who rests herein this night;
Bless Thou, O God, my dear ones
In every place wherein they sleep;

In the night that is tonight,
And every single night;
In the day that is today,
And every single day.

338 The homestead

O God, bless my homestead,
Bless Thou all therein.

O God, bless my kindred,
Bless Thou my substance.

O God, bless my words,
Bless Thou my converse.

O God, bless my errand,
Bless Thou my journey.

O God, lessen my sin,
Increase Thou my trust.

O God, ward from me distress,
Ward Thou from me misfortune.

O God, shield me from guilt,
Fill Thou me with joy.

And, O God, let naught to my body
That shall do harm to my soul
When I enter the fellowship
Of the great Son of Mary.

339 Blessing of the house

May God give blessing
To the house that is here;

May Jesus give blessing
To the house that is here;

May Spirit give blessing
To the house that is here;

May Three give blessing
To the house that is here;

May Brigit give blessing
To the house that is here;

May Michael give blessing
To the house that is here;

May Mary give blessing
To the house that is here;

May Columba give blessing
To the house that is here:

Both crest and frame,
Both stone and beam;

Both clay and wattle,
Both summit and foundation;

Both window and timber,
Both foot and head;

Both man and woman,
Both wife and children;

Both young and old,
Both maiden and youth:

Plenty of food,
Plenty of drink,
Plenty of beds,
Plenty of ale;

Much of riches,
Much of mirth,
Many of people,
Much of long life
Be ever there:

Both warrior and poet,
Both clay and beam;

Both gear and thong,
Both crook and tie;

Both bairn and begetter,
Both wife and children;

Both young and mature,
Both maiden and youth.

May the King of the elements
Be its help,
The King of glory
Be near it.

Christ the beloved,
Son of Mary Virgin,
And the gentle Spirit
Be pouring therein;

Michael, bright warrior,
King of the angels,
Watch and ward it
With the power of his sword;

And Brigit, the fair and tender,
Her hue like the cotton–grass,
Rich–tressed maiden
Of ringlets of gold;

Mary, the fair and tender,
Be nigh the hearth,
And Columba kindly
Giving benediction
In fulfilment of each promise
  On those within,
  On those within!

340 Blessing of a house

Be Christ's cross on your new dwelling,
Be Christ's cross on your new hearth,
Be Christ's cross on your new abode,
Upon your new fire blazing.

Be Christ's cross on your topmost grain,
Be Christ's cross on your fruitful wives,
Be Christ's cross on your virile sons,
Upon your conceptive daughters.

Be Christ's cross on your means and portion,
Be Christ's cross on your kin and people,
Be Christ's cross on you each light and darkness,
  Each day and each night of your lives,
  Each day and each night of your lives.

Death

341 The day of death

The black wrath of the God of life
  Is upon the soul of gloom as it goes;
The white wrath of the King of the stars
  Is upon the soul of the dumb concealments.

A perfect calm is on sea and on land,
  Peace is on moor and on meadow,
The King's joyful glance and smile
  Are to the feeble one down on ocean.

Day of peace and of joy
  The bright day of my death;
May Michael's hand seek me
  On the white sunny day of my salvation.

342 Happy death

Thou great god of salvation,
Pour Thy grace on my soul
As the sun of the heights
Pours its love on my body.

I must needs die,
Nor know I where or when;
If I die without Thy grace
I am thus lost everlastingly.

Death of oil and of repentance,
Death of joy and of peace;
Death of grace and of forgiveness,
Death of Heaven and life with Christ.

343 Death prayer

O God, give me of Thy wisdom,
  O God, give me of Thy mercy,
O God, give me of Thy fullness,
  And of Thy guidance in face of every strait.

O God, give me of Thy holiness,
  O God, give me of Thy shielding,
O God, give me of Thy surrounding,
  And of Thy peace in the knot of my death.

Oh give me of Thy surrounding,
  And of Thy peace at the hour of my death!

344 Death of unction

Death with unction and with penitence,
Death with joy and with forgiveness,
Death without horror or repulsion,
Death without fear or shrinking.

Dying the death of the saints,
The Healer of my soul by my side,
The death of peace and tranquillity,
And grant Thou me a good day of burial.

The seven angels of the Holy Spirit
And two attendant angels
Be shielding me, and be this night the night
Till brightness and summer–tide shall come!

345 I am going home with thee

I am going home with thee
  To thy home! to thy home!
I am going home with thee
  To thy home of winter.

I am going home with thee
  To thy home! to thy home!
I am going home with thee
  To thy home of autumn, of spring
    and of summer.

I am going home with thee,
  Thou child of my love,
To thine eternal bed,
  To thy perpetual sleep.

I am going home with thee,
Thou child of my love,
To the dear Son of blessings,
To the Father of grace.

346 The death dirge

Thou goest home this night to thy home of winter,
To thy home of autumn, of spring, and of summer;
Thou goest home this night to thy perpetual home,
To thine eternal bed, to thine eternal slumber.

Sleep thou, sleep, and away with thy sorrow,
Sleep thou, sleep, and away with thy sorrow,
Sleep thou, sleep, and away with thy sorrow;
Sleep, thou beloved, in the Rock of the fold.

Sleep this night in the breast of thy Mother,
Sleep, thou beloved, while she herself soothes thee;
Sleep thou this night on the Virgin's arm,
Sleep, thou beloved, while she herself kisses thee.

The great sleep of Jesus, the surpassing sleep of Jesus,
The sleep of Jesus' wound, the sleep of Jesus' grief,
The young sleep of Jesus, the restoring sleep of Jesus,
The sleep of the kiss of Jesus of peace and of glory.

The sleep of the seven lights be thine, beloved,
The sleep of the seven joys be thine, beloved,
The sleep of the seven slumbers be thine, beloved,
On the arm of the Jesus of blessings, the Christ of grace.

The shade of death lies upon thy face, beloved,
But the Jesus of grace has His hand round about thee;
In nearness to the Trinity farewell to thy pains,
Christ stands before thee and peace is in His mind.

Sleep, O sleep in the calm of all calm,
Sleep, O sleep in the guidance of guidance,
Sleep, O sleep in the love of all loves;
Sleep, O beloved, in the Lord of life,
Sleep, O beloved, in the God of life!

347 Joyous death

Give us, O God, the needs of the body,
Give us, O God, the needs of the soul;
Give us, O God, the healing balsam of the body,
Give us, O God, the healing balsam of the soul.

Give us, O God, the joy of repentance,
Give us, O God, the joy of forgiveness,
Wash Thou from us the lees of corruption,
Cleanse Thou from us the stain of uncleanness.

O great God, Who art on the throne,
Give to us the true repentance,
Give to us the forgiveness of sin —
Sin inborn and actual sin.

Give to us, O God, strong love,
And that beautiful crown of the King;
Give us, O God, the home of salvation
Within the beauteous gates of Thy kingdom.

May Michael, bright warrior of the angels,
Be keeping the evil enemies down;
May Jesus Christ the Son of David
Be giving us hospitality in the brightness of peace.

348 Joyous death

Give Thou to me, O God,
Each food that is needful for my body;
Give Thou to me, O God,
Each light that is needful for my mind;
Give Thou to me, O God,
Each salve that is needful for my soul.

Give Thou to me, O God,
Sincere repentance;
Give Thou to me, O God,
Whole-hearted repentance;
Give Thou to me, O God,
Lasting repentance.

Give Thou to me, O God,
The death of the priceless oil;
Give Thou to me, O God,
That the Healer of my soul be near me;
Give Thou to me, O God,
The death of joy and of peace.

Give Thou to me, O God,
To confess the death of Christ;
Give Thou to me, O God,
To meditate the agony of Christ;
Give Thou to me, O God,
To make warm the love of Christ.

O great God of Heaven,
Draw Thou my soul to Thyself,
That I may make repentance
With a right and a strong heart,
With a heart broken and contrite,
That shall not change nor bend nor yield.

O great God of the angels,
Bring Thou me to the dwelling of peace;
O great God of the angels,
Preserve me from the evil of the fairies;
O great God of the angels,
Bathe me in the bathing of Thy pool.

O great God of grace,
Give Thou to me the strong Spirit of powers;
O great God of grace,
Give Thou to me the Spirit undying, everlasting;
O great God of grace,
Give Thou to me the loving Spirit of the Lamb.

349 Joyous death

Death with oil,
Death with joy,
Death with light,
Death with gladness,
Death with penitence.

Death without pain,
Death without fear,
Death without death,
Death without horror,
Death without grieving.

May the seven angels of the Holy Spirit
And the two guardian angels
Shield me this night and every night
Till light and dawn shall come;

Shield me this night and every night
Till light and dawn shall come.

350 Supplication

I pray Peter, I pray Paul,
I pray Virgin, I pray Son,
I pray the twelve kindly Apostles
That I go not to ruin this night.

When the soul separates
From the perverse body,
And goes in bursts of light
Up from out its human frame,
Thou holy God of eternity,
Come to seek me and to find me.

May God and Jesus aid me,
May God and Jesus protect me;
May God and Jesus eternally
Seek me and find me.

Live Creatures

Birds, beasts, fishes and insects figure largely in the old lore of the people. All the live creatures with which they came in contact, large and small, wild and domestic, they were accustomed to regard with an observant and intelligent eye, and seldom without kindness and affection. The following are examples of the traditional lore of this kind: fables, beliefs, children's rimes and other verses, still more or less well known among the people.

The water–dog

The reciter was a man of much natural intelligence. The first part of what he said he gave from hearsay, but the account of the healing as fact; he had seen it done and done it himself, always successfully.

The dobharchu, an animal of the otter kind, is rarely seen and still more rarely caught, and many allege that it is a mythical creature like the sea–serpent and the mermaid. It has a white spot about the size of a florin on its breast. The reciter's account clearly supposes a difference between the *dobharchu* (water–dog), or *dobhran donn* (brown water–dog), and the *biast–dubh* (black beast, black otter); but these terms are sometimes synonymous.

The otter is plentiful in the Western Isles. It was for years preserved about the island of Rona, North Uist, and is consequently especially common there. The male otter is larger than the female, and much rarer.

The Water–Dog is the high–king of the Black Otters. He is but rare among creatures of sea and land; there is but one Water–Dog to every seven Black Otters.

A small bit of the hide of the Water–Dog is a charm upon a man in battle, and neither lead nor steel would overcome him all his life though the lead were showering on him like a fall of hailstones in the wild Wolf–month of winter. The Brown Water–Dog cannot be killed except through the white spot below his chin.

There are always seven Black Otters along with the Brown Water–Dog serving him day and night, and Oh! Thou King of knowledge! it is themselves who are attentive to him!

If a man were to put his tongue on the liver of a Black Otter his tongue has power to heal burning for all his life thereafter. The burn will not blister and will be whole in a moment.

Gravedigger beetle and sacred beetle

The following legend concerning the *Daol* (Gravedigger Beetle) and the *Cearrdubhan* (Sacred Beetle) is similar to that already given (see II:208–10 and especially II:208n.)

During the flight to Egypt, when Herod's men were in pursuit of the Holy Family, they asked those whom they passed whether they had seen Jesus. A farmer admitted that he had seen a family pass that way.

"When?" asked the pursuers.

"When this corn was being sown."

Now the corn had been sown the day before, but a miracle had been performed: the pursuers looked around, and behold the corn was ripe and yellow and ready for the sickle. As the soldiers were turning to go away the *Daol* came across the road and said:

Yesterday, yesterday
Went the Son of God by.

The *Cearrdubhan* however, with less regard for truth but more regard for charity, said:

Lie, lie, thou little thief!
Seven years without doubt,
I would give my word,
Since the Son of God went by.

Or according to another version he said:

Three Fridays after one another
Since the Son of God went by.

The *Daol* is therefore trampled on when seen, but the *Cearrdubhan* is merely turned on his back and not further molested.

The kestrel hawk and the red fox

Be not very anxious about a trifle. That thou hast grasped, grasp it well.

The Fox laid hold of the Kestrel, and the Kestrel said:

"Let me go! Let me go, and I'll lay thee an egg as big as thy paw!" But he did not let him go.

"Let me go, and I'll lay thee an egg as big as thy fist!" But he did not let him go.

"Let me go, and I'll lay thee an egg as big as thy head!" But he did not let him go an inch.

The wren

Conan Corr (the Wren) went with his twelve sons to the peat moss to pull a carrot. Conan grasped the carrot by the ear, and he was stamping his soles, and he was swaying it thither and swaying it hither, plough–casting it and peat–cutting it. White was his hue and red his cheek, but never did he take away the carrot from the smooth clasps of the ground, the fat rich carrot of the virtues and of the blessings.

"Come hither one warrior!" quoth Conan Corr. Conan and his son again grasped the carrot by the ear. They were swaying it thither and swaying it hither, and plough–casting it, and peat–cutting it.

So they did one after another, until the twelve sons took an ear–grip on the carrot. They all hauled once, and hauled twice, and hauled thrice on the ear of the carrot, and Conan and his twelve sons fell flat on their backs in the peat hag; but never did they take the carrot from out its firm foundation.

The cock

The domestic cock is sained throughout the Isles. It is perfectly trusted as an accurate time–keeper. Should a cock crow at an untimely hour it would cause uneasiness to the family. "If the big cock crows at an unmeet time some unfortunate mishap is to befall." The people differentiate, however, between the voice of the big cock and the voice of the little cock, between the crow of the young cock and the crow of the old cock. *An coileachan* (the little cock) is unreliable until he is twelve months old, but the big cock is remarkably reliable.

The cock is called by various endearing names: *am fear faire* (the watcher); *fear faire na h–oidhche* (the watcher of the night); *fear faire Chriosda* (Christ's watcher); *fear faire nan tràth* (the watcher of the hours); *fear bheannachaidh na maidne* (he who blesses the morning); *fear dhùsgadh nan naomh* (the wakener of the saints); *fear dhùsgadh nan creidmheach (creideach)* (the wakener of the believers); *fear choimheid na h–urnaigh* (the observer of prayer); *fear chuimhneachaidh Pheadair* (the remembrancer of Peter); *fear bhristidh nan geasa* (the breaker of the spells). Other phrases are: *guth fear ghabhail an rathaid* (the voice of him who takes the road); *coileach Chonnachd* (the cock of Connacht); *coileach Righ Chonnachdaich* (the cock of the King of Connacht).

No one will willingly be out and no one will willingly travel between midnight and cockcrow, *eadar mheadhon oidhche agus gairm choileach.* This time is known as *an tràth marbh, tràth marbh na h–oidhche* (the dead watch, the dead watch of the night). After the cock crows all is well, and the most timid will travel in the dark without fear or timidity. Highlanders dislike the voice of the redcock and still more that of the blackcock when travelling at night, but the voice of the domestic cock is hailed with joy as the voice of a friend, dispelling danger and darkness and all supernatural evil from the land.

To see a cluster of hens with no cock among them is a sure sign of evil impending in the family or the flock.

A cock cannot crow unless he is free to raise his head. If it be desired to prevent his crowing he is placed in a position where he must keep his head down. A cock so treated is called *coileach cùbaidh* (a depressed cock); *coileach crùbaidh* (a crouched cock); *coileach Chaluim Chille* (the cock of Columba).

Columba was travelling in Ireland. A disciple asked him at what time he was leaving.

"I am not leaving till cockcrow," said Columba. His emissaries brought this information to the King of Connacht, who commanded all the cocks of the townland to be placed under upturned tubs. This was done, unknown to Columba; death was the penalty for any who should inform him, for the King wished to annoy the Saint for denouncing his sins. The vigilant ear of Columba failed to hear the call of the morning cock, but his vigilant eye did not fail to see the glimmering of the morning, and he was up and away on his travels to tell the people of the life to come and of the hopes beyond the grave; not, however, before the King's servile men had time to annoy and to try him sorely. Columba cursed the cocks of that townland and left it as a ban that no cock should ever crow in that place. Nor has a cock of that townland ever crowed since then, and the curse is still upon them and shall remain till the day of doom. Even a cock from elsewhere becomes mute when brought to that townland.

The Roman Catholics of Barra attribute this deception to the Protestants of Tiree, the people of Tiree to the people of Connacht, and the Christians of Connacht to the Jews of Judea.

"The people of Connacht were not at all so guilty as those of Judea, glory to God in heaven and to saints on earth," said a bright beautiful woman of Connacht with an alluring smile, half doubtful of her own statement. Alas, none of us are at all as other people are!

A man died behind Ben More in South Uist. His son went to the townland to make arrangements for the funeral. The old man's body was laid out on the bier, in the upper part of the house. A girl of seven years, who had never spoken before, cried out: "Mother, mother, my grandfather is getting up!"

The woman was afraid (no wonder) at the girl speaking who had till then been dumb and at the thing she said, and she answered: "If this be thy first utterance it is time we moved!"

The woman and the rest of the family went into the *cùltaigh* (backhouse) and made fast the door with the *cnotag* (latch) and the *pollag.* The corpse got down from the bier, tried the door of the *cùltaigh,* and began to force it, calling out:

I am coming at you! I am coming at you!
I've got you anyhow!

As he could not force the door with the heavy stones behind it, he scraped and scratched away under the *comhla,* and had a big hole made there when the *coileach mór,* big cock, flapped his two wings and crowed. The corpse fell again dead on the floor, and was found there when the son came home.

A woman in Uist, a Roman Catholic, went to see a Protestant neighbour who was ailing. While they were together, the fowls on the rafters flew down to the floor and flew about as if pursued. There was no pursuit, however, and the woman, much amazed, looked at her sick friend for an explanation. The woman was dead.

A man in Uist was playing his pipes in the house during a great snow–storm. In the midst of the music the cock flew down from the spar and crowed loudly. The man kept on playing and the cock kept on crowing. The man's wife said: "Stop, John, there is something wrong."

Presently the priest came to tell John that his brother Malcolm had just perished, on account of the storm, in the lake near by.

Big Alexander, son of strong John, went out after midnight to gud the river (to drive fish into a trap or fish–weir). He met a man whom he did not know. The man was fair to see and spoke well.

"I myself will help thee, big Alexander, and we will divide the fish," said the stranger.

"I am willing," said big Alexander. They worked together and they worked well too. About the dead watch of the night the stranger said:

"It is time to divide, big Alexander."

"It is not time yet," said he, "there are more fish in the channel." They worked and they worked well, and in a while the stranger said: "It is time to divide, big Alexander."

"Oh it is not, it is not, there are more fish in the channel." They worked and they worked well, and in a little the stranger said: "It is time to divide, big Alexander."

"Yes, it is just time now," he answered, and scarcely was the word out of his mouth when the red cock crew, and at the first crow that the cock gave the stranger leapt from big Alexander's side and rushed away in red blazes of fire. Ever since that time none go out to gud the river save unbelievers without grace of God or fear of man. For who was this but the Fiend in human shape. Ever since that time no one goes out to gud the river at an unmeet time of the year (spawning time) or at an unmeet time of the night (the dead watch).

Columba and the flounder

Columba was one day in the strand of small–fry and he trampled on a beautiful little fair Flounder and hurt her tail. The poor little Flounder cried out as loud as she could:

Thou Colum big and clumsy,
With thy crooked crosswise feet,
Much didst thou to me of injury
When thou didst trample on my tail.

Columba was angry at being taunted with having crooked feet and he said:

If I am crooked–footed,
Be thou wry–mouthed.

And he left her that way.

The limpet

When the limpet opens her breast to drink the sun (as the people say), birds and beasts come to prey on her and sometimes get caught and are drowned. A limpet closed upon an oyster–catcher and pressed her imprisoned bill against the rock. The bird called out to her mate:

"What shall I do? what shall I do? what shall I do?
Lad of the red bill! lad of the red bill!"

"Hold on! hold on! hold on!
Till turns the tide of the sea."

This unwise advice led to the drowning of the oyster–catcher. A rat caught in the same way escaped, though maimed, because he bravely faced the difficulty. Gaelic lore is full of incitements to pluck and endurance.

"What shall I do? what shall I do?
Man of the black coat! man of the black coat!"

"Tear it off! tear it off!
Completely! completely! completely!"

The rat placed his three crooked claws in position, using the limpet as a fulcrum, and he took his life with himself though he left his foot with the limpet.

Dear is living to life;
I took with me my life,
Howbeit I left my paw
In the hard grip of the Limpet.

It will be observed that this was the black rat, indigenous to Britain, now nearly extinct. Only in Benbecula has the writer seen the black rat, and perhaps because of its rarity, perhaps because of its beauty, it never aroused in him the aversion which he has always felt towards the intrusive grey Hanoverian rat.

The rat

As our Blessed Lord went through Palestine feeding the poor and healing the sick there was an artful woman who pretended to Him that she possessed nothing in the world and pleaded for His aid, while at that very time she had a sow with a litter of piglets. The litter she carefully hid under an upturned tub while she went forth to plead her poverty to our Divine Lord. He paid no heed to her false talk and her pressing importunities. At length she was obliged to desist and went back to her house. Her first care was to go and feed the pigs. She lifted the lid of the tub and what was her horror to see a litter of nasty vicious gnawing creatures of a kind she had never known before. They rushed forth gnawing and devouring and destroying and would have destroyed the produce of the whole world had not our Blessed Lord created the cat to check them.

351 The cat

Creeping by night,
Creeping by night,
Creeping by night,
Quoth the grey Cat;

Creeping by night,
With neither star nor gleam,
Nor brightness nor light,
Quoth the grey Cat!

352 The dog

Dee do,
Said the white Dog,
Dee do,
Said the white Dog,
Dee do,
Said the white Dog,
Dee do
Often were we
From night–time till day
Happy and snug,
Said the white Dog!

353 The goldfinch

"Beauteous yellow Goldfinch,
I will spend a Sunday
Sweeping out thy chamber,"
Said the foolish yellow Hen.

354 The golden butterfly

Butterfly! Butterfly!
Whose the soul thou didst bear,
Butterfly! Butterfly!
Yesterday to heaven?

355 Lullaby

Thou art not the round–headed seal's blue cub,
Thou art not the sea–gull's grey chick,
Thou art not the otter's wry whelp,
Thou art not the lean cow's puny calf.

356 The salmon–trout

O soft smooth Salmon–Trout,
Who tookest the butter from Erin!
O soft fair Salmon–Trout,
Who tookest the cheese from Alba!

357 The mouse

Little mouse! little mouse!
Little mouse, kindly one!
Little mouse! little mouse!
Little mouse, beloved one!

Give thou to me
A little tooth gold–white,
Give thou to me
A little tooth silver–white,
And I will give to thee
In its stead, in return,
A little tooth beauteous white,
A little tooth of boy, bone bound,
A little tooth of maid, bone bound,
A little tooth of youngster laughing loud.

The Speech of Birds

358 The speech of birds

THE MAVIS SAID:
Little red lad!
Little red lad!
Come away home!
Come away home!
Come away home,
My dear, to your dinner!

What shall I get?
What shall I get?

A worm and a scrap of limpet!
A worm and a scrap of limpet!

Hurry up! Hurry up!
The night's coming!
The night's coming!
And the darkness!

ANOTHER MAVIS SAID:
Poor big Donald!
Poor big Donald!

Taste it!
Taste it!
Polish it off!
Polish it off!
Every drop!
Every drop!
O big Donald!

Who made your breeks?
Who made your breeks?
They're narrow!
They're narrow!

The tailor MacLucas!
The tailor MacLucas!
He spoiled them!
He spoiled them!

ANOTHER MAVIS:
Poor big Donald!
Poor big Donald!
Poor big Donald!
You are thirsty!
You are thirsty!
Drink it off!
Drink it off!
Every drop!
Every drop!

THE CORNCRAKE SAID:
O God of the powers!
O God of the powers!
Put food in the field!
Put food in the field!

THE CROW:
Sap of heart, sap of body,
Little black Robbie! quoth the Crow.

Sap of heart, sap of body,
Little black Robbie! quoth the Crow.

WITH ANOTHER NAME:
Sap of heart, sap of body,
Bonnie little dear Donald!
Sap of heart, sap of body,
Bonnie little dear Donald!

THE CUCKOO:
Said the Cuckoo to the Cockle,
"Where hast thou left thy bairns?
If thou didst keep thy house better,
Thy children would not thus be lost!"

THE PIGEON:
Gu–roo! Gu–roo! Gu–roo oo!
Not of my kin are you!
Not of my kin are you!

359 Voice of the swan

Gu vi gi,
Gu vi go,
Gu vi gi,
Loud *"guile!"*
The swans!

Voice of the swan,
Voice of the bird,
Voice of the swan
Upon the lake.

Gu vi gi,
Gu vi go,
Gu vi gi,
Loud *"guile!"*
The swans!

360 The swan

Guiliog i! guiliog o!
Guiliog i! guiliog o!
Guiliog i! guiliog o!
Voice of the swan, voice of the bird!

Voice of the swan, and she in the mist,
Voice of the swan, and she in sorrow,
Voice of the swan in the early day,
Voice of the swan upon the lake.

Voice of the swan, and she in the ocean,
Voice of the swan, and it so cold,
Voice of the swan, and it so keen,
Voice of the swan, and she in the ocean.

My one foot black,
My one foot black,
My one foot black
A–marching;
My one foot black
At mouth of brook,
My other plashing
Wounded.

361 The white swan

Columba went out
An early mild morning;
He saw a white swan,
"Guile guile,"
Down on the strand,
"Guile guile,"
With a dirge of death,
"Guile guile."

A white swan and she wounded, wounded,
A white swan and she bruised, bruised,
The white swan of the two visions,
"Guile guile,"
The white swan of the two omens,
"Guile guile,"
Life and death,
"Guile guile,"
"Guile guile."

Whence thy journey,
Swan of mourning?
Said Columba of love,
"Guile guile,"
From Erin my swimming,
"Guile guile,"
From the Fiann my wounding,
"Guile guile,"
The sharp wound of my death,
"Guile guile,"
"Guile guile."

White swan of Erin,
A friend am I to the needy;
The eye of Christ be on thy wound,
"Guile guile,"
The eye of affection and of mercy,
"Guile guile,"
The eye of kindness and of love,
"Guile guile,"
Making thee whole,
"Guile guile,"
"Guile guile."

Swan of Erin,
"Guile guile,"
No harm shall touch thee,
"Guile guile,"
Whole be thy wounds,
"Guile guile."

Lady of the wave,
   "Guile guile,"
Lady of the dirge,
   "Guile guile,"
Lady of the melody,
   "Guile guile."

To Christ the glory,
   "Guile guile,"
To the Son of the Virgin,
   "Guile guile,"
To the great High–King,
   "Guile guile,"
To Him be thy song,
   "Guile guile,"
To Him be thy song,
   "Guile guile,"
   "Guile guile!"

Harvesting

Fishing

From the manner in which Christ spoke of fish the people look upon fish as semi-sacred. The fish was a symbol of Christ Himself. Besides this, the people cherish many curious beliefs and customs and have many sayings and stories about fish and fishing.

A mother in Barra sent her two boys to fish. They came home with nothing, saying:

Narrow is a hook's point, little mother.

To this she promptly replied:

If narrow a hook's point,
Wide is the mouth of a spoon–net, little sons.

This woman was the wife of a schoolmaster in Barra. She was a native of Stirling, where no Gaelic is spoken, but after a year in Barra she spoke Gaelic well, and after two years she spoke it excellently. She used to reproach the people of Barra for not cultivating their flexible expressive language.

In Barra a fisherman will not wear clothing in which crotal is used. Crotal clings to the rocks, and were a fisherman to fall into the sea the crotal in his clothing would cling to the rocks in the bottom of the sea and prevent his coming to the surface.

In Barra the fishermen used to set their lines on New Year's Day. This gave them a claim for the season on the banks on which they set their lines. There the lines might remain, perhaps with only a few hooks attached, until St Bride's Day or thereabouts, marked with a buoy, that other lines might not be shot there and become entangled. No one else made claim to a place thus marked, for "ciad seilbh seilbh is fearr coir" (first possession has the best right). When the fishing season came these first hooks were taken up. The first hook of the season is then put down in the name of Father, Son and Holy Ghost (see also "Genealogy of Bride," I:70n).

When a man becomes a regular fisherman he is seized by his fellow boatmen and dipped in a convenient sea pool, to initiate him into the craft.

The *cailleach*

In those places where the crofters' fields are generally of a size and near each other, there is great striving to finish the harvest in time and not to be the last to have the corn cut. It was supposed that he who finished last had to support an invisible hag, *cailleach,* all the winter. It was the custom to bind up a handful of straw, the last sheaf of corn cut on the field, and to make it up into the likeness of a woman with docken and ragweed stalks, and tied with threads of various colours. This was called in Argyll, Perthshire, Uist, and other places the *cailleach.* When a man finished cutting his corn he sent the *cailleach* to a man who had not finished. This was considered a great insult to the recipients and was deeply resented, sometimes to the shedding of blood.

Caution had to be used in conveying the sheaf; usually a young man mounted on a horse passed the neighbour's uncut field at full gallop as if on urgent business, and threw the *cailleach* into the field on his course.

A man went on horseback in this fashion from Bornish to Milton in South Uist. After placing the *cailleach* he started to return. Two men on horseback set out after him, overtook him, and brought him back to Milton. They shaved his beard and hair and made "a clipping of bird and of fool"* on him, and sent him home.

Dùghall an Drorna, Dugall of the Ridge, sent the *cailleach* to "Pàdra" Nicolson, Cnoc na Moine, Benbecula. The messenger was caught, clipped, stripped, and sent home naked.

Other instances of violence done in consequence of sending the *cailleach* might be given. A crofter or tacksman would sooner see his best cow dead than see the *cailleach* on his harvest rig.

In Harris, Skye, and Glen Elg the last sheaf of the harvest is called the *gobhar bhacach* (halting goat). Dire evil and misfortune are predicted for the man on whom it falls:

Cattle–loss, death–loss, and mischance
Will befall the luckless one of the *gobhar bhacach.*

362 Abundance of seaweed

Come and come is seaweed,
Come and come is red sea–ware,
Come is yellow weed, come is tangle,
Come is food which the wave enwraps.

* *"Bearradh eoin is amadain air."* The phrase was originally *bearradh geòin (geòine)* (fool's tonsure, clipping in mockery).

Come is warrior Michael of fruitage,
Come is womanly Brigit of gentleness,
Come is the mild Mother Mary,
And come is glorious Connan of guidance.

363 Prayer for seaweed

Produce of sea to land,
  Produce of land to sea;
He who doeth not in time,
  Scant shall be his share.

Seaweed being cast on shore
  Bestow, Thou Being of bestowal;
Fruitfulness being brought to wealth,
  O Christ, grant me my share!

Cattle–Stock

The shieling

Lewis is the only place in Scotland, probably the only place in Britain, where the people still go to the àirigh (moorland shieling or mountain pasturage). Throughout Lewis the crofters of the townland go to the shieling on the same date each year, and they return from it on the same date each year. The sheep and cattle know their day as well as do the men and women, and on that day the scene is striking and touching: all the *ni* (flocks) are astir and restless to be off, requiring all the care of the people to restrain them and keep them together and in proper order. Should any event, such as a death and burial, cause the people to postpone the migration, the flocks have to be guarded day and night, or they would be off to their summer pastures by themselves.

Most of the shielings are several miles, some six or eight, some twelve or fourteen miles, from the townland homes. The moorlands are rough and rugged and full of swamps and channels, and the people use much care in guiding the cattle, especially the young ones not yet experienced in travelling. Even these, however, soon learn, being "gey gleg in the uptak," very quick of apprehension. It is instructive to see the caution with which the older animals travel over the rough channeled moors, daintily feeling their way when not sure of their ground. When they reach their camping ground the cattle and sheep soon spread themselves over the heather, being tired and hungry. While being milked the cattle eat the fodder which the girls and women have brought in creels.

This fodder is not so much grass as vegetables of various kinds, some of them of the most unpromising quality, such as nettles, dockens, ragworts, chickweed, common rushes and bulrushes. These the Lewis cattle eat with relish as a change from the heather and tussock–grass of the moorland. But it is still more curious to see them greedily eating fish–bones, especially the spinal bones of the cod and ling. There is nothing that a Lewis cow so much enjoys – not the most succulent clover nor the greenest corn in the blade. It is a common thing to find the side of a house partly or wholly covered with fish–bones, drying in the summer sun and becoming impregnated with the peat–reek which streams through the straw thatch. The bones are sometimes given to the cattle entire, but generally they are first more or less crushed between stones. Even so, it is difficult to conceive how the sharp spines fail to tear and injure the mouths, throats and stomachs of the cows. The people, however, say that no injury results; on the contrary, the fish–bones are a valuable food, and on a cold day nothing can be more wholesome. When a cow comes in wet, cold and shivering, a fish-bone is given her to chew. This chewing tries her to the utmost, and soon upon the point of every hair of her body stands a bead of perspiration, while from her rises a cloud of steam. The people are keen observers, and they follow the teaching of their forefathers, who studied nature with observant eyes and with intelligent interest.

The island of Berneray in Loch Roag is cut off by a deep channel some hundreds of yards wide, through which the tide runs rapidly and strongly Over this channel the people of the island swim their cattle, at high or low tide in order to avoid the worst currents. The calves are generally carried across in boats; but the calves are in a hurry to follow their mothers, and the mothers are in a hurry to be over the sound and on the moorland, and despite all precautions they dash into the sea and are out in the current, the calves rushing after them and struggling bravely with this new element. The masterful strength of the tide gives full scope to the strong experienced cow, but the weak, inexperienced calf is swept away like a leaf. Now is the time for the men in the boats: they pursue the calves over the stream and either draw them into the boats or lead them to land. Calves and cows having reached the shore safely, they shake the water from their shaggy backs, rush up the rocky beach, and are off to the moorland and their own pastures. It is worth going far to witness this exciting scene.

The shieling time is the most delightful time of the rural year, the time of the healthy heather bed and the healthy outdoor life, of the moorland breeze and the warm sun, of the curds and the cream of the heather milk. The young men come out from the townland in twos and threes and half-dozens to spend the night among the maidens of the shieling; some of them play the pipes or some other instrument, and the song and the dance and the merriment begin and are continued all night long under the moon on the green grass before the shieling door. I have heard old men and women waxing eloquent over these lightsome days and nights of their youth, and again sobbing and sighing over awakened memories too tender for words.

While the flocks are away at the moorland pastures the home pastures have grown rich and green, and on reaching home after a weary march and long fasting the cattle, like children, have to be restrained from eating too much. This good feeding produces good milking, and there is food for man and beast all autumn and winter through, and joy in house and byre.

Christmas for stock

Down to the middle of the nineteenth century it was customary in the Island of Lismore to give a special breakfast to all animals upon the farm on Christmas morning. Cattle and horses got a sheaf of corn in the stall, sheep got sheaves of corn spread out for them on the field, while pigs and poultry got special feeding of an appropriate sort. Even the birds of the air received a special feast. When a tree was at hand a sheaf of oats was suspended to a branch; otherwise a pole was put up and the sheaf tied to the top of the pole.

In Breadalbane it is said that the cows in the byres go down on their knees at midnight on Christmas Eve. The bees too leave their hives at three o'clock on Christmas morning, returning again immediately.

364 Driving the cows

Closed to you be every pit,
  Smooth to you be every hill,
Snug to you be every bare spot,
  Beside the cold mountains.

The sanctuary of Mary Mother be yours,
  The sanctuary of Brigit the loved be yours,
The sanctuary of Michael victorious be yours,
  Active and full be you gathered home.

The protection of shapely Cormac be yours,
  The protection of Brendan of the ship be yours,
The protection of Maol Duinne the saint be yours
  In marshy ground and rocky ground.

The fellowship of Mary Mother be yours,
  The fellowship of Brigit of kine be yours,
The fellowship of Michael victorious be yours,
  In nibbling, in chewing, in munching.

365 The driving

The protection of Odhran the dun be yours,
The protection of Brigit the Nurse be yours,
The protection of Mary the Virgin be yours
  In marshes and in rocky ground,
  In marshes and in rocky ground.

The keeping of Ciaran the swart be yours,
The keeping of Brianan the yellow be yours,
The keeping of Diarmaid the brown be yours,
  A–sauntering the meadows,
  A–sauntering the meadows.

The safeguard of Fionn son of Cumhall be yours,
The safeguard of Cormac the shapely be yours,
The safeguard of Conn and of Cumhall be yours
  From wolf and from bird–flock,
  From wolf and from bird–flock.

The sanctuary of Colum Cille be yours,
The sanctuary of Maol Ruibhe be yours,
The sanctuary of the milking Maid be yours,
  To seek you and search for you,
  To seek you and search for you.

The encircling of Maol Odhrain be yours,
The encircling of Maol Oghe be yours,
The encircling of Maol Domhnaich be yours,
  To protect you and to herd you,
  To protect you and to herd you.

The shield of the king of the Fiann be yours,
The shield of the King of the sun be yours,
The shield of the King of the stars be yours
  In jeopardy and distress,
  In jeopardy and distress.

The sheltering of the King of kings be yours,
The sheltering of Jesus Christ be yours,
The sheltering of the Spirit of healing be yours
  From evil deed and quarrel,
  From evil dog and red dog.

366 Columba's herding

May the herding of Columba
Encompass you going and returning,
Encompass you in strath and on ridge
And on the edge of each rough region;

May it keep you from pit and from mire,
Keep you from hill and from crag,
Keep you from loch and from downfall,
Each evening and each darkling;

May it keep you from the mean destroyer,
Keep you from the mischievous niggard,
Keep you from the mishap of bar-stumbling
And from the untoward fays.

The peace of Columba be yours in the grazing,
The peace of Brigit be yours in the grazing,
The peace of Mary be yours in the grazing,
And may you return home safe-guarded.

367 Sain for sheep

The sain placed by Mary
  Upon her flock of sheep,
Against birds, against dogs,
  Against beasts, against men,
Against hounds, against thieves,
  Against polecats, against marten-cats,
Against eye, against envy,
  Against disease, against *gaoban.*
In the hollow of your meeting,
  Be yours the aiding of God;
On the hillock of your lying,
  Whole be your rising.

368 Charm for stock

The charm placed of Brigit
  About her neat, about her kine,
About her horses, about her goats,
  About her sheep, about her lambs;

Each day and night,
  In heat and cold,
Each early and late,
  In darkness and light;

To keep them from marsh,
  To keep them from rock,
To keep them from pit,
  To keep them from bank;

To keep them from eye,
  To keep them from omen,
To keep them from spell,
  South and north;

To keep them from venom,
  East and west,
To keep them from envy
  And from wiles of the wicked;

To keep them from hound
  And from each other's horns,
From the birds of the high moors
  And from the beasts of the hills;

To keep them from wolf,
  From ravaging dog,
To keep them from fox,
  From *"Luath"* of the Fiann.

369 The Highland bull

THE HIGHLAND BULL
'Tis on the heather ridge I was born,
'Tis on the heather ridge I was born,
'Tis on the heather ridge I was born,
And on the milk of a beloved cow was reared.

THE LOWLAND BULL
'Tis on the floor of the big house I was born,
'Tis on the floor of the big house I was born,
'Tis on the floor of the big house I was born,
And on honey and beer and wine and grasses was reared.

The Highland bull turned on the Lowland bull and killed him.

370 The cow of blessings

When Colum Cille was dwelling in the Aoi (Iona), a poor little wretched woman came to put her trouble to him and to ask his advice, for Colum Cille was the world's head of wisdom and the head of healing of the universe.

The poor woman said: "My man died when he was coming home from the strand of periwinkles, and my son was drowned when he was swimming to the Isle of Women to visit his mother, and I am left with three orphans without pith or power. I have a lovely little heifer, but she will not give milk for the children and she will not take to her calf, and I know not under the white sun what to do or which way to turn."

Colum Cille said to the poor little woman: "I have made prattlings of cows and incantations of horses in my day and in my generation. I had them in a skin book, and I had the skin book in the window. The skin book was stolen from me, and I lost the charms for cattle and the incantations for horses, and I have none of them available this day. But I will make a rune for thee, poor little woman, which thou shalt sing to thy heifer, and before thou shalt have finished the rune the little heifer shall have taken to her calf. And the name of this rune is 'The Charm of the Wild Heifers.'"

And Colum Cille sang this charm to the poor little woman with the tears streaming down his cheeks:

My heifer beloved, be not alone,
Let thy little calf be before thee;
See yon bramble bush a-bending,
And bowing down with brambles.

He ho–li–vó 's a vó ri ag,
Ri ag vó, take to thy calf!

Coax thy pretty one to thyself,
Till thou sendest to the fold a herd;
Columba's tending shall be thine behind them,
He made this lilt for thyself.

Certain is the gentle proverb,
The cow of blessings is the cow of calves;
The cow of curses is the moorland cow,
That has never quenched our thirst.

Often afield is the calfless cow
Seldom within is the calfless cow,
Despised among cattle is the calfless cow,
Refuse among cattle the calfless cow.

Head to shoulder is the calfless cow,
Foot to mountain is the calfless cow,
At the edge of the fold is the calfless cow, .
Cow without profit is the calfless cow.

On crest of hill is the calfless cow,
On floor of glen is the calfless cow,
Ranging the upland goes the calfless cow,
Nor butter nor crowdie from the calfless cow.

In desert glens strays the calfless cow,
Ugly and bristling of shag is the calfless cow,
Leaper of walls is the calfless cow,
Dirt of byre is the calfless cow.

The black heifer is reconciled,
Thou wilt make lowing to thy pretty one;
Thou wilt come home with droves,
Thou wilt quench the thirst of hundreds.

My little black heifer thou! my little black heifer!
The same lot is mine and thine.
May thy little black calf not be lost to thee;
But mine only son beloved is beneath the sea.

He ho–li–vó 's a vó ri ag,
Ri ag vó 's a vó ri ag,
Ri ag vó 's a vó ri ag,
Ri ag vó, take to thy calf!

371 The milkmaid's blessing

The poor widow went home and she crooned the charm to the cow and the cow took to her calf. It was then that the woman sang a stave of thankfulness to Columba, and she said:

My blessing on Colum till doom,
Thou art the best son on whom wave (of baptism) was poured;
Bountiful to me was thy speech and thy love
When thou didst coax the brown heifer.

She moves not against me foot nor head,
She moves not against me hoof nor side;
She fills the pitcher for the children
After giving the calf his fill.

That is the Blessing: here is the Correction. Columba said:

Say no more to me of thy speech,
Small is my liking for thy sense;
Let not the flattery out of thy mouth,:
Small is its worth in the sight of God.

There has been no son of mother on earth
So good as the dear Son of heaven;
He created the creeping thing of the plain,
That which swims in the sea and the winged creature of the skies.

372 Fragment

"Leap the dyke" is the calfless cow,
Vexation of neighbours the calfless cow,
Curse of herdsman the calfless cow,
Head to rocky ground the calfless cow.

A useless head is the calfless cow,
A head of mischief is the calfless cow;
No shapely form has the calfless cow,
No increase has the calfless cow.

Head on high is the calfless cow,
Head without triumph is the calfless cow;
Worst of the byre is the calfless cow,
Worst of the herd is the calfless cow.

373 Prayer of the teats

Teat of Mary,
Teat of Brigit,
Teat of Michael,
Teat of God.

No malice shall lie,
No envy shall lie,
No eye shall lie
Upon my heart's dear one.

No fear shall lie,
No ill–will shall lie,
No loss shall lie
On my own "Mineag."*

No spell shall lie,
No spite shall lie
On her beneath the keeping
Of the King of the stars;
On her beneath the keeping
Of the King of the stars.

In sitting down to milk the cow the woman says or sings or intones a short rhythmical prayer:

Bless, O God, my little cow,
Bless, O God, my desire;
Bless Thou my partnership
And the milking of my hands, O God.

* Gentle.

Bless, O God, each teat,
Bless, O God, each finger;
Bless Thou each drop
That goes into my pitcher, O God!

After this prayer the woman sings songs and croons, lilts and lullabies, to cow after cow till all are milked. The secular songs and the religious songs of the people are mixed and mingled, song and hymn alternating in unison with the movements of the hands and the idiosyncrasies of the milker.

Nor is it less interesting to observe the manner in which the cows themselves differentiate between the airs sung to them, giving their milk freely with some songs and withholding it with others. Occasionally a cow will withhold her milk till her own favourite lilt is sung to her. The intelligence of these Highland cows is instructive and striking to the student of nature.

These differences are well known to the observant people themselves, who discuss them and discriminate between certain traits in the nature and character of their cows and horses and other animals.

Give the milk, my treasure!
Give the milk, my treasure!
Give the milk, my treasure!

Give the milk
And thou'lt get a reward:
Bannock of quern,
Sap of ale–wort,
Wine of chalice,
Honey and the wealth of the milk,
My treasure!

Give the milk
And thou'lt get a reward:
Grasses of the plain,
Milk of the fields,
Ale of the malt,
Music of the lyre,
My treasure!

Give the milk, my treasure!
Give the milk, my treasure!

Give the milk
And thou'lt have the blessing
Of the King of the earth,
The King of the sea,
The King of heaven,
The King of the angels,
The King of the City,
My treasure!

374 Give the milk, my treasure

Give the milk, my treasure,
Give quietly, with steady flow,
Give the milk, my treasure,
With steady flow and calmly.

375 Attracting an animal

The spell is placed in thy right ear
For thy good and not for thy harm;
Love of the land that is under thy foot,
And dislike of the land thou hast left.

My love has rest this night
Hard by the mountain ridges;
Thy fast binding in my bare hand,
An iron lock is upon thee, "Breast-white."

376 Milking croon

My cow will wait, my cow will stay,
My cow will wait for me,
My black sharp-headed cow will wait
On the top of the knoll for me.

Though others' cows should be out,
Though others' should be out,
Though others' cows should be out,
My dark cow will not be with them.

377 Give the milk, brown cow

Give the milk, brown cow!
Give the milk, brown cow!
Give the milk, brown cow,
  Abundantly and richly!

Give the milk, brown cow!
Give the milk, brown cow!
Give the milk, brown cow:
  Nobles are coming to the townland!

Give the milk, brown cow!
Give the milk, brown cow!
Give the milk, brown cow:
  MacNeill! MacLeod! MacCailein!

Give the milk, brown cow!
Give the milk, brown cow!
Give the milk, brown cow,
  For the heroes are thirsty!

378 Cattle croon

My little black one,
  Hó hi ri!
My little black one,
  A hó seó!
My little black one,
  Hó ri ri!
My little black one,
  A hó seó!

I'll not give thee to the big–mouthed folk,
I'll not give thee to the folk of the starvelings,
I'll not give thee to the rheumy–eyed folk,
'Tis with the Gael that thou shalt be!

I'd not give thee to the wheedler
Who has not yet found shame,
I'd not give thee to the mocker:
'Tis to the dairyman I'd give thee!

I'd not give thee to the cowherd
Lest folk should revile me:
'Tis with the farmers thou shalt be
Up in the fold of the shieling!

I'd not give thee to the fiddler
Nor at all to the claws of a tailor:
'Tis with the gentry thou shalt be,
Being milked up on the heights!

379 My brown cow

Ho my little cow, ho my brown cow!
Ho my little cow, ho my brown cow!
Little cow of my heart, dear, beloved,
Jewel of the white cows art thou.

Ho my little cow, ho my brown cow!
Ho my little cow, ho my brown cow!
Little cow of my heart, dear, beloved,
Thou seekest not calf nor calfling of me.

Ho my little cow, ho my brown cow!
Ho my little cow, ho my brown cow!
My little brindled cow, dear, beloved,
Safe thou wouldst cross the crest of the peaks.

Ho my little cow, ho my brown cow!
  Ho my little cow, ho my brown cow!
My sweet little cow, dear, beloved,
  With me thou wouldst cross the crest of the waves.

380 O hornless one

O hornless one, give thou the milk,
It is thy calf thou art bewailing,
O hornless one, give thou the milk.

Thou art of the seed of the white–shouldered kine
That my grandfather had in his fold.

Thou art of the seed of the beloved kine
That my people had in the glens.

Thou art of the seed of the proud kine
That the nobles of the Straths possessed.

But cease I from my crooning,
My love is in the linen shroud.

My calf is in the cold grave,
And he shall not stir in spring.

O cease I from my wailing,
Since my love is deep asleep.

O cease I from my wailing,
I do idly to lament.

381 Milking croon

Ho–an, ho–an, I'll lilt a croon;
Pour, little cow, milk of the pearlwort,
Herb of sweetness, herb of the Lord!
With aiding of Christ I culled the pearlwort,
And it will keep for me my milk aright.

The first flow for Columba of my love,
'Tis he closed for thee each pit and smoothed for thee each hill,
'Tis he who guided thee home tonight unharmed;
O the blessing of the poor upon my loving herdsman!
Pour, O pour, little cow, milk of the pearlwort for my dear companion!

Ho–an, ho–an, I'll lilt a croon;
Pour, little cow, milk of the pearlwort,
Herb of sweetness, herb of the Lord!
With aiding of Christ I culled the pearlwort,
And it will keep for me my milk aright.

The second flow for the weary pilgrim and the tender orphan;
There is no comfort for a little cow in an ill–kept fold;
Alas for him who would not aid pilgrim and tender little child;
Pour, little cow, milk of the pearlwort and of the sacred daisies!
Pour, O pour milk for the weary pilgrim and for the tender orphan!

Ho–an, ho–an, I'll lilt a croon;
Pour, little cow, milk of the pearlwort,
Herb of sweetness, herb of the Lord!
With aiding of Christ I culled the pearlwort,
And it will keep for me my milk aright.

The third flow for my goodman and my darling little boy;
May he be growing by day and may he be growing by night
With the sun of showers and with the moon of radiance!
Pour, little cow, milk of the pearlwort, the primrose and the shamrock benign!

Pour, O pour milk thick, rich and thick, that will give butter and curds
And fatness for my man and my lovely little boy!

Ho–an, ho–an, I'll lilt a croon;
Pour, little cow, milk of the pearlwort,
Herb of sweetness, herb of the Lord!
With aiding of Christ I culled the pearlwort,
And it will keep for me my milk aright.

The fourth flow ...

382 Charm of the butter

The charm made of Columba
To the maiden of the glen,
Her butter to make more,
Her milk to make surpassing.

Come, ye rich lumps, come!
Come, ye rich lumps, come!
Come, ye rich lumps, masses large,
Come, ye rich lumps, come!

Thou Who put beam in moon and sun,
Thou Who put food in ear and herd,
Thou Who put fish in stream and sea,
Send the butter up betimes!

Come, ye rich lumps, come!
Come, ye rich lumps, come!
Come, ye rich lumps, masses large,
Come, ye rich lumps, come!

383 Invocation at churning

Come, thou Calum Cille kindly,
Hasten the lustre on the cream;
Seest thou the orphans unregarded
Waiting the blessing of the milk–wave of the kine.

Stillim! steòilim!
Strichim! streòichim!
Send down the broken
And bring up the whole!

Come, thou Brigit, handmaid calm,
Hasten the butter on the cream;
Seest thou impatient Peter yonder
Waiting the buttered bannock white and yellow.

Stillim! steòilim!
Strichim! streòichim!
Send down the broken
And bring up the whole!

Come, thou Mary Mother mild,
Hasten the butter on the cream;
Seest thou Paul and John and Jesus
Waiting the gracious butter yonder.

Stillim! steòilim!
Strichim! streòichim!
Send down the broken
And bring up the whole!

Waulking

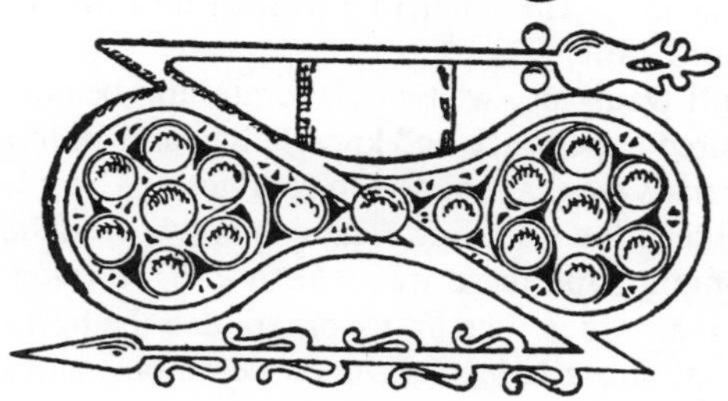

Five minor processes are involved in waulking. There is first the process of thickening the cloth; second the process of cleansing the cloth; third, the process of folding it; fourth, the process of giving it tension; and after these the rite of consecrating the cloth. All these processes are performed with care of eye and deftness of hand come of ability and experience.

During the work the women sing lively, stirring, emphatic songs. One sings a verse, all join in the chorus. The leader usually sits at the head of the waulking–frame; if she is advanced in life she is not allowed to work, in which case she sits a few feet back and in a line with the frame. The women keep time with their arms or feet.

Most of the songs sung are war–songs, love–songs, boating–songs, and hunting–songs. In all these the lovers or husbands or chiefs of the women form the subject of the song, which is fervid and personal to a degree. There are also perhaps impromptus, on some local topic, perhaps on the real or supposed love–affairs of one or more of the girls present. Perhaps the hunter who has looked in with his dog and his gun in passing, or the traveller with his staff and his plaid who has come to see and to listen, may form the subject of an impromptu song to a well–known air. In this case the women politely endow the subject of the song with many merits and good qualities, both mental and physical, which he, modest man, never knew he possessed.

When the process of waulking is completed the cloth is cleansed and washed with plenty of soap in a burn or stream if one is convenient. The cloth is carried to and from the water on a hand–barrow. After it is washed it is placed in folds, forming about a square of the cloth, and piled over one another. This process is called coinnleachadh, cur chlò air choinnlean. From these folds the cloth is rolled upon a piece of wood, round or flat as may be most conveniently got. This process is called *cornadh, cornadh a' chlò, cornadh an aodaich, cur a' chlò air chorn, cornaich an chlò.* The cloth is rolled slowly and carefully, bit by bit, hard and firm as the strong arms of the women can make it, in order that the tension may be evenly distributed. When the *cornadh* is completed and the end secured, the web of cloth is laid across the waulking frame. The ceremony of consecration is now performed, the first part solemnly, the second jubilantly. There are three celebrants, the oldest of them leading, the others following according to age. The first celebrant seizes the cloth and moves round about half a turn. Freeing her hands, she seizes it again and brings it round to complete the turn. With the first move the woman says, *"Cuirim car deiseal,"* ("I give a turn sunwise"); and with the second move, completing the circle, she completes the sentence, *"am freasdal an Athar,"* ("dependent on the Father"). The other two women turn the web similarly in name of Son and in name of Spirit.

Làn luathadh, a full waulking, was an elaborate and beautiful operation. It was complicated and required experience and knowledge, and on this account one or two or three women specialists were appointed to conduct it. There was a *bean luathaidh* (waulking woman) to lead the waulking. There was a *bean dhuan* (woman of songs or lilts) to lead the singing; and there was a *bean dhlighe* (woman of ceremony) to lead the processes in their order. The best workers and the best singers were chosen for the purpose, special stress being laid upon ceremony and upon music.

In the island of Coll there was a race of women called *"Clann Pheidirein,"* descendants of Peter, Patersons, who were famous through the generations for their knowledge of the formalities and the technicalities – and the melodies of the waulking. Before the people were evicted one or more of these women presided over every waulking in the island: The last of the family was Janet Paterson, Greosabal, aged eighty–two. She had all the processes of the waulking as no one else had, and carried them out as no one else could. These Mac Pheidirein women had a wonderful fascination over the workers and the singers at the waulking.

"The same song may not be sung twice at the same waulking. If the same song be sung twice, the cloth–mother will come and render the cloth as thin and streaky as it was before."

At the waulking in the island of Miu'alaidh, Mingulay, near Barra, in 1866, I asked a beautiful girl to sing a certain song over again. She blushed and looked confused and abashed, and the women looked in an embarrassed way at one another. The leader said that were they to sing the same song twice at the same waulking the cloth would become thin and streaky and white as *rùsg na caora* (the sheep's fleece) and there was no knowing what mischief might not befall the wearer of the cloth or the singer of the song. The hands of these girls were small, the fingers tapered, the arms muscular, the girls themselves of medium height, strongly made, well formed, muscular, and well mannered.

Casadh means hair or pile. *Casadh, basadh* and *basradh* all refer to the same operation, the process of raising a pile on the cloth. "The cloth is dragged hither and the cloth is drawn thither from side to side and from end to end of the frame or hurdle, and a pile raised on it with the women's palms."

384 Circuiting song

Hill! hill! hó! hillin ó!
Hill! is hó ro bhà ó!

Last night I got not a wink of sleep,
Hill! hill! hó! hillin ó!
This night I shall not get as much,
Hill! hill! hó! hillin ó!

Though she were tattered and brindled,
Her dusky cattle will fetch her out.

Though she were tattered and shaggy,
Fat and fair are her father's cattle.

Though she were wizened and shrivelled,
Fair and white are her horned cattle.

Though she were hungry and like death,
Oh my love the hidden windfall!

Though her eyes were watery, hollow,
And her mouth like amber, she'll get a lover.

But I lie snug, easy and sleepful,
Without cattle black or red or dappled.

Last night I got not a wink of sleep,
Hill! hill! hó! hillin ó!
This night I shall not get as much,
Hill! hill! hó! hillin ó!

385 Verses made at the waulking frame

Thou girl over there, may the sun be against thee!
Thou hast taken from me my autumn carrot,
My Michaelmas carrot from my pillow,
My procreant buck among the goats.

But if thou hast, it was not without help,
But with the black cunning of the dun women;
Thou art the little she–goat that lifted the bleaching,
I am the little gentle cow that gave no milking.

Stone in shoe be thy bed for thee,
Husk in tooth be thy sleep for thee,
Prickle in eye be thy life for thee,
Restless watching by night and by day.

May no little slumberer be seen on thy pillow,
May no eyes be seen upon thy shoulder,
But mayest thou sow them and Géige reap them,
And Morc garner them to the green barns!

386 Hand–smoothing

When the cloth is being piled they smooth it out with their palms and bless it:

To the Father,
To the Son,
To the Spirit.

Before they part, a mother of sons goes up to the man of the house, and making a courtesy to him she says to him:

Mayest thou wear the cloth
To shreds,
Mayest thou wear the cloth
To rags,

Mayest thou wear the cloth
With food and music
In every way
As we would fain have thee;

In thy modesty,
In thy health,
In thy friends,
In thy love,
In the grace of the Father,
In the grace of the Son,
In the grace of the Spirit,
In the grace of the Three of the elements.

387 Consecration of the cloth*

FIRST CONSECRATOR:
I give the sunwise turn
Dependent on the Father.

SECOND CONSECRATOR:
I give the sunwise turn
Dependent on the Son.

THIRD CONSECRATOR:
I give the sunwise turn
Dependent on the Spirit.

THE THREE:
And each sunwise turn
Dependent on the Three,
And each turn it takes
For the sake of the Three.

And each sunwise turn
Dependent on the Three.

* See also I:113.

388 Blessing

This is no second–hand cloth,
And it is not begged,
It is not property of cleric,
It is not property of priest,
And it is not property of pilgrim;

But thine own property,
O son of my body,
By moon and by sun,
In the presence of God,
And keep thou it!

Mayest thou enjoy it,
Mayest thou wear it,
Mayest thou finish it,
Until thou find it
In shreds,
In strips,
In rags,
In tatters!

Crafts

389 The counting of the shoemaking–tools

One awl one last,
Two awls two lasts,
Three awls three lasts,
Four awls four lasts,
Five awls five lasts,
Six awls six lasts,
Seven awls seven lasts,
Eight awls eight lasts,
Nine awls nine lasts;
  Awl and last,
  Wax and tallow,
  Hen's feather as a point
  To thrust it through the heel,*
  Stitches eighteen
  From snout above round about down to heel
  In the Gaelic shoe.

* Hen's feathers were used in place of bristles to push the strong thread through the thickest part of the shoe at the heel. Leather thongs or laces were sometimes used instead of waxed thread, and only one thread or lace was used instead of two, one on each side so as to make the tension equal. So Mr Alexander Stewart, of Ceann na Coille, Glen Lyon, informs the editor.

390 Choice of timber

Choose the willow of the streams,
Choose the hazel of the rocks,
Choose the alder of the marshes,
Choose the birch of the waterfalls.

Choose the ash of the shade,
Choose the yew of resilience,
Choose the elm of the brae,
Choose the oak of the sun.

391 Choice

These are said to be the best:

Boat of board–ends,
Shoe of welt–ends,
Stack of ear–ends,
Creel of rod–ends.

392 The farmer's food and footgear

Three pints of raw whey,
The fill of the cat's cogue of porridge,
A good thick round bannock
That has been half an hour in the ashes,
A trough of coalfish among every eight.
Every carcase and every pithless beast that falls on top of knoll or hillock or height, or in glen at mountain's foot, for wool and for skin.
That were the raiment, with shoe–soles of the hundred–thonged hide of the Brown Bull of Cuailnge, who would put nine cows in heat with the one bruling bellow.

St Kilda Poetry

Martin reports that the men and women of St Kilda had a genius for poetry, music and dancing, to all of which they were addicted. Dr Johnson, on the other hand, declared that no good poetry could come from St Kilda. The technique and diction of the following pieces would not satisfy Johnson, but they have other qualities that might please him. Though not old, they have a charming simplicity and intense feeling. They are some of several which the writer took down on 22nd May 1865 from the recitation of Eibhrig Nic Cruimein, Euphemia MacCrimmon, cottar, aged eighty–four years, who had many old songs, stories, and traditions of the island. I would have got more of these had there been peace and quiet to take them down, but this was not to be had among a crowd of naval officers and seamen and St Kilda men, women and children, and, even noisier than these, St Kilda dogs, mad with excitement and all barking at once. The aged reciter was much censured for her recital of these songs and poems, and the writer for causing the old woman to stir the recesses of her memory for this lore; for the people of St Kilda have now discarded songs and music, dancing, folklore, and the stories of the foolish past. We were silenced, but not subdued, and I fear that one of us was

Even in his penance
Planning sins anew.

Euphemia MacCrimmon said that the comhradh, or conversation, was composed by her own father and mother before they were married.

It was seldom that a St Kilda man died a natural death. When a St Kildan was asked: *"Ciod e am bàs a fhuair t'athair?"* ("What death did your father get?") the answer would too often be: *"Chaidh e leis"* ("He went over [the rock]"); sometimes *"Chaidh a bhàthadh"* ("He was drowned"): infrequently *"Fhuair e bàs cinn–adhairt"* ("He got a pillow–death, died in his bed").

Euphemia MacCrimmon's own father and her mother's father were on the rock *ag ianach,* hunting birds. The younger man was on a ledge below, seizing the birds, and the elder man on a ledge above, holding the rope. The fulcrum against which the latter held his feet suddenly broke away from the parent rock, precipitating the two helpless men into the seething Atlantic. Their bodies, when recovered, were much mangled, though the birds under their girdles had kept them afloat. These accidents caused much misery to the little community. Their distress was often rendered the more bitter that the wild sea around their rocky island often made it impossible to recover the dead, though the bodies could be seen buoyed up by the birds secured to them. The people are now either more cautious than their fathers were, or better provided, for accidents are fewer.

On one occasion eighteen men came from St Kilda to Uist for corn seeds for their crofts, their own scant crops having been destroyed by the storms of the previous autumn. They were taken to Balranald, one of the best and biggest and best known farms in the Western Isles, and there they got all they wanted. They then started out on their long and perilous homeward voyage which, alas, they never made, their frail coracle being swallowed up in the wild waves of the stormy Atlantic.

The St Kilda men's visit was long remembered, for it caused much amusement at the time; the artless simplicity, the peculiar words, and the lisping accent of the men were talked of long afterwards, but always kindly. If a question were asked of one of them, all the eighteen men would reply simultaneously, with one voice and one accord. Mrs MacDonald of Balranald asked:

"Do you have marriages and baptisms in St Kilda?"

"Oh my dear beloved, no, we have no marriages or baptisms, rather we are dying out. How shall we marry and baptize, did not the *bramach-innilt* die? and we cannot have children, and we are, my dear, like to die out."

"What is the *bramach-innilt?* It is, my dear, the female who attends to the woman who is sending children into the world."

Bramach-innilt, midwife, bondswoman, handmaiden, is the regular word in St Kilda for what others usually call *bean-ghlùin.* Ordinarily the *bean-shiùla* goes upon one knee, only in the remote island of Heisgeir the *bean tuisil (tuisilidh)* goes upon both knees.

393 St Kilda lilt

HE: Away bent spade, away straight spade,
Away each goat and sheep and lamb;
Up my rope, up my snare –
I have heard the gannet upon the sea!

Thanks to the Being, the gannets are come,
Yes, and the big birds along with them;
Dark dusky maid, a cow in the fold!
A brown cow, a brown cow, a brown cow beloved,
A brown cow, my dear one, that would milk the milk for thee,
Ho ro ru ra ree, playful maid,
Dark dusky maid, a cow in the fold!
The birds are a-coming, I hear their tune!

SHE: Truly my sweetheart is the herdsman
Who would threaten the staff and would not strike!
Dark dusky maid, a cow in the fold!
The birds are a-coming, I hear their tune!

HE: Mary, my dear love is the maid,
Though dark her locks her body is fragrant!

Dark dusky maid, a cow in the fold!
The birds are a–coming, I hear their tune!

SHE: Thou art my handsome joy, thou art my sweetheart,
Thou gavest me first the honied fulmar!
Dark dusky maid, a cow in the fold!
The birds are a–coming, I hear their tune!

HE: Thou art my turtle–dove, thou art my mavis,
Thou art my melodious harp in the sweet morning.
Dark dusky maid, a cow in the fold!
The birds are a–coming, I hear their tune!

SHE: Thou art my treasure, my lovely one, my huntsman,
Yesterday thou gavest me the gannet and the auk.
Dark dusky maid, a cow in the fold!
The birds are a–coming, I hear their tune!

HE: I gave thee love when thou wast but a child,
Love that shall not wane till I go beneath the earth.
Dark dusky maid, a cow in the fold!
The birds are a–coming, I hear their tune!

SHE: Thou art my hero, thou art my basking sunfish,
Thou gavest me the puffin and the black–headed guillemot.
Dark dusky maid, a cow in the fold!
The birds are a–coming, I hear their tune!

HE: The mirth of my eyes and the essence of my joy thou art,
And my sweet–sounding lyre in the mountain of mist.
Dark dusky maid, a cow in the fold!
The birds are a–coming, I hear their tune!

SHE: May the Being keep thee, the Creator aid thee,
The Holy Spirit be behind thy rope!
Dark dusky maid, a cow in the fold!
A brown cow, a brown cow, a brown cow beloved,
A brown cow, my dear one, that would milk the milk for thee,
Ho ro ru ra ree, playful maid,
Dark dusky maid, a cow in the fold!
The birds are a–coming, I hear their tune!

394 It was no crew of landsmen

It was no crew of landsmen
Crossed the ferry on Wednesday:
'Tis tidings of disaster if you live not.

What has kept you so long from me
Is the high sea and the sudden wind catching you,
So that you could not at once give her sail.

'Tis a profitless journey
That took the noble man away,
To take our one son from me and from Donald.

My son and my three brothers are gone,
And the one son of my mother's sister,
And, sorest tale that will come or has come, my husband.

What has set me to draw ashes
And to take a spell at digging
Is that the men are away with no word of their living.

I am left without fun or merriment
Sitting on the floor of the glen;
My eyes are wet, oft are tears on them.

395 St Kilda waulking song

I would make the fair cloth for thee,
Thread as the thatch–rope stout.

I would make the feathered buskin for thee,
Thou beloved and importunate of men.

I would give thee the precious anchor,
And the family gear which my grandfather had.

My love is the hunter of the bird,
Who earliest comes over misty sea.

My love the sailor of the waves,
Great the cheer his brow will show.

Plants

396

St Columba's plant

Armpit–package of Columba kindly
Unsought by me, unlooked for!
I shall not be lifted away in my sleep
And I shall not be thrust upon iron.

I will pluck the brown leafy one,
Herb found at a steep bank's foot;
Nor to man nor to woman would I give it
Without more than my thousand blessings.

I will pluck the brown handful,
The herb ordained of Christ;
'Tis it will set my milk aright,
'Tis it will make my cattle fruitful.

397

St Columba's plant

I will pluck my armpit–package,
Renowned plant of the fair women,
Plant of the joyful feast
That was in the delightful court of Fionn.

'Tis male plant, 'tis female plant,
Plant that would rear cattle and calf,
Plant of kindly wise Columba,
Lovely plant of the gentle women.

Better the reward of it under my arm
Than a crowd of calving kine;
Better the reward of its virtues
Than a herd of white cattle.

398 Silverweed

Honey under ground
Silverweed of spring.
Honey and condiment
Whisked whey of summer.
Honey and fruitage
Carrot of autumn.
Honey and crunching
Nuts of winter
Between Feast of Andrew
And Christmastide.

399 The club-moss

Thou man who travellest blithely,
Nor hurt nor harm shall befall thee,
Nor in sunshine nor in darkness
If but the club-moss be on thy pathway.

400 The ragwort

Thou ragwort! thou ragwort!
And thou woman who plied the ragwort!
If the dead of the grave should rise,
The plying of the ragwort would be remembered.

401 The gracious root

I will cull my gracious root
As Brigit culled it with her one hand,
To put essence in breast and gland of milk,
To put substance in udder and in kidney,
Butter and curd, fat and cheese,
Like stream pouring from breast of fortune,
Like honey distilling from the love on high.

Thou only anointed white One of the God of grace,
Keep Thou for me mine own,
Keep Thou to me the share of grace,
Keep Thou from me the goods of foes,
Keep Thou from me the folk of lies,
Keep Thou from me the [visiting] of death,
Keep Thou from me the [visiting] of harm,
Keep Thou from me the re–pairing,
Keep Thou from me the stillborn calf.

The plant of heathgrass be theirs,
The plant of substance be mine.

There is blessing in the crop,
There is fruitage in the kine,
There is honour in the pairing,
Thou only anointed white One of the God of grace.

In dependence on the God of life,
In dependence on the power of health,
Keep Thou for me my share desired,
Keep Thou for me my share beloved,
Keep Thou from me the visiting of bane,
Keep Thou from me the howling of foes.

Brigit came homeward
With butter, curd and cheese,
And she laid under the nine firm locks
The nine stocks securely —
The stock of the God of life,
The stock of the Christ of love,
The stock of the Spirit Holy,
The Triune of grace.

402 The primrose

Primrose, primrose
And wood-sorrel,
The children's food
  In summer;
Geimileachd, geimileachd,
Wine and plovers,*
The food of men
  In winter.

* Wine and plovers (the golden plover is the one meant) are the best of food. Hence the saying: "As good as wine and plovers."

403 The reed

Thou reed unblest,
Thou reed unholy,
Thou reed wherewith was given
The drink accurst;
Every wind that sobs
Over knoll and plain
Groans the death-groan
Through the reed accurst,
  Through the reed accurst!

404 Mountain yew, or juniper

I will pluck the gracious yew
  Through the one fair rib of Jesus,
In name of Father and Son and Spirit of wisdom,
  Against distress, against misfortune, against fatigue.

I will pluck the gracious yew
  Through the three fair ribs of Jesus,
In name of Father and Son and Spirit of grace,
  Against hardness, against pain, against anguish of breast.

I will pluck the gracious yew
  Through the nine fair ribs of Jesus,
In name of Father and Son and Spirit of grace,
  Against drowning, against danger, against fear.

405 The *monalan*

I will cull the *monalan,*
  Plant blessed of Christ,
Plant of wise Columba,
  Plant of Mary, plant of Brigit.

I will cull the *monalan,*
  Plant of rejoicing, plant of peace,
Plant of milk, plant of fatness,
  Plant of the nine essences.

I will cull the *monalan,*
  To the Three Who are in One,
To the Father, to the Son,
  To the Holy Spirit strong.

406 The pearlwort

I will cull the pearlwort
Beneath the fair sun of Sunday,
Beneath the gentle hand of the Virgin,
She who will defend me,
In the might of the Trinity
Who granted it to grow.

While I shall keep the pearlwort,
Without wile shall be my lips,
Without guile shall be mine eye,
Without hurt shall be mine hand,
Without pain shall be my heart,
Without heaviness shall be my death.

407 I will cull the pearlwort

I will cull the pearlwort
Beneath the fair sun of Sunday,
Beneath the hand of the Virgin,
In name of the Trinity
Who willed it to grow.

While I shall keep the pearlwort,
Without ill mine eye,
Without harm my mouth,
Without grief my heart,
Without guile my death.

408 Bog–myrtle

I am plucking thee,
  Thou gracious red myrtle,
In name of the Father of virtues,
In name of the Son Whom I love,
  In name of God's eternal Spirit.

For virtue of good man,
  For virtue of good span,
For virtue of good woman,
For virtue of good life,
  For virtue of good step.

For virtue of good love,
  For virtue of good leap,
For virtue of good cause,
For virtue of good life
  Without peril without reproach.

409 The shamrock

Thou shamrock of foliage,
  Thou shamrock entwining,
Thou shamrock of the prayer,
  Thou shamrock of my love.

Thou shamrock of my sorrow,
  Plant of Patrick of the virtues,
Thou shamrock of the Son of Mary,
  Journey's–end of the peoples.

Thou shamrock of grace,
  Of joy, of the tombs,
It were my wish in death
  Thou shouldst grow on my grave.

Justice

410

Prayer against ill report

I will close my fist,
  Fitly I hold the staff;
'Tis to efface evil speaking
  That I have come within.

The three sons of King Cluainnidh,
  And Manann son of King Lear,
And the young son of the King of the Green
Vesture,
  'Tis they shall set me free this night.

Fionn the Prince of the Fiann
  Shall deliver me from the lie,
And valiant Cumhall of the keen blades
  And Goll of the blows shall shield me.

Briain the melodious shall sain me,
  And Briais of virtue shall aid me,
And Columba, the Cleric,
  And Alexander, against venom.

The seven hosts of the Fiann
  With their keen blades shall shield me,
And the young son of the King of Greece
  Shall take the black lies from off me.

I shall go down with Fite,
   Brigit shall raise up my head;
'Tis to efface ill report
   That I have come hither.

411 Invocation for justice

I will go in the name of God,
   In likeness of deer, in likeness of horse,
In likeness of serpent, in likeness of king,
   Stronger am I than all persons.

The hand of God keeping me,
   The love of Christ in my veins,
The strong Spirit bathing me,
   The Three shielding and aiding me,
The Three shielding and aiding me;
   The hand of Spirit bathing me,
The Three each step aiding me.

412 Success of moot

Thou shalt arise early in the morning and go forth afield. Thou shalt betake thee to a boundary stream that shrinks not in heat, in drought, in parching of sun, in drouth of summer. And thou shalt dip thy face in the stream three times in succession. And after that thou shalt bathe thy countenance in the nine gentle rays of the sun. Thou shalt say thy prayer and proceed to the moot, and no matter nor might, between ground and sky, between heaven and earth, shall prevail against thee, shall have effect on thee, shall oppose thee, shall keep from thee that which is thine. And at the very beginning thou shalt utter this invocation, with a right and a calm heart, and thus shalt thou say:

In the name and in the dignity
   Of the glorious King of life;

In the name and in the dignity
   Of the sufficing Christ of love;

In the name and in the dignity
   Of the perfect Spirit of guidance;

In the name and in the dignity
   Of the might and aiding of the Three;

In the name and in the dignity
   Of the might and aiding of the Three:

I am bathing my face
   In the nine rays of the sun,
As Mary bathed her Son
   In the fermented milk of the *brac.**

* Reindeer, red deer. The reindeer was in Scotland until the beginning of the thirteenth century, probably later, and reindeer moss grows on the Scottish mountains. The reindeer is implied in the following fairy lullaby, known as *"Bainne nam fiadh:"*

On milk of deer I was reared,
On milk of deer was nurtured,
On milk of deer beneath the ridge of storms,
On crest of hill and mountain.

Charms for Healing

Thyroid gland

A gland in the throat of human beings and animals is called in Gaelic *brisgein,* in English the thyroid gland. It is sometimes imperfect in a child from birth, in which case the child is dwarfed in mind and body. To remedy this the people applied the *brisgein* (thyroid gland) of a sheep in the form of extract. A sheep born on *Là Fhéill Brighde,* St Brigit's Day, called *caora Bhrighde* or *caora Bhrighde mhin* (the sheep of Brigit, or the sheep of mild Brigit), was much sought for this purpose, but still more sought was a lamb born on this day, called *uan Brighde* or *uan Brighde nan ni agus nam beannachd* (the lamb of Brigit or the lamb of Brigit of the flocks and of the blessings). On the removal of the *brisgein* the sheep or lamb was sacrificed to Brigit.

Not the least curious thing about the old Gaelic remedies is that many of them have been adopted in medical practice. Dr Donald Munro Morrison, the youngest son of the famous poet and blacksmith of Harris, Iain Gobha na Hearadh, inherited his father's marvellous talent in mechanics and was also a distinguished student of chemistry; he remarked that the Highlanders had cures for all the common ailments of man and beast, but where or how they had acquired them he could not understand; he had analysed the plants, earths and other remedies they used, and in no instance were these misapplied, on the contrary their ingredients were those now used by practitioners in a more concentrated form.

Jaundice

A cure for jaundice practised in the Outer Isles was to place a lump of salt butter on the stomach of the sick man. The butter was held in place by bandages passing round the man's body, so fixed on all sides that none of the melting butter could flow away. After some hours the invalid was attacked by *gairiseann* (nausea) which continued until the butter was absorbed into the tissues. The jaundice then disappeared, and the patient became strong and healthy.

Cancer

From Thomas Ross, Inbhir Charsla, Inver Casslie, Sutherland, aged 96; 15th November 1905.

A man at Ullapool was famous for curing the *buirbean* (cancer), *silteach* (flow), and *tinneas an righ* (king's evil). He cured many men and women of these diseases.

We were living at Drochaid Sguideil (Conon Bridge). A cancer came in my sister's lip. Her lip was swelling and ever swelling, and the doctor said it was a bad case of cancer. My mother saw a man passing and went out and spoke to him. He came in and bathed his hands in a basin of clean cold water, and then bathed my sister's lip with this water. He told my mother to put the water in a bottle and to bathe my sister's lip with it at sunrise. My mother did as the man directed, and in three days the cancerous swelling disappeared, and never reappeared although my sister lived to old age. Everyone was surprised, and the doctor who said it was cancer was surprised. I do not remember the name of the man, and I never saw him before nor after, but I heard of him. My sister was Hanna Ross.

A cold poultice of hemlock was applied to a cancer sore. The hemlock plaster was so hot and so strong that it drew the cancer out from the bottom, the roots coming with the cancer as the roots come with the hemlock itself out of the ground.

This was effective when done in time. When the disease became soft nothing could cure it.

A police inspector in Glasgow had cancer in the lower lip. Instead of having it cut he went to his native home near Fort William. There a man applied a poultice of hemlock to the lip and extracted the cancer bodily. The patient told my informant that the pain was excruciating. The flesh containing the cancer came away, carrying the roots with it. These were very numerous and resembled the fine thready roots of hemlock, he could hear the sound of their breaking away. The patient placed the cancer in spirits and kept it for many years. My informant said that except for a hollow the man's lip seemed quite healthy and normal.

A man who had cancer in the lip or a woman who had cancer in the breast went to a rock on a hot sunny day. There he or she exposed the part affected to "The nine rays of the sun, in name of the God of life."

There was a long hymn appropriate to this subject, but it is now lost.

Madness

There were various cures for madness, some of them rough. On Di–Daorn là Chaluim Chille (Thursday the day of Columba), a strong man was to take the afflicted person behind him on the back of a grey horse at full speed and make a circuit round a *comharra criche* (march mark), and then round an immovable stone. Another cure common in the Isles was to tie a strong rope round the sufferer's waist and drag him behind a two–, four–, six–, eight–, or ten–oared boat, with all the speed the rowers could achieve.

Another was to dip him in Tobar Ma–Ruibhe (Maol Ruibhe's well) in Eilean Ma–Ruibhe (Maol–Ruibhe's isle), in Loch Ma–Ruibhe (Loch Maree). Men and women down to recent times, and possibly still, were brought from long distances to the sacred shrine of Maol–Ruibhe; in former days the pilgrimage was done openly, latterly by stealth.

Another famous place of cure was Poll Fhaolain (St Faolan's pool) in Strath Fillan; here are two pools partly separated by a projecting rock, the upper called "Poll nam Ban" (the pool of the women), the lower "Poll nam Fear" (the pool of the men). The patient was led sunwise round the pool, first in name of Father, secondly in name of Son, thirdly in name of Spirit, and then immersed in the pool in name of the Trinity. He was led to Teampall Fhaolain (St Faolan's church). A small stone basin was filled with *uisge coisrigte* (consecrated water), and poured over his head. He was stretched out with his back to the ground in the church, placed between two sticks, and bound in a simple ingenious way. If he extricated himself before morning there were hopes or recovery; if not, there was no hope. Sometimes he died during the night. The person who dipped the patient in the pool lifted three small stones from the bottom and threw them on a cairn near by; sometimes a coin was also thrown into the cairn. A mad infuriated bull was thrown into "Poll nam Ban" and thence sprang into "Poll nam Fear," since when both pools have lost their efficacy.

Saturday's autumn moon
Will take frenzy seven days.

New moon of Saturday
Will take madness three days.

A *gealachan,* from *gealach* (moon), is a moonstruck person, a lunatic, also a man walking by moonlight.

Childlessness

At Strolamas in Skye is a well called Tobar Cloinne or Tobar na Cloinne, the well of (the) children, the water of which conferred twin children upon a childless woman. The woman went to the well at dawn of day and drank of its water and appealed to its presiding deity, saying:

The water of the little fall on my forelock

* * *

Lift thou from me thine ill mischance,
Since the wish of the woman of hurry is on me.

At Elgol, some miles away, is a well of similar virtues. In this case the wife and the husband must go to the well, drink of its water, and appeal to the guardian god of the fountain to listen to their prayer and to confer issue on them.

Every district of Scotland had a *tobar slàinte* (healing fountain) whose water was clear and refreshing and whose situation was pleasing to the eye.

The plants *tri–bhileach* (valerian or marsh–trefoil), and *biolair Moire* (cress of Mary, water–cress) were given as a cure to childless women.

Children's cures

These lines, given to the writer by Dugall MacAulay, South Hacleit, Benbecula, are repeated to soothe a child that has been hurt, while the hurt is gently rubbed and at the mention of each creature is blown upon with the warm breath of the mother:

The fox's mouth

Mouth of this fox,
Mouth of that fox,
Beak of the moulting dove —
You'll be well before you marry!

Prickly sleep

Prickly sleep in my foot,
Put it in the grey dog;
The grey dog went through the townland
To seek milk for my foot.

Then the boy or girl who had the "prickly sleep" in his or her foot tramped, tramped, tramped, in imitation of the grey dog tramping through the townland in search of milk for the sleepy foot.

The uvula

John Mackenzie, smith, Aultbea, Ross, said: My uvula fell and for a day or two I could neither swallow anything nor speak a word. My mother sent a man to William Campbell to tell him of my condition and ask him to cure me. During the messenger's absence the uvula suddenly regained its position. The messenger on his return related that he had told William Campbell my name, and that Campbell went through a *rann* (rune), appealing to the Three Persons of the Trinity to raise the uvula and heal me. William Campbell performed this cure for many persons throughout this wide district during his long life; he had a great reputation for the cure and for the beautiful rune he sang for it.

A narrator at Meallan Thearlaich, Gairloch, said: My *cloch shlugain* (uvula) had fallen, and my mother went to a certain woman, who made *eòlas na ciche* (the charm of the uvula) for me, in my absence. The uvula returned to its place, and the time at which it returned agreed with the time at which the woman made the *eòlas.*

Margaret Mackenzie, "am Poll Glas," Polglass, Achiltibuie, Ross, performed the cure as follows. She went to the strand and brought thence what were called *na ciochagan tràghad,* uvulas from the strand. She hung them above the fire, which was on the floor (by some others they were placed on the *slabhraidh,* pot–chain). She recited a *rann* (rune), and raised the fallen uvula. This highly excellent woman had many charms and a *rann* for each. Her son Roderick has learned some of them from her.

Another name for the uvula is *an t–sineag.* There were some curious beliefs concerning it. There is a tuft of hair on the crown of the head that raises the uvula, whoever knows the tuft; by grasping the tuft a person can lift the uvula to its own place. There is a vein in the small of the wrist called "the wrist vein," and by driving the blood up the vein one can lift the uvula. The hiccough can be stopped by the same means.

Serpent's stone

This is a thing found among heather, especially old tall unburnt heather. It is alleged that the serpent goes round and round the clump of heather, emitting a froth or spittle from its mouth upon the clump without stop or pause. No one understands why this is. When the spittle emitted by the serpent on the heather plant cools and dries, the stuff grows as hard as a stone but as light as tinder. The serpent's stone is about the size of a pullet's egg and dark-grey in colour. Old people esteem it highly for its power in healing and for its power against fairy women. It was good for swelling or cut or bruise or festering in a person.

A boy was stung in the foot by a serpent. He ran to a stream and bathed his wounded foot. Then, running back to see whether the serpent had succeeded in reaching the water, he met it hastening to the stream. He cut it in five pieces, which he buried in a hole in the earth, closing this firmly with a sod. If this is not done the maggots produced by the rotting serpent fly about in the air, and should one of them strike a person in the face cancer will result. So said John Beaton, grandson of the famous "Fearchar Léigh," Farquhar the Physician, Dunvegan. It is said that the largest serpents in Scotland were in Mull. Goats were kept to reduce their numbers, and afterwards the big sheep practically killed them out, as they also killed out several plants indigenous to the soil, once well known, now never seen.

Cupping

Cupping was done in various ways. One way was to burn a little spirit in a tumbler, and having thus exhausted the air in the glass, to place it immediately upon the part affected. This raised a blister, which was then pricked.

Murdoch Maclean, Breinish, Lewis, performs the operation of cupping, and thereby cures people of rheumatism and other complaints. His instrument is a cow's horn, cast by the living animal. An air-opening is made by drilling through the point of the horn. Over the base is placed a piece of *streafon,* the membrane covering a calf at birth or the afterbirth, proverbially fine and tough.

Moireal Nic Leoid, Muriel MacLeod, crofter girl, aged twenty-six, described how Murdoch Maclean operated on her: When I was sixteen or seventeen I went to Berwick on Tweed as laundry-maid. I was strong and healthy and well grown, but the work was heavy and the food did not suit one who had been used plain simple fare. I became ill, and the doctor, unable to give me relief, advised me to go home, which I did. My symptoms were still distressing — if I leant forward my eyes filled with water and I could not see, and I had great pain and dizziness in my head. The doctors at Stornoway, Lochs and Tarbert treated me twelve times with the *cuileaga Spàinneach* (fly-blisters), but all to no purpose; if no worse, I was certainly no better. I then went to Murdoch Maclean. He placed the *ballan* (cup or horn) on the back of my neck, and sucked through it until he had raised a large lump. He pricked this lump with a needle. Replacing the *ballan,* he again sucked strongly and steadily. He applied the *ballan* in all five times, four times on the first night and once on the following night, this time upon the other side of my neck. He thus drew two saucers full of clear water streaked with blood. I felt severe pain, as though racked from head to foot. The marks of the *ballan* were deep in my flesh and the needle marks lasted a long time, but they were bathed and bandaged until they healed. I now feel as well and as healthy as I have ever felt in my life, and more than grateful to my kind benefactor Murdoch Maclean.

The dumb charm

The *Eòlas Balbh* is for taking the *goimh* out of *losgadh* (the smart out of a burn). The person who performs it breathes lightly upon the sore and moves his hand above it, turning slowly, and uttering a short prayer the while for assuaging the pain. The pain ceases immediately, and the wound heals almost as soon.

Whiteness

To cure *an gileas,* whiteness upon the tongue in infants, put the blood of a cockerel's comb upon the tongue, applying it with the cockerel's tail feathers. This will remove the *gileas* within a short time.

Stitch

Were a boy to get a *greim* (stitch) in his side in playing or running or jumping, he would lie on the ground with the sore side under. He would make the sign of the cross over the side affected, saying: "May the cross of Christ crucified be assuaging my pain."

Innumerable phrases and sayings of this nature are common among the people, Roman Catholic and Protestant alike: "Mary and Michael be with thee, little fellow."

God's fire (ringworm)

Teine Dé or *teine Diaidh,* "God's fire," denotes ringworm, for which there were many cures. Children bandied words over it, often in hot resentment. The following was a frequent rime in these encounters:

Ringworm be upon thy snout!
Thy mother-in-law brought forth a mouse;
Thou thyself broughtest forth the hatching,
Black snoutie of the growling!

Sore back

A child born feet foremost is made to walk along the back of a person suffering from a sore back.

Displacement of the heart

From Elspet Sutherland, crofter, Bay View Cottage, West Helmsdale: The following is a cure to replace the heart after fright: Go to a stream under a bridge over which the living and the dead pass. Take water from the stream in a wooden *cuach* (cup). Lift three stones from the stream in the name of the Father, of the Son, of the Spirit. One stone must be round to represent the head; one stone must be triangular to represent the heart; one stone must be oblong to represent the body. Put these three stones into the *cuach* of water and carry them home. Put the stones one by one into the fire until they are red–hot. Then take one stone out of the fire and place it in the water in the *cuach,* observing carefully for how long it fizzled in the water before it was cooled. Do the same to the second and the third stones. The stone which makes the most prolonged and mournful sound indicates the seat of trouble whether it be head, heart or body that is affected. [The account seems to be incomplete.]

Epilepsy

There are various cures for the falling sickness, or epilepsy. The juice of juniper berries is useful. A *famh* (mole) held up by the tail above the patient's breath until it dies relieves if it does not cure the disease. Corn and the points of the patient's nails are buried in the earth along with a live cock. If the living sacrifice of a live cock, drake or gander, buried alive where the epileptic fell, were made with the first attack, no second attack would ever occur.

An intelligent woman in Evanton, Ross, said: A boy whose sister had an epileptic fit came to fetch a black cock that my mother had. The cock was buried where the epileptic fell. The girl is now a middle–aged woman and has never had a recurrence of epilepsy since that day.

A minister in Ross writes: I mentioned to my mother–in–law the living burial of the black cock at Evanton. She said that she had seen a girl seized with an epileptic fit on the second floor of a house. Immediately a hole was made through the floor at the spot where the girl fell, a second hole through the floor below, and a hole dug in the earth beneath. Then a black cock was procured and lowered through the two floors and buried alive in the pit below.

Some years ago, a boat was crossing Loch Duthaich from Letterfearn to Dornie when a man in the boat had an epileptic fit. The other men turned back and brought out a live black cock with a stone in a sack. On regaining their former position they threw the sack into the sea. The man who had the fit has never had another.

The blood of a black cock was sprinkled on a person in whom was the demon of the falling sickness, and if a black cock could not be found high or low, near or far, the blood of a black cat was sprinkled instead.

When a child newly born into the world was being washed, a straw rope was twined three times sunwise round the infant's body, and this was done: "In name of Father; In name of Son; In name of Spirit; Three just and holy."

After that the straw rope was cut into three equal lengths, and so long as these pieces should not unite the child would be free from epilepsy.

Colic, or pining

From Catherine Maclean, crofter, Naast, Gairloch: A stranger came on a time to a house on a dismal dark night of winter, and asked for night's provision and shelter from the bitter storms without. The woman of the house said he could not get that, that she had no means of doing so. The man of the house said that he should get it; neither he nor any person of his people had ever sent a man away from the door.

The woman went out to the barn and prepared a bed for the stranger upon a heap of barley awns, and she bade him lie upon it. The stranger did as he was bid, and lay down upon the bed that the woman had made for him upon the heap of awns.

In the night the man of the house was struck by colic, and was nigh unto death.

The woman was in sore plight, seeing her husband going to eternity, and she with no way to keep him and no art to relieve him. She was shedding tears and wringing her hands, all alone by herself, not knowing under the sun what she should do or say. Then she remembered the man in the barn, went out, wakened the stranger, and asked him to come and help her. Dressing himself, he came in, and said:

A keen woman! a keen woman!*
And a generous husband dead;
Pining piercing him with pain
And Christ lying upon the awn.

Death to the microbe in the pining
Death to the colic that is bitter;
Whole may the hospitable man arise,
Christ Himself lying on the awn.

That woman never again refused hospitality to any person, nor yet did she put a poor man to sleep on barley awns. A pitiful thing it is if shelter from the storm be not given to the poor pilgrim and to the wayfarer.

The warble

The warble causes pain, loss and deterioration in cattle. The insect is difficult to kill. When the animal dies, however, the parasite dies with it — the tick dies with the sheep, the bot dies with the cow. Hence: "Kill thou the cow and I will overcome the bot." There were many cures and incantations for destroying this parasite.

413 Charm to constrain the evil eye

Four to work sickness with evil eye,
Man and woman, youth and maid;
Three to repel ill will,
Father and Son and Holy Spirit.

414 Repelling the evil eye

It is mine own eye,
It is the eye of God,
It is the eye of God's Son
Which shall repel this,
Which shall combat this.

* That is, quick to make refusal.

He who has made to thee the eye,
Surly lie it on himself,
Surly lie it on his affection,
Surly lie it on his stock.

On his wife, on his children,
On his means, on his dear ones,
On his cattle, on his seed,
And on his comely kine.

On his mares grey and brown,
On his geldings in the plough,
On his flocks black and white,
On his corn–barns, on his coarse meal.

On the little fairy women
Who are reeling in the knoll,
Who are biding in the heath,
Who are filling the cavities.

415 Countering the evil–eye

Make I to thee, thou cherished "Dubhag,"*
The charm of Mary, the charm of the King of all kings,
The most perfect charm that is in the world,
Which Thou hast given me, O God of all gods.

Against small eye, against large eye,
Against the eye of swift voracious women,
Against the eye of swift rapacious women,
Against the eye of swift draggling women.

Against mine own eye,
Against thine own eye,
Against the eye of the grey man
Who came yesterday to the door.

* Black One.

Whosoever has brought thee to sore straits
With eye, with malice, with jealousy, with envy,
May her life not be prolonged
On the surface of Loch Leargain.

May it lie on their own eyes,
May it lie on their own sorceries,
May it lie on their own jealousy,
May it lie on their own envy.

May it lie on their cow calves,
May it lie on their bull calves,
May it lie on their fold of young cows,
May it lie on their foaling mares.

May it lie on their little children,
May it lie on their big children,
May it lie on their bleating goats,
May it lie on their woolly sheep.

May it lie on their potent men,
May it lie on their pregnant women,
May it lie on their virile sons,
May it lie on their conceptive daughters.

May it lie on their back–head joints,
May it lie on their back–leg sinews,
May it lie upon each one of those things in the world
That these people love better than all else.

But be thy groan and thy grief,
Thy yawn and thy heaviness,
Thy sadness and thy tears,
Thy misery and thy lament,

Be they on the spoilers of the wings,
Be they on the beasts of the braes,
Be they on the searchers of the branches,
Be they on the withered heath of the hill–tops;

Be they on the rangers of the mountains,
Be they on the fishes of the currents,

Be they on the examiners of the boughs,
Since these themselves can best endure.

One third today;
Two thirds tomorrow,
And all thirds till doom
The day thereafter.

416 Countering the evil eye

Who shall lift the evil eye?
Who but Thou; O God of life!
By power of Peter, by power of Paul,
By power of the Three best in glory.

Pater of Mary, one,
Pater of Mary, two,
Pater of Mary, three,
Pater of Mary, four,
Pater of Mary, five,
Pater of Mary, six,
Pater of Mary, seven.

The might of the seven Paters of Mary
Be upon stones and upon trees,
Upon the wild ducks of the swamps,
Upon the withered trees of the copses.

Upon the creeping things of the plain,
Upon the bear of the lands,
Upon the blowers of the sea,
Upon the beasts of the holes.

Upon the brown stag of the mountain,
Upon the green grass beneath my sole,
Upon the birds of the wings,
Upon the fish of the waves;

Since they themselves can best endure,
And are most shapely of form.

417 Thwarting the eye

Twelve eyes against every malice,*
Twelve eyes against every envy,
Twelve eyes against every purpose,
Twelve eyes against every hope,
Twelve eyes against every intent,
Twelve eyes against every eye,
The twelve eyes of the Son of the God of life,
The twelve eyes of the Son of the God of life.

418 Thwarting the eye
(fragment)

May it lie upon their virile sons,
May it lie upon their conceptive daughters,
May it lie upon each of their worldly joys
That they themselves love best.

419 Charm for the evil eye

An eye was seeing thee,
A mouth has named thee,
A heart has thought of thee,
A mind has desired thee:

May Three Persons sanctify thee,
May Three Persons aid thee,
The Father and the Son
And the perfect Spirit.

Four have wrought thy hurt,
A man and a woman,
A lad and a maiden;

* I do not know what this represents unless it be the Twelve Apostles.

Three I set to oppose them,
Father and Son
And Holy Spirit.

Who is it that repels them?
Who is it that averts them?
The Three Persons of the Blessed Trinity,
The Three Persons of the Triune.

420 Charm for the eye

Peter and Paul and John,
Three most impressive of speech,
Arose to make the charm
In the protection of the city of heaven;

At the right knee of God the Father,
At the right knee of God the Son,
At the right knee of God the Spirit;

Against peering–eyed women,
Against keen–eyed men,
Against blear–eyed slender ones,
Against seven phantom fairies.

Four made to thee evil,
Four made to thee hurt,
Man and woman,
Youth and maid.

Three I set to check them,
Three I send to subdue them,
Father and Son
And Holy Spirit.

Four and twenty diseases
Inherent in men and beasts,

Inherent in man and woman,
Inherent in youth and maid.

May God search them, may God quash them,
May God scrape them, may God quench them,
From thy blood, from thy flesh, from thy urine,
From thy smooth fragrant bones;

From thy close veins, from thy hard kidney,
From thy pith, from thy marrow, beloved,
From this day forth and every day of them
Till the day thou shalt end thy life.

As Christ raised the fruit
Over the tops of the bushes,
May He lift from thee now
Each spell and ban and blindness;

As Christ removed the sleep
From the little son of the grave,
May He remove from thee, dear one,
Each frown, each envy, each malice.

421 Checking the evil eye

I make for thee charm
To check the evil eye;

Against the nine paths,
Against the nine tumults,
Against the nine crafty wiles,
Against nine slender women of faery;

Against the eye of bachelor,
Against the eye of old maid,
Against the eye of old man,
Against the eye of old woman.

If it be eye of man,
May it flare like pitch,
If it be eye of woman,
May she want her breast.

Flooding be to her water
And chilling be to her blood,
To her cattle, to her sheep,
To her people, to her wealth.

422 Repelling the eye

Rosary, one,
Rosary, two,
Rosary, three,
Rosary, four,
Rosary, five,
Rosary, six,
Rosary, seven,
Rosary, eight,
Rosary, nine:

The nine rosaries kindly
  Through the Holy Three
To lift from thee each illness,
  Each blindness, each affliction.

423 Charm for evil eye

I make for thee
  Charms for evil eye
In reliance on Peter and on Paul
  And on quiet Brigit my beloved.

Against eye of little man,
  Against eye of big man,
Against eye of man who travels
  The high road.

Against eye of bird that flies to sky,
  Against eye of bird that flies to sea,
Against eye of goose that passes by,
  Against eye of all the host;

Against eye of man red and harsh–spoken,
  Against eye of woman swift and loud–spoken,
Against eye of serpent red and venomous.

Salve, O kindly Calum Cille,
Salve, O holy Patrick of marvels,
Salve, O quiet Brigit of the Boyne,
Salve, O great Mary of the ringlets.

Whole be he who receives it,
Whole be thou giving it,
Whole be he after it,
Whole be thyself this night.

...
...

For the happiness and wealth
Of him who is there,
Man or woman, youth or maid,
Horse or cow, wife or children.

424 Charm for rose

Jesus and Mary were fugitives and travelling in the desert land of Egypt. And what but that they came to a little miserable bothy in the skirts of a glen. They went into the bothy seeking a drink of water, for they were parched with thirst in the hard shrivelled thirsty land. And who was dwelling in the bothy but a poor little wretched woman near dying with rose in her breast. The poor woman bared her breast to the Mary Mother to see if she could do aught for her or give her any sort of relief. Jesus asked His Mother to destroy the microbe, to reduce the breast, and give the woman peace. And this is the conversation that occurred between Jesus and His Mother:

MARY:
Behold, O Son, the pap,
Filled full with swelling;
Give Thou rest to the woman,
Bring Thou the microbe from out her tumour.

JESUS:
Behold thou her, O Mary,
Since it was thou who bore the Son;
Give thou rest unto the pap,
Relieve thou the woman.

MARY:
Behold Thou her, O Christ,
Since Thou art the King of power;
Give Thou rest to the woman,
Bring the destruction from out her tumour.

JESUS:
I will behold, said Christ,
And I will do as is thy wish;
I will make whole the pap,
And I will dissolve the tumour.

Whole be the woman,
Shrunken be the swelling.

425 Charm for rose

See, O Son, the udder,
Swollen by the rose;
Tell Thou that to Our Lady,
For 'tis she who bore the Son.

Get thee hence, thou rose,
Let me see the back of thy feet;
Whole be the udder,
Drained be the swelling.

Thou rose, dark red and swelling,
Hard, scabby and foul,
Leave the udder and the breast;
Reduce the swelling, behold the pap distressed.

426 Charm for rose

The charm made by Fionn son of Curnhall
For his own sister dear,
Against rose, against pang, against reddening,
Against surly creatures of the mountain;

Against the fairy elfin arrows,
Against elfin arrows charmed,
Against piercing arrows of fairy host,
Against harassing arrows on the journey;

In tryst of Father and Son of tears,
In tryst of perfect Spirit of might,
Refuse not the prayer to one in need,
And say it not on the Lord's Day.

427 Kidney of Mary

"Behold, O Mary Mother,
The woman and she near to death."
"Behold Thou her, O Christ,
Since it is of Thy mercy
To give rest to the child
And to bring the woman from her labour.

"Behold Thou her, O Christ,
Since Thou art the King of health,
Deliver the woman from death
And sain the innocent child,
Give Thou rest to the vine-shoot,
Give Thou peace to its mother."

428 Kidney of Mary

"Behold, O Mary, the woman,
And she beneath thy gracious pleasure;
Give freedom to the child,
Bring from death the woman."

"Behold Thou her, O Christ,
Since it is of Thy doing
To give freedom to the child,
To raise up the woman."

"I do as is thy wish,
Little Mother my Beloved;
Freedom I give the child,
From death I bring the woman."

429 Charm for swollen breast

Extinction to thy microbe,
Extinction to thy swelling,
Peace be to thy breast,
The peace of the King of power.

Whiteness be to thy skin,
Subsiding to thy swelling,
Wholeness to thy breast,
Fullness to thy pap.

In the holy presence of the Father,
In the holy presence of the Son,
In the holy presence of the Spirit,
The holy presence of compassion.

430 The charm of the toothache

The charm placed of Columba
About the right knee of Maol Iodha,
Against pain, against sting, against venom,
Against tooth disease, against bodily disease.

Said Peter unto James:
"I get no respite from toothache,
But it is with me lying down and rising
And leaping on my soles."

Said Christ, answering the problem:
"The toothache and the rune
Shall not henceforth abide in the same head."

431 Charm for sprain

He Who so calmly rode
The little ass fair of form,
Who healed each hurt and bloody wound
That clave to the people of every age:

He made glad the sad and the outcast,
He gave rest to the restless and the tired,
He made free the bond and the unruly,
Each old and young in the land.

He opened the eyes of the blind,
He awaked the step of the lame,
He loosed the tongue that was dumb,
He gave life to him that was dead.

He stemmed the fierce–rushing blood,
He took the keen prickle from the eye,
He drank the draught that was bitter,
Trusting to the High Father of heaven.

He gave strength to Peter and Paul,
He gave strength to the Mother of tears,
He gave strength to Brigit of the flocks,
Each joint and bone and sinew.

Soothing and salving
With the wort of Columba,
Soothing and salving
With the grace of the God of life.

Soothing and salving
With the wort of Columba,
Soothing and salving
With the grace of the Christ of love.

Soothing and salving
With the wort of Columba,
Soothing and salving
With the grace of the Holy Ghost.

Soothing and salving
With the wort of Columba,
Soothing and salving
With the grace of the Three in One.

Soothing and salving
In the strength of the sweet kisses
From the mouth and the lips
Of the Three clement and kind.

Soothing and salving
In the sign of the sweet kisses
From the mouth and the lips
Of the Three tender and mild.

Soothing and salving
In the shield of the sweet kisses
From the mouth and the lips
Of the musical choir of the saints.

432 Charm for sprain

In name of Father,
In name of Son,
In name of Spirit,
The Three of threes.

Bone to bone,
Vein to vein,
Balm to balm,
To the left foot.

Sap to sap,
Skin to skin,
Tissue to tissue,
To the left foot.

Blood to blood,
Flesh to flesh,
Sinew to sinew,
To the left foot.

Marrow to marrow,
Pith to pith,
Fat to fat,
To the left foot.

Membrane to membrane,
Fibre to fibre,
Moisture to moisture,
To the left foot.

The God of gods,
The Healer of healers,
The Spirit of eternity,
The Three of threes,
To the left foot.

433 The charm of the styes

The performance of the following charm is accompanied by a thrust towards the stye with a pin, a needle, or some other sharp-pointed instrument:

I repel thee, O stye,
By guidance of Father!
[Thrust]

I repel thee, O stye,
By guidance of Son!
[Thrust]

I repel thee, O stye,
By guidance of Spirit!
[Thrust]

By guidance of the Three of grace,
By guidance of the Three of kindness,
By guidance of the Three of mercy!

Simultaneously with the thrusting towards the stye, the following reproving lines are hissed through the teeth at the grig *or* grid *(microbe) in the eye. Whether from shame or from fright, the* grig *disappears and the swelling subsides immediately:*

Go back! go back! go back!
Go back! go back! go back!
Go back! go back! go back!
Thou thievish rascal of the stye!

What ever! ever! ever!
What ever! ever! ever!
What ever! ever! ever,
Thou microbe, brought thee here?

434 Charm of the stye

Thou microbe, microbe of the stye,
  What ever brought thee here?
Take thy feet with thee promptly,
  Or I promise thee extinction!

Take thy feet with thee, impudent!
  Take thy deceiving feet!
Take thy feet with thee, paltry,
  Or I will singe thy head for thee!

435 The charm of the warts

The reciter did not remember the rune. In order to charm away warts one procures naoi naoi glùnanan shop arbhair no feoir, *nine nine joints of stalks of corn or of hay. These are placed in a small bag and buried nine nine joint-lengths in the ground:*

In the name of Father,
In the name of Son,
In the name of Spirit,
The perfect Three of power.

As the joints decayed in the earth, the warts decayed in the air until none remained.

If the little bag containing the nine nine joints were thrown away, and another person took it up, the warts would be transferred to the finder. This, however, is not considered honourable, and is rarely done by the most careless boy or girl.

The nine-jointed stalk is:

The wisp of nine stalks
To make the warts retreat.

A woman of Upper Bornish, who had many warts on hands and feet, procured with time and trouble naoi naoi glùinean, *nine nine knees, that is, nine stalks with nine joints on each stem. These she buried in the ground, and as the knots of the straws decayed, the warts disappeared.*

As withered down the straws,
Withered till doom the warts.

Another cure was to rub dry rust upon the wart, or to apply moist rust to it. Those near the sea applied a poultice of the broad-leaved tangle to the wart. Even medical men will appreciate this cure from the iodine contained in the tangle.

"Go to the churchyard and dip the wart in water lying on a gravestone. The wart will disappear in a day or two."

"Rub the wart against the clothes of one who has committed fornication." A certain gentleman said that, having done this, he was utterly surprised to find the wart disappear in two days.

A wart was a good omen according to the sex of the person and the position of the wart:

The wart which the closed hand surrounds,
Fortunate is the youth who sees it;
The wart which the shoe surrounds
Fortunate is the maid who has it.

436 The charm of the scale

The reciter said: To turn back the growth and the grip and the pain of the cataract I make the charm of the cataract; and this is the manner of my making it. I go to running water over which the dead and the living have passed. I now lift a little basin of water on the lower side of the streamlet, and say:

I am lifting a palmful of water
In the holy name of Father
In the holy name of Son,

In the holy name of Spirit,
In the holy name of the Three
Everlasting, kindly, wise.

Certain that They will do to me
The thing that it becomes me to ask
The thing that accords with Their mind,
The thing that is causing pain,
The thing that is worthy to be done
Of the Trinity kindly and just.

I take the basin of water home, and three green blades of grass of the plain, and I put a piece of gold or a silver coin in the basin of water, and I dip blade after blade in the basin of water, and pray to:

God the Father,
God the Son,
God the Spirit,
For guidance and mercy and compassion.

I dip a blade of grass in the basin of water and draw the blade softly and gently across the cataract on the eyeball in the name of Father. And I dip a blade of grass in the basin of water and draw the blade softly and gently across the cataract on the eyeball in the name of Son. And I dip a blade of grass in the basin of water and draw the blade softly and gently across the cataract on the eyeball in the name of Spirit. And I ask the everlasting Trinity of life to grant me my prayer if it be Their own will so to do and if the asking be in accord with Their mind.

437 Blind seizure

The salve placed of Mary
To the eye of the salmon
That leaped with power
In the torrent of the river.

Against ...

Against ...

Pour, thou Brigit calm,
Pour, thou Mary mild,

Pour, thou Calum Cille,
Pour, thou Michael militant.

Pour, Thou King of life,
Pour, Thou Christ of peace,
Pour, Thou Spirit of laving,
Pour, O pour, Triune Three.

Thou Who didst create the orb,
And Who placed the pupil in the eye,
Search Thou the mystery within the lid,
Befriend Thou the sight, O God.

Turn Thou the evil of the orb,
Turn Thou the virus in the eye,
Turn Thou, O King of the eye,
And strengthen Thou the sight, O God.

Sanctify Thou this day the orb,
Sanctify Thou this day the eye,
Sanctify Thou this day the sight,
And befriend Thou the orb, O God!

The mote

Eoghan Macdougall, crofter, Meallaig, said: My brother and myself were herring-fishing over in Loch Hourn. A herring-scale stuck in my brother's eye and he was in severe pain. We went to a woman in Sgiathairigh, who possessed the Charm of the Mote, to get the mote removed from my brother's eye. The woman performed the Charm of the Mote, but although she did, the mote did not leave the eye. The thing left the woman utterly at a loss, and this vexed herself and surprised us, for the woman was famous throughout the countryside for the Charm of the Mote.

We left to come home. Coming over by Sanndaig my brother felt a sudden tremor and severe pain in his eye, as quick as a flash of lightning.

"It has gone!" said my brother.

"Has it," I said, "Mary, you were badly in need of that!"

I myself examined the eye and the herring-scale was beyond doubt gone. We gave thanks to the great God of life, to Christ, and to the gentle Mary Mother, and turned back on the track the way we had come.

The woman who had performed the charm saw the boat coming and met us on the beach. Before we were out of the boat the woman called to us that at last she had succeeded with the mote.

"It was wicked lack of faith that came on me and lay like a shadow on my soul; but I prayed the God of grace to aid and help me and to give my power back to me, and in His own loving-kindness and great goodness He did so. Look you, there is the mote that was in the eye," said the woman.

She had a little basin of water in her hand and the herring-scale on the surface of the water in the basin.

"That's the mote that was in your eye, Donald," she said.

Mary Macmillan was renowned in the countryside for removing the mote from a person's eye. Those who work with herring are apt to get a herring-scale in the eye, and herring-fishers used now and again to send for the woman to perform the charm for them.

Messages came to Mary Macmillan from far and near, and she never failed to remove the mote. She was beloved and respected throughout her long life, and herself and others believed in her occult powers.

A descendant of hers, Mary Cameron of Sgiathairigh, had Eòlas an Sguchaidh, the Charm for Sprain. She performed it with success for man and beast. I went to her from Ardchattan in Lorne, travelling up Glen Orchy, down the Black Mount, by the Moor of Rannoch, Lochaber, Fort William, through the Garbhchrioch (Rough Bound) and Arasaig on to Mallaig. Thence I took boat by night along the Linne Shléiteach (Sound of Sleat), past Cnoideart (Knoydart), and into Loch Shubhairn (Loch Hourn), arriving at Arnisdale late at night. Next morning I took boat for Sgiathairigh near Ceann Loch Shubhairn (Loch Hourn-head). I found Mary Cameron a pleasant and hospitable woman, but on no account would she repeat to me *Eòlas a' Chaimein,* though I tried every possible means to persuade her. She said that the *eòlas* was entrusted to her, for no foolish purpose, and she was not going to impart it for any foolish purpose to any person. On the following morning I took boat to Eilean Diaid (Isle Ornsay) to meet the steamer for Mallaig, whence by train to Edinburgh. It was a long, costly and, alas, disappointing journey, like many similar ones.

Christina Mackay, Bun Ilidh (Helmsdale), could remove the mote from the eye at a distance of many miles. She was a famous and a wonderful woman. Doctors derided her, but they could not deny her achievements.

William Polson, crofter and fisherman, Helmsdale, had the power to remove a mote from the eye without personal contact. On one occasion he found an insect peculiar to man in his mouth after the operation, after which he gave up doing the *caimein.*

William Ross, elder, Kincardine, Ross, could remove a mote from the eye many miles away. Like others who possessed this power, he could show the mote upon the point of his tongue, and often did this. He was an industrious and prosperous crofter, and an obliging neighbour. His people were known as "Na Gobhaichean," the smiths; "Gobhaichean Ruadha Achadh nan Gart," the red smiths of Achnagart, Strath Kyle.

Donald Murray, farm grieve, Arcan, Urray, near Dingwall, said: When I was a youth, I was bringing home a load of peats to a woman in Edderton, Ross. A bit of *culm* (dust) went into my eye. I told the woman about my eye.

"We will soon cure that," said she. Fetching a small basin of water, she said a rime over the water. I understood that she appealed to the great God Who created the eye to help her faith and to grant her request. I felt a sharp twitch in my eye and called out: "Dh'fhalbh e," (It has gone). She showed me a bit of peat *culm* floating on the water.

"That," said she, "is the *smùirnein* (mote) that was in your eye."

Alexander Campbell, Conon, said: My master said to me, "My wife cannot get a wink of sleep owing to a mote that has gone into her eye. Go you to Mrs Mackinnon in Arcan and ask her to take the mote *(durdan)* out of my wife's eye."

Mrs Mackinnon made the *eòlas,* and took a little tiny bit of corn husk out of her mouth and put it in a small basin of water in her hand... My good mistress had been working among sids, or corn husks, to make sowens. I marked the time when I left; it was half–past eight. Next morning my master said: "My wife is quite better; at half–past eight last night she cried out that the thing had left her eye. By the King Himself, Mrs Mackinnon is good!"

Kate Macphail, née Ross, cottar, Bishop's Kinkell, Conon Bridge, related how her brother suffered agony from a barley awn in his right eye. She went to Donald Mackinnon in Arcan, Urray, some four miles away. He made the charm and placed the awn on his tongue before her.

"That," said he, "is the *calg* (awn) that was in your brother's eye, and he has relief now."

That was so. Her brother felt a sudden twinge in his eye, and the thing was gone.

John Maclennan, crofter, said: My brother and I were working down in Fortrose. We were sitting, eating a hard biscuit for dinner. In play I struck my brother's hand from below and the half–eaten biscuit flew up in his face. A bit of it went into his eye. The medical man of the place failed to remove the mote and my brother suffered much for two days. Then I went to Mary Mackenzie in Bràigh Arcain (the upper part of Arcandeith in the Black Isle), near Tore Farm. She rose at once and made *Eòlas a' Chaimein* (the Charm of the Mote). She put three small pebbles in a small basin of clear clean water in name of the Three Persons of the Holy Trinity. She then drew a mouthful of water from the basin, but not finding the *caimean* she put out the mouthful of water in the ashes beside the fire on the floor. She did this a second and a third time, and felt in her mouth for the mote. She got the mote upon her tongue and poured that mouthful back into the basin.

"That is the mote that was in your brother's eye," she said to me. The woman had a rime in making the *caimean,* but I took with me only a word here and there of it. But I observed well that the woman prayed to the God of life to put on her tongue the mote that was in Donald Maclennan's eye.

Mr MacLeod, station–master, Diùirinis, Loch Alsh, saw practised a charm for removing a thing from the eye. A lad, while threshing in the barn, got a bit of straw in his eye. He told a neighbour, who went to a stream and filled his mouth with water therefrom, mentally repeating the words of *Eòlas a' Chaimein* with the water in his mouth. He then poured the water on the palm of his hand. He moved the water in his palm with a stalk of grass, and allowed it to leak through his fingers, and there remained on his palm a small bit of straw that came out of the eye. The youth did not know that the neighbour was performing the *eòlas,* but he felt the *caimean* leaving the eye. Mr MacLeod saw the thing done and heard *rann an eòlais,* the rime of the charm, but could not remember it.

Mr Donald Mackechnie, Edinburgh, the well-known and highly gifted writer in Gaelic, said: I was in a house in Jura (his native island) when a messenger came to ask the woman of the house to remove a mote from the eye of a man at a distance. The woman promptly got up and put water in a basin and said a short prayer in rhythmical form. She drew up a mouthful of water from the basin and having felt for something upon her tongue she poured back the water into the basin. Having carefully examined the water in the basin, she said:

"There is a small hair here. I do not know whether or not this is the mote that was in the eye of Donald Darroch; but whether it be or not, I know by myself that the mote has left the eye and the man has got relief."

We all looked in the basin and saw a small hair on the surface of the water. It looked like the hair of an eyelid or of an eyebrow. Donald Darroch's eyelids and eyebrows were fair, while the woman's were black. I made a mental note of the time, and having bade goodnight to the company I walked straight to the house of Donald Darroch. Without disclosing what I had seen in the house of John Blue, I discovered that Donald Darroch had had a small hair in his eye, which his wife had failed to remove, but that it had left the eye at the moment the woman made the charm. I have read many works of science and philosophy since then, but I have never chanced upon any explanation of how this occult power was obtained and used.

438 Charm for the mote

Christ upon the cross,
Mary upon her palm;
I am placing my trust
In the King of life
To put the mote that is in the eye
Here upon my palm.

In name of Father,
In name of Son,
In name of Spirit.

By the aiding of Christ,
By the greatness of the King
Am I doing this.

439 Charm for mote

Brigit, be by mine eye,
Mary, be my support,
Glorious King, be by my knee,
Loving Christ, be by my body.

The mote that is in the eye
Place, O King of life,
Place, O Christ of love,
Place, O Spirit Holy,
Place upon my palm.

May the King of life be giving rest,
May the Christ of love be giving repose,
May the Spirit Holy be giving strength,
May the eye be at peace.

O Brigit calm of the mantles,
O Mary mild of the poor,
O warrior Michael of the burnished swords,
Set the hurt at rest.

440 The mote

Christ upon the cross,
Mary upon her palm,
Brigit on her knee,
My prayer to the Creator
That this eye may find rest.

In name of Father,
In name of Son,
In name of Spirit
Do I this.

In reliance on the King,
In reliance on my Christ,
In reliance on Holy Spirit,
In reliance on the Three
Do I this.

441 Eye charm

The goading prick
Caught fast in rock,
Leap of belling elk,
The mote that is in the eye
Place, O King of life,
Gently on my tongue.

442 Eye charm

The stabbing prick
Caught fast in the eye,
Venom of the nine serpents,
Les of belling elk.

The mote of the eye
On which is my anticipation,
On which is my purpose,
On which is my expectation,
Place, O King of life,
Place, O Christ of love,
Place, O Spirit Holy,
Softly on my tongue.

443 The mote

Place, Thou King of peace,
Place, Thou Christ of the cross,
Place, Thou guiding Spirit,
This mote upon my palm.

The King be by my palm,
Christ be by my foot,
The guiding Spirit be by my knee,
The eye be at rest.

Grant, Thou King of the eyes,
Grant, Thou Christ of the cross,
Grant, Thou guiding Spirit,
Calm to the eye this night.

In name of the King of life,
In name of the Christ of love,
In name of the Spirit Holy,
Triune of peace.

444 Charm for the eye

In name of Father,
In name of Son,
In name of Spirit.

Triune, all alike in might, holy,
Triune, all alike in power, of wondrous works,
Triune, all alike in righteousness and love.

This is that which Christ wrote
When stretched upon the tree;
May Mary mild be by my hand,
May Brigit calm be by my head.

My trust is in the Being of life,
The mote that is in the blind eye,
That the true King of my devotion
Will gently place it hither on my tongue.

445 Charm for the mote

Mote of nine motes,
Awn of nine awns,
Pang of nine pangs,
  Leap of elk over adder.

The mote within the eye
Whereto my wishes lie,
Come, O King of life,
With me to withdraw it.

The seven bitches of the Fianna,
Let them attack the pain;
O Thou King of the clouds,
My desire were to withdraw it!

446 Charm for chest seizure

I will heal thee,
Mary will heal with me,
Mary and Michael and Brigit
Be with me all three.

Thy strait and thy sickness
Be upon the earth holes,
Be on the grey stones,
Since they have firmest base.

Be upon the birds of the sky,
Be upon the wasps of the knolls,
Be upon the whales of the sea,
Since they have swiftest body.

Be upon the clouds of the skies,
Since they are pronest to rain,
Be upon the stream of the river
Whirling to the wave.

447 Charm for chest seizure

Be the first third of thee upon the grey clouds,
Since they themselves have best power to move,
In name of Father and Son and Holy Spirit.

Be the second third of thee upon the headlong swamps,
Since they themselves have best power to suck,
In name of Father and Son and Holy Spirit.

Be the third third of thee upon the beauteous meads,
Since they themselves have best power to carry,
In name of Father and Son and Holy Spirit.

I am making thee now this charm,
Thou Donald son of Eoghan,
In name of Father, my two palms on the ground,
In name of Son, my two palms on the ground,
In name of Spirit, my two palms on the ground,
Three Who possess the heights.

448 Charm for chest seizure

Power of moon have I over thee,
Power of sun have I over thee,
Power of rain have I over thee,
Power of dew have I over thee,
Power of sea have I over thee,
Power of land have I over thee,
Power of stars have I over thee,
Power of planets have I over thee,
Power of universe have I over thee,
Power of skies have I over thee,
Power of saints have I over thee,
Power of heaven have I over thee,
Power of heaven and power of God have I over thee,
Power of heaven and power of God over thee.

A part of thee on the grey stones,
A part of thee on the steep mountains,
A part of thee on the swift cascades,
A part of thee on the gleaming clouds,
A part of thee on the ocean-whales,

A part of thee on the meadow–beasts,
A part of thee on the fenny swamps,
A part of thee on the cotton–grass moors,
A part on the great surging sea –
She herself has best means to carry,
The great surging sea,
She herself has best means to carry.

449 Charm for chest constriction

Jesus Christ bade Simon Peter
To fill His own people,
To teach His own people,
To shield His own people,
To succour His own people,
To save His own people
From robbers, from betrayers.

I am appealing to Thee,
I am praying of Thee,
Since Thou art the King of each good,
Since Thou art the King of heaven,
That Thou mayest lift each wasting,
Each weariness and weakness,
Each seizure and ailment,
Each soreness and discomfort,
Each malady and sickness
That adheres to this maiden.

Mayest Thou put them on the beasts of the heights,
Mayest Thou put them on the wild ones of the deserts,
Mayest Thou put them on the winged ones of the summits,
Mayest Thou put them on the monsters of the brine.

Mayest Thou put them on the streams of the glens,
Mayest Thou put them on the whales of the sea,
Mayest Thou put them on the crests of the bens,
Mayest Thou put them on the birds of the air.

I am praying of Thee keenly,
I am calling on Thee straitly;
That Thou mayest lift each stroke,
Each injury and bane.

As severs flood from flood,
As severs water from water,
As severs liquid from liquid
Throughout the vastness of the watery ocean,

As sunders haze from haze,
As sunders mist from mist,
As sunders cloud from cloud
In the depth of the great stormy sky,

As scatter *oin* from *oin,*
As scatter birds from birds,
May the God of guidance scatter this night
Each ill and affection that was ever in thy flesh.

It will cause them no harm,
And it will cause good to thee,
Thou dear Margaret Calder,
Mine own sister.

450 Charm for seizure

I trample on thee, thou seizure,
As tramples whale on brine,
Thou seizure of back, thou seizure of body,
Thou foul wasting of chest.

May the strong Lord of life
Destroy thy disease of body
From the crown of thine head
To the base of thy heel;

From thy two loins thither,
From thy two loins hither,
With the power of the Christ of love
And the Creator of the seasons;

With the aid of the Spirit Holy
And the whole Powers together,
With the aid of the Spirit Holy
And the whole Powers together.

451 Charm for consumption

I trample on thee, evil wasting,
  As tramples swan on brine,
Thou wasting of back, thou wasting of body,
  Thou foul wasting of chest.

May Christ's own Gospel
  Be to make thee whole,
The Gospel of the Healer of healers,
  The Gospel of the God of grace,

To remove from thee thy sickness
  In the pool of health
From the crown of thy head
  To the base of thy two heels,

From thy two loins thither
  To thy two loins hither,
In reliance on the might of the God of love
  And of the whole Powers together:
The love of grace!

452 Chest conflict

I trample on thee, thou slimy chest seizure,
As upon mountain land this night;
On thyself be thine arrow, O Géigean!
Intense and horrible is thy wounding.

The charm placed of Patrick the generous
On the mother of the king of Ibhir
To kill the beasts that fastened
Upon the veins of her heart.

Upon the four and twenty diseases
That were inherent in men and in beasts,
That were inherent in man and in woman,
That were inherent in son and in daughter.

Upon the running water of the mountain stream,
Upon the running water of the boundary stream,
Upon the rigid stones of the earth,
And upon the weakness of the heart.

Upon the ague,
Upon the whooping-cough,
Upon the fever,
Upon the wasting.

Upon the throat disease,
Upon the chest disease,
Upon the neck disease,
Upon the measles.

453 King's evil

May God heal thee, my dear;
I am now placing my hand on thee
In name of Father, in name of Son, in name of Spirit of virtue,
Three Persons Who compass thee ever.

Full healing be to thy red blood,
Perfect healing to thy soft flesh,
Another healing to thy white skin,
In name of the powers of the Holy Three,
In name of the powers of the Holy Three.

454 The charm of the swellings

Be this stroke upon the Màm of the Boar,
Be this stroke upon the Màm of Cluainidh,
Be this stroke upon the Màm of Coire Ghearraig,
In name of Father and Son and Holy Spirit.

[And each present says, Amen.]

Be this stroke upon the Màm of Diarmaid,
Be this stroke upon the Màm of the Hunts,
Be this stroke upon the Màm of Bàrasdal,
In name of Father and Son and Holy Spirit.

[And each present says, Amen.]

Be this stroke upon the Màm of Domhaillean,
Be this stroke upon the Màm of Gleann Eilg,
Be this stroke upon the Màm of Ràtagan,
In name of Father and Son and Holy Spirit.

[And each present says, Amen.]

455 Checking of blood

Checking of blood,
Incantation of blood,
Blood shall congeal,
Wound shall close.
Salve of Mary

Mother of Christ
Shield us,
Succour us.
In name of Father,
In name of Son,
In name of Spirit,
The holy Three of life
Spare us, aid us.

456 Checking of blood

Pater of God, one,
Pater of Mary, two,
Pater of God, three,
Pater of Mary, four,
Pater of God, five,
Pater of Mary, six,
Pater of God, seven.

Wherein the avail of these seven Paters?

In Christ the loving,
The holy Blood of powers.

(The name and designation of the person or animal)

Closed for thee thy wound,
And congealed thy blood.
As Christ bled upon the cross,
So closeth He thy wound for thee

In the eye of the loving Father,
In the eye of the loved Son,
In the eye of the Holy Spirit,
The Triune of power.

457 Charm for surfeit

For hill disease,
For wood disease,
For dark disease,
For light disease,
For fairy ill.

For *mil,*
For *malg,*
For belly,
For red–water,
For surfeit.

For evil disease,
For breast disease,
For milk and pairing,
To make thee whole,
O "Meilcheag!"

[Name the name of the cow]

458 The white cow

"Put thou in, O Calum Cille,
And heal the white cow;
Put thou in, O Calum Cille,
And heal the cow of water!

"Put thou in, O Calum Cille,
And heal the cow beloved;
Put thou in, O Calum Cille,
And heal my dear cow!"

"How so, O thick–tressed woman,
Am I to heal thy cow,
My one foot in the coracle,
My other foot on shore?"

Calum Cille came to the knoll,
He set his hand upon the cow;
He set his one foot in the coracle,
His other foot on ground.

"I myself break thy swelling,
I myself kill thine insect,
I lift from thee thy prickliness,
In name of the King of the ages!"

459 Charm for surfeit

Thou surfeit that art come hither
To the little bull yonder,
The foot of Calum Cille in the coracle
To decrease thy swelling,
To decrease thy prickliness,
To kill thy parasites,
To kill the pale worm,
To kill the brown worm,
To kill the beast of two liquids,
To kill the surfeit.

The nine wells of Mac an Lir,
To make thy blood stop;
The nine wells of Mac an Luin,
To make thy urine flow.

Great sea,
Red cascade,
Cease the blood,
Flow the urine.

460 Surfeit

The rune that Columba made
For the old woman's one cow,
For her swelling and her hide and her veins.

Four and twenty veins
Transverse in the cow,
Vein of heart, vein of liver,
Vein of kidneys...

With keen and cutting sword
That cleaves each red stroke

Be it put on stones,
Be it put on whales,
For the healing of the cow.

461 Charm for surfeit

The cure that Christ made
For the poor woman's one neat,
A foot on sea and a foot on land,
A foot in the coracle tonight.

* * *

Thine illness and thy heaviness
Be on the whales of the sea,
On woods and on trees,
On the black monsters of the deep,
And on the bears of the mountain.

May the God of life cure thee,
Thou dear quiet "Prugag,"
From this day and on each other day
To the day of the end of thy life.
Amen.

462 Surfeit

The rune made by Calum Cille
For an old woman's one cow,
Against the maggot,
Against the insect,
Against swelling,
Against pining,
Against the red disease
And against surfeit.

I will reduce the swelling,
I will cleave the prickly ball,
I will burn away the red disease,
I will kill the maggot,
And thou, brown cow,
Shalt be tomorrow on the knoll
Chewing thy cud;
Increase and milk–wave
In earnest of thy cure.

463 Charm for surfeit

I have a charm for the *muatan,*
I have a charm for the swelling,
I have a charm for the black ill,
I have a charm for the red ill
And for the surfeit.

The charm that Calum Cille made
For the old woman's one cow

* * *

Shake thou it from thee, "Cuanach,"
"Pur Chuanach!" "Pur Chuanach!" "Pur Chuanach!"
"Pur Chuanach!" My dear, come thou to me!

464 Charm for bruise

I have a charm for bruising,
I have a charm for blackening,
I have a charm for streaming
And for streaking.

I have a charm for disease known,
I have a charm for disease unknown,
I have a charm for disease of sorcery,
And for relief.

Be no venom nor complaint,
Be no blemish nor maggot
Upon thy four quarters,
Thou poor, precious beast,
That shall not be taken from thee
With the sigh of the north wind,
With cold running water
And urine of man tonight.

Bite and sip,
Chew and gulp;
If thou art to live, live;
If thou art not to live, begone;

If thou wilt come, come,
If thou wilt not come, abide;
If thou live, live,
If thou live not, so be it.

465 Charm for fleshworm

Death–verse of black insect,
Death–verse of evil insect,
Death–verse of wasting insect
Of every sort.

Fierce fleshworm
  Of many feet
That caused great pain
  Throughout flesh.

466 Charm for healing

I make for thee
Charm for horses,
Charm for cattle,
Charm for venom
And for...

Charm for worm,
Charm for wound,
Charm for ache,
Charm for sinew
And for displaced bone.

Death to thy pang,
Decay to thy worm,
Fullness to thy flow;
If pained thou art this day,
Blithe be thou tomorrow.

In name of the King of life,
In name of the Christ of love,
In name of the Spirit Holy,
Triune of grace.

467 Charm for chest disease

The hands of God be round thee,
  The eye of God be over thee,
The love of the King of the heavens
  Drain from thee thy pang.

Away! away! away!
  Dumbly! dumbly! dumbly!
Thy venom be in the ground,
  Thy pain be in the stone!

For a cure, they first blew on the finger–tips and then rubbed with the points of the five fingers the front of the shoulder; the galar toll *(chest disease) was before and behind the shoulder,* air chùl agus air bhial na gualainn.

The arrow which came with fright,
  Salt which heals pain,
The prayer prayed by Jesus Christ,
  To still the fairy arrow.

468 Charm for spaul

I have a charm for spaul,
I have a charm for bruising,
I have a charm for festering
  And for corruption.

I have a charm for disease of hip,
I have a charm for disease of haunch,
I have a charm for disease of spells
  And for the flux.

If good befell that,
May seven times better befall this,
And every complaint that might be thine
  And every ill, beloved.

Bite and sup,
Nibble and gulp,
If thou wilt live, live;
If thou'lt not live, begone!

469 Hide–binding

Teasel to tease thee,
Comb to comb thee,
Card to card thee,
Cat to scratch thee
In dole and in dolour;

And an old yellow hag,
Purring and taloned,
Putting on thee thy flecking,
Taking from thee thy hide–binding.

In peace and in comfort,
Full of marrow and sap,
Full of tallow and fat,
Full of pith and power,
Full of blood and flesh
May I see thee!

Be thy healing on the Being
Who created sea and land,
Who created man and neat,
Who created thee and me,
Thou hidebound one!

470 Charm

Living charm sent of quiet Brigit
To Patrick noble, beauteous,
For wound, for worm,
For gulping throat,
For rose, for swelling, for kidney,
For wounding, for festering,
For skin disease, for ulcer,
For serpent, for venom,

For illness in thy veins,
But be it for good and for excellence
  Upon thy flocks and upon thy herds;
If thou hast it up
Between the tips of thy two ears,
  Between the bases of thy two soles,
May it ebb from thee downward
As ebbs the ocean,
  Into the belly of the great whale
  And of beasts themselves,
  Till these divide each other;
As Jesus healed the people,
  It is in His nature to heal each of these distresses.

Miscellaneous

471 Baby boy

Baby boy fair art thou! fair art thou! fair art thou!
Baby boy fair art thou! turn thee hither.

My dear and my darling,
Thou wouldst climb the hill,
A lad at thy back
Holding hound upon leash.

Baby boy fair art thou! fair art thou! fair art thou!
Baby boy fair art thou! turn thee hither.

My dear and my love,
Thou wouldst climb the height;
Sure is thine hand
On Blàthbheinn out yonder.

My joy and my pride
Is the little foam of ocean,
A pleated kilt upon thee,
And red on the fawn.

My joy and my sense
Is the dusky son of Alpin;
With bow and with shield,
And thou hunting on the peaks.

Before a MacLeod came to Alba
Those heroes were saying
That our chief was renowned
In far Germany.

Before a MacLeod came from Lochlann,
Those stalwarts were battling;
None would say 'twas their poorness
  Has left us tonight so few.

Baby boy fair art thou! fair art thou! fair art thou!
Baby boy fair art thou! turn thee hither.

472 Mac Shiamain

Mac Shiamain sought to be at work;
He sought to be setting down,
He sought to be lifting up,
He sought to be active,
He sought to be blithe,
He sought to be diligent,
He sought to be mannerly,
But Mac Shiamain sought to be at work.

He'll bring wildcat from cairn,
He'll bring cormorant from crag,
He'll bring deer from height,
He'll bring seal from skerry.

He sought to be combing,
He sought to be carding,
He sought to be wool–smoothing,
He sought to be wool–anointing;
He sought to be praying,
He sought to be supplicating,
He sought to be bending
Knee and head to the Father;
And Mac Shiamain sought to be at work.

473 The vixen

Catherine's the wench
   Perverse and uncivil,
Unloveable, not plump,
   Graceless and dour;
'Tis my prayer each morning
To the court of the angels
That I be shielded from the hussy
   Headstrong and hard,
That she be not healthy
   Nor long-lived nor lasting!

'Tis my prayer each evening
Both Sunday and week-day
That the she-fool be stowed
   With the rabble of the graves;
Shortened be the life
Of herself and her people,
Her goats and her sheep,
   Her stock and her kine:
Be they stolen and plundered,
   Be they blasted and burned!

On her sheep be disease
Virulent, filthy,
With scab and with maggot,
   Rot and bloody flux,
Be they wasted by venom,
Be they sundered by dogs,
By honey-hound, by fierce wolf,
   By russet fox!

'Tis my prayer each hour
To the Crown of grace
That Catherine and her cows
   Be hapless and wan,
That she have no daughter nor son,
Her cows no calf nor milk,
No fatness and no cheer,

No comely look nor beauty,
But be each night and day
Sulky and glum.

Be her summer short,
Surly and grim,
Her winter long,
Flaying with cold,
Her spring snowy,
Shrivelled, hard,
Her autumn ice-sheeted,
Grievous, sullen,
Storm-harassed, disastrous,
Calamitous, evil,
Sharpening outward,
Shortening inward,
Dearth to southward,
Dearth to northward,
Dearth eastward and westward
I ask be hers eternally!

Dearth from below be hers,
Dearth from above,
Dearth from on high be hers,
Dearth from beneath,
Dearth be east of her,
Dearth be west,
Dearth be south of her,
Dearth be north,
The dearth of the seven
Miserable dearths
For ever and for ever
I ask be hers eternally!

I pray to Peter,
I pray to Paul,
I pray to James,
I pray to John,
To John the Baptist,
To Luke the Physician,

And to every saint
  And apostle that has followed them,
To kindly Columba
  And saintly Patrick,
To Mary mild
  And Brigit beloved,
To Ariel resplendent
  And to Michael of the blades,
To the Light of peace
  And to the Seer of the hills,
To guard and to keep me,
  On sea and on land,
From the vixenish wench
  In yonder town,
The vixenish wench
  In yonder town!

474 Melodious one of the mountains

My lover found me in my sleep,
I wearying for his coming;
I crouching beneath rough rocks,
Oh King! how shameful the condition.

I without understanding or reason,
Oh King! tearful was the awaking;
That grace for which I seek,
'Tis a breath of the Spirit of prayer.

It was Thou, O King Who art on the throne,
Who didst make for me the day in its season;
I in the wilderness of the mountains,
Thy warmth sheltered me from the cold.

Many are the ways of evil habits
To disturb the flesh of the sinful;
O Christ, ere I am laid in the tomb,
Place Thou the power of Thy righteousness within me.

Thou throned King of glory,
Thou great Being Who hast redeemed me
From the foolish ways of sin
To which my nature cleaves;

From the sins corrupt
Which have caused temptation to my soul,
From the sins deceiving
That would conquer me despite my will.

Though mine were the world
And all the wealth upon its surface,
Though mine were every treasure,
All pomp and all grandeur;

Though I should get and have them in my grasp,
I would give them all away,
If but the Father of salvation
Might with His arm encircle me.

O Thou great God enthroned,
Succour me betimes with Thy goodness;
Make my sins unclean
To part from me this night.

For the sake of Thine anguish and Thy tears,
For the sake of Thy pain and Thy passion,
Good Son of Mary, be in peace with me
And succour me at my death!

Thou art my precious Lord,
Thou art my strong pillar,
Thou art the sustenance of my breast:
Oh part Thou from me never!

For mine afflictions forsake me not,
For my tears' sake do not leave me!
Jesu! Thou likeness of the sun,
In the day of my need be near me!

Thou great Lord of the sun,
In the day of my need be near me;

Thou great Being of the universe,
Keep me in the surety of Thine arms!

Leave me not in dumbness,
Dead in the wilderness;
Leave me not to my stumbling,
For my trust is in Thee, my Saviour!

Though I had no fire,
Thy warmth did not fail me;
Though I had no clothing,
Thy love did not forsake me.

Though I had no hearth,
The cold did not numb me;
Though I knew not the ways,
Thy knowledge was around me.

Though I was in weakness,
The hinds showed me kindness;
Though I had no light,
The night was as the day.

Though I had no bed,
I lacked not for sleep,
For Christ's arm was my pillow,
His eye supreme was my protection.

Though I was forlorn,
Hunger came not near me,
For Christ's Body was my food,
The Blood of Christ, it was my drink.

Though I was without reason,
Thou forsookest me not a moment;
Though I was without sense,
Thou didst not choose to leave me.

Though the stones were diamonds,
Though they were dollars of gold,
Though the whole ocean were wine,
Offered to me of right;

Though the earth were of cinnamon
And the lakes were of honey,
Dearer were a vision of Christ
In peace, in love, in pity.

Jesu, meet Thou my soul!
Jesu, clothe me in Thy love!
Jesu, shield Thou my spirit!
Jesu, stretch out to me Thine hand!

475 Thou black cock

Ho ro, it is long, long,
  Ho ro, long it seems to us,
Long it seems that thou dost tarry,
  Thou black cock that speakst to us.

But wert thou but to come,
  My heart would beat fast with joy,
I should get sleep down in Crathie
  So long as a stone were in its ground.

Thou black cock that greetest us with joy,
  Gladsome the wood that hears thy voice;
When I enter my house at middle night,
  My loved little bird mourns me without.

A step that I took into the thorns,
  Christ was my comrade in the ditch;
He led me to a great highway
  With His mercy, His greatness, His beauty.

Thou man who setst me among the cairns
  And sentest the townland rabble after me,
'Twas thou didst help me to my straits,
  'Twas thou didst set me in conflict with the deer.

Thou woman who raisedst the din yonder
  And didst send the dogs upon my track,
I drank the milk of thy two breasts
  And I lay nine months within thy womb.

Early in the morning when I awakened
  I saw joyous stir in the house of the marriage;
My earnest hope is in the King of life
  That it be I who shall divine the light's meaning.

A glance that I cast behind my back,
  Enfolding guardians saw I at my helm,
Peter and Paul and John the Apostle,
  Their eye to the south, in converse close.

Three houses to which God has not gone,
  The feckless one's house without sense at its head,
The house of the slattern without luck or order,
  And the house of the wanton who sought not children.

The sky did awake and the earth did tremble,
  The grey heavy–bodied ocean was rent,
The star darkened and the wave roared,
  When the body of the Son of God was torn upon the cross.

Woe and woe for my plight this night!
  Poor the stock wherefrom I am fashioned,
The evil tree, decayed, without vigour or pith,
  Alas and alas, without richness or substance!

But Thou, O Christ, gentle Son of Mary,
  Thou Being Who puttest sap in wood,
Pour Thy grace into the bones unfruitful,
  Pour Thy light into the eyes of the blind!

Pour Thy dew into the joints unpliant,
  Pour Thy salve into the eyes without light,
Lead Thou my soul to the dwelling of the martyrs,
  Sustain my feet to the home of the saints!

476 The lullaby of the snow

Cold, cold this night is my bed,
  Cold, cold this night is my child,
Lasting, lasting this night thy sleep,
  I in my shroud and thou in mine arm.

Over me creeps the shadow of death,
  The warm pulse of my love will not stir,
The wind of the heights thy sleep–lulling,
  The close–clinging snow of the peaks thy mantle.

Over thee creeps the hue of death,
  White angels are floating in the air,
The Son of grace each season guards thee,
  The Son of my God keeps the watch with me.

Though loud my cry my plaint is idle,
  Though sore my struggle no friend shares it;
Thy body–shirt is the snow of the peaks,
  Thy death–bed the fen of the valleys.

Thine eye is closed, thy sleep is heavy,
  Thy mouth to my breast, but thou seekest no milk;
My croon of love thou shalt never know,
  My plaint of love thou shalt never tell.

A cold arm–burden my love on my bosom,
  A frozen arm–burden without life or breath;
May the angels of God make smooth the road,
  May the angels of God be calling us home.

A hard frost no thaw shall subdue,
  The frost of the grave which no spring shall make
    green,
A lasting sleep which morn shall not break,
  The death–slumber of mother and child.

Heavenly light directs my feet,
The music of the skies gives peace to my soul,
Alone I am under the wing of the Rock,
Angels of God calling me home.

Cold, cold, cold is my child,
Cold, cold is the mother who watches thee,
Sad, sad, sad is my plaint,
As the tinge of death creeps over me.

O Cross of the heavens, sign my soul,
O Mother of breastlings, shield my child,
O Son of tears whom a mother nurtured,
Show Thy tenderness in death to the needy.

477 Late it was I saw yestreen

Late it was I saw yestreen
A red–robed man upon the glen;
My heart rejoiced at his step,
Methought it was thyself I saw.

Methought it was thyself I saw,
Hunter of venison of the dun deer,
Traveller of the heaths and hills,
Hunter of a thousand mighty stags.

Hunter of a thousand mighty stags,
May gentle Brigit be close to thee,
May gentle Mary guard thy body,
Fair white Michael guard thy head.

478 Sleep has forsaken me

Sleep has forsaken me since Shrovetide,
Often I turn
In hope to see thy speeding ship
On black–blue ocean.

Surpassing swift thy bark grey–timbered
From the slope of Lochlann,
Each plank of her smooth as the swans' plumage
On a loch's billows.

Of Alba's three prime warriors one far faring,
This grieves me sore,
Far afield without folk or dwelling
In the Isle of Man.

Would, Oh King! that thy grief's burden
Were spread in thy land,
Upon each man his share, and on me
Full share of three!

Love of youths art thou on a morning early
In van of battle,
Love of women in mirth of evening
When harp is playing.

This I would ask, a blade in thy right hand
In a narrow pass,
There encountering them who hate thee,
Blood blinding them.

There would come the carrion–crow and raven
At the dawn's breaking,
Would drink their fill from the pools
Brimming, blood–red.

479 The Macleods' petition

Wind from the west
On the tooth of Neist,
Wind and more,
Mist and rain;
Sea concealing
Earth and heaven;
Clan Donald
On broken planking,
No shred of sense left them —
I pity not their bawling!
  Skiff crank and narrow,
Masts tall and stout,
Sails coarse and bulging,
Cargo of empty barrels,
Spindrift flying
Up to heaven,
Brine blinding them,
And Cuan nan Gallan free to them.
  Bilge to thwarts,
Bailer brittle,
Sails ripping,
Fog suffocating,
Snow choking,
Sea swelling,
Men straining,
And every orifice gaping.
  Crew weak-handed,
Haughty, ignorant,
Big of speech,
Small of sense,
Scant of reason,
Blind of action,
Ugly of form,
Without respect to God or men!

480 The Cats are come on us

The Cats are come on us,
The Cats are come on us,
The Cats are come on us,
The Cats are come on us,
They are come on us.

To break in upon us,
To lift the spoil from us,
To steal the kine from us,
To cudgel our horses,
To strip bare our houses,
They are come on us.

They are come, they are come,
They are come, they are come,
They are come, they are come,
They are come in the ill hour,
They are found amidst us.

The Cats are come, Cats are come,
The Cats are come, Cats are come,
The Cats are come, Cats are come,
The Cats are come in the evil hour,
Their stroke is upon us.

The children of wicked men
In storm and in wind
Are in the heathery hollows,
Their blood on the field,
Their shafts by their sides,
And their quivers well filled.

The Cats are come on us,
The Cats are come on us,
The Cats are come on us,
The Cats are come on us,
They are come upon us.

For murder and for mauling
They are come,
For howling and for hazard
They are come,
For pillage and for plunder,
In rain and in wind,
To lift the calving kine
  They are come upon us.

The Cats are come,
The Cats are come,
The Cats are come,
The Cats are come,
Cats are come on us,
The Cats are come in the evil hour,
  Their stroke is upon us.

To drive the calving kine,
To lift away the sheep,
For blood and for wrath,
For weeping and for wailing,
For blood and for wrath,
Marching on Thursday,
  They are come upon us.

481 Little bird

Little bird! O little bird!
I wonder at what thou doest,
Thou singing merry far from me,
I in sadness all alone!

Little bird! O little bird!
I wonder at how thou art,
Thou high on the tips of branching boughs,
I on the ground a–creeping!

Little bird! O little bird!
Thou art music far away,
Like the tender croon of the mother loved
In the kindly sleep of death.

482 Thou speckled troutling

Thou speckled little beauteous troutling,
Where is the lover of my love?
Is he beyond the boisterous waves,
Holding combat with heroes?

Thou speckled little beauteous troutling,
Where is the lover of my mind?
Is he out on the gloomy mountain
Along with the "Gruagach" of the cairn?

Thou speckled little beauteous troutling,
Where is the lover of my heart?
Is he in the Isle of Youth,
Along with Osgar, Connlaoch and Fraoch?

Thou speckled little beauteous troutling,
Where is the lover of my breast?
Is he in Alba or in Erin,
Or behind the sun asleep?

Thou speckled little beauteous troutling,
Is the Son of the Virgin with my love?
And may I my sorrow leave
In the River that fails not for aye?

Waulking Songs

483 The apple tree

O apple tree,
Apple branch,
Apple tree,
Tree of apples.

When thou goest to the wood to strip it,
Recognise the tree which is mine there,
The tree of softest, sweetest apples,
The branching pear-like tree full of apples,
Its roots growing and its top bending.

I have a tree in the Green Rock,
Another tree hard by the garden gate;
If Mackay were but here,
Or the redoubtable Neil, his brother,
My dower would not go unpaid,
With milch kine and heifers in calf,
With sheep black-faced and white,
And with geldings for the ploughing.

A versatile man is Mackay,
He can make silk of May wool,
And satin of heather if need were;
He can make wine of mountain water.

An ingenious man is Mackay,
He can dry grain without fuel,
It is with his fists he bruises it.

Mackay of the gusseted coat
Would not require heavy armour;
Rider of the chestnut horses,
He would put golden shoes on their hooves,
Traverser of the broken ground.

My dear, my love is the valiant youth,
I would go with thee through the branchy wood,
I would fashion and sew thy shirt
With slender needle and pure–white thread;
I would wash it thereafter
On slippery slab in the bright river;
I would dry it on the tips of the branches,
I would place it folded in thy page's hand.

O apple tree, may God be with thee,
May the moon and the sun be with thee,
May the east and west winds be with thee,
May everything that ever existed be with thee,
May every bounty and desire be with thee,
May every passion and divinity be with thee,
May great Somerled and his band be with thee,
May everyone, like myself, be with thee.

My dear, my love is the sportive youth,
Who would dance vigorously, merrily, spiritedly;
On the tops of the bens we would be mirthful,
On the brae of the glens we would be [gay.]
At the base of the bens we would be [cheerful.]
On the top of the waves we would be [sportive.]

484 The apple tree

O apple tree, apple branch,
O apple tree o ho,
Apple tree, flourishing apple tree,
O apple tree o ho.

O apple tree, may God be with thee,
May moon and sun be with thee,
May east and west winds be with thee,
May the great Creator of the elements be with thee,
May everything that ever existed be with thee,
May great Somerled and his band be with thee.

I have a tree in the Fowling Rock,
And another tree hard by the garden gate.

When thou goest to the wood to strip it
Recognise the tree which is mine there,
The branching pear-like tree full of apples,
Its base firmly rooted and its top bending,
The tree with softest and sweetest apples.

An ingenious man is Mackay,
He can dry grain without fuel,
With his feet he removes the awns,
And with anger he bruises it.
A versatile man is Mackay,
He can make silk of May wool,
He can make wine of mountain water,
He can make butter of the pure-white foam.

If Mackay were but here,
Or the redoubtable Neil, his brother,
My dower would not be unpaid,
Milch kine and heifers in calf would be there,
Sheep black-faced and white would be there,
Geldings would be there for ploughing
And goats going to mountain pastures.

Mackay of the gusseted coat
Is the rider of chestnut horses,
Rider of the slender steeds,
Who would put shoes of gold on their hooves,
Who traversed the broken ground.

My dear, my love is the sportive youth,
Who would dance lightly, royally, spiritedly,
On the top of the waves we would be sportive,
At the base of the bens we would be cheerful.

My dear, my love is the splendid youth
Who is out in the great branchy wood,
With thee I would cross the Irish Sea.

485 Hugh son of Archibald the clerk

Thou tall man from the Coolin hills,
Strong art thou, mighty thy blow;
My seven curses on thy foster–mother
That she did not press on thee with knee or elbow
Before thou didst slay all the brothers!

I was last night in the house of delirium,
I am tonight in the house of carnage;
I got my share of the large cow,
The fattest and the finest cow.

The cook asked me to eat something:
"Thou churl, wilt thou not look in thy letter?
See yonder three on the bier,
And that other one in the coffin,
And Angus being lashed at Dùn an Sticir."

Dun Donald was taken with the fever,
An ill way did he pass the crisis,
Being pursued with cold dirks,

The great hounds putting him to flight,
The lean spare swift hounds
Driving him under the hooves of gentlemen's horses.

Thou woman yonder who didst vent thine anger,
Who didst loudly clap thy hands,
My little child is unbaptized,
If thou wert a sister to Hector,
To brown-haired John or handsome Angus.

The Great Vicar came from the Lowlands
And did not find one of the brothers alive;
He found Marion and he found Mary,
And he found me, wretch that I am —
I was not of the number (of the dead).
Would that I would see my mother
Running from place to place,
Without shelter or place to rest,
Because of how ill she lamented the brothers.

Be quiet, thou woman without sense or understanding!
They are sons to me, if they are brothers to thee;
From my womb they were delivered,
It was my own knee that succoured them,
It was my linen shirt they wetted,
It was the milk of my breasts they swallowed.

I raised the wall and I filled the corn-yard,
Not of the clean dry barley,
Or of the white mealy oats,
But of the young men of my clan.

Tall Hugh, son of Archibald the Clerk,
Where thou liest down, arise not whole!
May the news of thy death reach the women of Sleat,
May thy entrails be in the tail of thy shirt,
And may I have my share in it!

A ro ho lail eo eile
Him bo ho laoil eo
Ro ho no lail eo eile
Him bo ho laoil eo.

486 Rowing song of the oaken galley

My treasure among the men of the sun,
I have seen thee not today nor yesterday.
I have seen no man thy like,
Except thou come, O John son of James,
In thy youth before death has struck thee.
Thou wast the grandson of Roderick the generous,
And great–grandson of Torquil of the keen blades,
Seed of the woman who won esteem;
Thou hast left my spirit grieving and tearful.

'S na hada hia hi 's na hi ho hua.

My treasure among the men of the oar–banks,
When thou wouldst go to thy boat
That was the work that well became thee,
Thy lads would be in the oar–bank,
Thyself wouldst be at thy boat's helm,
A champion–like, valiant, powerful man.

'S na hada hia hi 's na hi ho hua.

My treasure and my ransom and my dower is
Young John, son of James, of the full round eyes,
Blue is thine eye, and it is no mockery,
Yesterday thou didst sail through the Sound of Harris,
And my own good wish to thee for thy safe coming.

'S na hada hia hi 's na hi ho hua.

My treasure among the men of the mountain,
When thou wouldst go to the peaks
Truly thy lodging would not be empty,
But with slender–muzzled gun
Or with the knobbed bow of yew,
Breaking bones wherever it struck,
Welcoming ever him of the belling.

'S na hada hia hi 's na hi ho hua.

My treasure among the men of the sea,
I saw thee passing downward by;
Mayest thou enjoy the tressed maiden of the snood,
Daughter of the lord of Glen Shee,
Of kindred wide–spread and many,
A bright form from the vine–slope art thou,
Thou shalt get a fold of jet–black cattle.

'S na hada hia hi 's na hi ho hua.

My treasure among the men of deftness,
When thou wouldst turn to sailing
She would catch the breeze between the sheets,
The creak of the oars was music for thee,
Rudder behind her and a valiant, skilful man
Steering her in her proper course.

'S na hada hia hi 's na hi ho hua.

My treasure and my ransom and my hoard
Are the men of the black and brown locks
Who would pound the ocean,
Who would souse her oaken timbers,
Who would drink red wine in waves
And who would carry off a spoil.

'S na hada hia hi 's na hi ho hua.

My treasure and my ransom and my dower,
When thou wouldst go to sea
Truly thy hand was not found feeble
Though thou wast but a child;
Wooden pins would be twisted from her oaken planks,
She would shed the rove from every rivet's head;
Thy craft was not decayed,
And thy sailing was not inshore.

'S na hada hia hi 's na hi ho hua.

My treasure and my ransom and my hoard,
Beauty of head grew richly on thee,
Hair in luxuriant precious locks
Well combed, of goodly cut;
And were I a bard I would make an oar-song,
And were I a carpenter I would make ships,
And here behind thee I needs must abide.

'S na hada hia hi 's na hi ho hua.

487 Young John son of Macneil

Ho ho eile ho i o hu o,
Ho hi o hu o,
Ho ho eile ho i o hu o.

I am the poor woman
Who has been harried,

Ho hi o hu o.

It is not my cattle
Or my horses,
Or that my corn-stacks
Have been scattered;
It is not that my corn-yard
Has gone up in flames,

Or that my mows
Have been plundered;
It is not that my daughter
Has died in childbed,
That drives a woman
To lament a space;

It is not that has harried me,
But that my courtier
Is in prison in Glasgow,
And that they are threatening
To send him to England,
Or to Edinburgh
Of the hundred fashions.
Were a ransom accepted
For my child,
The cattle would not be
Adown the glens;
Horses would not be
Carrying seaweed;
There would be no white
Sheep on the hills.
Goodly son of MacNeil
Once of the Castle,
It is my hand that
Used to bathe thee,
It is my knee that
Used to nurse thee,
It is my breast that
Used to swell thee.
Goodly son of MacNeil
From the tower and the Castle,
Thou didst kill the colonel,
Thou didst wound the captain;
Thou didst bring thine own
Force home with thee,
The host with brown hair
And curling locks;
Thou didst leave the Lowlanders

Dead without life,
The host with polls
Red and bristly.
I am tortured
And tormented,
In my mansion,
In my storehouse;
My sleeping-chamber,
My bedroom:
Though woe is me for that,
It is not what has harried me!

488 Waulking song

Hug oireannan o hi a bho,
Hi ri ri o hi ri a bho.

Last night it was I did not sleep.
Though my morning rising was early,
It was not that I had slept much,
But I was worrying about the stirks since the night was long,
And worrying about all in my charge.

Heavy is thy sleep, James,
When thou didst not reach me today or yesterday.

I would escort a company in along the hillside.
Young gallant, thou didst wrap me in thy plaid,
But though thou didst, I gave thee the slip.
It was not that I hated to have thy kiss,
But for fear of my fair fame in the morning,
For fear of the fault-finder and the parson.

I escorted a company past the cattlefold,
I thought that they were gentlemen;
They were but contemptible churls.
They reached the mouth of the cave;
My own three brothers were asleep there;

They thrust their cold dirks in them;
My own palms were a cup to them,
Drawing water to their cold wounds;
I had thrown away the cogue and lost the spancel.

A boat was seen entering the narrows,
A woman in its stern ever weeping,
A woman in its prow with hair dishevelled.
I asked them the reason for their weeping.
"It is not a lament for the calves,
Nor a lament for the lean stirks,
Nor a lament for the pairs of sheep,
But my three sons are lost in the battle,
And the three brothers are on either side of them."

489 Waulking song

Sad, sad am I,
Climbing the hill and descending it.
My heart fell since many a day,
Fiddle nor harp will raise it,
Nor war-pipe of the shrill reeds.
It was I who had the brothers
Who would gamble, drink and pay,
Who would play at backgammon
And with white and speckled cards,
And with white ivory dice.
My foster-mother said to my Saviour
That it was not Friday that was rearing them,*
But the Monday at the beginning of the quarter,
Or the Lord's Day, the Sabbath day.
The witch killed Coll and Ranald,
And little Hector, the son of the...

* It was unlucky to count things on a Friday (Nicolson, *Gaelic Proverbs,* 407; J.G. Campbell, *Witchcraft and Second Sight in the Scottish Highlands,* 299).

Would, O King, that she would come,
With her hand wounded and her leg broken,
Seeking a leech in every port,
And no leech in the land but I;
By my hand, I would take courage,
I would bend bone and draw blood;
When I would close thy coffin's lid,
I would pile earth on the brink of thy tomb.

Son of the generous John of Moidart,*
I am the poor sorrowful tearful woman;
It is not for the fewness of my cattle.
Like the generous John of Moidart
Ships went not under sail for thee,
The Red Hand did not go into action for thee,
But white trimmed staves.
Son of the generous John of Moidart,
No lying dirge was chanted over thee;
Woe is me that thou art being shrouded;
I saw a day when there was need of thee;
The day of Cnoc nan Dos thou wast keen;
The day of Kilsyth thou wast active,
Thou didst spill blood and cut sinews,
Thou didst leave the enemy badly mangled,
Women taking leave of their senses,
Men being bandaged as was needful.

There is no sleep for me; I lie awake,
I cannot make merry or divert myself;
I have seen thy wood being stripped,
The rider of the black horse was in the van,
The rider of the sable steed.

The rider of the prancing well-shod charger
With his golden spurs and his boots that would not crack.

* Donald, eleventh of Clan Ranald, who died in Canna in 1686. He had played a distinguished part in the Civil War in Scotland and Ireland.

Sad, sad am I, climbing
The hill and descending it.

Hill–irinn o ho huill o ro bha ho,
Hill–irinn e ho ho ro huill o ho ro.

490 Waulking song

'Twas late that I heard the hunt
Between Bay Head and the ford,
Not voice of wrangling nor voice of hound,
But voice of woman on the crest of her joy.
A band of young men after me,
And if it was thyself who didst choose them,
Thou didst take the worst and reject the choice
And refuse the youth of skill and courage.
A good reaper on a harvest day,
Thou shalt go to the hill where the hunt will be,
Thy dog and thy lad shall be after thee,
And thou shalt take the deer from the forefront of the herd.

My petition to the King of the sun
That thou be not destroyed in right nor in wrong,
In exchange of sword nor of shield,
Nor at the drinking of deceiving beer.

I gave my love to the son of the weaving–woman,
Spouse of the womanly maidens,
'Tis to thee I'd trust my life
Going around Rubha na Gaillinn,
And going on land at Port na h–Eala

E ho hao ri ho ho gu,
E ho haoi ri ri hao ri ri,
Hi ho ri ri,
E ho hao ri ho ro,
E ho hao ri ri o.

491 Duncan Mac Cuilcein

It is Duncan Mac Cuilcein
Who has brought a flood on every road;

Who has brought a flood on every place
Though the Judgment has not yet come.

There was neither timber nor iron
Nor anything that could be dragged

But was down in the Back Ford
With the scouring of the stream.

I shall see Diarmaid's Chapel
A fishing–rock yet,

And if the Rough Ford rises
There will be corn unbound.

I shall see Teisteamal of the barley
With the water in its midst,

And the Chapel of the Clan MacColl
With the sea about its breached walls.

Where is the cornyard or the kiln
Or the place where my father was?

It is not of that I complain
But the resting–place of the bones.

E ho i bho i a bho,
A hoill a bho,
E ho i a bho hi ri ho ro,
E ho i a bho hoill a bho ho ro.

492 A missing knife

Na ho i eadh ho ho ill a bhi,
Na ho ibh o ha o ri ho a ro,
Na ho hao ri o bho leathag.

I lost the beautiful knife
  On Sunday just past,

It was no longer than a needle
  And it was better than a sword.

It fell among the rushes
  And I have not found it yet;

I am tired searching for it
  At the foot of the slope.

I would not give it on loan
  To mother or father,

Or to Angus MacDiarmid —
  Were he to ask, he would not get it.

493 Waulking song

I ho haoi ri ho ro.

My love is to thee, son of the laird of Sórasdal!
I hate the man who has cast thee down,
And against him who destroyed his country
That will yet come to be reckoned,
The Campbells will be driven out,
And the rabble of the sowens scattered.

Sad that I and my chosen love
Were not in yonder wood arising;
Well would I wash thy shirt,
I would dry it on the tips of the boughs,
I would set it clean in thy page's hand.

Sad that I and the splendid youth
Were not on the summit of the sharp steep peaks,
With no living man beholding us.
In good repute we would come home,
The red snood would be folded by,
The peaked kertch would come into fashion.

494 A St Kilda waulking song

Hill hu hill ho,
Hill ho ro bha ho,
Hill hu hill ho,
Thou wouldst be my support didst thou come.

I should prefer to all the cattle I have got
To be in St Kilda plucking the guillemots,
Hill hu ho

Along with the grey–billed solan goose
Which snatches the fish from the surface of the current.
Hill hu ho

Thou youth with the top–boots,
Thou wilt go to the byre before I can sit down.
Hill hu ho

Thou wouldst dance strongly and vigorously,
Without ever bending thy knees.
Hill hu ho

Thou wilt bring the fulmar and the garefowl,
And the cormorant from the point of the cape.
Hill hu ho

Thou wilt go to the great mainland of Kintail
Along with Ivar of Ardbrae.
Hill hu hill ho

495 Little sister of love

Little sister of love,
Art thou asleep?

Ill–i–rinn is ho ro,
Ill–i–rinn is ho ro.

If thou art, thou
Hast no cause;

Take that with thee if thou hast heard it.
Hi–ibh o ho hi,
Na hi hiuraibh o ro hi.

The brother of ours
Who was in Ireland,

O hoireann o ho ro i
Hoireann o hi ri eile.

Yesterday early they had
Upon the staves.

I was beside them
And the rest not seeing me;

Awhile on the ground I was,
Awhile on horseback,

And awhile from their sight
In a green veil folded.

Little sister of sisters,
Art thou asleep?

Take that with thee as thou hast heard it.
Hi–ibh o ho hi,
Na hi hiuraibh o ro hi.

The brother of ours
Who was in Ireland,

Yesterday they had him
Upon the staves.

496 Little sister, my love

Little sister, my love
Art thou asleep?

Ill–i–rinn is ho ro,
Ill–i–rinn is ho ro.

The brother of ours
Who was in Ireland,

Hi–ibh o ho hi,
Na hi hiuraibh o ro hi.

The brother of ours
Who was in Ireland,

Ill–i–rinn is ho ro,
Ill–i–rinn is ho ro.

Yesterday early they had
Upon the staves.

Hi–ibh o ho hi,
Na hi hiuraibh o ro hi.

Yesterday early they had
Upon the staves.

Ill–i–rinn is ho ro,
etc.

I was beside them
And the rest not seeing me,

Awhile on the ground I was,
Awhile on horseback,

And awhile from their sight
In a green veil folded.

I shall give thee a sign
Of thy dream:

The great byre that
Holds the cattle,

It will be tomorrow
In red flames;

And that little child
Thou hast in thine arms,

Thou wilt find him dead
At the edge of thy bed.

Take that home with thee
As thou hast heard it.

The brother of ours
Who was in Ireland,

Yesterday they had him
Upon the staves.

Another version:

Little sister, my love, art thou asleep?
  O hoireann o ho ro i.
If thou art, thou hast no cause;
  I hoireann o hi ri eile.
The brother of ours who was in Ireland,
They had him yesterday in the kirktown.
I was there and the rest not seeing me,
Awhile I was on foot and awhile on horseback,
And awhile shrouded in satin.

Little sister, my love, Catriona,
You have left me on a wild moorland,
A rugged moorland with the rest seeking me.
Little sister, my love and darling,
You will set out early in the morning
And you will find my bones in the hollow;
You will see the colour in the plaiding,
And my mother's brooch hard by it.

Another version:

Little sister of my love, hu ru,
Art thou asleep, hu ru,
Still, my dear? hao ri a hu,
Do not be silent, hu ru!
I shall give a sign, hu ru,
To thee of thy dream, hu ru,
The corn, hao ri a hu,
Thou hast in the barn, hu ru,
It is the bailiffs, hu ru,
Who will scutch it, hu ru!
That byre, hu ru,
In which the cattle are, hu ru,
Will go up in flames, hao ri a hu,
And be burnt to cinders, hu ru!

The spouse thou hast, hu ru,
In thy bed, hu ru,
Will be dead tomorrow, hao ri a hu,
Early in the morning, hu ru!
What will waken thee, hu ru,
Before daybreak, hu ru,
Is the clangour of weapons, hao ri a hu,
And the din of battle, hu ru!

497 Seathan son of the King of Ireland

Woe to him who heard of it and did not tell it,
  Hu ru na hur i bhi o,
Woe to him who heard of it and did not tell it,
  Na bhi hao bho hao bhi o an.*
That my darling was in Minginish;
If thou wert, my love, thou hadst returned long since:
I would send a great ship to seek him there,
With a famed crew, fresh and bright and expert,
Young men and lads would be there,
He would visit here when he returned,
I would spend a festal day dallying with him,
I would sit on a knoll and engage in sweet converse,
I would curl thy hair as I did oft–times,
I would lie in thy arms and keep the dew from thee,
I would wash a fine–spun shirt full white for thee
So long as any water remained in the pool,
And I would dry it on a moorland branch.

But Seathan tonight is a corse,
A sad tale to the men of Scotland,
A grievous tale to his followers,
A joyous tale to his pursuers,
To the son of the Hag of the Three Thorns.

Dear Seathan of the tranquil eyes,
Oft didst thou redden the hillocks:
It was not with the blood of cattle or horses,
Or the blood of the swift deer,
Or the blood of the roe in a nook of the corn–field,
But the blood of thine enemy bent on strangling thee.

When I thought thou wast giving chase,
Thou wast dead in the conflict,
Borne on the shoulders of the young men,
And on the point of being buried.

* Each line of the song is repeated, followed by half the refrain.

When I thought thou wast in Galway,
Thou wast dead without breath,
Borne on the shoulders of manly men,
And as cold as the mountain snow.

My love thy right hand, though now cold,
Oft did I have it, seldom was it away from me,
Oft did I have a present from it,
And never with aught that was mean,
It was not with stick or cudgel,
It was not with abuse or quarrelling,
But with green satin and fine silk,
With the noblest of gifts.

O brown–haired Seathan, calf of my love,
I would go far away with thee, my love,
I would go with thee through the branchy wood
Where the birds are wont to warble,
I would cross the Irish Sea with thee
Where the swelling ocean surges,
I would cross the Sea of Greece with thee,
The haunt of swarthy corsairs.

I and Seathan traversing mountains,
I was weak, but Seathan was strong,
I could endure but little clothing,
A russet coat to the middle of my thigh,
A kerchief of fine pure–white linen,
As I fared with my darling Seathan.

O Seathan, Seathan, bereft of life,
Own son to my king from Tyrconell,
Oft have I lain beneath thy cloak;
If I did, it was not in a homestead,
But in a green hollow in a tree–sheltered field,
Under the slope of the rugged blue peaks,
The wind from the mountains sweeping over us,
The wind from the glens with a sough taking
Its fill of the first burgeoning of spring.

Many a glen and ben we traversed,
I was in Islay and in Uist with thee,
I was in Sleat of the yellow–haired women with thee,
I was in Iona of the nuns with thee,
I was in the land of birds and eggs with thee,
I was in Ireland, I was in Liutha with thee,
I traversed Bhreathann and Bhruthann with thee,
I traversed the Continent and A'Mhuthairn with thee,
I traversed the Boyne, I traversed Munster with thee,*
I heard Mass in Cill Chumha with thee,
I heard the music of the fairy–mansions with thee,
I drank a draught from the well of wandering with thee,
I was the day before yesterday and last year with thee,
I was from cape to cape with thee,
I was in Kildonan of the pines with thee,
I was three years on the hills with thee.

I kept watch for a day in the treetops with thee,
I kept watch for two days in the sea wrack with thee,
I kept watch for a night on a sea rock with thee,
I kept watch, my love, and I did not regret it,
Wrapped in a corner of thy tartan plaid,
The spindrift ever breaking over us,
Water that is very pure, cool and wholesome.

My love is Seathan of the tranquil eyes,
I would lie with thee on an uneasy bed,
A bed of heather with my side on stones;
Dearer Seathan in a coil of heather rope
Than a king's son on bed of linen;
Dearer Seathan behind a dyke
Than a king's son in silks on deal flooring,

* The translation of some of these place names is quite tentative. Liutha probably represents older Letha, which meant both Brittany (Welsh *Llydaw)* and Latium. A' Mhuthairn may represent Munster, but as Munster also occurs here, it may be equated, somewhat arbitrarily, with A' Mhaoirne, the Mearns.

Though he should have a restful bed
Which had been well-planed by wrights,
And protected by power of druids;
Dearer Seathan in the birch wood
Than to be in Magh Meall with Airril,
Though he had satin and silk under his feet,
And pillows lustrous with red gold.

If Seathan were seen as he arose
In shade of hill on a May morning,
A short kilt to the middle of his thigh,
A narrow black belt about his tunic,
His foster-mother's love, his wife's darling,
The sight seven times dearest to his own mother,
A secret lover he is to me.

O brown-haired Seathan, thou gentle hero,
Small is the place in which I would put thee,
I would put thee on the very top of my head,
I would put thee between my breasts,

Between Bride and her soft kerchief,
Between a young maiden and her snood,
Between a fair virgin and her silken mantle,
Between myself and my shirt of linen.

But Seathan is in the lonely chamber,
Without drinking of cups or goblets,
Without drinking of wine from splendid silver tankards,
Without drinking of ale with his cronies and gentlemen,
Without drinking to music, without kiss from seductive woman,
Without music of harp, without listening to melody,
But strait bands on his shoulders,
And looped bands on the bier poles.

I am a sister of Aodh and yellow-haired Brian,
I am a kinswoman of Fionn son of Cumhall,
I am the wife of brown-haired Seathan, the wanderer,

But alas! for those who said I was a joyous wife,
I am a poor, sad, mournful, sorrowful wife,
Full of anguish and grief and woe.

My father put me in a distressing place
On that night he made a wedding-feast for me,
Alas, O King! that it were not my lyke-wake,
That the linen shroud had not been cut for me,
That the pine planks had not been polished for me,
That the loops had not been tied on me,
That I had not been hidden in the mould,
For fear I should be alive on earth.
There is many a table where I shall be slighted,
Where my teeth shall no more chew bread,
Where my spoon shall no more draw,
Where my knife shall no more cut,
Where my fancy shall no more linger.

If Seathan could be but redeemed
The ransom could be got like rushes,
Silver could be got like ashes,
Gold could be got on the fringe of meadows,
Wine could be got like spring water,
Beer could be got like a cool verdant stream;
There would not be a goat in rock or stony upland,
There would not be a young she-goat in meadow,
There would not be a sheep on rocky shelf or mountain top,
There would not be cattle on plain or in fold,
There would not be pig or cow in pastures;
The salmon would come from the seas,
The trout would come from the river-banks,
The geldings would come from the rushes;
There would not be a black or white-shouldered cow
High or low in the fold,
At the edge of township or in stall,
That I would not send, my love, to redeem thee,
Even to my green plaid,
Though that should take the one cow from me,

And it was not the one black cow of my fold,
But herds of white–shouldered cattle,
Of white–headed, white–backed, red–eared cattle.

But Seathan is tonight in the upper town,
Neither gold nor tears will win him,
Neither drink nor music will tempt him,
Neither slaughter nor violence will bring him from his doom,
Neither tumult nor force will wake him from his slumber;
And my heart is broken and distraught,
My tears flow like a well,
Uneasily I sleep on a pillow,
For thou hast no one who pities thee
Save me, running to and fro.

O Seathan dear! O Seathan dear!
I would not give thee to law or king,
I would not give thee to the gentle Mary,
I would not give thee to the Holy Rood,
I would not give thee to Jesus Christ,
I would not, for fear I would not get thee myself.

O Seathan, my brightness of the sun!
Alas! despite me death has seized thee,
And that has left me sad and tearful,
Lamenting bitterly that thou art gone;
And if all the clerics say is true,
That there is a Hell and a Heaven,
My share of Heaven — it is my welcome to death —
For a night with my darling,
With my spouse, brown–haired Seathan.

The other women did not have the song so perfectly, but in a fragmentary state. This is that part of it which Mary Henderson in Morvern knew:

Woe to him who heard of it and did not tell it,
That my darling was in Minginish;
He would visit here when he returned,
And I would spend a festal day dallying with him.

Many a ben and glen we traversed,
I was in Islay and in Mull with thee,
I was in Ireland and in London with thee,
I was in the land of the nuns with thee.

I slept for a night on a sea rock with thee,
I did, my love, and I did not regret it,
Wrapped in a corner of thy tartan plaid,
The spindrift ever breaking over us,
Water that is very pure, cool and wholesome.

Alas! for those who said I was a joyous wife,
For I am a poor, sad, mournful, sorrowful wife,
Uneasily I sleep on a pillow,
For thou hast no one who pities thee,
Save me, running to and fro.

And this is that part of it which Jessie Matheson, Kilmuir, Skye, knew:

Woe to him who heard of it and did not tell it,
That my darling was in Minginish;
He would visit here when he returned,
He would spend a festal day in dallying with me,
I would sit on a knoll and engage in sweet converse with thee,
I would curl thy hair as I did oft–times.

But Seathan is tonight a corse,
A sad tale to his followers,
A joyous tale to his pursuers.

My love thy right hand, though now cold,
Oft did I have it, seldom was it away from me,
And never with aught that was mean,
But often with noble gifts.

My love is Seathan of the tranquil eyes,
I would lie with thee on an uneasy bed,
A bed of heather with its side on stones.

Thou art red Seathan of the hills,
And not with barley or oats
But the blood of the deer wounded by thee.

Seathan is tonight in the upper chamber,
Uneasily I sleep on a pillow,
For thou hast no one who pities thee,
Save me, running to and fro.
If I could but ransom Seathan
I would not leave a cow in the fold,
I would leave neither black nor red of them,
Though that should take my only cow from me,
And not the one black cow of my fold
But herds of the white-shouldered cattle,
Of the white-headed, white-backed, red-eared cattle.

The Sweet Sorrow

Eight versions of Am Bròn Binn (The sweet sorrow) were collected by Dr Carmichael. Here only versions A and B are given. For published versions see: *Leabhar na Féinne,* 208; *Clàrsach na Coille* (1st ed.), 263; Henderson, "Arthurian Motifs in Gadhelic Literature" in *Miscellany in Honour of Kuno Meyer,* 18–33; *Reliquiae Celticae,* i.368; Miss Frances Tolmie's Collection *(Journal of the Folk-Song Society,* vol. iv), no.90.

In some versions the following lines are included, but they do not properly belong. They are the prophecy made to MacDonald of Sleat, by his follower, Maclean of Boreray, before the battle of Leac a' Li, fought against the Macleans. Maclean of Boreray secretly sympathised with the Macleans and he hoped that this forecast, purporting to have been revealed to him in a dream, would discourage the MacDonalds and contribute to their defeat:

O Dùn Dubh! O Dùn Dubh!
Beautiful sunny knoll far from the sea,
Early shall the cuckoo call
On thy shoulder, O Dùn Dubh!

O Dùn Dubh! O Dùn Dubh!
On thee shall much blood be spilt;
On thee shall be slain the Red Knight
Before sword is returned to its black sheath.

O Leac a' Li! O Leac a' Li!
On thee shall peace be proclaimed;
It is the Clan Maclean who shall have victory
Over the host that invades their land.

498 The sweet sorrow

A day that Arthur of the waves
Went to the hill of triumphs to hunt,
There was seen coming from the plain
A maid of fairest form under the sun.
There was a harp in the hand of the young damsel
Of sweetest kiss and brightest mien;
And sweetly though she played the harp,
Sweeter the voice which accompanied it.
It was at the sound of her sweet harpstrings
That the king sank into gentle sleep;
And when he awoke from his slumber,
Quickly his hand reached for his weapons.
Concerning the girl who had played the music,
Who had not been seen alive or dead,
Sir Gawain spoke right generously:
"I shall go myself to seek her for thee,
Myself, my lad and my hound,
The three of us the woman to seek."
He set off with his lad and his hound,
And with his fair, white-sailed, lofty ship.
He was seven months at sea
Ere he saw solid earth
Where he could bring the ship to land.
He saw in the brightness of the sea
Stones of price with green water-cress,
Windows of glass on the gable,
Plenteous there were cups and horns.

Sir Gawain was at its base,
A black chain was suspended from above,
And the chain which did not quiver
Carried him aloft at a run.
He saw the tender gentle maid
On a chair of gold within,
A carpet of silk beneath her soles,
And the hero greeted her fair face.

"Has God blessed thee, man?
Deep is the love that has brought thee across the waves;
If the lord of this castle be in health
He knows no mercy or pity."
"I am most impatient that he comes not,
I shall do battle with him speedily."
"How wouldst thou do that when thou
Art not the best warrior under the sun?
For no weapon will draw blood from the man
But his own bright white sword."
"Let us promote speech and abate wrath,
Let us lay a trap for the giant;
Let us steal his sword from the man,
So will we take off his head."
I saw newly come from the sea
A young warrior wounded by weapons;
He had a golden spur on his right foot,
Full elegant were his dress and form.
He had another spur about his left foot
Of royal silver or inlaid gold;
I made to seize his spur,
But if I did, it was not good sense;
He grasped his weapon and to be
Near him was to be a dead man.

"A truce! a truce! great warrior,
I am alive and near my weapons,
Tell me of a truth thy tidings,
Who thou art or what thy name."
"I am the victorious fortunate Bile,
It is I who shall have the house of melody;
Is there any doubt I shall be king?
Over against me were the Greeks.
It is I shall have the wife
With fairest cheek and whitest teeth,
It is I shall have the ship
Which will leave the wash behind;
It is I shall have the horse

Which swiftest struck hoof on grass,
It is I shall have the hound
Which malice or violence will not affect."
They moved to the house on the rock,
There thou canst verify my tale;
That is how I rode the horse
Of swiftest and most prancing pace.
Riding furiously across the ocean,
Cantering over the surface of the sea,
I saw the hound–loving battalion of three
In close combat about the woman.
I shall still the combat,
I shall take it on myself to check them,
The three brothers, my sad tale!
In sad combat about the woman.
I am the hero who was never affrighted,
The eldest son of the King of France;
By me fell the two sons of the King of Greece,
It is they themselves who killed the third one.
If thou desirest to take me with thee,
Dig a grave for the King of Greece's children;
That is how I dug the grave,
Since it is the work of a madman
To dig, at the request of a captive woman,
A grave to please herself.
She leapt down into the pit,
The wise woman of fairest hue;
The soul sprang out of her body,
Alas! tonight it is woe.
If only I had then a leech,
I had used him at that time,
I had brought her to life once more,
I had not left my love in the grave.
On the mount of the way of the true words,
On Thy right hand, O Son of God,
May I be on the Day of Doom.
That is the end of my tale,
And how the Sweet Sorrow was sung.

499 The sweet sorrow

The King of Britain saw in his sleep
The woman of fairest hue under the sun,
And he would rather be beloved of her
Than have converse with a man like himself.

Then spoke Sir Gawain right generously,
"I shall go myself to seek her for thee,
Myself, my lad and my hound,
The three of us the woman to seek."

Seven weeks and three months
I was weary traversing the sea
Ere harbour or land was won
Or a place where the ship might lie.

Nearing the edge of the rough sea
A smooth azure castle was seen,
It had windows of glass facing the waves,
And plenteous there were cups and horns.

When they won in to its base
A black chain came down;
Neither fear nor trembling seized me,
I went up on it at a run.

The young white–coifed lady was seen
On a chair of gold within,
A carpet of silk beneath her soles;
I greeted her fair face.

"O gallant who has come from the sea,
Cool is thy greeting to us;
Come, place thy head on my knee,
That I might play the harp to thee and sing."

A harp there was in the lap of the fair young damsel,
Of bluest eye and whitest teeth,
And sweetly though she played the harp,
Sweeter than that the song from her lips.

He fell into a deep sleep
After voyaging on the rough sea
...
...

She took the sharp sword from his baldric,
And she swept off his head by stealth;
That is the end of my tale
And how the Sweet Sorrow is sung.

Fairy Songs

500 **Fairy song**

Away, John, away!
  A ho a hau.
Away, John, away!
  A ho a hi.

Make for the house,
  A ho a hau.
Swift as the arrow.
  A ho a hi.

Away, John, away,
  With the speed of thy feet,
And come not back
  With a host to the land.

Away, John, away!
  A ho a hau.
Away, John, away!
  A ho a hi.

501 Fairy song

O little Morag,
A-climbing bens,
Descending glens,
A-climbing bens,
O little Morag,
A-climbing bens,
Tired thou art,
And the calves lost.

502 Fairy song

Girdle beloved, rise not,
  Hu ru bhi hu ho.
If thou rise I shall be tearful,
  Hu ru bhi hu ho.
  Ho hoile a bha ho hi,
  Ocha ro chall eile.
If thou rise not I shall be lightsome,
I shall be merry, I shall be joyful,
If thou leave me free to stride,
Free to sport and free to leap,
Free to ride on holiday.

503 Fairy song

'Tis I that am pained
For the woman that was in Dùn Trò.

  Aparain duibh o hi ho,
  Ro hu ill o ho.

Where I lost my brothers
And my three young babes.

Aparain duibh o hi ho,
Ro hu ill o ho.

My father and my mother
Are laid under the sod.

Aparain duibh o hi ho,
Ro hu ill o ho.

504 Fairy song

The bairnies of this townland,
This townland, this townland,
The bairnies of this townland
Will be romping on a knoll.

Romping, romping,
Romping on a knoll,
Romping untiringly,
Romping without pause.

I would not give my laddie,
My laddie, my laddie,
I would not give my laddie
For twenty white kine.

I'd rather have thee in the meadow,
In the meadow, in the meadow,
I'd rather have thee in the meadow
Than any of thy kindred's bairns.

Dainty and cream I'll give to thee,
And the white milk of the gentle cows;
Wine of the wort I'll give to thee,
So thou come home with me to the knoll.

505 The fairy

I left in the doorway of the bower
My jewel, the dusky, brown, white–skinned,
Her eye like a star, her lip like a berry,
   Her voice like a stringed instrument.

I left yesterday in the meadow of the kine
The brown–haired maid of sweetest kiss,
Her eye like a star, her cheek like a rose,
   Her kiss has the taste of pears.

506 The hunter and the fairy

Over the cattle I will not watch,
Over the cattle I will not be,
Over the cattle I will not watch,
For my joy is in the fairy hill.

Though I have ceased from the cattle–herding,
A little trouble is on my mind,
That my courtly lover will go from me,
And my green–clad child in the fairy hill.

But thou man who closed to me my door
And robbed me of my pleasure,
Without seed, without luck, without joy be thou —
Ill is the thing which thou hast done!

Though I am tonight in this townland,
I sorrow to be telling it —
'Tis many a place where are my friends,
And some of them in the low land.

Though I am tonight in this abode,
It is not my love to be therein —
'Tis many a place where are my friends,
And some of them in the fairy hill.

But thou man who rangest rough grounds,
And who hast banished my comely looks,
My hope fell altogether from me
At seeing thee in the fairy hill.

But thou man who rangest yonder,
Bear a farewell from me and tell it,
Bear word unto the dairymaid
That I am she who has condemned her.

And thou man whose are my children,
'Tis thyself who hast left me forlorn;
If thy hand be raised against them,
My malison on thee, thou shalt lose it.

507 The hunter and the fairy woman

There was a young lad once who had a fairy sweetheart. She would be meeting him on the hill and in the glen. His foster–mother was finding fault with him, and she told him: "If thou shun her not, she will put an end to thee."

But the lad was trysting with the maiden as he had been before.

"If thou wouldst ask of her about the fairy flax," said his mother, "and what it is that makes the calves notch–eared." He did that.

"What makes the calves notch–eared?" he asked.

"Because their mother shuns the fairy flax," said she. He told this to his foster–mother. The lad plucked the fairy flax, and he put it upon his sister's clothing on the morrow. The fairy woman met him, and gave him hearty greeting, and sat near him on the knoll, but she could not come close to him.

Thou maiden there, and thou gracious maiden,
Thou maiden to whom I have given my love,
Were this day as yesterday,
Thou hadst not got the smooth fairy flax beneath thy foot.

The lad left her, and he married a mortal woman. She was pregnant, and past the time when the child should come, and there was no word of the child being born. She had carried the child a long year, but if she had, for all that there was no word of its being born. The hunter went up the glen, and who met him at the knoll but the little woman coming round the end of the knoll.

"Is it not long since that day!" said she.

"O King, it is long indeed since that day!" he said.

"How is thy wife — without lack or loss?" said she.

"Oh, she is very well, without lack or loss as thou wouldst say," said he.

"What is the matter of thy tidings, or what thy journey, O hunter, that thou comest to the mountains in the heat?"

"I have not a word myself, but I saw a poor little creature as I was coming across the ridge, and truly I pitied her."

"What creature was that?" said she.

"It was a doe sending a fawn unto the world, and she not succeeding."

"O King and O choice one, I wonder at that myself, a doe sending a fawn unto the world, and she not succeeding, though the fairy flax was under her foot! Who knows but it is thine own wife that is there?"

"Oh, it is not she, it is not she at all," said he.

"Well, I will give thee a fair and potent girdle, and thou shalt put it about her middle, and the child shall come unto the world."

The hunter went home in haste, and he took with him the girdle - the fairy woman's girdle. There was an old tree-stump by the river's side, and the hunter placed the girdle about the stump, to see how it would fare. The tree-stump shattered in four parts from top to bottom.

He went home and took the girdle with him, and he put the girdle on the top of the fire. He plucked the fairy flax, and he put a plaster of it under the woman's two soles, and the child came unto the world without toil or trouble to its mother.

The woman grew heavy and pregnant again, and she was near her time. The hunter went to the townland seeking a midwife, and whom saw he but the fairy woman behind a rock, and a sweet strain of music in her mouth. The hunter stood still listening to her, and the croon that she had was this.

The woman of the white palms
At home is being shrouded;
Margaret, Roderick's daughter,
The kindly woman, generous-natured;
The young wife of ringlet locks,
Who well knew to be modest,
The young wife of twining locks,
Who dwelt in the Brae.

The hunter listened to no more, but returned home, and found his wife dead before him.

Yon is the other thing,
Na hi ho ho hu ho
Yon is the other thing.
Na ho hi na ho a ro nailinn.

508 The hunter and the fairy woman

A ranger of the forest was living in a mountain far afield, and what but he was wooing a fairy sweetheart in the glen. He would be meeting her on his going and coming, and speaking with her. But if he was, what of that? – the hunter left the fairy woman, and he married a girl of the children of men. The fairy woman was in pain and in grief and in sorrow, but if she was, she gave no sign, until the hunter's wife grew sick with the sickness that is better than health, and until the time came for her to be delivered; and when it came, she put death in her mouth. When the man's wife came to childbed, he went to seek a midwife, and if he did, who met him but the fairy woman in the breast of the knolls at the glen's foot as of wont. She blessed him in words mild, mannerly, and he returned her blessing in the like words, and if they were not better, they were no whit worse.

"What are thine own tidings, O hunter?" said the fairy woman.

"Not a word have I rare or strange," said the hunter, "but one thing that pained me as I came down the mountain, to see a goat putting forth a kid into the world, and she not succeeding."

"Well, that seems strange to myself, a goat putting forth a kid into the world, and she not succeeding, though the smooth fairy flax was under her foot. – But whither art thou thyself going today, hunter of the hill? – I am sure that not without cause hast thou left thine own soft, obese, sallow wife."

"I am going to the townland to seek a midwife for my wife, and she in the cold clasps of death."

"Well, thou needst go no further," said she. "I will give thee a gauzy gossamer girdle to place around the loins of thy wife that would bring her back from death to life though the nine deaths were in her mouth."

The hunter gave no sign, but sat down by the well to drink a draught. She brought sleep upon him, and she sat by his side and sang in his ear:

  Hi ri ri ri u o,
  Hao ri o hiu ri ri bho ho.
'Tis ill work for a traveller
  Hi ri ri ri u o.
To stay and to dally,
  Hao ri o hiu ri ri bho ho.
And ill deed for a journeyer
To be sleeping on cairns,
While the young wife of ringlet locks
Is being shrouded at home.
My counsel, gallant youth,
To shun me had served thee better,
For there lies betwixt my hands
That which would wound thee without weapon,

And would leave thy shirt,
A part gleaming–white, a part of it red!
It is time for me to go homeward
To the field of review,
Where are the comely men
And sweet–voiced women tending them.

But thou Murdo son of John,
Thou wast the heart of generosity,
Thou wast the hunter of the hinds
On the day of bright sun!
Going about the high hill–slope,
Thou wouldst bring down a herd of them,
Ascending the rough summit,
'Tis I would follow after thee!
There was a time when thy promise
Was as the life of the sun to me,
And when to me thy kiss was sweeter
Than to drink in the sunbeam.

The fairy woman gave the gauzy gossamer girdle to the hunter, and he set out to return; but he remembered the goat and the fairy flax, and he took the fairy flax home to his wife. He placed the smooth blessed fairy flax beneath her on the floor–bed, and immediately she was whole. He then placed the fairy woman's girdle on a round pillar–stone before the door, and the pillar burst asunder in fragments. What was it, beloved of men, but the fairy woman seeking to destroy the hunter's wife. The fairy women are like the world women, cold and keen and cutting to her who has come between themselves and the heart of the son of man. God be between us and the envy of every fairy woman and every world woman so long as we are in the worldly frame!

509 The fairy lover

What, my love, shall I do with thee?
What food and clothing give to thee?
I fear lest thou should take the hiccough
  And thou not on thy mother's breast!

Alas and alas now for myself!
Thou hast broken the cockles of my heart!
'Twere better, plainly, to be in the grave
  Than watch over thy wailing.

I had rather than all my store,
I had rather than all my living,
I had rather than thy breast–milk
  That thou wert beside thy mother!

I'll carry thee home to the fairy bower,
Where thou shalt have food in plenty,
Meal and milk, cream and butter,
  And the milking of the cow–folds.

510 Mór, my beloved

  Ill o bha ho,
  Ill o bha hau.

I rose betimes,
I rose reluctant,
I rose betimes –
  Better that I had not risen!
'Twas my utter reaving
  That sent me forth!

The calf of my calf,
The calf of my calf,
The calf of my calf
  Lies by a knoll's side,
Without fire,
  Without comfort or shelter!

The mist was in the hill,
The mist was in the hill,
The mist was in the hill
  And on the scree,
When there fell in with me
  The fair–faced maiden.

'Tis the milk-white brown maid,
'Tis the milk-white brown maid,
'Tis the milk-white brown maid
  Who bore the son to me,
Though not tenderly
  Has she fostered it!

O Mór, my beloved,
O Mór, my beloved,
O Mór, my beloved,
  Turn to thy little son!
Cold is the place
  Where thou hast left him!

Cold is the spot,
Cold is the spot,
Cold is the spot
  On the lip of the hollow!
Cold is my calf
  By the side of a hillock!

O Mór, my beloved,
O Mór, my beloved,
O Mór, my beloved,
  Turn to thy little son,
And thou shalt get from me
  The pretty little speckled beads!

Cold is the night,
Cold is the night,
Cold is the night
  Tonight for a little boy,
And he without clothing
  By a knoll's side!

Thou shouldst get wine,
Thou shouldst get wine,
Thou shouldst get wine
  And all thou wouldst have,
Thou shalt get from me
  The trout at the loch-side.

The calf of my love,
The calf of my love,
The calf of my love
  Is by a knoll's side,
With never a fire,
  Cold, without shelter!

I would give thee silk,
I would give thee silk,
I would give thee silk
  And all thou wouldst have,
O Mór, my beloved,
  Turn to thy little son!

I would kill for thee the deer,
I would kill for thee the deer,
I would kill for thee the deer,
  And all thou wouldst have,
Save that I would rise not
  With thee in the morning!

O Mór, my beloved,
O Mór, my beloved,
O Mór, my beloved,
  Turn to thy little son!
Cold is the place
  Where thou hast left him!

511 Mór and the fairy lover

The mist was on the hill,
The mist was on the hill,
The mist was on the hill,
  And on the scree,
The mist was on the hill
And in the glen
When there met me
  The comely maiden.

'Tis the bright, brown–haired one,
'Tis the bright, brown–haired one,
'Tis the bright, brown–haired one,
  Who bore the son to me;
'Tis the bright, brown–haired one
Who bore the child,
Though not gently
  Did she nurse it.

  Ill o hu o
  Ill o hu o
  Ill o ro ho

Little brown–haired Mór,
Little brown–haired Mór,
Little brown–haired Mór,
  Come back to thy son!
And thou shalt get the beautiful
  String of trout from me.

Alas and alas,
And alas and alas!

Cold is the blast,
Cold is the blast,
Cold is the blast
  Beside a hillock!
Without fire,
  Without comfort or shelter!

Alas and alas,
And alas and alas!

Thy small soft mouth
Against my old grey snout,
As I sing sadly
  Beside a hillock!
Without fire,
  Without comfort or shelter!

512 The fairy lover

Little lad, ho! and merry little lad!
  Dear lad o! dear lad o!
Little lad, ho! and merry little lad!
  Last night didst thou keep me waking.

My sweetheart promised to be at my bidding,
  He promised it today and he promised it yesterday;
Though thou come not till the Monday of Doom,
  Long life be to the mouth of guile!

And thou mother there, and thou other mother,
  What, my beloved, my calf, my child?
More painful it is than the ant's bite,
  My brothers have slain my first sweetheart.

Thou gentle sister and foster–sister,
  Woe to her who should tell her secret to thee!
Sooner didst thou let out my tale
  At thy mouth than at thy knee!

I shall not go till the Monday of Mondays,
  I shall not go to the fold of the lambs,
Nor yet shall I go to the fold of the calves,
  Since not lasting is my life.

Thou rowan tree there by the door,
  On thee shall I go to the graveyard;
The wrights shall come from Dùn Dealga,
  Let there be made for me a comely bier.

My own brothers are coming
  On the nimble, swift horses –
May sharp knives pierce their hearts,
  And their bodies' blood flow from them in flood!

The curse that I made to my brothers
  In the passion that was in my heart,
Let it lie upon the brindled meadows
  And on two thirds of the deer of yonder glen!

513 The fairy lover

Why is not come the calf of my delight,
  The calf of my delight, the calf of my delight,
Why is not come the calf of my delight
  To keep the visit with me?

I was last night in the Meads of the Fold,
  The Meads of the Fold, the Meads of the Fold,
I was last night in the Meads of the Fold,
  Drinking the beer with the beguiling one.

I'll be this night in the Meads of the Kine,
  The Meads of the Kine, the Meads of the Kine,
I'll be this night in the Meads of the Kine,
  Eating the May–time crowdie.

Sad that I were not in the Meads of the Trees,
  The Meads of the Trees, the Meads of the Trees,
Sad that I were not in the Meads of the Trees,
  With none there but my darling!

Sad that I were not in yonder glen,
  In yonder glen, in yonder glen,
Sad that I were not in yonder glen,
  Where I fell in love with the beguiling one!

514 The secret lover

There was a girl who had a secret lover. Her brother went to the mountain to hunt. When the lad came home from the hill he said to his sister, and she replied:

"I saw the dearest one yesterday,
Who was asking for thee truly."
"How was my love,
When he remembered me?"

"I was smiting him sorely,
To the north and to the south,
With my bright sword and my axe,
With my left hand and with my right."

"If thou hast slain the dear Oscar,
Arise and wash thy hands;
May that be the final washing
From which thy body and bones will bleach.

"May there be no tops on thy rushes,
May there be no butter on thy milk,
Or a month–old child in thy house
To take the weariness from his mother."

Then her mother said:

"Mayst thou be split like the freshwater salmon
Between thy two breasts and thy belly,
And may the poisonous serpent be beside thee...!"

The girl then said:

"The ill–wish I made for my brother,
Let it not be on him it rests at all,
But on the rugged brindled hills
And on two thirds of the deer of yonder glen."

Next day in the early morning the rugged brindled hills were in riven fragments through the glen and two–thirds of the deer were dead.

515 My father and mother will kill me

"My father and mother will kill me,
My sister and brother will kill me,
Displeasure of kindred and friends will be to me,
If thou lettest me not home as I came.

It was last night that I heard
That my love was surrounding me,
And since thou hast got me to the fold,
Beloved, let me home as thou foundest me."

* * *

"Though thy father and mother should kill thee,
Though thy sister and brother should kill thee,
Though displeasure of kindred and friends should be to thee,
Thou shalt not go home as thou camest forth."

"O my love, my dear Donald,
O my dear, my dear Donald,
O darling of men, my dear Donald,
O my love, let me home to my own!"

516 Fairy song

Three squirrels, three little mavises,
A brindled mavis at their head.
Ho a ho hala gu math!

My mother's cattle are on the moors,
Their leader has forsaken them.

Three squirrels, three little mavises,
A brindled mavis at their head.
Ho a ho hala gu math!

If I were near the wild pastures,
I would avenge that on the children who forsook them.

Three squirrels, three little mavises,
A brindled mavis at their head.
Ho a ho hala gu math!

517 The carlin of Beinn Bhreac

The carlin of Beinn Bhreac ho,
  Bhreac ho, Bhreac ho,
The carlin of Beinn Bhreac ho,
  The tall carlin of the mountain spring.

I would not let my herd of deer,
  My herd of deer, my herd of deer,
I would not let my herd of deer
  Go nibble the grey shells of the shore.

They had rather their own cress,
  Their cress ho, their own cress,
They had rather their own cress
  That grew on the spur of the high hills.

I am a carlin ranging bens,
  Ranging bens, ranging glens,
I am a carlin ranging bens,
  Trying to see the best glen.

Climbing up the mountain top,
  The mountain top, the mountain top,
Climbing up the mountain top,
  I found not the white pin.

I found not, I lost, I found,
  I found not, I lost, I found,
I found not, I lost, I found,
  I found not the white pin.

I never wore an upper shoe,
  An upper shoe, an upper shoe,
I never wore an upper shoe,
  What I got was the short hose.

I never wore a garment,
A garment, a garment,
I never wore a garment,
Until the fair–haired gallant rescued me.

I never set fetter,
A fetter, a fetter,
I never set fetter
On black or red cow in the herd.

I am the carlin who is light,
I am the carlin who is light,
I am the carlin who is light,
Alone on the spur of the cairns.

518 The fairy woman and the hunter

The carlin of Beinn Bhreac, ho ro,
Bhreac ho ro, Bhreac ho ro,
The carlin of Beinn Bhreac, ho ro,
The tall carlin of the mountain spring.

I would not let my herd of deer,
My herd of deer, my herd of deer,
I would not let my herd of deer
Go seek grey shells upon the strand.

They had rather the cresses green,
The cresses green, the cresses green,
They had rather the cresses green
That grew on the mead of the glorious springs.

519 The fairy woman's lullaby

Ho! soft art thou,
  Smooth thou, soft thou!
Well I love thee,
  Smooth thou, soft thou!

Well I love thee,
  Smooth thou, soft thou!
Under the plaid,
  Smooth thou, soft thou!

Well I love thee,
  Smooth thou, soft thou!
In the morning
  Soft-white, red-bright.

Well I love thee,
  Smooth thou, soft thou!
I to companion thee,
  I to lull thee.

I to fill thee
  With the fondnesses,
I to fill thee
  From the breast of thy mother.

Soft thou! soft thou!
  Soft my little love!
Soft as silk to thee
  The heart of thy mother!

520 The fairy woman's lullaby

Ho do ro sonnie,
  Ho do ro kiddie,
Behind the ridges
  At the berries.

Hal hal aoirinn,
Hal hal aoirinn,
Hal hal aoirinn,
  The goats in the fold.

Hiu bhidil hiu bhi,
Hiu bhidil hiu bhi,
Hiu bhidil hiu bhi,
  The sheep in the misty ben.

I would range the darkling
  With the hunter of my love,
I would range the night
  Through wood and through heath.

MacLeod's Lullaby

The reciter, James son of Colin (James Campbell), crofter, Ceann Tangabhal, Barra (26th September 1872) said: "MacLeod of Dunvegan got a child by the fairy woman; and because he would not receive herself, she sent the child home to him. But though she put him away, she was missing the child and she went to see him. The child was with MacLeod's foster–nurse, and the fairy woman seized hold of the child, and she was hushing and caressing and fondling and nursing and rocking him back and fore, intending to snatch him from her and to sweep him away with her to the fairy mound."

Another reciter, Donald MacQuien, cottar, Ferinlea, Skye, said, 1860: "The young heir of MacLeod of Dunvegan was lifted up from his cradle and out of the castle. There was no knowing between earth and sky or in the land of the living who had lifted the child or how he had been lifted or where he had been taken. There was no knowledge or information under the white sun of the seasons. But suspicion lay on the fairy woman, for she was always lifting infants who had not been baptized and women who had not been purified, when she got a chance or opportunity. There was no one on hill or at homestead, in strath or on moor, on house hillock or castle lawn, who was not out in search of the beautiful little child, the young heir of MacLeod of Dunvegan. Search was made high and low, hither and yon, but nothing was heard or seen of the child who had been lost.

"In going past a beautiful green heathery knoll at the base of the green corry of the hinds, the young daughter of MacCrimmon, MacLeod's haughty piper, heard singing in the knoll, for her young ear was as acute for music as the young ear of the mavis of the branches — the young girl heard a crooning music in the green heathery knoll. Immediately the girl thrust the needle, which was in her breast after darning her father's hose, into the ground. The smart girl — and by my word that is what she was! — placed her ear to the long thread to see what she would hear, and she heard clearly enough music in the fairy mansion — the mansion of the slim fairies — as if a mother were singing a lullaby to a little child.

"Every day and night people were set to watch the entry to the fairies' round hillock, just as people used to be sent to watch the entry to the lair of the wicked carnivorous wolf. On Hallowe'en, in contrast to all other nights, the mound of the slim fairies opened, and there quickly poured forth pell–mell a disorderly giddy swarm like schoolchildren just dismissed.

"The watchers forthwith entered the mound and there the young heir of MacLeod of Dunvegan was found, joyous jolly, mirthful merry, sweet–voiced. He was sitting on the knee of a mortal woman whom the fairies had 'lifted' from her pallet when the attendant women were heavy of head and sleepy of eye. MacLeod's young heir was lifted on the warriors' shoulders, attended by his nurse, and the child was brought home under the white banner fluttering in the breeze, the plumed pipes waking the melody of the rocks' echo to the loud shouts of the men and the clamorous laughter of the women."

521 The fairy woman's lullaby

My little dun buck thou,
Offspring of the lowing cow,
For whom the Mull cow lows,
My darling and my fair one,
My soul and my delight!
Thou art not of the race of Clan Donald,
But of a race dearer to us —
The race of Leod of the galleys,
The race of the weighty saplings,
The race of the breastplates,
Norway was thy patrimony!

Faire fire
Thou art not the calf of
Faire fire
The old shrivelled cow,
Faire fire
Thou art not the little kid
Faire fire
Whom the she–goat brought forth,
Faire fire
Thou art not the lamb
Faire fire
Whom the sheep brought forth,
Faire fire

Thou art not the foal
Faire fire
Of a lean old mare,
Faire fire
Though thou art not,
Faire fire
Thou art my calf!

Fairim firim obh obh!
May I not hear of thy wounding,
May I not see thy tears,
Until thy shoes are holed,
Until thy nose grows sharp,
Until thou duly becomest grey
As hoar as the clouds,
Until thy day becomes dark
Within the precincts of Dunvegan!

Be the plighted truth with us!
The fairy maid seized her chance,
Be the plighted truth with us!
When the snow was on the tree,
Be the plighted truth with us!
When the mist was in the glen,
Be the plighted truth with us!
When the brook was in spate,
Be the plighted truth with us!
When the goat was without kid,
Be the plighted truth with us!
When the cuckoo was without young,
Be the plighted truth with us!
When the hedgehog could not be found,
Be the plighted truth with us!
When the summit of the Coolin could not be seen,
Be the plighted truth with us!
When thy foster-mother was blind,
Be the plighted truth with us!

Hug o regretful,
The young women of the village,

Hug o regretful,
Dejected and tearful,
Lamenting the child,
Traversing the wood
And their white breasts
Overflowing with milk.

My treasure and my delight,
By theft I won thee
In the dead of night,
Without light or glimmer,
Without candle or candlestick.
Thou hast been with me since last year,
And thou art my treasure,
And thou wilt be this year
Fresh and lively
On my shoulder through the village!

Thou art my child
Sweet enticing,
With rattling breastplate,
Thou art the chieftain
Of spirited horses.
Thou art my child
Ruddy and stout,
My fatness and plenty,
My soft rushes
Wherein my cows are wont to be.

Would that I might see thy cattle-fold
High up on the mountain slope,
A fine green collared coat
About thy shoulders, and a shirt.

Would that I might see thy team of horses
And men following it sowing seed;
There was always a merry hum throughout thy hall
With the quaffing of beer and wine.

522 The lullaby of the MacLeod child

My magnificent child,
Striking of quivers,
Of mail–clad youths,
Of chieftains,
Of spirited steeds,
My little child, my little child!

Thou art my child
Ruddy and plump,
Lusty and noble,
My armful of yew,
My soft bulrush, my soft bulrush!

Thou art my joy,
My delight and my care,
My gaiety and my cheer,
My little child, my little child!

Thou art my child,
Last year thou wast under my girdle,
Plant of fertility,
Plant of fertility,
My womb did bear thee,
My breast suckled thee,
My knee reared thee,
My little child, my little child!

Thou art my child,
And thou wilt be this year
Fair and playful
On my shoulder,
As I go blithely
About the homestead,
My little child, my little child!

Would that I could see thy cattle–fold
High up on the mountain's upper slope,
Thy horse–teams after thee,
And winnowers with their thin green coats
With thy household sowing seed,
My little child, my little child!

Would that I could see and hear
Thy piercing voice on mountain face,
Thy lofty sail breasting the wave,
That my lad should be swimming in the pool,
That my offspring should excel all in the deer–forest,
My little child, my little child!

O Son of the Virgin,
May I not see his sorrow!
O Son of the Virgin,
May I not hear his wounding!

O Son of the Virgin,
May he duly grow grey
On the soil of Dunvegan,
My little child, my little child!

My magnificent child,
Striking of quivers,
Of mail–clad youths,
Of chieftains,
Of spirited steeds,
My little child, my little child!

Thou art not of Clan Kenneth,
Thou art not of Clan Conn,
Thou art of a seed we held dearer,
Thou art of a seed we held dearer —
The seed of Leod of the ships, the swords and the breastplates,
Norway was thine ancestors' patrimony,
My little child, my little child!

523 The fairy woman's lullaby

The fairy woman was lulling the child, designing to entice him home with herself to the fairy dwelling.

Carefree little suckling,
My little yellow-haired child
Who would remain seated,
Who would eat the eggs,
No stain on his shirt,
Which would not need to be washed,
He would get that
And many treasures!

Fill the wine in a thin slanting stream,
Then fill the beer,
Fill the wort speedily,
And it would not be the worse
Of a little ale;
Copious wine
From the precipitous glens;
A handful of sordid silver
Most unlovely.

A child conceived by a young woman
To a youth of renown.

My love is the comely helmsman
Whose frame is never clad by aught
Save a jet-black coat with goodly nap
And a soft wisp of a shirt.

My skirmisher,
My lucky one,
My roving one,
My sportive one!

My courteous one among ladies,
My thick strong luxuriant oats,

Turning it, sowing it, harrowing it,
Reaping it every year.

My heart's darling,
My sense's delight,
Lids of my eyes
On an early May morning!

Thou art the darling of my desire,
My satisfying armful,
Sun of my love
On the feast day!

Calf of my esteem,
Ocean of my love!
Beside the cold hills
I myself found thee.

Ho my treasure,
He my treasure,
Ho my treasure,
A branch of the summer branches.

Darling of youths
Fresh and famed,
Vigorous sapling,
The desire of comely women.

Thou wouldst climb, thou wouldst descend,
Thou wouldst climb, thou wouldst descend,
Thou wouldst climb, thou wouldst descend,
The mountain where feats are performed.

Thou art my bread and my meat,
My carolling and my music,
My ale-wort and my beer,
My fowl and my eggs.

My little child, my little child,
My little child, my little child,
My little child, my little child,
My little child who chatters.

Son of the brown–haired lady
Who never touched bowl or milk–pail,
Who never lowered her hand to baking,
Who never raised her laugh in the cattle–fold.

Silk and satin,
Yellow satin,
Silk down to the shoes,
Satin to the elbows —
Thou wouldst get that and many treasures!

Would that I might see thy spouse,
A white swan, in early May,
Coming with her brood over the Irish Sea,
Thy younglings making music in far places.

My little child, my little child,
My little child who chatters,
My little child among the rocks,
I myself would give thee eggs!

Thou art the seed of the sons of the waves,
Thou art the seed of the bent bows,
Thou art the seed of the bay horses,
Thou art the seed of the swords and ships.

Thou art the seed of the host of the tempest,
Thou art the seed of the host of fury,
Thou art the seed of the host of warriors,
Thou art the seed of the host of my love.

Thou art the seed of the compact domain,
Thou art the seed of the weighty Mull men,

Thou art the seed of Cormac and Conn,
Thou art a seed we held dearer,

Tender scion, soft and comely,
Tender scion, soft and brown-haired,
Tender scion, soft and fair,
Tender soft scion, thou art mine!

Another version:

Thou art my tender comely scion,
Thou art my tender brown-haired scion,
Thou art my tender fair scion,
My tender scion, thou art mine!

Thou art the treasure of the MacLeod women,
Thou art the music of the Mull women,
Thou art the support of the MacNeil women,
Thou art the darling of the Macvurich women.

Ho my child,
He my child,
Ho gogag orrai,
Ho my child!

My darling who was,
My darling who is,
Calf of fair women,
Love of fairy women!

Thou art sun to my bosom,
Thou art my trout stream,
Thou art my white geese,
Thou art my ocean gull!

My thick sturdy tawny oats
Being planted every year,
My powerful numerous horse-teams,
My young heifers going wild.

With their green coats of goodly nap,
With their white sewn shirts
Full of pleats from fist to elbow,
Their sheen like snow on the cold bens' slope.

Ho my child,
He my child,
Ho my child,
He my child!

Pass across the offspring,
Pass across the offspring! –
There was no one at home
But a bald scurvy fellow,

An old carlin toasting herself,
An old carle sunk in sleep,
A darling of a child no bigger than a fist,
And the young woman stitching linen.

Thou art my tender comely scion,
Thou art the seed of Colla, the seed of Conn,
Thou art my tender comely scion,
Thou art the seed of the compact clan!

Ho my child,
He my child,
Ho my child,
He my child!

My tender scion,
My garlic in rocks,
My tender scion,
My linen–in–press!*
My tender scion,
Were it not for the mole on thy palm,
We would lift thee away with us!

* A plant name, perhaps.

524 The fairy woman's lullaby

Bhog bhog bhire
Bhog bhog bhire
Bhog bhog bhire
Thou art not the calf
Bhog bhog bhire
Bhog bhog bhire
Bhog bhog bhire
Of an old lean cow!
Bhog bhog bhire
Bhog bhog bhire
Bhog bhog bhire
Thou art not the lamb
Bhog bhog bhire
Bhog bhog bhire
Bhog bhog bhire
Which the sheep brought forth!
Bhog bhog bhire
Bhog bhog bhire
Bhog bhog bhire
Thou art not the chick
Bhog bhog bhire
Bhog bhog bhire
Bhog bhog bhire
Last hatched in the brood!
Bhog bhog bhire
Bhog bhog bhire
Bhog bhog bhire
Thou art not the blue cub
Bhog bhog bhire
Bhog bhog bhire
Bhog bhog bhire
Of the round-headed seal!
Bhog bhog bhire
Bhog bhog bhire
Bhog bhog bhire
Though thou art not,

Bhog bhog bhire
Bhog bhog bhire
Bhog bhog bhire
Thou art my calf!
Bhog bhog bhire
Bhog bhog bhire
Bhog bhog bhire
My womb bore thee,
Bhog bhire bhog
Bhog bhire bhog
Bhog bhire bhog
My breast suckled thee,
Bhog bhire bhog
Bhog bhire bhog
Bhog bhire bhog
My knee nursed thee;
Bhog bhire bhog
Bhog bhire bhog
Bhog bhire bhog
Thou art fair,
Bhog bhire bhog
Bhog bhire bhog
Bhog bhire bhog
Thou art mine!

525 MacLeod's lullaby

He is my sweet delightful child,
Seven times sweet and delightful,
He is the shoulder of swords and hauberks
Who grew not feeble.

He is my ruddy child,
Chubby ruddy cheerful,
My cuckoo fledgeling of the braes,
It were my delight to gain thee,

Since I have given my all,
My beauty and my pride, with thee,
My milch kine on meadows
And my white sheep on uplands.

Hug ogag oirre
The young women of the township
Hug ogag oirre
Taking thee to the greenwood,
Hug ogag oirre
With their curling locks,
Hug ogag oirre
Carrying thee off by stealth,
Hug ogag oirre
Through moor and fell
Hug ogag oirre
Carrying thee off last night,
Hug ogag oirre
With their swelling breasts,
Hug ogag oirre
Carrying thee off in the night,
Hug ogag oirre
And they overflowing with milk,
Hug ogag oirre
Without light or glimmer.

Fire faire, I shall do about thee,
Combs for your head I shall do about thee,
Elegant plaids I shall do about thee,
Fine tartans I shall do about thee.

Thou art not the calf, etc.

Fire fire, I shall do about thee,
A little shirt of white linen I shall do about thee,
A little shirt of white silk I shall do about thee,
A fine white little shirt I shall do about thee,
Thou tender scion, thou art mine!

Thou tender scion, my womb gave thee birth, etc.

526 The fairy woman

Thou art my famous child,
Hi ri hill lium
Most dexterous under arms,
Chall o ro hi ho

Well do dirk and targe become thee,
Hi ri hill lium
And speckled shield with red bosses.
Chall o ro hi ho

My fragrant starry child,
Hi ri hill lium
Heir to a famous heritage,
Chall o ro hi ho

Thou wilt climb the slopes,
Hi ri hill lium
Thou wilt bring us booty.
Chall o ro hi ho

Thou art the seed of the warrior host,
Hill hi hill lium
Thou art the seed of the furious host,
Chall o ro hi ho

Thou art the seed of the tempestuous host,
Hill hi hill lium
Thou art the seed of my beloved host.
Chall o ro hi ho

Thou art the seed of Colla, the seed of Conn,
Hill hi hill lium
The seed of weighty strife art thou,
Chall o ro hi ho

Thou art the seed of Cormac, the seed of Coll,
Hill hi hill lium
A seed we held dearer.
Chall o ro hi ho

My womb gave thee birth,
Hi li ri lium
My knee reared thee,
Chall ho ro hi ho

My breast suckled thee,
Hi li hill lium
My tender scion.
Chall ho ho ro hi ho

Carefree little sleeper,
Tranquil little sleeper,
Helpless little sleeper,
Were it not for the mole on thy foot
We would lift thee away with us!

My heart's darling,
My sense's delight!
It was behind the cold hills
That I found thee!

Fairies

Dialogue between a fairy woman and a mortal woman

These dialogues between the fairy woman and the world woman are on the recognized lines of intercourse between fairies and mortals. No advantage in smartness of language is to be permitted to the fairy; if it be, she is able to exercise her will on the mortal with whom she contends — "Give her an inch, and she will take an ell." One is reminded of Lochiel and the witch who tried to exhaust him in walking with her "Ceum ann, Eoghain!" ("Step on, Ewen!") (II:191n.; J. Gregorson Campbell, *Witchcraft and Second Sight,* pp.198–201). The contest of wit between Michael Scott and the witch–nag that carried him on his journey to Rome is another case in point; his errand was successful because his wit in reply silenced the witch.* The least advantage allowed to the witch is fatal.

A fairy woman came to where a mortal woman was nursing a little child. She stood stubbornly, stiffly, starkly, before the child, peering and staring at it straight in the face. At last she said:

"Comely is thy child, woman," quoth the fairy woman.
"Comely is every lucky worldling," said the nurse.
"Green is thy child, woman," said the fairy woman.
"Green is the grass, but it grows," said the nurse.
"White of skin is thy child, woman," said the fairy woman.
"White of skin is the snow of the peaks," said the nurse.
"Pretty and golden are thy child's locks, woman," said the fairy woman.
"Pretty and golden is the daisy of the plain," said the nurse.
"Sharp and cutting is thy tongue, woman," said the fairy woman.
"It was never set to a grindstone," said the nurse.

When the fairy woman saw that the mortal woman would not yield her an inch here nor there, down nor up, she turned the back of her head to her and departed by the way she had come, and never did herself nor any of her people come again upon that ground. Oh she came not, beloved, ever again that way, the black nor the white of her ever ever again. The fairies are little lovely daring dignified creatures, with green raiment. If they get an inch they will take an ell, and there is no gainsaying them. Poor little creatures are often daring and dignified and manful. Think of the wren himself, how brash and bold he comes and sits on the windowsill until I give him food! When he gets the food he makes his bob to me and is off, and I see neither the black nor the white of him until he grows hungry again, or until bad weather and hard times and scarcity of food come, and he brings one or two of his numerous little family to me in search of food. The poor little creature lives but from hour to hour, from hand to mouth, from day to day, as I do myself. It is matter for thought, the work of creation and the goodness of the great God of the elements to His creatures, great and small; and I! I! I am one of them!

* See J. Gregorson Campbell *Superstitions of the Scottish Highlands,* 85, 296; *Waifs and Strays of Celtic Tradition,* i.46–53.

527 The fairy woman and the child

"De di thou! de di thou!
My quiet little child thou!
De duibhe! de duibhe!
My gold-haired little child thou!
How pretty thy prattle!

My gold-haired little child,
'Tis thou wouldst sit straight
When eating the eggs,
When taking the crowdie —
'Tis I would be eager!

Thy shirt I would wash
As white as a sunbeam,
As the snows of the mountain,
And could I get thee for my own,
'Tis I would be eager!

Oh 'tis I found the treasure
When I found last year,
When the apples were gathering,
That thou wast fine and plump —
My fair lap-burden thou!"

528 The fairy and the pot

A woman came to a house in Vallay, and the goodwife said to her: "Whence art thou come, woman?"

"I am come from Buchain,
I am come from Bàchain,
I am come from Gabasdal,
From the Loch of the Little Bird,
From the Loch of the Big Bird,
And from the Big Division
In Vallay.

"I am come to ask for the cauldron to boil meat," said she with a dignified air. The goodwife knew not what to say to her, and she went to an old man who was in

the townland, and she told him how it was, and how she was coming every day for the pot and taking it away with her. "Say thou this to the little woman when she comes again:

"A pot deserves a bone,
And to be brought home whole;
A smith deserves coal
To heat cold iron."

The woman forgot this one night, and the pot never again came home from the fairy hill. The fairy woman went off with the pot in her hand and the lilt from her mouth, and this is the verse that she had:

"Over the cattle I will not watch,
Over the cattle I will not be;
Over the cattle I will not watch,
For my joy is in the fairy hill.

Though I have given up the herding,
My mind is somewhat troubled,
That my gentle lover will leave me,
And my pale child in the fairy hill."

529 Host hound

O alas for me now!
O alas for me now!
O alas for me now,
Since thou shalt come to me never!

Brown frolicking hound,
Fairy fawning hound,
White frisking hound,
Ranging bens, ranging bens!

Hound dappled, red,
Hound of seven slumbers,
Hound of notched ears,
Hound son of "Truagh,"
Ranging bens, ranging bens!

530 The fairy woman

Grind the quern, little wifie,
Grind the quern, little wifie,
Grind the quern, little wifie,
And thyself shalt get the little bannock.

Coat upon Toll–a–Ghunna,
Cloak upon Toll–a–Ghunna,
Clothing upon Toll–a–Ghunna,
Mischief take the ugly one!

There's many a man across in Mull,
Many a man who is no man,
There's many a man that's lacking gear
Who is sorry for an ugly one.

Coat upon Toll–a–Ghunna,
Cloak upon Toll–a–Ghunna,
Clothing upon Toll–a–Ghunna,
Mischief take the ugly one!

My curse upon the winnowing–floor,
My curse upon the winnowing–post,
Seven curses upon Toll–a–Ghunna
If she make more grinding!

Coat upon Toll–a–Ghunna,
Cloak upon Toll–a–Ghunna,
Clothing upon Toll–a–Ghunna,
Mischief take the ugly one!

531 Prayer for protection

Christ be between me and the fairies,
  My frown upon each tribe of them!
This day is Friday on sea and on land —
  My trust, O King, that they shall not hear me.

Fairy Changeling

532 The fairy changeling

The fairies would be lifting children unbaptized and carrying off women uncleansed and leaving old men and old women in their place.

There was a woman in the upland of Benbecula who bore a fine big child. But the midwife was in a hurry, and she forgot to put the consecration on the child, and the watching–women were sleepy, and neglected to burn the old leather shoes and to place the little drops (in baptism upon the child's forehead). And the outcome of that was that the fairies came down and lifted the child with them high on their shoulders, and out they went by way of the hen–hole, leaving an ancient changeling in the child's place. The child that was left was thriving neither by day nor yet by night, for all that he was eating and drinking and putting away without stop or stay, without rest or pause. It is he who was eating and drinking, swallowing up and putting away, but if he was, what of that? There was neither thriving nor growth on him, not an atom. The poor woman knew not what to say or do — she knew not in the world. Every last woman who would come to the house, and if they were not many they were not few, would say to the poor woman: "Is not thy child small, goodwife!" "Is not thy child wan, goodwife!" "Is not thy child green, goodwife!" "Is not thy child sallow, goodwife!" "Is not thy child the sorrow, goodwife!" — the same dismal drone of disaster from every last one of them, like the scream of the seagulls at the skate. The poor woman was vexed to distraction with them, without relief or remission, and she not knowing what she should say or do. But she thought to herself that she would go to an old man who was in the townland, and lay her problem before him, and get counsel from him.

She did that, and she told the man about the child, every word, every turn, how he was eating and drinking without stop or stay, without rest or pause, and for all that and despite it had neither thriving nor growth on his head nor his legs, on his form nor his frame — how that when she would go to the well the milk–pitcher would be drained, when she would go to the cattlefold the cake would be eaten, when she would go to the moor the butter–basket would be made away with, and not a living creature on the bare flat of the floor save the child in the cradle.

The kindly old man listened mildly, mannerly, to the woman's words, and he said to her: "It is an ancient changeling thou hast, poor woman. The midwife has been forgetful and the watching–women neglectful, and the fairies have come and lifted thy child away with them, and have left an ancient changeling in his place. Go thou home, poor unhappy little woman, and do not betray thyself in any way. Go to the strand and bring home a good supply of shellfish of every sort, and after parboiling the shellfish, scatter the shells on the bare flat of the floor around the hearthstone. Leave the changeling in the cradle, and go out as if thou wert going to the well for a stoup of water. Go not far away, and keep an eye and an ear behind the door to see what thou shalt see or hear. After that, thou shalt go to the shellfish strand, and place the changeling stretched out at the margin of the wave, and put a slumber-croon in his ear to send him to sleep. When the first wave of the rising tide strikes him the changeling will wail, but take nothing to do with him and do not betray thyself at all, that thou hast seen aught or heard a cheep. When thou reachest home thou shalt find thine own soft pretty youngster there in the cradle."

The woman went home, and she did as the old man bade, and she left nothing forgotten. She went to the strand and brought home the fill of a big creel of shellfish of every sort. She parboiled the shellfish and spread and scattered the shells on the bare flat of the floor around the hearth as the old man bade. Then, "I am going to the well," said the woman, "and see thou, my dear, if thou canst have a pleasant sleep until I come back."

"I will, mamma," said the changeling, and he closing his two poor little eyes in the pleasant sleep. She went out with a pitcher in her hand, and she closed the door behind her. She put eye and ear to the peg-hole in the door to see what she should see or hear.

Instantly, as soon as she turned her back to the door on going out, the changeling took a standing leap out of the cradle, and where did he land but among the shells on the floor.

"Ov! ov! ov! my feet cut and injured with the shells!" said the changeling, speaking to himself. "Ov! ov! I have been living since I was born and never before in the creation have I seen such shells — never never have I seen them, O merciful Mary of grace! Shells here and shells yonder, shells up and shells down, everywhere I put my foot!"

The changeling gazed to and fro, up and down, here and yonder, at the shells. He began to make a rime about them.

The croon of the shells

Brown crab, cockle, oyster,
Mussel, bruiteag, limpet,
Bearded mussel, *miasag,* scallop —
Alas my reaving, my heels!

Lobster, squid, green crab,
Red crab, seashore flea,
Cowrie, *maighdeag,* little limpet —
Alas my wounding, my heels!

Whelk, whorl, barnacle
Have pained me to my bones,
And the crafty sea urchin —

So many a prickle in my heels!

Slender sand–eel and razor–fish,
Hose–fish, black–snout, limpet...

But he had got no opportunity to put a finish to the croon of the shells when he heard the noise of the woman's footsteps as she came home with a pitcher of water. That sent the changeling in a vigorous standing leap back to the cradle, and he closed his poor little eyes in a drowse of sleep.

"Didst thou see, my darling, who ate the butter or who devoured the bannock or who drank the milk today?"

"I saw nothing, mamma — I was fast asleep in the cradle until thyself didst wake me coming in with the water."

"Thou wast, my treasure, it is thou who wast asleep — sound asleep!"

"The height of the spring tide is today, and thou shalt come with me to the strand of shellfish to see if I can get a boiling for the hens, and thou shalt get pullets' eggs from me," said the woman to the fairy changeling.

"Yes, I will come, mamma," said the changeling, pleased and willing.

The woman placed the fairy changeling in the small creel and put the sling over her head. She lifted him high on her shoulders and departed for the strand of shellfish with a step light and jaunty, and the fairy changeling in the small creel on her back. She laid the pigmy sprite quietly and gently down at the margin of the wave by the shallow ripples, and said to him: "Sleep thou, my pretty treasure, sleep, beloved of men, in the smooth soft plaid beside the wave, and I will sing thee the pretty croon and raise the melody for thee while I am working at the shellfish."

"I will sleep, mamma," said the pigmy sprite, and he closed his little tiny eyes in a pleasant placid slumber and gave forth a heavy sleepy snore.

The croon of the shellfish gathering

Sleep thou by the wave's side,
   Sleep thou, my love,
Sleep thou by the wave's side,
   Till I cease from the shellfish gathering.

Goats' milk I'd give thee,
   And sheep's milk I'd give thee,
And milk of mares I'd give thee,
   My love, wert thou mine own!

Beer and wort I'd give thee,
   And the white barley of the plains,
And wine of the chalice I'd give thee,
   My love, wert thou mine own!

The plucks and *sguithim* I'd give thee,
And the lapwings' yellow eggs,
And the autumn carrot I'd give thee,
My love, wert thou mine own!

Sweet maize I'd give thee,
Earthnut, lard and whiting,
And the spring tansy I'd give thee,
My love, wert thou mine own!

Milk and feast–fare I'd give thee,
Cheese and crowdie and mild whisky,
And kail dressed with butter I'd give thee,
My love, wert thou mine own!

Rough–meal porridge I'd give thee,
And honey and foaming milk,
And goodly sowens I'd give thee,
My love, wert thou mine own!

The first thing the trickster knew on awaking was the first wave of the rising tide driving in below and above him at the margin of the wave. The changeling uttered the wail of death at the pitch of his voice, and he made a lightning leap to his feet upon the bare flat of the strand. The woman did not betray at all that she had seen or heard him, nor so much as raised her head, but kept on singing her slumber–croon and lifting the shellfish. But in the twinkling of an eye the changeling's screechings were like the seagull at herring fry. The fairies lifted the changeling on the tops of their palms away with them to the fairy hill.

The woman sped swiftly home, and the foot that was hindmost was the foot that was foremost as she traversed the path. The poor pitiable woman found her own fair little child there before her in the cradle. A cleric was found, and the child was baptized, and neither fairy nor elf nor pigmy sprite ever came again to trouble him.

533 The croon of the shellfish gathering

There was a woman in Upper Bornish who had a child unthriving and bloodless. The woman would have the child in the cradle while she herself was working about the house. When she would go out, she would find the milk drunk and the house higgledy–piggledy and in disorder. Though she would give him the world of food and of drink, it was not putting bloom on his face nor fat on his frame — he was not growing an atom for all that she was giving him and doing for him, and she knew not what to do or to say about the business. So this is what she did, she went to an old man who was in the townland, and she told him how things were, and she sought advice of him.

"It is a changeling thou hast in the cradle, my poor woman," said the man.

"O Mary and O Son, thinkest thou it is?" said the woman. "O food and clothing, what shall I do about him now?" said she.

"Take home," said the old man, "a good pile of shells from the strand of shellfish, and scatter them hither and thither over the floor. Go thyself into a hiding-place where thou shalt not be observed, and see what thou shalt see or hear."

The woman went out as though she were going for a creel of peats. She climbed up on the top of the wall of the house, and she gazed down the smoke-hole to see what in fortune she should see. The big shambling changeling then arose from the cradle, and he went across and opened the chest and drank the milk.

*"Uv! uv! uv!" said he, "my feet are cut and my sight destroyed. Over a hundred years have I been living in the knoll, and never have I seen such a lifting as this!"**

"Lifting!" said the woman, "lifting of thy mischief be upon thee!" said she who was above.

The big shambling changeling went back to the cradle as smartly as his feet would take him, and he shut his eyes, making the world believe that he was fast asleep. The woman came home as though she were come with a creel of peats.

"Hast thou had a wink of sleep since I left thee, my dear?" said the woman.

"Yes, mamma, I have slept all the time since thou wentest."

"Hast thou seen or noticed anyone about the house today?"

"I have seen not and heard not a whisper today," said the child.

"Well, my love, thou shalt go along with me tomorrow to the strand of cockles," said she.

"Yes," he said, "and I shall get a cowrie."

"Thou shalt, and a soft fat limpet. Mischief, mischief on the man who would kill his craggy skittering wether while thou, thou soft fat limpet, art bursting full of fatness on the rock!"

Early next morning the woman girt herself up to go to the strand of sand-eels. She put the child in the little creel on her back, and she took the crook in her hand by her side, and she departed, and out she went down the strand. It was nearly low water, and she put off the little creel and set it on the margin of the wave, and she began to lull the child. And this was the lullaby that she sang to him:

Sleep thou by the wave's side,
  Sleep thou, my darling,
Sleep thou by the wave's side
  Till I cease from the shellfish gathering.

By the wave's side, by the wave's side,
  By the wave's side ever,
By the wave's side, with the billow's sound
  In the ear of my little pup beloved.

* That is, rearing, treatment of a child?

Though I myself should go to the well,
  That were no drink for my darling;
I would milk for him my herd of goats,
  And I would gather my sheep to the milking.

534 The fairy changeling

The big shambling changeling was found crouching, round and hunched, in the child's cradle. He was lifted thence and thrown outside the door of the house, and the door was shut.

"Now is it not a pity that I have not my hammer and my anvil!" said the little old fairy man when he got the soles of his two little feet beneath him on the solid ground. They looked into the cradle, and under the little old fellow's head they found two poor tiny little pebbles. These they took up and cast about his feet, and he was bidden to make off and take his feet thence or worse would befall him.

"Ov! ov!" said he, "my feet hurt by the bad people!" — when the poor little pebbles were thrown about his little bare naked feet without shoe or stocking, without buskin or hose. But he raised the melody in his mouth and made up the hillside and across the mountain to the Corry of the Fairies. Merrily, cleverly, he scaled the summit, his lilt in his mouth and his tune flowing free, and by my mantle indeed, O Mary of grace! it is himself that had the hand for music!

I spent last night in the house of ale,
I spent last night hearty and blithe,

I spent last night in the house of thatch,
This night I'll be in the fairy knoll.

They gave me wine, they gave me milk,
They gave me cream and dainty,
They gave me the combs of honey,
And they gave me the breast-milk.

The Washing–Woman

The Luideag (little shaggy or hairy female one), or *Luideag bheag a' chliabhain* (the little shaggy sprite of the basket), is one of several names, varying in different districts, for the *bean–nighidh* (washing–woman), who washed the *léin* or *léineag* (shirt), of a man destined to die in battle. In Barra she was also called *glaistig, glaisteag, glaislig.*

While washing the shroud she wailed piteously the death–song. When spoken to she never replied, and could only be approached by stealth. Her appearance always portended death or disaster *(sgiorradh).* Lochan nam Breac Dubh, the lakelet of the black trout, between Sleat and Broadford in Skye, is among the places where she had been seen and heard.

535 Luideag of the river

There was a widow in Barra and she was living near Léig. She was left with one son and no more. The lad's name was Roderick, and he was a kind, polite, affable, capable, hard–working lad, liked and respected by everybody.

There was another widow in Tangasdal and she had two sons. Roderick was the name of the two sons, and they were fine lads and of good repute. The sons of the widow in Tangasdal were called the "two Rodericks." They and Roderick, the son of the widow in Léig, were constant companions.

There was a large skiff going from Barra to Glasgow with barley and rye, mutton and beef, butter and cheese, the produce of the year. The two Rodericks and Roderick of Léig went to Glasgow on the skiff with their own produce. The Barra skiff reached Clyde and each one sold his own goods as he best knew how, and they did well.

The widow of Léig was out early one morning in the grey dawning of the day attending to the cattle, and she heard a tiny wee whimpering as of a poor tiny wee pup crying for its mother, and a splashing as of the dunlin washing itself in the pool; but she could not see anything. She looked to her and from her, up and down, hither and yon, and she spied a tiny wee figure of a woman down at the ford of Abhainn Bhàn (White River). Who was this but Luideag of the River standing on a grey stone at the edge of the water, washing a shirt and singing a lament.

The Luideag had the appearance of age, but if so, who could make out her age or her period? Her visage had become swarthy and her skin tanned like brambles at New Year, and she was as old as the mountain mist. The poor creature was so busy lustring the shirt and lamenting all those who were to perish that she was quite oblivious of anything around her. The widow came softly and silently behind her and seized the Luideag in her arms.

"Confound thee, little carlin!
Confound thee, little carlin!
Confound thee, little carlin!
What has brought thee here?"

"To wash the shirt of the two Rodericks
And the shirt of Roderick thy son;
There is many a lair in the seas,
Though every cave beneath sea–ledge is not a tomb."

"Is that the linen (shirt) I planted,
And the linen I plucked?
The linen I shrank,
And the linen I beetled?
The linen I softened,
And the linen I hardened?
The linen I heckled,
And the linen I combed,
Soft and elegant?
The linen I spun,
And the linen I wove?
The linen I steeped,
And the linen I washed?
The linen I decked,
And the linen I sewed?
The linen I bleached
On the grass of the green?
Ochone! ochone!
My plight and my torment!

The linen I consecrated
With my scalding tears
To the One Son of God
For my only lambkin!
O wifie
Of the three marvels,
I wonder
What has sent thee to the eddying stream!"

"Thou hadst need of that,
Poor little woman!
The two Rodericks will be drowned,
But thy lambkin will make the shore."

When the men were returning home from Clyde a mist came over them and the clouds of the heavens burst, with spindrift and ground-drift and a driving hurricane, and the Barra skiff was reduced to matchwood on the Cairn of Coll. Every man inside the skiff was lost except Roderick the son of the widow of Léig. He reached the shore still alive, but little more.

There was a farmer's daughter in Rubha Mhàil in Coll and she was out early on the morning after the storm in search of her father's sheep. It filled the girl with dread and terror to see the fragments of the vessel among the rocks and the tidal wrack, and a mingled mass of men. She saw one young lad in the clefts of the rocks, his hands, his feet and his head dripping blood, but seeming still to have the vital spark in him. The girl placed her mouth to the lad's mouth and her hand to his heart to see if there was any throb or life or breath in him, and there was. The girl carried the lad home on her back, and she placed him softly and quietly on the bed.

"Here," said the girl to her father, "is my morning jetsam, and see now that you treat him well." And the people did treat the lad well, and if the rest did so the daughter of the house treated him especially well.

"Where my pain is, there is my helping hand, where my love is, there is my resort," the girl would say when she was missing and could not be found. She never stopped applying plasters to his wounds and providing delicacies for the lad's palate.

The lad grew well — that he did — after having been thrown on Rubha Mhàil in Coll and having been found by the farmer's daughter without life or breath in his body, sea-borne jetsam among the rocks.

The lad now wished to come home to Barra to see his mother, to see how she was, and he did not know on earth what he would do with the girl who had nursed him to life from death, or how he would take her with him, or how he could possibly leave her behind him.

"Where thou art, there shall I be, and where thy home is, there shall my home be, and where thy people are, there shall my people be," said the girl, the dew of tears coursing on her cheek.

"O that cannot be," said the lad, "seeing my mother has but a small tumbledown house — a poor little hut, of poor appearance outside and of scant comfort inside. I shall go home to little Barra and I shall build a better hut and when it is finished I shall come back and lift the net."

"Well would suffice me a side of the house of her who sewed thy shirt and embroidered thy linen," said the girl.

"O that cannot be," said the lad, "I am only a poor lad, the son of a widow, and all the wealth my mother has is two white hummel cows and a pair of horses and two brace of horned sheep." — There were no two ways about it but that the farmer's daughter would go with the widow's son to Barra, and she went with him.

To trust a man is a woman's duty
If she is wise, and if not 'tis no novelty;
The trust consists in maintaining it
And the purpose of God in fulfilling it.

A wedding and wedding-feast was made for Roderick, the son of the widow of Léig in Barra, and for the daughter of the farmer of Rubha Mhàil in Coll. The woman's father sent a large skiff full of cattle and sheep and goods of every kind home to Barra with his daughter. The couple reared a fine family and their descendants are living in Barra to this day.

536 Ewen of the little head

"Nigheag," the washing-nymph, is called "Nigheag nan Allt," the washing-nymph of the streams, "a' Bhean-nighidh," the wash-woman, "Léinteag," she of the shirts, "Lointeag," she of the lake, "Cointeag," she of the wailing, and by other names. At a stream or at a lake she washed the shirt and wailed the dirge of those doomed to die, seeming always to be absorbed in her task, and always causing anxiety and sorrow to those who heard and saw her.

Eóghan a' Chinn Bhig, Ewen of the Little Head, saw the Nigheag washing. He watched her intently for a time, then crept stealthily nearer and nearer till he came up close behind her. Her breasts troubled her as she stooped to wash, and now and then she would throw them over her shoulder, as African and Indian women do when travelling. Eóghan a' Chinn Bhig set the nipple of Nigheag to his mouth and sucked her breast and having done this he said:

"Thou thyself and myself are witnesses
That I am thy first fosterling, Nigheag."

"By the hand of thy father and thy grandfather, Eóghan,
It is timely for thee, little son, that I am."

Eóghan then asked Nigheag whose shroud she was washing and whose dirge she was wailing. And she answered him:

I am washing the shrouds of the fair men
Who are going out but in shall never come,
The death–dirge of the warlike men
Who shall go out and fall in the field.

I am lustring the linen of the fair men
Who shall go out in the morning early
Upon the well–shod grey steeds
And shall not come back in season due.

"Shall I win victory on the field, Lointeag?" said Eóghan of the Little Head.

"Thou shalt, fosterling, if thou get from thy wife without asking butter with thy breakfast in the early morning, going to the battle."

"And shall I myself come living from the fight, little foster–mother?"

"Thou shalt, if thy wife bless thy suit of cloth."

Nigheag went away plumping (plopping) across the lake, but before she went she left a ban upon Eóghan of the Little Head, that his ghost should be running before his people before the death of the men and making hubbub and confusion above Loch Buie whenever a Maclaine chief should die. And the reason of that was his being impudent, because of his unmannerliness in putting his hand to her breast, a thing that is forbidden — that a man should put his hand upon the pap of a woman.

Ever since then Eóghan a' Chinn Bhig is seen and heard prancing and marching above Loch Buie before the death of a Maclaine of Loch Buie.

Eóghan did not get butter without asking, his wife being notoriously stingy; and at this disappointment he stormed furiously. His muime–altraim *(fostering nurse), was the first to enter the room when he got into his* triubhais mharcachd *(riding breeches). As was customary on such an occasion, the woman said:*

Enjoy and wear the cloth,
Thou love of my heart, Eóghan.

But to his muime, *in return for her affectionate good wishes, Eóghan said:*

Mayest thou not enjoy thy health,
Thou ugly old woman of the devil!

The muime *however, was not surprised, being more than accustomed to these family traits.*

Eóghan was killed in the battle that ensued. "The scalp of his head was struck off in the combat." According to some, this was how he acquired his nickname; according to others, his head was by nature unusually small.

Innumerable doings and sayings are attributed to Eóghan. When his mother's body was being carried to the place of burial he called out to those who were carrying it: "Do not raise my mother so high, lest she should be seeking the habit."

Seventy years ago boys and girls within a radius of seventy miles from Mull dreaded to hear of Eóghan a' Chinn Bhig and of his headless riding and heedless doings — a source of much pleasurable excitement of which the boys and girls of the present day, it is to be feared, are deprived. When sounds of unexplained origin are heard, that is "Eóghan of the Little Head making much ado and uproar."

Augury

Translated "augury" in Volume II, "divination" is perhaps better, but *frìth* is concerned with matters which, though physically unseen, are contemporary. A brief account of the *frìth* has been given already (II:194n.)

Frìth is a term of deep and wide meaning, signifying the sight of the unseen, the divination which enables the *frìtheir* (augur), to see into the unseen. It consists in looking forth towards the sea or towards the land to observe signs of good or ill to man or beast, in health or in sickness, at home or abroad, when the fate or state of the object of the quest is not known by natural means. It was made with much care and prayer and meditation, by men specially endowed and inspired. The gift of *frìtheireachd* was inherited; sometimes it appeared in one member of a family but not in others, and sometimes it disappeared from a family to reappear later, like the *taibhse.* It survived in the Western Isles until within modern times, but is not now practised, though there are those who are said to have inherited the gift but do not use it for fear of the ridicule of their neighbours and the anathema of the ministers. The clergy were much averse to the practice, and stamped it out along with the rest of the picturesque lore of the people. The descendants of those who practised it are still called "Clann an Fhrìtheir," the children of the seer.

The *frìth* was known among the people by various names, such as *frìth Mhoire,* augury of Mary; *frìth an teampaill,* augury of the temple; *frìth Bhrighde,* augury of Brigit; *frìth an tobair,* augury of the well.

To make the *frìth* across stream, lake, or sea is difficult, and across a wide or deep sea most difficult. The *siol sidh* (race of fays) has more power under water than above water, under the foundations of the sea than under the foundations of the land; and the *sìol sìdh* interferes with the current of man's thoughts and thwarts man's mind and wishes. The sea is more sacred and mysterious than the land, and contains inhibiting spirits not known ashore; therefore, an informant said, the *frìth* cannot so well be made across the sea "because there is a sort of fairies under the sea, and the *frìth* is hard to read."

The signs are many and varied, and only some examples of them can be given. They are called *rathadach* and *rosadach,* lucky and unlucky, fortunate and mischievous. The sight of a man, especially a brown man, is in itself good; a man coming or looking towards the seer is an excellent sign. A man standing, or a beast rising, indicates that the person who is the object of the quest is casting off the sickness from which he has been suffering. A man going away from the seer is unfortunate. A man lying down indicates sickness or the continuance of sickness in the object of the quest. A beast lying down indicates death. A woman, in particular a fair, brown, or black woman, is fortunate, and a woman standing is very good. A woman passing or coming is not bad. At the sight of a woman coming, the seer should cross himself. A woman going is unfortunate. A light–red woman is bad, and a deep–red woman very bad. "A man should sanctify himself (cross himself) were he to see a woman with red hair while making the *frìth.* Red hair is mischievous. Red was the colour of Judas who betrayed Jesus the Son of Mary," said a woman reciter. A cock coming or looking towards the seer is excellent. A bird approaching indicates news.

Among other signs that are *rathadach* (lucky), are the following: a bird, a bird on the wing, especially the dove or pigeon, the *lacha Lochlannach* (or widgeon), the *lacha Mhoire* (duck of Mary or mallard), the *fosgag Mhoire* (Mary's lark or skylark), the *Gille Brighde* (or oyster–catcher), the first stonechat on grass; a dog; a horse; a foal, calf, or lamb if fronting the seer; a sheep, especially good for beginning a journey. The duck is a specially good sign concerning sailors; if it is seen, they are safe from drowning. The duck is a blessed bird, for it covered our Lord, when the hen exposed Him, under the straw on the knoll when the man was threshing his corn. The *glaisean* (sparrow), is not lucky but blessed. It is a sign of the death of a child. Three or four of these always come before the death of a child, and return each day until the death, not reappearing after it.

Fowls without a cock, the first stonechat on rock or road, the crow, the grey crow, the hooded crow, the rook, especially if approaching — all these are *rosadach* (harmful). Still worse is the raven, especially if approaching: it is a sign of death. The lapwing or green plover is a bad sign for Protestants, having betrayed the Covenanters among the hills. The meadow pipit signifies the death of a child; three of these singing near a door are singing the requiem of a child within. The grey or ringed plover singing near a house in the dusk is singing the death–song of a person within. The hen is a very ill sign, for the hen exposed the Lord to His enemies in the heap of corn. The pig, when its back is towards the seer, is an ill sign for all but Campbells; when facing him it is indifferent. The cat is bad, being a sign of witchcraft; but it is not bad for the Clann Chatain (Mackintoshes and Macphersons). The goat is bad, especially for one beginning a journey — he should defer it.

A white horse (indicates) land,
A grey horse ocean,
A bay horse burial–place,
A brown horse sorrow.

Each buidhe (a dun horse), indicates Clann Choinnich (MacKenzies).

The writer has a small pebble of red quartz which was used in making the *frìth* and in other forms of occult science. It is called "Clach Bheag nan Tursanan," the little stone of the quests [?]. It belonged to the Macleans of Coll, by whom it was much prized and religiously kept. It came down to them from remote antiquity. A member of the Coll family gave it to Mary MacInnes, cottar, Taigh a' Gheàrraidh, North Uist, in gratitude for service she had rendered, and she gave it to me. It was used in the *frìth* for discovering the body of Donald Maclean of Coll when he was drowned in the Sound of Ulva.

Donald Maclean was engaged to be married to one of the two daughters of Sir Allan Maclean of Innis Choinnich. He was on his way to Innis Choinnich, and with him in the boat were several friends, including an English gentleman and Maclean of —. The latter quarrelled with Donald Maclean about the lady to whom he was engaged. The boat, much overladen, was upset and sank under them. Only one man escaped; he climbed to the top of the mast, which was above water. Maclaine of Loch Buie demanded that he should come down and give place to his betters. "You have been long enough over me in this world — we shall be even in the next," was the answer. The death of Donald Maclean of Coll caused regret throughout the country, for he was known through Dr Johnson and Boswell. He greatly endeared himself to all who knew him and very specially so to his own people of Coll.

A man in Lochs, Lewis, went to Australia in search of fortune. He was to send home for his wife and three children as soon as he could command means for the purpose. A year passed, two years, three years, and still no news or message came from the man. Then the wife went to a certain woman. The woman asked how long it was since the man left. She then went into a trance and was to all appearance dead and was oblivious of all around her. She opened her eyes and said: "Thy husband is in such a place and not where thou didst fancy. He is safe and sound but has not prospered and has not written to thee, but he will write to thee now and without delay."

Three months after that a letter came from the man in which he said to his wife: "Didst thou go to Mary daughter of Neil on such a day and at such an hour? I was stricken as I was never stricken before and was like to die for full twenty minutes. No one expected I should live. I saw Mary daughter of Neil before me in the flesh as completely as ever I saw thee, and she spoke to me... I have not prospered in this country more than has many another man of my kind."

My informant, — Maclean, Ord, Ross, on 21st August 1909, is an educated and highly respected man; he is convinced of the truth of what he told me.

From John MacRury, crofter, Tolorum, Benbecula.

There was a man in Baile Mhanaich in Benbecula, whose name was Duncan MacInnes, but he was called Duncan Alan's son, and oftener Alan's son. He was a man who was famed for augury, and people would be coming to him from far and near from every place. Four men were storm–driven from (Uig in) Lewis; no one had the least knowledge what had happened to them, or where they were, in an isle of the sea or in the depths of the ocean. No wreckage came on shore and nothing belonging to their boat was seen.

Men went to the Flannan Isles, but saw nothing. People advised their friends to send a messenger to Alan's son in Benbecula. It is easier to go to Canada today than it was to go from Uig to Benbecula at that time. The messenger arrived at his journey's end, and Alan's son received him kindly and treated him courteously after his journey and his wandering.

Alan's son told the man that it was late that night for an augury, and that he would make an augury early in the morning; and that he did. Alan's son told the messenger that his friends were safe and sound in St Kilda of all places, and that at that very moment they were skinning a mart along with the St Kilda people, and that they would come home in March, when the days should lengthen and the late winter be past.

All this fell out in every particular as Alan's son saw in his presage. The men who had been storm–driven were astonished enough when they were told that they had been skinning a hornless dun mart one cold day of late winter in St Kilda, over forty miles away across the ocean. The men had been driven from their own home in the beginning of the dark depth of winter. And with the severity of the elements and the intensity of the storm they did not get back home until the end of March had come. The people of St Kilda had been very kind to them, but despite that and notwithstanding they were seven times bitterly tired of their prison, and no wonder.

537 *Frìth Mhoire* (Augury of Mary)

The people's accounts of the manner of divination agree in substance but vary in detail. The frìth *is made on the first Monday of the quarter. It is made in the morning, before sunrise, with fasting, with prayer, with meditation, and in the name of the Virgin Mary — "praying to Mary the Mother of Christ for the prosperity of the* frìth." *Some say that the* frìtheir *has head and feet bare. He says, intones, or sings the* "Fàilte Mhoire," *(Hail Mary) and then the proper hymn of the* frìth, "Fàilte na Frìthe" *or* "Frìth Mhoire." *Some say that while doing so he walks sunwise around his fire, which is in the middle of the floor of the house, and that he walks thrice around it, once in name of the Father, once in name of the Son, once in name of the Holy Spirit:*

God before me, God behind me,
God over me, God below me,
I on Thy path, O God,
Thou, O God, in my steps.*

The Son of the King of life
Be my stay behind me,
To give me eyes to see all my quest,
With His love before me,
With His grace which dims not,
Holding His death in my vision ever.

* Compare III:320f. For the last line of the second verse an alternative is: "Which shall never be darkened."

He then goes with closed or blindfolded eyes to fàd–buinn (fàd–bacain, maide–buinn) an taighe *(the doorstep of the house), and places a hand on each jamb. He appeals again to the unseen all–seeing God to grant him his request. He opens his eyes, and looking steadfastly before him, without moving his eyes or his eyelids to right or to left, upwards or down, he carefully notes all he beholds. According to some, he crosses the threshold and goes sunwise around his house, keeping his gaze always before him as described, and saying or chanting the hymn. From the nature and position of the objects within his sight, he draws his conclusions.*

538 Augury

The augury mild Mary made for her Son,
The Queen–maiden gazed downward through her palm;
"Sawest thou glimpse of the King of life?"
The fair Queen–maiden said that she saw.

"I see Christ, of curling locks,
In the Temple of the King of hosts,
Disputing with the frowning doctors,
A while before the court closed."

539 Augury

The augury Brigit made for her Foster–son,
She made a pipe within her palms:
"I see the Foster–son by the well's side,
Teaching the people assuredly.

I set the augury towards the well,
And truly that was righteous work,
The King of kings teaching the people,
Yonder see I Christ assuredly."

540 *Frìth*

The man or woman performing the augury or divination forms the fingers of the left hand into a tube. He or she blows through this tube in the name of the Three Persons of the Trinity, and then says the rune.

I am going without
To the doorstep of my house
In the holy name of God
Stronger of sight than all.

I go out in the name of God,
I come in in the name of the Son,
I walking in thy path, O God,
Thou, O God, upon my doorstep.

God before me, God behind me,
God over me, God beneath me,
God within me, God without me,
The God of marvels leading me.

The augury that Mary made for her Son,
That Brigit breathed through her palm;
Hast thou seen the augury, guiding maid?
The young maid said that she had.

Message of truth without message of falsehood,
That I myself may see
The semblance, joyous and mild,
Of all that is amissing to me.

Mac Gille Chaluim of Raasay

Iain Garbh Mac Gille Chaluim Ratharsaidh (of Raasay) was drowned in April 1671 on his way home from visiting the Earl of Seaforth in Lewis. It is said that he was drowned through the machinations of his own *muime* (foster–mother) who employed several famous witches to raise the tempest in which he was drowned. These were "Spog Bhuidhe," ("Yellow Foot,") of Màiligir in Skye; "Gormshuil," ("Blue–eyed,")* from Cràcaig in Skye, and "Doideag Dhubh," ("Black Doideag,") from Duart in Mull.

Iain Garbh's foster–mother lived in Trondaidh, usually known as Trondaidh a' Chuain, a small remote island lying north of Trondarnis, Trotternish, Skye. It is not known, though the matter is often spoken of, why his foster–mother was offended with Iain Garbh.†

Iain Garbh left Loch Sealg in Lewis on a day clear and calm, with not a cloud in the sky. The *muime* saw her *dalta* (foster–son) coming, and she put milk in a *miosair mhor* (large vessel) and a *miosair bheag* (little vessel) floating in the milk. She herself was a milkmaid in the island, and she placed the calf–herd *(buachaille laogh)* in the door of the *àirigh* (sheiling) where he could see both Iain Garbh's birlinn and the two vessels, large and small. She herself stood by the fire with her foot in the *slabhraidh* (pot–chain) reciting incantations.

Immediately after she began her incantations the little vessel floating in the large vessel began to sway to and fro like the pot–chain over the fire. The herd–boy called out that the little boyne was going round *deiseil* (sunwise) in the big boyne, and then being violently agitated and going round *tuathail* (widdershins) and shaking the side of the big boyne, and then capsizing and floating bottom upwards. At this same moment Iain Garbh's boat disappeared, and the boy saw no more of it.

When the galley was between Sgeir Mhaol and Trondaidh a' Chuain, three ravens were seen hovering about the boat in the raging storm. Soon afterwards twenty birds flew into the boat and assumed the form of frogs *(muileacha–màg, mealacha–màg)*. All the witches of Scotland were there, and all as busy as busy could be; but

* "Gormshuil" represents, rather, the old name "Gormlaith."

† See *Trans. Gael. Soc. Invss.*, xxix.270; xxxvi.392.

they could not sink the galley until Iain Garbh said: "What the big brindled one (i.e. the devil) brought you here?"

Then Iain Garbh became distracted from the number of ravens flying about and the number of frogs leaping aloft. Then a huge raven lighted on the gunwale *(beul–mór)* beside him, and he drew his sword from its sheath to kill it, and in his fury he drove the sword down through the gunwale and clove the boat right to the keel, in which the sword stuck.

Some say that the first intimation of the drowning came to the witches of the Minigeig *(buidsichean Mhonadh Mhiongaig)* in the north of Atholl. Others say that Iain Garbh's spirit came to his wife, and she told her dream to his mother. The spirit said:

Friday came the wind
And stirred itself to rage and fury;
Tell thou to the mother of my body
That it was the evil ones who brought death.

This was repeated thrice. When Iain Garbh's mother was told she said: "My heart's darling is lost."

A *seanchaidh* (storyteller) in Fiskavaig, Skye, related (30th December 1861): Iain Garbh's foster–mother drowned him for the sake of money, and no sooner had she drowned him than she repented. Iain Garbh and his wife used to go from Raasay to Harris without a living person but themselves together. She would be at the helm and he at the sails. Once on a time when they were going to Harris and sailing along the coast of Trotternish, Iain Garbh fell out into the sea from the bow of the boat. The boat was going at speed and the sea was high, and just as he was going past her quarter his wife seized him by the topmost bunch of the hair of his head.

"Good gripping to you!" said he.

"Let the warrior have no care," said she, "I have my own wager on the mark."*

She put the boat up into the wind and took him aboard. Was not that the woman who had the grip?

Women are often in the form of cats when going about as witches. A gentleman in South Uist was out hunting in the *sliabh sheilg* (mountain of the hunt). A heavy shower came down and he took shelter in a sheiling. The gentleman saw a cat on the top of the wall of the bothy, and he raised his *musg* (gun) to kill it. He tried two or three times, but each time, although the powder in the pan flashed, the shot did not go off. He thought the cat was uncanny and he put a silver stud in the gun and was raising it to his eye when the cat changed into the form of a woman well known to him.

"Is it thou, Mary?" said he.

"It is," said Mary. "What a great grudge thou hast against me! Be patient," said she, "and I shall tell thee the reason why I am in the guise of a cat."

* The expression has the second meaning: "My own love is on the dear one."

And she told him that she and many other women were drowning the great Mac Gille Chaluim of Raasay when he was coming home from Lewis.

"The Great Mac Gille Chaluim is on the verge of death in the vicinity of Rubha Hùnais. His galley was full of cats and he was chasing them with his great broadsword, slashing them here and mauling them there, when he struck the sheet-rope a blow with his sword and the galley capsized. It is his own foster-mother who forced me to go there, and we were there a great swarm of cats."

541 Iain Garbh's lament

The same seanchaidh recited the following lament, ascribed to Iain Garbh's wife:

As I sit on the beach
Without joy or gladness,
Never more shall I raise a blithe song
After the Friday of my woe.

Never more shall I raise a blithe song
After the Friday of my woe,
Since my world was overthrown,
Since my kinsmen went to the depths.

Since my world was overthrown,
Since my kinsmen went to the depths,
Gille Caluim the younger
And Great John, my sorrowful tale.

There is many a white-coifed lady
Who tearfully mourns,
And many a fresh gracious maid
Sprung from tenants and commons.

Thy greyhounds are unstirring,
Without wagging or rejoicing,
Without welcome from the noble
Whose forebears were manly.

Without coursing or huntsmen,
  Without trek to the hill,
To the heights of the hunt,
  To the rough peaks of the Coolin.

Ho ro hill o ro ho
  Hill o hill uil ill ho ro
Hill o ro bha hi.

MacVurich

542 MacVurich's three wishes

The old people used to say that God gave MacVurich Mór of Stiligarry three wishes when he was born.

Once upon a time MacVurich Mór was returning to Uist from Moidart, from Castle Tirrim, a route he not infrequently travelled, and what happened but that he was lying somewhere in the Rough Bounds or in the Small Isles – Canna, Rum or Eigg. Early one morning MacVurich heard the goodman of the house where they were staying asking his wife what day it was.

"Arise, girl, for the howl of the east wind has deafened me," said the woman. MacVurich understood that the good woman was tired of them and by my soul it was no wonder! He called out to his lads to rise immediately and that they would put to sea, and they arose. A soft warm wind came and they hoisted the smooth speckled towering sails to the tops of the tall enduring masts of wood. They gave her stern to land and her prow to sea. They set a course for Uist, piled on every stitch they had aboard and set off. There was a harsh, grating noise from her prow and foam in her wake, and the galley was making excellent speed.

But now there was only a low slow moan of wind, and it was not long before the breeze died away and its speed forsook the ship. The men were sticking knives in the masts and whistling for wind, but what of that? No wind was coming or anything like it.

At last his son said to MacVurich Mór: "Ask a wind, father, for goodness knows when we will reach home with this dawdling."

"Dost thou ask me, son?" said MacVurich.

"Yes," said his son. It was then MacVurich said:

East wind from the smooth rocks
As a prayer to the King of my love!
A brisk wind from the Rough Bounds
As a prayer to the Lord of the elements!
A wind without ceasing or veering or slacking,
That would do no harmful deed to us!

Then the lad without sense said:

Soft and dumb thine asking, father,
And the day fast forsaking us,
The sun is setting upon Hekla
And not a third of the distance behind us.

"Hast thou said it to me, fellow?" quoth MacVurich Mór in anger; and he said:

If there be wind in cold hell
To raise a wave from her red side,
O irascible Conan, send it after us
In sparks of fiery fire.

There burst upon them a stark storm and cruel sea. It seemed likely that the ship would be sent to the abyss and the men to eternity. His son asked MacVurich to give calmness to the wind and rest to the sea and peace of soul and body to themselves.

"O father, father, weaken the wind or we are with the shellfish of the deep."

"Thou blockhead, thou who didst ask me to seek the wind, away with thy senseless talk. I would not ask the third request of my God should she go to the tangles of the deep," said MacVurich.

The lashing dashing sea rose in peaks steep and towering and sank in glens low and ugly, the red seaweed of the abyss coming up and the brown whelks of the deep giving cracks on the black thole-pins of the galley. Fear and dread fell on the crew until they were blind and deaf, of no use to themselves and of no use to others. They were fainting with fear on this side and on that, fore and aft, not one of them able to lift his head or stretch his hand to defend or succour himself though the pursuit were close on him, all that is save MacVurich Mór and his own servant Finlay. When it was calm everyone was making fun of Finlay — he was the butt of their ridicule hither and thither, up and down; but when the storm came Finlay was the only hero among them — there was no one else who would do a hand's turn but he. MacVurich was steering the vessel and striving to keep her dry, and Finlay was baling and striving to keep the bilge-water down, and by my soul, they had their work cut out in this extremity! But Finlay was strong and sturdy and as MacVurich would steer Finlay would bale. Then it was that MacVurich said:

From me MacVurich, from me Mac Mhairich,
From me Mac Annd and Mac Cùsbaig,
From me Mac Ceileig, from me Mac Ceallaig,
From me every boaster and coward,
From me the Campbells, from me the Macleans,
From me the vagrants and scum,
From me Mac Iogaire, from me Mac Cogaire,
From me every outcast but Finlay.

When the men came ashore they were so weak and weary that they could not put a foot under them. A hound came out of the ship and it lay down beside a lamb, without troubling the lamb. MacVurich Mór said:

The son of the hound and the son of the lamb
In the cold friendship of the snow,
It is the storm of the waves and the roar of the sea
That have made you lie down side by side.

Another version:

MacVurich Mór of Stiligarry had three requests.

He was once lying at Canna, as he often was when back and fore between Uist and Moidart. Early one morning he heard the lady of the house shouting to the maid: "Get up! get up! girl, the wind beating on the east window has deafened me."

MacVurich understood that the woman was tired of himself and his men — and O Mary and O Son, it is certain that she had cause! MacVurich called out to his lads: "Get up! get up! lads, the lady of the house is tired of us."

The lads jumped to their feet, and one of them said: "Go on, then, ask for a wind, for there is not a breath from the sky."

MacVurich replied and said:

East wind from the smooth rocks
As a prayer to the King of the elements! —
A following breeze without faintness or slacking,
That would do no harmful deed to us.

"Softly, feebly, bashfully hast thou asked for the wind," said one of the lads.

"Sayest thou so, fellow?" said MacVurich in anger, and he made his second request:

From the heights of the bens
To the depths of the glens,
Which will take hair from a horse
And moor-grass from the ground,
Which will take heather from the hill
And willow from the root,
Which will take the limpet from the rock
And the eagle from its eaglet:
Brown Donnan, send it after us
Howling and raging
In blazing sparks of fire!

Then the wind came, and that was the wind, and the sea rose, and Mary, Mother of grace, that was the ugly sea — the vessel at one time showering the black whelks from the draught seaweed at the bottom of the sea, the next time up on the very tops of the mountainous seas! There was none who was not stretched on the vessel's floorboards amid the bilge-water she was shipping astern except MacVurich Mór himself and a half-wit called Finlay. When they reached Loch Eynort (Loch Skipport?), a lamb was lifted out, and a dog jumped out and lay down beside the lamb on the bare pebbly beach. MacVurich looked at the two and said:

The son of the hound and the son of the lamb
Lying down on the same field,
It is ocean storm and raging sea
That afflicted you among your foes.

543 Big MacVurich and the monster

Big MacVurich was out in the hill hunting for venison. He got a royal stag, and after gralloching the stag he slung the venison on his back. The man had to pass to the left of Loch Druidibig with the royal stag on his back.

In a cranny at the edge of the loch what should the man see but a tiny little creature. He lifted the poor little creature away with him in his breast and thus brought home the monster's whelp. Hardly had he brought it home than the monster came to the window and called out with a loud angry voice: "Out with my whelp, Big MacVurich!"

"For a bargain, monster."

"Out with my whelp, Big MacVurich, or the highest stone in thine ugly dwelling shall be the lowest stone in its foundation."

"For a bargain," said MacVurich.

"What is thy bargain, thou dirty rascal?" said the monster.

"That thou build me a causeway across Loch Stadhlabhal on which my peats may be brought home and on which my cattle and sheep, my horses and goats, may pass back and fore without a white or red one among them."

"Alas! alas!" said the monster, "though hard the saying, it is better to fulfil it," said she.

In the dead of night the monster came and called out at the window:

"That is ready, Big MacVurich; out with my bouncing boy."

"No, except for a bargain," said Big MacVurich.

"Let me hear thy terms, thou wicked man," said the monster.

"That thou bring home every single peat I have on the hill slope and make a stack of them on the hill at the end of the house."

"Alas! alas! though the causeway was hard, harder still is it to bring the peats home and make them into a stack at the end of the house. But though the saying is hard, it is better to fulfil it," said she, setting out to the hill.

The monster then came a third time and called out at the window:

"Big MacVurich, out with my bouncing yellow boy, that is done."

"Not yet, except for a bargain," said Big MacVurich.

"Let me hear thy bargain, thou wicked man," said the monster.

"That thou build me a dwelling-house with nine couples in its roof, thatched with birds' feathers, and no two feathers of the same hue."

"Hard is the form of thy bargain, MacVurich," said the monster.

"Hard is the form of necessity, monster," said MacVurich.

The monster laid the foundations of the house neatly, and began on the mason-work; and Mary, Mary! 'tis herself that had the hand for it! There was but the one song coming from her mouth, she was ever crooning and murmuring thus:

Stone on top of stone,
 Stone on top of two;
Set the stones thus
 And the wall will be complete.

Stone on top of stone,
 Grey stone by its side;
Stone on top of stone,
 Grey stone to build it.

Stone in front of stone,
 Stone in front of two;
Stone in front of stone,
 And the wall will be up.

Stone on top of stone,
 A peg placed in the hole,
Layer upon layer
 From the top to the base.

Beam set to beam,
 Divot upon divot,
Pole upon pole,
 To keep out the drip.

Feather upon feathers
 From the inside,
Gravel, divot, wooden wattle
 From the outside.

Gravel, divot, wooden wattle
 To the roof of the deceiver's house,
The sudden destruction of the serpent
 On the scoundrel's vaulted roof.

Every timber in the wood save the wild fig,
 Every timber in the wood save the wild fig,
Every timber in the wood
 To the house of treachery
Save the aspen of the cross and the wild fig.*

* The wild fig is "crossed" *(air a chrosadh)* probably because of the incident near Bethany. *Critheann chroinn:* the aspen of the cross.

See *Trans. Gael. Soc. Invss.,* xxvi.264; *An Duanaire,* 123ff; *Celtic Monthly,* iii.44; cf. *History of Clan Macrae,* 5; *Urquhart and Glenmoriston,* 424–5.

Thus she sang and sought until the house was finished. There was not a brood–bird in the beautiful blue sky that did not come with a feather to help with the thatching of the house, out of compassion for the monster.

The monster then came some time before cock–crow and she called out at the window and said: "That is done, MacVurich; out with my whelp."

"Here is thy whelp, thou great crafty monster, and let me not see thine eye or thy nose, thy paw or thy face, on this ground ever again."

And so saying MacVurich Mór of Stiligarry thrust the great monster's brat out at the window.

"Alas! alas!" said she, "though the other conditions were hard, this is the worst predicament of all." And she lifted the whelp on to her shoulders. The monster placed her brat on her back and she set off with a mighty stride singing this song:

Far from me is the base of Beinn Eadarra,
   Far from me undoubtedly is Bealach a' Mhorghain,
The back of the hills, the slope of the passes,
   The base of the cliffs and Bealach a' Mhorghain.

Miscellaneous

544 The auspicious day

Thou man who wouldst travel tomorrow,
 Illinn ho ro hu o hu o
Tarry a little as thou art,
 Hillirinn ho ro hu o hu o
 Hillinn o i hu o ho i
 Ho hiura bhi hu o hu o
 Hill o a bha hillinn o ro
Till I make a shirt of thread for thee;
There is waiting and waiting for that:
The lint was sown but has not grown,
The wool is on the sheep of the wasteland,
The loom is in the wood of Patrick,
The beam is in the highest tree,
The shuttle is with the King of Spain,
The bobbin is with the Queen,
The weaver is not born to her mother.
Thou man who wouldst travel tomorrow,
Thou shalt not go on Monday nor shalt thou go on Tuesday,
Wednesday is tormenting, hurtful,
On Thursday are temptation and turbulence,
Friday is a day of rest,
Saturday is to the Mary Mother,
Let the Lord's Day praise the High King.
Thou man who wouldst travel strongly,
Thou shalt not go on Monday, the end of the quarter.

Thou man who wouldst travel lightly,
There is red blood upon thy shirt;
Not blood of roe nor blood of deer,
But blood of thy body and thou full of wounds.

545 The brave men

The brave men are
On the flat of the moor,
And the beautiful women
On the flat of the glen,
With their grey plaids
And their pure-white feet,
And though sweet is the [flesh]
It is venison I sought.

O hi ri-ag ho ro-ag ho ro
Sna hi ri ri ri-ag ho ro ho hu

My love are the households
On whom gloom would not settle,
Who would procure venison
Where lead would not reach the birds,
And who would not require powder
To wake them into activity,
The killers of the solan goose —
Much fair fame is theirs to tell of.

O hi ri-ag ho ro-ag ho ro
Sna hi ri ri ri-ag ho ro ho hu

But a man of Clan Farquhar,
I would not leave thee neglected in a corner,
Seeing I am so persuaded
That thy conduct is faultless;

Thou wouldst bring the razor-bill
From the ledges of the Dunan,
And didst thou but get practice
Thou wouldst harry the fulmar.

O hi ri–ag ho ro–ag ho ro
Sna hi ri ri ri–ag ho ro ho hu

And a man of Clan Donald,
'Twere not right to rebuff him;
Thou art fashioned like a bull,
Thick of neck and broad of shoulder;
If I be not mistaken
Thou art the mightiest of thy clan —
Stouter the calf of thy leg
Than a well–matured body!

O hi ri–ag ho ro–ag ho ro
Sna hi ri ri ri–ag ho ro ho hu

546 Giùran

Giùran son of Giùran is
The unsheather of swords,
The ranger of the countryside
And the scourge of black Saxons;
And despite all the resentment,
The gossip and talk,
Giùran son of Giùran is
My love of them all.

I spent a year in delirium
Awaiting thy love;
I spent a year in a fever,
My word! I had cause;
My mother was wrangling,
My father was enraged,
But Giùran of heroic deeds
Is the dearest in the world to me.

I spent more than a year
   In the fever of thy love;
I spent more than a year,
   My word! 'twas not a trifle;
My father was cursing,
   My mother was weeping,
But Giùran of the hostages
   Is my darling of men.

547 Mhiog! Mhag! Ho!

Mhiog! mhag! ho!
The communion of the five *mags.*

I shall not make communion with Earc
Nor with the Son of the Red Earl
Until the ant shall bring a sack
   Hi hiura bhi hoireann o
Of the heady malt across the ocean.

Mhiog! mhag! ho!
The communion of the five *mags.*

I shall not make wooing with Earc
Nor with the son of the Red Earl
Until the speckled bee shall bring
   Hi hiura bhi hoireann o
The honey in its grasp across the meadow.

Mhiog! mhag! ho!
The communion of the five *mags.*

I shall not make pleasantness with Earc
Nor with the Son of the Red Earl
Until the speckled salmon shall give

Hi hiura bhi hoireann o
The three struggles in the pen of the lambs.

Mhiog! mhag! ho!
The communion of the five *mags.*

I shall not make poet's minstrelsy with Earc
Nor with the Son of the Red Earl
Until the speckled little bee shall bring
Hi hiura bhi hoireann o
A band of troops upon the flagstone of the tombs.

Mhiog! mhag! ho!
The communion of the five *mags.*

I shall not make repose with Earc
Nor with the Son of the Red Earl
Until yonder mountain below shall come
Hi hiura bhi hoireann o
To keep peace with yonder mountain above.

Mhiog! mhag! ho!
The communion of the five *mags.*

I shall not make pleasantness with Earc
Nor with the Son of the Red Earl
Until Fionn prince of the troops shall come
Hi hiura bhi hoireann o
To keep justice with Art of triumphs.

Mhiog! mhag! ho!
The communion of the five *mags.*

Mourning

Mourning–woman

In Tiree the tuirimeag or *bean–tuirim, bean–tuiream* (mourning–woman) was found until the middle of last century. The *bean–tuiream* followed the body, every now and then striking the coffin with her hands like a drum, and making all the din possible, and keeping time with the movements of the men. All the virtues of the dead, and a few more, were mentioned and extolled, and the genealogy for many generations praised and lauded.

There was some ill feeling between the last mourning–woman and a neighbour called Domhnall Ruadh, Red Donald. At their last encounter the woman said: "I will make thee live after thy death, Red Donald." The man died and the mourning–woman took her place at the head of the funeral procession according to custom. Beneath her cloak she carried a cat, and at the end of each verse of her elegy the cat called out. The young were amused, but the older were shocked to see the woman's malice and her misuse of her position. She was never again asked to mourn at a funeral, and the custom finally died out through her unseemly conduct. The aged narrator of this, Donald MacDonald, crofter in Manal, Tiree, quoted the saying:

A wicked woman will get her prayer,
Though her soul shall not get mercy.

A verse of the woman's elegy will suffice:

Thou art gone, thou art gone!
Thou art gone and hast remained not!
We shall see thee no more,
Black evil Donald!

In Lismore the place over which, whether by design or by accident, a funeral procession travels is ever after considered sacred and has a right of way.

In Barra a corpse is left forty–eight hours above ground, in Uist from three to five nights.

The *séis, séisig* or *séisig–bhàis,* death–mourning, or death–music, was the mourning in the house after the death. The *tuiream, tuirim* (lament) was the mourning in the open after the journey to the place of burial.

Piping. John MacDonald, Strombane, Lochmaddy, used to pipe after funerals in North Uist. I knew John MacDonald, a famous piper; he died about twenty years ago [dated 21st June 1904].

Gul, gal (weeping or sobbing) was applied to professional mourning. This has fallen into disuse in Scotland, though it is still practised in Ireland, where it is called *caoineadh* (keening). The writer prevailed upon a woman in Barra to give a practical illustration of this lost and almost forgotten art. The burial was that of a crofter–fisherman who died young; his house was in Lag nan Druisean, the Hollow of the Brambles, lying below Heaval, the highest hill in Barra. The scene was remarkable; below and right before us on its tidal rock stood the magnificent ruin of Ciosmal Castle, the ancient residence of MacNeil of Barra, and beyond this for twelve miles out to sea lay one behind another the isles of the Atlantic, usually wild and foamy, like lions at bay, this day peaceful and calm as lambs tired of play. The *bean–tuirim* (rehearsing– or lamenting–woman) was tall and handsome, though somewhat gaunt and bony, with long features and long arms. At first she was reluctant to sing, but by degrees she came to use her magnificent voice to the full and the result was striking in the extreme. She and I followed the body as it was carried in simple fashion on three staves by a man at either end of each. The woman rehearsed the grief, the bitter grief, of the winsome young widow, the cries, the bitter cries, of the helpless young children, asking, plaintively asking, who would now bring them the corn from the breird, the meal from the mill, the fish from the sea and the birds from the rocks? Who indeed? No one now, since he was laid low. She then rehearsed the sorrows of the poor and the needy, the friendless and the aged whom he had been wont to help. Who would help them now? Who indeed? No one now, since he was laid low.

Catherine Pearson, Ceann Tangabhal, Barra (24th September 1872), said: There was a midwife and a mourning–woman in each townland in Barra. And it was an obligation on the people of each townland to find each woman of the sort in summer grass and winter fodder to the satisfaction of the bailiff on the sword's edge. And the people might not see one of these suffer loss or want more than her fellow, in order that each of them should be able to do her duty when it came to her, and alas for her who should not – she was the woman of the hard fate!

548 Dirge

Whom have you there upon the staves?
Whom but my supporting shoulder,
Whom but my utter burning,
Whom but my close succour,
Whom but my burning coal of loss,
Whom but my darling and my treasure,
  Whom but the sap of the sap of my heart.

549 Threnody

Mary MacLeod the poetess, Màiri nighean Alasdair Ruaidh, lived for a time in Benbecula at Aird near Nunton, the house of Clan Ranald. A sister who lived with her died there, and her body was taken to Rodel in Harris for burial. On the way through North Uist, a professional bean–tuirim *(mourning–woman) accidentally met the funeral procession and instinctively joined in weeping and wailing, like to break her heart. After a while at this, the woman asked in an aside:*

But, O King of the world
And King of wondrous power,
What was the clan–name
Of my utter burning?

that is, of the dead person who was causing her such grief. The person she addressed happened to be Mary MacLeod, the sister of the deceased, and she at once replied:

Wert thou, my dear, in Kilmuir,
Or in Eynort of the solemn processions,
Or in Rodel of the bare tombstones,
It would not be asked what was thy surname!

550 Death–lament

Although thou hast died,
Love, thou hadst not needed to die;
Still uam, still am.

Thy little kebbocks of cheese
Had been placed on the withe;
Still uam, still am.

Thy little kegs of butter
Had been smoothed by thy hand;
Still uam, still am.

And thy little chests of meal
Had been pressed by thy foot.
Still uam, still am.

Where shall we go to make our plaint
When we are hungry on the round?
  Still uam, still am.

Where shall we go to warm ourselves
When we are chilled with cold?
  Still uam, still am.

Where shall we go for shelter
Since thy hearth is now dead?
  Still uam, still am.

Whom shall we resort to and visit
Since thy house, love, is cold?
  Still uam, still am.

Although thou hast died,
It was not thy wont to be gloomy;
  Still uam, still am.

Well mightest thou have stayed
To give crowdy to folk.
  Still uam, still am.

But, O gentle loved Mary,
Be thou kind to my love.
  Still uam, still am.

551 Mackintosh's lament

It is I am the wife of sorrow,
Wearing the cap of dolour,
Since all men have come to know
That on its crown is the favour.

It is I am in dire distress
Since in the earth they laid thee;
Carry my blessing with earnestness
To the tower of the high stones.

It is I who am sad
Since the beginning of the year;
Yet would I not have seek my hand
The son of earl or peer.

The day is bright and sunny,
There is music on the meadows,
There is wine in plenty there —
That will not banish my gloom.

Yet shall I not go to wedding,
Never more to feast or to fair,
'Twas in the beginning of springtide
I received the arrow that pierced me.

Beloved was my sweetheart,
Beauteous branch of the clustering locks,
More fragrant than cinnamon
To me the breath of thy mouth.

Beloved was my courtier,
Loveliest branch of the country,
Like the garden of apples
Was thy dalliance and mirth.

It is thou who wouldst dance evenly
When they played to thee the music,
And thou wouldst not bend the grass-blade
Beneath the point of thy high shoe.

Hunter of the deer thou,
Of the grilse on the waterfall,
Of the capercailzie on the bough,
While the white bird thou wouldst kill.

My love and my joy
Both early and late,
At feast and at fair,
'Tis thy arrow that pierced me.

It is I who was gay,
Mirthful and merry-eyed,

It is I who am now sad
Since my treasure lies under the sod.

The wines for thy wedding
They went to thy wake;
Ah King! but I was tearful
While the measures were being drained.

'Tis I am the woman of tears
Every morning as I arise,
Bearing the kertch
Each feast-day and Sabbath.

'Tis I am the maid of great grief
Whom none again will recognise
Since this time last year
When the ring was put on me.

'Tis I who am in sore distress,
Often the tears flow from mine eyes,
I missing the noble sapling,
The gallant rider of comely steeds.

I was a maid, I was kertched,
I was veiled and mated;
Alas, alas, what befell me
All in the space of a day!

I was snooded, I was kertched,
I am a poor, tearful widow,
The wound of wounds is paining me grievously,
No plaster can avail me.

Beloved is my sweetheart,
Beloved while I live,
Beloved on earth
And in the kingdom of the High King.

My love and my desire art thou,
My love and my harp of music art thou,
My love art thou and my devoted one,
My hope for thee is in Paradise.

Young Ewen, thou art fallen,
Young Ewen, thou art fallen,
Young Ewen, thou art fallen
In the breach of the wall.

Alas, alas, thou art fallen,
Alas, alas, thou art raised,
Alas, alas, thou art fallen
In the breach of the wall.

The bald–faced horse threw thee,
The bald–faced horse raised thee,
The bald–faced horse threw thee
By the site of the wall.

Oh! an I were there,
Oh! an I were there,
Oh! an I were there,
I would have grasped thine hand.

Rider of the prancing black steed,
Prancing black steed, prancing black steed,
Rider of the prancing black steed,
The white steed tore thee.

Young Ewen, thou art fallen,
Young Ewen, thou art fallen,
Young Ewen, thou art fallen
In the breach of the wall.

552 Mackintosh's lament

Thou art being lifted on the bier,
  Thy converse is not heard,
In a coffin slender, shapely,
  Of pine the fairest.

Ubh ubhanaich! oich oicheanaich!
Ubh ubhanaich! oich oicheanaich!
Ubh ubhanaich! oich oicheanaich!
Ubh ubhanaich! And ochan, ochan,
  my affliction!

Thy being placed in the grave
  Has turned my gladness to sorrow,
Has turned my eyes to weeping,
  Has darkened hope and strength to me,
Has turned my day to wailing,
  Has turned my night to mourning,
Nor was there a string within my heart
  That was not daunted all at once.

Ubh ubhanaich! oich oicheanaich!
Ubh ubhanaich! oich oicheanaich!
Ubh ubhanaich! oich oicheanaich!
Ubh ubhanaich! And ochan, ochan,
  my affliction!

The black steed and the dun steed
  Lie prone upon the plain,
The black steed and the dun steed
  Lie prone upon the plain,
The black steed and the dun steed
  Lie prone upon the plain,
And Mackintosh without stirring,
  Unable to succour his kin.

Dead in my arms! dead in my arms!
Dead in my arms! dead in my arms!
Dead in my arms! dead in my arms!
The beautiful son of the mountains!

Thou King of life and angels,
Keep Thy promise to the wicked,
Bare the edge of Thy sword,
Press against the people of rapine!
The dastards who slew my love
In the fresh glory of youth,
And who awakened my soul to anguish,
O King of the Sun, do thou pursue them!

For the sake of Him who was crucified,
O King, sharpen now Thy face to them,
Crown Thou Thy will upon the assassins,
Keep now Thy sharp blade alive!
Behold Thou me in mine agony,
Behold Thou the wounds of my country,
Seize Thou the wolf in his lair
And exact a double vengeance!

Thou Mackintosh of manly mien,
The beauty spot was on thy brow,
Lyre and viol were in thy house
And crowd and harp of melody;
Maidens and heroes were wont to be
In thy proud plenteous halls,
While thy pipes sounded passionately
Following the rout with thy sons beloved!

Thou Lachlan the gracious! thou Lachlan the gracious!
Thou Lachlan the gracious! thou Lachlan the gracious!
Thou Lachlan the gracious! thou Lachlan the gracious!
Thou Lachlan the gracious! till doomsday thou wilt not stir!

Variant of the last verse:

Streamers and banners would be
In the pursuit on the heath with thee,
While the wail of thy pipes sounded furiously
As the sons of evil were being slaughtered.

Lachlan is in his sleep! Lachlan is in his sleep!
Lachlan is in his sleep! Lachlan is in his sleep!
Lachlan is in his sleep! Lachlan is in his sleep!
Till doomsday he will not waken!

553 Beautiful Margaret

The chair of my mother is void, cold and empty,
My father who loved me is sleeping in the tomb;
I am travelling the wilds to no purpose on earth,
Since I have now none of my kindred but a sister without pity.

The chair of my mother is void, cold and empty,
My father who loved me is dwelling in the tomb;
I am travelling the heights all alone upon earth,
Since in the world there is none of my kindred save a sister without pity.

She sought and I gave her the cause of my distress,
Since I had none under the sun to whom to reveal my secret;
But this I felt, and it brought the flood to mine eyes,
That sooner will a secret come through the mouth than through the knee.

Never prosper the thing in which thou puttest thy love,
Nor ever fall the dew on the earth of thy garden,
Nor ever sing the lark over thy dwelling,
Nor ever behold thine eye the form beneath thy girdle.

May the worm and the maggot possess thy store,
May the moth and the belly–worm work within the lid of thy chest;
Were there hearing of the prayer of a sister sobbing and mourning,
Avenged would be her tears even upon thy children.

May the marten and the harrier be plundering thy fowls,
May the fox and the wolf be bartering thy sheep,
May madness and blindness be searching out thy horses,
May murrain and spring–losses be sundering thy kine.

I am travelling the sheilings, I am travelling the heights,
I am travelling the places frequented of my love;
I am travelling the groves and the corries and the woods
From the base of the mountains to the crest of the hills.

I am watching the passes and traversing the hollows,
To see if I behold my lover who was gracious and kind;
I see not thee, my love, I see not glimpse of thee
On the tops of the mountains nor at the edge of the sea.

I am visiting the streams and I am visiting the rivers,
I am visiting the bowers, the rock–shelves and the caves,
To try if I can see thy form, to try if I can hear thy voice;
I see and hear nought but the sorrowing of the sea.

554 Lullaby

The nest of the raven
Is in the hawthorn rock,
My little one will sleep and he shall have the bird.

The nest of the seagull
Is in the rock of droppings,
My little one will sleep and he shall have the bird.

The nest of the ptarmigan
Is in the rough mountain,
My little one will sleep and he shall have the bird.

The nest of the mavis
Is in the bonnie copse,
My little one will sleep and he shall have the bird.

The nest of the blackbird
Is in the withered bough,
My little one will sleep and he shall have the bird.

The nest of the skylark
Is in the track of "Dubhag,"*
My little one will sleep and he shall have the bird.

The nest of the pigeon
Is in the red crags,
My little one will sleep and he shall have the bird.

The nest of the wild–duck
Is in the bank of the lakelet,
My little one will sleep and he shall have the bird.

The nest of the cuckoo
Is in the hedge–sparrow's nest,
My little one will sleep and he shall have the bird.

The nest of the sealark
Is in the level shingle–beach,
My little one will sleep and he shall have the bird.

The nest of the tealduck
Is in the breast of the tree,
My little one will sleep and he shall have the bird.

* A cow.

The nest of the lapwing
Is in the hummocked marsh,
My little one will sleep and he shall have the bird.

The nest of the kite
Is high on the mountain–slope,
My little one will sleep and he shall have the bird.

The nest of the wren
Is in the rock thicket,
My little one will sleep and he shall have the bird.

The nest of the plover
Is in the wooded copse,
My little one will sleep and he shall have the bird.

The nest of the red–hen
Is in the green red–tipped heather,
My little one will sleep and he shall have the bird.

The nest of the starling
Is under the wing of the thatch,
My little one will sleep and he shall have the bird.

The nest of the heath–hen
Is in the marshland mound,
My little one will sleep and he shall have the bird.

The nest of the curlew
Is in the bubbling peat–moss,
My little one will sleep and he shall have the bird.

The nest of the oyster–catcher
Is among the smooth shingles,
My little one will sleep and he shall have the bird.

The nest of the heron
Is in the pointed trees,
My little one will sleep and he shall have the bird.

The nest of the bullfinch
Is in the wood of the dell,
My little one will sleep and he shall have the bird.

The nest of the stonechat
Is in the garden dike,
   My little one will sleep and he shall have the bird.

The nest of the rook
Is in the tree's top,
   My little one will sleep and he shall have the bird.

555 Sain mine own lover in the field

Thou youth who goest in the chase,
There was a time when I was thy chosen one,
The maiden now pillowed by thy face,
Once methought she was not thy choice.

      I ag eile bho i o
      Bho hi ro ho hug o
      I ag eile bho ro
      Bho hi ro ro ro
      Hao ri o hu

Thou man the most comely who moves on plain,
Much noble blood is kin to thee;
O Thou who wast crucified above the others,
Sain mine own lover in the field!

      I ag eile bho i o
      Bho hi ro ho hug o
      I ag eile bho ro
      Bho hi ro ro ro
      Hao ri o hu

A sprightly fellow is the stag
In the brindled bower dwelling,
Yet though strong and sturdy be his bound,
He cannot aye escape from death.

I ag eile bho i o
Bho hi ro ho hug o
I ag eile bho ro
Bho hi ro ro ro
Hao ri o hu

My loved one is beauteous and fair–shapen,
A hand of valour which a blade well becomes,
A man welcoming, mild, generous, liberal,
Blithe, mannerly, pleasant of temper, well–endowed.

I ag eile bho i o
Bho hi ro ho hug o
I ag eile bho ro
Bho hi ro ro ro
Hao ri o hu

556 Hogmanay verse

Tonight is the hard night of Hogmanay,
I am come with a lamb to sell —
The old fellow yonder sternly said
He would strike my ear against a rock.

The woman, better of speech, said
That I should be let in;
For my food and for my drink,
A morsel due and something with it!

557 Hogmanay rime

The rime that follows is for lads that have no other rime.

I have no dislike to cheese,
   I have no disgust of butter,
But a little sip of barley bree
   I am right willing to put down!

558 The song of Hogmanay

Tonight is the last night of the year,
   Be generous to me in the dwelling,
As I come to sing my Hogmanay song,
   Give to me timely heed.

The wedding–feast of the black lad of the snuff
   Is a cause of pondering in the place;
Were I among the rabble,
   Many an ugly fellow there would be.

Some at flattery, some at lies,
   Some at words unwonted,
Others devouring the gizzards
   Of the wheezy grey fowls;

Some of them fixing their back–teeth
   In the back joints of the cattle,
And some of them hunkering down
   In a corner on a heap of potatoes.

They are from every quarter of the land,
   The hungry ones of the corners and the cairns;
'Tis the rumbling of their bodies has brought
   Three of them, at any rate, to this place.

[One brought] the chicken here from Lewis,
  A ragged–foot from Kintail,
A great clumsy lout that was in Tiree
  Who ate the milk–pail–cover in Balemartin.

Since it is not worth my telling
  The state of this country with yon rabble,
I hope that I shall get a morsel,
  And that there will be butter and cheese on it.

I pray for you sweethearting and peace
  Until a year from this time, O friends,
And since my feet are bare,
  Open to me the fastening of the door.

559 There is music in the marriage house

There is music in the marriage house,
There is ale, there is speaking;
But were there remembrance of the good that was,
'Tis the good that was which would be.

560 Glen Liadail

Glen of my heart is Glen Liadail,
  A glen that is not wild to see,
A glen whereto the world resorts,
  A glen wherein are fields and shelter.

I will go into thee, thou green glen,
  And I will go from thee as I went in,
Under compact of the safeguard of the great ones,
  Who would travel the plain as well as the glen.

Ascending the Fairy–Hill of the Pass,
  I saw a sight of the sun,
Going sunwise around Ni Ruairidh's Grave,
  Where the spectres rise.

561 The King of Sionn

The candle hard and round
Which I am now set to hold
In the smoke of the wick:
  Once that was not my custom;

But to be scaling the steeps,
And ranging the corries,
And visiting the hills
  And the hollows beloved;

Traversing the breast of Beinn a' Bheithir,
Traversing the breast of Beinn a' Cheathaich,
Going with my father and my grandfather
  Hunting hinds and grown stags.

It was not a smoky bonfire
To which I at first was used,
But a house without ashes or dust,
  The blithe castle of my father and mother.

562 A fragment

The roar of battles on the hillock of Samhain
  Above me;
The weeping of the women on the haugh of the river
  At the entrance to this plain.

Women bereft, a rugged bed,
  Fierce the contest
That will come after it, that will come heavily on them,
  Fierce the contest.

563 The hare

Whoever reads my testimonial,
I was unquestionably virtuous,
Without gloom or servility
  In my nature.

I would not eat rank grass,
What was food for my kind
Was the fine herbs
  Of the moorlands.

My cap, though it be reddish,
Was beloved by gentle ladies,
And my haunch, though cold,
  By gentlemen.

'Tis a sad tale to tell
That I am tonight laid low
And that my brain-pan
  Is being mangled,

After they had removed my coat
Right down to my paws,
And roasted my carcase
  On embers.

Not thus was I at
The Martinmas season
Frisking and sporting
  Mid the rough hills.

Without thought at that time
That the villain would come
With his gin to ensnare me
   In the gloaming.

I was at home on the heaths
Where my father and ancestors
Were sportive, merry
   And spirited;

Nibbling the blades of grass
On rounded slopes and moors,
Though I fell into the snare
   Which was grievous for me.

564 Oisean's servants

Oisean was blind but he used to go out every night to attend to the cattle. He always had a gillie and a servant.

The gillie went out and he came in and said:

It is outside the heavy rumbling is,
   Heavy rainfall from the tops of the trees;
I cannot hear the heaving of the waves
   For the heavy showers showering from the trees.

The storms are coming from the east,
   White snow and a black deluge;
What has left the plain so cold
   Is severe fall and drift of snow.

The trees of the forest are quaking,
   Their tops have become a black mass,
The snow is truly killing the birds:
   That is what it is like outside.

Said the girl:

Arise, Oisean, to look to
   The white–shouldered, white–footed cattle,
The cold wind of the thaw
   Is bending the branches of the nut wood.

The lads got a water–tub. They were in front of Oisean. There was one behind Oisean who had a hold of him by his ears guiding him to the cattle. The girl had a brushwood broom and she was dipping the brush–wood in the tub and sprinkling the water in Oisean's face. When they reached the cattle they left Oisean and the guide there. The night was very fine.

"I understand what it is," said Oisean; and Oisean never again sent anybody out at night to look after the cattle.

565 Oisean's nine skewers

Oisean had nine skewers in his stomach to restrain his appetite. He was getting the food of fifteen men and he could lift a lintel above a door which fifteen warriors could not manage.

"That was the best feat," said they.

"If the people inside gave me the food of sixteen men, that were no feat," said Oisean.

566 The finger–compassing

Who is before me?
Who is behind me?
Who is beneath me?
   God and the Lord.

Who upholds me?
The Three of power,
Father and Son
   And Spirit of peace.

Farewell

The Fairy and the Hunter

Fare thee well, brown hunter of the hill, farewell to thee for ever on this side of the mountain stream and the side beyond the river, the day I see thee and the day I see thee not, the day thou huntest the forest deer and the day, beloved one, thou huntest none.

Alexander Carmichael

Editorial Note on the present edition

Alexander Carmichael's magnificent collection of Gaelic oral folklore, charms, songs, hymns and incantations, owes its survival in written form not only to his own lifetime's work but also to the dedicated efforts of later editors: his daughter, Ella; his grandson, James Carmichael Watson (Volumes III and IV); and lastly Angus Matheson for his careful preparation of Volumes V and VI.

The principal aim of this edition is to present Carmichael's collection in a readable and accessible form to the non–Gaelic speaking world. To this end, I have had to compress material from five of the original volumes between the covers of one single volume, and sacrifices have sadly but necessarily had to be made. Omissions include the several biographical and memorial tributes to the succeeding editors. The loss perhaps most regretted has been Carmichael's own Gaelic glossary at the end of Volume II, though some material has been borrowed from this where helpful. Lack of space also forced the omission of the full list of Carmichael's reciters and informants for Volumes I and II, though a good number of these are identified in the relevant notes.

Here, the verses themselves make up the main body of the book, with most of Carmichael's prose descriptions as endnotes. However, some of the accounts of the folklore and the practices accompanying use of the verses have been reorganized as introductions to relevant sections.

For the sake of readability, variants and queries — a concomitant aspect of oral tradition — have been removed or simplified in the poetry, and a small number of Carmichael's original notes have been deleted or abbreviated. Gaelic words have been glossed where kept; where there is no accompanying gloss, the sense is unclear. Orthography and quotations are for the most part left as in the original editions.

To provide ease of reference, numbering in the present edition runs consecutively throughout the entire collection, corresponding to Carmichael's original sequence in Volumes I and II (nos. 1–216) but departing from it in Volume III (in subsequent volumes no numbering was provided). A concordance has been added in this revised edition (1994) so that items can be traced back to the original five volumes.

C J Moore
February 1994

Index to themes in the notes

(numbers refer to the Note number)

Notes

VOLUME I

1 Old people in the Isles sing this or some other short hymn before prayer. Sometimes the hymn and the prayer are intoned in low tremulous unmeasured cadences like the moving and moaning, the soughing and the sighing, of the ever-murmuring sea on their own wild shores.

They generally retire to a closet, to an out-house, to the lee of a knoll, or to the shelter of a dell, that they may not be seen nor heard of men. I have known men and women of eighty, ninety, and a hundred years of age continue the practice of their lives in going from one to two miles to the seashore to join their voices with the voicing of the waves and their praises with the praises of the ceaseless sea.

2 This poem was taken down in 1866 from Mary Macrae, Harris. She came from Kintail when young, with Alexander Macrae, whose mother was one of the celebrated ten daughters of MacLeod of Rararsay, mentioned by Johnson and Boswell. Mary Macrae was rather under than over middle height, but strongly and symmetrically formed. She often walked with companions, after the work of the day was done, distances of ten and fifteen miles to a dance, and after dancing all night, walked back again to the work of the morning fresh and vigorous as if nothing unusual had occurred. She was a faithful servant and an admirable worker, and danced at her leisure and carolled at her work like *Fosgag Mhoire,* Our Lady's Lark, above her.

The people of Harris had been greatly given to old lore and to the old ways of their fathers, reciting and singing, dancing and merry-making; but a reaction occurred, and Mary Macrae's old-world ways were abjured and condemned.

The bigots of an iron time
Had called her simple art a crime.

But Mary Macrae heeded not, and went on in her own way, singing her songs and ballads, intoning her hymns and incantations, and chanting her own *port-a-bial,* mouth music, and dancing to her own shadow when nothing better was available.

I love to think of this brave kindly woman, with her strong Highland characteristics and her proud Highland spirit. She was a true type of a grand people gone never to return.

3 Duncan Maclellan, crofter, Carnan, South Uist, heard this poem from Catherine Macaulay in the early years of this century. When the crofters along the east side of South Uist were removed, many of the more frail and aged left behind became houseless and homeless, moving among and existing upon the crofters left remaining along the west side of the island.

Among these was Catherine Macaulay. She wandered about from house to house, and from townland to townland, warmly welcomed and cordially received wherever she went, and remained in each place longer or shorter according to the population and the season, and as the people could spare the time to hear her. The description which Duncan Maclellan gave of Catherine Macaulay, and of the people who crowded his father's house to hear her night after night, and week after week, and of the discussions that followed her recitations, were realistic and instructive. Being then but a child he could not follow the meaning of this lore, but he thought many times since that much of it must have been about the wild beliefs and practices of his people of the long long ago, and perhaps not so long ago either. Many of the poems and stories were long and weird, and he could only remember fragments, which came up to him as he lay awake, thinking of the present and the past, and of the contrast between the two, even in his own time.

I heard versions of this poem in other islands and in districts of the mainland, and in November 1888 John Gregorson Campbell, minister of Tiree, sent me a fragment taken down from Margaret Macdonald, Tiree. The poem must therefore have been widely known. In Tiree the poem was addressed to boys and girls, in Uist to young men and maidens. Probably it was composed to a maiden on her marriage. The phrase *eala dhonn,* brown swan, would indicate that the girl was young — not yet a white swan.

5 The three poems which follow were obtained from Dr Donald Munro Morrison in 1889, a few days before he died. Dr Morrison heard them from an old man known as "Coinneach Saor" (Kenneth the Carpenter) and his wife, at Obbe, Harris. These aged people were habitually practising quaint religious ceremonies and singing curious religious poems to peculiar music, evidently ancient. In childhood, Dr Morrison lived much with this couple and in manhood recorded much of their old lore and music. These however he noted in characters and notations of his own invention which he did not live to render intelligible to others. This is extremely regrettable as Dr Morrison's wonderfully wide, accurate and scientific attainments, deep knowledge of Gaelic, of music and of acoustics, were only surpassed by his native modesty of mind and tender benevolence of heart. He was a distinguished medallist in several subjects at the University of Edinburgh.

14 The reciter said that this poem was composed by a woman in Harris. She was afflicted with leprosy, and was removed from the community on the upland to dwell alone on the seashore, where she lived on the plants of the plains and on the shellfish of the strand. The woman bathed herself in the liquid in which she had boiled the plants and shellfish. All her sores became healed and her flesh became new — probably as the result of the action of the plants and shellfish.

Leprosy was common everywhere in medieval times. In Shetland the disease continued till towards the end of last century. Communities erected lazar-houses to safeguard themselves from persons afflicted with leprosy. Liberton, now a suburb of Edinburgh, derives its name from a lazaretto having been established there.

The shrine of St James of Compostella in Spain was famous for the cure of leprosy. Crowds of leper pilgrims from the whole of Christendom resorted to this shrine, and many of them were healed to the glory of the Saint and the enrichment of his shrine. In their gratitude, pilgrims offered costly oblations of silks and satins, of raiments and vestments, of silver and gold, of pearls and precious stones, till the shrine of St James of Compostella became famous throughout the world. The bay of Compostella was famed for fish and shellfish, and the leper pilgrims who came to pray at the altar of the Saint and to bestow gifts at his shrine were fed on those and were healed, according to the belief of the period, by the miraculous intervention of the Saint. As the palm was the badge of the pilgrims to Jerusalem, the scallop-shell was the badge of the pilgrims to Compostella: "My sandal shoon and scallop shell."

20 Proverbs anent law and justice abound in Gaelic, as: "Crooked and straight is the law;" "A witling may give judgment, but who will give justice?" "Like the justice of the fox, crooked, cunning, corrupt."

The administration of law and justice throughout the Highlands and Islands before the abolition of heritable jurisdictions was inadequate — men being too often appointed to administer justice not from their fitness but from their influence. Probably the feeling of distrust engendered by this absence of even-handed justice evoked these poems from the consciousness of the people and led them to appeal their cause to a Higher Court.

The litigant went at morning dawn to a place where three streams met. And as the rising sun gilded the mountain crests, the man placed his two palms edgeways together and filled them with water from the junction of the streams. Dipping his face into this improvised basin, he fervently repeated the prayer, after which he made his way to the court, feeling strong in the justice of his cause. On entering the court and on looking round the room, the applicant for justice said mentally, sometimes in an undertone:

God sain the house
From site to summit;
My word above every person,
The word of every person below my foot.

The ceremonies observed in saying these prayers for justice, like those observed on many similar occasions, are symbolic. The bathing represents purification; the junction of three streams, the union of the Three Persons of the Godhead; and the spreading rays of the morning sun, divine grace. The deer is symbolic of wariness, the horse of strength, the serpent of wisdom, and the king of dignity.

24 This poem was taken down at Creagorry, Benbecula, on the 16th December, 1872, from Janet Campbell, nurse, Lochskiport, South Uist. The reciter had many beautiful songs and lullabies of the nursery, and many instructive sayings and fables of the animal world. These she sang and told in the most pleasing and natural manner, to the delight of her listeners. Birds and beasts, reptiles and insects, whales and fishes talked and acted through her in the most amusing manner, and in the most idiomatic Gaelic.

Her stories had a charm for children, and it was delightful to see a small cluster of little ones pressing round the narrator, all eyes, all ears, all mouth, and all attention, listening to what the bear said to the bee, the fox to the lamb, the harrier to the hen, the serpent to the pipet, the whale to the herring, and the brown otter of the stream to the silvery grilse of the current. Those fair young heads, now, alas! widely apart, probably remember some of the stories heard at Janet Campbell's knee better than those they afterwards heard in more formal schools.

26 The night prayers of the people are numerous. They are called by various names, such as: *Beannachadh Beinge,* Bench-Blessing, *Beannachadh Bobhstair,* Bolster Blessing, *Beannachadh Cluasaig,* Pillow Blessing, *Beannachadh Cuaiche,* Couch Blessing, *Coich Chuaiche,* Couch Shrining, *Altachadh Cadail,* Sleep Prayer; and other terms. Many of these prayers are become mere fragments and phrases, supplemented by the people according to their wants and wishes at the time.

It is touching and instructive to hear these simple old men and women in their lowly homes addressing, as they say themselves, *"Dia mor an dul, Athair nan uile bheo"* (the great God of life, the Father of all living). They press upon Him their needs and their desires fully and familiarly, but with all the awe and deference due to the Great Chief whom they wish to approach and to attract, and whose forgiveness and aid they would secure. And all this in language so homely yet so eloquent, so simple yet so dignified, that the impressiveness could not be greater in proudest fane.

38 The Soul Shrine is sung by the people as they retire to rest. They say that the angels of heaven guard them in sleep and shield them from harm. Should any untoward event occur to themselves or to their flocks, they avow that the cause was the deadness of their hearts, the coldness of their faith, and the fewness of their prayers.

50 It is known that a form of baptism prevailed among the Celts previous to the introduction of Christianity, as forms of baptism prevail among pagan people now. Whenever possible the Celtic Church christianized existing ceremonies and days of special observance, grafting the new on the old, as at a later day Augustine did in southern Britain. Immediately after its birth the nurse or other person present drops three drops of water on the forehead of the child. The first drop is in the name of the Father, representing wisdom; the second drop is in the name of the Son, representing peace; the third drop is in the name of the Spirit, representing purity.

If the child be a male the name *Maol-domhnuich,* if a female the name *Griadach,* is applied to it temporarily. *Maol-domhnuich* means "tonsured of the Lord," and *Griadach* is rendered Gertrude. When the child is ecclesiastically baptized — generally at the end of eight days — the temporary is superseded by the permanent name. This lay baptism is recognized by the Presbyterian, the Anglican, the Latin, and the Greek Churches. If the child were not thus baptized it would need to be carefully guarded lest the fairies should spirit it away before the ecclesiastical baptism took place, when their power over it ceased. The lay baptism also ensured that in the event of death the child should be buried in consecrated ground.

51 Death blessings vary in words but not in spirit. These death blessings are known by various names, such as: *Beannachadh Bais* (Death Blessing), *Treoraich Anama* (Soul Leading), *Fois Anama* (Soul Peace), and other names familiar to the people.

The soul peace is intoned, not necessarily by a cleric, over the dying, and the man or the woman who says it is called *anam–chara* (soul–friend). He or she is held in special affection by the friends of the dying person ever after. The soul peace is slowly sung — all present earnestly joining the soul–friend in beseeching the Three Persons of the Godhead and all the saints of heaven to receive the departing soul of earth. During the prayer the soul–friend makes the sign of the cross with the right thumb over the lips of the dying.

The scene is touching and striking in the extreme, and the man or woman is not to be envied who could witness unmoved the distress of these lovable people of the West taking leave of those who are near and dear to them in their pilgrimage, as they say, of crossing *abhuinn dubh a bhais* (the black river of death), *cuan mor na duibhre* (the great ocean of darkness), and *beanntaibh na bith–bhuantachd* (the mountains of eternity). The scene may be in a lowly cot begrimed with smoke and black with age, but the heart is not less warm, the tear is not less bitter, and the parting is not less distressful, than in the court of the noble or in the palace of royalty.

According to the old people, when a person gives up the ghost the soul is seen ascending like a bright ball of light into the clouds. Then it is said:

The poor soul is now set free
Outside the soul–shrine;
O kindly Christ of the free blessings.
Encompass Thou my love in time.

54 This little prayer is said by old men and women in the islands of Barra. When they first see the new moon they make their obeisance to it as to a great chief. The women curtsey gracefully and the men bow low, raising their bonnets reverently. The bow of the men is peculiar, partaking somewhat of the curtsey of the women, the left knee being bent and the right drawn forward towards the middle of the left leg in a curious but not inelegant manner.

The fragment of moon–worship is now a matter of custom rather than of belief, although it exists over the whole British Isles. In Cornwall the people nod to the new moon and turn silver in their pockets. In Edinburgh cultured men and women turn the rings on their fingers and make their wishes. A young English lady told the writer that she had always been in the habit of bowing to the new moon, till she had been bribed out of it by her father, a clergyman, putting money in her pocket lest her lunar worship should compromise him with his bishop. She naively confessed, however, that among the free mountains of Loch Etive she reverted to the good customs of her fathers, from which she derived great satisfaction!

55 Christmas chants were numerous and their recital common throughout Scotland. They are now disappearing with the customs they accompanied. Where they still linger their recital is relegated to boys. Formerly on Christmas Eve bands of young men went about from house to house and from townland to townland chanting Christmas songs. The band was called *goisearan* (guisers), *fir–duan* (song–men), *gillean Nollaig* (Christmas lads), *nuallairean* (rejoicers), and other names. The “rejoicers” wore long white shirts for surplices, and very tall white hats for mitres, in which they made a picturesque appearance as they moved along singing their loudest. Sometimes they went about as one band, sometimes in sections of twos and threes. When they entered a dwelling they took possession of a child, if there was one in the house. In the absence of a child, a lay figure was improvised. The child was called *Crist, Cristean* (Christ, Little Christ). The assumed Christ was placed on a skin, and carried three times round the fire, sunwise, by the *ceannsnaodh* (head of the band), the song men singing the Christmas Hail. The skin on which the symbolic Christ was carried was that of a white male lamb without spot or blemish and consecrated to this service. The skin was called *uilim.* Homage and offerings and much rejoicing were made to the symbolic Christ. The people of the house gave the guisers bread, butter, crowdie, and other eatables, on which they afterwards feasted.

The three poems which follow were taken down from Angus Gunn, Ness, Lewis, then over eighty-four years of age. Angus Gunn had been a strong man physically and was still a strong man mentally. He had lived for many years in the island of North Roney, and gave a graphic description of it, and of his life there. He had much oral lore which he told with great dramatic power.

58 These carols were sung by a band of men who went about from house to house in the townland. The band selected a leader for their singing and for their actions throughout the night. This leader was called *fear-duan* (song-man), and the others were called *fir-fuinn* (chorus-men). When they had sung their carols at a house, two or three bannocks were handed out to them through a window.

The song-man got half of every bannock so received, and the other half went to the chorus-men.

63 This rune is still repeated in the Isles. Rarely, however, do two persons recite it alike. This renders it difficult to decide the right form of the words.

The walls of the old houses in the West are very thick — from five to eight feet. There are no gables, the walls being of uniform height throughout. The roof of the house being raised from the inner edge of the wall, a broad terrace is left on the outside. Two or three stones project from the wall at the door, forming steps. On these the inmates ascend for purposes of thatching and securing the roof in time of storm.

The *gillean Callaig* (carollers or Hogmanay lads) perambulate the townland at night. One man is enveloped in the hard hide of a bull with the horns and hoofs still attached. When the men come to a house they ascend the wall and run round sunwise, the man in the hide shaking the horns and hoofs, and the other men striking the hard hide with sticks. The appearance of the man in the hide is gruesome, while the din made is terrific. Having descended and recited their runes at the door, the Hogmanay men are admitted and treated to the best in the house. The performance seems to be symbolic, but of what it is not easy to say, unless of laying an evil spirit. That the rite is heathen and ancient is evident.

67 This poem was repeated the first thing on the first day of the year. It was common throughout the Highlands and Islands. The writer has heard versions of it in many places.

69 *Diardaoin, Didaoirn* (the day between the fasts, that is, Thursday) was St Columba's Day — *Diardaoin Chaluim-chille* (St Columba's Thursday) — and through him the day of many important events in the economy of the people. It was a lucky day for all enterprises — for warping thread, for beginning a pilgrimage, or any other undertaking. On Thursday eve the mother of a family made a bere, rye, or oaten cake into which she put a small silver coin. The cake was toasted before a fire of rowan, yew, oak, or other sacred wood.

On the morning of Thursday the father took a keen-cutting knife and cut the cake into as many sections as there were children in the family, all the sections being equal. All the pieces were then placed in a *ciosan* (a beehive basket) and each child blindfold drew a piece of cake from the basket in name of the Father, Son, and Spirit. The child who got the coin got the crop of lambs for the year. This was called *sealbh uan* (lamb luck). Sometimes it was arranged that the person who got the coin got a certain number of the lambs, and the others the rest of the lambs among them. Each child had a separate mark, and there was much emulation as to who had most lambs, the best lambs, and who took best care of the lambs.

Maundy Thursday is called in Uist *Diardaoin a brochain* (Gruel Thursday), and in Iona *Diardaoin a brochain mhoir* (Great Gruel Thursday). On this day people in maritime districts made offerings of mead, ale, or gruel to the god of the sea. As the day merged from Wednesday to Thursday a man walked to the waist into the sea and poured out whatever offering had been prepared, chanting:

> O God of the sea,
> Put weed in the drawing wave
> To enrich the ground,
> To shower on us food.

Those behind the offerer took up the chant and wafted it along the sea-shore on the midnight air, the darkness of night and the rolling of the waves making the scene weird and impressive. In 1860 the writer conversed in Iona with a middle-aged man whose father, when young, had taken part in this ceremony. In Lewis the custom was continued till this century. It shows the tolerant spirit of the Columban Church and the tenacity of popular belief, that such a practice should have been in vogue so recently.

The only exception to the luck of Thursday was when Beltane fell on that day:

> When the Wednesday is Hallowmas
> Restless are the men of the universe;
> But woe the mother of the foolish son
> When Thursday is the Beltane.

70 The Genealogy of Bride was current among people who had a latent belief in its efficacy. Other hymns to Bride were sung on her festival, but nothing now remains except the names and fragments of the words. The names are curious and suggestive, as: *Ora Bhride* (Prayer of Bride), *Lorg Bhride* (Staff of Bride), *Luireach Bhride* (Lorica of Bride), *Lorig Bhride* (Mantle of Bride), *Brot Bhride* (Corslet of Bride), and others. *La Feill Bhride* (St Bridget's Day) is the first of February, new style, or the thirteenth according to the old style, which is still much in use in the Highlands. It was a day of great rejoicing and jubilation in olden times, and gave rise to innumerable sayings, as "Feast of the Bride, feast of the maiden;" "Melodious Bride of the fair palms;" or:

> Thou Bride fair charming,
> Pleasant to me the breath of thy mouth,
> When I would go among strangers
> Thou thyself wert the hearer of my tale.

There are many legends and customs connected with Bride. Some of these seem inconsistent with one another, and with the character of the Saint of Kildare. These seeming inconsistencies arise from the fact that there were several Brides, Christian and pre-Christian, whose personalities have become confused in the course of centuries — the attributes of all being now popularly ascribed to one. Bride is said to preside over fire, over art, over all beauty, *fo cheabhar agus fo chuan* (beneath the sky and beneath the sea). And man being the highest type of ideal beauty, Bride presides at his birth and dedicates him to the Trinity. She is the Mary and the Juno of the Gael. She is much spoken of in connection with Mary, generally in relation to the birth of Christ. She was the aid-woman of the Mother of Nazareth in the lowly stable, and she is the aid-woman of the mothers of Uist in their humble homes.

It is said that Bride was the daughter of poor pious parents, and the serving-maid in the inn of Bethlehem. Great drought occurred in the land, and the master of the hostel went away with his cart to procure water from afar, leaving with Bride a stoup of water and a bannock of bread to sustain her till his return. The man left injunctions with Bride not to give food or drink to anyone, as he had left only enough for herself, and not to give shelter to any one against his return.

As Bride was working in the house two strangers came to the door. The man was old, with brown hair and grey beard, and the woman was young and beautiful, with oval face, straight nose, blue eyes, red lips, small ears, and golden brown hair, which fell below her waist. They asked the serving-maid for a place to rest, for they were footsore and weary, for food to satisfy their hunger, and for water to quench their thirst.

Bride could not give them shelter, but she gave them of her own bannock and of her own stoup of water, of which they partook at the door; and having thanked Bride the strangers went their way, while Bride gazed wistfully and sorrowfully after them. She saw that the sickness of life was on the young woman of the lovely face, and her heart was sore that she had not the power to give them shade from the heat of the sun, and cover from the cold of the dew.

When Bride returned into the house in the darkening of the twilight, what was stranger to her to see than that the bannock of bread was whole, and the stoup of water full, as they had been before! She did not know under the land of the world what she would say or what she would do. The food and the water of which she herself had given them, and had seen them partake, without a bit or a drop lacking from them!

When she recovered from her wonderment Bride went out to look after the two who had gone their way, but she could see no more of them. But she saw a brilliant golden light over the stable door, and knowing that it was not *dreag a bhais* (a meteor of death), she went into the stable and was in time to aid and minister to the Virgin Mother, and to receive the Child into her arms, for the strangers were Joseph and Mary, and the child was Jesus Christ, the Son of God, come to earth, and born in the stable of the hostel of Bethlehem. When the Child was born Bride put three drops of water from the spring of pure water on the tablet of His forehead, in name of God, in name of Jesus, in name of Spirit. When the master of the inn was returning home, and ascending the hill on which his house stood, he heard the murmuring music of a stream flowing past his house, and he saw the light of a bright star above his stable door. He knew from these signs that the Messiah was come and that Christ was born, for it was in the seership of the people that Jesus Christ, the Son of God, would be born in Bethlehem, the town of David. And the man rejoiced with exceeding joy at the fulfilment of the prophecy, and he went to the stable and worshipped the new Christ, whose infant cradle was the manger of the horses.

Thus Bride is called *ban-chuideachaidh Moire* (the aid-woman of Mary). In this connection, and in consequence thereof, she is called *Muime Chriosda* (foster-mother of Christ); *Bana-ghoistidh Mhic De* (the godmother of the Son of God); *Bana-ghoistidh Iosda Criosda nam bann agus nam beannachd* (godmother of Jesus Christ of the bindings and blessings). Christ again is called *Dalta Bride* (the foster-son of Bride); *Dalta Bride bith nam beannachd* (the foster-son of Bride of the blessings); *Daltan Bride* (little fosterling of Bride), a term of endearment.

John the beloved is called *Dalta Moire* (foster-son of Mary), and *Comhdhalta Chriosda* (the foster-brother, literally co-foster, of Christ). Fostership among the Highlanders was a peculiarly close and tender tie, more close and more tender even than blood. There are many proverbs on the subject, as: *Fuil gu fichead, comhdhaltas gu ceud* (blood to the twentieth, fostership to the hundredth degree). A church in Islay is called *Cill Daltain* (the Church of the Fosterling).

When a woman is in labour, the midwife or the woman next her in importance goes to the door of the house, and standing on the doorstep, with her hands on the jambs, softly beseeches Bride to come:

> Bride! Bride! come in,
> Thy welcome is truly made,
> Give thou relief to the woman,
> And give the conception to the Trinity.

When things go well, it indicates that Bride is present and is friendly to the family; and when they go ill, that she is absent and offended. Following the action of Bride at the birth of Christ, the aid-woman dedicates the child to the Trinity by letting three drops of clear cold water fall on the tablet of his forehead (see "The Baptism Blessing," I:50).

The aid-woman was held in reverence by all nations. Juno was worshipped with greater honour than any other deity of ancient Rome, and the Pharaohs paid tribute to the aid-women of Egypt. Perhaps, however, appreciation of the aid-woman was never more touchingly indicated than in the reply of two beautiful maidens of St Kilda to John Macdonald, the kindly humorist, and the unsurpassed seaman and pilot of Admiral Otter of the West Coast Survey: "Oh! ye loves of the domain and of the universe, why, King of the moon and of the sun! are ye not marrying and ye so beautiful?" "Oh! thou love of men, how can we marry? Has not the knee-wife died!"

On Bride's Eve the girls of the townland fashion a sheaf of corn into the likeness of a woman. They dress and deck the figure with shining shells, sparkling crystals, primroses, snowdrops, and any greenery they may obtain. In the mild climate of the Outer Hebrides several species of plants continue in flower during winter, unless the season be exceptionally severe. The gales of March are there the destroyers of plant-life. A specially bright shell or crystal is placed over the heart of the figure. This is called *reul-iuil Bride* (the guiding star of Bride), and typifies the star over the stable door of Bethlehem, which led Bride to the infant Christ. The girls call the figure *Bride, Brideag* (Bride, Little Bride), and carry it in procession, singing the song of *Bride bhoidheach oigh nam mile beus* (Beauteous Bride, virgin of a thousand charms). The *banal Bride* (Bride maiden band), are clad in white, and have their hair down, symbolising purity and youth. They visit every house, and every person is expected to give a gift to Bride and to make obeisance to her. The gift may be a shell, a spar, a crystal, a flower, or a bit of greenery to decorate the person of Bride. Mothers, however, give *bonnach Bride* (a Bride bannock), *cabag Bride* (a Bride cheese), or *rolag Bride* (a Bride roll of butter). Having made the round of the place the girls go to a house to make the *feis Bride* (Bride feast). They bar the door and secure the windows of the house, and set Bride where she may see and be seen of all. Presently the young men of the community come humbly asking permission to honour Bride. After some parleying they are admitted and make obeisance to her.

Much dancing and singing, fun and frolic, are indulged in by the young men and maidens during the night. As the grey dawn of the Day of Bride breaks they form a circle and sing the hymn of *Bride bhoidheach muime chorr Chriosda* (Beauteous Bride, choice foster-mother of Christ). They then distribute *fuidheal na feisde* (the fragments of the feast) — practically the whole, for they have partaken very sparingly, in order to have the more to give — among the poor women of the place.

A similar practice prevails in Ireland. There the churn staff, not the corn sheaf, is fashioned into the form of a woman, and called *Brideog* (little Bride). The girls come clad in their best, and the girl who has the prettiest dress gives it to Brideog. An ornament something like a Maltese cross is affixed to the breast of the figure. The ornament is composed of straw, beautifully and artistically interlaced by the deft fingers of the maidens of Bride. It is called *rionnag Brideog* (the star of little Bride). Pins, needles, bits of stone, bits of straw, and other things are given to Bride as gifts, and food by the mothers.

Customs assume the complexion of their surroundings, as fishes, birds, and beasts assimilate the colours of their habitats. The seas of the *Garbh Chriocha* (Rough Bounds) in which the cult of Bride has longest lived, abound in beautiful iridescent shells, and the mountains in bright sparkling stones, and these are utilised to adorn the ikon of Bride. In other districts where the figure of Bride is made, there are no shining shells, no brilliant crystals, and the girls decorate the image with artistically interlaced straw.

The older women are also busy on the Eve of Bride, and great preparations are made to celebrate her Day, which is the first day of spring. They make an oblong basket in the shape of a cradle, which they call *leaba Bride* (the bed of Bride). It is embellished with much care. Then they take a choice sheaf of corn, generally oats, and fashion it into the form of a woman. They deck this ikon with gay ribbons from the loom, sparkling shells from the sea, and bright stones from the hill. All the sunny sheltered valleys around are searched for primroses, daisies, and other flowers that open their eyes in the morning of the year. This lay figure is called Bride, *dealbh Bride* (the ikon of Bride). When it is dressed and decorated with all the tenderness and loving care the women can lavish upon it, one woman goes to the door of the house, and standing on the step with her hands on the jambs, calls softly into the darkness, "Bride's bed is ready." To this a ready woman behind replies, "Let Bride come in, Bride is welcome." The woman at the door again addresses Bride, "Bride! Bride, come thou in, thy bed is made. Preserve the house for the Trinity." The women then place the ikon of Bride with great ceremony in the bed they have so carefully prepared for it. They place a small straight white wand (the bark being peeled off) beside the figure. This wand is variously called *slatag Bride* (the little rod of Bride), *slachdan Bride* (the little wand of Bride), and *barrag Bride* (the birch of Bride). The wand is generally of birch, broom, bramble, white willow, or other sacred wood, "crossed" or banned wood being carefully avoided. A similar rod was given to the kings of Ireland at their coronation, and to the Lords of the Isles at their instatement. It was straight to typify justice, and white to signify peace and purity — bloodshed was not to be needlessly caused. The women then level the ashes on the hearth, smoothing and dusting them over carefully. Occasionally the ashes, surrounded by a roll of cloth, are placed on a board to safeguard them against disturbance from draughts or other contingencies. In the early morning the family closely scan the ashes. If they find the marks of the wand of Bride they rejoice, but if they find *lorg Bride* (the footprint of Bride), their joy is very great, for this is a sign that Bride was present with them during the night, and is favourable to them, and that there is increase in family, in flock, and in field during the coming year. Should there be no marks on the ashes, and no traces of Bride's presence, the family are dejected. It is to them a sign that she is offended, and will not hear their call. To propitiate her and gain her ear the family offer oblations and burn incense. The oblation generally is a cockerel, some say a pullet, buried alive near the junction of three streams, and the incense is burnt on the hearth when the family retire for the night.

In the Highlands and Islands St Bride's Day was also called *La Cath Choileach* (Day of Cock-fighting). The boys brought cocks to the school to fight. The most successful cock was called *coileach buadha* (victor cock), and its proud owner was elected king of the school for the year. A defeated bird was called *fuidse* (craven), *coileach fuidse* (craven cock). All the defeated, maimed, and killed cocks were the perquisites of the schoolmaster. In the Lowlands *La Coinnle* (Candlemas Day), was the day thus observed.

It is said in Ireland that Bride walked before Mary with a lighted candle in each hand when she went up to the Temple for purification. The winds were strong on the Temple heights, and the tapers were unprotected, yet they did not flicker nor fail. From this incident Bride is called *Bride boillsge* (Bride of brightness). This day is occasionally called *La Fheill Bride nan Coinnle* (the Feast Day of Bride of the Candles), but more generally *La Fheill Moire nan Coinnle* (the Feast Day of Mary of the Candles) — Candlemas Day.

The serpent is supposed to emerge from its hollow among the hills on St Bride's Day, and a propitiatory hymn was sung to it. Only one verse of this hymn has been obtained, apparently the first. It differs in different localities:

Early on Bride's morn
The serpent shall come from the hole,
I will not molest the serpent,
Nor will the serpent molest me.

Other versions say:

The Feast Day of the Bride,
The daughter of Ivor shall come from the knoll,
I will not touch the daughter of Ivor,
Nor shall she harm me.

On the Feast Day of Bride,
The head will come off the *caiteanach,*
The daughter of Ivor will come from the knoll
With tuneful whistling.

The serpent will come from the hole
On the brown Day of Bride,
Though there should be three feet of snow
On the flat surface of the ground.

The "daughter of Ivor" is the serpent; and it is said that the serpent will not sting a descendant of Ivor, he having made *tabhar agus tuis* (offering and incense) to it, thereby securing immunity from its sting for himself and his seed for ever.

On the day of Bride of the white hills
The noble queen will come from the knoll,
I will not molest the noble queen,
Nor will the noble queen molest me.

These lines would seem to point to serpent-worship. One of the most curious customs of Bride's Day was the pounding of the serpent in effigy. The following scene was described to the writer by one who was present:

"I was one of several guests in the hospitable house of Mr John Tolmie of Uignis, Skye. One of my fellow-guests was Mrs MacLeod, widow of Major MacLeod of Stein, and daughter of Flora Macdonald. Mrs MacLeod was known among her friends as

'Major Ann.' She combined the warmest of hearts with the sternest of manners, and was the admiration of old and young for her wit, wisdom, and generosity. When told that her son had fallen in a duel with the celebrated Glengarry — the Ivor MacIvor of Waverley — she exclaimed: 'Good thou art my son! good thou art my son! thou the white love of thine own mother! Better the hero's death than the craven's life; the brave dies but once, the coward many times.'

"In a company of noblemen and gentlemen at Dunvegan Castle, Mrs MacLeod, then in her eighty-eighth year, danced the reel of Tulloch and other reels, jigs, and strathspeys as lightly as a girl in her teens. Wherever she was, all strove to show Mrs MacLeod attention and to express the honour in which she was held. She accepted all these honours and attentions with grace and dignity, and without any trace of vanity or self-consciousness. One morning at breakfast at Uignis someone remarked that this was the Day of Bride. 'The Day of Bride,' repeated Mrs MacLeod meditatively, and with a dignified bow of apology rose from the table. All watched her movements with eager curiosity. Mrs MacLeod went to the fireside and took up the tongs and a bit of peat and walked out to the doorstep. She then took off her stocking and put the peat into it, and pounded it with the tongs. And as she pounded the peat on the step, she intoned a *rann* (rune), only one verse of which I can remember:

This is the day of Bride,
The queen will come from the mound,
I will not touch the queen,
Nor will the queen touch me.

"Having pounded the peat and replaced her stocking, Mrs MacLeod returned to the table, apologising for her remissness in not remembering the Day earlier in the morning. I could not make out whether Mrs MacLeod was serious or acting, for she was a consummate actress and the delight of young and old. Many curious ceremonies and traditions in connection with Bride were told that morning, but I do not remember them."

The pounding in the stocking of the peat representing the serpent would indicate destruction rather than worship, perhaps the bruising of the serpent's head. Probably, however, the ceremony is older, and designed to symbolise something now lost.

Gaelic lore is full of sayings about serpents. These indicate close observation: "He has the ear of a serpent" (he hears keenly but does not speak); "The witch-woman is crooked as the serpent"; "The tail is the least harmful of thee, the trick of the serpent venomous."

Though smooth be thy skin,
Venomous is the sting of thy mouth;
Thou art like the dun serpent,
Take thine own road.

The beauteous woman, ungenerous,
And she full of warm words,
Is like the brindled serpent,
And the sting of greed is in her.

The people of old practised early retiring, early rising, and diligent working:

Supper and light the Night of St Bride,
Sleep and light the Night of St Patrick.

The dandelion is called *bearnan Bride* (the little notched of Bride), in allusion to the serrated edge of the petal. The linnet is called *bigein Bride* (little bird of Bride). In Lismore the oyster-catcher is called *gille Bride* (page of Bride):

Poor page of Bride,
What cheeping ails thee?

In Uist the oyster-catcher is called *Bridein* (bird of Bride). There was once an oyster-catcher in Uist, and he was so elated with his own growing riches that he thought he would like to go and see something of the great world around him. He went away, leaving his three beautiful, olive-brown, blotched black-and-grey eggs in the rough shingle among the stones of the seashore. Shortly after he left the grey crow came hopping round to see what was doing in the place. In her peering she saw the three eggs of the oyster-catcher in the hollow among the rocks, and she thought she would like to try the taste of one of them, as a variant upon the refuse of land and shore. So she drove her strong bill through the broad end of an egg, and seizing it by the shell, carried it up to the mossy holm adjoining. The quality of the egg was so pleasing to the grey crow that she went back for the second, and then for the third egg. The grey crow was taking the last suck of the last egg when the oyster-catcher was heard returning with his usual fuss and flurry and hurry-scurry. He looked at his nest, but there were no eggs there — no, not one, and the oyster-catcher knew not what to do or say. He flew about to and fro, hither and thither in great distress, crying out in the bitterness of his heart: "Who drank the eggs? Who drank the eggs? I never heard the like! I never heard the like!"

The grey crow listened now on this side and now on that, and gave two more precautionary wipes to her already well-wiped bill in the fringy, friendly moss, then looked up with much affected innocence and called out in deeply sympathetic tones: "No, nor heard we ourselves that, though we are older in the place."

Bride is said to preside over the different seasons of the year and to bestow their functions upon them according to their respective needs. Some call January *am mios marbh* (the dead month), some December, while some apply the terms, *na tri miosa marbh* (the three dead months), *an raithe marbh* (the dead quarter), and *raithe marbh na bliadhna* (the dead quarter of the year), to the winter months when nature is asleep. Bride with her white wand is said to breathe life into the mouth of the dead Winter and to bring him to open his eyes to the tears and the smiles, the sighs and the laughter of Spring. The venom of the cold is said to tremble for its safety on Bride's Day and to flee for its life on Patrick's Day. There is a saying:

Bride put her finger in the river
On the Feast Day of Bride
And away went the hatching mother of the cold,
And she bathed her palms in the river
On the Feast Day of Patrick
And away went the conception mother of the cold.

Another version says:

Bride put her palm in it,
Mary put her foot in it,
Patrick put the cold stone in it,

alluding to the decrease in cold as the year advances. In illustration of this is the saying: "Mary put her fingers in the water on Bride's Feast Day and the venom went out of it, and on Patrick's Feast Day she bathed her hands in it and all the cold went out of it."

Poems narrating the events of the seasons were current. That mentioning the occurrences of Spring begins:

The Day of Bride, the birthday of Spring,
The serpent emerges from the knoll,
"Three-years-olds" is applied to heifers,
Garrons are taken to the fields.

In Uist the flocks are counted and dedicated to Bride on her Day:

On the Feast Day of beautiful Bride
The flocks are counted on the moor.
The raven goes to prepare the nest,
And again goes the rook.

Nest at Brigit, egg at Shrove, chick at Easter,
If the raven has not he has death.

The raven is the first bird to nest, closely followed by the mallard and the rook. It is affirmed that:

As far as the wind shall enter the door
On the Feast Day of Bride,
The snow shall enter the door
On the Feast Day of Patrick.

In Barra, lots are cast for the *iolachan iasgaich* (fishing-banks), on Bride's Day. These fishing-banks of the sea are as well known and as accurately defined by the fishermen of Barra as are the qualities and boundaries of their crofts on land, and they apportion them with equal care. Having ascertained among themselves the number of boats going to the long-line fishing, the people divide the banks accordingly.

All go to church on St Bride's Day. After reciting the virtues and blessings of Bride, and the examples to be drawn from her life, the priest reminds his hearers that the great God who made the land and all thereon, also made the sea and all therein, and that *cuilidh Chaluim agus cuilidh Mhoire* (the treasury of Columba and the treasury of Mary, that is, the wealth of sea and the plenty of land) are His gift to them that follow Him and call upon His name, on rocky hill or on crested wave. The priest urges upon them to avoid disputes and quarrels over their fishing, to remember the dangers of the deep and the precariousness of life, and in their fishing to remember the poor, the widow and the orphan, now left to the fatherhood of God and to the care of His people. Having come out of church, the men cast lots for the fishing-banks at the church door. After this, they disperse to their homes, all talking loudly and discussing their luck or unluck in the drawing of the lots. A stranger would be apt to think that the people were quarrelling. But it is not so. The simultaneous talking is their habit, and the loudness of their speaking is the necessity of their living among the noise of winds and waves, whether on sea or on shore. Like the people of St Kilda, the people of Barra are warmly attached to one another, the joy of one and the grief of another being the joy and grief of all.

The same practice of casting lots for their fishing-banks prevails among the fisher-folk of the Lofoten Islands, Norway.

From these traditional observations, it will be seen that Bride and her services are near to the hearts and lives of the people. In some phases of her character she is much more to them than Mary is.

Dedications to Bride are common throughout Great Britain and Ireland.

72 Magnus was descended from Malcolm Canmore, King of the Scots. Earl Magnus and his half-brother Earl Hakon ruled the Northern Isles, and while they were in agreement with one another there was peace and plenty within those isles. But dissensions arose. Magnus was eminently handsome, beneficent and beloved. Hakon was lacking in these qualities, and he became morose and jealous of his brother.

The two brothers met at the Thingstead in Lent, Hakon being there for offensive, and Magnus for defensive, purposes. Wisdom prevailed, however, and war was averted. To confirm the peace Hakon invited Magnus to meet him in Pasch week in the church of Egilsay, the brothers agreeing to limit their retinue to two warships each. Magnus observed the agreement and came with two ships, but Hakon brought eight, with their full complement of armed men.

His people wished to defend Magnus, but he refused to allow the spilling of blood, or the perilling of souls. Magnus submitted to his brother three proposals. First, that he should go to his relative, the King of the Scots, and never return; second, that he should go to Rome or to Jerusalem and never return; or third, that he would submit to be maimed, gouged, or slain. Hakon spurned all the proposals save the last, and Magnus was put to death on Easter Monday, 1117, to the great grief of his people.

The place where Magnus was slain had been a rough, sterile moor of heath and moss, but immediately Magnus was put to death the moor became a smiling grassy plain, and there issued a heavenly light and a sweet odour from the holy ground.

Those who were in peril prayed to Magnus and were rescued, and those who were sick came to his grave and were healed. Pilgrims flocked to his tomb to keep vigil at his shrine, and be cured of their leprosy of body or of soul.

St Magnus had three burials — the first in the island of Egilsay where he was slain, and the second at the intercession of his mother, Thora, in Christ Church in the island of Birsa. During imminent peril at sea Earl Rognvald prayed to Magnus for deliverance, and vowed that he would build a minster to his memory more beautiful than any church in those lands. The prayer was heard, and Rognvald built and endowed, to the memory of the holy Magnus, the cathedral church of Kirkwall. Thither the relics of the saint were brought and interred, and the cathedral became the resort of pilgrims who sought the aid of St Magnus.

At the battle of Anglesey, between Magnus Barefoot, his brother Ireland, his cousin Haco, and the Earls of Chester and Shrewsbury, Magnus recited the Psalter during the conflict. The victory of his northern kinsmen was attributed to the holy Magnus.

73 *Bealltain* (Beltane) is the first of May. On May Day all the fires of the district were extinguished and *tein eigin* (need-fire) produced on the knoll. This fire was divided in two, and people and cattle rushed through for purification and safeguarding against *ealtraigh agus dosgaidh* (mischance and murrain) during the year. The people obtained fires for their homes from this need-fire.

The practice of producing the need–fire came down in the Highlands and Islands to the first quarter of this century. The writer found traces of it in such distant places as Arran, Uist and Sutherland. In 1895 a woman in Arran said that in the time of her father the people made the need–fire on the knoll, and then rushed home and brought out their *creatairean* (creatures), and put them round the fire to safeguard them, *bho 'n bhana bhuitsich mhoir Nic–creafain* (from the arch–witch Crawford).

The ordeal of passing through the fires gave rise to a proverb which I heard used by an old man in Lewis in 1873: "Ah Mary! sonnie, it were worse for me to do that for thee, than to pass between the two great fires of Beall."

75 On the first day of May the people of the crofter townland are up betimes and busy as bees about to swarm. This is the day of migrating, *bho baile gu beinn* (from townland to moorland), from the winter homestead to the summer sheiling. The summer of their joy is come, the summer of the sheiling, the song, the pipe, and the dance, when the people ascend the hill to the clustered bothies, overlooking the distant sea from among the fronded ferns and fragrant heather, where neighbour meets neighbour, and lover meets lover. All the families of the townland bring their different flocks together at a particular place and drive the whole away. This miscellaneous herd is called *triall* (procession), and is composed of horses, cattle, sheep and goats. In the *triall* the sheep lead; the cattle follow according to their ages; then come the goats, and finally the horses, with creels slung across their backs laden with domestic gear of various kinds. The men carry burdens of spades, sticks, pins, ropes, and other things that may be needed to repair their summer huts, while the women carry bedding, meal, and dairy utensils. About their waists the women wear a cord of wool, or a belt of leather called *crios–feile* (kilt girdle), underneath which their skirts are drawn up and fastened, to enable them to walk the moor with greater ease. These crofter women appear like Leezie Lindsay in the old song:

She kilted her coats of green satin,
And she kilted them up to the knee.

When the people meet, they greet each other with great cordiality, as if they had not seen one another for months or even years, instead of probably only a few days before. There are endless noises in the herd: sheep bleat for their lambs, lambs for their mothers, cows low for their calves, and the calves respond, mares neigh for their foals, and foals whinny in reply to their dams as they lightly skip and scamper, curveting in and out, little dreaming of coming work and hard fare. The men give directions, several at a time; the women knit their stockings and sing their songs, walking free and erect as if there were no burdens on their backs or on their hearts, nor any sin or sorrow in the world so far as they are concerned.

Ranged along on either side of the procession are barefooted, bareheaded comely girls and sturdy boys, and sagacious dogs who every now and then, and every here and there, have a neck–and–neck race with some perverse young beast, unwillingly driven from his home, for, unlike his elders, the animal does not know or does not remember the pleasures of the heathery knoll, the grassy dell or fronded glen, and the joyous freedom of the summer sheiling. All who meet them on the way bless the *triall,* and invoke upon it a good day, much luck and prosperity, and the safe shepherding of the Son of Mary on man and beast.

When the grazing ground is reached, the loads are laid down, the huts repaired, fires kindled and food made ready. The people bring forward their stock, each man his own, and count them into the fold. The herdsman of the townland and one or two more men stand within the gateway and count the flocks as they enter. Each crofter is restricted in his stock on the common grazing of the townland. He may, however, vary the number and the ages of the species and thus equalise a deficit in one species by an excess in another. Should a man have a *barr–suma* (oversoum), he may arrange with a man who has a *di–suma* (undersoum), or with the townland at large, for his extra stock. Every facility is given to a man in straits, the consideration of these intelligent crofting people towards one another being most pleasing.

The grazing arrangements of the people, complex to a stranger, but simple to them–

selves, show an intimate knowledge of animal and pastoral life. Having seen to their flocks and to the repairing of their huts, the people resort to their sheiling feast. This feast consists principally of a male lamb, without spot or blemish, killed that day. Formerly this lamb was sacrificed, now it is eaten. The feast is shared with friends and neighbours; all wish each other luck and prosperity, with increase in their flocks:

> Beside each knoll
> The progeny of the sheiling cows.

The frugal feast being finished and the remains divided among the dogs, who are not the least interested or interesting actors in the day's proceedings, every head is uncovered and every knee is bent as they invoke on man and beast "the shepherding of Abraham, of Isaac, and of Jacob."

Protestantism prevails in Lewis, Harris, and North Uist, and the people confine their invocations to the Trinity:

> The Shepherd that keeps Israel
> He slumbers not nor sleeps.

Roman Catholicism prevails in Benbecula, South Uist, and Barra, and in their dedicatory hymn the people of these islands invoke, besides the Trinity, St Michael of the three-cornered shield and flaming sword, patron of their horses; St Columba of the holy deeds, guardian of their cattle; Bride of the clustering hair, the foster-mother of Christ; and the golden-haired Virgin, mother of the White Lamb.

As the people intone their prayers on the lonely hillside, literally in the wilderness, the music of their evensong floats over glen and dell, loch and stream, and is echoed from corrie and cliff till it is lost on the soft evening air.

76 The Feast Day of Mary the Great is the fifteenth day of August. Early in the morning of this day the people go into their fields and pluck ears of corn, generally bere, to make the *Moilean Moire.* These ears are laid on a rock exposed to the sun, to dry. When dry, they are husked in the hand, winnowed in a fan, ground in a quern, kneaded on a sheepskin, and formed into a bannock, which is called *Moilean Moire* (the fatling of Mary).

The bannock is toasted before a fire of faggots of rowan, or some other sacred wood. Then the husbandman breaks the bannock and gives a bit to his wife and to each of his children, in order according to their ages, and the family raise the *Iolach Mhoire Mhathar* (the Paean of Mary Mother) who promised to shield them, and who did and will shield them from scath till the day of death. While singing thus, the family walk sunwise round the fire, the father leading, the mother following, and the children following according to age.

After going round the fire, the man puts the embers of the faggot-fire, with bits of old iron, into a pot, which he carries sunwise round the outside of his house, sometimes round his steadings and his fields, and his flocks gathered in for the purpose. He is followed without as within by his household, all singing the praise of Mary Mother the while.

The scene is striking and picturesque, the family being arrayed in their brightest and singing their best.

77 St Michael is spoken of as *brian Micheil* (god Michael):

> Thou wert the warrior of courage
> Going on the journey of prophecy,
> Thou wouldst not travel on a cripple,
> Thou didst take the steed of the god Michael,
> He was without bit in his mouth,
> Thou didst ride him on the wing,
> Thou didst leap over the knowledge of Nature.

St Michael is the Neptune of the Gael. He is the patron saint of the sea, and of maritime lands, of boats and boatmen, of horses and horsemen throughout the West. As patron saint of the sea St Michael had temples dedicated to him round the coast wherever Celts were situated. Examples of these are Mount St Michael in Brittany and in Cornwall, and Aird Michael in South and in North Uist, and elsewhere. Probably Milton had this phase of St Michael's character in view. As patron saint of the land St Michael is represented riding a milk-white steed, a three-pronged spear in his right hand and a three-cornered shield in his left. The shield is inscribed *Quis ut Deus,* a literal translation of the Hebrew "Micha-el." Britannia is substituted for the archangel on sea and St George on land.

On the 29th of September a festival in honour of St Michael is held throughout the Western Coasts and Isles. This is much the most imposing pageant and much the most popular demonstration of the Celtic year. Many causes conduce to this — causes which move the minds and the hearts of the people to their utmost tension. To the young the Day is a day of promise, to the old a day of fulfilment, to the aged a day of retrospect. It is a day when pagan cult and Christian doctrine meet and mingle like the lights and shadows on their own Highland hills.

The Eve of St Michael is the eve of bringing in the carrots, of baking the *struan,* of killing the lamb, of stealing the horses. The Day of St Michael is the Day of the early Mass, the day of the sacrificial lamb, the day of the oblation *struan,* the day of the distribution of the lamb, the day of the distribution of the *struan,* the day of the pilgrimage to the burial-ground of their fathers, the day of the burial-ground service, the day of the burial-ground circuiting, the day of giving and receiving the carrots with their wishes and acknowledgments, and the day of the *oda* — the athletics of the men and the racing of the horses. And the Night of Michael is the night of the dance and the song, of the merry-making, of the love-making, and of the love-gifts.

Several weeks previously the people begin to speak of St Michael's Day, and to prepare for St Michael's Festival. Those concerned count whose turn it will be to guard the crops on St Michael's Day and to circuit the townland on St Michael's Night. The young men upon whom these duties fall arrange with old men to take their place on these occasions. As the time approaches the interest intensifies, culminating among the old in much bustle, and among the young in keen excitement.

Three plants which the people call carrots grow in Uist: the *daucus carota,* the *daucus maritimus,* and the *conium.* The *daucus carota* is the original of the cultivated carrot. The *daucus maritimus* is a long slender carrot, much like the parsnip in appearance and in flavour, and is rare in the British Isles. The *conium* (hemlock) resembles the carrot, for which it is occasionally mistaken. It is hard, acrid, and poisonous.

Some days before the festival of St Michael the women and girls go to the fields and plains of the townland to procure carrots. The afternoon of the Sunday immediately preceding St Michael's Day is specially devoted to this purpose, and on this account is known as *Domhnach Curran* (Carrot Sunday). When the soil is soft and friable, the carrots can be pulled out of the ground without digging. When, however, the soil is hard, a space is dug to give the hand access to the root. This space is made in the form of an equal-sided triangle, technically called *torcan* (diminutive of *torc,* a cleft). The instrument used is a small mattock of three prongs, called *tri-meurach* (three-fingered) *sliopag* or *sliobhag.* The three-sided *torcan* is meant to typify the three-sided shield, and the three-fingered *sliopag,* the trident of St Michael, and possibly each to symbolise the Trinity. The many brightly-clad figures moving to and fro, in and out, like the figures in a kaleidoscope, are singularly pretty and picturesque. Each woman intones a rune to her own tune and time irrespective of those around her. The following fragment was intoned to me in a soft, subdued voice by a woman who had gathered carrots eighty years previously:

> *Torcan* fruitful, fruitful, fruitful,
> Joy of carrots surpassing upon me,
> Michael the brave endowing me,
> Bride the fair be aiding me.
>
> Progeny pre-eminent over every progeny,
> Progeny on my womb,
> Progeny pre-eminent over every progeny,
> Progeny on my progeny.

Should a woman find a forked carrot, she breaks out into a more exultant strain that brings her neighbours round to see and to admire her luck:

> Fork joyful, joyful, joyful,
> Fork of great carrot to me,
> Endowment of carrot surpassing upon me,
> Joy of great carrot to me.

There is much rivalry among the women who shall have most and best carrots. They carry the carrots in a bag slung from the waist, called *crioslachan* (little girdle), from *crios* (a girdle). When the *earrasaid* was worn, the carrots were carried in its ample folds. The women wash the carrots and tie them up in small bunches, each of which contains a handful. The bunches are tied with three-ply thread, generally scarlet, and put in pits near the houses and covered with sand till required.

The people do not retire to rest on the Eve of St Michael. The women are engaged all night on baking *struain,* on household matters, and on matters personal to themselves and to others, while the men are out and in watching their horses in the fields and stables. It is permissible on this night to appropriate a horse, wherever found and by whatever means, on which to make the pilgrimage and to perform the circuiting:

> Theft of horse of the Feast of Michael,
> Theft that never was condemned.

The people act upon this ancient privilege and steal horses without compunction, owners and stealers watching and outwitting and circumventing one another. It is obligatory to leave one horse with the owner to carry himself and his wife on the pilgrimage and to make the circuiting, but this may be the worst horse in the townland. No apology is offered or expected for this appropriation provided the horse be returned uninjured; and even if it be injured, no adequate redress is obtained. The Eve of St Michael is thus known as *feasgar faire nan steud* (the evening of watching the steeds); *feàsgar furachaidh nan each* (the evening of guarding the horses); *oidhche crothaidh nan capull* (the night of penning the mares); *oidhche glasadh nan each* (the night of locking the horses) — hence also *glasadh na Feill Micheil* (the locking of the Feast of Michael).

A male lamb, without spot or blemish, is slain. This lamb is called *Uan Micheil* (the Michael Lamb).

A cake called *struan Micheil* is made of all the cereals grown on the farm during the year. It represents the fruits of the field, as the lamb represents the fruits of the flocks. Oats, bere, and rye are the only cereals grown in the Isles. These are fanned on the floor, ground in the quern, and their meal in equal parts used in the struan. The struan should contain a peck of meal, and should be baked on *uinicinn* (a lambskin). The meal is moistened with sheep's milk, the sheep being deemed the most sacred animal. For this purpose the ewes are retained in milk till St Michael's Eve, after which they are allowed to remain in the hill and to run dry. The struan is baked by the eldest daughter of the family, guided by her mother, and assisted by her eager sisters. As she moistens the meal with the milk the girl softly says:

> Progeny and prosperity of family,
> Mystery of Michael, protection of Trinity.

A *leac struain* (struan flag), brought by the young men of the family from the moorland during the day, is securely set on edge before the fire, and the struan is set on edge against it. The fire should be of *crionach caon* (sacred faggots), such as the faggots of the oak, the rowan, the bramble, and others. The blackthorn, wild fig, trembling aspen, and other "crossed" woods are avoided. As the struan gains consistency, three successive layers of a batter of cream, eggs, and butter are laid on each side alternately. The batter ought to be put on with three tail feathers of a cockerel of the year. But in Uist this is generally done with a small bunch of bent-grass. This cake is called *struan treo* (family struan); *struan mor* (large struan), and *struan comachaidh* (communal struan). Small struans are made for individual members of the family by mothers, daughters, sisters, and trusted servants. These are known as *struain beag* (little struans), *struain cloinne* (children's struans), and by the names of those for whom they are made. If a member of the family be absent or dead, a struan is made in his or her name. This struan is shared among the family and special friends of the absent one in his or her name, or given to the poor who have no corn of their own. In mixing the meal of the individual struan, the woman kneading it mentions the name of the person for whom it is being made:

Progeny and prosperity to Donald,
Mystery of Michael, shielding of the Lord.

The individual struans of a family are uniform in size but irregular in form, some being three-cornered, symbolic of the Trinity; some five, symbolic of the Trinity, with Mary and Joseph added; some seven, symbolic of the seven mysteries; some nine, symbolic of the nine archangels; and some round, symbolic of eternity. Various ingredients are introduced into the small struans, as cranberries, bilberries, brambleberries, caraway seed, and wild honey. Those who make them and those for whom they are made vie with their friends who shall have the best and most varied ingredients.

Many cautions are given to her who is making the struan to take exceptional care of it. Ills and evils innumerable would befall herself and her house should any mishap occur to the struan. Should it break before being fired, it betokens ill to the girl baking it; if after being fired and before being used, to the household. Were the struan flag to fall and the struan with it, the omen is full of evil augury to the family. A broken struan is not used. The *fallaid* (dry meal remaining on the baking-board after the struan is made) is put into a *mogan* (footless stocking), and dusted over the flocks on the following day — being the Day of Michael — to bring them *piseach agus pailteas agus pronntachd* (progeny and plenty and prosperity), and to ward from them *suileachd agus ealtraidh agus dosgaidh* (evil-eye, mischance, and murrain). Occasionally the *fallaid* is preserved for a year and a day before being used.

On the morning of the Feast of Michael all within reach go to early Mass.

They take their struans with them to church to be blessed of the *pears eaglais* (priest). At this festal service the priest exhorts the people to praise their guardian angel Michael for his leading and their Father God for His corn and wool, fruits of the field and fruits of the flocks, which He has bestowed on them, while the foodless and the fatherless among them are commended to the fatherhood of God and to the care of His people.

On returning from Mass the people take the *biadh Micheil* (Michael food), *biadh maidne Micheil* (Michael morning food). The father of the family places the struan "on a board as white as the chalk of the rock or the snow of the hill." He then takes:

A knife keen, true,
Without stain, without dust,
Without smear, without flaw,
Without grime, without rust,

and having made the sign of the cross of Christ on the tablet of his face, the man cuts the struan into small sections, retaining in the parts the form of the whole. And he cuts up the lamb into small pieces. He places the board with the bread and the flesh on the centre of the table. Then the family, standing round, and holding a bit of struan in the left hand and a piece of lamb in the right, raise the *Iolach Micheil* (triumphal song of Michael), in praise of Michael, who guards and guides them, and in praise of God, who gives them food and clothing, health, and blessing withal. The man and his wife put struan into one *ciosan* (beehive basket), and lamb into another, and go out to distribute them among the poor of the neighbourhood who have no fruits nor flocks themselves. Nor is this all.

"It is proper that every husbandman in the townland should give, on the day of the St Michael Feast, a peck of meal, a quarter of struan, a quarter of lamb, a quarter of cheese, and a platter of butter to the poor and forlorn, to the despised and dejected, to the alms-deserving, and to the orphans without pith, without power, formed in the image of the Father everlasting. And the man is giving this on the beam of Michael as an offering to the great God of the elements who gave him cattle and sheep, bread and corn, power and peace, growth and prosperity, that it may be before his abject, contrite soul when it goes thither. And the miserable, the poor, the tearful, the alms-deserving helpless ones, and the orphan, will raise the triumphal song of Michael, giving fame and laud to Michael, the fair hero of power, and to the Father all-blessed and powerful, blessing the man and the woman in their sons and in their daughters, in their means, fame, and lot, in their cattle, and in their sheep, in the produce of their herds, and in the produce of their lands. These are the people who are called 'the humane men,' 'the compassionate men,' and 'the good women,' 'the generous women,' who are taking mercy and compassion on the poor, and on the tearful, on the dejected and the despised, on the miserable alms-deserving, and on the orphans without pith, without power, without support, without breast-staff, without leaning-rod, formed in the image of the Father all-creative. And the surpassingly white angels of God, with their foot on tiptoe, their eye on the horizon, their ear on the ground, their wings flapping, their bodies trembling, are waiting to send announcement of the deed with a beat of their wings to the King of the throne everlasting."

After the father and mother have distributed their gifts to the poor, the family mount their horses and set out on their pilgrimage to perform the circuiting of St Michael's burying-ground. None remain at home save the very old and the very young, to whom is assigned for the day the duty of tending the sheep, herding the cattle, and guarding the corn. The husband and wife ride on one horse, with probably a boy astride before the father and a girl sideways beside the mother, filling up the measure of the horse's capacity. A girl sits *culag* (behind her brother), or occasionally behind the brother of another girl, with her arm round him to steady her. A little girl sits *bialag* (in front of a brother), with his hand lovingly round her waist, while with his other hand he guides the horse. A little brother sits *culag* (behind his elder brother) with his two arms round him.

The people of the different hills, glens, islands, and townlands join the procession on the way, and all travel along together, the crowded cavalcade gaily clad in stuffs and stripes and tartans whose fineness of texture and brilliancy of colouring are charming to see, is impossible to describe. The air is full of salutations and cordialities. Even the whinnying, neighing, restive horses seem to know and to feel that this is the Day of their patron saint the holy archangel:

The valiant Michael of the white steeds
Who subdued the dragon of blood.

On reaching their destination the people crowd into and round the simple prayer-house. The doors and windows of the little oratory are open, and the people kneeling without join those kneeling within in earnest supplication that all may go well with them for the day. And commending themselves and their horses to the leading of the valiant, glorious archangel of the cornered shield and flaming sword, the people remount their horses to make *cuartachadh a chlaidh* (the circuiting of the burial ground).

The great crowd starts from the east and follows the course of the sun in the name of God, in the name of Christ, in the name of Spirit. The priest leads the way riding on a white horse, his grey hair and white robe waving in the autumn breeze. Should there be more than one priest present they ride abreast. Should there be higher dignitaries they ride in front of, or between the priests. The people follow in a column from two to ten abreast. Those on horseback follow immediately behind the priest, those on foot behind these. The fathers of the different townlands are stationed at intervals on either side of the procession, to maintain regularity and to guard against accidents. All are imbued with a befitting reverence for the solemnity of the proceedings and of the occasion. Families, friends, and neighbours try to keep together in the processional circuiting. As they move from left to right the people raise the *Iolach Micheil,* song of Michael the victorious, whose sword is keen to smite, and whose arm is strong to save. At the end of the circuit the *culag* gives to her *bialag* a handful of carrots, saying:

Progeny and prosperity on thy lying and rising.

The *bialag* acknowledges the gift in one of the many phrases common on the occasion:

Progeny and peace on the hand that gave.
Issue and peace on my love who gave.
Progeny and plenty without scarcity in thy dwelling.
Wifehood and motherhood on my brown maid.
Endowment and prosperity to my love who gave.

Greetings, courtesies, and gifts are exchanged among the people, many of whom have not met since they met at the circuiting. The most prized courtesy, however, is a *culag* round the burial-ground, and the most prized gift is a carrot with its customary wishes and acknowledgments. Those who have no horses readily obtain them to make the circuiting, the consideration of those who have for those who have not being native and habitual.

Having performed the professional pilgrimage round the graves of their fathers, the people hasten to the *oda* — the scene of the athletics of the men and the racing of the horses. The games and races excite much interest. The riders in the races ride without bonnet, without shoes, clothed only in a shirt and *triubhais bheag,* small trews like football trousers. All ride without saddle, some without bridle, guiding and driving their horses with *steamhag chaol chruaidh,* a hard slender tangle in each hand. Occasionally girls compete with one another and sometimes with men. They sit on either side as may be most convenient in mounting. They have no saddle, and how they retain their seat is inconceivable. Some circuiting goes on all day, principally among the old and the young — the old teaching the young the mysteries of the circuiting and the customs of the olden times. Here and there young men and maidens ride about and wander away, converting the sandy knolls and grassy dells of the fragrant *machair* into Arcadian plains and Eden groves.

On the night of St Michael a *cuideachd* (ball), is held in every townland. The leading piper selects the place for the ball, generally the house of largest size and of evenest floor. Every man present contributes a sixpence, or its equivalent in farm produce, usually in grain, towards paying the piper if he be a married man; if not, he accepts nothing. Several pipers, fiddlers, and players of other instruments relieve one another during the night. The small bets won at the *oda* during the day are spent at the ball during the night, no one being allowed to retain his luck.

The women put their bunches of carrots into white linen bags with the mark of the owner. Having filled their *crioslachain,* they leave the bags in some house convenient to the dance-house. As their *crioslachain* become empty during the night they replenish them from the *falachain* (hidden store). When a woman comes into the dance-house after refilling her *crioslachain,* she announces her entrance with a rhyme, the refrain of which is:

It is I myself that have the carrots,
Whoever he be that would win
them from me.
It is I myself that have the treasure,
Whoso the hero could take them from me.

At the circuiting by day and at the ball at night, youths and maidens exchange simple gifts in token of good feeling. The girls give the men bonnets, hose, garters, cravats, purses, plaids, and other things of their own making, and the men give the girls brooches of silver, brass, bronze, or copper, knives, scissors, snoods, combs, mirrors, and various other things. Some of these gifts are mentioned in the following verses:

The promises

My lover gave to me a knife
That would cut the sapling withe,
That would cut the soft and hard,
Long live the hand that gave.

My lover promised me a snood,
Ay, and a brooch and comb,
And I promised, by the wood,
To meet him at rise of sun.

My lover promised me a mirror
That my beauty I might see,
Yes, and a coif and ring,
And a dulcet harp of chords.

He vowed me those and a fold of kine,
And a palfrey of the steeds,
And a barge, pinnacled white,
That would safely cross the seas.

A thousand blessings, a thousand victories
To my lover who left me yestreen,
He gave to me the promise lasting,
Be his Shepherd God's own Son.

The song and the dance, the mirth and the merriment, are continued all night, many curious scenes being acted, and many curious dances performed, some of them in character. These scenes and dances are indicative of faraway times, perhaps of faraway climes. They are evidently symbolic. One dance is called *Cailleach an Dudain* (carlin of the mill-dust). This is a curious character-dance. The writer got it performed for him several times.

It is danced by a man and a woman. The man has a rod in his right hand, variously called *slachdan druidheachd* (druidic wand), *slachdan geasachd* (magic wand). The man and the woman gesticulate and attitudinise before one another, dancing round and round, in and out, crossing and recrossing, changing and exchanging places. The man flourishes the wand over his own head and over the head of the woman, whom he touches with the wand, and who falls down, as if dead, at his feet. He bemoans his dead *carlin,* dancing and gesticulating round her body. He then lifts up her left hand, and looking into the palm, breathes upon it, and touches it with the wand. Immediately the limp hand becomes alive and moves from side to side and up and down. The man rejoices, and dances round the figure on the floor. And having done the same to the right hand, and to the left and right foot in succession, they also become alive and move. But although the limbs are living, the body is still inert. The man kneels over the woman and breathes into her mouth and touches her heart with the wand. The woman comes to life and springs up, confronting the man. Then the two dance vigorously and joyously as in the first part. The tune varies with the varying phases of the dance. It is played by a piper or a fiddler, or sung as a *port-a-bial* (mouth tune) by a looker-on, or by the performers themselves. The air is quaint and irregular, and the words are curious and archaic.

In his *West Highland Tales,* Iain F. Campbell of Islay mentions that he saw *cailleach an dudain* danced in the house of Lord Stanley of Alderley. He does not say by whom it was danced, but probably it was by the gifted narrator himself. In October 1871, Mr Campbell spent some time with the writer and his wife in Uist. When driving him to Lochmaddy, at the conclusion of his stay, I mentioned that there were two famous dancers of *cailleach an dudain* at Clachan-a-ghluip. We went to their bothy, but they were away. The neighbours told us that they were in the direction of Lochmaddy. When we reached there we went in search of them, but were unsuccessful. Some hours afterwards, as I was coming up from the shore after seeing Mr Campbell on board the packet for Dunvegan, I saw the two women racing down the hill, their long hair and short dresses flying wildly in the wind. They had heard that we had been inquiring for them. But it was too late. The packet, with Mr Campbell on board, was already hoisting her sails and heaving her anchor.

Another dance is called *cath nan coileach* (the combat of the cocks); another, *turraban nan tunnag* (waddling of the ducks); another, *ruidhleadh nan coileach dubha* (reeling of the black-cocks); another, *cath nan curaidh* (contest of the warriors), where a Celtic Saul slays his thousands, and a Celtic David his tens of thousands. Many dances now lost were danced at the St Michael ball, while those that still remain were danced with much more artistic complexity. The sword-dance was performed in eight sections instead of in four, as now. The reel of Tulloch was danced in eight figures with side issues, while *seann triubhas* contained much more acting than it does now. Many beautiful and curious songs, now lost, were sung at these balls.

The young people who have individual struans give and receive and share them the night through, till sleep overcomes all.

Chiefs and chieftains, tacksmen and tenants, men and women, old and young, rich and poor, mingle in the pilgrimage, in the service, in the circuiting, in the games and races, in the dancing and the merry-making. The granddame of eighty and the granddaughter of eight, the grandsire of ninety and the grandson of nine, all take much interest in the festival of St Michael. The old and the young who do not go to the ball entertain one another at their homes, exchanging struans and carrots and homely gifts in token of friendship and neighbourliness. The pilgrimage, the service, the circuiting, and the games and races of the *oda,* once so popular in the Western Isles, are now become obsolete. The last circuiting with service was performed in South Uist in 1820. It took place as usual round Cladh Mhicheil, the burial-ground of Michael, near the centre of the island. The last great *oda* in North Uist was in 1866, and took place on the customary spot, Traigh Mhoire (the strand of Mary), on the west side of the island.

> But all that has gone like a vision,
> Like the breaking of a bubble on the surface of the sea.

The Michael lamb is sometimes slain, the Michael struan is sometimes baked, and the carrots are occasionally gathered, but the people can give no account of their significance. Probably the lamb and the struan represented the first-fruits of the flock and the fields, the circuiting and the sunwarding, ancestor-worship and sun-worship, and the carrots of the west the mandrakes of the east, "given in the time of the wheat-harvest."

The wives of husbandmen carried struans to the castles of the chiefs, and to the houses of the gentlemen in their neighbourhood, as marks of goodwill. This was one of the many links in the social chain which bound chief and clansmen, proprietor and tenant together. In the past the chiefs and gentlemen and their families joined the people in their festivals, games and dances, secular amusements and religious observances, joys and sorrows, to the great good of all and to the stability of society. In the present, as a rule, the proprietors and gentlemen of the Highlands and Islands are at the best but temporary residents, if so much, and generally strangers in blood and speech, feeling and sympathy, more prone to criticise than to help, to scoff than to sympathise. As a result, the observances of the people have fallen into disuse, to the loss of the spiritual life of the country, and of the patriotic life of the nation.

Throughout the Highlands and Islands special cakes were made on the first day of the quarter. As in the case of the struan, a large cake was made for the family and smaller cakes for individual members. So far as can now be ascertained, these cakes were round in form. They were named after their dedications. That baked for the first day of spring was called *bonnach Bride* (bannock of Bride); that for the first day of summer, *bonnach Bealltain* (Beltane bannock); that for the first day of autumn, *bonnach Lunastain* (Lammas bannock); and that for the first day of winter, *bonnach Samhthain* (Hallowtide bannock). The names of the individual cakes were rendered into diminutives to distinguish them from the family cake, while the sex of the person for whom they were intended was indicated by the termination, as *Bridean* (masculine diminutive), *Brideag* (feminine diminutive), after Bride; *Bealltan, Bealltag,* after Beltane; *Luinean, Luineag,* after Lammas; and *Samhnan, Samhnag,* after Hallowmas. The people repaired to the fields, glens, and corries to eat their quarter cakes. Where eating them, they threw a piece over each shoulder alternately, saying: "Here to thee, wolf, spare my sheep; there to thee, fox, spare my lambs; here to thee, eagle, spare my goats; there to thee, raven, spare my kids; here to thee, marten, spare my fowls; there to thee, harrier, spare my chickens."

As may be seen from some of the poems, the duty of conveying the souls of the good to the abode of bliss is assigned to Michael. When the soul has parted from the body and is being weighed, the archangel of heaven and the archangel of hell preside at the beam, the former watching that the latter does not put "claw of hand nor talon of foot near the beam." Michael and all the archangels and angels of heaven sing songs of joy when the good in the soul outweighs the bad, while the devil howls as he retreats.

79 This poem was obtained from Janet Currie, Staonabrig, South Uist, a descendant of the Mac Mhuirichs (corrupted into Currie) of Staoligearry, the famous poet-historians to the Clanranalds. She was a tall, strong, dark-haired, ruddy-complexioned woman, with a clear, sonorous voice. Her language was remarkably fluent and copious, though many of her words and phrases, being obsolete, were unintelligible to the stranger. I took down versions of the poem from several other persons, but they are all more or less corrupt and obscure. Poems similar to this can be traced back to the eighth century.

82 The kindling of the fire is a work full of interest to the housewife. When "lifting" the fire in the morning the woman prays, in an undertone, that the fire may be blessed to her and to her household, and to the glory of God who gave it. The people look upon fire as a miracle of Divine power provided for their good — to warm their bodies when they are cold, to cook their food when they are hungry, and to remind them that they too, like the fire, need constant renewal mentally and physically.

84 Peat is the fuel of the Highlands and Islands. Where wood is not obtainable the fire is kept in during the night. The process by which this is accomplished is called in Gaelic *smaladh;* in Scottish, smooring; and in English, smothering, or more correctly, subduing. The ceremony of smooring the fire is artistic and symbolic, and is performed with loving care. The embers are evenly spread on the hearth — which is generally in the middle of the floor — and formed into a circle. This circle is then divided into three equal sections, a small boss being left in the middle. A peat is laid between each section, each peat touching the boss, which forms a common centre. The first peat is laid down in name of the God of Life, the second in name of the God of Peace, the third in name of the God of Grace.

The circle is then covered over with ashes sufficient to subdue but not to extinguish the fire, in name of the Three of Light. The heap slightly raised in the centre is called *Tula nan Tri* (the Hearth of the Three). When the smooring operation is complete the woman closes her eyes, stretches her hand, and softly intones one of the many formulae current for these occasions.

Another way of keeping embers for morning use is to place them in a pit at night. The pit consists of a hole in the clay floor, generally under the dresser. The pit may be from half a foot to a foot in depth and diameter, with a flag fixed in the floor over the top. In the centre of this flag there is a hole by which the embers are put in and taken out. Another flag covers the hole to extinguish the fire at night, and to guard against accidents during the day. This extinguishing fire–pit is called *slochd guail* (coke– or coal–pit). This coke or charcoal is serviceable in kindling the fire.

88 The preparation of the seed–corn is of great importance to the people, who bestow much care on this work. Many ceremonies and proverbs are applied to seedtime and harvest.

The corn is prepared at certain seasons of the year, which are seldom deviated from. The rye is threshed to allow the soft wind of November and December to winnow the seed; the oats to allow the cold winds of January and February to winnow the seed; and the bere to allow the sharp winds of March and April to winnow the seed. All these preparations are made to assist Nature in the coming Spring. Three days before being sown the seed is sprinkled with clear cold water, in the name of Father, and of Son, and of Spirit, the person sprinkling the seed walking sunwise the while.

The ritual is picturesque, and is performed with great care and solemnity and, like many of these ceremonies, is a combination of paganism and Christianity.

The moistening of the seed has the effect of hastening its growth when committed to the ground, which is generally begun on a Friday, that day being auspicious for all operations not necessitating the use of iron.

89 The day the people began to reap the corn was a day of commotion and ceremonial in the townland. The whole family repaired to the field dressed in their best attire to hail the God of the harvest.

Laying his bonnet on the ground, the father of the family took up his sickle, and facing the sun, he cut a handful of corn. Putting the handful of corn three times sunwise round his head, the man raised the *Iolach Buana* (reaping salutation). The whole family took up the strain and praised the God of the harvest, who gave them corn and bread, food and flocks, wool and clothing, health and strength, and peace and plenty.

When the reaping was finished the people had a trial called *cur nan corran* (casting the sickles), and *deuchain chorran* (trial of hooks). This consisted, among other things, of throwing the sickles high up in the air, and observing how they came down, how each struck the earth, and how it lay on the ground. From these observations the people augured who was to remain single and who was to be married, who was to be sick and who was to die, before the next reaping came round.

91 When it is necessary to provide a small quantity of meal hastily, ears of corn are plucked and placed in a net made of the tough roots of the yellow bedstraw, bent, or quicken grass, and hung above a slow smokeless fire. The bag is taken down now and again to turn the ears of corn. This net, however, can only be used for bere or barley; rye and oats, being more detachable, require the use of a pot or *tarran* to dry them. This mode of drying corn is called *fuirireadh* (parching), and the corn *fuirireach* (parched). The meal ground from the grain is called *min fhuiriridh* (parched meal). Bread made of meal thus prepared has a strong peaty flavour much relished by the people.

92 The quern songs, like all the labour songs of the people, were composed in a measure suited to the special labour involved. The measure changed to suit the rhythmic motion of the body at work, at times slow, at times fast, as occasion required. I first saw the quern at work in October 1860 in the house of a cottar at Fearann-an-leatha, Skye. The cottar-woman procured some oats in the sheaf. Roughly evening the heads, and holding the corn in one hand and a rod in the other, she set fire to the ears. Then, holding the corn over an old partially dressed sheepskin, she switched off the grain. This is called *gradanadh* (quickness), from the expert handling required in the operation. The whole straw of the sheaf was not burnt, only that part of the straw to which the grain was attached, the flame being kept from proceeding further. The straw was tied up and used for other purposes.

Having fanned the grain and swept the floor, the woman spread out the sheepskin again and placed the quern thereon. She then sat down to grind, filling and relieving the quern with one hand and turning it with the other, singing the while to the accompaniment of the whirr! whirr! birr! birr! of the revolving stone. Several strong sturdy boys in scant kilts, and sweet comely girls in nondescript frocks, sat round the peat fire enjoying it fully, and watching the work and listening to the song of their radiant mother.

In a remarkably short space of time the grain from the field was converted into meal, and the meal into bannocks, which the unknown stranger was pressed to share. The bread was good and palatable, though with a slight taste of peat, which would probably become pleasant in time.

The second time I saw the quern at work was in January 1865, in the house of a crofter at Breubhaig, Barra, and it reminded me of Mungo Park's description of a similar scene in Africa. The quern was on the floor, with a well-worn cowhide under it. Two women sat opposite one another on the floor with the quern between them. The right leg of each was stretched out, while the knee of the other leg formed a sharp angle, with the foot resting against the kneejoint of the straight leg. A fan containing bere lay beside the women, and from this one of them fed the quern, while the other relieved it of the constantly accumulating meal. Each woman held the *sgonnan* (handle) with which they turned the quern, and as they turned they sang the Quern Blessing here given, to a very pretty air. Then they sang an impromptu song on the stranger, who was hungry and cold, and who was far from home and from the mother who loved him.

When mills were erected, the authorities destroyed the querns in order to compel the people to go to the mills and pay multure, mill dues. This wholesale and inconsiderate destruction of querns everywhere entailed untold hardships of thousands of people living in roadless districts and in distant isles without mills, especially during storms. Among other expedients to which the more remote people resorted was the searching of ancient ruins for the *pollagan* (mortar mills) of former generations. The mortar is a still more primitive instrument for preparing corn than the quern. It is a block of stone about twenty-four inches by eighteen by eight. The centre and one end of this block are hollowed out to a breadth of about six or eight inches, and a depth of four or five, leaving three gradually sloping sides. The grain is placed in this scoop-like hollow and crushed with a stone. When sufficiently crushed, the meal is thrown out at the open end of the scoop, and fresh grain is put in to follow a similar process. When using the mortar, the woman is on her knees, unless the mortar is on a table.

The meal obtained by this process is called *pronn, pronnt, pronntach, min phronntaidh* (bruised meal), to distinguish it from *gradan, gradanach, min ghradain* (quick meal), *min bhrath, min bhrathain* (quern meal), and *min mhuille* (mill meal). The crushed meal of the primitive mortar is similar in character to the crushed meal of modern commerce.

The quern and mortar are still used in outlying districts of Scotland and Ireland, though isolatedly and sparingly.

93 The milking songs of the people are numerous and varied. They are sung to pretty airs, to please the cows and to induce them to give their milk. The cows become accustomed to these lilts and will not give their milk without them, nor, occasionally, without their favourite airs being sung to them. This fondness of Highland cows for music induces owners of large herds to secure milkmaids possessed of good voices and some "go."

It is interesting and animating to see three or four comely girls among a fold of sixty, eighty, or a hundred picturesque Highland cows on meadow or mountain slope. The moaning and heaving of the sea afar, the swish of the wave on the shore, the carolling of the lark in the sky, the unbroken song of the mavis on the rock, the broken melody of the merle in the brake, the lowing of the kine without, the response of the calves within the fold, the singing of the milkmaids in unison with the movement of their hands, and of the soft sound of the snowy milk falling into the pail, the gilding of hill and dale, the glowing of the distant ocean beyond, as the sun sinks into the sea of golden glory, constitute a scene which the observer would not, if he could, forget.

100 Being a pastoral people, the Highlanders possess much pastoral poetry. The greater part of this is secular with fragments of sacred poetry interspersed. The herding runes are examples of these purely pastoral poems. They are sung by the people as they send their flocks to the pastures, or tend them on the hills, glens, or plains. The customs vary in details in different districts, but everywhere is the simple belief that the King of shepherds watches over men and flocks now as of old, "the same yesterday, today, and for ever."

When a man has taken his herd to the pasture in the morning, and has got a knoll between himself and them, he bids them a tender adieu, waving his hand, perhaps both hands, towards them, saying:

The herding of Bride to the kine,
Whole and well may you return.

The prosperity of Mary Mother be yours,
Active and full may you return.

The safeguard of Columba round your feet,
Whole be your return home.

Be the bright Michael king of the angels
Protecting, and keeping, and saving you.

The guarding of God and the Lord be yours
Till I or mine shall see you again.

The help of Coivi to you.

Travelling coire, travelling copse,
Travelling meads long and grassy,
The herding of the fair Mary
Be about your head, your body, and aiding you.

When these patriarchal benedictions are intoned or chanted, and the music floats over moor and loch, the effect is charming to the ear of the listener.

107 The marking of the lambs is done on Thursday, being St Columba's Day. Upon no account would the people mark their lambs on Friday, or in any manner draw blood on that day. Nor till lately would they use iron in any form on Friday. A blacksmith in Benbecula, a Protestant, an excellent man and an admirable tradesman, never opened his smithy on Friday. He maintained that "that was the least he could do to honour his Master."

When the lambs are marked, the people collect the bits taken out of their ears, and carefully bury them beyond the reach of beast or bird. They say that a plant, which they call *gearradh-chluasach* (literally, ear-cuts, ear-clips) grows from them. This plant is generally found growing where a carcase has been buried, and when ripe, it is cut, tied up in a bunch, and suspended from the *casan ceanghail,* couple above the door of the lamb-cot, and dedicated to:

The fair-white Mary of lasting graces,
For luck of sheep and love of lambs.

The marks made on the ears of sheep and lambs are varied and descriptive in name, as: *barr, beum, cluigean, cliopan, cliopadh, crocan, corran, duile, meaghlan, meangan sgolta, slios, snathad, sulag, toll.* These marks and their modifications are said to number over 250 in the island of Benbecula, in the island of North Uist over 480, and in the island of South Uist over 500. The people know all these marks and modifications at a glance.

When a man marries, it is considered a good omen of the union when the marks on his own sheep and those on the sheep brought him by his wife are nearly alike, and the necessary change easily effected.

The small native sheep have a long tuft of wool called *sguman* coming down the face. They are hardy, picturesque little animals, almost wholly free from the innumerable diseases which the larger but softer breeds of sheep have brought in their train. The sheep is regarded with a veneration which is not extended to the cow or other animals.

108 When a man has shorn a sheep and has set it free, he waves his hand after it and says this blessing.

109 During the winter months the women of Highland households are up late and early at *calanas* – this comprehensive term embracing the whole process of wool-working from the raw material to the finished cloth. The process is an important factor in the internal economy of a Highland family. The industry of these women is wonderful, performed lovingly, uncomplainingly, day after day, year after year, till the sands of life run down. The life in a Highland home of the crofter class is well described in the following lines:

In the long winter night
All are engaged,
Teaching the young
Is the grey-haired sage,
The daughter at her carding,
The mother at her wheel,
While the fisher mends his net
With his needle and his reel.

Calanas is an interesting process. The wool is carefully sorted and the coarser parts put aside. It is then washed and laid out to dry, and again examined and teased, and all lumps and refuse taken out.

If the wool is meant to be made into very fine cloth, it is drawn on combs of specially long teeth; if into ordinary cloth, it is carded on the cards without going through the combs. After carding, the wool is made into *rolagan* (rowans), and spun into thread, which is arranged into hanks. At this stage the thread is generally dyed, although occasionally the wool is dyed after the teasing process and before being carded.

The work of dyeing requires much care and knowledge and practical skill. It is done with native plants gathered with patient care from the rocks and hills, moors and fields and lakes, and with certain earths. When it is considered that a thorough knowledge of plants is necessary, their locality, their colouring properties, whether of root, stem, or leaf, and the stage of growth or decay, it will be understood that those who use them need much intelligence. All Highland women are practical dyers, some more skilful than others. From infancy they are trained in *calanas,* and in plants and dyeing; the whole clothing, including the blankets, of the household being dependent upon their skill and industry. Are there any other women in any class who can show such widespread skill and intelligence as these Highland women show wool-working and dyeing operations?

Home-made tartans and other fabrics, made many generations, sometimes centuries, ago, are not only wonderfully fine in texture, but all the different colours are remarkably bright and beautiful.

The Celts must have had an eye for colour in very early times. The Book of Kells is said by experts to be the most beautiful illuminated manuscript in the world. It is believed to have been written in the Columban monastery of Iona, and to have escaped the Norse destruction of manuscripts and been carried to the Columban monastery of Kells. Not only are the forms of the initial letters in the manuscript marvellously intricate and artistic, but the different pigments used in colouring are still bright and beautiful and fresh, while the colouring of copies made during this century is already sickly and faded.

The pattern of the tartan or other cloth to be woven is first designed on a small piece of wood, the thread being placed on the wood according to the design proposed. This is called *suidheachadh* (setting). It is a work that requires patient care and skill in order to bring out the pattern correctly.

The Chant of the Warping is feelingly

intoned by the women in warping the web. When a word or a phrase has struck their minds, they stop singing in order to emphasise the sentiment in a word or a phrase of their own, beseeching Mary's beloved Son to give them strength to observe His laws. These pious interjections and momentary stoppages may not add to the beauty of the singing, but they do to the picturesqueness.

111 *Imirt, iomairt, iumairt, umairt* is cloth striped lengthwise, not crosswise. While the warp of the *iomairt* is composed of stripes of various colours, the weft is confined to one — generally light blue, dark blue, or black. This cloth was confined to women's use, in the *earasaid,* the *tonnag,* the *guaileachan,* and the petticoat. Setting the *iomairt,* like setting other warp, and setting the eggs, and many other operations of the people, was done on Thursday, that being the day of St Columba. Framing the web is a work of much anxiety to the housewife, and she and her maidens are up very early to put the thread in order.

The thread of the *iomairt,* like that of the tartan, was very fine, hard-spun and double twisted, rendering the cloth extremely durable.

112 In the Outer Isles women generally do the weaving, while in the Inner Isles and on the mainland it is usually done by men.

In Uist, when the woman stops weaving on Saturday night she carefully ties up her loom and suspends the cross or crucifix above the sleay. This is for the purpose of keeping away the brownie, the banshee, the *peallan,* and all evil spirits and malign influences from disarranging the thread and the loom. And all this is done with loving care and in good faith, and in prayer and purity of heart.

113 Formerly throughout the Highlands and Islands the cloth for the family was made at home. At present home-made clothing is chiefly made in the Islands, and even there to a lesser extent than formerly.

After the web of cloth is woven it is waulked, to thicken and strengthen and brighten it. The frame on which the cloth is waulked is a board some twelve to twenty-four feet long and about two feet broad, grooved lengthwise along its surface. The frame is called *cleith* (wattle), and *cleith-luaidh* (waulking-wattle), probably from its having been originally constructed of wattle-work. The waulking-frame is raised upon trestles, while the waulking-women are ranged on seats on either side, about two feet of space being allowed to each woman. The web is unrolled and laid along the board. It is then saturated with ammonia, warm water, and soap suds, and the women work it vigorously from side to side across the grooves of the frame, slowly moving it lengthwise also, that each part of the cloth may receive due attention. The lateral movement of the cloth is sunwise. Occasionally the waulking-board is laid on the ground instead of on trestles, and the women work the cloth with their feet instead of with their hands.

Generally the waulking-women are young maidens, a few married women of good voice being distributed among them. They sing as they work, one singing the song, the others the chorus. Their songs are varied, lively, and adapted to the class of work. Most of them are love-songs, with an occasional impromptu song on some passing event — perhaps on the casual stranger who has looked in, perhaps a wit combat between two of the girls about the real or supposed merits or demerits of their respective lovers. These wit combats are much enjoyed, being often clever, caustic, and apt.

A favourite subject at these waulkings is Prince Charlie, and a favourite song is *"Morag"* (little Marion), the endearing term under which the Prince is veiled. The words of the song are vigorous and passionate, and the air stirring, while the subject is one to fire the hearts and imaginations of the people even at this distance of time, and notwithstanding the spoliations, oppressions, and butcheries inflicted on their fathers through their adherence to *Morag.*

The song begins as follows:

And ho ro Morag,
Ho ro na ho ro darling,
And ho ro Morag.

Beauteous Morag of the clustering locks,
To sing of thee is my intent.
If thou art gone beyond the sea,
Prithee hasten home to me.

Remember, bring a band of maidens,
Who will waulk the red cloth firmly.

When the women have waulked the cloth, they roll up the web and place it on end in the centre of the frame. They then turn it slowly and deliberately sunwise along the frame, saying with each turn of the web:

This is not second clothing.
This cloth is not thigged.
This is not the property of cleric or priest.

Another form is:

Division one, division two, division three, division four, division five, division six, division seven, division seven.

This is not cloth for priest or cleric,
But it is cloth for my own little Donald of love,
For my companion beloved, for John of joy,
And for Muriel of loveliest hue.

Each member of the household for whom the cloth is intended is mentioned by name in the consecration. The cloth is then spat upon, and slowly reversed end by end in the name of Father and of Son and of Spirit till it stands again in the centre of the frame. The ceremony of consecrating the cloth is usually intoned, the women, hitherto gay and vivacious, now solemn and subdued, singing in unison. The woman who leads in the consecration is called *coisreagan* (consecrator or celebrant). After the cloth is waulked and washed it is rolled up. This is called *coilleachadh* (stretching), *coilleachadh an aodaich* (stretching the cloth), a process done with great care in order to secure equal tension throughout the web.

The operation of waulking is a singularly striking scene, and one which Highlanders cherish wherever situated.

114 A young man was consecrated before he went out to hunt. Oil was put on his head, a bow was placed in his hand, and he was required to stand with bare feet on the bare grassless ground. The dedication of the young hunter was akin to those of the *maor* (the judge, the chief, and the king) on installation.

Many conditions were imposed on the young man, which he was required to observe throughout life. He was not to take life wantonly. He was not to kill a bird sitting, nor a beast lying down, and he was not to kill the mother of a brood, nor the mother of a suckling. Nor was he to kill an unfledged bird nor a suckling beast, unless it might be the young of a bird or beast of prey. It was at all times permissible and laudable to destroy certain clearly defined birds and beasts of prey and evil reptiles, with their young.

115 This hymn was sung by the hunter when he went away in the morning, and when he had bathed his hands and face in the junction of the first three streams he met.

116 This hymn was sung by a pilgrim in setting out on his pilgrimage. The family and friends joined the traveller in singing the hymn and starting the journey, from which too frequently, for various causes, he never returned.

117 On Christmas Day the young men of the townland go out to fish. All the fish they catch are sacred to the widows and the orphans and to the poor, and are distributed among them according to their necessities.

There is a tradition among the people of the Western Isles that Christ required Peter to row 707 strokes straight out from the shore when He commanded him to go and procure the fish containing the tribute-money. Following this tradition, the old men of Uist require the young men to row 707 strokes from the land before casting their lines on Christmas Day. And whatever fish they get are cordially given to the needy as a tribute in the name of Christ, King of the sea, and of Peter, king of fishermen. This is called *dioladh deirc* (tribute-paying), *deirce Pheadair* (Peter's tribute), *dioladh Pheadail* (Peter's payment), and other terms. This tribute-paying on Christmas Day excites much emotional interest, and all try to enhance the tribute and in various ways to render the alms as substantial as possible.

The whiting and the haddock of the same size bear a strong resemblance to one another. There are differences, however. The haddock has a black spot on each side of its body above the pectoral fin, while the head of the whiting is more elongated than that of the haddock. Children and strangers are taught to differentiate between the two thus:

A black spot of the haddock,
A long snout on the whiting.

The people of Uist say that the haddock was the fish in whose mouth Peter found the tribute-money, and that the two black spots are the marks left by Peter's fingers when he held the fish to extract the money from its mouth. The crew of young men who get most haddocks on Christmas Day are looked upon during the year as the real followers of the King of fishers. There is, therefore, considerable emulation among the different crews.

The haddock is called *iasg Pheadail* (Peter's fish), and *iasg Pheadair runaich* (the fish of loving Peter); and a family of birds *peadaireach, peitirich* (Peter-like, petrels) because in their flight they seem to be walking on the sea.

The tradition as to rowing 707 strokes is curious and interesting. The only other similar tradition which I know is of the wars between the Fomorians and the Milesians in Ireland. Both were invaders — the Milesians earlier, the Fomorians later. When the Fomorians landed in Ireland the Milesians were already established, and the result was a long-continued war, till both sides were exhausted and tired of the strife. During a temporary truce it was agreed that the Fomorians should retire to the sea and row straight out 707 strokes from land, and if they succeeded in landing again they were to be allowed to remain and enjoy their hard-won honours. Whether for good or for ill to Ireland, the Fomorians effected a landing a second time, and settled in the south and west of the island.

The Irish were pagan at the time, and the tradition of the 707 strokes being imposed by Christ on Peter must have been inserted in the Fomorian tradition after Ireland became Christian.

118 Sea prayers and sea hymns were common amongst the seafarers of the Western Islands. Probably these originated with the early Celtic missionaries, who constantly traversed in their frail skin coracles the storm-swept, strongly tidal seas of those Hebrid Isles, oft and oft sealing their devotion with their lives.

Before embarking on a journey the voyagers stood round their boat and prayed to the God of the elements for a peaceful voyage over the stormy sea. The steersman led the appeal, while the swish of the waves below, the sough of the sea beyond, and the sound of the wind around blended with the voices of the suppliants and lent dignity and solemnity to the scene.

There are many small oratories round the West Coast where chiefs and clansmen were wont to pray before and after voyaging. An interesting example of these is in the island of Grimisey, North Uist. The place is called Ceallan, cells, from *ceall* (a cell). There were two oratories within two hundred yards of one another. One of the two has wholly disappeared, the other nearly. The ruin stands on a ridge near the end of the island looking out on the open bay of Ceallan and over the stormy Minch to the distant mountains of Mull and Morven. The oratory is known as Teampull Mhicheil (the temple of St Michael). The structure was simple but beautiful, while the remains are interesting and touching from their historical associations. Tradition says that the oratory was built by Eibhric (Euphemia or Amie), sole daughter and heiress of Ruaraidh, the son of Alan, High Chief of Lorn.

Amie, the daughter of Ruaraidh, married in 1337 John of Islay, Lord of the Isles. The two being related, they were granted a dispensation by Pope Benedict XII. The Lady Amie had three sons.

About the year 1358 John of Islay discarded Amie, and married Margaret, daughter of Robert Steward, and granddaughter of Robert Bruce. When the Lord of the Isles came south to celebrate his marriage with the Lady Margaret, one hundred and eight ships full of kinsmen and clansmen, chiefs and chieftains, came in his train. Such a sight had never been seen in Scotland before, and people came to the Clyde from long distances to see this large fleet. The power and influence indicated by this enormous retinue created much comment and envy among the nobles of the south and even at the Court.

The Lord of the Isles retained possession of the extensive territories of the Lady Amie, disposing of them afterwards to his several sons.

The discarded lady took to a religious life, building and restoring oratories, churches, nunneries, monasteries, and castles throughout her ancestral lands. St Michael's Temple at Ceallan was one of these. In this little sanctuary built for the purpose the Lady Amie offered prayers and thanks before and after voyages to her kindred in Lorn.

John, Lord of the Isles, was a man of much munificence, like all those princely Macdonalds. He gave largely to the Church, earning for himself from the priests of the period the name of "The Good John of Islay." He was buried in Iona in the year 1386, in splendour and magnificence never surpassed, if ever equalled, in the case of the many kings of the five nationalities buried there.

About two years after his father's death, Ranald, the eldest surviving son of the Lady Amie, handed over the lordship of the Isles to Donald, eldest son of the Lady Margaret, who afterwards fought the battle of Harlaw. The ceremony of installing a Lord of the Isles usually took place at Loch Finlaggan in Islay, the principal seat of the Macdonalds, where the ruins of their castle, chapel, and other buildings are still to be seen, as well as the stone with the footmarks cut in it upon which the chief stood when, before the "gentlemen of the Islands" and Highlands, he was proclaimed "Macdonald" and "High Prince of the seed of Conn." But it was at Kildonan in the island of Eigg that Ranald gave the sceptre into the hand of Donald, who thus became eighth Lord of the Isles. The account given of the ceremony by Hugh Macdonald, the Seanchie of Sleat, is interesting as representing the usual manner of installing a king, chief, or other dignitary among the Celts:

"At this the Bishop of Argyll, the Bishop of the Isles, and seven priests were sometimes present, but a Bishop was always present, with the chieftains of all the principal families and a Ruler of the Isles. There was a square stone seven or eight feet long, and the tract of a man's foot cut thereon, upon which he stood, denoting that he should walk in the footsteps and uprightness of his predecessors, and that he was installed by right in his possessions. He was clothed in a white habit to show his innocence and integrity of heart, that he would be a light to his people and maintain the true religion. The white apparel did afterwards belong to the poet by right. Then he was to receive a white rod in his hand intimating that he had power to rule, not with tyranny and partiality, but with discretion and sincerity. Then he received his forefathers' sword, or some other sword, signifying that his duty was to protect and defend them from their enemies in peace or war, as the obligations and customs of his predecessors were. The ceremony being over, Mass was said after the blessing of the Bishop and seven priests, the people pouring their prayers for the success and prosperity of their new-created lord. When they were dismissed, the Lord of the Isles feasted them for a week thereafter, and gave liberally to the monks, poets, bards, and musicians. You may judge that they spent liberally without any exception of persons."

Other accounts differ but slightly from the above, as when Martin says that "the young chief stood upon a cairn of stones, while his followers stood round him in a circle, his elevation signifying his authority over them, and their standing below their subjection to him, also that immediately after the proclamation the chief druid or bard performed a rhetorical panegyric setting forth the ancient pedigree, valour, and liberality of the family as incentives to the young chieftain and fit for his imitation."

Martin speaks of this ceremony of installing a chief as prevalent in the eighteenth century.

VOLUME II

122 When this charm is applied, the point of a knife or a needle, or the tongue of a brooch or of some other sharp instrument, is pointed threateningly at the part affected. The part is then spat upon and crossed three times in the names of the three Persons of the Trinity, whether it be the breast of a woman or the udder of a cow. The legend says that Mary and Jesus were walking together when Mary took rose (erysipelas) in her breast, and she said these words to Jesus.

126 The teeth of ancient human skeletons found in stone coffins and other enclosures, and without enclosures, are usually good and complete. This is in marked contrast to the teeth of modern human remains, which are generally much impaired if not wholly absent. But there must have been toothache and even artificial teeth in ancient times, as indicated by the mummies in Egypt and the toothache charms and toothache wells in the Highlands. One toothache charm and one toothache well must suffice to illustrate this. The toothache well is in the island of North Uist. It is situated 195 feet above the sea, at the foot of a hill 757 feet high, and nearly three miles in the moorland from the nearest townland. The place is called Cuidh–airidh, shieling fold, while the well is variously known as Tobar Chuidh–airidh, well of the shieling fold; Tobar an deididh, well of the toothache; Tobar na cnoidh, well of the worm; and Tobar cnuimh fhiacail, well of the tooth worm; from a belief that toothache is caused by a worm in the tooth.

The general name of the well is Tobar Chuidh–airidh, well of the shieling fold, to distinguish it from other healing wells throughout the Isles. The pilgrim suffering from toothache must not speak, nor eat, nor drink, after beginning the pilgrimage till after three draughts of the well of Cuidh–airidh are drunk in name of God, and in name of Christ, and in name of Spirit.

Some persons profess to derive no relief, some profess to derive partial relief, and some profess to derive complete relief from toothache after drinking the water of the well of Cuidh–airidh.

127 The following scene was described to me by Angus MacEachain, herdsman, Staonabrig, South Uist, one of the chief actors in the episode.

The daughter of a farmer in the neighbourhood was ill with jaundice. The doctor of the parish was attending her, but she was becoming worse instead of better, and her end seemed near. Her distressed parents sent for Aonas nan gisrean, Angus of the exorcisms, and he came. The man examined the girl and announced that she was possessed of the demon of the jaundice, but that he would expel the demon and cure the girl.

He requested the mother to put on a big fire, the sisters to bring a tub of clear cold water, and the father to bring the plough irons, evil spirits being unable to withstand iron. All this was promptly done. The exorcist placed the plough irons in the fire, displaying much solicitude that they should be red–hot. The room was darkened and the eyes of the patient were bandaged that the eyes of the body might be subjective to the eyes of the mind. Directed by the exorcist, the mother and sisters placed the back of the girl to the front of the bed, and laying it bare left the room, the man securing the door after them. Making a clanging noise with the plough irons as if to drive away the jaundice demon, the man replaced the share in the fire and put the coulter in the water.

Then pretending to take the red–hot share out of the fire, he took up the icy–cold coulter and placed it along the spine of the patient, loudly commanding the demon to depart. The girl screamed in evident agony, calling on the Mother of Christ and on the Foster–mother of Christ, and on her own mother, to come and rescue her from the brutal treatment of black Angus the father of evil, the brother of demons, and to see how her blood was flowing in streams and her flesh was burnt off her back, laying her backbone bare. While loudly calling to the jaundice demon to depart, the expert exorcist threw the red–hot share into the tub of water, adding to the already abundant noise in the room. Against the remonstrances of the father, who said that Angus knew what he was about, the mother and sisters burst open the door, calling on Mary Mother to rescue the maltreated girl, and on Calumcille to redress her wrongs.

"Whether the cure was due to her simple faith in the exorcist or to the shock to her nervous system I do not know," continued the narrator, "but in a few days the girl was up and about. She is grateful, but shy of me ever since, probably remembering the hard things she said. She will always believe that I exercised some occult power over the jaundice demon. The case of this girl was as bad as any I have seen. She had been an attractive, comely girl, with a winning expression and a clear complexion, but she had become yellow–black instead of rosy–red."

Angus MacEachain told of this and similar cases with much humour, but without a smile on his lips, though his eyes sparkled, and his countenance glowed with evident appreciation of the scenes.

133 *Fath–fith* and *fith–fath* are interchangeable terms and indiscriminately used. They are applied to the occult power which rendered a person invisible to mortal eyes and which transformed one object into another. Men and women were made invisible, or men were transformed into horses, bulls, or stags, while women were transformed into cats, hares, or hinds. These transmutations were sometimes voluntary, sometimes involuntary. The *fith–fath* was especially serviceable to hunters, warriors, and travellers, rendering them invisible or unrecognisable to enemies and to animals.

Fionn had a fairy sweetheart, a daughter of the people of the mounds, but Fionn forsook her and married a daughter of the sons of men. The fairy was angry at the slight put upon her, and she placed the wife of Fionn under the *fith–fath* spell in the form of a hind of the hill. The wife of Fionn bore a son in the island of Sanndraigh in Loch–nan–ceall in Arasaig. The mother possessed so much of the nature of the hind that she licked the temple of the child when he was born, but she possessed so much of the nature of the woman that she only gave one lick. But hair like the hair of a fawn grew on the part of the temple of the child which the tongue of the hind–mother had touched. And because of this patch of fawn's hair on his temple the child was called "Oisein," the fawn.

While still a boy Ossian followed Fionn and the Feinne to the hunting–hill to chase the mountain deer. In the midst of the chase a magic mist darker than night came down upon the hunters, blinding them from one another and from their surroundings — no one knew where was another or where he was himself. Hunt–wandering came over Ossian, and he wandered wearily alone, and at last found himself in a deep green glen surrounded by high blue hills.

As he walked along he saw a timid hind browsing in a green corrie before him. And Ossian thought to himself that he had never seen a creature so lovely as this timid hind, and he stood gazing upon her with joy. But the spirit of the hunt was strong upon Ossian, and the blood of the hunter was hot in his veins, and he drew his spear to throw it at the hind. The hind turned and looked at Ossian and gazed upon him with her full wistful grey eyes, more lovely and alluring than the blue eyes of love.

"Do not hurt me, Ossian," said the hind. "I am thy mother under the *fith–fath* in the form of a hind abroad and in the form of a woman at home. Thou art hungry and thirsty and weary. Come thou home with me, thou fawn of my heart."

And Ossian accompanied the hind step by step till they reached a rock in the base of the hill. The hind opened a leaf in a door in the rock where no door seemed to be, and she went in, and Ossian went in after her. She closed the door–leaf in the rock and there was no appearance of a door. And the graceful hind became transformed into a beautiful woman, like the lovely woman of the green kirtle and the locks of gold. There was light in the bower in the bosom of the ben like the light of noontide on midsummer day. Nor was it the light of the sun, nor was it the light of the moon, nor was it the light of the star of guidance.

His mother prepared food and drink and music for Ossian. And she placed food in a place of eating for him, and she placed drink in a place of drinking for him, and she placed music in a place of hearing for him. Ossian took of the food and of the drink and of the music till he was full satisfied — his seven full satiations. After feasting, Ossian said to his mother:

"I am going, mother, to see what Fionn and the Feinne are doing in the hunting–hill."

And his mother placed her arm around his neck and kissed Ossian with the three kisses of a mother, and then she opened the door–leaf in the door of the bower and allowed him out. When she closed it there was no appearance of a door in the rock.

Ossian had been feasting on food and drink and music in the bower with his mother for the space of three days, as he thought, but he had been in the bower for the space of three years instead. And he made a song, the first song he made, warning his mother against the men and the hounds of the Feinne.

In his *Leabhar Na Feinne,* Iain Campbell of Islay says that he had received fourteen versions of this song of Ossian. Six of these had been sent to him by the present writer. One of these versions was obtained from Oirig Nic Iain — Effric or Effie Mac Iain — lineally descended, she said, from Alexander Mac Iain, chief of the massacred Macdonalds of Glencoe.

Effric Mac Iain was not tall, but she was very beautiful, intelligent, and pleasant. I obtained a silver brooch from her which, she said, had come down like herself through the generations from the massacred chief of Glencoe. The brooch is circular and beautifully chased, though much worn.

134 The charm *(sian* or *seun)* is occult agency, supernatural power used to ward away injury, and to protect invisibly. Belief in the charm was common, and examples of its efficacy are frequently told. A woman at Bearnasdale, in Skye, put such a charm on MacLeod of Bearnaray, Harris, when on his way to join Prince Charlie in 1745. At Culloden the bullets showered upon him like hail, but they had no effect. When all was lost, MacLeod threw off his coat to facilitate his flight. His faithful foster-brother Murdoch Macaskail was close behind him and took up the coat. When examined it was found to be riddled with bullet-holes. But not one of these bullets had hurt MacLeod!

A woman at Bornish, South Uist, put a charm on Allan Macdonald of Clanranald when he was leaving to join the Earl of Mar at Perth in 1715. But Clanranald took a lad away against the will of his mother, who lived at Staonabrig, South Uist. The woman implored Clanranald to leave her only son, and she a widow, but he would not. Then she vowed that "Ailean Beag" (Little Allan), as Clanranald was called, would never return. She baked two bannocks, a little bannock and a big bannock, and asked her son whether he would have the little bannock with his mother's blessing, or the big one with her cursing. The lad said that he would have the little bannock with his mother's blessing. So she gave him the little bannock and her blessing and also a crooked sixpence, saying: "Here, my son, is a sixpence seven times cursed. Use it in battle against Little Allan and earn the blessing of thy mother, or refrain and earn her cursing."

At the battle of Sheriffmuir, blows and bullets were showering on Allan of Clanranald, but he heeded them not and for every blow he got he gave three. When the strife was hottest and the contest doubtful, the son of the widow of Staonabrig remembered his mother's injunction, and that it was better to fight with her blessing than fall with her cursing, and he put the crooked sixpence in his gun. He aimed and Clanranald fell. His people crowded round Clanranald weeping and wailing like children. But Glengarry called out: "Today for revenge, tomorrow for weeping!" and the Macdonalds renewed the fight. Thirsting for revenge they fell upon the English division of Argyll's army, cutting it to pieces and routing it for several miles.

When Clanranald's father was asked whom he wept and watched, his only reply was: "He was a man yesterday."

Allan Macdonald of Clanranald was called "Ailean Beag," Little Allan, in contradistinction to some of his predecessors who had been exceptionally big men. If apparently short of stature, he was exceedingly broad and powerful, active, gallant of bearing, and greatly beloved by his people.

After the failure of Dundee in 1689 Clanranald lived in France for several years. There he made the acquaintance of Penelope, daughter of Colonel Mackenzie, governor of Tangiers under Charles II. Clanranald married Penelope Mackenzie and brought her home. He also brought a French architect, French masons, and French freestone to build a new house at Ormacleit. The house took seven years in building and was occupied for seven years. On the night of the battle of Sheriffmuir, when its owner was killed, the house was burnt to the ground through the kitchen chimney taking fire. Some days previously Lady Clanranald had told some guests that she had had a vision that her eyes melted away in scalding water and that her heart burned up like a live coal, and she feared some dire double disaster was to befall her.

The great ruins of Ormacleit stand high and picturesque on the monotonous far-reaching, machairs of the Atlantic side of South Uist. The gables are high-pointed, and the wings being at right angles to the main building, the ruins show to admirable advantage in the long level landscape. The freestone forming the corners, doors, and windows is of peculiar hardness, and of a blue tint.

The farm of Ormacleit had been tenanted during many years by Mr John Maclellan, whose wife was Miss Penelope Macdonald, a kinswoman of Flora Macdonald and of her chief Clanranald. Mrs Maclellan was a lady of great beauty, excellence, historical knowledge, and good sense. She had the happiness, a few years before she died, of handing to her chief and relative, Admiral Sir Reginald Macdonald of Clanranald, some jewellery that had been found in the ruins of the castle. The jewellery in all probability had been the property of Penelope Mackenzie, the lady of the gallant Clanranald of the '15, and for whom Penelope Macdonald had been named.

138 The people quote many proverbs relating to love and to love charms. "Lunacy and love are twins;" "Alike are the complaint of love and the complaint of madness;" "Love will close a thousand eyes but waken five thousand jealousies."

The lucky bones are the joint of the big toe of the right foot and the nail-joints of the left foot of an old man. These are said to be the first part of the human body to decay.

140 The results of the evil eye appear in yawning and vomiting and in a general disturbance of the system. The countenance assumes an appearance grim, gruesome, and repulsive.

This formula for removing the effects of the evil eye is handed down from male to female, from female to male, and is efficacious only when thus transmitted. Before pronouncing it over the particular case of sickness, the operator proceeds to a stream, where the living and the dead alike pass, and lifts water, in name of the Holy Trinity, into a wooden ladle. In no case is the ladle of metal. On returning, a wife's gold ring, a piece of gold, of silver, and of copper, are put in the ladle. The sign of the holy cross is then made, and this rhyme is repeated in a slow recitative manner — the name of the person or animal under treatment being mentioned towards the end.

In the case of an animal a woollen thread, generally of the natural colour of the sheep, is tied round the tail. The consecrated water is then given as a draught, and sprinkled over the head and backbone. In the case of a cow the horns and the space between the horns are carefully anointed.

The remnant of the water, no drop of which must have reached the ground previously, is poured over a corner stone, threshold flag, or other immovable stone or rock, which is said to split if the sickness be severe. Experts profess to distinguish whether it be a man or a woman who has laid the evil eye: if a man, the copper adheres to the bottom of the upturned ladle, significant of the many turns in a man's dark wily heart; if a woman, only the silver and gold adhere, the heart of a woman being to that of man — not in this case, "as moonlight unto sunlight and as water unto wine" — but as gold and silver to copper and brass. Old women in the Highlands say that if men's hearts were laid bare they would be found to contain many more twists and turns and wiles than those of women.

154 The exorcism of the stye is variously called *Cunntas an t-Sleamhnain* (Counting of the Stye), *Eolas an t-Sleamhnain* (Exorcism of the Stye), and *Eoir an t-Sleamhnain* (Charm of the Stye).

When making the charm the exorcist holds some sharp-pointed instrument, preferably a nail, or the tongue of a brooch or buckle, between the thumb and forefinger of the right hand. With each question the operator makes a feint with the instrument at the stye, going perilously near the eye. The sensation caused by the thrusting is extremely painful to the sufferer and even to the observer.

The reciter assured the writer that a cure immediately follows the operation. Possibly the thrusting acts upon the nervous system of the patient.

Ordinarily the exorcist omits mentioning the word "stye" after the first two times, abbreviating thus:

Why came the two here
Without the three here?

After the incantation the Lord's Prayer is intoned, and the following is repeated:

Pater one,
Pater two,
Pater three,
Pater four,
Pater five,
Pater six,
Pater seven,
Pater eight,
Pater nine,
Pater one
And eight,
Pater of Christ the kindly
Be upon thee tonight,
Pater of the Three of life
Upon thine eye without harm.

This seems to indicate that the Lord's Prayer was originally repeated nine times.

159 The figwort is known as *farach dubh, farach donn, farum, forum, fothlus, fotlus, lus nan cnapan, lus nan clugan, clugan, cluganach, lus an torranain, torranach,* and *torranan.* The names are descriptive: *farach dubh* (black mallet), *farach donn* (brown mallet); *farum* and *forum* are probably forms of *farach. Fothlus* and *fotlus* (crumbs, refuse, scrofulous), *lus nan clugan* (plant of the clusters), *lus an torranain* (plant of the thunderer). Probably *tarrann, torrann, torranan, tarranan,* are variants of Taranis, the name of the thunder god of the Gauls.

On the mainland the figwort is known for its medicinal properties, and in the islands for its magical powers. On the mainland the leaf of the plant is applied to cuts and bruises, and the tuber to sores and tumours. In the islands the plant was placed on the cow fetter, under the milk boyne, and over the byre door, to ensure milk in the cows.

Having intoned the incantation of the *torranan,* the reciter said:

"The *torranan* is a blessed plant. It grows in sight of the sea. Its root is a cluster of four bulbs like the four teats of a cow. The stalk of the plant is as long as the arm, and the bloom is as large as the breast of a woman, and as pure white as the driven snow of the hill. It is full of the milk of grace and goodness and of the gift of peace and power, and fills with the filling and ebbs with the ebbing tide. It is therefore meet to cull the plant with the flow and not with the ebb of the restless sea. If I had the *torranan* it would ensure to me abundant milk in my cow all the year. Poor as I am, I would rather than a Saxon pound that I had the blessed *torranan.* I went away to John the son of Fearachar, who knows every plant that comes through the ground, to see if he would get me the *torranan* of power. But John's wife said 'No,' and that I was only an *oinig,* a silly woman. The jade!"

John Beaton, known as John, son of Fearachar, son of John, son of Niall Dotair, Neil the Doctor, was a shepherd by occupation but a botanist by instinct. He knew Gaelic only, and he knew no letters, but probably he knew more about plants and plant habitats and characteristics than any other man in Scotland. He lived in close communion with Nature, and loved plants as he loved his children — with a warm abiding love which no poverty could cool and no age could dim. A Gaelic proverb says: *Bu dual da sin* (That was hereditary to him); and *Sgoiltidh an dualchas a chreig* (Heredity will cleave the rock); and again *Theid dualchas an aghaigh nan creag* (Heredity will go against the rocks). John Beaton was a striking confirmation of these sayings, being descended from a long line of botanists and botanical doctors who left their impress on the minds and on the language of their fellow-countrymen. He was descended from the Beatons of Skye, who were descended from the Beatons of Islay. They in turn were descended from the Beatons of Mull, who are said to have come down from Beatan, the medical missionary of the Columban Church of Iona. These Beatons produced many eminent men, among them James Beaton, Archbishop of Glasgow, and his still greater nephew David, the Cardinal Archbishop of St Andrews, and through the Barons Livingstone of Bachuill, Lismore, David Livingstone, physician, missionary, traveller and explorer. Mary Beaton, mentioned in the song of the Queen's Four Maries, was also of these Beatons:

Last night there were four Maries,
This night there shall be but three;

There was Marie Beaton and Marie Seaton
And Marie Carmichael and me.

The people of Mull say that this Mary Beaton was of the Mull family, but the distinguished scholar, the late Hector Maclean, and other Islay men, claimed that she was of the Islay Beatons. The Beatons were hereditary *leighean* (physicians) to the Lords of the Isles and to other great insular and mainland chiefs. They were also physicians to the Kings of Scotland, whom they visited periodically. Payments for some of these visits are recorded in the Exchequer Rolls.

The Beatons left many manuscripts on medicine and on medicinal plants. Some of these are in the Advocates' Library, some are in private possession, and many are known to have been lost. Some of the most beautiful sculptured stones in Iona, Mull, Islay, and elsewhere, are over the tombs of Beatons.

Several of the Beatons of Mull and Islay went to Paris and other continental cities to complete their medical and theological studies. Some of these remained abroad and rose to positions of distinction. The name is still to be met with in France in the French form of Béthune. One of the Beatons on returning to Scotland retained that form of the name. He settled in Fife. A descendant of his settled in Skye as leech to MacLeod of MacLeod, founding the Skye branch of the family. One of this family was known as Fearachar Leigh, Fearachar Lighiche, Farquhar the Physician. He held the small estate of Husabost, near the mouth of Dunvegan Loch, for his services. He had a medical manuscript valued at sixty milch cows; and so careful was he of this manuscript, that when he himself came up to Dunvegan by boat he sent a trusted manservant on horse-back round by land with the manuscript. John Beaton, the shepherd of Uist, was descended from this Fearachar Leigh.

John Beaton was too old and too rheumatic to move from home, but he described the *torranan*, its flower, leaf, stalk, and root, and its situation in Benmore, to his son and the writer, with marvellous fullness and accuracy, though he had not been to Benmore nor seen the *torranan* for many years previously. He said that there were only two plants of it there, and that these were near one another on Benmore and overlooking the sea. He explained the various medicinal uses of the plant, but smiled at its alleged magical powers.

This was in 1877. John Beaton died in 1881, aged ninety-two, one of nature's scientists and of nature's gentlemen. In 1896 his son, Fearachar, sent me the two plants from Benmore in South Uist. One of them I gave to Professor Bayley Balfour of the University of Edinburgh, who kindly identified the plant for me.

The following tradition is current in Uist: the Pope sent Torranan to teach the people of Ireland the way of salvation. But the people of Ireland would not receive Torranan, whom they beat and maltreated in various ways. Torranan prayed to God to deliver him from the Irish, and shook the dust of Ireland off his feet. He betook himself to his coracle and turned it sunwise, in name of God, and in name of Christ, and in name of Spirit, praying the *Teora Naomh,* Holy Three, to send him when and where and whichever way they listed and had work for him to do — but not again to Ireland. The man was driven about hither and thither on the wild waves in his frail coracle no one knows how long or how far. But an Eye was on his prow, and a Hand was on his helm and the tide, and the wind, and the waves combined to take him into the little creek of Cailigeo in Benbecula.

The island of Benbecula is situated between the islands of South Uist and North Uist, its axis being at right angles to the axis of these islands — one end on the Minch, the other on the Atlantic. It is fordable on both sides when the tide is out, hence the Gaelic name Beinn-nam-faoghla (ben of the fords). The hill indicated in the name is near the centre of the island and nearly in a direct line between the fords. It is called Ruaidh-bhal, Ruaival (red hill), from the Gaelic *ruadh* (red), and the Norse *fell* (a hill). Ruaival is the only hill in Benbecula. It is cone-shaped, flat and level on the top, and 409 feet in height. The sloping sides are flushed with heather, while the flat summit is green and grassy. The summit commands an extraordinary view of fords and channels, islands, peninsulas and mainlands, seas and lakes, and of moors and machairs broken up and dotted over in the most marvellous manner with shallow pools, tarns, and lakes scattered broadcast beyond count, beyond number. Probably the world does not contain anything more disorderly than the distribution of land and water in and around Benbecula.

When Torranan was ascending the round red hill of Ruaival to survey his surroundings and to ascertain his whereabouts, his breast was sore from thirst, for he had had no water to drink since leaving Ireland. And Torranan prayed to God for water to quench his thirst, and lo! the red rock before him rent asunder, and from the fissure a clear rill of cold water issued. Torranan thus pre-experienced the truth of Goethe's words:

At his appointed time revolving,
The sun these shades of night dispels,
The rock, its rugged breast dissolving,
Gives up to earth its hidden wells.

The water was fair to see and pleasing to taste, and Torranan drank his *seachd sath* (seven satiations), and he blessed the rill from the rent rock and called it "Gamhnach," farrow cow. "And Torranan beseeched the great God of the elements that the Gamhnach might never go dry." And ever since then all pilgrims who go to the Gamhnach and drink of the rill give a choice green leaf to the "farrow cow" in memory of its refreshing drink to the holy man who came to teach the people of Innis Cat, Isle of the Caty, the way of salvation.

The man rejected of the people of Ireland became the accepted missionary of the people of Uist. He wished to build his prayer-house on Cnoc Feannaig, the knoll of the hooded crow, within sight and hearing of the wild waves of Cailigeo where he had been driven ashore from his perilous voyage. Accordingly he began to gather stones to build himself a prayer-house on the knoll. But the stones that Torranan collected on the knoll during the day, the spirits transferred by night to the island in the lake adjoining. After a time Torranan gave up the unequal contest, saying that it was not meet for him to set his will against the will of God as revealed by His angels. Then Torranan built his prayer-house on the little island within hearing but not within seeing of the green seas and white waves of Cailigeo. And when the house was made Torranan dedicated the labour of his hands and the subject of his prayers to God and to Columba.

The lake containing the islet on which the seafarer built his oratory is now lowered, and what was formerly an island is now a peninsula jutting into the lake. The oratory said to have been built by Torranan is a ruin. The ruin shows an extension of the original building. This extension is said to have been made by Amie, daughter of Ruairi mac Allan, High Chief of Lorn, and wife of John of Islay, Lord of the Isles. Shell lime is used in the extension ascribed to the Lady Amie, but not in the original structure ascribed to Torranan. Captain Thomas, R.N., to whom the antiquities and archaeology of the Outer Hebrides owe much, said that the part of the church ascribed to Torranan might well belong to the Columban period. The Columban churches are believed to have been usually constructed of wattles. But there were no wattles nor wood of any kind in Uist so late as Columba's time. Consequently, in this and similar situations the Columban brethren and followers had to depart from their usual practice, and build of stone.

The lake containing the peninsula on which Torranan built his prayer-house, dedicated to Columba, is called Loch Chaluim-chille, Columba's Loch. It only covers an area of some few acres and is of no great depth. Cairns and crosses studded the many knolls and hillocks surrounding the lake. But no trace of cairn nor of cross now remains. These pious offerings of a grateful people and of a bygone age to the memory of the saint have been secularised and utilised in making roads and in building culverts.

A religious house was afterwards built on Cnoc Feannaig, where Torranan had wished to build his prayer-house. It is now, and has been for centuries, a dwelling-house, and is probably the oldest inhabited house in Scotland.

Torranan is represented on the West in the island of Tarransey, Tarran's island. In this small rocky glaciated island of the Atlantic there were two small churches, of which nothing now remains but the foundations, with a small burying-ground attached to each. The churches are beautifully situated on the seashore near one another, and look across to the ice-rounded mountains of Harris and Uist, while in the faraway blue distance are seen the serrated calcined hills of Skye. One of these simple churches with its burying-ground was dedicated to St Tarran and called Teampull Tharrain, the Temple of Tarran, and Cladh Tharrain, the burial-place of Tarran. The other church and burying-ground were dedicated to St Ce, or Keith, and were called Teampull Che, the Temple of Ce, and Cladh Che, the burial-place of Ce. The temple and burying-ground of Tarran were exclusively for the use of women, while the temple and burying-ground of Ce were exclusively for the use of men. This rule could not be violated with impunity. If the body of a man were buried in St Tarran's, or the body of a woman in St Ce's, the guardian spirits of the temples and burying-grounds thrust forth the obtruded corpse during the night, and it was found in the morning lying stiff and stark above ground. In North Uist there is a tall obelisk called Clach Che, the stone of Ce. St Ce is represented on the East by Beinn Che (Ben-achie), the hill of Ce; Innis Che (Inchkeith), the island of Ce; and Dail Che (Dalkeith), the plain of Ce.

Palladius is the name usually assigned to the missionary sent by the Pope to the Irish and rejected by them. Skene thinks that Ternan was a disciple of Palladius, with whom he is confounded. "Ternan was buried at Liconium or My Toren of Tulach Fort-chirn, in Ui Felmada, and Druim Cliab in Cairbre." Skene thinks that Liconium was the old name of Banchory-Ternan on the river Dee in Aberdeenshire.

The feast of St Ternan is the 12th of June. Like St Brendan of Clonfert, St Ternan was a seafarer, visiting many countries. He is spoken of as "Torranan lasting, deedful, over a wide shipful sea." Many popular stories and distinctive names attach to him.

The plant named after him is popularly supposed to grow only near the sea which Torranan loved. The small rill from which Torranan obtained a drink is named Gamh-nach, farrow cow, that is, a cow that does not carry a calf, but which gives milk of good quality and continuous but small in quantity. At present the blade of any grass or the leaf of any plant is given to the Gamh-nach in offering. Probably it was permissible for pilgrims who came to drink the water and to worship the Gamhnach, to offer only the leaf of the *torranan* to the rill. Another curious thing is that two streams into which the Gamhnach runs are called "na Deatha-chan," the Dees, and that two lakes into which these streams flow are called "Loch nan Deathachan fo dheas," the Loch of the Dees to the south; and "Loch nan Deatha-chan fo thuath," Loch of the Dees to the north. *Dee* and *deathachan* are plurals of *dia,* god. Were these rivers worshipped as gods?

St Ternan forms a connecting-link bet-ween the Dees of Benbecula and the Dee of Aberdeen.

165 St John's wort is known by various names, all significant of the position of the plant in the minds of the people: *achlasan Chaluim-chille* (armpit package of Colum-ba); *caod Chaluim-chille* (hail of Columba); *seun Chaluim-chille* (charm of Columba); *seud Chaluim- chille* (jewel of Columba); *allus Chaluim-chille* (glory of Columba); *alla Mhoire* (noble plant of Mary); *alla-bhi, alla-bhuidhe* (noble yellow plant). Possibly these are pre-Christian terms to which are added the endearing names of Mary and Columba.

St John's wort is one of the few plants still cherished by the people to ward away second-sight, enchantment, witchcraft, evil eye, and death, and to ensure peace and plenty in the house, increase and prosperity in the fold, and growth and fruition in the field. The plant is secretly secured in the bodices of the women and in the vests of the men, under the left armpit. St John's wort, however, is effective only when the plant is accidentally found. When this occurs the joy of the finder is great, and gratefully expressed:

St John's wort, St John's wort,
Without search, without seeking!
Please God and Christ Jesu
This year I shall not die.

It is specially prized when found in the fold of the flocks, auguring peace and prosperity to the herds throughout the year. The person who discovers it says:

St John's wort, St John's wort,
Happy those who have thee,
Whoso gets thee in the herd's fold,
Shall never be without kine.

There is a tradition among the people that St Columba carried the plant on his person because of his love and admiration for him who went about preaching Christ, and baptizing the converted, clothed in a garment of camel's hair and fed upon locusts and wild honey.

169 The people of Uist say that the hateful aspen is banned three times. The aspen is banned the first time because it haughtily held up its head while all the other trees of the forest bowed their heads lowly down as the King of all created things was being led to Calvary. And the aspen is banned the second time because it was chosen by the enemies of Christ for the cross upon which to crucify the Saviour of mankind. And the aspen is banned the third time because ... [here the reciter's memory failed him]. Hence the ever-tremulous, ever-quivering, ever-quaking motion of the guilty hateful aspen even in the stillest air.

Clods and stones and other missiles, as well as curses, are hurled at the aspen by the people. The reciter, a man of much natural intelligence, said that he always took off his bonnet and cursed the hateful aspen in all sincerity wherever he saw it. No crofter in Uist would use aspen about his plough or about his harrows, or about his farming implements of any kind. Nor would a fisherman use aspen about his boat or about his creels or about any fishing-gear whatsoever.

170 Some of the people say that the four-leaved shamrock is the shamrock of luck. Others maintain that the shamrock of luck is the five-leaved shamrock. This is a very rare plant and much prized when found.

The shamrock of luck must be found, like many of the other propitious plants *gun sireadh, gun iarraidh* (without searching, without seeking). When thus discovered the lucky shamrock is warmly cherished and preserved as an invincible talisman.

Seamarag nan buadh (shamrock of luck), is often lovingly called *seamarag nam buadh agus nam beannachd* (shamrock of luck and of blessing).

It is also called *seamarag nan each* (horse shamrock), *seamarag nan searrach* (foal shamrock), *seamarag an deocain* (shamrock of the *deocan), seamarag an deocadain* (shamrock of the *deocadan),* and simply *deocan* and *deocadan.*

Immediately after birth the foal throws up a pale soft substance resembling a sponge or the seed-cells of the cod. This sponge-like substance coughed up by the newly-born foal is variously called *deocan, deocadan, deocardan.* The people bury this in the ground, believing that the lucky shamrock grows from it as the nettles grow from human remains, whether buried in the pure shelly sand on the sea-shore or in the pure peat moss on the mountainside.

172 The *mòthan* (I am not sure what the plant is — perhaps the bog-violet?) is one of the most prized plants in the occult science of the people. It is used in promoting and conserving the happiness of the people, in securing love, in ensuring life, in bringing good, and in warding away evil.

When the *mòthan* is used as a love-philtre, the woman who gives it goes upon her left knee and plucks nine roots of the plant and knots them together, forming them into a *cuach* (ring). The woman places the ring in the mouth of the girl for whom it is made, in name of the King of the sun, and of the moon, and of the stars, and in name of the Holy Three. When the girl meets her lover or a man whom she loves and whose love she desires to secure, she puts the ring in her mouth. And should the man kiss the girl while the *mòthan* is in her mouth be becomes henceforth her bondsman, bound to her everlastingly in cords infinitely finer than the gossamer net of the spider, and infinitely stronger than the adamant chain of the giant.

The *mòthan* is placed under parturient women to ensure delivery, and it is carried by wayfarers to safeguard them on their journeys. It is sewn by women in their bodice, and by men in their vest under the left arm. An old woman in Benbecula said:

"I gave the blessed *mòthan* to red Roderick son of Ranald of Lewis from the South-end (of Uist), and he on his journey to Lochmaddy to be tried before the sheriff, and he got off although he was as guilty of the guilt as the son of a sinner."

"But, Christina, why did you give the *mòthan* to the man when you knew that he was guilty? I think myself it was not right of you to go and do it!"

"O food and clothing! thou dear one of my heart, and thou loved one of my people, I could not myself go and refuse him. He beseeched to me, and he swelled to me, and he vowed to me, and he placed a thing in my hand, and oh! King of the moon, and of the sun, and of the beautiful, sublime stars, what could I myself say or do, and the bad man in his black trouble, in his red difficulty, and in his hard plight!"

I remembered Bacon and was silent.

To drink the milk of an animal that ate the *mòthan* ensures immunity from harm. If a man makes a miraculous escape it is said of him: "He drank the milk of the guileless cow that ate the *mòthan.*"

180 In making the incantation of the red water, the exorcist forms her two palms into a basin. She places this basin under the urine of the cow or other animal affected, and throws the urine into water, preferably running water, to carry away the demon of the complaint. Having washed her hands in clean cold water, the woman forms them into a trumpet. She then faces the rising sun, and intones the incantation through the trumpet as loudly as she can.

184 The fox was the plague of the people of the Highlands, killing their sheep as the wolf killed their cattle, and as the foumart killed their fowls. From the wildness of the land and the sparseness of the people, the Highlands were the natural habitat of beasts and birds of prey and other noxious creatures, which took the people much time and trouble to subdue.

Much could be written of the intelligence of the fox. One of the tales illustrating this intelligence is known as *Sionnach na Maoile,* the Fox of the Mull [of Kintyre]. This fox never committed destruction near his home — always going considerable distances to make his raids, sometimes ten or twenty miles. He caused much injury to the sheep that he attacked, and to the dogs that chased him. When pressed, the fox leaped over a certain precipice and the dogs leaped over after him. The dogs were found dead on the rocks below, but not the fox, who in due time turned up as before.

Nothing could be seen from above nor from below the precipice to account for the immunity of the fox. No shelf or ledge could be seen whereon the fox could leap, and the people were puzzled. But the fox-hunter was not satisfied, and procuring ropes, he went down the precipice and examined it carefully. He found a sapling mountain ash growing out of the rock, and marked as if to distinguish it from the saplings of ordinary ash, bramble, plane, and other woods which were growing in the neighbourhood. And he found that by bending the marked mountain lash to a certain degree from its perpendicular and at a certain angle to the plane of the precipice, it touched a narrow thread-like sinuous ledge that might yield a precarious footing to a cat, to a marten, or possibly to a fox. This ledge led away to other ledges up and down the cliff. The fox-hunter cut the marked sapling, securing it, however, in its place. When the next havoc of the sheep had occurred, and the next pursuit of the fox had followed, the fox was found dead at the foot of the precipice, the marked mountain ash in his mouth! Choosing the tough mountain ash sapling in preference to the other less tough saplings showed sagacity, leaping from the precipice and seizing the sapling in mid-air to arrest his fall showed courage, and taking the precipice at an angle by which to get the sapling to land him in the only possible spot showed intelligence of a high order in the fox. The scene of this story has ever since been called Creag an t-Sionnaich, precipice of the fox.

The conduct of this fox gave rise to many sayings of the people: "as crafty as the red fox of the Mull of Kintyre;" "as cunning as the fox of the Mull;" "as great-great-great-grand-fatherish as the fox of the Mull;" "He will lead you over the cliff as the fox led the hounds."

186 Flat moorland is generally intersected with innumerable reins, channels and ditches. Sometimes these are serious obstacles to cattle, more especially to cows, which are accurate judges. When a cow hesitates to cross, the person driving her throws a stalk or a twig into the ditch before the unwilling animal and sings the *Feith Mhoire,* Vein of Mary, to encourage her to cross, and to assure her that a safe bridge is before her. The stalk may be of any corn or grass except the reed, and the twig of any wood except the wild fig, the aspen, and the thorn. All these are forbidden, or "crossed" as the people say, because of their ungracious conduct to the Gracious One. The reed is "crossed" because it carried the sponge dipped in vinegar; the fig-tree because of its inhospitality; the aspen because it held up its head haughtily, proud that the cross was made of its wood, when all the trees of the forest — all save the aspen alone — bowed their heads in reverence to the King of glory passing by on the way to Calvary; and the thorn-tree because of its prickly pride in having been made into a crown for the King of kings.

Notwithstanding, however, the wand of safety and the hymn of the herdsman, a cow driven against her will sometimes sinks into the ditch while crossing. This may necessitate the assistance of neighbours to extricate her from her helpless position. Hence the proverb: "It is the man of the cow himself who shall go into the ditch first." The practice of throwing down the wand and repeating the hymn gave rise to a proverb among the more sceptical of the people: "Thou wilt not make a 'vein of Mary' upon me at all, sonnie."

190 This incantation is said over an animal suffering from surfeit. It is repeated three times, representing the Three Persons of the Trinity. If the surfeit is from eating too much grass or from drinking too much water, the cow or other animal affected begins to chew the cud on being appealed to. If the animal does not begin to chew the cud, the cause of swelling must be sought for otherwise, and the appropriate incantation applied.

191 An evil eye or an evil spirit is powerless across water, especially across a running stream or a tidal water. Black Sir Ewen Cameron of Lochiel was at feud with Mackintosh of Moy about lands in Lochaber. Great Gormul of Moy, the celebrated witch, wished to destroy Lochiel, the foe of her chief and of her race. But, though she nursed her wrath and pursued her course day and night, she could not accomplish her purpose, as running water lay between herself and the object of her hatred. Lochiel knew this, and, although brave to recklessness, he prudently kept out of the way of the witch-woman. But on one occasion when Lochiel was returning from a conference at Inverness, great Gormul saw him far away on the blue horizon; but, if far away was he, not long was she in reaching him:

GORMUL
Step on, beloved Ewen.

LOCHIEL
Step on thou thyself, carlin,
And if it be necessary to take the step,
A step beyond thee for Ewen.

Sir Ewen Cameron was one of the bravest men in Albain, and one of the best walkers in Gaeldom. Many a brave Saxon man he met without quailing, and many a hero he laid low, but this froward woman was trying him severely, and he was anxious to be rid of her with the least delay of time and the least betrayal of fear. The witch-woman observed this; and the more desperately he pressed on space, the more she pressed on him, while she herself appeared to be only making *cas ceum coilich feasgar fann foghair agus a sgroban lan* (the footstep of a cock on a gentle autumn eve when his crop is full).

GORMUL
Step on, thou beloved Ewen,
And oh! King Goileam and King Geigean!
Long indeed since that day!

LOCHIEL
Step on thou thyself, carlin,
And if the step must be taken,
A step beyond thee for Ewen.

Remembering that occult power could not operate across running water, Lochiel suddenly swerved aside to the first stream he saw and plunged into it. The witch, chagrined at the escape of the prey she had thought safe, immediately called after him:

GORMUL
The wish of mine heart to thee,
Thou best-beloved of men, Lochiel.

LOCHIEL
The wish of thine heart, carlin,
Be upon yonder grey stone.

The pillared grey stone on the bank of the river to which Lochiel pointed with his sword rent from top to base. Gallant courtier though he was, Sir Ewen Cameron waited to show but scant courtesy to great Gormul of Moy.

The influence of an evil spirit commanded by an evil mind is believed to retard or wholly to prevent butter from coming upon the cream in the churn. This evil influence was used by one woman against another in order to spirit away the butter from her neighbour's churn to her own churn. This, however, could only be done if no stream ran between the two women. A fire for kindling carried across a stream, however small, loses its occult power and is ineffective in spiriting away milk, cream, butter, or other milk product.

The following story was told me in 1870 by Mór Macneill, cottar, Glen, Barra. Sometimes the substance is spirited out of the milk, nothing being left but the semblance. On one occasion a household in Skye were at the peat-moss making peats, none remaining at home but the housewife and a tailor who was making clothes for the father and the sons of the house.

The housewife was up in the *ben* churning, and the tailor was down in the butt sewing. He sat on the meal-girnel, cross-legged, after the manner of tailors. Presently a neighbour woman came in and asked for a kindling for her fire. She took the kindling and went her way. When she went out, the tailor leaped down, and taking a live cinder from the fire, placed it in the water-stoup below the dresser, and with a bound was back again cross-legged on the meal-girnel sewing away as before.

In a little while the woman came back saying that she failed to kindle her fire, and asked for another kindling, which she took. The tailor leapt down again and took another live cinder out of the fire and put it in the water-stoup below the dresser, and, with a spring to the meal-girnel, resumed his work. The woman came a third time saying that she had failed to kindle her fire, and for the third time she took a kindling and went her way. As soon as she had left, the tailor leapt down, and taking a live cinder from the fire, placed it in the water-stoup as he had done before, and then springing to the top of the meal-girnel sat cross-legged sewing as if nothing unusual had occurred.

Towards evening the housewife came down in sore distress, saying:

"O Mary and Son, am I not the sorely shamed woman, churning away at that churn the live-long day till my spirit is broken and my arms are weary, and that I have utterly failed to bring butter on the churn after all! O Mary! Mary, fair Mother of grace! what shall I do when the people come home? I shall never hear the end of this churning till the day of my death!"

"Place thine hand in the water-stoup below the dresser and see if thy butter be there," said the tailor. And with that the woman placed he. hand in the water-stoup as directed, and three successive times, and each time brought up a large lump of butter as fresh and fair and fragrant as the beauteous buttercups in their prime. The clever tailor had counteracted the machinations of the greedy neighbour woman by placing the live cinders in the water-stoup.

192 The nun referred to is Brigit, of whom Broccan's Hymn says: "She was not a milkmaid of a mountainside; she wrought in the midst of a plain." The second stanza is an echo of one of the miracles attributed to her in the same hymn: "when the first dairying was sent with the first butter in a hamper, it kept not from bounty to her guests, their attachment was not diminished," explained further as follows:

"Brigit serving a certain wizard was wont to give away much butter in charity. This displeased the wizard and his wife, who came on her without notice. Brigit had only a small churning ready and she repeated this stave:

My store-room, a store-room of fair God, a store-room which my King has blessed, a store-room with somewhat therein.
May Mary's Son, my friend, come to bless

my store-room which my King has blessed, a store-room with somewhat therein.
May Mary's Son, my friend, come to bless my store-room. The Prince of the world to the border may there be plenty with Him.
O my Prince, who hast power over all these things! Bless, O God — a cry unforbidden — with thy right hand this store-room.

She brought a half churning to the wizard's wife.
'That is good to fill a big hamper!' said the wizard's wife.
'Fill ye your hamper,' said Brigit, 'and God will put somewhat therein.'

She still kept going into her kitchen and bringing half a making thereout and singing a stave of these staves as she went back. If the hampers which the men of Munster possessed had been given to her she would have filled them all. The wizard and his wife marvelled at the miracle which they beheld. Then said the wizard to Brigit:

'This butter and the kine which thou hast milked, I offer to thee; and thou shalt not be serving me but serve the Lord.'

Said Brigit: 'Take thou the kine, but give me my mother's freedom.'

Said the wizard: 'Behold thy mother and the kine; and whatsoever thou shalt say, that will I do.'

Then Brigit dealt out the kine to the poor and the needy; and the wizard was baptized and he was full of faith."

193 These and other poems were obtained from Isabella Chisholm, a travelling tinker. Though old, Isabella Chisholm was still tall and straight, fine-featured and fresh-complexioned. She was endowed with personal attraction, mental ability and astute diplomacy of no common order. Her father, John Chisholm, is said to have been a "pious, prayerful man," terms not usually applied to his class.

Isabella Chisholm had none of the swarthy skin and faraway look of the ordinary gipsy. But she had the gipsy habits and the gipsy language. variously called "Cant," "Shelta," "Romany," with rich fluent Gaelic and English. She had many curious spells, runes,and hymns, that would have enriched Gaelic literature, and many rare words and phrases and expressions that would have improved the Gaelic dictionary.

194 The *frìth* (augury) was a species of divination enabling the *frìtheir* (augurer) to see into the unseen. This divination was made to ascertain the position and condition of the absent and the lost, and was applied to man and beast. The augury was made on the first Monday of the quarter and immediately before sunrise. The augurer, fasting, and with bare feet, bare head, and closed eyes, went to the doorstep and placed a hand on each jamb. Mentally beseeching the God of the unseen to show him his quest and to grant him his augury, the augurer opened his eyes and looked steadfastly straight in front of him. From the nature and position of the objects within his sight, he drew his conclusions.

Many men in the Highlands and Islands were famed augurers, and many stories, realistic, romantic, and extremely curious, are still told of their divinations. The people say that the Virgin made an augury when Christ was missing, and that it was by means of this augury that Mary and Joseph ascertained that Christ was in the Temple disputing with the doctors. Hence this divination is called *frìth Mhoire* (the augury of Mary); and *frìtheireachd Mhoire* (the auguration of Mary).

The *frìth* of the Celt is akin to the *frett* of the Norseman. Probably the surnames Freer, Frere, are modifications of *frìtheir* (augurer). Persons bearing this name claim that their progenitors were astrologers to the kings of Scotland.

195 This poem was obtained in 1891 from Malcolm Macmillan, crofter, Grimnis, Benbecula. Macmillan was then an old man. He heard this and many other poems when a boy from old people who, when evicted in Uist, emigrated to Prince Edward's Island, Nova Scotia, Cape Breton and other parts of the Canadian Dominion, and to Australia. These old people took great quantities of traditional Gaelic lore with them to their new homes, some of which still lingers among their descendants. Many original and translated songs of the Highlands and Islands are sung among these settlers, whose hearts still yearn towards their motherland.

199 This verse, the only verse of the poem he could remember, was obtained from John Kane, a native of Ireland. John Kane had many traditional stories of St Columba showing that he "being dead yet speaketh." These stories were vivid and graphic, the probable and the improbable, possible and impossible, blending and diffusing throughout.

200 The following lines are whispered by mothers into the ears of sons and daughters when leaving their homes in the Outer Isles for the towns of the south and for foreign Lands.

Probably they are the last accents of the mother's voice — heard in the faraway home among the hills clothed with mist or on the machair washed by the sea — that linger on the Gaelic ear as it sinks in the sleep that knows no waking.

201 The two following poems were got in Kintail. They are obscure in themselves, and the dialect of Kintail in which they were recited increases their obscurity. The reciters repeated them as one poem, but were uncertain whether they were one or two poems.

203 The people believed in omens of birds and beasts, fishes and insects, and of men and women. These omens were innumerable, and a few only can be mentioned.

The fisher would deem it a bad omen to meet a red-haired woman when on his way to fish; and were the woman defective in mind or body, probably the man would return home muttering strong adjectives beneath his breath. On the other hand, it was lucky for a girl to find the red hair of a woman in the nest of certain birds, particularly in the nest of the wheatear.

The red hair of a woman,
The grey beard of a man,
Are love and luck to the sloven
Who gets them in the nest of the wheatear.

208 There are many curious legends and beliefs current in the Isles about the *cearr-dubhan,* or sacred beetle. When his enemies were in search of Christ to put Him to death, they met the sacred beetle and the gravedigger beetle out on a foraging expedition in search of food for their families. The Jews asked the beetles if they had seen Christ passing that way. Proud to be asked, and anxious to conciliate the great people, the gravedigger promptly and volubly replied:

"Yes, yes! He passed here yesterday evening, when I and the people of the townland were digging a grave and burying the body of a field-mouse that had come to an untimely end."

"You lie! you lie!" said the sacred beetle; "it was a year ago yesterday that Christ the Son passed here, when my children and I were searching for food, after the king's horse had passed."

Because of his ready officiousness against Christ, the gravedigger is always killed when seen; while for his desire to shield Christ, the sacred beetle is spared, but because he told a lie he is always turned on his back. The sacred beetle is covered with a strong integument like a knight encased in armour. Consequently he is unable to resume his position, and he struggles continually, waving his feet in the effort to touch something which will assist him to rise. It is unlawful to pass by the sacred beetle without putting him on his back, but should he succeed in righting himself, it is unlawful to molest him further.

In some places the gravedigger is killed because otherwise he will profane the grave of the grandmother of the person who passes him by.

The following somewhat similar legend is also current in Uist:

The anti-Christians were pursuing Christ, wishing to kill Him. Christ came to a townland where a crofter was winnowing corn on the hillock. The good crofter placed Christ under the heap of grain to conceal Him from his enemies. The crofter went into the barn to bring out more grain to place over Christ to hide Him more effectually. In his absence the fowls attacked the heap of corn under which Christ was hidden. They were round the heap and over the heap — hens and ducks feeding as rapidly as they could. The ducks contented themselves with eating and tramping the corn. Not so the hens: they scattered the corn about with their feet as they ate, so that the hidden Christ was exposed to view when the crofter returned. In consequence of this disservice to Christ in His distress, it was left as a heritage to the hen and to her seed for ever that she should be sever–toed; that she should be confined to land; that she should dislike hail, rain, sleet, and snow; that she should dread thunder and lightning; that dust, not water, should be her bath; that she should have no oil with which to annoint herself and preen her feathers; and finally, that she should have only one life and only one joy in life — the joy of land.

And because the duck contented herself with eating the corn without exposing the person of Christ, it was left to her and her descendants ever more that she should be web–footed, and not be confined to land; that she should rejoice in hail and rain and sleet and snow; that she should rejoice in thunder and lightning; that water not dust should be her bath; that she should have oil with which to anoint herself and preen her feathers; that she should have three lives and three joys — the joy of earth, the joy of air, and the joy of water; nay, a fourth life and a fourth joy — the joy of under the water; that she should be most dressed when the hen was most draggled; that she should be most joyous when the hen was most miserable; that she should be most hopeful when the hen was in most despair; that she should be most happy when the hen was in most dread; that she should dance with joy when the hen quaked with fear. When the hen hears thunder she trembles as the aspen and hurries home in terror, screaming and screeching the while. Hence the saying:

Thine heart is quivering
Like a hen in thunder.

The converse is true of the duck. When she hears thunder she rejoices and dances to her own *port–a–bial* (mouth music). This gave rise to the saying:

Thou art like a duck
Expectant of thunder.

211 The swan is a favourite bird and of good omen. To hear it in the morning fasting — especially on a Tuesday morning — is much to be desired. To see seven, or a multiple of seven, swans on the wing ensures peace and prosperity for seven, or a multiple of seven years.

In windy, snowy, or wet weather swans fly low, but in calm, bright, or frosty weather they fly high; but even when the birds are only specks in the distant blue lift above, their soft, silvery, flute–like notes penetrate to earth below.

Swans are said to be ill–used religious ladies under enchantment, driven from their homes and forced to wander, and to dwell where most kindly treated and where least molested. They are therefore regarded with loving pity and veneration, and the man who would injure a swan would thereby hurt the feelings of the community.

A woman found a wounded swan on a frozen lake near her house, and took it home, where she set the broken wing, dressed the bleeding feet, and fed the starving bird with lintseed and water. The woman had an ailing child, and as the wounds of the swan healed the health of the child improved, and the woman believed that her treatment of the swan caused the recovery of her child, and she rejoiced accordingly and composed this lullaby to her restored child.

212 There were many religious houses throughout the Isles. Two of these were in Benbecula: one at Baile–mhanaich, Monks'–town, and one at Baile–nan–cailleach, Nuns'–town. These houses were attached to Iona, and were ruled and occupied by members of the first families of the Western Isles. Probably their insularity secured them from dissolution at the time of the Reformation, for these communities lingered long after the Reformation, and ceased to exist simply through natural decay.

It is said that two nuns had been visiting a sick woman. When returning home from the moorland to the townland, they heard the shrill voice of a child and the soft voice of a woman. The nuns groped their way down the rugged rocks, and there found a woman soothing a child in her arms. They were the only two saved from a wreck — the two frailest in the ship.

The nuns took them home to Nunton. The woman was an Irish princess and a nun, and the child an Irish prince, against whose life a usurper to the throne had conceived a plot. The holy princess fled with the child-prince, intending to take him for safety to Scandinavia. The two nuns are said to have composed the two following poems.

One version of the story says that the child grew up and succeeded to the throne in Ireland; another that he died in the North Sea, and that he was buried in North Ronaldsay, Orkney.

During the three centuries of the Norse occupation there was much cordial communication between Scotland and Ireland, and much, but not cordial communication between Ireland and Scandinavia. Norsemen infested the east of Ireland and west of Scotland. There were plots and counterplots and wars innumerable between invaders and invaded, the ends of the beam ascending and descending in sore quick succession. Ultimately the Irish succeeded in inflicting a crushing defeat on the Scandinavians at the battle of Clontarf.

Clontarf is situated on Dublin Bay, a few miles below the city. It is a low-lying plain of much extent and great fertility. In the adjoining sea is a spit or bar emitting curious sounds during certain conditions of tide and wind. The sounds resemble the bellowing of a bull, and hence the name Cluain tarbh, Clontarf, the plain of bulls.

The famous battle of Clontarf was fought on Good Friday, 23rd April, 1014. The Irish were led by their celebrated warrior-king, Brian Boroimhe, monarch of all Ireland, and the Danes by their Celto-Danish Prince, Earl Sigurd. There was indescribable havoc on both sides. The slaughter, as seen from the walls of Dublin, is described as resembling the world of mad reapers in a field of corn. Earl Sigurd fell. This was foretold him by his mother, Audna, daughter of Carroll, King of Ireland, when she gave him the "Raven Banner of Battle" at Skidda-myre, now Skidden, in Caithness.

Audna told Sigurd that the Raven Banner would always bring victory to the owner, but death to the bearer. At the battle of Clontarf every man who took up the Raven Banner fell. At last no one would take it up. Seeing this, Sigurd himself seized the banner, saying: "'Tis meetest that the beggar himself should bear his bag."

Immediately thereafter Sigurd fell, and with him the Norse power in Ireland. The victorious Irish slaughtered the defeated Danes with all the concentrated hate of three centuries of cruel wrong. The fall of Earl Sigurd was made known to his friends in the North through the fore-knowledge of the Valkymar, the twelve weird sisters of Northern Mythology, of whom Gray sings in his "Fatal Sisters."

214 A curious ceremony was current in the Island of Lismore. When several boys gathered together, two boys seized a third by the head and heels, and swaying him from side to side sang this eerie chant over him.

After more questions and more answers, the boy was carried round in procession sunwise to a wailing march, in which all the boys joined. The boy was then laid upon a rock or knoll for an altar. After more singing and more ceremonial the victim was laid in some convenient hollow for a grave, to the music of another eerie lament and the laughter of the boys. The writer was an actor in this boyish drama, but what the drama represented he does not know.

215 *Am breid* (the kertch or coif), was a square of linen formed into a cap and donned by a woman on the morning after her marriage. It was the sign of wifehood as the *stiom* (snood) was the emblem of maidenhood. The linen of the kertch was pure white and very fine. The square was arranged into three angles symbolic of the Trinity, under whose guidance the young wife was to walk. From this it is called *currachd tri-chearnach* (three-cornered cap). The kertch was fastened to the hair with cords of silk or pins of silver or of gold. It is said to have been very becoming and picturesque. It is mentioned in many of the sayings of the people as: *breid ban* (white kertch); *breid cuailean* (hair kertch); *breid beannach* (pinnacled kertch); *breid an crannaig* (kertch on props); *breid cuimir nan crun* (the shapely coif of the crowns); and *breid cuimir nan tri crun* (the shapely coif of the three crowns). It is also spoken of in many songs:

Never on thee be seen kertch
Upon feast-day or church-day,
And never be seen thy children
Going to the temple of baptism.

Were I to obtain to myself
Thee with the blessing of the clerics,
It is I who would be joyous
At seeing on thee thy kertch
The first Sunday.

Her hair in coils, curled, curved,
And in clustered folds has my beloved,
And though beautiful it seems within the snood,
It would not look worse beneath the kertch.

Well becomes thee the white kertch,
Placed pinnacle-wise,
And cords of the fine silk
Binding it upon thee.

The song from which this last verse is quoted had curious wanderings and narrow escapes — from Lochaber to Lahore, from Lahore to Lochalsh, and from Lochalsh to Skye and Uist. It was taken down at Howmore, South Uist, from Peggie Macaulay, better known as Peggie Robertson and "Peigi Sgiathanach" (Skye Peggie). She came from "brindled Sleat of the beautiful women," and well upheld the reputation of her native place, for she was a tall, straight, comely brunette, with beautiful brown eyes and hair "like raven's plumage, smoothed on snow." She had accompanied her master and mistress, Captain and Mrs Macdonald, Knock, Skye, on a visit to Sir John Macrae, Airdantouil, Lochalsh. Sir John was famed for his symmetry, bravery, and accomplishments. He inherited the musical talents of the MacLeods of Raarsey, and could play a phenomenal number of musical instruments. He was wont to say that there was no music for the house equal to Highland music, nor instrument for the field equal to the Highland bagpipe.

Sir John had been military attaché to his cousin, the Marquis of Hastings, when he was Governor-General of India. From Sir John Macrae, Peggie Macaulay heard the words of this song and an account of how he got them. Sir John said that when in India he was sent with despatches to a distant fort. As he was nearing the gate under cover of night, he was surprised to hear a Gaelic song once heard in childhood and often sought since. When he reined in his horse to listen, the sentry stopped his song and challenged. The answer was given in Gaelic, and the sentry was surprised in his turn. Macrae was just in time to rouse the Governor from his fancied security and to lead the garrison to repel an attack, in which the singer Eoghan Cameron fell after killing seven sepoys single-handed.

Sir John Macrae died soon after Peggie Macaulay heard him singing the song, and she died soon after the song was taken down from her dictation by the present writer. Sir John Macrae called this song, *treas taladh na h-Alba* (the third lullaby of Alban), and as sung by bright Peggie Robertson it merited praise.

VOLUME III

217 Reciter: Catherine MacNeill, cottar, Breubhaig, Barra.

The reciter, Catherine daughter of Murdoch, said: "I heard this rune from old women in the long ago of the world ... That rune would be upon the nurse's tongue till she was finished of bathing the little infant.

"There were many curious customs among the old people; but strangers began to come into the country, and they began to mock the people of the country, and the beautiful customs of the country were allowed bit by bit to drop, and some of them to be lost. There are not many people who would stand to be made fun of by people of more learning than themselves, not many at all."

219 From Mary MacNeill, crofter.

220 Reciter: The wife of Donald, son of Eoghan, crofter, Bernera (Barra Head), Barra.

"I heard this with my mother, peace to her soul, when I was young, but a poor tiny little urchin out and in at the threshold as lightsome and foolish as the birds of the air. O Mary Mother, little heed I gave these things at the time, and little did I think that you would come, dear one, to seek them today, after four score years. My dear mother was telling the ways of the townland to a woman who was in the hill–land, and though I was small and foolish at the time, I was keeping an ear on her talk. And this is what my dear mother said to the woman who came home."

221 The reciter said: "These, my dear one, were the words of the womb–woman, and lovely, methinks, was her language, and beautiful it was to hear her. O Mary of grace, many a beautiful thing had the people who are gone, though it is not much of these that can be gleaned today. No, my dear one, they do not exist. The gentle Christian folk are gone who took an interest in the old things, good and venerable, of their country. I remember myself, though I was little at the time, when the Christian folk crowded into one another's houses, telling tales and histories, invocations and prayers, singing hymns and songs, runes and lays, sweet, beautiful and soft. Many a goodly thing there was — O many a goodly thing there was among the old people who are gone. The good people of that day lived not on senseless babbling — no, my dear one, they disdained gossip and scandal. The old people conversed about the state of the world and about the changes of the weather, about the moon and the sun, about the stars of the sky, about the ebbing and flowing of the sea, about the life in the depths of the ocean, and about the hot and the cold lands of the earth. We children would be sitting on the bare flat of the floor, not uttering a syllable, nor moving a hand, lest we should be put out of the house were we not mannerly. O King! 'tis there would be the talk!"

"You can hear nothing of that today, goodwife," said I.

"No, my dear, no, it does not exist. The dear Christian folk who gave heed to it are beyond the river, where I myself shall shortly be. O Mary of grace, mayest thou give me thy two arms around mine everlasting soul when going over the black river of death whither my beloved have gone to rest!"

222 From Catherine Maclennan, née MacDonald, crofter, Achadh nam Breac, Moydart.

"My mother was always at work, by day helping my father on the croft, and by night at wool and at spinning, at night clothes and at day clothes for the family. My mother would be beseeching us to be careful in everything, to put value on time and to eschew idleness; that a night was coming in which no work could be done. She would be telling us about Mac Shiamain, and how he sought to be at work. If we were dilatory in putting on our clothes, and made an excuse for our prayers, my mother would say that God regarded heart and not speech, the mind and not the manner; and that we might clothe our souls with grace while clothing our bodies with raiment. My mother taught us what we should ask for in the prayer, as she heard it from her own mother, and as she again heard it from the one who was before her.

"My mother would be asking us to sing our morning song to God down in the back–house, as Mary's lark was singing up the clouds, and as Christ's mavis was singing it yonder in the tree, giving glory to the God of the creatures for the repose of the night, for the light of the day, and for the joy of life. She would tell us that every creature on the earth here below and in the ocean beneath and in the air above was giving glory to the great God of the creatures and the worlds, of the virtues and the blessings, and would we be dumb!

" My dear mother reared her children in food and clothing, in love and charity. My heart loves the earth in which my beloved mother rests."

226 From Catherine Maclean, crofter, Naast, Gairloch.

227 The narrator said: "In my own time, and before we were put out of Ben More, there was much of old lore and old customs and old ways of thought among the old people — prayers and charms, songs and hymns, tales and music and dancing from Monday to Sunday. Whatever the people might be doing, or whatever engaged in, there would be a tune of music in their mouth. When they would arise in the morning — and Mary mild, early rising and early astir were the people of that day! — there could always be heard a man here and a woman there, a lad yonder and a maiden at hand with a cheerful strain of music in the mouth of each; whether they would be shaking corn in the kiln or feeding cattle in the byre, fetching in a stoup of water or bringing home a creel of peat, from each one's mouth came his own croon. It might well be that no person would be seen, but their voices would be heard up and doing, here and there throughout the townland, a joyful song in the mouth of every one. O Mary Mother, sweet indeed it was to hear them early on a spring morning, speeding their labour, the thrush here in the thicket, the mavis yonder in the rock, the lark aloft in the sky, the radiant golden-yellow sun illumining the high slopes of the mountains and bathing the surface of the waves, the seagull seeking the seed, and the porpoise raising the spray and blowing yonder in the Sea of Canna. O Mary and O Son, sweet, sweet it was to be seeing and to be hearing them, sweeter than the trash and the gadding of useless folk at the present time, who have neither music nor song nor prayer nor work in them, nor much of any good thing whatever, but only a tittle-tattle of talk and rubbishy rants that run through the world."

228 From Mary Gillies, crofter, Morar, 1st September 190?:

Mary Gillies was an old woman, ill and suffering. Like most of her kind, she was unlettered, but endowed with much natural intelligence. She was polite and well mannered, and most desirous to share her limited food and her unlimited lore with the stranger. The poor are ever hospitable and generous.

She was tall, erect and stately. Her face was oval, her features fine, and her brown hair abundant. Notwithstanding her sufferings, she was still beautiful in her age, and in her youth she must have been very beautiful. Mary Gillies sang this poem in a recitative voice. The effect was charming, but the poem was difficult to follow. The music and rhythm were good, but these disappear in the process of writing.

Folklore reciters, not being accustomed to being stopped become confused with the interruptions of writing. When they are allowed to proceed in their own way, music and poetry and pleasure flow back, and all rejoice.

229 When the people of the Isles come out in the morning to their tillage, to their fishing, to their farming, or to any of their various occupations anywhere, they say a short prayer called *"Ceum na Corach,"* "The Path of Right," "The Just or True Way." If the people feel secure from being overseen or overheard they croon, or sing, or intone their morning prayer in a pleasing musical manner. If, however, any person, and especially if a stranger, is seen in the way, the people hum the prayer in an inaudible undertone peculiar to themselves, like the soft murmur of the ever-murmuring sea, or like the far-distant eerie sighing of the wind among trees, or like the muffled cadence of faraway waters, rising and falling upon the fitful autumn wind.

232 The following poem was taken down from the recitation of Dugall MacAulay, cottar, Creagorry, Benbecula. MacAulay is an old man, full of old songs and hymns, runes and incantations. These he heard from his aunt and mother, who were full of song and story, natural and supernatural, and of old lore of the most curious kind. The reciter called the poem *"Altach Shomhairle,"* Somhairle's or Somerled's Petition, and *"Altach Shomhairle Mhic Calmain,"* The Supplication of Somhairle or Somerled MacCalman. He said that Somhairle Mac Calmain was a good man, moving about doing no harm, asking nothing and always getting enough. In his travels he was always crooning these little hymns to himself. This description might fit MacAulay himself, save that he seldom leaves his wind-swept moorland home.

238 Reciter: Catriona Bheag (Little Catherine) MacDonald, cottar, Borve, Barra.

239 Reciter: Roderick MacDonald, Manal, Tiree.

The aged reciter said: "This rune is good on sea and on shore, in peril of sea and in distress on land. Many the black journey and many the bad man in extremity on sea and in danger on land to whom this prayer has brought relief. And it is I who can say that, considering

From how many a danger and peril,
Pounding sea and drowning sea,
Thou hast delivered me safely
For the sake of the Prayer of Distress.

"And that was true for me, considering how many a wave has gone over my head in the course of my life! Thou King of the moon and of the sun and of the fragrant stars, Thou Thyself knowest, Thou Thyself knowest, O compassionate God of life!"

240 From Alexander MacDonald, crofter, Borve, Barra.

246 Reciter: Catherine MacNeill, Ceann Tangabhall, Barra.

The reciter said: "The man around whom the charm shall go shall no be killed in battle nor drowned in sea. The charm is a blessed thing. Brigit set the charm about her Foster-son and Mary set the charm about her Son. Many a man has been preserved from peril in field of battle and from drowning in sea in consequence of the charm's being set around his person and around his body.

"The man around whom the charm shall go and the woman who sets the charm go to a hidden glen, far away or near at hand, where no eye shall see them but the eye of the God of all life, nor ear hear them but the ear of the God of glory, unless the little chirpers of the bushes or the fays of the knolls or the gnomes of the rocks see or hear them. The man around whom the charm should go, recited Credo and Pater Noster and the Prayer of Mary Mother. It was necessary that the man around whom the charm should go, should have a right heart and good thoughts and a clean spirit. If he had not, my dear, the charm was of no efficacy to the man, nor would there be wave of fruit for the woman. There would not, my dear, O there would not, no virtue in the charm for him nor wave of fruit for her."

247 From Mary Cameron, cottar, Borve, Barra, 16th June 1901.

248 *Caim* (encompassing), is a form of safeguarding common in the west. The encompassing of any of the Three Persons of the Trinity, or of the Blessed Virgin, or of any of the Apostles or of any of the saints may be invoked, according to the faith of the suppliant. In making the *caim* the suppliant stretches out the right hand with the fore-finger extended, and turns round sunwise as if on a pivot, describing a circle with the tip of the forefinger while invoking the desired protection. The circle encloses the suppliant and accompanies him as he walks onward, safeguarded from all evil without or within. Protestant or Catholic, educated or illiterate, may make the *caim* in fear, danger, or dis-tress, as when some untoward noise is heard or some untoward object seen during the night.

The caim is called *caim Dhé, caim Chriosda, caim an Spioraid, caim Mhoire, caim na Cro Naoimhe, caim na Cro Naoimhe agus nan naomh am flathas, caim Mhicheil, caim nan naodh aingeal, caim nan naomh agus nan naodh aingeal, caim Chaluim Chille* (the encompassing of God, of Christ, of the Spirit, of Mary, of the Holy Rood, of the Holy Rood and of the saints in heaven, of Michael, of the nine angels, of the saints and of the nine angels, of Columba); and to these may be added the customary epithets, as *caim Dhé nan dùl, caim Mhicheil mhil nam buadh, caim Chaluim Chille chaoimh* (the encompassing of the God of the creatures, of Michael militant the victorious, of Columba the kindly). It is also called *caim na corraig* (the encompassing of the forefinger), and *caim na còrach* (the encompassing of righteous-ness).

251 From Ann Livingstone, crofter, Bay, Taynuilt, Lorne.

252 From Roderick MacNeill, cottar, Mingulay, Barra.

"On the Night of the Gifts the good-wives used to put the bannock-stone into the laps of their girl-children as a symbol of Brigit, since she was the first woman who took Christ the Son of God into her lap. There is a dear hymn concerning this, but I do not remember it. I have lost my memory since I lost my means and since my people were scattered — some of them in Australia, and some of them in Canada, and some of them mouldering in the dust. Oh the turns of the hard world! Many a trick does it play, and so it was with me. My fresh new house was burned over my head, and I burned my hands in rescuing my dear little children. Oh the suffering of the poor folk! The terrible time that was! The land was taken from us, though we were not a penny in debt, and all the lands of the townland were given to the Lowland farmer beside us. He had always been wishing to have them, and he never stopped until he got them."

255 Reciter: Mary MacDonald, crofter, Greater Bohuntin, Lochaber.

The form *Moire,* Mary, is confined to the Blessed Virgin. It is used even in Protestant districts as an asseveration, as *"Moire tha," "Moire chan 'eil"* ("by Mary it is," "by Mary it is not"). "Be still, children, be quiet, children, you would cause the mild Mary of grace to sin!" This was said by a woman in Protestant Skye to her grand-children.

In the Flight to Egypt Mary met a milk-maid going to the *eadradh* milking. She asked the milkmaid to hold the Child a while as her arms were weary. The woman rudely refused, saying that she was in a hurry to milk her cows. Then Mary met another milkmaid going to the *eadradh,* and asked her to hold the Child a while as her arms were weary. The woman took the Child, nursed Him and fondled Him and sang songs to Him till Mary was rested, and then went on her way. This woman had twice as many cows to milk as the other, yet she was done of the milking in half the time; she had four times as much milk as the other for her cows gave twice as much milk. We should show compassion to our fellow-creatures even though at inconvenience to ourselves.

256 From Mary Maclellan, née Mac-Donald, crofter, Beoraidh, Morar.

257 From Ann Macdonald, a native of Lochaber, lately returned from Australia after an absence of many years, a woman full of native wit and humour. A very similar poem was obtained from Catherine MacNeill, cottar, Breubhaig, Barra, a woman of wit and humour, of clearness of head and goodness of heart.

258 Cf. "Counteracting the evil eye," II:142.

259 From Ann Livingstone, née Mac-Callum, crofter, Taynuilt.

A woman in South Uist said: "A great great day, the day of the Feast of St Michael, my dear, a day the like of which we shall never see again. Every little and big, every young and old, every male and female in the country was away at the *Oda,* not a person in the house save an old man or an old woman or an innocent little child without sin or sense. Gentle Mary of grace, it was on them there was the whirling of mind! Round the burial-ground of the Church of Michael the people were as thick as are the barnacle-geese on the Plain of Miogadan on the great day of migration. There was not a hill nor a townland, a bay nor a promontory between the Ford of Gramasdal and the Stack of Eriskay but was pouring out its people to Michael's Point on the day of the *Oda.*

"O Mary, Mary, the thick crowd of folk that would be there, small and great, high and low! There was the same eager stir among all the horses, young and old. You would get the eye so lively, the ear so pointed, the foot so swift and the spirit so lightsome. Oh by the Book itself, you would think the old aged horses were young horses, and the young horses that had never been at the *Oda* were old horses, for they were as much agog as those that had often been there. It was as though it were natural to them, as it is natural to the cattle of the shieling and to the birds of the sea to migrate on their own appointed day. O Mary of grace, the instinct and nature that the great Being of life has placed in every creature created by His own blessed hands! — from the son of man to the horses of the *Oda,* from the cattle of the shieling to the birds of the plain!"

Strùbhan

Strùbhan, strùdhan, strùthan, the St Michael cake. When the word stands alone the stress is on the first syllable and the *u* is long. In the phrase *strubhan Micheil,* the stress is on the first syllable of *Micheil,* the other stress is reduced and the *u* shortened. Even when the word is used alone, *Micheil* is understood, for the word is applied to no other thing.

The woman who baked it threw a bit of the dough into the *bealaidh* (hot embers), saying: "Here to thee devil, thine own share." This bit was called *taois an donais* (the devil's dough); *toinn (teom) an t-sionnaich* (the fox's twist or oblation), and *mir a' mhadaidh ruaidh* (the fox's bit). What this represented the narrator did not know, but she thought it might be to buy off the fox from killing the sheep (cf. i. 209).

Curran Micheil

The carrot was a symbol of deep and high significance, appealing to the sacred instincts of the people as no other plant did. It symbolised fertility, offspring, children. The carrot was given by a woman to a man, rarely by a man to a woman. Girls and women were and are in the habit of gathering wild carrots on the sandy plains; when one gets a bifurcated carrot she rejoices greatly, crying out in the fullness of her heart:

Little cleft one! little cleft one!
Joy of carrot surpassing to me!
Little cleft one! little cleft one!
Fruitage of carrot surpassing to me!

Michael militant will give me seed and fruit,
Calm Brigit will give me passion
Fite Fith will give me wine and milk,
And Mary mild will give me aid.

In some districts the word is *torcan,* a diminutive from *torc,* a cleft, cut or opening, of V-shape.

A place in North Uist is called Gearraidh nan Curran, the Grassland of the Carrots; immediately before the Feast of St Michael girls and women from all parts of North Uist would crowd thither for wild carrots and for enjoyment.

Feast of St Michael

The following notes from Father Allan MacDonald, taken from a letter dated Dalibrog, 21st December 1898, may be added to the account of the Feast of St Michael:

"The implement for digging up the carrots I hear called *sleibheag;* I am told that it was the same as was used for digging up the roots of the *cairt leamhna* (bitter vetch). In Barra some call it *spleacan,* the *ea* having the same sound as in *fead.*

"The women tied up the carrots into bunches with a thread. Each bunch was of such circumference as to fill up the circle made by the thumb and forefinger joining each other at the tips. The women had many such bunches prepared for the ball of St Michael's Night. They hid them in the neighbourhood of the dancing-house, and they went out from time to time during the night to fetch a bunch. On coming into the ballroom with a bunch each of them said:

It is I that have the carrots,
Whoever he be that can take them from me.

"Even in Benbecula the going to the St Michael's races was called *dol a Chille Mhicheil* (going to St Michael's church). I do not know if there was such a dedication in Benbecula; my informant, a native of Benbecula, never heard of such a dedication.

"The *strùbhan* that was made for a person away from home was kept carefully awaiting him even though three months were to elapse before his return. A woman tells me that her father and brothers were away sailing in a smack at St Michael's, and that her mother duly made the cakes and kept them carefully for them till they returned home.

"The religious functions most commonly assigned by the people here to St Michael are his meeting of the souls of the elect at the moment of death, and his presiding at the balance where the soul's good and bad works are weighed."

St Connan's Fair and St Michael's Day

Ann Livingstone, née MacCallum, of Taynuilt, was already old when I came to know her in 1882, but she was still full of the songs and rimes, the hymns and ballads and traditions, of her native Gleann Conghlais, Glen Kinglass, on Loch Etive. With graphic power and pathetic interest she described the people of her own district and her own day, simple, noble, and neighbourly, the men big and powerful, the women strong and handsome, whom to see was to admire and to know was to love.

She described minutely the famous "Féill Chonnain," St Connan's fair in Glen Orchy. To this the people of the surrounding districts came to sell their native produce, and strangers to buy cheese and butter, beef and mutton, clothes and tartans, linens and garters, plaidings and blankets, and swords in their time. From Callander, Doune, Stirling, Perth and other towns of the south men came with horses bearing panniers filled with knives, pistols and every sort of hardware. Booths were erected, and the *féill* lasted several days. It created much stir among the people. There were games and athletics during the day and dancing and singing during the night. A sort of industrial exhibition was held, to which the neighbourhood contributed of its best, for the competition was keen. The arts most exemplified were wood-carving, sword-making, leather-tanning, wool-dyeing, garter-making, tartan-making, hose-knitting, weaving and wool-working in general. The judges were brought from afar to ensure impartiality and to avoid disputes.

Many men of the surrounding districts were "in the wars of the Stuarts and in the wars of the French." Their courage being high, their losses were heavy; and those who returned found their people dead or driven out, their houses down, their home desolate, and themselves without where to lay their heads. Sheep had taken the place of people, to be in their turn replaced by deer, and the glens once full of innocence and merriment are now desolate and dumb.

It was, however, the *Féill Micheil,* Feast of St Michael, that evoked the higher and nobler instincts of the people. Ann Livingstone spoke of the customs of the *Féill Micheil* more from tradition than from observation, for they had fallen into disuse before her time; but as bearing on the customs of the Outer Isles (see i.198ff), those of the inner glens may be mentioned as related by this intelligent and educated woman.

The *strùbhan Micheil* or *bonnach Micheil,* Michael *struan* or cake, was baked on St Michael's Eve by the wife or daughter of the house. It was three-sided. The meal was moistened with sheep's or goat's milk. The cake was placed before the bright peat fire on the middle of the floor, and one side and then another was coated with batter of eggs and cream. While the *strùbhan* or *bonnach* was toasting, the *fallaid* (dry meal on the baking-board) was gathered and dusted over the flocks assembled for the purpose. In the morning the father of the family cut the bannock into small pieces of the form of the whole, and gave a piece to his wife and to each of his children, to each of his household, and to all his dependants about the place.

The farmers gave a fourth of a *strùbhan,* a fourth of a plate of butter and a fourth of a cheese to the poor about them; "and the man and wife bestowed this on the Michael beam (balance) that it might be before their souls at the time of going over the gleam of the river." If a man had no *strùbhan* himself he bought one to give away to the poor and the needy, framed in the likeness of the Father everlasting. The farmer's wife took a *strùbhan* to the house of the superior as a sign of friendship and protection. The sheep and the goats were milked till St Michael's Eve, and then were allowed to run dry.

On St Michael's Day the people rode about singing *rainn* (rimes), the women giving carrots to the men and wishing them "progeny and prosperity, triumph and increase, and fame and fortune to the day of their death and after it." The men were giving presents to the women. There were balls and dancing on that evening, all the people gathering in the biggest barn, and young men crossed the hills to join the dancing in other straths.

Leanabh Micheil

A child who came opportunely was called *leanabh Micheil* (child of Michael); *conail Micheil* (procreant of Michael); *curran Micheil* (carrot of Michael), and by other terms indicative of the faith of those who prayed at the saint's shrine.

Michael was besought by women, who went sunwise round his enclosure praying his aid and singing his hymn. Mares were led sunward around his burial-ground, the leader singing the hymn of Michael Militant, subduer of the dragon and patron saint of horses. The sunwarding was done under cover of darkness that none might see:

Where was no babbler nor gaddler
To give twaddle to the world.

Michael's Brian

Brian was the name of Michael's steed, famed for its swiftness and its whiteness. Michael's Brian was:

As white as the snow of the peaks,
As white as the foam of the waves,
As white as the cotton of the meads,
And nearly as white as the angel
victorious.

Michael's Brian was:

As swift as the swallow of the spring,
As swift as the wind of March,
As swift as the deadly levin,
And nearly as swift as the shaft of death.

A derivative of Brian is the feminine "Brianag." *Bilean Brianaig bial mo ghaoil* (the lips of Brian, the mouth of my love) is a phrase alike in meaning to *binneas Brianaig* (the melody of Brianag).

Brianag was as fair as the sun of the
seasons,
Brianag was as musical as the harmony
of the bards
Brianag was as gentle as Brigit of the
herds,
And nearly as sweet as the mother's lips.

263 Reciter: Peggy MacCormack, née MacDonald, crofter and nurse, Aird Bhuidhe, Loch Boisdale, South Uist.

Ob (or Iosab), the father of Brigit, used to draw water to the town getting payment for each vessel. He had a long way to go to the loch every day, and he could not be back until late. When Ob would set out early in the morning, he would leave a vessel of water with Brigit for her own use and the needs of the house until he should come home at night. In the late evening came two persons to the door, a man and a woman, and the woman asked for a drink of water.

"I cannot give thee a drink without payment for it," said Brigit. The two went away without food or drink, without music or hospitality, without anything in the world being given to them. Late at night Ob came home with a cart of water as usual, and Brigit gave him his supper, and they went to their sleep as they were wont. In the middle of the night a great noise was heard outside, as it were the omen–roar of a river.

"Get up, Brigit, and look out, for I am hearing a noise like the omen–roar of a river," said her father to Brigit.

Brigit got up, and clothed herself, and looked out to see whether she could see what the noise meant. What was there but a great beautiful river flowing down past the house! Brigit returned and told her father within what she had seen and heard without.

"Was there anyone here today?"

"There was," said Brigit, "a man and a woman."

"Did they receive aught?"

"No, not a taste," said Brigit. "The woman asked for a drink of water, but I would not give her a drop without payment, as thou didst bid me, father, and they went away."

"Look out, to and fro, and see what more thou shalt see or hear, or whether the prophecy is come to pass upon the world."

Brigit went out and looked about, to and fro, and returned within upon her track.

"There is a light in the stable, father," said Brigit. Ob leaped with a standing–leap out of his bed and quickly clothed himself. Brigit went down to the stable, and she knelt on her two knees, and she took the King of the elements into her bosom, and she raised Him in her arms when He came unto the world. And that is the reason that a woman's head is in four divisions and a man's head in three divisions. The Son of the God of the elements might not be born and come into the world as the children of men are born and come into it; it was a miracle from beginning to end, Jesus Christ's coming from heaven to earth.

That is how I heard it among the old folk of the *ceilidh* when I was young. But, O Mary of grace! long indeed is the time since then, though short it has been in passing.

See also "Genealogy of Bride," "Bride the aid–woman," I:70, 71.

265 When a girl goes out at night to the well, she croons a hymn variously called *Rann Tobair* (Rune of the Well); *Caim Moire* (Shelter of Mary); *Caim Moire Màthar* (Shelter of Mary Mother), and by other names. The maiden lilts the rune in the firm belief that the protecting arm of the

Mary Mother is shielding her from ill and mishap, natural and supernatural.

270 The reciter, Dugall MacAulay, said that he always crooned this little hymn to himself when leaving his house upon an errand of whatever kind, and that he always derived comfort from it. He learned it from his mother and from her sister, who lived with his mother, These two old women had innumerable hymns, songs, stories and fables, sayings and proverbs, full of wisdom and beauty, almost all of which died with them.

271 The reciter, Dugall MacAulay, cottar, Hacleit, Benbecula, said that he always recited this little prayer to himself *"fo m'anail"* ("under my breath") when he went upon a journey, however short the distance, however small the matter of his errand.

272 Reciter: Malcolm Sinclair, fisherman, Baile Phuill, Tiree.

This was the name of a charm worn upon the person to safeguard the wearer against drowning at sea, against disaster on land, against evil eye, evil wish, evil influences, against the wrongs and oppressions of man and the wiles and witcheries of woman, against being lifted by the hosts of the air, and against being waylaid by the fairies of the mound.

Such a charm might consist of a word, a phrase, a saying, or a verse from one of the Gospels, and from this came the name, "Gospel of Christ." The words were written upon paper or parchment, and were often illuminated and ornamented in Celtic design, the script being thus rendered more precious by the beauty of its work and the beauty of its words.

The script was placed in a small bag of linen and sewn into the waistcoat of a man and the bodice of a woman, under the left arm. In the case of a child the bag was suspended from the neck by a linen cord. Linen was sacred because the body of Christ was buried in a linen shroud, and there are many phrases which indicate the special esteem in which lint was held (see OE Vol.II pp.319f). The blue flax was used medicinally (cf OE Vol. II pp.332, 353), especially for stomach complaints, and also as a safeguard against invisible dangers.

The blue–eyed one of the fairy woman
Be to shield me and to keep me
From the hosts (of the air) and from faery,
From ill–will and from ill–deed.

There were three thefts from which there was no absolution "in the world here or in the world yonder ... It would need three priests three times to bring from out of Purgatory the thief of salt or the thief of seed or the thief of flax."

In giving *Eolas Sguchadh (Sgiucha) Féithe* (the Charm for the Burst Vein), an intelligent woman in Kincardine, Ross, gave me a piece of the linen thread which she uses in her operations. It consists of three threads of three ply each, with three knots upon each thread (cf IV:413n., 431n.) These threads were wound around the injured limb. The thread is of fine linen, and it was applied:

In name of Father, in name of Son,
In name of Spirit.

273 Reciter: Ann Mackinnon, crofter, Sorasdal, Island of Coll.

274 From Mary Maclean, crofter, Manal, Island of Tiree.

275 From Mary MacDonald, crofter, Staoinibrig, South Uist, who possessed the second sight.

282 From Mary Mackintosh, née Smith, Gearraidh na Moine, South Uist.

The reciter of this poem and of other poems in this work was a woman of great natural courtesy and intelligence. She was full of songs and hymns, runes and rimes, and of various kinds of literary lore of much interest. Her husband was a tailor, a man of good presence and much modesty, and her father was Patrick Smith, crofter, of Leth Mheadhonach, South Uist. Patrick Smith was rich in literary matter of great and varied interest and excellence. Mr Campbell of Islay, Mr Hector Maclean, and the present writer took down many pieces of prose and of poetry from him. He was equally interested in both, but especially in old heroic tales in prose or verse. During the winter nights his house used to be filled with young and old listening to stories and poems rehearsed in simple idiomatic Gaelic.

His son, John Smith, inherited some of his father's lore but none of his diction. I took down some stories from him, as did also Dr George Henderson. Some forty years after I had first visited Patrick Smith I visited his old home again. His grandsons and granddaughters were full of modern so-called education, and of self-sufficiency, and of unabashed disdain for their unlettered old grandfather and for his traditional lore. Unasked they showed their own advancement by singing music-hall songs and ditties and by reciting music-hall slang and vulgarities. The contrast between the present and the past was strongly illustrated. The difference between the quiet, simple dignity and repose of unlettered old Patrick Smith and his forward, aggressive, talkative grandchildren was as grievous as it was striking. Not less striking was the contrast between the beautiful and elevated old lore of the old man and the vulgar modern literature of the young people.

My heart did sorely weep,
Though simply I did smile.

283 From Mary Macmillan, crofter, Lianacuidh, South Uist, 1872.

292 When a son or a daughter is leaving home in the Western Isles, the event is warmly felt, for the feelings of the people are deep and strong, if silent and subdued. Friends and neighbours come to say farewell to the pilgrim, and to pray for peace and prosperity in the adopted land. Before crossing the threshold of the old home, a parting hymn is sung, all joining in the pilgrim song. It is sung or chanted or intoned or recited in slow measured cadences, pleasing and peculiar, though perhaps difficult for the stranger to follow. The scene is striking and impressive, and the stranger who is allowed the privilege of being present feels indeed the depths of a mother's love and the strength of a father's affection. An aged woman in Uist said:

"By the Book, love, you would not seek but listen to them although your own heart were full and overflowing and you striving to keep down the tears. O thou Mary of grace! O thou Mother of sore sorrow! Many the tearful eye that I have seen in my day and in my generation."

Friends and neighbours come with bonnets, stockings, gloves, plaiding *(clò)* and the like, the parting gifts of the makers, who consecrated their heartfelt offerings with the tears of their eyes and the prayers of their hearts. These parting scenes are less common now than they were in the past. And yet those people of warmest emotion in safety are of coolest composure in danger. The writer observed this many times during his long residence in those stormy Isles of the Atlantic. Many times among those wild seas, among bristling rocks, roaring reefs and mountainous waves, when death appeared inevitable, the people have remained cool and calm, neither cry nor clamour from man or woman, but only the murmured prayer for the soul and the tear for those behind.

293 From Mór Maclellan, née Morrison, Beoraidh Mhor, Morar.

The reciter said: "When a member of a family was leaving home for a time or for ever, the *"Dùil Deora"* (Pilgrim's Hope), was sung by the family. The pilgrim bathed his face in warm milk, preferably in sheep's milk; the sheep being sacred to Christ. During the flight to Egypt, the Mary Mother bathed her Son in *bainne beannaichte na brac."* [the blessed milk of the *brac,* a term of uncertain meaning.] (Cf. I:20ff)

296 From Ann MacDonald, Lochaber, who died in Leith Poorhouse.

The following prayer was said immediately before Confession. It was sung, chanted or intoned by the members of the family, sometimes separately, sometimes together. The prayer was sung slowly and solemnly, the father and mother pressing upon their children to confess their sins, and to ask forgiveness for the past and strength for the future, and to allow no false shame nor foolish pride to prevent them from making a "good" confession. And here the reciter said:

"There was a woman in Lochaber, and she made special mention to the priest of her pride, which she said she found it difficult to subdue. The priest advised her. The woman listened till the priest was done, and then with an air of dignity said: 'God and men know that I have a right to be proud — I am a MacDonald!'

"The good priest could scarcely restrain his laughter, as much at the manner as at the words of the woman."

297 Reciter: Mór MacNeill, cottar, Castlebay, Barra.

299 From Mary MacLeod, Naast, Gairloch.

303 The people addressed invocations to the sun, moon, and stars. Men and women saluted the morning sun and hailed the new moon. The practice prevailed over the British Isles, nor is it yet obsolete, though now a matter of form more than of belief. The people hailed the morning sun as they would a great person come back to their land; and they hailed the new moon, *"lochran mór an àigh"* (the great lamp of grace), with joyous welcome and acclaim. The sun was to them a matter of great awe, but the moon was a friend of great love, guiding their course upon land and sea, and their path wherever they went. The reciter, Mór MacNeill of Barra, said:

"In the time of my father and of my mother there was no man in Barra who would not take off his bonnet to the white sun of power, nor a woman in Barra who would not bend her body to the white moon of the seasons. No, my dear, not a man nor woman in Barra. And old persons will be doing this still, and I will be doing it myself sometimes. Children mock at me, but if they do, what of that? Is it not much meeter for me to bend my body to the sun and to the moon and to the stars, that the great God of life made for my good, than to the son or daughter of earth like myself?"

Mór MacNeill was poor and old and alone, but she was bright of mind and clean of person, and she was full of old songs and hymns, of old runes and traditions. She was capable, too, and could give an account of the faith that was in her.

In leaving the Isles, the writer went to say goodbye to the people who had all been so good and kind, so courteous and hospitable to him, and of whom the poorest of the poor were not the least near to his heart. When saying goodbye to me, Mór MacNeill ceased speaking, and taking my hand in her two hands, kissed it and watered it with her tears, and curtseying low, said: "And you are now going away and leaving your people and your country, dear one of my heart! Well, then, whole may you be, and well may it go with you, every way you go and every step you travel. And my own blessing go with you, and the blessing of God go with you, and the blessing of the Mary Mother go with you, every time you rise up and every time you lie down, until you lie down in sleep upon the arm of Jesus Christ of the virtues and of the blessings — of the virtues and of the blessings!"

304 To sea-faring people like those of the Western Isles the light and guidance of the moon is a matter of much interest and importance, often indeed a matter of life or death. Sun, moon and stars are all addressed for practical purposes. The moon was of more concern than the sun, for by day, whether the sun was visible or not, the people could thread their way through their intricate tortuous reefs and rocks, fords and channels. But they could not do this on a moonless night except at the peril of their lives. This is one reason for the many odes and hymns addressed to the gracious luminary of the night. In the extremity of danger at sea an old man at the helm may be heard crooning to himself:

Glory be to Thee, O God of life,
For the guiding lamp of ocean;
Be Thine own hand on my rudder's helm
And Thy love behind the billows.

306 Reciter: Isabel MacNeill, cottar, Ceann Tangabhall, Barra.

"When I see the new light, I am right to raise my eyes, to bend my head, and to bow my knee, giving praise to the God of life that I have seen the moon of moons once more. Many a one has crossed over the black river of death since thou didst come before, though I am left here still in the world of the living, on the earth of repentance; many a one that, O white moon of the seasons!

In my father's time there was not a man in Barra but would take off his head-covering to the white sun of the day, nor a woman in Barra but would incline her body to the white moon of the night. Old men in this countryside do so still. I myself do so at times, though the children make fun of me.

I think myself that it is a matter for thankfulness, the golden–bright sun of virtues giving us warmth and light by day, and the white moon of the seasons giving us guidance and leading by night."

307 From Ann Maclellan, crofter, Meallaig Mhor, Morar.

309 From Una MacDonald, crofter, Buaile Dhubh, Iochdar, South Uist.

The following verses were addressed to the new moon when first observed. They were sung by the company of women, maidens, and perhaps men and boys, with impressive effect. At the summer shielings there might be a dozen or two dozen women and girls, with a sprinkling of men and boys, singing and dancing, carolling and prancing, upon the green grass under the shining light of the moon, the moonbeams shimmering upon the clear lake below, while the fleecy clouds moved slowly above, showing the blue, beautiful sky in the faraway distance, with the projecting rocks and the heath–clad everlasting hills at hand. The "hooch–ing" of the men, the clapping of the girls, the mouth–music of the women, and the reverberations in the rocks combined with the surroundings to make up a picture that can neither be described nor forgotten.

313 From Mary Mackintosh, née Smith, Leth Mheadhonach. South Uist.

314 The aged reciter said: "When a person sees the new moon, he ought to make reverence to it, and to make the cross of Christ over the tablet of his heart, and to say the rune in the eye of the God of glory Who sees all."

315 These fragments [of the morning hymn to the sun] were obtained from a man of ninety–nine years in the south end of South Uist, and from another in Mingulay, one of the outer isles of Barra.

316 From John MacNeill, cottar, Buaile nam Bodach, Barra.

318 Reciter: Malcolm Macmillan, merchant, Balivannich, Benbecula.

319 Reciter: Malcolm Macmillan, merchant, Balivannich, Benbecula.

320 This rune is said by travellers at night. Any person saying it from the heart will be sained and safeguarded from harm. He will not be molested by the *fuath*, the *gruagach*, the *peallag*, the *ban–sith*, the *bean–nighidh*, nor by *fridich nan creag*, nor by any spirit in the air, in the earth, under the earth, in the sea, nor under the sea. The imprecation *"Guma h–anmoch dhuit!"* ("May you be late!") is still reckoned as specially evil.

"Do you see anything, little son?"

"I see nothing, father."

"Do you see anything now, little son?"

"I see nothing, father."

"Do you see anything at all now, little son?"

"I see nothing at all, father."

"By Mary, you see nothing! There is not so much sense in your head or in your snout or in your eye that you would see a bogle or anything else of the ill work of the night!"

This conversation took place between a father and the little son on his back as they were passing through a spot of evil reputation. When the father passed the dreaded hollow he put down his boy and ran as hard as he could. The boy overtook and passed him. When he reached home, the boy fell in the door exhausted. Immediately after the father came up and stumbled over the motionless boy lying in the doorway. Thinking that this was the bogle at last, the father yelled, rousing the boy without and the mother within. The frightened man gave his son a cuffing and a severe scolding for leaving him to the mercy of the bogles.

"You little sack of hide, to go and leave your father to be eaten by the bogles of Lag Onair and the marsh–spirit of the night!"

326 From Peigidh Nic Cormack (Peggy MacCormack) née MacDonald, Aird Bhuidhe, Loch Boisdale, Uist.

The reciter said that this and similar hymns used to be sung in her father's house at Airigh nam Ban in Uist. Crofters then held the land now occupied by sheep. The people were strong, healthy and happy, and enjoyed life to the full in their simple homely ways. They had sheep and cattle, corn, potatoes, and poultry, milk, cheese, butter and fish, all in sufficiency. They were good to the poor, kind to the stranger, and helpful to one another, and there was nothing amiss. There were pipers and fiddlers in almost every house, and the people sang and danced in summer time on the green grass without, and in winter time on the clay floor within.

"How we enjoyed ourselves in those faraway days — the old as much as the young. I often saw three and sometimes four generations dancing together on the green grass in the golden summer sunset. Men and women of fourscore or more — for they lived long in those days dancing with boys and girls of five on the green grass. Those were the happy days and the happy nights, and there was neither sin nor sorrow in the world for us. The thought of those young days make my old heart both glad and sad even at this distance of time. But the clearance came upon us, destroying all, turning our small crofts into big farms for the stranger, and turning our joy into misery, our gladness into bitterness, our blessing into blasphemy, and our Christianity into mockery. O dear man, the tears come on my eyes when I think of all we suffered and of the sorrows, hardships, oppressions we came through."

330 Reciter: Dugall MacAulay, cottar, Hacleit, Benbecula.

332 Reciter: Mary MacRae, cottar, Camas Luinge, Kintail.

The reciter said: "After I have closed my door and put out my cruisie (lamp) and gone to my bed, I beseech the Being of life and the God of grace, and say this verse to Him."

334 The reciter said that she heard this hymn, and many other hymns and songs, tunes and melodies, when a child, from her father John MacNeill and from her mother Mary Maclean. Her parents had innumerable songs and hymns, chants and melodies, which they taught to their children. She, however, was but a child when her parents died, and she remembers but fragments of what they taught to her and her brothers and sisters. The woman taught all that she could remember of her childhood's prayers and hymns and harmonies to her own ten children, most of whom are now dead. The woman said that she often thought over those old songs and airs, hymns and tunes, that she heard in her childhood and never heard again since, and that they appear to her very peculiar and very different from anything that she had ever heard since then. She thinks that most of them must have been very old; they were very weird and very beautiful.

336 The reciter, Catherine Macphee, cottar, Aird Mhór, Iochdar, Uist, said: "Many a thing I have seen in my own day and generation. Many a thing, O Mary Mother of the black sorrow! I have seen the townships swept, and the big holdings being made of them, the people being driven out of the countryside to the streets of Glasgow and to the wilds of Canada, such of them as did not die of hunger and plague and smallpox while going across the ocean. I have seen the women putting the children in the carts which were being sent from Benbecula and the Iochdar to Loch Boisdale, while their husbands lay bound in the pen and were weeping beside them, without power to give them a helping hand, though the women themselves were crying aloud and their little children wailing like to break their hearts. I have seen the big strong men, the champions of the countryside, the stalwarts of the world, being bound on Loch Boisdale quay and cast into the ship as would be done to a batch of horses or cattle in the boat, the bailiffs and the ground-officers and the constables and the policemen gathered behind them in pursuit of them. The God of life and He only knows all the loathsome work of men on that day.

"The women would be singing these verses at time of going to sleep. The people of that day were full of hymns and prayers, full of music and songs, full of joy and melody and innocent merriment. By the Book itself, you would not ask but to be hearing them, however long the night, however wild the weather, however miry the road, however dark the night going home-ward. That was our school, and we had no other. There was but one school in South Uist between the Stack of Eriskay and the Isle of Floday, near forty miles' journey, with three ferries to make, three sounds to cross. That was very different from the children of today — a school at every door.

"But the people of that day were strong and healthy, active and industrious, in a way that those of today are not, whether men or women. They are not, my dear; I myself draw your notice to that. A great change of life has come into the countryside — every-one observes that. Much tea is drunk and much flour is eaten nowadays. There was nothing of that in my own time or in my mother's time. There was nothing but butter and cheese and crowdie, dairy-produce and milk, and beer of heather-tops, oat-bread, barley-bread and rye-bread, porridge and milk, meat and flesh, gruel and broth. That is all changed today, my dear, and this has its visible effect and its result. Everything nowadays is sold for the sake of lowland food without worth or pith. Think you is there any kind of jam in the town of Glas-gow that is not found today in Uist? Not one! In my day there was no jam except the kind that we made ourselves of brambles, of blaeberries, and of our own black and red currants. The people of today have not so much as a rose-bush. The men have taken to sloth, and they have neither kail nor carrots, nor even a garden. Since the folk were cast out to the streets of Glasgow and to the woods of Canada and to the peat-hags, the gardens have stopped.

"O Mary Mother, we see the effect and the result! The young women of today have neither bone nor body, nor the growth proper to women. If they make a trip to the lowlands they come home stuffed full of airs and pride, and who but they? They go to Mass and to church to show themselves off, and who but they? With a knot on their breast, a *polonaise* (fancy gown) on their back, a picture-hat on their head, and a sunshade in their hand held above their head, and Mary Mother! who but they? — looking down on the mothers that bore them, be-cause they had nothing of that sort and it did not exist in their time! May God give them sense! It is themselves who would need that, and who would need to go to the knoll to see if the fairy woman would bestow the wisdom and grace of womanhood upon them.

"In my mother's time and in my own time no shoe nor bonnet, no skin-sandal nor cap went on foot or on head of lad nor of lass in the countryside until they were big gawks of girls or tall striplings of lads. No, nor would headgear nor footgear go on lad nor on lass save on holiday or Sunday or special day like that. Not a rag of clothing nor a shred of leather was coming into the countryside, but each family making clothes and linen, leather and shoes, for themselves. By the Book itself, beautiful was that, the work of their hands!

"Every maiden in the countryside went forth on holiday and Sunday without cap or head-covering save a big comb in the back of her hair and a satin snood from ear to ear, showing the world's people that she was still free of wedlock and of baptism and the cares of a family. If there was a young woman who had lost being a maiden without becoming a wife (but rare was that, my dear), there would be neither snood about her ears nor fillet about her head. It might not be. They were hard, hard, on the wretched young woman of misfortune.

"The goodwives of the countryside went forth on holiday and on Sunday with a coif of linen about their heads, as white as the mountain cotton or with a cap of linen as white as the snow of the hill. They wore gowns on their persons and cloaks about their shoulders of stuff or of *iomairt* (striped cloth; see I:111n) or of tartan, the wage-work of their own hands. And Mary Mother, they were a beautiful sight compared with the half-clad slovenly rag-covered women of the present day! Each young girl wore a shoulder-plaid or a waist-plaid of her own clan, of thread as slender and fine, and of colours as bright and pleasing, and cloth as beautiful and tasteful as you could see with your eye.

"O King of the moon and the sun, many is the change that has come on the country in my own time. I remember when the folk of the countryside would be going to the *Oda* held at St Michael's Point on the day of St Michael's Feast. I myself was at the *Oda* time and time again; and 'tis there was the sight of people. Folk from every hill and township, moor and plain, island and head–land in the countryside, and the world itself of horses! There was no knowing whence they were come or from what places they were still coming — no knowing under the bright sun of powers. O Mary of grace, what a dear day we had there! with horse–riding and circuiting and wrestling, with youngsters getting seats behind the rider, with giving of carrots, with greeting and welcome of folk!

"And the night of St Michael's Feast! That was the delightful night in Uist! A ball and dancing, music and songs, beer and feast–fare by every doorpost. And the young girls' hidden stores! and no knowing under the sun when or where they had got the carrots — no knowing!"

339 From Alexander Maclean, Manal, Tiree.

340 This poem was chanted over a new house, or over a new family in a new house.

341 The old people had a great desire for good weather at the death and burial of a person. It was a good sign that the elements should be at peace at that time. There were two reasons for this. If there was peace on earth it was a sign that there was peace in heaven and a welcome for him who had gone and that the King of all creatures was at peace with him and His own two mighty arms open to take the immortal soul home to Himself. And if there was peace on earth this gave opportunity to friends and kindred to come to the burial and take farewell of the body in the natural earth and in the grave of the fathers.

If the weather was bad it was a sign that God was wroth. And the bad weather kept friends and kindred from coming to the burial.

If the day was wet or misty it was a sign that the King of the elements was pouring wrath on the earth. If the day was black, dark and stormy it showed that God, the Creator of all creatures, was pouring the black wrath of His grief on the soul of him who had gone. If it was a day of snow this was a sign that the white wrath of God was upon the bruised soul that had gone over the black river of death.

342 Happy death

The lovable little infant
Will go through the pains of Purgatory
As the valorous dove
Through the darkness of the skies.

They call Purgatory *Ifreann nan aithreacha naomh* (the Hell of the holy fathers). The holy fathers are detained in Purgatory but for a moment of time to be fanned, and fumed, and freed of all earthly contaminations. They are fanned by the white wings of the fair angels of heaven:

Till they are whiter than the swan of the songs,
Till they are whiter than the seagull of the waves
Till they are whiter than the snow of the peaks,
And whiter than the white love of the heroes.

After that the holy fathers fly through the unseen space like the lightning–fire through the clouds, and sit upon the right hand of the Father of Heaven Whom they served upon earth.

"O that you and I, beloved of my heart, could claim their help in freeing us of the impurities of earth!"

In the Roman Catholic communities of the west, *"bàs sona"* (happy death) is a phrase frequently heard among the people. When these words are used they imply that the dying person has been confessed and anointed, and that the death–hymn has been intoned over him. Under these conditions the consolation of the living in the loss of the loved one is touching. The old people speak of *bàs sona* with exultant satisfaction, and would wish above all things on earth that *bàs sona* may be their own portion when the time comes for them to go. The hymn which follows is one of many which used to be sung by the Catholics of the Western Isles.

343 Reciter: Barbara MacPhee, cottar, Drimsdale, Uist.

345 I obtained four or five versions of this poem in Lewis. A sacred hymn and a secular song, through being sung to the same air, had become confused. The following are some of the lines of the secular song:

Bonnet and feather and tartan and plaid,
Bonnet and feather and tartan and plaid,
Bonnet and feather and tartan and plaid,
The dress that sits bravely on the Sons of
 the Gael.

Yet! yet! yet shalt thou see it,
Yet! yet! yet shalt thou see it,
Yet shalt thou see the pride and the joy
 of it,
White and red ribbons about thine ears
 streaming.

The tune was played at funerals in Lewis, Harris and Skye down to Disruption times. I spoke to people who had heard it played at a funeral at Aoidh, in Lewis. They said that the scene and the tune were singularly impressive — the moaning of the sea, the mourning of the women, and the lament of the pipes over all as the body was carried to its home of winter, to its home of autumn, of spring and of summer; never could they forget the solemnity of the occasion, where all was so natural and so beautiful, and nature seemed to join in the feelings of humanity.

347 From Malcolm Macmillan, crofter, Grimnish, Benbecula.

348 From Ann MacDonald, widow, from Lochaber.

VOLUME IV

354 This is a rime which children repeat on seeing the *Dealan-Dé* (Golden Butterfly) which is said to be the angel of God come to bear the souls of the dead to heaven.

If the Yellow Butterfly be seen in a house where lies a corpse, and if it goes across the corpse in the chest of sleep (coffin) or upon the bier, the soul of that corpse is safe in heaven. This is not true of all, but only of the Yellow Butterfly.

John MacRury, Tolorum, Benbecula, said: "Tradition says that there was never a Yellow Butterfly on earth until Christ came forth from death and rose up from the tomb. The true Yellow Butterfly, they say, came out of the Holy Tomb, and that Yellow Butterfly spread throughout the world. The true Yellow Butterfly was never seen among wicked men, among evil company, evil speech, evil deeds, things hateful, things shameful, things vicious.

There are many kinds of Butterfly, but the kind we speak of is not so plentiful. The true Yellow Butterfly is near half an inch in length, and stouter about the body than any other kind, covered with very pretty down or plumage, very small about the tail, more so than any other kind under the sun. The top of his head is like a king's crown with a fringe around it. His hue is half-way between fine gold and the white snow of the hill. He is always seen in summer, quiet and peaceful, without heat or flurry, above the corpses of infants or of other good people. It is a good sign to see the Yellow Butterfly upon a corpse or near a corpse. They say that every furrow and streak in his wings and in his head and in his body is exactly in the manner of those that were in the sacred corpse and body of the Saviour lying in the linen shroud."

355 Seals. (v.OE Vol.IV p.13ff) Another informant, Angus Morrison, Suainebost, who was blind, told me (16 November 1887) that the *ron mór* (great seal) has its cub about 10 November, and the cub is cream-coloured. The male great seal is called *cullach,* the female *biast* or *piast.* When the female is bringing forth, the male attends her most assiduously; she strikes him on the head and tries to drive him away, but without effect: he is exultant. The seals used to cub in Sùlasgeir, not in Rona, as this was inhabited.

The seals are people under spells. In the face they resemble people as closely as one herring resembles another. The eye and the gaze of the eye are like the eye and the gaze of a person. There is no doubt that the seals are people under spells.

There are two tribes of seals, a tribe of small seals and a tribe of great seals, the tribe of elves and the tribe of giants. The two tribes do not consort with one another. And more than that, the same region is not the home of both. The small seals keep to the narrows and to the straits and to the sea lochs that indent the land. Hence the small seal is called the strait seal or the loch seal, as well as the elf seal.

The great seal does not come to the sea lochs nor to the little narrow straits nor to the inner islands; not at all. It keeps to the open sea and to the outer islands and to the skerries and bays of the great ocean.

There is a great difference between the two kinds in nature, habit and size. The small seal bears its cub about midsummer; the cub is grey at its birth and has short hard bristles like its mother. The great seal bears its cub about midwinter; the cub is white in colour like a sheep unshorn and has long smooth hair. This colour and hair remain about two months. Then the cub casts this hair and dark-blue and blackish-grey bristles come in its place. *Moineis* or *bainis* is the term applied to a female seal and *briomal* to a male seal.

The Uist people used to kill and eat seals. Seal-meat was accounted wholesome. The people of the west of Uist were called *"na briomail"* or *"na briomalaich"* ("the seals" or "the seal-people"). Those of the east of Uist were called *"na bàghaich"* ("the bay-people") because they dwelt among the bays.

Hoilisgeir is a rock, or rather reef, a mile and a half from land on the coast of South Uist. Within recent memory it summered three sheep, but now the winter waves sweep over the islet and it summers none. It has always been a resort of the great seals, which crowd on it like a flock of sheep. In pairing-time the males fight for the females as do the male deer. These fierce fights are seen and heard from land, the seals' fierce roars resounding like those of wild bulls or lions at bay. In calm weather the seals of Hoilisgeir roar loudly, and when the people hear them they know that a storm is coming and prepare accordingly.

The daughter of the King of the Land of Waves

There was formerly a man in Aird an Runnair in North Uist who was called Red Roderick of the Seals. He was out one night fishing from the rock, and he heard such sweet delightful music as his ear had never heard. The man followed the music and softly and dumbly listened to it, and he was sure that never in the mortal body had he heard the like. He saw the musicians clearly, a fine stately company dancing while one of them played music. They were fairly decked in the silk of Galway and the satin of France.

Over in a rocky cleft he saw a heap of things black and black-grey, speckled and speckled-grey, as they might be the hides of cattle. What was here but the skins of the seals which they had doffed at the dance. The man stood gazing at this play, not knowing under the gentle Mary Mother what it was or whither he would go.

The music ceased. Roderick went across in haste and put a skin under his great cloak and stood to see what would happen next. Each and every seal took a covering and did it on, and they rushed down to the sea one after another as children might be seen dispersing from the schoolhouse, without heed one to another. One maiden stood: the loveliest brown-haired maid on whom eye of man ever gazed in the great world. The maiden's person was comely, straight and shapely as a moorland rush, her skin as white as the snow of one night on the crests of the peaks, her brown entwining hair of the glorious aspect of the sun, and her two eyes warm like two honied dew-drops on the tips of the bushes. The man was thinking to himself that never in the mortal body nor in the thought of night had he seen a blood-drop so fair as the brown-haired maid.

She was wringing her hands and shedding tears, ranging up and down, hither and thither, searching for her garment, for the garment was lost. She saw not a glimpse of it, for it was under the man's great coat.

The woman's beauty fired his heart and softened his breast, and he went over, his bonnet in his hand, and inquired of her what she lacked. She flamed like the sun-beam arising in the summer's dawn, every drop of blood in her body in her bright face.

"I have lost my beautiful garment and have not a shadow of knowledge where it may be."

"Come with myself, dear maiden, and I will give thee a garment in its place."

The brown-haired maid of beauty went home step for step with Red Roderick. He went to the shop and bought a suit for her and the maiden put it on.

"I am," said she, "the daughter of the King of the Land of Waves under spells. My mother died and my father brought home another in her place. My step-mother said that I was in her way and asked the floor-messenger to carry me to the strand and there leave me. The woman did as she was bid and struck my forehead with the magic wand and I fell into a swoon. The first I knew on waking was that a great band of seals was around me arraying me with every finery that is best in the land of the waves. I should have been thus for ever were it not that thou didst greet me in the name of the King of all creatures."

A cleric was found and the maiden was baptized and married without more delay.

She bore three handsome shapely sons to the man, but the seals' nature was in them. After a number of years she said:

"I am going, Roderick. Give me my garment, for I failed to say farewell to the folk of my love and affection at the dancing. They will not carry me away since the blessed water is on my face and forehead. Give thou support to my three sons and rear them in love and tenderness. Thanks to thee for thy kindness, but take care that thou kill no seal all thy days lest thou shouldst kill my mother or my brother or my sister on the skerry. Leave my covering on the beach and hide thyself where they shall not see thee. On this side of the stream, farewell."

The night of the dancing came and the seals danced heartily as of wont in the half-light of the moon. They did not touch her, for the blessed water was on her forehead.

357 The little boy or girl who lost a tooth said: "Little mouse, little mouse, give me a white tooth of gold (or silver) and I will give thee a white tooth of bone." (Or the bargain may be the other way about.) After that the child placed the fallen tooth in a chink of the wall of the house, there to remain until the mouse should replace it with the little tooth of white gold or the little tooth of white silver. And the boy or girl visited the chink many times a day to see if the little mouse had brought the promised tooth.

Similarly when hair was cut, at the waxing of the moon, the child from whom the hair was taken placed a lock of it in the hole of a wall as high as the hand could reach. After that the little owner of the lock was to grow with the growing moon until the little head reached as high as the little hand had reached before. The child went every now and then to measure the head against the hair in the wall. Those hopes! And those disappointments!

The *luch fheoir* (field-mouse) was believed to exert a bad influence. A child who stepped across a field-mouse would stop growing and would remain a dwarf. Hence to a small person of dwarfish form is said: "It is thou who gavest the clumsy leap over the field-mouse;" "It is thou who gavest the mouse-leap," that is, the little leap in growing.

To place the sieve on a child's head had the same effect; hence the sayings, applied as those above: "The sieve was placed upon thine head." "It is thou who gavest the sieve-leap," a small leap in growing.

To count the teeth of a comb will have the same effect, and will cause untimely death. The child's age will not exceed the number of teeth in the comb.

359 From Alexander MacDonald, piper, Loch Aoineart, South Uist.

The following are some examples of the attempts of the people of the Western Isles to reduce the notes of the swan to articulate sounds and visible signs.

The old pipers could play and whistle many imitations of the song of the swan, the long-tailed duck, the lark, the merle and the mavis, and other birds of our western coasts, some of them only visitors, whether of summer or of winter.

I have seen men and women, boys and girls, who could sing and croon and whistle imitations of birds so effectively that the birds themselves stood still and listened, turning their heads this way and that to ascertain whence the sound came, and tentatively, inquiringly, cautiously drawing nearer to it.

362 The people of the Western Isles are greatly dependent upon seaweeds for the manuring of their lands. The soil, being for the most part either peaty or sandy, and containing little lime, mineral salts, etc., is poor and infertile unless constantly refreshed by seaweed, which, though rather poor in quality, is available in large quantity. Seaweed is detached by the action of storms and thrown upon the shores by the prevailing westerly winds. The scarcity of seaweed caused by a prolonged calm period is a serious matter; the people watch and hope and pray for the coming of seaweed, and are anxious at the prospect of impending famine. When the seaweed comes they rejoice and sing hymns of praise to the gracious God of the sea Who has heard their prayers.

The people have a simple, effective way of clearing the ground of large boulders. They kindle a good fire of their best peats on the top of the stone. When the stone is sufficiently heated they pour cold water on it, and the boulder breaks into manageable fragments. If they wish to split the stone in a particular direction, for lintels, corner-stones and the like, they extend the fire in that direction, along the natural cleavage if possible. The stone being heated and the fire swept aside, two parallel banks of plastic boulder-clay are hastily laid along the line of the fire. Into this improvised channel a continuous stream of cold water is poured, when the rock splits, invariably along the required line.

Another method the old people had was to drill short holes at intervals along the given line, generally along the stratum. Into these holes they drove wedges of dry wood, and then left them to the rains. Under moisture the wedges expanded so much that their combined pressure along the whole line was enough to split stratified granite.

In their present depressed condition the people do not practise the old ingenuity of their fathers.

It is worthwhile to record the answer given to the writer by a man conveying *brùchda dubh* (seaweed for manure) from the shore to the *mointeach* (moor). The man stood fully six feet tall. He was leading one horse, while another horse was tied to its tail. Each horse had two creels slung across its back.

"Why do you not have the horses harnessed to carts instead of creels?" said I. "One horse and cart would carry as much as six with creels."

"It is thus we have been since God created the world, and Mary Mother! it is certain that thus we shall be until the world comes to an end — until the day of judgment!"

364 The man or woman, youth or maiden, who goes *a' saodach (saodachadh) a' chruidh,* driving the cows, to the morning pastures, sings a song to the flock as they move leisurely along. The melody is very pleasing to man and evidently to beast. The song commends the cattle to the keeping of Mary the mild, to the keeping of Brigit the fair, and to the keeping of Michael the valiant, whose sword is sharp but whose shield is strong. The song is sung in slow measured cadences charming to hear; and it is interesting to see the measured tread of the older cattle keeping time with the well-known music. The native intelligence of the Highland cattle has often been noticed by strangers.

The person who goes to bring the cattle home probably meets them coming on their way. When they come in sight, the man or woman, youth or maiden, addresses them in a rich variety of endearing terms, and as he draws nearer he strikes up a song of welcome to the cattle, *fàilte a' chruidh,* to which they respond with a low modulated moan, sometimes breaking forth into a bellow. Some cow has hustled her way to the front, and the rest follow her as a leader. The bull always brings up the rear.

Occasionally a young animal during the day separates himself from the herd and remains, after they have gone homeward, grazing in some hidden hollow, oblivious of the approach of night. The herdsman, fearing that the truant may have been caught in a bog or fallen over a rock, searches high and low, near and far. At last coming in sight of him, he addresses him in terms and tones different from those he used to the others. The animal stops grazing and looks up; it is only for a moment: he is off at his hardest, taking the nearest way for home, over a lakelet, across a river, over whatever obstacle may lie in his path. *"Tuigidh an cù a choire féin"* (The dog understands his own fault.)

368 Reciter: Archibald Currie, shoemaker.

370 From Catherine MacNeill, Ceann Tangabhall, Barra.

373 The woman who gave this divided the four teats of the cow according to four different purposes. She said that the milk of each teat possessed qualities peculiar to itself. The milk of one contained more butter, the milk of another more casein, the milk of another more sugar, and the milk of a fourth more fat, than the milk of the other teats.

For each of the four she had a different name. The two front teats together were called *tosdaidh* (fronts), and separately *tosdaidh toisgeil (toisgeal)* and *tosdaidh doisgeil (doisgeal)* or *tuathail* (right and left fronts). The two after–teats she called *tondaidh,* and each separately *tondaidh toisgeil (toisgeal)* and *tondaidh doisgeil (doisgeal)* or *tuathail.*

The four teats were dedicated to four individuals, sometimes four members of the family, sometimes four saints.

378 From Mary MacRae, dairymaid, North End, Harris.

Mary used to sing this croon to the cattle when she would be milking them in the fold or at the shieling.

379 Mary Macneill was known as Màiri Raghaill, Ranald's Mary, or Màiri ni Raghaill, Mary daughter of Ranald. She had been *ceanna–bhanachaig* (head milkmaid), for fifty–five years with the Macneills of Barra. Feeling herself become too frail for her work, she left Eolaigearraidh and went to live in a little bothy by herself. When General Macneill came home from the wars, he asked Màiri ni Raghaill to come and sit at the gateway of the fold, watching the calves go in and out.

"The eye of Mary daughter of Ranald is putting lustre and fatness upon my calves," he was wont to say.

This woman was full of song and story. My informant said: "Scores and scores, hundreds and hundreds of songs of fairies and of the world, lilts of shieling, of cows and of milking had Mary daughter of Ranald. The crossest cow that was ever in MacNeill's fold, Mary could quiet her and make her give milk to calf and to milkmaid. She had a musical voice and a rare way with her."

Almost all the many songs and lullabies that this wonderful woman knew died when she died or when the evicted people of Barra were scattered over northern Canada.

382 Reciter: Kate MacNeill, pauper, Breubhaig, Barra.

The *crannachan,* a kind of churn, is a cylindrical vessel of staves. Its lid is detachable and has a hole in the centre with a cuplike lip. Through this hole passes a staff or plunger with a perforated disc fixed to its lower end. The plunger is called *loinid, simid, ceann–simid, maide maistridh.* The cuplike lip of the hole is designed to intercept any cream that may come up with the plunger in the process of churning.

The *crannachan* supplanted churns of other types. One of these was the *cuinneag* (stoup). This too was circular and built of staves, but it was much wider at the base than at the top. It had no plunger. The cream having been put in, the mouth of the vessel was covered with the dressed skin of lamb, sheep, kid, goat, or calf, and tightly bound with a cord of linen or leather. This covering was called *bùilig, bùilich, bùileach.* The *cuinneag,* thus secured, was placed on a bench, bed, table or other suitable place, and the process of churning consisted in agitating it rapidly to and fro.

The *crannachan* (staff–churn) was felt to be an innovation.

Since lost is the stoup
Not seen is the covering,
New–fangled fashions
Having come to the land,
But standing at a staff–churn
With the length of a sailyard
Of a stick driven hard
Down to its base.

Cuman, crathadair, imideal, simideal, meadar, muidhe, cùdainn, currasan: these were the names of other churns superseded by the *crannachan,* some of them, however, denoting vessels used for various domestic purposes besides churning.

The *imideal* is more properly the skin, otherwise called *bùilig.*

Milking–cogue and cord and covering of skin
Right round the *Lùb* of Teamradal.

The meaning is that these were numerous around the *Lùb* (Bend) of Teamradal, Loch Carron.

383 Reciter: Isabel MacEachainn, cottar, Bunessan, Mull.

384 The circuiting song is sung by the maidens around the waulking frame, the matrons taking no part beyond an occasional lift with the chorus. As the song goes round every maiden present has an opportunity of trying her talent at impromptu verse. In these verses the girls banter one another about their lovers or supposed lovers, their merits and demerits, mental and physical endow–ments, virtues and defects of any kind coming in for special attention. Some of these impromptus are clever and amusing, and some occasionally bitter. The following song was sung by a maiden whose lover was said to have left her for one endowed with more substance.

385 The following lines were composed at the waulking frame by a young woman to her successful rival.

387 From Duncan Cameron, police con–stable, Morven, a man who was full of valuable old lore.

394 Eighteen men of north St Kilda went to Boreray to fetch wethers. They were eighteen weeks storm–stayed in Boreray. There was left at home in St Kilda only one man called Calum (Malcolm). The women of the island were so displeased with Calum that they were making tunes and verses and songs to him, one woman putting him down and another bringing him up, one woman dispraising him and another praising him.

396 St John's wort. See II:165n for the sense of "armpit package."

398 The *brisgein* (root of silverweed) is often mentioned in the old songs and sayings, for it was much in favour among the people.

The blest silverweed of spring,
One of the seven breads of the Gael.

The feeding silverweed,
One of the seven most excellent breads that through the ground.

The root was much used throughout the Highlands and Islands before the potato was introduced. It was cultivated, and so grew to a considerable size. As certain places are noted for the cultivation of the potato, so certain places are remembered for the cul–tivation of silverweed. One of these was Lag nan Tanchasg in Paible, North Uist, where a man could sustain himself on a square of ground of his own length. In dividing com–mon ground, the people lotted their land for *brisgein* much as they lotted their fishing–banks at sea and their fish on shore. The poorer people exchanged *brisgein* with the richer for corn and meal, quantity for quan–tity and quality for quality. The *brisgein* was sometimes boiled in pots, sometimes roasted on stoves, and sometimes dried and ground into meal for bread and porridge. It was considered palatable and nutritious.

399 *Garbhag an t–sléibhe,* fir club–moss, grows wild on the hill; it is of much efficacy in the home and on the journey — you will not go astray if you find it without searching.

400 The ragwort or ragweed was much prized by the old people. They stored it among the corn to keep away mice. *"Lus na Frainge,"* the tansy, was also used for this purpose.

The fairies (some say the *sluagh,* host) sheltered beside the ragwort in stormy nights; and the fairies rode astride the ragwort in voyaging from island to island, from Alba to Erin, from Alba to Manainn, and home again.

In the Outer Isles, for want of better material, the stem of the ragwort was used for making creels. It was also used as a switch for cows, horses and children. The following is the verse addressed by the first wife to the second wife for ill–using the children of the mother in the grave.

401 From Isabel MacEachainn, cottar, Bunessan, Mull.

402 The primrose is mentioned in many of the rimes of the people. It was much relished by children.

405 Isabel MacEachainn said: "A blessed plant is the smooth *monalan.* The Virgin Mary, the Mother, the Queen of the world, the glory of the universe, carried the smooth *monalan* in her bosom for the space of two years, when she went to Egypt with the Child of her body in her arms, Jesus Christ the Son of the living God. Ever since that time the blessed smooth *monalan* is called:

Plant of Mary loved,
Plant of Christ holy.

"Great is the virtue that is in the plants of the ground and in the fruit of the sea, were we but to hold them in esteem and turn them to good use — O King, great indeed! The Being of life never set a thing in the creation of the universe but He set some good within it — He never did. O King, many a good is in the soil of the earth and in the depth of the sea, did we but know to make good use of them — many and many a good, O Thou perfect King of life!"

406 Reciter: Isabel MacEachainn, Bun–eissan, Mull.

The *mòthan* or *mòlus* (pearlwort), is rare, and is found in the moorland and the hill. It has five– or six–pointed leaves and red roots.

It is a *lus beannaichte* (blessed plant), according to some, because it was the first plant on which Christ placed His foot when He came to earth; according to others, because it was the first plant on which he placed His foot after He rose from the dead; and a third reason given is that He lay on it when He was out and away from His enemies.

It was used, and is still to some extent used, for purposes varying according to the district or island. If placed over the *arddoras* (lintel of the door), it prevents the *sluagh* (airy host) from entering the house and from beguiling and spiriting away any of the household. When placed under the right knee of a woman in labour it has a soothing spiritual effect on the woman, ensures her relief, and secures to her and her child immunity from being spirited away by the fairies. When the *mòthan* is so used, the marriage ring and every other ring must be removed from the hand of the woman on the floor–bed, in order that the influence of the plant may not be checked or diverted.

It is used in many districts for a love–philtre. If a girl be kissed by her lover while even a small piece of the *mòthan* is in her mouth, the lover is ever after her adoring slave. Love–sick maidens wet their lips or drink the juice of the *mòthan* to entice the loved one. In this case the plant is placed in *uisge sèimh* (still or silent water), and the juice pressed out of it and then drunk. The person who draws the water must observe silence from the time of setting out to the time of returning from the well, whence the name *uisge sèimh.* It is drawn from a sacred well. In Ardchattan this was Tobar Bhao–dain, St Baodan's Well, close to Team–pall Bhaodain, St Baodan's church, behind the ancient Priory. In Nigg, near the town of Aberdeen, the holy well was Tobar Mhoire, Mary's Well, usually called the Lady's Well. Still or silent water for healing and enticing was taken from this well in recent years and may perhaps still be taken.

A small bag containing the *mòthan* and an iron nail is put under the milk boyne; the virtue of the plant joined to that of the iron avails much. When placed in the fore hooves of the bull when with the cow, the *mòthan* sains the cows milk from having its *toradh* (substance) spirited away, and her calf from mischance and mishap. A cow that ate the pearlwort is sained, and no evil influence can affect her or the calf she carries or the milk she gives or the man, woman or child that drinks the milk.

Two women went to the fold to spirit away the substance (of the milk). One of them went towards a big spreading brown cow beside the hillock on the edge of the fold, chewing her cud and ruminating, but who, my dear, could tell of what she was thinking in her mind? The woman's companion observed her and called to her: "Thou needst not, dame, go near the big spreading brown cow, she has eaten the pearlwort on the moor."

The woman turned on her tracks and approached a big black white–backed cow on a round hillock in the upper part of the fold, chewing her cud, drinking the moon and sucking the breeze. The ill women then did their will with this cow and all the others save the cow that ate the pearlwort, and not an atom of substance did they leave! Oh, not an atom of substance did the ill women leave!

My dear old informant told me this in good faith, and expressed satisfaction that the women's evil design had been in one case thwarted. I suggested that the two wicked women were going to do the false milking. She acknowledged that that might be so, but maintained that in any case the *mòthan* was a blessed plant full of charms and virtues to man and beast, and that it had been blessed by Christ Son of the Mary Mother and by Bride the Foster–mother and by Calum Cille the best beloved of men and the most potent of saints. The narrator and the writer fell into a general discussion about the power of saints, the wickedness of the false milking, the evil spiriting away of substance, and the efficacy of the pearl–wort. Of all these the aged reciter told many stories with the realism, vividness and con–viction of all her kind. It is impossible to realise, without having experienced it, the charm, the power, the fascination of these old–world narrators over an audience. They were able men and women, with a courtesy and a politeness of manner all their own, and full of old–world ways and learning. May peace and blessing be with them for ever!

The *saobh bhleoghan* (false milking), mentioned above was a kind of theft sev–erely punished, first by being buried alive, upstanding, in the gateway of the fold, so that the cows going in and out might trample over the woman's body in contempt; this was modified to the taking off of the right arm from the shoulder, then from the elbow, then from the wrist. In the island of Vallay, North Uist, is a small deep hollow in the ground caused by the sinking of the ground as the body of the upright victim decayed and fell to the bottom of the cylindrical grave.

407 The following version is from the Rev. Dr Kenneth MacLeod, who says: "I do not know the *monalan* plant. Is it the same as the *mòthan?* I have heard many times about the *mòthan* — here is one of them."

410 From Una MacDonald, crofter, Buail Uachdrach, Iochdar, South Uist.

This poem was recited to expel ill–will and to counteract bad report and evil speaking. The man suffering from these went to the *mòd* or court held on the hill or knoll without or in the house within. He had his staff in his grasp and his wit upon his tongue, and looking round defiantly upon those present, he said his rune in the full assurance that it would obtain a hearing and be efficacious.

411 Reciter: Catherine MacNeill, pauper, Breubhaig, Barra.

Thou shalt go fasting early in the morning and thou shalt come to a boundary stream of three branches. Thou shalt bathe thy forehead in the stream:

In name of Father,
In name of Son,
In name of Spirit,
In name of the Three. Amen.

Thou shalt say then this verse.

A woman made this charm when going to a court, knowing that there were enemies ahead and against her. The poor woman raised her head and looked yonder upon the town that was before her where the court was to sit, knowing that there was no one alive in the land of the living upon her side but the loving God of life. The poor unhappy one, oppressed in soul and body, said:

Black is yonder town,
Blacker men therein ;
I am the white swan,
Queen over them.

413 The first Monday of the quarter
On the first Monday of the quarter the household was early astir. They were blessed with water got from a wise woman, or with water got from a woman who had the bridle of the water–horse. That day was a specially good day for checking evil eye, and for drawing lovers to one another, and, alas! for parting.

The first Monday of the quarter was a favourite day for the men and women of the evil eye to practise their *dubh–cheilg* (black guile, black art). This was the day on which the men and women of the *frìth* (augury) cast their visions, and the men and women of the witchcraft spirited away the milk from the cows. It was unsafe to lend on this day, lest the luck of the house should go with the thing lent and never come back.

The first Monday of the quarter,
Take care that luck leave not thy dwelling.
The first Monday of the spring quarter,
Leave not thy kine neglected.

Some men observed this advice so closely that they kept their cattle indoors all day, letting them out for water only at nightfall, lest an evil eye should see them. No eye but the eye of the owner was allowed to see them, *"eagal gun laigheadh sùil orra"* (lest an evil eye should lie on them).

Repelling the evil eye

William Mackenzie, mason, said: "My father was ploughing in the spring when a man came over across the loch seeking oat-seed. The man got what he wanted and went homeward the way he had come, thanking my grandfather for the favour.

"No sooner had the man turned his back on the house and homestead than the mare fell down by the gelding's side in the plough, to all appearance dead on the field. She stretched out her head and her legs in the furrow. My father supposed the mare to be dead, and he ran in to the kiln where my grandfather was shaking grain and winnowing seed.

'It is the eye of Donald, son of John, that has lain on the poor beast,' said my grandfather.

'Son of the big fellow! that was ill done of him after you gave him the oat-seed,' said my father.

'Most likely the poor fellow could not help it,' said my kindly grandfather. 'Go and make the man return, that he may repel the eye.'

"My father ran as fast as his two feet would carry him and called to Donald, son of John, as he was going to the boat with the sack of oat-seed on his back. The man returned with shame and confusion, with disgrace and flushing of cheek, saying that he could not in the least degree help what had befallen the mare.

"Donald, son of John, went three times sunwise around the mare, singing a rune of aiding, and praying the eternal Trinity of power to repel the eye that had lain upon the mare. No sooner had the man uttered the rune than the mare raised her head and set down her legs and put her four hooves under her and stood upon her shanks straight and erect. She shook herself and put her shoulder to the plough and drew the plough in the drill as though there were nothing wrong.

"Donald, son of John, was filled with shame and confusion by what had happened, and said that he could no way help its happening."

Charm for the evil eye

Mary Ross, pauper, Bonar Bridge, said: "To counteract evil eye you will rise early in the morning and go to a boundary stream over which the living and the dead have passed. You will lift a little palmful of water from the lower side of the pathway (bridge),

In the name of Father,
In the name of Son,
In the name of Spirit,
The Triune of power.

"And you will return home upon the track with the little palmful of water in the vessel and you will sprinkle the water, pure, cold, surpassing, upon the backbone of the animal on which the evil eye has rested. And every whit of this you will do

In the eye of God,
In the love of Jesus
In the heed of Spirit,
The Trinity of power.

"And the little drop of water in the vessel you will pour behind the fire-flag. And every whit of this you will do in the eye and in the love of the Trinity above you. And if you do, I will go bound and bonded that your animal will be whole and healthy, and that he will rise on his four feet, and that he will begin to nibble the grass under his feet, without moan in his head or pain in his body, and that he will obtain victory over the wicked woman who put the evil eye on him.

Thy strait be on the fire-flags,
Thine ailment on the wicked woman."

The charm of the threads

The incantation of the threads was made to a sick animal, generally a cattle-beast. The threads were in the form of a cord of three ply and of three colours. The number was symbolic of the Trinity. The colours used were black, symbolic of the condemnation of God; red, symbolic of the crucifixion of Christ; and white, symbolic of the purification of the Spirit.

The cord was applied thrice around the tail of the animal affected and tied in a threefold loop of ingenious construction, resembling the device of the trefoil in masonry. With the first turn, the operator spat upon the cord in the name of God the Father, with the second in the name of Christ, with the third in the name of the Spirit.

In February, 1906, a man from Benbecula came to the island of Grimisey, North Uist, to buy a horse. Passing a crofter's house he saw a beautiful horse, praised it and went on. He was hardly out of sight when the horse became ill, rolling on the ground in evident agony. Knowing that the stranger was reputed to have the evil eye, the owner of the horse hurried to a woman credited with power to counteract the evil. The woman twined with her teeth three threads of three ply and of different colours, and bade him tie these, one after the other, round the root of the horse's tail in name of Father, in name of Son, in name of Spirit, Triune of power. The man did so, and he had barely completed his work when the horse rose, shook himself and began to browse.

The woman said that she inherited the power from her father, a good man of few words and of many prayers. She said that she knew immediately on beginning her prayer whether the illness was due to natural causes or to the evil eye. In the former event, she prescribed natural cures; in the latter, she countered it through prayer. The evil eye of a man was more difficult to counteract than that of a woman, being, though less venomous, more powerful.

She declared that when she emerged from the struggle of counteracting the eye, she was mentally exhausted and had to rest for some days. She added that she felt sure that, were she to cease communing with God, He would immediately withdraw His gift and His countenance from her.

The writer knew the woman well, and can testify that she was a highly excellent woman, beloved and respected throughout a wide district.

There is a saying:

Luthan and *cruthan*
Come from the root of the evil eye.

The following lines were copied by the Rev. Archibald MacDonald, of Kiltarlity, from the Records of the Presbytery of Kintyre and Islay, dated at Kilvorow in Arran, 11th November 1697:

> Milcolm MacIlvoil [Malcolm Macmillan] being called compeired and confessed he practised a charm (with a stringe and some words he spoke within the compasse of the stringe) for the rickets, possession, and any other sudden distemper, which he did practice by putting a lint thread to his breath and repeating the following words within the compasse of it, viz., *Cuirim cumorich Dhia umid sluadh dall harrid do dhion vo gach gabhidh soisgeul Dhia na grais o mullach gu lar umid. Ga ghraichidh na fir hu 7 na millidh na mnaih thu.* [The editor has not been able to verify the quotation.]

The lines may be rendered as follows:

I place the protection of God about thee
Blind folk over thee (?);
Mayest thou be shielded from every peril –
May the Gospel of the God of grace
Be from thy crown to the ground about thee.
May men love thee
And women not work thee harm.

When cattle are sent to pasture or brought from pasture the person in charge of them leaves one or two animals behind to follow. This wards off the evil eye, the stock not being complete before the herdsman.

When a person praises an animal the man in charge of it promptly praises it more warmly. Were a stranger to say: "Beautiful is the broad brown cow that is leading the herd;" the herdsman would reply: "Mary Mother, she is beautiful indeed! There is not a cow in any herd in the country so beautiful as she!"

A little boy at Leitir of Loch Duthaich fell under the power of the evil eye. No one knew what to do in the matter, and the father went to a woman at the head of Loch Carron to have the evil eye counteracted. He took with him a *luideag léine* (rag of a shirt), belonging to the boy. The woman performed the counteraction of the evil eye and told the father that his child was now restored and laughing on his mother's knee. But the woman herself became ill, and very ill, and was on the brink of death, and no one knew what to do or what to say or how to save her. She was ill for a day and a night, and then recovered. She said that she was always ill after performing the counteraction, whether for man or for beast.

414 From Catherine MacNeill, pauper, Breubhaig, Barra.

Man or woman on whom evil eye had fallen, a cure was made for him by saying a rune above him and binding it about the wrist. There was another cure — three mouthfuls of cold water in which a silver coin had lain; the first mouthful was in the name of the Father, the second in the name of the Son, the third in the name of the Spirit.

416 Reciter Kate Cameron, cottar, Kiltarlity, Inverness-shire.

You go with a clay crock till you reach running water over which the living and the dead cross. You must not open your mouth to person nor to animal nor to any created thing from the time you go away till the time you return home. On the lower side of the bridge on which the living and the dead go across, you shall go on your right knee, and you shall lift a palmful of water in the hollows of your hands into the crock saying thus:

I am lifting a little drop of water
  In the holy name of the Father;
I am lifting a little drop of water
  In the holy name of the Son;
I am lifting a little drop of water
  In the holy name of the Spirit.

You shall put a small bedewing of water in the two ears of the person or of the neat whereon the evil eye has lain, and down the spine of the animal on which the illness is, and you shall say:

Shake from thee thy harm,
Shake from thee thy jealousy,
Shake from thee thine illness,
  In name of Father,
  In name of Son
  In name of Holy Spirit.

The rest of the water must be poured on a grey stone or on a fixed rock that fails not. The name of the person or of the animal must be mentioned the while the water is applied.

419 From Dugall MacAulay, Hacleit, Benbecula.

The reciter said: Thou shalt kneel on thy two knees and thou shalt say thy two Credos and thy Pater Noster in the sight of the God Who created thee, in the love of the Christ Who purchased thee, in the heed of the Spirit Who cleansed thee. Thou shalt make a thread, dark-grey (?) or dusky-grey or dun-grey, of the colour of the cadder, and thou shalt say this verse.

420 Reciter: Mary Mathieson, cottar, Malacleit, Uist, aged 69; 17th March 1871.

422 From Mrs Ann Moore, née MacDougall, Thurso.

Mrs Moore was but a young girl when she heard this rime from Mary MacNicoll, Bail Ur, Lismore, who was then an old woman. She was known as *"màthair Dhùghaill Ruaidh,"* mother of Red Dugall, a poor lunatic. Whether or not the moon had in fact aught to do with his disease, it is certain that he was most violent at the full of the moon. He was unusually strong at all times, but when his paroxysms were at their worst he had to be bound with the strongest ropes, for ordinary plough reins he broke like straws. The most fractious child in Lismore became meek at the mere mention of Dùghall Ruadh.

423 Reciter: Isabel MacEachainn, cottar, Bunessan, Mull.

424 From Margaret MacDonald, cottar, Ob, Harris.

The old Highland people maintained that there were twenty-four diseases inherent in man and in beast:

Four and twenty dreg diseases
Inherent in man and in beast.

The people said also that all diseases affecting themselves and their flocks were caused by *fridich bheaga bhideach bhrònach, làn nimhe neamha agus nàimhdeis,* (microbes small, minute, miserable, full of spite, venom and hostility).

How they inherited these diseases the people do not know, but they think it to be probably through their own and their fathers' long continuance in offending God that these family afflictions came about, some families and animals being more afflicted than others.

It was instructive to hear these unlettered men and women talking about *fridich* (microbes), *gridean* (bacteria), *fineagan* (mites), and other animalcules hereditary to man and beast.

The young people who are "educated" do not believe in these *seann rolaistean briagach,* old lying romances, as they call them.

425 Reciter: Ann O Henley, cottar, North Boisdale, South Uist, 24th April 1873.

The reciter was of the famous tribe of "Tochradh Nighean a' Chathanaich," the Dowry of the Daughter of O'Kane, who became the wife of Aonghus Og, Young Angus, son of Aonghus Mór, Big Angus, prince of Innse Gall, the Hebrides, who died in Islay and was buried in Iona in 1326 (Book of Clan Ranald, Reliquiae Celticae, ii.158f).

The dower the lady obtained from her father when she left Ireland was a following of twenty-four gentlemen of good birth, a great acquisition to her lord when men and not sheep or deer were the strength of a chief.

These men included the names of Martin, Mac Cuithein, Steel, O Hianlaidh and others. Some of them were not well liked in the country according to the testimony of old native people.

The reciter said that this charm was good for swelling in the breast of a woman, and in the udder of a cow or mare, sheep or goat. She had cured all these by means of the *eòlas* (charm) many times. The rune had to be repeated three times over the part affected, in the name of the Three Persons of the Holy Trinity.

426 From Duncan MacEachainn, crofter, Staghlaigearraidh, South Uist.

The reciter was a man of much ability and intelligence, of observant eye and retentive memory. He was one of a band of pilgrims from Scotland who went to see the Pope, and he brought home a most informative account of his experiences. He described the person, vesture and jewels of the Pope minutely, but he was more impressed by the Pope's kindliness in speaking to him. Archbishop MacDonald interpreted between the Pope and the Gaelic-speaking crofters, and he reported that the Pope was much impressed by the dignity, good sense, and good feeling of the simple crofter from the Western Isles.

427 Kidney of Mary; *tearna Moire,* saving of Mary. This is a square thick Atlantic nut, sometimes found indented along and across, the indentations forming a natural cross on the nut. It is occasionally mounted in silver and hung around the neck as a talisman. Every nurse has one which she places in the hand of the woman to increase her faith and distract her attention. It was consecrated on the altar and much venerated.

429 From Catherine Maclean, crofter, Naast, Gairloch.

Jesus and His Mother were travelling, and in the passing by they went into a house to rest. Who was dwelling in the cottage but a poor widow and three orphans without pith or power. And the poor widow was suffering hard pain from swelling in the breast, and the breast itself was near bursting with swelling.

Jesus asked His Mother to destroy the microbe in the pap, and to give peace to the breast and health to the woman. But His Mother said to Christ, "Do Thou, O Son, destroy the microbe in the pap. It is Thou Thyself, O Son of tears and of sufferings, Who hast received from the Father in heaven power to perform healing on earth."

There are many things that are crossed (forbidden) and not becoming to do, and it is forbidden to a man to place his hand on a woman's breast. But Christ gave us an example in this matter, as He gave us in many another. Christ blew the warm breath of His mouth on the tortured breast, and He stretched His gentle hand thither over the pap, and He said this verse.

No sooner had the Physician of virtues and of blessings uttered these words of power and of virtue than the microbe died, the swelling subsided, and the woman was whole.

Many a great and good thing Christ did on earth, and especially to poor women who were suffering pain and tribulation and shame, in silence of head and in soreness of heart. Many a one that!

I was living in Moray, and I healed the breast-swelling of ten or twelve women while I was there. The people used to mock me, saying that I had witchcraft. But I had no witchcraft, nor anything in creation except the power that God gave me, the God of life and of the worlds, to Whom I prayed to increase my love, to confirm my earnestness, to bless my words and to strengthen my hands. And God did that; the glory be to Him and not to me!

431 Reciter: Isabel MacEachainn, cottar, Bunessan, Mull.

Sprain is variously called *sguchadh, sguthadh, sgiuchadh, sgochadh, sguch, sguth, sgiuch, sgoch, siachadh, siach*; *sguchadh féithe* (sprain of sinew); *sguchadh lùthaidh* (sprain of joint); *siachadh féithe* (strain of sinew), and *siachadh lùthaidh* (strain of joint).

Eòlas an sguchaidh, the knowledge or charm of the sprain, is the invocation repeated during the rubbing of the injured limb. In this rubbing an extract of St John's wort or some other specific is applied, to moisten and relieve the part. Rubbing and singing proceed together; the rubbing is done soothingly and skilfully, and the hymn is sung tenderly and sympathetically. The hymn is punctuated throughout with something like a snort, or a small emission of breath between the slightly opened teeth.

The man or woman who operates provides himself or herself with a three-plied cord of hard lint, lint being sacred to Christ. This he divides into three parts of equal length. He makes a hard knot on the first part, breathing on it and touching the knot with his lips in the name of God the Father. He makes a second knot, touching it with his lips in the name of God the Son, and a third knot, touching it with his lips in the name of God the Spirit. He then ties the cord round the limb in the name of the Sacred Father, of the Sacred Son, of the Sacred Spirit. So with the second and third parts of the cord. There are thus thrice three knots upon the cord altogether. The cord is called *tolm.*

With some, the cord is passed through the mouth and left in the mouth during the recital of the rune. The knot is drawn in the mouth, the first knot when the operator appeals to God the Father, the second when he appeals to God the Son, the third when he appeals to God the Spirit. With others, the knot is in the mouth while the operator utters the name of the man or woman or animal being treated. One operator used no knots.

This and every other charm is performed in reliance on the power of God, never on the performer's own skill.

Another treatment was described as follows. The sign of the cross is made in soot upon the sprain in name of the Three Who hang on the pot-chain. The soot is left on the foot or on the hand until it gradually disappears.

433 *Grig, grige, grid, gride,* are similar in meaning and denote a mite, a tiny insect or animalcule, a microbe. The old people speak of *grig an neònain* (the microbe of the stye) as they speak of *grig na niosgaid* (the microbe of the boil), *grige lionnrachaid* (the microbe of suppuration), and of various kinds of swellings.

> Ugly microbe, mother of mischief.
>
> Tis smaller than a mite,
> The virulent mother of enmity.

It was interesting and instructive to listen to these unlettered old men and women describing "how the hatching-mother of the *grig* brought up her bad brood, causing gall and venom in the blood and flesh of people ... How the hatching-mother of the *grig* got into the blood and flesh of a person and grew there it was not easy to understand nor easy to explain; but one thing, where there were ill care and ill keeping the hatching, *grig* was there, running from person to person and from house to house like the wont of the ill tale (as ill tidings are wont to do)."

The stye has a variety of names: *neòn, neònan, neònagan*; *leòn, leònad, leònadan, leòna, leònag, leònagan*; *sleòn, sleònan, sleònagan*; *sleamh, sleamhnan, sleamhnagan,* etc.

A certain plant, which the writer has not identified, was called *lus na sùla* or *lus nan sùl,* the plant of the eye or the eyes; the eye was bathed with the essence obtained by bruising the plant.

The method of curing the stye varied from district to district; the most usual method has been described already (see "The counting of the stye," II:154). Another method was to rub a finger–ring round and round the stye while repeating a rime thus:

Stye one, stye without one,
Stye two, stye without two,

and so on up to nine, eighteen or twenty–four, without once stopping or drawing breath. It is certain that styes were cured, but perhaps by the long–continued rubbing rather than by the charm.

Eòlas nan Neòn, the charm of the styes, must be confided by a man to a woman and by a woman to a man.

434 Another method of charming a stye is to twirl a glowing splinter of wood around before the eye, while counting out the *eòlas* without taking breath. The counting is from one to seven, from one seven to two sevens, from two sevens to three sevens, then down from three sevens to two sevens, from two sevens to one seven, and from one seven to one. The performer then threatens the *grig* with the fiery splinter, saying this verse.

436 Cataract, or scale on the eye, is called *gulm, gulman, lann, lannan.* The writer has met several persons on the mainland who possessed knowledge of the cure.

Alexander Urquhart, a tailor near Loch Ewe, Gairloch, said: I place a blade of grass, a piece of gold or a silver coin in a basin of clear cold water fresh from the well. The vessel must not be put on earth nor on stone nor on aught but wood. The grass and the gold or the silver are drawn across the scale on the eye. Then the eyelid is held back with the finger, and the water in the basin is poured into the eye, to clear the sight and to remove the scale. I have cured twelve men and women of the *gulm* in my time; some of them came to me from long distances. I have never accepted payment for relieving a fellow–creature of pain; some men have sent me messages of thanks, and some women have sent me stockings as a gift.

Isabel Chisholm, crofter, Mealabhaig, Gairloch, said: The *gulm* (cataract) grows on the eyeball of a person. It resembles in hue and in form a herring scale. If the cataract is allowed to go forward, it will spread over the eyeball and take away the sight of the eye and the person will be blind.

437 Jesus and His Mother were walking by the side of a river in the Holy Land. And what but it was a gentle autumn evening, the sun about to sink in the depth of the ocean, scattering gold–yellow and gold–red upon the crests of the mountains and upon the surface of the waves. And in the meeting of day and night, what but a white–bellied salmon leaped with a great rush up the rough bed of the stream. Christ noticed that the salmon was wanting the sight of an eye, and He desired the Mary Mother to give the sight of the eye back to the salmon. And the Mary Mother gave the sight of that eye back to the salmon, and the sight of that eye of the salmon was as good as that of the other eye.

At the time of making the Blind Eye, the woman will say the Creed of Mary with the lips of her mouth and with the cords of her heart. And the woman will place the cross of Christ the Son of God upon the blind eye, and she will put a spittle upon the cross of her own palm, and she will place the spittle upon the blind eye in the name of the God of life and in the name of the Christ of love and in the name of the Spirit Holy, Who are guiding her eye and her mind and her tongue when searching the blind eye.

438 This charm was got in November 1905 from Peggy Ross, of over seventy years of age, wife of John Maclean, crofter, Achadh nan Gart, Slios a' Chaolais (Kyle–side), Kincardine, Ross.

The woman got a basin of water, and filled her mouth with water out of a bowl or small basin, saying:

Thou Christ on the cross.

She then put the water back into the basin from her mouth. She then filled her mouth again with water, saying:

I am placing my trust
In the Ring of life.

She then put the water back into the basin. She then drew up a third mouthful, saying (here the person is named, and the right or left eye specified):

That that which is in the ... eye of ... come out therefrom.

The sister of the woman, older than she, was sent out while the ceremony was being performed, as no other woman must be present. The husband and son of the operator were allowed to remain. The sister came in again immediately after, and sat beside the operator while the latter went over the *eòlas* a second time. She went over it several times in order to ensure that I had it rightly noted down.

The woman said that she had removed the *smùirnein* (mote) many many times by this *eòlas* from the eyes of people still living, and also from the eyes of cows and horses. Some of the people were far away, in Edinburgh and Glasgow, while she was in Achadh nan Gart.

She believes in this as firmly as that she must die, and so do the others of the family.

439 From William Maclean, gillie and gamekeeper, Alness, formerly in Boath, near Alness.

Maclean was tall, deep-chested, broad-shouldered and sinewy of frame, a handsome, powerful man in his day, but suffering from rheumatism. He had his big Bible open before him, from which he said he derived much comfort.

He said: There was a man in the place where I was and a small particle of barley awn went into his eye when he was winnowing on the green field outside. The man was suffering sore pain, and I pitied him from my heart. I said to myself: "Who knows but that the Being of life will help me to take the mote from his eye if I perform the Eye Charm that the blessed woman, Mór MacAndrew, taught me when I was young?"

I said the rune, and I prayed the Being of life to bring the mote out of the man's eye. God listened to my voice and He brought the mote from the man's eye, and He placed the mote upon my tongue. I placed the awn that came on to my tongue in the little basin that was in my hand.

That was the first time that I attempted to take it out; but many a time have I done it since.

You drink a mouthful of water from a small basin and pray to the God of life to bring the mote out of the man's eye and to place it on your tongue. You put back the mouthful of water in the little basin in your hand time after time, until you get the mote on your tongue — three times in succession, according to the Three Persons of the Trinity. You draw up the water in name of Father, in name of Son, in name of Spirit, in name of the powerful Holy Trinity, and say: "Donald MacDonald, the fruit of this be thine," — the name of the man for whom you are making the charm.

If one holds the tip of the tongue in the eye of a frog, one will have power to take the mote out of a person's eye with the tip of the tongue.

441 Reciter: Isabel Chisholm.

443 The reciter, Isabel Calder, crofter, Tulloch, Bonar Bridge, Sutherland, says that she got the power of the Eye Charm from her father Finlay Calder.

Her father was famous throughout his district for his occult powers. Without personal contact with the sufferer, he could remove a mote from the eye and stop bleeding; he could also cure chest-contraction. All these cures he performed many times, never unsuccessfully. He always prayed that the mote in the eye might be placed upon his tongue, and this always happened. On one occasion, however, he found that the mote which was removed from the eye to his tongue was an insect. From the disgust this caused him he contracted jaundice. After this he prayed the great God of life to place the mote from the eye upon his hand, instead of upon his tongue, and this always happened. The reciter gave many examples, from her father's experience and from her own, of the removal of the mote by means of occult powers. These mysterious manifestations are beyond the writer's power to explain.

Finlay Calder is spoken of throughout his district as a good man, and as a good Christian of marvellous miracles. He died at the age of seventy-two years. How he exercised such powers no one can explain, but the people of his district explicitly maintain that he did so.

The reciter says that she herself always feels a bitter, disagreeable taste in her mouth after performing the cure.

444 Reciter: Isabel Calder, crofter, Tulloch, Bonar, Creich, Sutherland.

445 This charm is for removing a mote from an eye, whether it be the eye of a person or of an animal. The woman will say the Credo of Mary in her heart, and she will make the cross of Christ on the eye, and the woman will lick the eye with the tongue. And nothing of this will the woman do in her own strength, but altogether in the strength of the living God Who created the eye and established its form.

446 Reciter: Eoghan Maclennan, farmer, Achadh an Tobair, Resolis, Ross.

The "chest seizure" was much dreaded throughout the Highlands and Islands. In the old Statistical Account of Scotland the Rev. Dr Thomas Bisset of Logierait says: There is a disease called *glacach* by the Highlanders, which, as it affects the chest and lungs, is evidently of a consumptive nature. It is also called "the MacDonalds' disease," because there are particular tribes of MacDonalds who are believed to cure it with the charms of their touch and the use of a certain set of words. There must be no fee given of any kind. Their faith in the touch of a MacDonald is very great.

The disease is still called *tinneas, glac* or *glacach nan Domhnallach* or *Chlann Domhnaill,* according to some of my informants, for the reason given by Dr Bisset, according to others, because a certain sept of the MacDonalds were peculiarly liable to it. In Skye the complaint is called *glagach nan Domhnallach.* Other names are *glacach* (*cleacach*), *glac, na glacaich, na glacaichean* (seizure or the seizures); *glacach cléibhe,* etc., (chest seizure or seizures); *caitheamh* (consumption); *iomairt* (struggle), *iomairt cléibhe* (chest struggle); *cuinge cléibhe* or *cuingeach chléibhe, a' chuingleach* or *a' chunglach, cuingealach* or *cuigealach cléibhe* (constriction or chest constriction); *coilleas* or *coillteas, na coilleasaichean* or *na coillteasaichean, calltmas, an corran, cliatha, cliathanan*; *na clisichean cléibhe* (the chest spasms); *an galar toll* (the hollow disease); *cuidichean* or *cuidichean cléibhe.* The charm for counteracting it is called *eòlas nan glacach, eòlas nan lac, eòlas nan glacaichean cléibhe, eòlas na caitheimh, eòlas iomairt cléibhe, eòlas a' chorrain, eòlas a' ghalair tholl,* etc.

In this disease, according to the narrators, the bones of the thorax close together and press upon the heart, lungs and liver, constricting them and reducing their blood supply, and causing consumption and death. To counteract this, a powerful but well controlled massage is applied. The person who operates grasps and clutches and fingers and rubs the patient to and fro, up and down, this way and that, hither and thither.

"He is taking the flesh and the bones and the sinews and the joints asunder, and rubbing oil or butter or cream into the sick person, and driving it through the hardness. All this is a great work, but to do this rightly is work of hands and head and heart — Mary, that is the work indeed! And with that, it is men's hands that can better deal with the chest seizure than the hands of women. Not many women have a grip so hard and so firm and so powerful as a man's grip. Time and again I have seen myself, under the hand of the God of life, winning a person from death from the chest seizure."

The patient's arms are worked in all directions, his knuckles meeting behind his back. His shoulder-blades are pressed and worked to and fro, and every fibre of the upper part of his body is thoroughly roused. The rubbing may be continued for an hour and administered daily or several times daily for a week, two weeks, or more. Girls and women are supposed to be particularly liable to this disease. Children of both sexes who seemed to be threatened by it, or whose physical development was not satisfactory, were made by their parents to perform *cleasa nàdair,* physical drill or remedial exercises of various kinds, such as travelling hand by hand from one couple to another of the barn roof.

The liniments used are various. *Blonag mhuc gun leaghadh* (unmelted hog's lard), *armadh cloimh* and *li armaidh,* oil for smearing wool, drawn seal oil, the oil of the *corra ghritheach* (heron or crane), the oil of deer's horns, *ola dhurn mhart* (neat's-foot oil), strong spirits and *garbh ghucag* (foreshot), are all good.

This does not exhaust the physical treatment. The patient is advised to drink milk warm from the cow; in Tiree they have home-made *crogain chriadh* (clay crocks), into which they milk the cow, and the patient drinks the milk straight from the crock. He is made to eat fat (or tender) meat cut small and fine, to live in the open air, and to keep *ri cùl gaoithe 's ri aghaidh gréine* (at the back of the wind and in the face of the sun). The patient comes to live in the house of the person who works the cure, and remains there until a cure is effected. No charge is ever made for either the treatment or the lodging, these kindly people doing it all, as they say, for the love or Him Whose example they are following.

The *eòlas* is transmitted from man to woman and from woman to man. The person who performs the treatment places his two palms on the floor or ground before beginning. On finishing, he must wash his hands in water, in running water if possible. A man who was in the way of "making the *glacaichean*" had the habit of placing his hands on his hips each time he took them off the patient. He suffered much from this, not knowing why, till one day a *bean shiubhail* (travelling woman) came the way. The woman told him that he should always rinse his hands in cold water, in a running stream. The man did as the woman enjoined, and suffered no more trouble.

Some of the men and women who "do the *glacaichean*" profess to be able to transfer the complaint from one person to another. The mother of William Maclennan, Bog an Dùraidh, was removing the seizure from a man when another man present derided her.

"Will you let me put the seizures on yourself, good man?" said the woman.

"Deed and indeed, I will, and as much as you like of them — as much as ever you can."

"Stretch yourself on the table," said the woman, "and open the breast of your shirt."

The mocker stretched himself on the table and opened his breast from top to bottom. The woman, instead of putting the seizures upon the floor as she was wont, put them on the upper part of the man's breast, until he was calling out and imploring with pain. The original patient sprang up, lithe of limb and ready of tongue, and said: "Here now, sonnie, the carle's hump upon the derider!" The mocker was going about from place to place and from doctor to doctor in search of healing, but no healing could he find. Repentant of heart and apologetic of mien he came to the woman whom he had been reviling, and she relieved him as he asked. After that he had nothing but praise where before he had only scorn and blame.

447 Reciter: Eoghan Maclennan, farmer, Achadh an Tobair, Resolis, Ross.

448 Reciter: Isabel MacEachainn, cottar, Bunessan, Mull.

449 Reciter: Isabel Calder, crofter, Tulloch, Bonar Bridge, Sutherland.

451 From Malcolm Sinclair, cottar, Baile Phuill, Tiree.

453 From John Mackay, crofter, Kinlochewe, Ross.

The aged reciter said: It is the seventh son that heals the king's evil, and none can heal it but he. The healer places his right hand upon the head of the person that is ill, and says this verse.

From Donald Mackay, crofter, Brora, Sutherland:

Neil Sutherland, crofter, Brora, was a seventh son. He was famed for curing the king's evil. Men and women came to him from distant places to be healed. He never sent any person away unhealed or unhappy.

The man would go out in the early morning, without breaking fast or silence, and would go to a well of pure cold water facing the north. And he would go upon his two knees over the well, and lift up a cup of water from the well:

> In name of God,
> In name of Jesus,
> In name of Spirit,
> The Trinity of power.

Then the man would return home and sprinkle the cup of pure cold water on the sore of the sick person:

> In name of Father,
> In name of Son,
> In name of Spirit,
> The laving Three of power.

And the man would command the *grid* (microbe) in the sore to depart and not return again. And the sore of the king's evil would heal, and the *grid* would never more come back.

Neil Sutherland and the stranger would then wash their hands in warm water, and they would break the fast of the night–hours like two kindly friends. There was no fee nor reward passing that way nor this. Neil Sutherland was an upright man, narrow to himself but broad to others.

From Donald Mackay, crofter, Brora, Sutherland.

Neil Sutherland, crofter, Brora, was a seventh son. He was famed for curing the king's evil. Men and women came to him from distant places to be healed. He never sent any person away unhealed or unhappy.

The man would go out in the early morning, without breaking fast or silence, and would go to a well of pure cold water facing the north. And he would go upon his two knees over the well, and lift up a cup of water from the well:

> In name of God,
> In name of Jesus,
> In name of Spirit,
> The Trinity of power.

Then the man would return home and sprinkle the cup of pure cold water on the sore of the sick person:

> In name of Father,
> In name of Son,
> In name of Spirit,
> The laving Three of power.

And the man would command the *grid* (microbe) in the sore to depart and not return again. And the sore of the king's evil would heal, and the *grid* would never more come back.

Neil Sutherland and the stranger would then wash their hands in warm water, and they would break the fast of the night–hours like two kindly friends. There was no fee nor reward passing that way nor this. Neil Sutherland was an upright man, narrow to himself but broad to others.

454 *Màm,* a low rounded swelling hill, is commonly used of various swellings on the body, as *màm sléisne* (swelling in the groin), *màm achlais* (swelling in the armpit), *màm seic, màm sic,* also *maidhm seic* (rupture), *màm amhcha* (swelling in the neck, mumps). The rite of curing the *màm* was common throughout the Highlands and Islands, though differing more or less from place to place.

In the north–western mainland there are many hills called "Màm" with some qualifying term, and the object of the incantation is to transfer to such hills the swelling on the patients body. These hills must be know to the operator himself, and must be places over which the living and the dead have passed.

The operator provides himself with a pin, a needle, or the tongue of a brooch, a block of wood, a basin of clean cold water, and an axe. He makes the sign of the cross on the tablet of his face and on the tablet of his heart, and says the Prayer of the Lord, the Prayer of Mary, and *Eòlas nam Màm,* the incantation of the swellings. He divides the swelling into three imaginary sections, each subdivided into three, making nine in all. This is called *àireamh nam màm* (numbering the swellings). He lays the needle upon each section as he proceeds. He takes the axe and dips its edge into the water in the basin. He swings the axe over his head and aims a blow with all his might at the needle, which is held by an assistant upon the appropriate section of the swelling. At the moment of apparent contact the axe is arrested as if by some unseen power, and it touches the needle only gently. Its edge falls at right angles to the needle, so that a cross is formed. The axe is then diverted to the block of wood on the floor, into which it is driven with force, while *fear bualadh nam màm* (the striker of the swellings) utters the appropriate part of the incantation *"Biodh sin air Màm Ràtagain"* (Be that upon the Màm of Ràtagan). After three successive strokes, on three successive sections of the swelling, the operator intones the names of the Three Persons of the Trinity, and then rests to draw breath. This is therefore done three times, until each of the nine sections has been treated, and nine hills have been named, both the sections and the hills being taken sunwise.

Bualadh nam màm, striking the swellings, is extremely trying to the nerves of the beholder, and still more so to those of the patient, who knows that instant death may follow failure to stay the axe. The nervous system must be considerably affected. It is said that the operation is successful, the swelling subsiding as it proceeds.

The *eòlas* was obtained from Angus Gillies, crofter, A' Mhormhach, Arasaig, on St Michael's Day, 1909, from Flora Maclennan, née Matheson, Dornie, Kintail, and from others. It was also obtained in Mull, where there are twelve hills called "Màm" — Màm Doire Chuilinn, Màm Liorainn, Màm Bhreabadail, Màm an Tiompain, Màm Brathadail, Màm an Lochain, Màm Chlachaig, Màm an t-Snodanaich, Màm na Croise, Màm Thapaill, Màm Dhoire Dhubhaig, Màm Gaoithe.

In the Outer Isles there are no hills called "Màm," and the operation of cure is confined to the use of the needle or other sharp-pointed instrument, as in curing the stye. The instrument was pointed frowningly at the swelling nine times, and after each thrust the operator said:

Thy pang be in the ground,
Thy pain be in the earth.

455 Mary Gordon, aged one hundred and three years, spinster, Crasg Éagais, Beauly, says that she heard these lines from a man in Strath Spey nearly a century ago (6th August 1909).

Casgadh fala (checking of blood) connotes the power of certain persons to stop the escape of blood from man or beast without any sort of manipulation, without personal contact, and even at a distance. Belief in this power is now obsolete in the Isles, but is still common in Caithness and Sutherland and the mainland of Ross and Inverness-shire. The accounts of such cures and the runes now given are but a few of many which the writer gathered in these districts. It was always emphasised that the *eòlas* must be performed with faith and earnestness, by one of upright life and pure heart. Those who perform it are following the example of Christ, as are those who cure mote in the eye, consumption, burst vein, and other ailments. The *eòlas* is without effect on an unbaptized person, nor has it any effect if the performer should take food or drink, even a mouthful of water, without giving thanks. Most of those who perform the *eòlas* use a plant, usually the *cearban-feòir* or *cearbanach* (crowfoot), sometimes some other plant; one informant said that he covered the plant with his bonnet while uttering the rune; but the opinion was expressed that the plant was not an essential part of the cure. Like the other occult powers, this power is transmitted from man to woman and from woman to man, with few exceptions. A narrator in Inverness-shire was under a promise to transmit the power to none but his daughter; she, however, refused to have it. He himself had learned it from a woman long ago; the woman told it to a *fòd mòna* (clod of peat) upon her floor, and he took up the *eòlas* as she sang it through, a long and obscure rune. Some of the runes are prefaced by the Lord's Prayer, others by the Apostles' Creed.

The writer overtook a man on the highroad from Strath Carron to Ardgay, Ross. The man seemed to be a crofter. He was well clad, well mannered and well informed, but I omitted to ask his name. He said: A man mending horse-harness drove the needle right through the palm of his hand. A woman present withdrew the needle. The blood spurted out against the opposite wall of the room. The woman pointed the needle towards the floor of the room, saying:

In name of the King of life,
In name of the Christ of love,
In name of the Spirit Holy,
The Trinity of each helpless one.

Be thy bane within the ground,
Be thy pain within the hill!
Wholeness be to the wound,
Rest be to the hurt!

The woman had hardly uttered these words, with evident earnestness, when the bleeding suddenly stopped. All present were awe-stricken. The scene was striking and solemn. I immediately remembered the words of Christ: "Whatsoever ye shall ask in My name, that will I do;" and again: "If ye have faith as a grain of mustard seed."

[First name not given] Ross, Altas, Sutherland, said: I saw my father perform blood-checking for a man on the other side of the water (the Kyle of Sutherland). The man had been threshing and the flail had struck him on the nose. The nose began to pour blood, and the men completely failed to stop the blood. The man's sons came across the water at imminent peril of drowning, in the height of a storm and in the middle of the night. My father said: "I cannot stop the blood until daylight comes and I can see the plant — the night is as black as pitch."

"I will light the lantern, father, and go out with you."

"You are right, daughter," said my father, and he rose from his bed, though he was aged. My father and I went out to the garden in the teeth of the storm, and my father plucked the crowfoot in the name of the Three Persons of the Trinity, and we went inside again. My father went on his two knees and prayed earnestly to the God of life to grant him his prayer and to stop the blood. When he got up he said to the man's sons: "The blood has stopped and your father is well."

The lads departed. I went across on the morrow, and the man was asleep and the blood had stopped.

Mrs Mackenzie, Bail Eoghain, Kiltearn, Ross, said: When a girl of twelve or fourteen I was subject to profuse bleeding at the nose. Hitherto my mother had been able to control this bleeding, but on this occasion she failed, and I was thought to be bleeding to death. My mother hurried me away to the house of Alexander Maclennan. When we entered the house Mr Maclennan asked my name. He offered up a short rhythmical prayer, and suddenly the blood stopped. There was no personal contact — Mr Maclennan was on the other side of the room. Mr Maclennan was a highly excellent man and well known through the district for his power of stopping blood. I have seen many wonderful things done in London hospitals by skill and science; but this was a miracle obtained through prayer.

John Cameron, aged 76, shoemaker, Alness, Ross, said (27th November 1905): I got the *eòlas,* knowledge of how to cure, from Hector Munro, the horse-doctor here. I wished to have it in order to do good to my fellow-men. Many times in my long life I have stopped bleeding in men and women, boys and girls.

One fast-day a man came running up from the distillery crying: "John Hall's son's arm has been torn off at the elbow. He is ebbing of blood, and I have been sent up to ask you to be so good as to check the blood."

I performed the charm on the spot, and told the man to go back and see whether the blood had stopped. He went, and returned, and told me that the blood had stopped. Then I went down, and we put lint on the arm, and the arm healed.

The same man said: John Stewart was bleeding to death, and a man came to ask me to stop the bleeding. I ran for the doctor. The doctor came and treated the man, but without effect — the blood came pouring out as before. The doctor then said to me: "I can do no more, Cameron, stop you the blood." But I said: "Neither you nor I can save him, for he is ebbed of blood." The man died almost at once.

John Cameron described his *eòlas* thus: I lift a little water in a small basin, and say slowly and solemnly:

In name of God,
In name of Jesus,
In name of Spirit,
Triune of power.

I make the charm, and say:

I am checking the blood
Of Donald Munro, Alness
In name of the Father,
In name of the Son,
In name of the Spirit.

A man must live near to his God before he can stop bleeding; without that he does not receive the power.

Nurse A.B., in the house of Thomas Ross, Rosehall, Sutherland, 14th November 1908, said: The case (one of childbirth) was tedious and difficult. I could do nothing by myself — I was waiting for the doctor, and very anxious the while. The patient's mother filled a small basin with water, and into this water she put a number of rings and brooches of gold and silver, which she stirred about in the basin. She then held the basin to her dying daughter's lips, and made her drink three mouthfuls of the water, each mouthful in the name of Father, of Son, and of Spirit, the Three Persons of the Holy Trinity *(Tri Pearsa na Trianaid chaoimh chumhachdaich)*. Soon after that the child came. Then the doctor came, and soon all was well. But the child was born before the arrival of the doctor, and the birth was as gentle and as easy as any I have ever seen. How the trinkets in the water could affect the case I do not pretend to know, but that some occult power was at work in the whole matter I am certain. I had often heard about the rings, brooches, pins and other jewels of that sort, but never before or since did I see them save in that case, and that case itself caused me wonder and in plenty.

This nurse was an active capable woman with a good professional reputation in her district. [It is to be understood that the trouble was haemorrhage.]

456 Anna Nic Aonghuis, Ann MacFinish, crofter, Auchterneed, Strathpeffer, learned this *eòlas* from her father, Alexander, who was known far and wide for his power to stop bleeding in men and women, cattle and horses.

457 From Duncan MacEachainn, farmer, Staghlaigearraidh, South Uist.

The reciter said: This charm is for a cow that went to the hill and ate too much grass and moorgrass without digesting it. Then the cow would swell, and would die unless she were relieved. That is the *tairbhein,* and this is the charm.

An tairbhein, an tarbhan, was the name applied to the condition of a cow or other cattle–beast which was swollen by a surfeit of undigested food. One reciter said that it was like the *greim mionaich* (colic) in man or woman, but was peculiar to *ni* (cattle). Another said that it was akin to *teas broilein* (heat in the manyplies). A reciter said that Mary Mackenzie, Badfearn, Aultbea, Ross, cured a badly swollen stirk, the property of the reciter's father. She walked thrice *deiseil* (sunwise) around the beast, reciting a rune in name of "Dia nan dùl," the God of life, "Criosd caomh," beloved Christ, and the Spirit of laving — one Person in the course of each of the three circuits.

458 From Isabel MacEachainn, cottar, Bunessan, Mull.

The reciter was learned in folklore, traditional songs and hymns, charms and incantations, and stories and traditions of her native island. At first she was reticent, but by degrees reciter and writer became friends. At parting she said that when I came again she would give me all the lore she had, which she admitted would take me many days to write down. A few weeks thereafter Isabel MacEachainn died, and with her died volumes of valuable tradition and folklore.

Isabel MacEachainn said that a widow woman at Tabal, Mull, had a cow ill with the *tarbhan* (swelling from surfeit), and she was wringing her hands and beating her breast to see her beloved cow in pain. At that moment she saw Calum Cille, Columba, and his twelve disciples in their *curachan* (little boat or coracle), rowing home to Iona. The widow ran down to the *rudha* (point), and hailed Calum Cille, and asked him to heal her cow. Calum Cille never turned a dull ear to the poor, to the penitent, to the distressed, and he came ashore and made the *òra* to the white cow, and the white cow rose upon her feet and shook herself and began to browse upon the green grass before her.

"Go thou home, *brònag,* and have faith in the God who made thee and in Christ the Saviour who loved thee and died for thee, and in thine own self, and all will go well with thee and with thy cow."

Having said this, Calum Cille rejoined his followers in the *curach* and resumed his journey to Hi.

"There was no one like Calum Cille, no

one, my dear. He was big and handsome and eloquent, haughty to the over-haughty and humble to the humble, kind, kind to the weak and the wounded."

460 From Roderick MacLeod, shepherd, Cul na Creige, Coigeach, Ross. 18th August 1908.

Roderick MacLeod said: Columba had power to heal men and cattle and horses and goats. There was no healer in Scotland nor in Ireland nor in any part of the world who could excel or surpass his hand. A godly and a great man was Columba, and his fame was known far and wide throughout the world. He walked in the way of God and of Christ each step that he took, each place he was in. An outstanding soldier like David.

462 Reciter: Mary Murchison, crofter, Diùirinis, Loch Alsh; 20th September 1909.

463 Reciter: Catherine Maclean, crofter, Naast, Gairloch.

464 Reciter: John Sinclair, Thurso, Caithness.

465 From Alexander Cameron, the Bard of Turnaig, Gairloch; 13th September 1909.

Mr Cameron wrote twenty years after this (26th July 1929): The *fiollan fionn* was a small worm which moved between the flesh and the skin, and caused great pain. It was sometimes to be seen moving under the skin. A man told me that he had taken the beast out of his thigh with a knife. That was the *fiollan fionn*. This man was an elder in the Free Church, but he is dead these three and twenty years. I myself never saw the charm practised, but I have heard that others believed strongly in it.

The way was to pluck three little blades of grass in the name of the Holy Trinity, and to put them in a bottle, and to pour a good big wave of water over them and to shake the crock. This was poured on the painful part, and these words were said.

466 From Mary Macmillan, crofter, Lianacuidh, Iochdar, South Uist, 1872.

468 The following charm is for the cure of spaul, usually called black spaul, in cattle.

469 From Mary MacDonald, crofter, Tosgaig, Applecross, Ross.

Craicneadh (hide-binding) is a disease of cattle, chiefly of cows. The complaint is variously known as *tart* (dryness); *tart broilein* (dryness of the manyplies); *craicneadh* (the state of being skin-bound or hide-bound, shrivelling); hence an animal suffering from the disease is called *craicneach, cracnach,* from *craiceann* (skin or hide).

To counteract the complaint a decoction of a certain plant is given to the animal. Should this fail, the animal's back is scarified till blood comes. The instruments used in scarifying are the teasel, the comb, the card and the cat — the cat being drawn by the tail. All these are drawn against the hair of the animal, which is tied by the head to a stake, and maddened by the pain lunges frantically with head, horn and hoof.

471 Reciter: John Pearson, cottar, Ceann Tangabhall, Barra, 2nd June 1870.

This lullaby, though recorded in Barra, seems from its reference to Blàthbheinn to belong to Skye. Like most Gaelic lullabies, it is difficult to render intelligibly into English. The child is described as *"Ailpeineach ciar"* (a dusky son of Alpin), and in view of this and of the mention of Blàthbheinn, he was most probably a son of Mackinnon of Strath. These Mackinnons are elsewhere termed "Ailpeinich," and one of them is addressed *"a mharbhtháir bhric Bhláithbheinne"* (thou freckled slayer of Blàthbheinn) in the Gaelic MS. lii.33b in the National Library of Scotland. The term "Ailpeineach" is applied also to the MacAlpines, the MacGregors, the Grants, the Macnabs, the MacAulays of Ardincaple, and the MacQuarries, all of which clans and septs claimed descent from Kenneth MacAlpine.

The final word of the refrain, "thou," is strongly stressed.

472 From John Morrison, Rucaidh, North Uist.

"Mac Shiamain" means "son of straw-rope," from *siaman,* a cord or rope, particularly one of straw, grass, etc., here taken as a thing often useful to a tidy man. The name is made up to hint at the character of the person: Mac Shiamain is the good husbandman, diligent and God–fearing (cf. iii.24f).

It seems doubtful whether the second verse properly belongs to the poem.

474 The subject of this poem is variously known as "Fionnghal nam Fiadh," Flora of the Deer; "Sorch an Or–fhuilt," Clara of the Golden Hair; "Binneach nam Beann," the Melodious One (or the Crazed One) of the Mountains; and by other names. I have taken down several versions, in South Uist and elsewhere.

The girl was young and beautiful, *"nighean dhuin uasail,"* the daughter of a gentleman, but poor. She had many who admired her, but she gave the love of her heart and the devotion of her being to one alone. The mother of this young man, however, interfered, and pressed her son to marry another, a girl of wealth. In urging this upon him his mother said:

Son, gentility is a heavy burden
On the land where the kine are not.

To this the son answered:

Mother, where the cattle are got
Good manners are not got with the wife.

Many–tongued rumour said that in deference to his mother the young man was going to marry her choice. Whether he had wavered or had only appeared to waver, the proud sensitive girl resented the implied slight. She lost her reason and became wildly insane. She was bound with cords and secured in the *cùlaist* (back–house), but broke the cords, tore off her clothing, and escaping through the window fled to the hills.

It is said that all creatures except man are partial to the insane and weak–minded. The maiden of the golden hair joined the deer in the mountains, travelling with them during the day and sleeping with them at night. She became almost as fleet of foot as the deer themselves; the people of the country were pursuing her, but in vain. If at any time she seemed to tire or falter, the deer looked round and wistfully gazing at her awaited her coming.

The golden hair of the girl grew so long that it covered her person like a mantle, while thick soft hair grew over her body like the soft fur of the spotted fawn, or like the soft fur of the white cub of the seal, and thus nature, ever compassionate, enabled her to withstand the summer heat and winter cold. With what food she sustained herself is not known, but it was supposed that she lived on berries and nuts in their season and possibly on hind's milk.

By degrees all the people in pursuit of the girl retired except her lover. He said he would go to *frith nam fiadh,* the forest of the deer, alone, but not alone return. After many days of wandering and many nights of sleeplessness the young man returned to his *sgairte falaich* (hiding–cleft) among the rocks; and there he found his golden–haired guest lying sound asleep, "white angels guarding her, my dear." Covering the beautiful form with the soft plaid warm from his own body, the young man waited and watched. When the girl opened her blue eyes and saw her lover, she addressed him by name and thanked him for his many kindnesses to her, not least the last.

"I am now going to die, Iain," she said, "and you will take me down to the townland and to the home of our childhood, and lay me to sleep beside my mother and among the dust of the kindred." And having sung this song for the ear of her lover she died in his arms.

And the young man put all the strength of his nature and all the energy of his manhood into himself and carried the girl's body to the homestead of the glen. After giving the poem to others the young man laid himself down and died beside the maiden. The two were buried side by side in the burial–place of the green glen of their fathers, at the foot of the blue hills of the red hen, the dun deer, the brown eagle and the white ptarmigan, and beside the clear stream of the silvery salmon that runs wailing and laughing and leaping day and night towards the heaving, mourning, everlasting sea. And from their two graves two weeping willows grew and twined round one another, stem and branch and bough. And the dusky merle and the mottled mavis sang their morning elegies and their noonday coronachs and their evening lullabies.

475 The following poem was taken down at Baile Mhic Nill, Barra, in June 1901.

Baile Mhic Nill, "MacNeill's town," is the native name of the place also called Bàgh a' Chaisteil by the natives, and rendered "Castle–bay" by strangers. The reciter of the poem was Isabella MacDonald, wife of Alexander MacDonald, tinker. The woman was a Stewart from Lewis, her husband from Assynt.

Some ten or twelve days after Alexander MacDonald and his wife and family came to Baile Mhic Nill, James MacDonald, brother to Alexander, arrived with his wife and family. The meeting of the two brothers and of their two families was cordial and touching in the extreme. James MacDonald set up his tent close to that of Alexander, on the bare bleak rocky hillock, exposed to all the winds that blew. Both tents were torn and tattered, ill adapted to shelter the inmates from the wind and rain, hail and snow coming in from the cold Atlantic. The inmates themselves were no whit better, being extremely ill clad, as well as ill kempt and ill washed. Notwithstanding all this, the tinkers themselves, men and women were tall and handsome, well–featured and lithe of limb, and their children ruddy and healthy. As my wife remarked at the time, the contrast in condition between the ragged tents and clothing and the handsome healthy look of the people was striking; and the manners of the people were in full keeping with the best of their appearance. When I placed a *duais* in the woman's hand, she at once stood straight up and with dignity and firmness declined it, saying that it would take away the pleasure she had had in giving her old songs to the *duin uasal.* I urged that I should feel shy of coming again if she did not accept it, but she and her husband, *am beul a chéile,* in one another's mouth, said that I was welcome to come if I proffered nothing.

This has been my invariable experience of these wandering tribes of the weary feet and moving homes, driven hither and thither, from post to pillar, by county authorities and landed proprietors. A little more thought for their needs, a little more consideration for their inherited idiosyncrasies, would lead to fewer crimes, real or imaginary, laid to the charge of tinkers. I have seen many tinkers and observed their ways; I have taken down thousands of their Shelta words, hundreds of their stories and scores of their songs, and I have found them always well mannered and well behaved, much preferable to the residuum of towns, fit to compare, mentally, morally and physically, with any class of the community. Nor have I ever heard of a farmer regretting consideration shown to them.

The reciter said that the poem was composed at Garbhath Mór, in Badenoch. The composer had been confined, and lay on the *leaba làir* (floor–bed). Her husband had brought home a lamb from the hill to offer sacrifice for the safe delivery of his wife. Having tied the lamb's feet he placed its neck upon a block and struck off its head with an axe and placed the lamb upon a fire on the knoll.

There were two boys in the house who keenly watched the proceedings. In imitation of their father, the elder boy placed the neck of the younger upon a block on the floor near their mother. The mother watched the boys with anxiety, but was too weak to move and too afraid to cry out, until she saw the elder boy raise the axe to his shoulder as the father had done.

She sprang from the bed, diverted the blow, but diverted it from the neck of the boy upon the block to the neck of the infant in her arms. When she saw what had occurred, her reason fled; she sprang to her feet and with lightning speed flew to the hills and joined the deer. There she grew as fleet of foot, as sharp of sight, as keen of scent and as wild of nature as the wild deer themselves.

Many efforts were made to capture the woman, but they availed nothing and were at last discontinued. When the deer came down from the heights above to the straths below, the woman was in their midst, feeding wherever they fed and moving wherever they moved. When the crofters sent their dogs to drive the deer from their corn, the woman was the first to see and to hear, the first to flee and to lead the way up the steep corries, over the deep chasms and along the narrow devious passes to the mountain summits beyond, never slipping, never tripping, never hesitating however great the speed, however difficult the way. The mother of the insane woman was persistent in hounding the deer with the dogs and in driving them from the straths to the mountains. For whenever she saw the deer and her daughter in their midst, she became possessed and acted accordingly.

By the law of the times it was permissible for the insane woman's husband to marry again after seven years. The man was going to avail himself of this law. The day and hour of his marriage arrived, the people were in their places, and the ceremony was about to begin, when the man's wife appeared in their midst and took her place beside her husband. All was surprise and confusion, no one knowing what to do or say. The *pears-eaglais* (cleric) who was to perform the marriage, examined the woman, and finding her sane and sensible, dispersed the people.

The woman was well clothed and wisely spoken, but where she had obtained her clothing, not to mention her reason, no one understood. She was covered with fine fur or soft down, "like the cub of the grey seal of the ocean or the fawn of the red hind of the mountains."

The poem is unequal in rhythm and irregular in measure, evidently incomplete, and difficult to translate. Although composed inland, it contains many island phrases, probably because island reciters have substituted known words for those which they did not understand. I have often found a reciter replacing an unknown word or phrase in this way.

476 The following poem was taken down by John Macnab, student of divinity, Glen Orchy, from Pàra Mór Domhnallach, Big Peter MacDonald of Glen Coe.

The night after the massacre of Glen Coe officers and soldiers were out searching the hills and dales for any stray fugitives who might have escaped the massacre. Hearing the sound of the pipes, they followed it, thinking that this might be some MacDonald guiding his friends to safety. Eager to wreak their vengeance on the clan they hated, they followed the piping through mud and mire, swamp and stream, snow wreath and rock cleft, till they reached a distant tarn among the high mountains. Here the music sank down in the depths of the tarn and died softly away as dies the eerie sough of the western wind.

The people maintain that the piper was one of the good fairies of the mound.

Beaten and battered by the storm, with baffled rage in their hearts and curses on their lips, the soldiers returned. They heard upon the wind the screaming of a child. The officer in command called out to the nearest soldier: "Go and put a twist in the neck of that brat."

As the man neared the place from which the screams were coming, he heard the one most beautiful music that ever ear heard, music more beautiful than the lip of the fairy women in the knoll. Who was this but a young mother who had escaped the massacre, lulling her child to sleep the sleep of death amid the snow?

The soldier remembered her whom he had left at home beside the fire with a little beautiful beloved babe upon her breast, singing a quiet croon of sleep to him, and the blood of Clan Donald in the veins of both. And it chanced that the gentle croon of music that the child's mother was singing in the snow was the very same music as he had last heard when he left his kin and his home many a day and year before that. The soldier wrapped the woman and her child in his plaid, gave them what food and drink he had, and left them to overtake his comrades. On the way he came upon a wolf devouring the body of a woman who had escaped alive from the scene of the massacre. He slew the wolf and showed the officer the blood upon his sword. By the mercy of God and through the soldier's compassion mother and child survived. Descendants of the child are still living, and the tradition is current and believed throughout the districts of Appin and Lochaber.

478 Reciter: The wife of Angus son of Lachlann, Acha-Da-Dheardail, Eigg, whose mother had been a servant at Gruilinn with Raghall Dubh, Black Ranald, who was a son of the poet Alexander MacDonald and published a famous anthology of Gaelic poetry in 1776. When Raghall Dubh heard the song, he said: "It is a pity I had not heard it before I published the book."

479 Reciters: Archibald Maclellan, master-mariner, Loch Boisdale, South Uist; John Pearson and Catherine Pearson, cottars, Ceann Tangabhall, Barra, 14th March 1873; and others in Kintail in 1903.

480 This *piobaireachd* (pipe–tune) is composed upon a cattle–raid by the Cats, but it is not said upon whom the raid was made. The Cats may have been either members of the Clann Chatain or members of the Cat tribe whose name is preserved in the English name Caithness and in the Gaelic names "Cataibh," Sutherland, and "Cataich," men of Sutherland. The Earl of Sutherland was styled "Morair Chat," Lord of the Cat–folk; the Duke of Sutherland is "Diùc Chat," Duke of the Cat–folk.

481 Reciter: Flora Maclennan, Dornie, Kintail.

482 "In the holy wells of the Isles there lived, through generations, a trout which in the thoughts of the folk was accounted pious as a monk and worldly–wise as a druid. To such a trout went the maid of the song for tidings of her absent lover." (Kenneth Mac–Leod, *The Road to the Isles,* p.200). The poem is charming in the original, but though it embodies an old idea it cannot itself be old.

VOLUME V

483 From Marion MacNeil (Marion daughter of Alexander son of Fair Roderick), cottar, Ceann Tangabhal, Barra, 8th March 1869. Cf. J.L. Campbell *Gaelic Folksongs from the Isle of Barra,* 36, 53–4; *Eilean Fraoich,* 65. Mr Campbell has an unpublished version from the Donald MacCormick Collection (South Uist, 1893), entitled *Craobh an Iubhair*.

484 It was his sweetheart who made this song to Mackay of the Rinns in Islay.

485 From — Cameron, crofter, Leideag, Barra, July 1902.

The song refers to the rooting out of the Macvicars in North Uist by Uisdean mac Gille–easbuig Chléirich (Hugh MacDonald, grandson of Donald Gruamach, 4th of Sleat). Donald, Am Piocair Mór, and his youngest son John (Iain Donn) held Baleshare and Eaval. Angus (Aonghus Mhannta) had Baleloch, Balemartine and Balelone. Donald (Domhnall Odhar) had Carinish and Cladach Carinish. Hector (Eachann) had Kyles Bernera, Baile Mhic Phàil and Baile Mhic Conain. His window helped with the capture of Uisdean. Mór and Màiri were probably daughters of Am Piocair Mór. See *Clan Donald,* iii.30–48. The song was composed by a third daughter, name unknown. Earlier reference than *Clan Donald* is Cameron, *History and Traditions of the Isle of Skye,* 53–55.

486 From the manuscript of the Rev. Angus Macphail, a native of Barvas, Lewis, and Free Church minister of Kilmartin, Argyll. The poem was written down from the recitation of an old man in Lewis.

The subject of this song appears to have been Iain Og mac Sheumais, son of James MacDonald of Castle Camus. His son was the famous warrior Domhnall mac Iain 'ic Sheumais, ancestor of the MacDonalds of Kingsburgh. Iain Og mac Sheumais was killed in Mull in 1585. It would appear from the song that his mother was of the MacLeods of Lewis. See *Collectanea de Rebus Albanicis,* 11; R.C. MacLeod, *MacLeods of Dunvegan,* 85; Mackenzie, *History of the MacLeods,* 25; *Clan Donald,* iii.231, 469, 499.

487 From Marion daughter of Alexander MacNeil (Alexander son of Fair Roderick), Ceann Tangabhal, Barra, 2nd December 1870.

The reciter said: "It was his foster–mother who composed this song to Young John, son of MacNeil of Barra. John Og son of MacNeil was pursued, and he was caught landing from a fishing skiff, and he was carried away prisoner to Glasgow. The death they inflicted on him was to put him in a barrel, and to let the barrel roll down the mountainside, either in Edinburgh or in England. There were spikes thrust through the barrel, and when the barrel reached the foot of the mountain John Og son of MacNeil was dead."

Cf. W.C. Mackenzie, *The Western Isles,* 180. This is no doubt John Og MacNeil of Barra who was taken prisoner to Glasgow in

1610 and then transferred to the Tolbooth of Edinburgh, where he died (*The Clan MacNeil,* 67–9; *Miscellany of Maitland Club,* iii.30).

488 From Mary Macrae, dairywoman, Harris. Cf. Craig, *Orain Luaidh,* 96; K.N. MacDonald's *Puirt-a-Beul,* 46; *Gesto Collection,* App. 22; *An Gàidheal,* March 1951, 22. There is a version in the Maclagan MSS, printed in *The Highland Monthly,* i.211, which ascribed it to "Bean Mhic Mhàrtuinn na Leitireach," that is, the wife of MacMartin of Letterfinlay in Lochaber (Maclagan MSS., nos. 129 and 117).

489 From the wife of Donald Macintosh, tailor, South Boisdale, South Uist.

490 From Mary Boyd, crofter, Glen, Barra.

491 The daughter of Donald son of Cathan Mac Mhuirich of Stadhlaigearraidh composed this song to Duncan Mac Cuilcein. Duncan Mac Cuilcein built the first mill in Uist. In order to get water for the mill he closed the outflow of the lochs; and the water of these rose, and the lochs spread out at either end, this way and that, everywhere, until every place was covered and submerged around Hogh Mór.

492 From Mary Macmillan, crofter, Lianacuidh, Iochdar, South Uist.

493 The following was the first song to be sung at the waulking in Coll.

494 The song was composed by a maiden of St Kilda, who had been carried away and married in Lewis. She was not happy in Lewis, and yearned for her native home and her St Kilda lover.

495 There were two sisters and one brother in a family in Barra. The brother went over to Ireland. One of the sisters died, and her spirit came back to tell the living sister that their brother had died In Ireland.

Cf. Frances Tolmie's Collection (*Journal of the Folk-Song Society,* Vol. iv), No.21; two versions contributed by Rev. John Macrury to *Trans. Gael. Soc. Invss.,* xvi.105; Air in Patrick MacDonald's Collection, No.1. See also Amy Murray, *Father Allan's Island,* 124, and J. Gregorson Campbell, *Witchcraft and Second Sight in the Scottish Highlands,* 179.

496 Variants on the theme of verse 495.

497 This song was obtained from a number of singers: from Mór MacNeil (daughter of Alexander son of fair-haired Roderick), cottar, Ceann Tangabhal, Barra; from Mary MacDonald and Mary the wife of Angus Campbell, cottars in Mingulay, Barra, on Saturday 22nd May 1869; from Mary Ferguson, Carinish, North Uist, a poor miserable woman but full of music and old lore, on 29th May 1869; from Mary Boyd, Glen, Barra; from Mary Macrae, crofter, Dunan, Letterfearn, Glen Shiel, on 22nd August 1903; from Mary Henderson, Morvern (sister of the great Ann); from Jessie Matheson (Mrs Cameron), nurse, Oban, a native of Kilmuir; from a *"cailleach Chnoideartach,"* old woman from Knoydart, whose name is not recorded, High Street, Oban; and from Janet MacLeod, the Schoolhouse, Island of Eigg, January 1905. It is Janet MacLeod's song that is printed first below, with variants of other versions in the margin.

Mór MacNeil said: This lament was composed by his wife for Seathan son of the King of Ireland. Seathan was a great marauder, killing and plundering in every quarter as he best got the chance. He was an outlaw and fugitive and his wife hid him in hope of sending his pursuers past and saving his life for herself.

Mary MacDonald and Mary wife of Angus Campbell. These two women sang the lament together and separately — in the latter case one sang the refrain and the other the lament. Both sang the whole of the refrain at the end of each line. One of them was carding and one of them spinning, and each had a strong sweet voice and right well could they sing.

Mary Macrae sang the song as though at the waulking frame, and sang it finely, and it was a pleasure to one to listen to her.

Mary Ferguson who heard this from an old man who was in Baile Sear (Baleshare), and the old man heard the lament in a fairy bower inside a heather–clad hill: The man was one day pulling heather for ropes out in the hill. The day was warm and sultry. And the man heard the most beautiful melody that he had ever heard with his two ears. He sat down in the shadow of the hill away from the warm rays of the sun and listened carefully to the melody. When the man came home in the evening with a load of rope–heather on his back, he related word for word what he had heard without changing a syllable. The man sang the song as he had heard it from the fairy in the fairy dwelling. The folk of the townland came out to listen to him, and by the Book it was worth that.

The man's name was John son of Angus MacAulay in Baile Sear. It was at the Black Hill of the River of the Fishing that the man was pulling the heather when he heard the music. The Black Hill was always uncanny and to the present day people do not like to go near it.

Kenneth MacLeod and the Collector were together in Eigg in January 1905, in search of traditional lore, and this is the conversation that took place between the two and Janet MacLeod:

We. Where did you hear this song?

Answer. I have heard it from many a person, and many a time have I myself sung it lustily at the waulking frame. My father's people, the tribe descended from the Counsellor, were famous for old songs and things of that kind — was it not about them it was said that they never forgot any poetry or lore, but were constantly adding to the cairn? And when my father came to Trotternish, whether or not he brought any property with him from MacLeod's Country, he at least brought with him enough poetry and lore to fill the world.

We. That legacy was not worth much!

Answer. Was it not? I would not say so! Everything that endures is good. "Shared gold goes not far, but a shared song lasts a long time." A gold coin does not go far in company, but a good song will suffice for a whole world of people. But what I was going to say was that "Seathan son of the King of Ireland" was the choice of waulking songs. The women today have only fragments of it; when I first remember, "Seathan" by itself would be sufficient to complete the waulking, however tough the cloth. I myself remember but little of it today, compared with what I knew when no waulking was complete without me — it is not through vainglory I say it, but though many a lad was matched with me, I never left one of them in obscurity (unsung). I detest what I dislike, and indeed I would consider it no small disgrace that a poor lad should be matched with me and that I would not raise him above the rest in the forefront of a verse.

We. But who was Seathan?

Answer. Who but the son of the King of Ireland. But according to the tale he was not at all as good as the song makes him out to be. The man he would not kill in the north he would kill in the south, and the rapine he would not commit in the west, he would commit that and more in the east. At last every town and village was on his track in pursuit of him, and he was three years an outlaw, and three years in *caim* and three years among *dàimh.*

We. Three years in *caim?* What is that?

Answer. That he was under the protection of the church, in Cill Chumhann (the Narrow Church), wherever that is, and that he could not be touched.

We. And three years among *daimh?* What on earth is that?

Answer. That his wife had him hidden and that not even the tiny mouse knew where he was.

We. And was he caught at last?

Answer. He was indeed, by his own clumsiness and the snares of women. There was a hag in Ireland called the "Hag of the Three Thorns" and she loathed Seathan. She was a sister of the King of Ireland, and she hoped, if Seathan could be got out of the way, that her own son would be the king's heir. She was a wicked witch, and there was a deadly venom in each of the thorns. "You go," she said to her son, "and get the six strongest men in the five great provinces of Ireland, and at sunset we shall all arrive at Seathan's house." This was done. At sunset Seathan's wife was in the cattlefold, and her place in the house was hardly cold before the "Hag of the Three Thorns" was inside on the floor. "Seathan, my love," said she, "a boar's bristle has wounded my finger; come and let blood." Seathan sprang quickly from his hiding-place, and in a trice the warriors were upon him, and though five of them were killed, the sixth man gave his death-blow to Seathan.

After the song was sung, the conversation continued:
Query. Where are Liutha and Breathann and Bruthann?
Answer. In Ireland, I think — many a queer name there is there.
Query. And where is Magh Mell?
Answer. Goodness and the fairies only know, but it seems that it was a beautiful, merry place, where there was no sin or sorrow, and where a change would be no improvement.
Query. Who was yellow-haired Brian?
Answer. A renowned warrior in Ireland, and methinks he was a king.
Query. And Airril?
Answer. The topmost grain of the whole world in beauty of person and virtues of heart.

For printed versions, see: *Trans. Gael. Soc. Invss.,* xiii, 204–8; Frances Tolmie's Collection *(Journal of the Folk-Song Society,* Vol. iv), No.51; Craig, *Orain Luaidh,* 118–20.

499 Reciter: John MacLeod, crofter, Iochdar, South Uist, 10th January 1865.

There was once a king called King Arthur. He had many goodly Gaels at his court and in his following, every one of them surpassing the other in hardihood, pride and valour. The King saw a dream about a beautiful young maiden and he told his warriors what he had seen and the substance of his dream. One of the warriors, Sir Gawain, offered to set out in search of the woman, and he departed, and he was a long long time away before he discovered her; but he found her at last in a castle in the very middle of the sea. On a certain occasion Sir Gawain offended her and she slew him. Who should it be but a wicked witch sitting in a limpet shell! She had a grudge against Sir Gawain and she caused King Arthur to dream about herself. She caused the King of Britain to fall into a sleep and slumber, that she might get an excuse to destroy the fine hero, Sir Gawain of the Horns (Goblets) (=Sir Gawain of Cornwall?). And the wicked woman without ruth or mercy got that. "A wicked woman will get her wish, though her soul will get no mercy."

500 A man searching in the hill for sheep heard this *òran sidh* in Creaga Gorma, Hèathabhal, Barra. The fairy woman in the rocks was grinding at the quern while singing the song. The man could remember only a small fragment of what the fairy woman sang.

On fairies see *The Fairy-Faith in Celtic Countries* by W. Y. Evans Wentz (Oxford University Press, 1911).

501 Two girls in Iochdar were out feeding their father's cattle, and they heard music in the fairy hill of Croise Beaga. The children put their ears to the side of the hill, and within the fairy bower they heard the sweetest music that ear ever heard, and this was the lull-song that the fairies were singing.

502 A woman was out herding the cattle in the Isle of Sandray, and she heard this fairy song in the great fairy mound.

503 From a black-haired fine-featured intelligent woman in Miughalaidh, Mingulay. The woman first sang this very sweetly, and then dictated it with great intelligence.

Roderick MacDonald heard this lament beneath his house in Bernera one night when he was lying awake. The fairy woman was singing it as she ground at the quern under Roderick's floor. Roderick's house was on a fairy mound, and many a night the fairies would not let him sleep, but were at music and at dancing and at reels and at blowing and at sport and at all merry-making without rest or repose or halt or stillness of head or of foot in the knoll. With the uproar and with the discomfort Roderick had perforce to build his house in another spot, where the fairies no more troubled himself or his household.

504 This fairy song was heard in a fairy mound in Mingulay.

506 A deer-hunter of the hill found a sorrowful little woman in a rocky nook at the foot of the mountain. She was naught but a sorrowful little tiny fairy woman, and as pretty as a picture. She was weeping and lamenting, grieving and sorrowing, sobbing and sighing, like to break her heart. The hunter inquired of her the cause of her sorrow, and she told him that the big world-ling had put the steel above the lintel of her bower when she was out seeking a pitcher of water, and she could not get into her own house. The hunter lifted the dear lovely little mild modest woman of curling coiling hair on the tops of his palms and the summit of his shoulder, and he took her home, and he had her herding the cattle. The hunter of the deer kept the little woman fairy of the knoll with himself, and she was tending the flocks. When the fay would be at the cows she would be mourning and sorrowing, and she could be heard afar off.

507 Narrator: Catherine MacNeil, cottar, Breubhaig, Barra, 18th July 1902.

508 Narrator: Mary MacMillan, crofter, Iochdar, South Uist.

509 The narrator of this story and singer of the song was a woman of seventy or eighty years, above middle height, mild, dignified and vivacious when speaking. Her figure and complexion were such as a court lady might envy. She had never been out of her native Uist, and had never heard a word of English except once when the lowland factor, who knew no Gaelic, damned her for not speaking English when she went to pay her rent.

Never a word of English had she heard but that, and although she did not know what it meant, it made her frame tremble.

"The wicked man gave me the scowl of death because I had no English for him. I had not, oh! I had not any English for the wicked man, there was no English in my time. But I had the rent for him, and he took that. Never was I or the man I had a penny in debt to factor or to landlord — never were we, though I was left a young orphan with a large family about my hand and about my foot. My father and my two brothers and the man of my house were drowned off the Point of Muck on the voyage to Glasgow with a cargo of grain and cattle, and I was left very young with orphans without pith or power about my hand and about my foot. The boat was heavy and the sea high, and she sank beneath their feet, while the people of the Isle of Muck looked on without power to help or rescue them. I was left with helpless children, but the God of the elements was merciful to me, and the people of the townland were good and kind towards me. Never yet was my rig left neglected on the day of ploughing, on the day of sowing and harrowing, or on the day of reaping, until the children grew up — never yet, oh! never yet was it left neglected, thanks be to Him and to His Son Jesu Christ!"

A farmer's daughter was once herding her father's big cattle and small stock in Trosairigh in the upland of Corry Corodale in Uist. The day was warm and sultry, and what but a drowse of sleep and a load of slumber fell upon the girl. When the herd awoke the cattle were a-missing. The herd had no tidings of the cattle, and the cattle had no tidings of the herd. But as it drew towards evening the cattle came home, sauntering at their own sweet leisure, and the girl came home with a hasty step after them. She came, my dear, oh! she came, and neither herself nor others knew where she had been — O Mary Mother, neither she herself nor others knew at all where she had been!

But three quarters after that the girl bore a son. The girl herself knew not, nor did others know, who was father to the child, no, neither the girl herself nor others knew at all who was father to the child. But there was a fair green fairy knoll in the upland of the Corry, full of fairies, oh! a great troop of the fairy folk with their fine green mantles and their gallant handsome costumes. Men suspected one of these.

The girl was advised to go to an old man who was in the townland and to seek and to take counsel of him. The girl did that, and the counsel which the man furnished to her was that she should go and leave the child hard by the green mound wherein the slumberers rested and where the drowse and overmastery of sleep had fallen upon her, and remain in hiding, and overlook and overhear to discover whatever she might see or hear.

The girl did every whit as the old man bade, and left the child by the mound, and went herself into hiding. The child was wailing, a thing not his wont, when his mother was going to leave him hard by the mound at the approach of the night.

Then a poor tiny little dweller in the fairy bower came forth from the beautiful green mound, with a green mantle and a well-fitting distinctive garb about his form and about his frame. The fairy lifted the child into his bosom, and began to beguile and coax and assuage it, singing airs and strains and mouth-tunes to it, and Mary Mother! his music and mouth-tunes were such as ear had never before heard in the land of the living, so lightsome and melodious, so blithe and seductive were they!

510 A fairy lover fell in with Mór early one morning when she was out with the cattle, and it would seem that pretty little Mór and the sly slender fay came to know each other, and that a son child was born of Mór as the consequence of the knowledge that was between them. Mór knew not what to do with the fairy's child, and she went to seek counsel of an old man who was in the townland. On this man's advice she left the child where she had got it, and herself went into hiding near the place. The child was wailing, and who came to lull it but the fairy out of the green fairy knoll in the breast of the glen, and he set to beguiling it and coaxing it, to assuaging it and lulling it, and this is the lull-song that the fairy had.

Cf. *Trans. Gael. Soc. Invss.*, xv.154, xix.41, xxxvii.191; *An Duanaire,* 95; Frances Tolmie's Collection, No.7; *Gesto Collection,* App., 20; *Story and Song from Lochness-side,* 238; Amy Murray, *Father Allan's Island,* 13-14.

511 Said Janet Currie, née MacDonald, wife of Archie Currie, cobbler, Aird na Mona, Iochdar, 8th April 1869:

The daughter of a farmer in Ormacleit used to go out to Benmore to Coire Mhic Iain with fodder for the cattle. Every day the girl went out she found a string of trout beside the lochlet, and she used to bring the little string of trout home, and not a living soul knew who was leaving the trout or where they were coming from. One fine day a handsome young fellow met the girl and he greeted her heartily in soft fair-spoken words, and the girl answered the young man in gentle courteous words.

The youth had a string of fish in his hand and he told the maiden to come and cleanse his hair for him and that she would get the string of fish. The youth sat down on a knoll and the girl sat beside him. He put his head in the girl's lap and he fell fast asleep. The girl was fingering the youth's head and what was she finding there but water weeds. She understood that it was the water-horse she had to do with and her heart started with fear she understood that he was not a right canny man. She took her scissors from her pocket and cut the girdle of her coat and she left the coat under the head of the man who was sleeping and made off home at speed. The girl was bed-ridden for three years with the fright she got.

She was then one summer's day sunning herself on the knoll behind her father's house, playing with the little children and the sunbeams, and who should she see coming but the water-horse in the guise of a man. Her heart leapt from her with fear and she was dead.

It was said that it was when the fairy creature woke from his sleep he made this lullaby; but who knows — who indeed? The girl had a child by this fairy creature and it was the latter who made this lullaby, and a young girl heard it one day when she was seeking calves in the hill.

512 There was a young girl who had fallen in love with a fairy. She was pining and wasting away, and her mother said to her sister: "Slàine, I will reward thee, and do thou find out what is troubling Sorcha. Sorcha will be going out at dusk every evening and coming home none knows when. See thou, my dear, canst thou discover it for me, and by the Book itself, I will reward thee well for it."

"What is worrying thee, Sorcha? There is trouble on thy mind, and do thou tell me what is the cause of thy trouble," said Slàine.

"Sooner will it come out at my knee than at my mouth," and she took great oaths that never would she reveal her sister's secret. Sorcha told her sister that she had a fairy lover in a fairy knoll behind the mountain, and that he would be singing fairy music to her in the Glen of the Grove of the Copses. Slàine told this word for word to her mother, and if she did not make over-much of it, she did not make over-little. And her mother told it to her brothers, and her brothers went in pursuit of the fairy, and they slew him. That was when the girl sang this song. The brown-haired maiden fell to grief and breaking of heart, and she withered away like the white lily under the black frost.

Another narrator said: "Her step-mother would be sending forth her own daughter along with the daughter of the wife who was before her.

"And the tell-tale would come home and relate that a fairy would be coming to keep company with her sister, to herd the sheep, and to fold the lambs, and to protect herself from the wolf, and to protect the small stock from the red fox. Her step-mother told this to her sons, and they went in pursuit of the fairy, and they slew him, and they spilled his blood upon the ground. The brown-haired ringleted maiden fell to grief and breaking of heart, and she withered away like the white lily under the black frost."

Cf. *Leabhar na Féinne,* 211; *Trans. Gael. Soc. Invss.,* xv.156; *An Duanaire,* 93; *MacDonald Collection of Gaelic Poetry,* 331; Rev. Duncan MacCallum's Collection *(Co-Chruinneacha Dhàn, Orain,* etc.: Inverness, 1821), 69.

513 There was a farmer's daughter in the Croe (Cattle-fold) of Kintail, and she was visiting the fairy of the green knoll in the upper part of the glen at the bottom of Sgurr Urain. Her mother was noticing a change in her, that the girl's mind was troubled — that though her body was here her heart was yonder, and none knew what should be done with her. When the girl would go out in the morning to tend the cattle, she would not come home until late.

Early in the morning one feast-day her father told the girl that she had better go to Mass today and that he himself would tend the cattle. He did that. When he reached the pasture he went into hiding in a cleft of a rock whence he could see the fairy mound. The man was not long in the cleft of hiding when he saw the fairy mound opening and a poor tiny little mannikin opening the leaf of the door and placing a hand on each door-post. The fairy man cast a glance up and down, here and there, if perchance he might see the girl, since he saw the cattle; but he saw not a sight of her. Then the fairy began to sing this little lilt, while the girl's father listened to him. And that was the singing of the quick notes!

"Son of this one and of that other," said the girl's father, "if I bring it not upon thee that thou shalt not go thence in thy life's span!" And he leaped down towards the knoll. But if he leaped, he saw neither fairy nor fairy mound, and he fancied that a mist had come over his eyes and that he was under spells. And by Mary and her Son, I fancy myself that that is what he was under.

515 This song was composed by a girl who went to the *sliabh* (mountain moor) to look after her father's cattle. While searching for the cattle the girl met a *leannan sidh* (fairy lover) who wished to carry the girl to his *brugh* (dwelling) and to keep her there whether she would or not.

516 The fairies caught a girl who was out on the hill herding her mothers cows, and they carried her away to the *brugh sidh* (fairy bower). But her companions came safely home, and composed this fairy song.

517 The wonderful woman who sang this song and many other songs to the writer has been described earlier (I:2f). Mary Macrae, known as Màiri Bhreac, Màiri Bhanchaig, was dairywoman with Alexander Macrae of Hùisinis, Caolas Stiadar, Harris. In her ninety-ninth year she was hale, strong and comely, having been ill but once in her life, and that with smallpox. She had been always an active and excellent worker, bright, cheerful, and good-humoured, and these qualities she retained to the end of her days. She sang this song with remarkable effect, as if she were in her nineteenth rather than her ninety-ninth year.

She attended church every Sunday, no matter what the weather might be. If the tide was out she came across Tràigh Chliamain, St Clement's Strand, which shortened the way, though wet; if the tide was in she had to come round the bay, which made the distance much longer. One stormy day of wind and snow the minister, Mr Charles Maclean, expected no one to come out in such weather; but, lest any should, he went down to the church. To his astonishment he found Mary in her usual place, alone in the church.

"Mary, Mary, what has brought you out on such a day, and all alone?"

"To hear the word of God being read and expounded to me, Mr Charles; and I am not alone at all, Mr Charles."

"Are you not, poor Mary?" and the minister glanced round the church, if by chance he might see somebody but he saw no one at all.

"I am not alone at all, Mr Charles; far from it. There were three dear and loved friends with me every step of the road coming."

"Were there now? I do not see them, Mary! Who or where are they?"

"Yes, there were three dear kind friends with me every step of the way — the Father and the Son and the Spirit were with me every step of the way," said Mary. Mary Macrae and the answer she gave, though she had not a word of schooling in her head and she was close on a hundred years old, made the minister think as nothing before or since.

Alexander Macrae, whose dairywoman Mary Macrae was, had come from Aird an t-Sobhail, Kintail, to live in Harris, and was known as "Fear Hùisinis," the laird of Hùisinis. His brother was Sir John Macrae, who was on the staff of his cousin, the Marquis of Hastings, Governor- General of India. Sir John, who was an able musician, sent to his brother for this song, and played it before Queen Victoria upon the pipes.

Mary Macrae, dairywoman, said that this song was sung by a woman whose mind was deranged by a sudden fright when she was but newly risen from childbed. She fled to the hills and lived in the *frìth* (forest) with the deer, going with them wherever they went. The people of the townland often saw and followed her, but they could not keep her in sight, far less catch her. At length a *brocair* (fox-hunter) found her asleep and came upon her from behind. "The hunter twined her long hair around his left arm, and she had no wish to flee. My love on himself! was he not brave!" said poor old Mary. The sudden start she got put back her heart in its place, and she became quiet and gentle. The hair of her head reached down to her heels, and her body was covered all over with downy hair, a touching sight to see. The hunter put his *breacan-guaille* (tartan shoulder-plaid) about her, and she came home with him quite quietly. This happened in Lochaber.

Cf. *An Gàidheal,* ii.369; *Gesto Collection,* 17; *An Duanaire,* 121; *Story and Song from Lochness-side,* 231; Macdougall and Calder, *Folk Tales and Fairy Lore,* 240; *West Highland Tales,* ii.369.

518 Narrator: John Fraser, of Lochaber, street porter, Edinburgh, 16th July 1883.

Donald Cameron was a famous hunter in Lochaber, where there were hunters at that time. Big young Donald the man was called among his kindred and his friends. He was a right stalwart fellow and a good hand at need in hill and in townland. He was out one day hunting the deer, and being tired with traversing bens and glens and corries, he sat down on the breast of the glen and fell asleep. He heard a soft gentle voice at his side, and the voice said: "Art thou asleep, young Donald?"

"Not now," said young Donald, leaping to his toes. Then young Donald beheld there before him the one woman fairest of mien and mould on whom eye of mother's son ever lay — brown russet locks floating down about her beauteous girdle white as the cotton of the moor, and her white breasts floating upon her bosom as the white seagull on the crest of the waves.

The woman spoke and said: "It grieves me sorely, young Donald, that thou art so wholly bent on shooting the hinds."

"I have never fired at a hind where I could find a stag," said young Donald.

"Well has that served thee, young Donald; but thy sharp-pointed shaft is in my haunch since Wednesday last, and little did I expect it would be thou who wouldst do it to me, O young Donald, considering how many a day thou and I have spent together, eating dainty and sucking honey in the breast of the wood, O young Donald!"

Young Donald knew not in the sun's

circuit or the darkling of the world what to say or to think of the maiden's talk.

Then the mist of the mountains sank down upon the glen, and young Donald could not see so far as the length of the bow in his hand until the mist lifted; and when it did, he could see not a glimpse of the maiden — not so much as a glimpse, and he never saw her more.

Who was here but a young hind in *"fàth fith"* in the guise of a woman. Now she was high on the breast of the corry — the Corry of the Stirk — leading her herd, with the unvaried musical belling for a song in her mouth. Young Donald thought this the finest music that he had ever heard since he was born, and I myself believe it surely was.

She would be singing while she went at their head; and there is old tradition in Lochaber to the present day that it is herself who had the hand at singing, whether she were on the side of a hill–slope, on the steep of a mountain, or on a corry's breast.

519 Reciter: Donald MacIain, piper, Eriskay, Uist, 24th April 1869. Donald MacIain was a good piper and an agreeable man, and said he was descended from a MacIain who escaped from the massacre of Glen Coe.

520 Reciter: Donald MacIain, piper, Eriskay, Uist, 24th April 1869.

521 MacLeod's lullaby. Cf. MacDougall and Calder, *Folk Tales and Fairy Lore,* 104–11; Frances Tolmie's Collection *(Journal of The Folk Song Society,* Vol. iv), No.20; *Waifs and Strays of Celtic Tradition,* v.141; *An Gaidhal* (1872), i.235; *Celtic Magazine,* xi.366; T.D. MacDonald, *Puirt mo Sheanmhar,* 5.

526 Reciter: Anne Campbell, crofter, Stiligarry, South Uist (Anne Macinnes, wife of Angus Campbell), 29th January 1875. Also from Ann Maclellan, cottar, Mointeach an Iochdair, South Uist, 1865.

A child was born — some say in Dun–borve, some in Dunvegan, some in Duntulm; I do not know which, — but a child was born, as I heard and as I was told. No sooner was the child born than the fairy woman came to lift the poor little creature away with her to the fairy mound. She came softly and silently, gently and politely, unheralded unseen and unnoticed, to lift the poor little infant away with her on the top of her shoulder home to the fairy mansion at the foot of the corrie in the brae of the glen. The beautiful mischievous little woman stood on the level floor, looking at the tiny little child straight in the face. Thus she stood and said to herself: "The prettiest little child in the world! The most lovable darling on earth! The most engaging little sleepy one in the world!" said she thrice, one after the other, as if she were not at all tired of praising him.

The child was very pretty indeed and the mischievous little woman stood looking at him who could not turn or stir or move, like the poor little bird under the glance of the serpent — she stood there, my dear, on the level floor of the house, without stirring or moving, looking at the tiny little child in the cradle. She then stretched out her tiny beautiful hands under the soft chubby arms of the infant in the cradle to lift him away with her to the fairy mound. She did, my dear; but she did not succeed. She could not stir or move the soft chubby sleeping one in the cradle, she could not raise so much as to let air pass between him and the ground.

"Ho ho! what is this?" said she, as if the matter did not please her. But as if she understood what was wrong she sniffed the air with her little shapely nose like a beauti–ful little roe in the fastness of the wood.

The matter did not please her, nor did it ever please any of her kind. What, dearest of men, but there was a *lias* on the sole of the infant's foot!

"What sort of thing is a *lias,* Anne?" said I.

"With your leave, my dear, it is a charm, a beauty–spot, a mole on a person's skin. Anyone who has that, neither fairy nor mortal will ever win him as long as he lives."

The beautiful little fairy was troubled, for it was her heart's desire to lift the fine pretty child in the cradle away home with her to the fairy mound. But she did not succeed and it is well that she did not. But though she did not succeed and did not manage to lift him, the beautiful mischievous little woman would come to the house at every season every other day to gaze at the fair little sleeping one in the shelter of the cradle. She would come and sing songs and lullabies in the tiny soft ear of the beautiful little child. The beautiful mischievous little woman would come and stand there declaiming musical rigmaroles of sweeter modes than the mavis of the branches. Ear never heard, as I have been told, sweeter music than the music of the beautiful little creature from the fairy mound. Ear never heard, never in the world.

Anne Campbell is a bright beautiful woman and a sweet singer, alert and intelligent, full of old-world songs and ballads and of old-world tales and traditions, as were her father and mother. She herself said: "I heard the lullaby and this tradition when I was a poor little toddling child on the knee of my mother — the peace of loving Christ be to her beloved soul!" Her mother's songs and stories, like those of all Highland mothers, were about hosts and fairies, birds and beasts, seals and fishes, and about what all these said to one another before the sins of man rendered them speechless. As Anne Campbell told these stories and sang these songs, it was easy to understand the fascination they exercised over the minds of old and young.

527 The fairy woman came into the house, and she seized the child in the cradle as though he were her own, and she began to lull him and nurse him and sing this melody to him.

The fairy woman set the child in the door, and she was fain to carry him off, and she said to the child's mother: "Is not thy child red, woman?"

"He has come from a big fire."

"Is not thy child green, woman?"

"The grass is green, and it grows."

"Is not thy child heavy, woman?"

"Every fruitful worldling is heavy."

"Is not thy child pinched, woman?"

"He is as the God of grace created for him, and be thou going, thou brazen hussy without manners, thou shalt not lift my child this year."

"Thou hadst need of that, little woman, that thou hadst the three answers for me, or there is no knowing in the hard shrivelling world what would befall thyself and thy child," said the fairy woman, as she went home to the knoll.

528 Narrator: Flora MacRae, Camas Luinge, Kintail 18th August 1903.

There was a woman dwelling in this cold desolate glen up yonder who would be spinning for the fairy woman. When the woman took the spinning home to the fairy in the fairy hill, the fairy would say: "This is much and good, but not all my share is here." The woman was affronted, and she could not understand what the fairy meant every wisp and shred that she was getting from the wool she was taking home to the fairy, and she could not understand what was lacking. The woman went to an old man who was in the townland and told him her trouble. "Art thou scraping the distaff tuft?" said the man. The poor woman went home, and she scraped the distaff tuft, and she took that home to the fairy. "If ill befall thee, may worse befall the mouth that taught thee!" said the fairy. The fairy never again gave the woman a scrap of work. She wed to pay her very well.

The fairy woman used to come seeking the loan of a pot, and she used to get it too. When the woman would hand over the pot she would say:

A pot deserves a bone
And to be brought home whole;
A smith deserves coal
To heat cold iron.

The pot would come home with something in it. One day there was when the pot did not come home, and the woman went to seek it. She seized the pot and swept it away (in much displeasure), not a syllable coming from her mouth. Then said the fairy, as she gazed after her:

Thou dumb woman there and thou dumb
woman,
Who art come to us from the land of the
cormorants,
She seized the pot with her evil claw –
Loose the noose and let slip the Fierce!

That was done, and the dog leaped after the woman and seized her by the back of the leg. She screamed, and was dead.

Cf. J.F. Campbell, *West Highland Tales*, (2nd ed.), ii.54–5; J. Gregorson Campbell,

Superstitions of the Scottish Highlands, 58; *Celtic Review,* v.155ff; *Béaloideas,* xv.244.

529 The *cù sidh* (fairy dog) followed horses from Loch Gearraidh nan Capall to Baile Mhàrtainn thinking that he had the *each-uisge* (water-horse). The fairy dogs pulled the tails out of the horses.

530 There was a woman in Mull, and she was expecting the men home for their food, but the bannocks were not baked and the food was not ready. She was hurried and flurried, running thither and scurrying hither, and she not knowing under hard fortune what she should say or do, but determined that her purpose should be served. The grain was not yet parched, the meal not ground, and the bannocks not baked and the food not cooked.

"O King of the world and of power, O food and clothing of men, if I had now a woman of the little folk to better my hand and to hasten my foot!" said the woman. She put off the cloak she wore at milking and querning, and she ran out of the house, and she cast a glance to and fro to see whom she might see or take note of.

There came home a woman of the little folk, and put on herself the coat and cloak and clothing of her who went out. She seized a sheaf, and she parched the grain, and winnowed it. She sat at the quern and she spread her two legs about it, and she cast a glance over her shoulder to that side and a glance over her shoulder to this, and plenty was the conceit of her. The grinding began, and began the talk and the music.

Cf. J. Gregorson Campbell, *Superstitions of the Scottish Highlands,* 189.

531 Cf. Henderson, *Survivals in Belief among the Celts,* 18; J. Gregorson Campbell, *Witchcraft and Second Sight in the Scottish Highlands,* 299.

535 The *Luideag.* Cf. J. Gregorson Campbell, *Witchcraft and Second Sight in the Scottish Highlands,* 208; *Superstitions of the Scottish Highlands,* 42; "A Washer at the Ford," *Aberystwyth Studies,* iv.105ff.

536 Cf. *Waifs and Strays of Celtic Tradition,* ii.238-40: Thànaig mi air cùlaibh na cailliche agus rug mi air ceann na ciche le m' bheul, agus thubhairt mi rithe, "Fhianais ort fhéin, a bhean, gur mise dalta do chiche deise." *Id.* iii.50, 269; J.G. McKay, *More West Highland Tales,* i.501; *Guth na Bliadhna,* ix.195. Cf. also M.A. O'Brien on the expression "sugere mammellas," *Etudes Celtiques,* iii.372. Cf. also J. Gregorson Campbell, *Witchcraft and Second Sight in the Scottish Highlands,* 111-19; *An Teachdaire Gaelach,* August 1830; Nicolson, *Gaelic Proverbs,* 410. The early Irish war-goddess, Morrigan, is sometimes described as the washer at the ford.

537 When Christ was not to be found Mary made an augury to discover Him. "Mary made a tube of her palms and looked through this and saw Christ in the temple disputing with the doctors." Then Mary and Joseph went to the temple and there found Christ as Mary had foreseen.

Mary and Brigit were loving friends. It was the husband of Brigit who brought Jesus the water to wash the feet of His disciples. When Christ was again not to be found Mary asked Brigit to make an augury for His discovery, and Brigit made the augury as Mary asked. She made a tube of her hands as Mary had done and looking through the tube saw Christ sitting at a well. Brigit and her husband went to the well and there found Christ sitting as Brigit had seen Him.

For *frith,* see Henderson, *Survivals in Belief among the Celts,* 223; William Mackenzie in *Trans. Gael. Soc. Invss.,* xviii.103-8 (from information largely supplied by Father Allan MacDonald).

540 Cf. Henderson, *Survivals in Belief among the Celts,* 223.

541 For the historical account of the drowning of Iain Garbh see James Fraser's *Polichronicon* under the year 1671. Traditional accounts, attributing the tragedy to witchcraft, are given in *Clàrsach na Coille,* 290, and in J. Gregorson Campbell's *Witchcraft and Second Sight in the Scottish Highlands,* 25. For versions of the song see: Maclean Sinclair, *Gaelic Bards,* i.95; *Songs of the Hebrides,* ii.102; *An Gaidheal,* vi.280; *Gesto Collection,* App.17; *MacDonald Collection,* 155.

543 A conflation of many MS. versions, some of them fragmentary.

544 There was a youth before now and he prepared to go away, and to leave his country and his people, and to place the wrangling world under his head. The youth was the only son of his mother. The mother's heart was full of grief and of sorrow, full of tears and of weeping, her only son to be leaving her, and she not knowing how she would contrive to keep him with herself.

The kindly youth said to his mother: "What day now, mother, shall I go? Which is the auspicious day of the week, at all?" Then the mother of the youth answered and spoke the verse that follows.

The poor woman kept her son with herself, and he never forsook her till he closed her eyes when she went over the black river of death.

From Christine Gillies, Dùn Gain–mheachadh, Benbecula. Also from Mary MacDonald, wife of Alexander MacNeil, Ceann Tangabhal, Barra, 25th September 1872. Mrs MacNeil spoke of the mother's *taibhse,* vision of the second sight.

545 Some disease occurred among the wild birds of St Kilda, greatly lessening the food supply of the people of the island. The following poem was made on that occasion.

546 This is in the measure of another old song beginning:

About Loch Creran
I shall never go
Without bow and arrow
And two–handed sword.

For other versions, see *Scottish Highlander,* 4th December 1885; *An Deò Gréine,* vi.193.

547 Catherine MacAulay had the curious belief that she could convert storms into calm by singing this song. Her voice was strong and sonorous, yet melodious and delightful to hear. "By the Book, Mr Carmichael, you would travel many miles to hear her. You never saw such a stir as she created in the midst of our *baile* (townland) when her turn came in the circuit at the ceilidh."

Catherine MacAulay's family, along with several others, was evicted from Benmore, the young and strong being sent to Nova Scotia, the old and frail being sent to live upon the people of the plains of Uist. The representative of the Gordon estates declared before the Crofters' Commission and again before the Deer Forest Commission that there had been no people in Benmore, that is, upon the east side of South Uist. The writer, however, has a list of families who had been evicted from Benmore. This list gives their various destinations, and was compiled by the Reverend Donald MacColl, priest of the parish during many years, a man of outstanding ability and integrity. [The original list is now in the possession of Mr J.L. Campbell of Canna.]

According to Duncan Maclellan, a reliable informant, Catherine MacAulay could relate many vivid and interesting stories of Prince Charlie during the time when he was among the crofters of Ben–more. I took notes of some of these.

Cf. *Mac Og an Iarla Ruaidh,* Sinclair's *Oranaiche,* 175; *Leabhar na Féinne,* 212.

The Reverend John MacAulay, grandfather of Lord Macaulay, was minister of South Uist in Prince Charlie's time. He was a highly capable man but obstinate in his opinions and an anti–Jacobite. When he came to know that the Prince had left Benmore for Stornoway he sent a messenger to his father, the minister of Harris, and his father sent a messenger to his son, a solicitor at Stornoway. When the minister of Harris came to know that the Prince was in the Island of Scalpay he hurriedly got together a crew of his kinsmen and retainers and hurried away at midnight to seize him. The Prince was staying in the house of Donald Campbell, tacksman of Scalpay, a dependant of the House of Argyll.

Campbell had men on watch around the island. In the early morning one of these reported that a boat from Miabhaig a' Chuain was making for Scalpay. Campbell got up, took his *claidhe–mór* (big two–handed sword) and hurried down to meet the boat, which was that of the minister of Harris and his kinsmen. In the discussion which followed Campbell declared that the Prince was indeed in his house, and that, while he himself was in principle no friend to every claim of the House of Stuart, he would fight and die for the fugitive who was a guest in his house. The minister and his party eventually retired.

Cf. J.L. Buchanan, *Travels in the Western Hebrides,* 65–67.

550 This lament or dirge *(séisig–bhàis, tuirim–bhàis)* was composed in Barra towards the end of the eighteenth century. A family of one son and two daughters were left orphans, and were devoted!y attached to each other. The son was carried off through the night by the press–gang, and was either mortally hurt in the struggle or was killed soon after. Thereafter the sisters lost their reason in part, and went about from house to house and from island to island. The people were kind to them, and MacNeil of Sandray was especially good to them. When he died they composed several laments for him, of which this is one. The sisters were known as Na Goimhseagan or Na Gòragan.

Cf. *Poetry of Badenoch,* 229. See reference to the coronach in *Minutes of the Synod of Argyll,* i.61; Scotland and Scotsmen (from the *Ochtertyre MSS.),* ii.429–33. Cf. III:345, 346.

551 Cf. *Killin Collection,* 46; *An Gàidheal,* ii. (1873), 168; *Celtic Monthly,* iii.137; *Celtic Magazine,* ii.235; *Macdonald Collection,* 336; *Gillies Collection,* 204 (=Maclagan MS, No.61).

552 This lament was written down for me by the late Mr Paul Cameron, Blair Atholl, from the dictation of Anne Forbes, Blair Atholl. Versions were afterwards obtained from Mr James Macpherson, Union Bank, Edinburgh; Sholto Douglas, cab–driver, Stockbridge, Edinburgh, and others. Sholto Douglas was a native of Blair Atholl, and knew that district well; he was a well–built, intelligent, and respectable man, and spoke Atholl Gaelic admirably.

553 Reciter: Duncan Cameron, policeman, Loch Aline, Morvern.

The laird of Brolas in Mull had two tall good–looking daughters. Elizabeth was the name of one of them, Margaret that of the other. Though the family were but poor, they were noble, as was natural to the Macleans:

> The dignity of the MacDonalds,
> The conceit of the Macleans.

Said a lady in Mull:

> Although I am poor I am noble,
> As were natural to a Maclean.

Wooers were coming the way, gallants noble and half–noble (well–born and half well–born). Though they did not satisfy the daughters, Elizabeth took to one of these. Margaret would not cast an eye on a suitor, not so much as an eye, and none knew what should be done with her. Elizabeth was seeing trouble on Margaret's face, and was questioning her, in hope that she would tell her the cause of her sorrow, promising that the secret would come sooner out of her knee than out of her mouth. Margaret told her that she had a secret lover, one of the MacDonalds, but that since the MacDonalds and the Macleans were at odds, she feared that mischief would happen.

"Last night I dreamed and the night before that I dreamed that my sweetheart was dead, and I am in a sorry plight, for I am going away with him tonight," said Margaret. Elizabeth was anxious for Margaret's sake, and told this to her own sweetheart.

> It is no secret
> When three have heard it.

Elizabeth's sweetheart told this to the men who were coming to win Margaret, and they lay in wait for MacDonald, and they killed him when he was going off with the girl. Margaret took her lover in her arms, and from that spot she could not be taken, alive or dead, of her will or against her wish.

> The lovely maid was found in sorrow,
> And living she could not be torn from
> her love –
> Mouth to mouth and breast to breast,
> As the clasp of a tendril round an aged
> stock.

But the girl was seized and plucked away on the very summit of men's shoulders.

The Macleans were no way for letting the girl, so stately and fine and handsome as she was, go with the MacDonalds. The girl lost her reason, and was going about throughout Mull in hopes that she might get word of her sweetheart. She got none. She would come under no house–roof nor take a morsel of food, but her feet ever on the move and the same cry ever on her lip: "Hast thou seen my sweetheart?"

Margaret was found dead in the brae of Ben More, without colour on flesh, without hue on blood (wasted and bloodless), so had she dwindled and pined away. Margaret's father and mother died of grief and hurt and heartbreak, and Elizabeth lost the sight of her eyes with mourning and lamenting. The men who killed MacDonald left the country, and never showed up again.

555 From Kirsty Gillies, cottar, Dun Gainmheachadh, Benbecula.

557 Cf. J. Gregorson Campbell, *Witchcraft and Second Sight in the Scottish Highlands,* 236.

558 From John MacRury, Tolorum, Benbecula.

559 This verse was uttered by a maiden whose lover had forsaken her and was arranging, with the usual feast and merrymaking, a marriage with another girl in the townland:

The words were repeated to the errant lover, and he said: "That is true, thou best beloved!" and took up his plaid, staff and bonnet and returned whence he had come.

Cf. *Waifs and Strays of Celtic Tradition,* v.97, where the verses are said to be by Mairearad Bhòidheach (see "Beautiful Margaret," V:553) to her sister, Ealasaid Odhar.

560 From John Maclellan (Iain Bàn), aged 82 years, crofter, Hàcleit an Iochdair, Benbecula.

Old John Maclellan had a great many old poems and songs, got from his father and mother. He had many Ossianic lays, very full and finished, and containing old words and phrases not in other versions known to the writer; but these, owing to pressure of other work, I was not able to take down.

Glen Liadail or Liathadail is a glen in South Uist, adjoining Corodale. No one dared to go into Glen Liadail without singing the song to propitiate *daoine beaga a' ghlinne,* "the little folk of the glen." The only persons who could go were Clann 'ic Iosaig, the MacIsaacs, better known as Clann 'ic 'ille Riabhaich, the clan of the son of Gille Riabhach, the brindled lad. There are some of this clan in South Uist, who call themselves Mac Iosaig, MacIsaac, and some in North Uist, who call themselves Mac–Donald.

Reilig Ni Ruairidh, the burial place of the daughter of Roderick, is in Benmore, near Liadal. It was the custom of the women of Benmore to pour libations of milk on Reilig Ni Ruairidh when milking their cows in the neighbourhood. One day, however, a woman of less faith than her neighbours said: "I will not pour another drop on the Grave of Ni Ruairidh — I see no reason for it."

Her woman companions pressed the poor woman not to break the honoured custom and not to refuse the milk, or she would see what would befall herself or her goods or her kindred.

"Be that as it will," she said, "I will not offer up another drop to the Grave of Ni Ruairidh." Soon after that her son was killed by a leap which he made. The place where the lad made the leap is called to this day "the Leap of the son of John son of Alan."

Mr J. L. Campbell of Canna has drawn my attention to the reference to this glen in Martin Martin, *A Description of the Western Islands of Scotland,* 152 (4th ed., 1934): "There is a valley between two mountains on the east side [of South Uist] call Glenslyte [sic], which affords good pasturage. The natives who farm it come this with their cattle in the summer time, and are possessed with a firm belief that this valley is haunted by spirits, who by the inhabitants are called the great men; and that whatsoever man or woman enters the valley without making first an entire resignation of themselves to the conduct of the great men will infallibly grow mad. The words by which he or she gives up himself to these men's conduct are comprehended in three sentences, wherein the glen is twice named, to which they add that it is inhabited by these great men, and that such as enter depend on their protection ... there had happened a late instance of a woman who went into that glen without resigning herself to the conduct of these men, and immediately after she became mad...." It is clear from this and from the poem that *daoine beaga a' ghlinne* should be *daoine mora a' ghlinne,* the great men of the glen. An alternative form of Reilig Ni Ruairidh is Reilig nan Ruairidh.

561 Sionn was king of Sionn, or as some say king of Sionnaidh, or as others say king of Sionnachan (all these names are connected with *sionnach,* a fox). The Race of Sionn were the hardest to outwit between earth and sky in the four mighty quarters of the great world. They were as crafty as the foxes themselves, for these were the tribe from which they came and they were of the one stock. They were full of spells and of charms and of sorceries, full of tricks and of incantations, full of wile and guile and cunning, and there was no besting them.

The Big Young Son of the King (Knight) of the Hunt was out in the hill chasing the grown stags, and what did he come upon, my dear, but a beautiful young damsel in the niche of a rock in the breast of the cliff. The brown-haired maiden was wrapped in slumber in the warmth of the sun, in the remoteness of the couch of the mountains. The Big Young Son of the Knight of the Hunt spoke to the russet-haired damsel at the foot of the thickets and in the breast of the bushes. The maiden parted the lids of her two smiling blue eyes and looked at the sweetheart of the Hunt straight in the face, but she did not open her two soft fair tender warm red lips.

The Big Young Son of the King of the Hunt lifted the russet-haired damsel on the very summit of his shoulder and took her home to his father's and his mother's house. It was not the best thanks that he got for that deed from his mother, and it was not good praise that his father gave him.

The brown-haired maid bore a son to the Big Young Son of the Knight of the Hunt, and they sent for the parish priest to come and baptize the child. The man came to the house and put the water upon the little guest that had come home and baptized the child that was between the Big Young Son of the Knight of the Hunt and the daughter of the King of Sionn.

Summons was sent over the kingdom far and wide to come to the baptism and the great company came to the house to see the russet-haired damsel and the brown-haired maid; they came, and people came to see the brown-haired maiden from every corner of the kingdom.

The Lady of the Hunt set the brown-haired maid, daughter of the King of Sionn, standing on a pedestal at the head of the feast, and put a wick-candle in her hand to make sure that the world's people should have sight of the russet-haired damsel, daughter of the King of Sionn. The business did not please the russet-haired damsel and though she had never hitherto spoken, she spoke now [this verse] and she spoke well.

Some words in the translation are doubtful. Cf. J. Gregorson Campbell, *Witchcraft and Second Sight in the Scottish Highlands,* 107–8.

562 Hector (son of Alexander) MacLeod, cottar, Lianacuidh, Iochdar. St Michael's Day 1872.

563 From John Ewen MacRury, crofter, Tolorum, Benbecula. December 1894.

564 From Dugald MacDonald, Manal, Tiree. This is more probably a half-remembered version of the story of the night spent by the Bard O'Daly in the house of the farmer Gille-Brighde. See *Highland Monthly,* ii.432. But cf. *Waifs and Strays of Celtic Tradition,* iv.102–3.

Concordance

The following concordance refers the reader to items and to sources for section notes where they occur in the original edition (OE).

Volume I

Invocations

No.	OE page
1	3
2	5
3	7
4	13
5	15
6	19
7	23
8	27
9	29
10	31
11	33
12	35
13	37
14	39
15	43
16	45
17	47
18	49
19	51
20	53
21	55
22	57
23	59
24	61
25	65
26	67
27	69
28	71
29	73
30	75
31	77
32	79
33	81
34	83
35	85
36	87
37	89
38	91
39	93
40	95
41	97
42	99
43	101
44	103
45	105
46	107
47	109
48	111
49	113
50	115
51	117
52	119
53	121
54	123

Seasons

No.	OE page
55	127
56	133
57	135
58	139
59	141
60	143
61	145
62	147
63	149
64	151
65	153
66	157
67	159
68	161
69	163
70	164
71	177
72	179
73	183
74	187
75	190
76	195
77	198
78	213
79	217
80	223
81	225

Labour

No.	OE page
82	231
83	233
84	235
85	237
86	239
87	241
88	243
89	247
90	249
91	251
92	252
93	259
94	261
95	263
96	265
97	267
98	269
99	271
100	273
101	275
102	277
103	279
104	281
105	283
106	285
107	289
108	293
109	295
110	301
111	303
112	305
113	306
114	311
115	315
116	317
117	319
118	322
119	329
120	331
121	333

Volume II

Incantations

No.	OE page
122	3
123	5
124	7
125	9
126	11
127	13
128	15
129	17
130	19
131	19
132	21
133	22
134	26
135	33
136	35
137	37
138	39
139	41
140	43
141	45
142	49
143	53
144	55
145	57
146	59
147	61
148	61
149	63
150	65
151	67
152	69
153	71
154	73
155	75
156	75
157	77
158	77
159	78
160	87
161	91
162	93
163	95
164	95
165	97
166	99
167	101
168	103
169	105
170	107
171	109
172	111
173	113
174	115
175	115
176	117
177	117
178	119
179	119
180	121
181	123

Volume V

Index

of titles and *first lines* (where different)